Time Out

London

timeout.com/london

Time Out Guides

Time Out Guides Ltd
Universal House
251 Tottenham Court Road
London W1T 7AB
United Kingdom
Tel: +44 (0)20 7813 3000
Fax: +44 (0)20 7813 6001
Email: guides@timeout.com
www.timeout.com

Published by Time Out Guides Ltd, a wholly owned subsidiary of Time Out Group Ltd. Time Out and the Time Out logo are trademarks of Time Out Group Ltd.

Previous editions 1989, 1990, 1992 and annually from 1994 to 2013.

10 9 8 7 6 5 4 3 2 1

This edition first published in Great Britain in 2014 by Ebury Publishing.
A Random House Group Company
20 Vauxhall Bridge Road, London SW1V 2SA

Random House Australia Pty Ltd 20 Alfred Street, Milsons Point, Sydney, New South Wales 2061, Australia

Random House New Zealand Ltd 18 Poland Road, Glenfield, Auckland 10, New Zealand

Random House South Africa (Pty) Ltd Isle of Houghton, Corner Boundary Road & Carse O'Gowrie, Houghton 2198, South Africa

Random House UK Limited Reg. No. 954009

Distributed in the US and Latin America by Publishers Group West (1-510-809-3700)

For further distribution details, see www.timeout.com.

ISBN: 978-1-84670-323-2

A CIP catalogue record for this book is available from the British Library.

Printed and bound in China by Leo Paper Products Ltd.

The Random House Group Limited supports The Forest Stewardship Council® (FSC®), the leading international forest-certification organisation. Our books carrying the FSC label are printed on FSC®-certified paper. FSC is the only forest-certification scheme supported by the leading environmental organisations, including Greenpeace. Our paper procurement policy can be found at www.randomhouse.co.uk/environment.

FSC
www.fsc.org
MIX
Paper from responsible sources
FSC® C020056

Contents

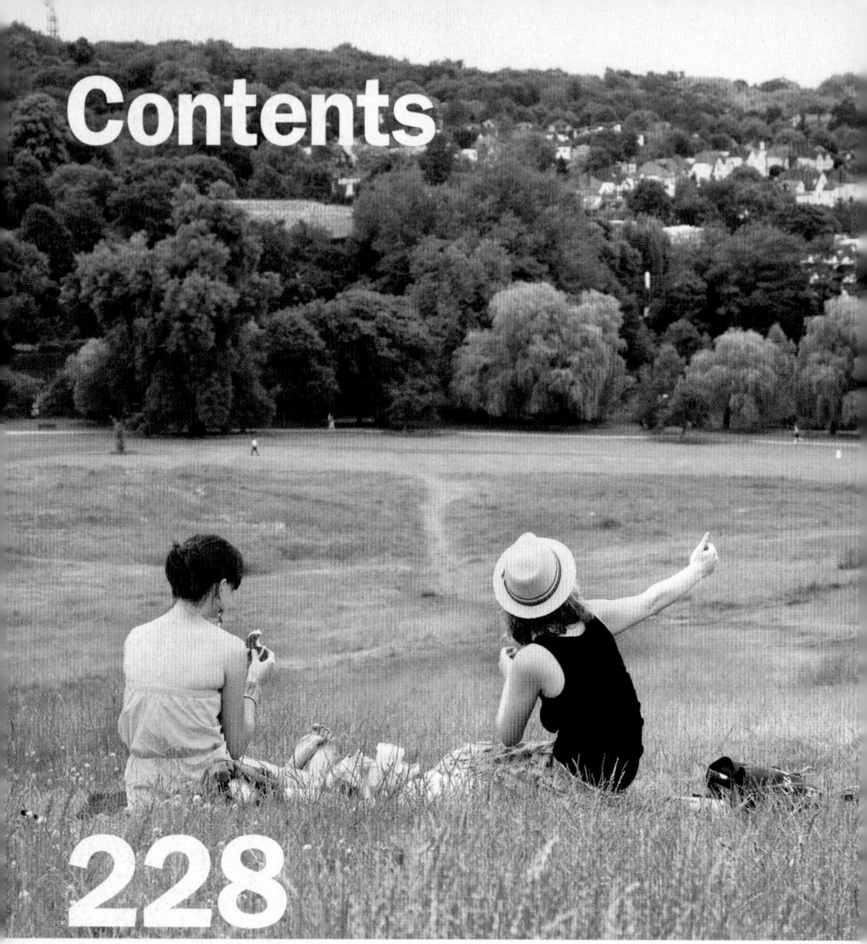

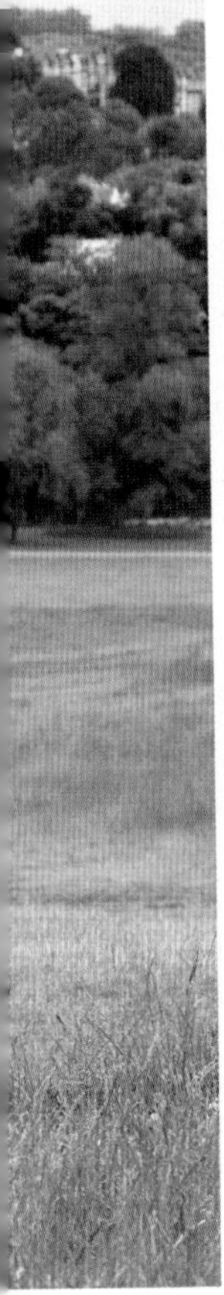

In Context 310

Essential Information 336

Maps 388

Time Out London

Editorial
Editor Simon Coppock
Deputy Editor Ros Sales
Listings Editor Olivia Rye
Proofreader Marion Moisy
Indexer Rebecca Knott

Editorial Director Sarah Guy
Management Accountant Margaret Wright

Design
Senior Designer Kei Ishimaru
Designer Thomas Havell
Group Commercial Senior Designer Jason Tansley

Picture Desk
Picture Editor Jael Marschner
Deputy Picture Editor Ben Rowe
Freelance Picture Researcher Lizzy Owen

Advertising
Managing Director of Advertising St John Betteridge
Advertising Sales Deborah Maclaren, Helen Debenham @ The Media Sales House

Marketing
Senior Publishing Brand Manager Luthfa Begum
Head of Circulation Dan Collins

Production
Production Controller Katie Mulhern-Bhudia

Time Out Group
Chairman & Founder Tony Elliott
Chief Executive Officer Tim Arthur
Publisher Alex Batho
Group IT Director Simon Chappell
Group Marketing Director Carolyn Sims

Contributors
London's Top 20 Simon Coppock. **London Today** Pete Watts. **Itineraries** Simon Coppock. **Diary** Simon Coppock and contributors to *Time Out London* magazine. **Explore** Simon Coppock. *Restaurants, Pubs & Bars* Sarah Guy, contributors to *Time Out London Eating & Drinking*. *Shopping & services* Anna Norman, contributors to *Time Out London* magazine. **Children** Emma Perry. **Film** Simon Coppock. **Gay & Lesbian** Paul Burston. **Nightlife** Jonny Ensall, Ben Walters, Simon Coppock. **Performing Arts** Andrzej Lukowski, Lyndsey Winship, Simon Coppock. **Escapes & Excursions** Simon Coppock. **History** Simon Coppock. **Architecture** Simon Coppock. **Hotels** Simon Coppock, Ros Sales. **Essential Information** Olivia Rye. **Additional research** Carol Baker.

Maps JS Graphics Ltd (john@jsgraphics.co.uk).

Cover and pull-out map photography Steve Vidler/Alamy

Back cover photography Clockwise from top left: Rob van Esch/Shutterstock.com; antb/Shutterstock.com; Kiev.Victor/Shutterstock.com; citizenM hotel Bankside; Dutourdumonde Photography/Shutterstock.com

Photography Pages 2, 190, 194 pcruciatti/Shutterstock.com; 4, 228 Oliver Knight; 5 (top), 96, 150 Dan Breckwoldt/Shutterstock.com; 5 (middle left), 135 antb/Shutterstock.com; 5 (middle right), 193 Paul Clarke; 5 (bottom), 344 (left), 350, 358 Simon Brown; 7, 14 (middle), 303, 388/389 Kamira/Shutterstock.com; 10 (left) Caruso St John and Tate; 10/11, 26 (bottom right), 168 (bottom right), 198, 264, 276, 302 (left) Jonathan Perugia; 11, 13 (bottom), 199, 329 (bottom right) Ed Marshall; 13 (top), 15 (bottom), 16 (bottom), 91 (bottom), 136/137, 186, 299, 330 (bottom), 332 (right) Kiev.Victor/Shutterstock.com; 14 (top), 44, 115, 121, 148, 209, 357 (top) Britta Jaschinski; 14 (bottom), 195, 321 chrisdorney/Shutterstock.com; 15 (top), 23, 335 (top) Padmayogini/Shutterstock.com; 16 (top) Tim Motion; 16 (middle) Patricia Niven; 17 (top) QQ7/Shutterstock.com; 17 (bottom) Marc de Groot; 18/19 Celia Topping; 20 Ron Ellis/Shutterstock.com; 21, 27 (bottom), 60, 64 (top), 82, 111, 126, 144 (top and bottom right), 158, 176, 184, 187, 204 (top right), 222, 226, 231, 232, 256 Rob Greig; 24 irisphoto1/Shutterstock.com; 24/25 (top), 252, 310/311 Andrew Brackenbury; 24/25 (bottom), 48 cristapper/Shutterstock.com; 25 Thilo Weimer; 26 (top), 56 Tupungato/Shutterstock.com; 26 (bottom left), 61, 247, 251 Tove K Breitstein; 27 (top) BasPhoto/Shutterstock.com; 30/31 Nick Ballon; 35 (top), 300 (left) Olivia Rutherford; 35 (bottom) Bill Selwyn; 37 Nando Machado/Shutterstock.com; 40 (top), 260, 263, 278 (left) Heloise Bergman; 40 (bottom) Clive Totman; 42/43 (top) anshar/Shutterstock.com; 42/43 (bottom), 44/45 (bottom), 65, 107, 161, 204 (left and bottom right) Ming Tang-Evans; 45 Peter Kindersley; 46/47 Scott E Barbour/Getty Images; 48/49, 92 Simon Leigh; 50, 178 Claudio Divizia/Shutterstock.com; 51 Abramova Elena/Shutterstock.com; 55, 122, 131, 246, 262, 270, 300 (right), 329 (bottom left) Michelle Grant; 62, 243 (left) Alys Tomlinson; 63 i4lcocl2/Shutterstock.com; 64 godrick/Shutterstock.com; 66 Dutourdumonde Photography/Shutterstock.com; 66/67 Justin Kase zsixz/Alamy; 68 Bokic Bojan/Shutterstock.com; 73 Phil Ashley; 76, 81 Bucchi Francesco/Shutterstock.com; 79 Hélène Binet/Caruso St John and Tate; 84 Luis Santos/Shutterstock.com; 84/85 pio3/Shutterstock.com; 87, 180, 206, 235, 240 Ben Rowe; 93 Luke Hayes; 98, 140 Michael Franke; 99 Richard Booth; 100 (bottom) Magnus Andersson; 100/101 watchlooksee/Getty Images; 106 Hayley Harrison; 112, 116, 143, 212, 290 Scott Wishart; 113 Justin Barton; 118, 239 Paula Glassman; 123 Maremagnum/Getty Images; 132 (left) Kate Elliott; 132 (right) Dennis Gilbert; 136 Susie Rea; 144 (left) Fiona Hanson; 149 Lee Mawdsley; 157 John Sturrock; 163/164 Oli Scarff/Getty Images; 164 Anibal Trejo/Shutterstock.com; 168 (left) Martin Charles; 170 Andreas von Einsiedel; 171, 202, 203, 248 Elisabeth Blanchet; 172 irish1983/Shutterstock.com; 175 Ratikova/Shutterstock.com; 177 Alex Rumford; 181 r.nagy/Shutterstock.com; 188 (bottom) ZSL; 188/189 nito/Shutterstock.com; 196 (bottom) Jael Marschner; 196/197 Eddy Galeotti/Shutterstock.com; 213/214 Nadiia Gerbish/Shutterstock.com; 216, 218, 258, 259 Bikeworldtravel/Shutterstock.com; 224 Alex Morris Visualisation Ltd; 227 ODA; 233 Lisa Payne; 236 David Poultney; 238 Anthony Webb; 243 (right) Tricia De Courcy Ling; 244/245 Mark Oxley; 253 Featureflash/Shutterstock.com; 254 Everett Collection/Rex Features; 257, 261 Mike Kear; 265 Seb Barros; 271 Abigail Lelliott; 280 Tony Nandi; 283 Miller Hare; 284 Joe Plommer; 287 Pete Le May/Shakespeare Globe Trust; 290 (top) Johan Persson; 290 (bottom), 291 Brinkhoff/Mögenburg; 292 Benedict Johnson; 293 Belinda Lawley; 294/295 stefbennett/Shutterstock.com; 298 Terence Mendoza/Shutterstock.com; 301 © 2011 Warner Bros. Ent./Harry Potter Publishing Rights © J.K.R.; 302 (right) Cedric Weber/Shutterstock.com; 304 (left) Ioana Marinescu; 304 (right) Jodi Warren; 305 (top) Daniel Clements Photography; 305 (bottom) Carlos Dominquez; 306 David Fowler/Shutterstock.com; 307 (top) Mark Yuill/Shutterstock.com; 307 (bottom) CBCK/Shutterstock.com; 308 (top) Walencienne/Shutterstock.com; 308 (bottom) Ian Trotter; 309 Alexandra Reinwald/Shutterstock.com; 312 Harry Todd/Getty Images; 315 Time & Life Pictures/Getty Images; 317 (top) Alisdair Macdonald/Rex Features; 318 Hulton Archive/Getty Images; 322 H. F. Davis/Topical Press Agency/Hulton Archive/Getty Images; 326/327 Solnechnaja/Shutterstock.com; 328 Claudio Divizia/Shutterstock.com; 330 (top) Alastair Wallace/Shutterstock.com; 331, 332 (left) Patrick Wang; 333 Agnese Sanvito; 339 Joakim Blockstrom; 346 Nikolas Koenig; 349 Tom Sullam; 360 Mads Perch; 363 (top left, top right and bottom right) Chris Tubbs

The following images were supplied by the featured establishments: pages 29, 34, 57, 69, 91 (top), 95, 147, 155, 162, 168 (top right), 179, 183, 223, 250, 267, 269, 274, 278 (right), 288, 317, 335 (bottom), 336/337, 338, 342, 344 (right), 345, 347, 351, 353, 354, 357 (bottom), 363 (bottom left)

About the Guide

GETTING AROUND

Each sightseeing chapter contains a street map of the area marked with the locations of sights and museums (❶), restaurants (❶), pubs and bars (❶), and shops (❶). There are also street maps of London at the back of the book, as well as an overview map of the city and a tube map. In addition, there is now a detachable fold-out street and tube map inside the back cover.

THE ESSENTIALS

For practical information, including visas, disabled access, emergency numbers, lost property, useful websites and local transport, see the Essential Information section. It begins on page 336.

THE LISTINGS

Addresses, phone numbers, websites, transport information, hours and prices are all included in our listings, as are selected other facilities. All were checked and correct at press time. However, business owners may alter their arrangements at any time, and fluctuating economic conditions can cause prices to change rapidly.

The very best venues in the city, the must-sees and must-dos in every category, have been marked with a red star (★). In the Explore chapters, we've also marked venues with free admission with a FREE symbol.

PHONE NUMBERS

The area code for London is 020, but within the city, dialling from a landline, you only need the eight-digit number as listed. From outside the UK, dial your country's international access code (011 from the US) or a plus symbol, followed by the UK country code (44), 20 for London (dropping the initial zero) and the eight-digit number as listed in the guide. So, to reach the British Museum, dial +44 20 7323 8000. For more on phones, including information on calling abroad from the UK and details of local mobile phone access, *see pp374-375.*

FEEDBACK

We welcome feedback on this guide, both on the venues we've included and on any other locations you'd like to see featured in future editions. Please email us at guides@timeout.com.

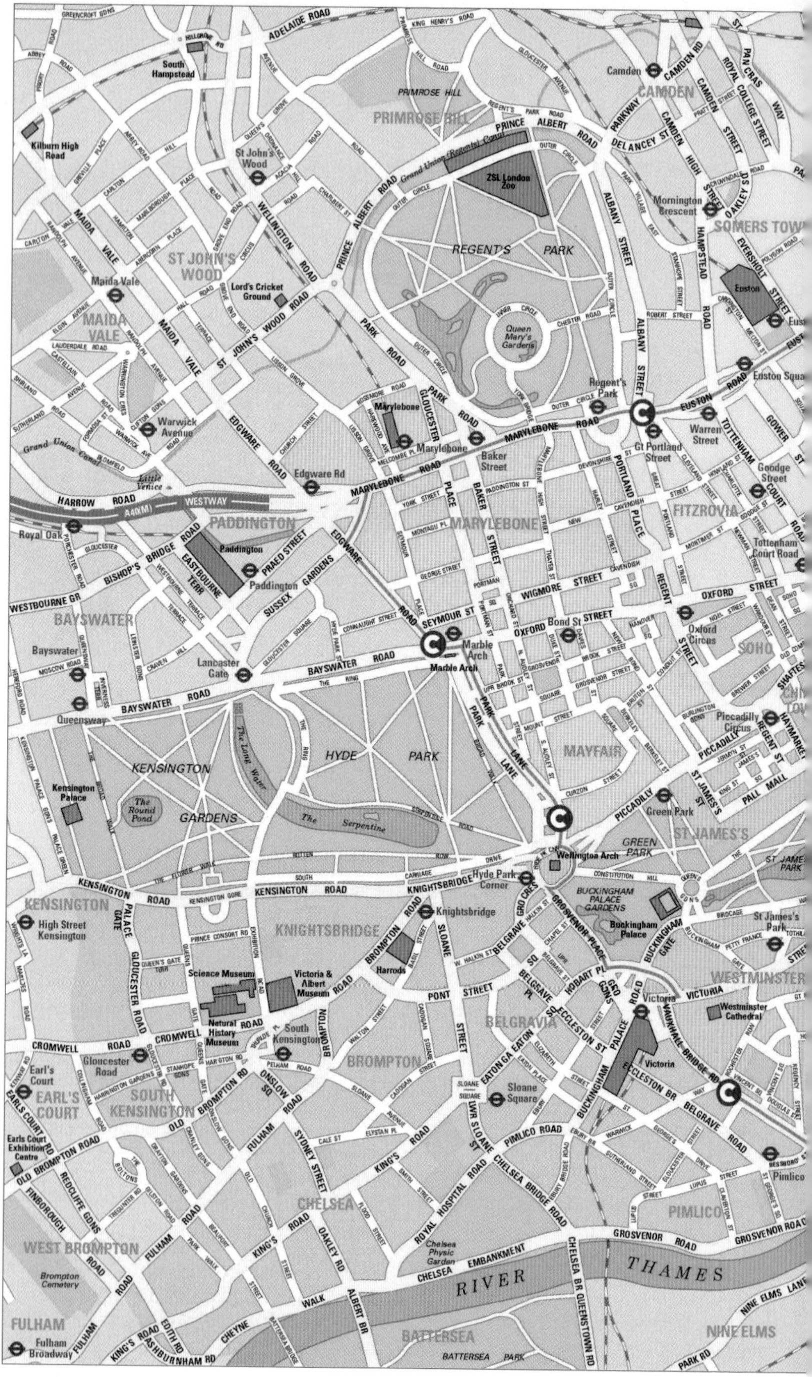
ADELAIDE ROAD
South Hampstead
Kilburn High Road
PRIMROSE HILL
Camden
CAMDEN
CAMDEN RD
ROYAL COLLEGE STREET
PARKWAY
DELANCEY ST
CAMDEN HIGH STREET
PRINCE ALBERT ROAD
Grand Union (Regent's) Canal
ZSL London Zoo
OUTER CIRCLE
REGENT'S PARK
Queen Mary's Gardens
INNER CIRCLE
ALBANY STREET
Mornington Crescent
HAMPSTEAD ROAD
SOMERS TOWN
EVERSHOLT STREET
Euston
Euston Square
EUSTON ROAD
St John's Wood
ST JOHN'S WOOD
WELLINGTON ROAD
Lord's Cricket Ground
ST JOHN'S WOOD ROAD
PRINCE ALBERT ROAD
PARK ROAD
MAIDA VALE
Maida Vale
Warwick Avenue
Grand Union Canal
Little Venice
EDGWARE ROAD
Marylebone
MARYLEBONE ROAD
Baker Street
Regent's Park
Gt Portland Street
PORTLAND PLACE
Warren Street
TOTTENHAM COURT ROAD
GOWER STREET
Goodge Street
FITZROVIA
Tottenham Court Road
Edgware Rd
HARROW ROAD
WESTWAY
A40(M)
PADDINGTON
Paddington
PRAED STREET
Royal Oak
BISHOP'S BRIDGE ROAD
EASTBOURNE TERR
SUSSEX GARDENS
MARYLEBONE
BAKER STREET
WIGMORE STREET
OXFORD STREET
REGENT STREET
Oxford Circus
SOHO
WESTBOURNE GR
BAYSWATER
Bayswater
Lancaster Gate
BAYSWATER ROAD
SEYMOUR ST
Marble Arch
Bond St
Queensway
HYDE PARK
KENSINGTON GARDENS
The Long Water
The Round Pond
Kensington Palace
The Serpentine
PARK LANE
MAYFAIR
Piccadilly Circus
PICCADILLY
Green Park
GREEN PARK
ST JAMES'S
PALL MALL
Wellington Arch
Hyde Park Corner
KENSINGTON ROAD
KNIGHTSBRIDGE
Knightsbridge
KENSINGTON
High Street Kensington
BUCKINGHAM PALACE GARDENS
Buckingham Palace
BUCKINGHAM GATE
St James's Park
WESTMINSTER
Harrods
Science Museum
Victoria & Albert Museum
Natural History Museum
South Kensington
BROMPTON ROAD
SLOANE STREET
PONT STREET
BELGRAVIA
Victoria
VICTORIA STREET
Westminster Cathedral
CROMWELL ROAD
Gloucester Road
Earl's Court
EARL'S COURT
SOUTH KENSINGTON
BROMPTON
Sloane Square
ECCLESTON BR
BELGRAVE ROAD
Pimlico
PIMLICO
Earls Court Exhibition Centre
OLD BROMPTON ROAD
FULHAM ROAD
KING'S ROAD
CHELSEA
ROYAL HOSPITAL ROAD
CHELSEA BRIDGE ROAD
GROSVENOR ROAD
Chelsea Physic Garden
CHELSEA EMBANKMENT
RIVER THAMES
WEST BROMPTON
Brompton Cemetery
FULHAM
Fulham Broadway
CHEYNE WALK
ALBERT BR
BATTERSEA
BATTERSEA PARK
CHELSEA BR QUEENSTOWN RD
NINE ELMS
NINE ELMS LANE
PARK RD

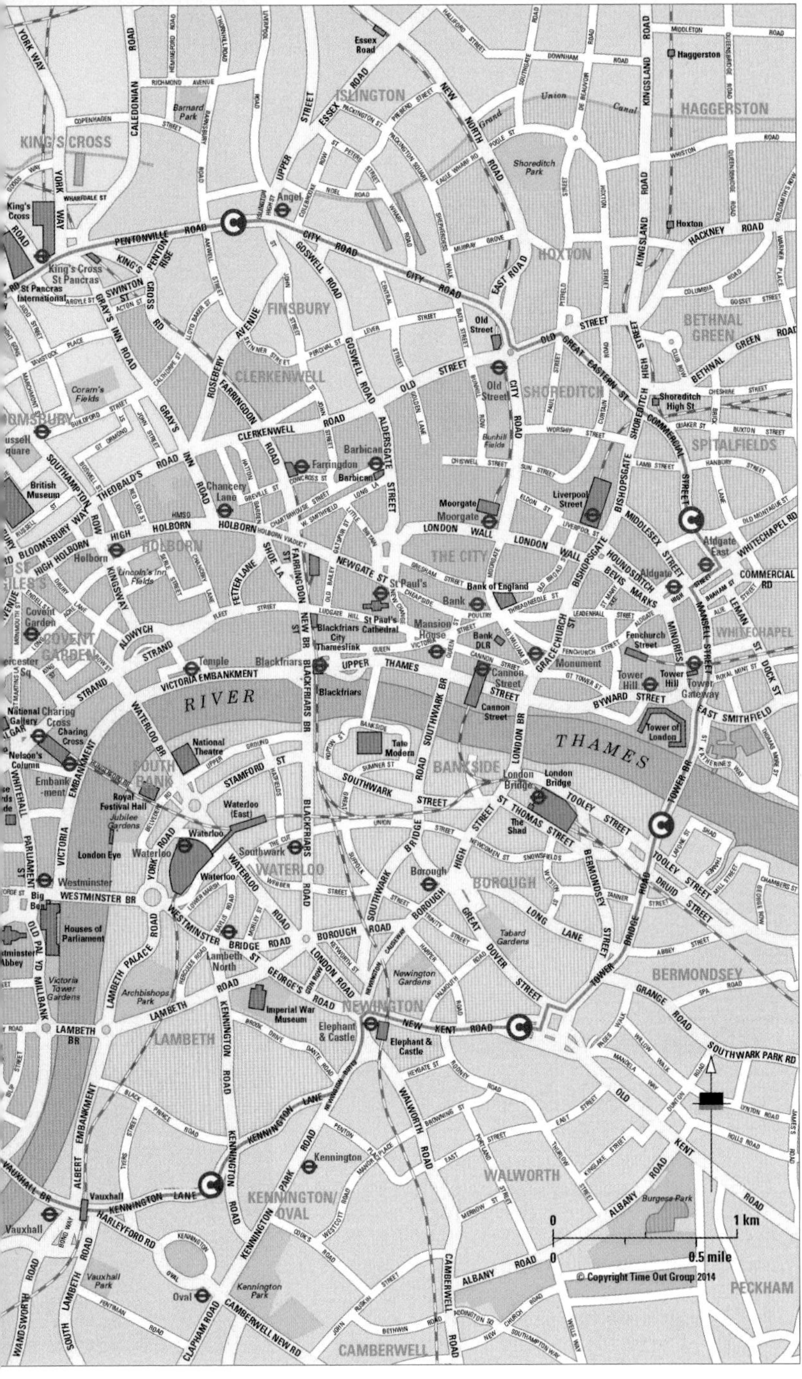

London's Top 20

From real ale pubs to historic sights, we count down the capital's finest.

1

1 Tate Britain
(page 77)

Since it opened in 2000, Tate Modern (*see p56*) has got all the plaudits, but the recent refurbishment of the original Tate nudged it ahead of its bombastic younger sibling in our affections: lovely premises and the whole chronological span of British art since 1545 to walk through.

2

2 Victoria & Albert Museum (page 90)

Stroll into the V&A's main entrance – that grand hall with the strangely beautiful glass chandelier – and the scale of this museum of art and design, its artful combination of stately historical context and cutting-edge modern design, is already apparent. It's gallery after grand and gorgeous gallery, and all with less hubbub than the neighbouring NHM (*see p87*) or Science Museum (*see p90*).

4

3 Berners Tavern (page 159)

Jason Atherton is one of London's hottest chefs. Already in possession of a Michelin star at his first solo restaurant, Pollen Street Social, last year he opened three more. Our tip for a luxury blow-out is the Berners, a grand setting for his playful and appealing dishes.

4 Broadway Market (page 210)

If you want to see what the latest trends are, head to Broadway Market on a Saturday – the perfect nexus of gourmet food stalls, quirky independent shops and people in whatever the look is in east London that week.

5 British Museum
(page 150)

This is one of the world's great museums – a compendium, in fact, of key artefacts from many of the world's cultures, from the Rosetta Stone and monumental Mesopotamian sculpture to Egyptian mummies and even an Easter Island head. Every visit uncovers further revelations, from working clocks to a trickling fountain.

6 The Shard
(page 63)

The Shard was an immediate icon of contemporary London, a slender pyramid so tall it's visible from almost everywhere. The admission is steep, nearly £25 each for adults, but the views are revelatory: don't look to the horizon, but down at the Thames, the Tower – the whole plan of the city spread out beneath your feet.

7 St James's Park
(page 80)

One of the city's joys is its chain of central parks, from Kensington Gardens and Hyde Park through Green Park to St James's. The last is our favourite. Why? It's the prettiest, has lovely lakes for waterfowl – not just ducks, but pelicans too – and nestles between Buckingham Palace and Horse Guards Parade.

8 Cock Tavern
(page 235)

These are great days for beer drinkers. A few years back, the microbrewery trend took off in London, and pubs were suddenly full of varied and interesting local brews. In fast gentrifying Hackney, the Cock is one of the best of a new breed – a popular and unfussy pub, serving faultless beer.

9 Liberty
(page 115)

Liberty isn't quite our favourite shop here – that accolade goes to Selfridge's (*see p107*) – but it is the most London, with its unique combination of up-to-the-minute fashion with those characteristic prints, of high Victorian, Tudor revival premises with modern shopping attitude.

9

10 Shakespeare's Globe
(page 286)

London's West End is a powerhouse of international theatre, but the best bargain is undoubtedly seeing some Shakespeare authentically staged at the Globe. It costs only £5 if you're prepared to stand as a 'groundling' for the performance. For a different, but equally scintillating night out, try the Globe's new Sam Wanamaker Playhouse – lit only by candles.

10

11 Tower of London
(page 186)

When William the Conqueror wanted to symbolise his control of the city – and the country – in 1078, he built the White Tower, now the castle's central keep. It was witness to many of the key events in London's history and is now a fabulous showcase for the Crown Jewels, as well as giving a home to the traditionally dressed 'Beefeaters' (Yeoman Warders) and their ravens.

11

12 Southbank Centre
(page 282)

Since Jude Kelly took over as artistic director – blessed with a refurbished Royal Festival Hall at the centre of the Southbank Centre's cluster of arts venues – she has given the place a new coherence, with events themed across all arts and venues, and buzzy events and markets all round the Centre.

13 Greenwich
(page 212)

The colonnades of Wren's Old Royal Naval College draw you into historic Greenwich Park, a fine introduction to London's most expansive UNESCO World Heritage Site, which combines the National Maritime Museum, an art gallery, an historic sailing ship and the Prime Meridian.

14 Changing the Gurard
(page 41)

Almost everyone who comes here wants to see some old-fashioned pomp and pageantry. We can't guarantee a sighting of the Queen, but we can provide the Changing the Guard. Either join the throng at Buckingham Palace, or do as we suggest and head to the less-crowded version at nearby Horse Guards Parade.

15 Royal Botanic Gardens, Kew
(page 299)

Its origins reach back to 1759, when royal plant collector Queen Caroline began developing a garden, but Kew keeps up to date with temporary alfresco sculpture exhibitions and a focus on learning about plant habitats and the environment. But relax: this isn't a visit to the classroom, it's time well spent strolling in a huge and gorgeous garden.

20

16 St John
(page 170)

This simple, relaxed restaurant – still one of the city's finest – can serve itself a healthy portion of responsibility for changing Britain's reputation for terrible food. Its owner, Fergus Henderson, pretty much invented 'modern British' cooking: striking combinations of well-sourced ingredients, traditional but out-of-favour cuts of meat and offal ('nose-to-tail' cooking) – it sounds so obvious now.

16

17 St Paul's Cathedral
(page 176)

Wren's masterpiece has a significance way beyond its undoubted technical excellence. Born out of the Great Fire, it became an image of hope for Londoners as the Blitz flattened everything around it. Now it graces royal weddings, state funerals and tourist itineraries alike with flamboyant grandeur.

15

18 Westminster
(page 73)

The grand buildings of Parliament Square – collectively recognised as another UNESCO World Heritage Site – are mostly Victorian, but their core is ancient: the heart of the Houses of Parliament is a medieval Great Hall, almost every British monarch has been crowned in the Abbey, and they sit on Thorney Island, one of the city's two original sites.

19 XOYO
(page 268)

A decade or so before it was discovered by hen parties and post-office drinking mobs, the wasted industrial buildings of Shoreditch made up the coolest slice of clubland in the country – perhaps the world. XOYO gives a flavour of what was: industrial-not-terribly-chic decor, great music, and… what else do you need?

20 The Thames
(page 48)

The broad and muddy serpent of river that divides our city is the reason London is where it is, and was through seaborne trade the source of its wealth. Ponder its importance from Waterloo Bridge or on board a boat tour (*see p29*) or Thames Clipper (*see p367*), or bone up on what the MP John Burns described as 'liquid history' at the Museum of London Docklands (*see p241*).

London Today

Peter Watts on a city foolish locals love to hate.

Perhaps it's the climate, but Londoners can be a pretty cynical breed; we have a tendency to gripe constantly at the city's flaws and failings. But there comes a time – usually after reading more carefully about what's on offer around their new dream home – when even the most disgruntled Londoner must applaud what has gone on around them over the past few years. Yes, there are outrageous living costs, an over-ambitious mayor, a chaotic transport system and miserable weather, but London continues to prosper in a manner shared by no other city in Europe. London's secret is the way it combines continued artistic adventurousness and a sharp nose for cool with huge piles of cash to fund the fun stuff and keep London exciting, even for those who cannot claim lifestyles anywhere near as luxurious as the one per cent of Paternoster Square, home of London's Stock Exchange.

PINK'S

New Bus for London. *See p23.*

FROM TOP TO BOTTOM...

Let's start with the good news. In 2013, London boasted record visitor numbers, with an estimated 16 million arrivals pumping more than £3bn into the city's economy, making it the most popular city in the world for tourists. With typical get-go, London capitalised on the acclaim it received for staging such a fine Olympics in 2012, and hammered home its advantage with an aggressive worldwide marketing campaign that promised a rare combination of great restaurants, museums, galleries, shops, history and royal babies. And London made good on the promise, epitomised by exhibitions that ran almost concurrently through the summer of 2013 – Pompeii at the British Museum and David Bowie at the V&A, two very different subjects, but equally brilliant, ambitious and entertaining in scope and scale. The city even delivered the royal baby it promised.

As this suggests, London's arts scene remains strong, despite continued cutbacks. Galleries and museums are becoming more innovative in fund-raising and attention-grabbing, and larger establishments continue to expand. The British Museum has finally opened a dedicated exhibition space, Tate Modern's vast extension is due to open in 2016, the Imperial War Museum and Wellcome Collection have had major refits, while an extensive redevelopment of the Southbank Centre is in the offing. Similarly, London's auction houses and private galleries are thriving, as London's 4,224 'ultra-high net worth' residents (that's those with more than £19m in the bank, including 54 billionaires) fill their Chelsea townhouses and lateral high-rise Belgravia apartments with the very best, or at least the very latest, in contemporary art, so they have something nice to look at for the six weeks a year they spend in the city.

At the other end of the scale, almost as a direct response to the manicured tastes of the invisible but ubiquitous millionaires who are said to populate the vast luxury developments around Hyde Park, London continues to experience a boom in grittier fare like street art, fast food and craft beer. The hot-dog-shack-and-gallery-in-an-abandoned-factory-in-Peckham trend shows little sign of abating, as 'hipsters' (a disparaging term for fun-seeking twenty-somethings who have the indecency to boast taste, imagination and a little disposable income) continue to supplement a burgeoning economy in cheap, filling, Yank-inspired tucker. London's brewing scene – again influenced by America, but with a significant nod to London's long tradition of beer-making – is also prospering, with more than 60 breweries supplying a city that five years ago boasted only two. For these and other reasons – not least of which is the fact that the city is a key staging post for any touring band or DJ – London continues to be a magnet for Europe's young creative types in fields as varied as fashion and technology.

'Crossrail, Europe's largest single construction project, is cutting a high-speed east–west swathe through the city, and will make the centre of London even more accessible.'

...AND INSIDE OUT

As London's population continues to swell, its infrastructure is growing with it. Crossrail, Europe's largest single construction project, is cutting a high-speed east–west swathe through the city, and will make the centre of London even more accessible when limited services begin in 2015 (full opening is due for 2018). A north–south Crossrail 2 is already being proposed. Also planned is an extension of the Northern Line of the Underground to Battersea and Nine Elms, due to open in 2020 and intended to serve one of London's biggest regeneration areas, incorporating Battersea Power Station, New Covent Garden Market and a new US Embassy. Cycling continues to grow in popularity despite some well-publicised accidents in those parts of London where the car, or lorry, still dominates. In 2015, London will also be able to boast some 24-hour tube services, a belated acknowledgement of the value of the night-time economy.

Mayor Boris Johnson.

This then, is the good news; incontrovertible evidence that London continues to innovate and expand, still scarred by the atmosphere of stagnation that befell the city in the 1980s. It is an exciting city for the young and the rich, and offers great opportunities for those seeking to escape the entropy of many European economies. Life is hard for the poor – as it is everywhere – but also increasingly for professionals with families, who have moved back to the city from the suburbs, regenerating failing districts but putting tremendous strain on housing, education and their own stretched finances. It is largely to them that the politicians are talking when they mention the 'cost of living crisis', as prices rise faster than wages, a problem suffered by many, but which the relatively wealthy middle-classes are apt to shout about the loudest – and use their vote to try to change.

OWN IT.
PRESENT THIS AD AND RECEIVE A COMPLIMENTARY
SOUVENIR WITH £25 PURCHASE IN THE ROCK SHOP
Not valid with any other offers, one per person per visit
Offer expires 31/05/2015. Valid only at london location
OPENING HOUR
RESTAURANT
MON-THURS 11.30–00.30 • FRI-SAT 11.30–01.00 • SUN 11.30–22.3
ROCK SHOP
MON-SAT 9.30–23.30 • SUN 9.30–23.0
Hard Rock CAFE
150 OLD PARK LAN
020 7514 1700 • HARDROCK.COM
/HARDROCKCAFELONDON /HARDROCKLONDON
#HARDROC
©2014 Hard Rock International (usa), inc. All rights reserved. Seetheshow

Emirates Air Line cable car.

THE MOTHER OF ALL DEMOCRACIES

With a general election in 2015 and a mayoral election in 2016, this is a particularly itchy time for politicians, who want to ensure their own re-election while jockeying for position should there be any major change of power in their respective parties. London's mayor since 2008, Conservative maverick Boris Johnson, is known to have prime ministerial ambitions and remains one of the country's most popular politicians, thanks to his knack for a cutting soundbite and despite his limp record at City Hall.

Some big things have happened on Johnson's watch – the Olympics, expansion of the Overground rail network and Crossrail in particular – but the mayor had little to do with any of them, beyond his remarkable ability for exploiting any situation for the maximum publicity, both for himself and by extension his city.

Johnson's own innovations have been less successful, although his New Bus for London – a sort of grumpy Iron Man version of the classic 1950s Routemaster – has been a popular if expensive addition to the London milieu. Johnson loves a gimmick (his latest being the Garden Bridge, a leafy pedestrian bridge between Temple and the South Bank, tentatively planned for 2017), so there is a danger he will be defined by the unwanted and underused sponsored cable car that criss-crosses the Thames pointlessly between North Greenwich and the Royal Docks. That's why Johnson has been so keen to build a new airport for London. His dream, typically, has been to plonk one on an island in the middle of the Thames to the east of London, an imaginative idea nicknamed 'Boris Island' but not one that has met with much approval among aviation experts, who prefer an expansion of existing capacity at Heathrow to meet increased demand.

Johnson could yet pull off his airport scheme (starchitect Norman Foster's plans to create a huge infrastructural hub just outside the city are at least cogent), and it would be foolish to discount the personal charm, networking skills and sheer energising pizzazz that will make him such a hard act to follow. Since the formation of the Greater London Authority in 2000, London has had just two mayors. They are at opposing poles politically, but share certain characteristics – namely, an enthusiasm for nose-tweaking, wild schemes and bold statements – that set them apart from the suited banalities that usually pass for politicians in this country. Quite what that means for the 2016 mayoral election is unclear, but it's no surprise that among the names being proposed is Eddie Izzard, a stand-up comedian with a taste both for the surreal and for women's clothing. If any city would elect him, it's London.

Itineraries

Let our step-by-step planner help you fall in love with London.

Day 1

10AM Start the day in **Trafalgar Square** (*see p68*). The centre of London is an impressive sight, especially when it isn't too full of tourists snapping pictures of themselves with the lions: check out the bright blue cockerel on the Fourth Plinth. The masterpieces of the **National Gallery** (*see p68*) – an encyclopaedia of Western art – are on the pedestrianised northern side of the square.

10.45AM Head south down Whitehall, keeping an eye out for the cavalryman on sentry duty. You should arrive in time to see Horse Guards with shiny swords and helmets go through the daily **Changing the Guard** (*see p41* **Stunning Ceremonials**; it's an hour earlier on Sunday). After the ceremonials, head through the parade ground into **St James's Park** (*see p80*) to feed the ducks and admire **Buckingham Palace** (*see p80*) at the end of the lake.

NOON Just out of the park's southern corner is Parliament Square. Admire the tobacco-yellow stone of **Westminster Abbey, Parliament** and the **Queen Elizabeth Tower** ('Big Ben' to most visitors) – this is a UNESCO World Heritage Site. Next cross Westminster Bridge for County Hall, the **London Eye** (*see p51*) and a stroll east along the South Bank. This walk is modern London's biggest tourist cliché, but it's still great fun. The area around the **Southbank Centre** (*see p50*) is busy with places to eat.

3PM Go with the flow past the ace rep cinema **BFI Southbank** (*see p256*) and the **National Theatre** (*see p285*) to **Tate Modern** and **Shakespeare's Globe** (for both, *see p286*), and finish your afternoon by crossing the Millennium Bridge for the slow climb up to the 17th-century architectural masterpiece **St Paul's Cathedral** (*see p176*), right by St Paul's tube station.

8PM Enough history and culture. Head north into Clerkenwell for brilliant food: modern British at **St John** or fusion at **Modern Pantry** (for both, *see p170*). If you're in town at the weekend and still have some energy, join the queue for enduringly cool superclub **Fabric** (*see p265*).

Clockwise from top left: **Changing the Guard**; **Westminster Abbey**; **Fabric**; **Tate Modern**.

Day 2

10AM Ready for one of the world's finest museums? You betcha – and you'll be early enough to miss most of the crowds. The **British Museum** (*see p150*) is so full of treasures you may not know where to begin: try left out of the middle of the covered courtyard for monumental antiquities, including the Parthenon Marbles.

NOON Wander south to the boutiques around Seven Dials until lunch. **Great Queen Street** (*see p141*) is a good option if you didn't try St John; **Wahaca** (*see p143*) and **Homeslice** (*see p142*) are cheaper for a quick snack. **Covent Garden Market** (*see p138*) is here, but the excellent **London Transport Museum** (*see p138*) or a coffee on the lofty terrace of the **Royal Opera House** (*see p138*) are better reasons to linger.

3PM If the weather's fine and you're interested in how London has been changing, head to Bank station and get the DLR: it will take you to the **Olympic Park** (*see p237*) or the **Royal Docks** (*see p241*), with plenty of walking opportunities in the redeveloped former industrial hinterland. If it's rainy, Covent Garden tube is the right line for South Kensington's trio of powerhouse museums: the **V&A, Natural History Museum** and **Science Museum** (for all, *see pp87-90*). If there's any walking left in you, head to Hyde Park for the grandiloquent **Albert Memorial** (*see p87*) and Kensington Gardens for the Zaha Hadid-redesigned **Serpentine Sackler** gallery (*see p93*). Now you need food: take on a refined refuel at **Le Café Anglais** (*see p94*).

9PM Not yet ready for bed? All you need do is get back on the Central (red) underground line and head to the **East End** (*see pp196-211*): Liverpool Street station is the gateway to bleakly nondescript Shoreditch and its plethora of concept cocktail bars. The young-at-heart can then join wispily moustached hipsters and their retro-styled molls on the Overground from Shoreditch High Street to Dalston Junction for a taste of **Dalston's nightlife** (*see pp267-269*).

Top: **Covent Garden Market**; **Selfridges**. Bottom: **Natural History Museum**; **Dalston Superstore**.

Shopping Around

COVENT GARDEN & SOHO
Shops around the former flower market have improved markedly over the last few years, but Neal Street and around Seven Dials rule for streetwear. In Soho, pedestrianised Carnaby Street is a key area for trainers.

OXFORD STREET
London's commercial backbone, Oxford Street heaves with department stores and big chains, which spill on to Regent Street. Marylebone has small shops selling everything from jewellery to artisan cheeses.

NOTTING HILL
Best known for Portobello Road market, Notting Hill also has posh boutiques, as well as rare vinyl and vintage clothes shops.

MAYFAIR & ST JAMES'S
This patch retains bespoke tailors, specialist hatters, cobblers and perfumers, but Bond Street glitters with jewellers and Mount Street packs in niche designer labels.

CHELSEA & KNIGHTSBRIDGE
King's Road is now pretty bland, but boutiques line Sloane Street and mix with deluxe department stores on Knightsbridge.

THE EAST END
Visit on Sunday for the Columbia Road market and the best of Spitalfields, or on Saturday for Broadway Market at its busiest. Brick Lane and its offshoot Redchurch Street have great vintage clothes and home goods.

CAMDEN
The formerly grungy markets, still a natural habitat for under-25s, have grown up a bit – notably with food stalls at the Lock.

LONDON FOR FREE

Not everything in the city need cost the Mint.

MUSIC TO OUR EARS
There are a vast number of free gigs every week. They range from rock and pop at pub venues and in stores, notably at Rough Trade East, via lunchtime sessions at churches, including the atmospheric Union Chapel and, for classical, St Martin in the Fields and St James's Piccadilly. The National Theatre, Barbican and Southbank Centre all host regular foyer gigs, and don't miss the free Sunday afternoon organ recitals at St Paul's Cathedral.

CULTURE GRATIS
All the key venues (the British Museum, both Tates and all three South Kensington museums are just the start) are free, as are many smaller ones (including the Soane's, Wallace, Grant and Horniman) and many prestigious private art galleries, including White Cube Bermondsey, the Saatchi and the South London Gallery.

FREE RIDERS
See the Changing the Guard at Buckingham Palace or Horse Guards Parade – early risers can catch the cavalry ride out through Hyde Park at 10.30am daily (9.30am Sundays). There are also mounted sentries on duty all day at Horse Guards and St James's Palace.

FOUNTAINS & SUMMER FUN
When the sun appears, roll up your trousers in the lovely fountain courtyards at Somerset House and Granary Square. Summer is also great for free alfresco theatre: try Greenwich & Docklands Festival or the Scoop near Tower Bridge.

PARK LIFE
London has a delightful array of green spaces, several surprisingly central. Don't neglect the charming smaller spaces such as the City's Postman's Park, nor the wild acres of Hampstead Heath.

Guided Tours

BY BICYCLE

The **London Bicycle Tour Company** (1A Gabriel's Wharf, 56 Upper Ground, South Bank, SE1 9PP, 3318 3088, www.londonbicycle.com) runs a range of tours in central London, while **Capital Sport** (01296 631671, www.capital-sport.co.uk) offers gentle cycling tours along the Thames. For self-starters, 'Boris Bikes' – available for hire and return at docking stations across town – can be an affordable option (*see p368*).

BY BOAT

City Cruises: Red River Rover *7740 0400, www.citycruises.com. Rates from £15.30.* Hop-on, hop-off river journeys.

Jason's Trip Canal Boats *www.jasons.co.uk. Rates £14 return; £13 reductions.* Narrowboat tours from Little Venice to Camden.

London Kayak Tours *0845 453 2002, www.londonkayaktours.co.uk. Rates from £19.99.* Guided tours from Tower Bridge or Hampton Court Palace, or on the Regent's Canal, from March to October.

Thames RIB Experience *7930 5746, www.thamesribexperience.com. Rates £34-£48; £20-£29 reductions.* One of several speedboat tour companies: zoom from the Embankment to Canary Wharf (50mins) or the Thames Barrier (80mins), and back.

BY BUS

Both of these companies offer multiple hop-on hop-off stops near the key central London sights. The tickets include a river cruise.

Big Bus Company *7233 9533, www.bigbustours.com. Rates from £29; £12 reductions; free under-5s.*

Original London Sightseeing Tour *8877 1722, www.theoriginaltour.com. Rates £26; £13 reductions; £91 family; free under-5s.*

BY AIR

Adventure Balloons *01252 844222, www.adventureballoons.co.uk. Rates from £189.* Flights run at dawn on weekdays from late April to mid August.

London Helicopter Tour *7887 2626, www.thelondonhelicopter.com. Rates from £150.* Half-hour flights from Redhill in Surrey along the Thames and back.

BY CAR

Black Taxi Tours of London *7935 9363, www.blacktaxitours.co.uk. Rates £140-£150.* Tailored 2hr tours for up to five.

Small Car Big City *7585 0399, www.smallcarbigcity.com. Rates £54-£549.* Themed tours in a classic Mini Cooper – for half an hour or the entire day.

ON FOOT

For free, self-guided walking tours head to **www.walklondon.org.uk** or the Royal Geographical Society's **www.discoveringbritain.org/walks/region/greater-london**, and try the themed audio walks from the **Guardian** newspaper (www.guardian.co.uk/travel/series/london-walks).

Good choices for paid group tours include **And Did Those Feet** (8806 4325, www.chr.org.uk), **Performing London** (01234 404774, www.performinglondon.co.uk), **Silver Cane Tours** (07720 715295, www.silvercanetours.com) and **Urban Gentry** (8149 6253, www.urbangentry.com). **Original London Walks** (7624 3978, www.walks.com) provides an astonishing 140 different walks on a variety of themes. Idiosyncratic outings follow **old London maps** (www.londontrails.wordpress.com), trace a pun-ishing route throug the city's history via its **public conveniences** (www.lootours.com), look at the **vanished docks** (www.tiht.org.uk) or journey through the **art scene** (www.foxandsquirrel.com and streetartlondon.co.uk/tours). **Unseen Tours** (www.sockmobevents.org.uk) are a terrific initiative: they are led by homeless guides, who bring their own stories and close-up perspectives to well-known landmarks and the quirkier nooks and crannies of the city.

London Kayak Tours.

Diary

Your guide to what's happening when.

Notting Hill Carnival. *See p37.*

Forget about British reserve. Festivals and events play ever more elaborate variations on the age-old themes of parading and dancing, nowadays with ever-larger sprinklings of arts and culture. Some are traditional, some innovative, from the outdoor spectacle of the Greenwich & Docklands International Festival to the splendid ritual of the Changing the Guard. Weather plays a part in the timing, with a concentration of things to do in the warmer – and sometimes drier – months of summer, but the city's calendar is busy for most of the year. Indeed, some of the most enjoyable events take place in winter – Bonfire Night, for example.

All year round

For the **Changing the Guard**, *see p41* **Stunning Ceremonials**.

Ceremony of the Keys

Tower of London, Tower Hill, the City, EC3N 4AB (3166 6278, www.hrp.org.uk). Tower Hill tube or Tower Gateway DLR. **Date** 9.30pm daily (advance bookings only).

Join the Yeoman Warders after-hours at the Tower of London as they ritually lock the fortress's entrances in this 700-year-old ceremony. You enter the Tower at 9.30pm and it's all over just after 10pm, but places are hotly sought after – apply at least two months in advance; full details are available on the website.

Gun Salutes

Green Park, Mayfair & St James's, W1; Tower of London, the City, EC3. **Dates** 6 Feb (Accession Day); 21 Apr & 14 June (Queen's birthdays); 2 June (Coronation Day); 10 June (Duke of Edinburgh's birthday); 14 June (Trooping the Colour); State Opening of Parliament (*see p33*); Lord Mayor's Show (*see p40*); Remembrance Sunday (*see p40*); also for state visits.

There are gun salutes on many state occasions – see the list of dates given above for a complete breakdown of when the cannons roar out. A cavalry charge features in the 41-gun salutes mounted by the King's Troop Royal Horse Artillery in Hyde Park at noon (it takes place opposite the Dorchester Hotel; *see p353*), whereas, on the other side of town, the Honourable Artillery Company ditches the ponies and piles on the firepower with its 62-gun salutes (1pm at the Tower of London). If the dates happen to fall on a Sunday, the salute is held on the following Monday.

Spring

League Cup Final

Wembley Stadium, Stadium Way, Middx HA9 0WS (www.capitalonecup.co.uk). Wembley Park tube or Wembley Stadium rail. **Date** early Mar.

Less prestigious than the FA Cup, the League Cup is a knockout football competition with a 50-year history – but widely regarded as the annual trophy that's 'better than nothing'. Still, the winners do get to play in the UEFA Europa League.

★ Kew Spring Festival

Kew Gardens, Surrey TW9 3AB (8332 5655, www.kew.org). Kew Gardens tube/rail, Kew Bridge rail or riverboat to Kew Pier. **Admission** £16; £14 reductions; free under-17s. **Date** early Mar-May.

Kew Gardens is at its most beautiful in spring, with five million flowers carpeting the grounds.

'LONDON'S
BEST MUSICAL'
ANGIE GREAVES – MAGIC FM
THE
BODYGUARD
THE MUSICAL
FOR THE BEST SEATS WITH NO BOOKING FEES
visit www.thebodyguardmusical.com or call +44 (0)1142 239 752
ADELPHI THEATRE
London Evening Standard
SAVOY
SWAROVSKI
new kid
magic

National Science & Engineering Week

Various venues (7019 4937, www.britishscience association.org). **Date** mid Mar.
From the weird to the profound, this annual week of events engages the public in celebrating science, engineering and technology.

St Patrick's Day Parade & Festival

7983 4000, www.london.gov.uk. **Date** mid Mar.
Join the London Irish out in force for this annual parade through central London followed by toe-tapping tunes in Trafalgar Square. Held on the Sunday closest to 17 March.

Oxford & Cambridge Boat Race

River Thames, from Putney to Mortlake (www.theboatrace.org). Putney Bridge tube, or Barnes Bridge, Mortlake or Putney rail. **Date** Apr.
Blue-clad Oxbridge students (dark blue for Oxford, light blue for Cambridge) race each other in a pair of rowing eights, as they have done since 1829, but now watched by tens of millions worldwide. Experience the excitement from the riverbank – along with 250,000 other fans.

La Linea

Various venues (@LaLineaFest, www.comono.co.uk). **Date** early Apr.
A contemporary Latin music festival, featuring everything from brass bands to flamenco guitar, held over a fortnight in April.

★ Virgin London Marathon

Greenwich Park to the Mall via the Isle of Dogs, Victoria Embankment & St James's Park (7902 0200, www.virginlondonmarathon.com). Blackheath & Maze Hill rail (start), or Charing Cross tube/rail (end). **Date** mid Apr.
One of the world's elite long-distance races, the London Marathon is also one of the world's largest fundraising events – nearly 80% of participants run for charity, so zany costumes abound among the 36,000 starters. Held on a Sunday.

FA Cup Final

Wembley Stadium, Stadium Way, Middx HA9 0WS (www.thefa.com/thefacup). Wembley Park tube or Wembley Stadium rail. **Date** mid May.
The oldest domestic knockout tournament is an annual highlight for many international football fans. For all that the competition – which began in 1871 – has lost a little lustre for the top teams, who all fear being defeated by lowly opposition, it retains the capacity to surprise.

Covent Garden May Fayre & Puppet Festival

Garden of St Paul's Covent Garden, Bedford Street, WC2E 9ED (7375 0441, www.punchand judy.com/coventgarden.htm). Covent Garden tube. **Date** mid May.

All-day puppet mayhem (10.30am-5.30pm) devoted to celebrating Mr Punch at the scene of his first recorded sighting in England in 1662. Mr P takes to the church's pulpit at 11.30am. Held on a Sunday.

> **IN THE KNOW DO MORE**
>
> The free weekly *Time Out* magazine has salient highlights of festivals and events. See the website, www.timeout.com, for comprehensive listings. Events can be cancelled and dates may change with little notice, so do check before making plans.

State Opening of Parliament

Palace of Westminster, SW1A 0PW (7219 4272, www.parliament.uk). Westminster tube. **Date** May.
Pomp and ceremony attend the Queen's official reopening of Parliament after its recess, an event that marks the formal beginning of the Parliamentary year. She arrives (at about 11.15am) and departs in the state coach, accompanied by troopers of the Household Cavalry.

Chelsea Flower Show

Royal Hospital, Royal Hospital Road, Chelsea, SW3 4SR (www.rhs.org.uk). Sloane Square tube. **Date** late May.
Elbow through the huge crowds to admire perfect blooms, or get ideas for your own plot, with entire gardens laid out for the show, as well as tents with their walls packed with endless varietals. The first two days are reserved for Royal Horticultural Society members and tickets for the open days can be hard to come by.
► *The show closes at 5.30pm on the final day, but the display plants are sold off to the public from around 4.30pm.*

★ Epsom Derby

Epsom Racecourse, Epsom Downs, Surrey KT18 5LQ (01372 726311 information, 0844 579 3004 tickets, www.epsomdowns.co.uk). Epsom Downs or Tattenham Corner rail. **Date** early June.
The world's most famous horse race on the flat, the Derby, is run over a distance of one and a half miles, but crowd-watching is a large part of the fun, with the race accompanied by all manner of hoopla.

Summer

Spitalfields Music Summer Festival

Various venues (7377 1362, www.spitalfields music.org.uk). **Date** June.
A series of mainly classical concerts in June, based at Christ Church Spitalfields, as well as local venues including Shoreditch Church and Spitalfields Market. The festival returns in December each year.

PUBLIC HOLIDAYS

Good Friday
Fri 18 Apr 2014, Fri 3 Apr 2015

Easter Monday
Mon 21 Apr 2014, Mon 6 Apr 2015

May Day Holiday
Mon 5 May 2014, Mon 4 May 2015

Spring Bank Holiday
Mon 26 May 2014, Mon 25 May 2015

Summer Bank Holiday
Mon 25 Aug 2014, Mon 31 Aug 2015

Christmas Day
Thur 25 Dec 2014, Fri 25 Dec 2015

Boxing Day
Fri 26 Dec 2014, Mon 28 Dec 2015

New Year's Day
Thur 1 Jan 2015, Fri 1 Jan 2016

Field Day

Victoria Park, Victoria Park Road, Hackney, E3 5SN (www.fielddayfestivals.com). **Date** June.

One of the best music festivals in London, with a left-field booking policy. Acts range from weird pop and indie rock to underground dance producers and folk musicians. Held over a weekend.

London Festival of Architecture

Various venues (www.londonfestivalof architecture.org). **Date** June.

An entertaining mix of talks, discussions, walks, screenings and other events, always gathered under a punchy theme ('Capital' for 2014).

Meltdown

Southbank Centre, Belvedere Road, Southbank, SE1 8XX (www.southbankcentre.co.uk). **Date** mid June.

The Southbank Centre invites a guest artist to curate a fortnight of gigs, films and other events. David Bowie, Ornette Coleman, Richard Thompson, Patti Smith and, most recently, UNKLE's James Lavelle are among the previous curators.

Opera Holland Park

Holland Park (7361 3570, www.operaholland park.com). **Date** June-Aug.

A canopied outdoor theatre hosts a season of opera, including works aimed at children.

Clockwise from above: **BBC Proms** (*see p37*); **Royal Ascot**; **Lovebox Weekender**.

Open Garden Squares Weekend
www.opensquares.org. **Date** mid June.
Secret – and merely exclusive – gardens are thrown open to the public for this horticultural shindig. You can visit roof gardens, prison gardens and children-only gardens, as well as a changing selection of those tempting oases railed off in the middle of the city's finest squares. Some charge an entrance fee.

Tennis: Aegon Championships
Queens Club, Palliser Road, West Kensington, W14 9EQ (7386 3400, www.queensclub.co.uk). Barons Court tube. **Date** mid June.
The pros tend to treat this week-long grass-court tournament as a summer warm-up session for world-famous Wimbledon (*see right*).

Royal Ascot
Ascot Racecourse, Ascot, Berks SL5 7JX (0844 346 3000, www.ascot.co.uk). Ascot rail. **Date** mid June.
Major races include the Ascot Gold Cup on the Thursday, which is Ladies' Day. Expect sartorial extravagance and fancy hats.

★ Greenwich & Docklands International Festival
Various venues (8305 1818, www.festival.org).
Date late June.
This annual week of outdoor arts, theatre, dance and family entertainment is consistently spectacular. Events take place at the Old Royal Naval College and other sites, including Canary Wharf and Mile End Park.

LIFT (London International Festival of Theatre)
Various venues (7968 6800, www.liftfest.org.uk). **Date** June.
An extraordinary number of performances (nearly 90 in just under a month), under the inspirational directorship of Mark Ball.

Pride London
Various venues (www.prideinlondon.org).
Date late June.
A week-long celebration of the LGBT community, with the Parade held on the Saturday. In 2014 the Parade on 28 June commemorates the 45th anniversary of the Stonewall Riots in New York. *Photo p37.*

City of London Festival
Various venues (0845 120 7502 tickets, www.colf.org). **Date** late June-mid July.
A wide array of classical in a variety of genres, with an emphasis on classical music and jazz. Many concerts are held in unusual venues (historic churches, handsome courtrooms, ancient livery companies); there's always a strong programme of free events.

★ Wimbledon Tennis Championships
All England Lawn Tennis Club, Church Road, Wimbledon, SW19 5AE (8971 2700, www.wimbledon.org). Southfields tube. **Dates** 23 June-6 July 2014; 29 June-12 July 2015.
Getting into Wimbledon requires considerable forethought. Seats on the show courts are distributed by a ballot, which closes the previous year; enthusiasts who queue on the day may gain entry to the outer courts – and even get rare tickets for Centre Court. You can also turn up later in the day and pay reduced rates for seats vacated by spectators who've left the ground early.

Lovebox Weekender
Victoria Park, Victoria Park Road, Hackney, E3 5SN (www.mamacolive.com/lovebox).
Date mid July.
Expect some of the best names the London nightlife scene has to offer, over two days in myriad themed stages, tents and arenas.

Somerset House Summer Series
Somerset House, the Strand, WC2R 1LA (7845 4600, www.somersethouse.org.uk/music). Temple tube. **Date** July.

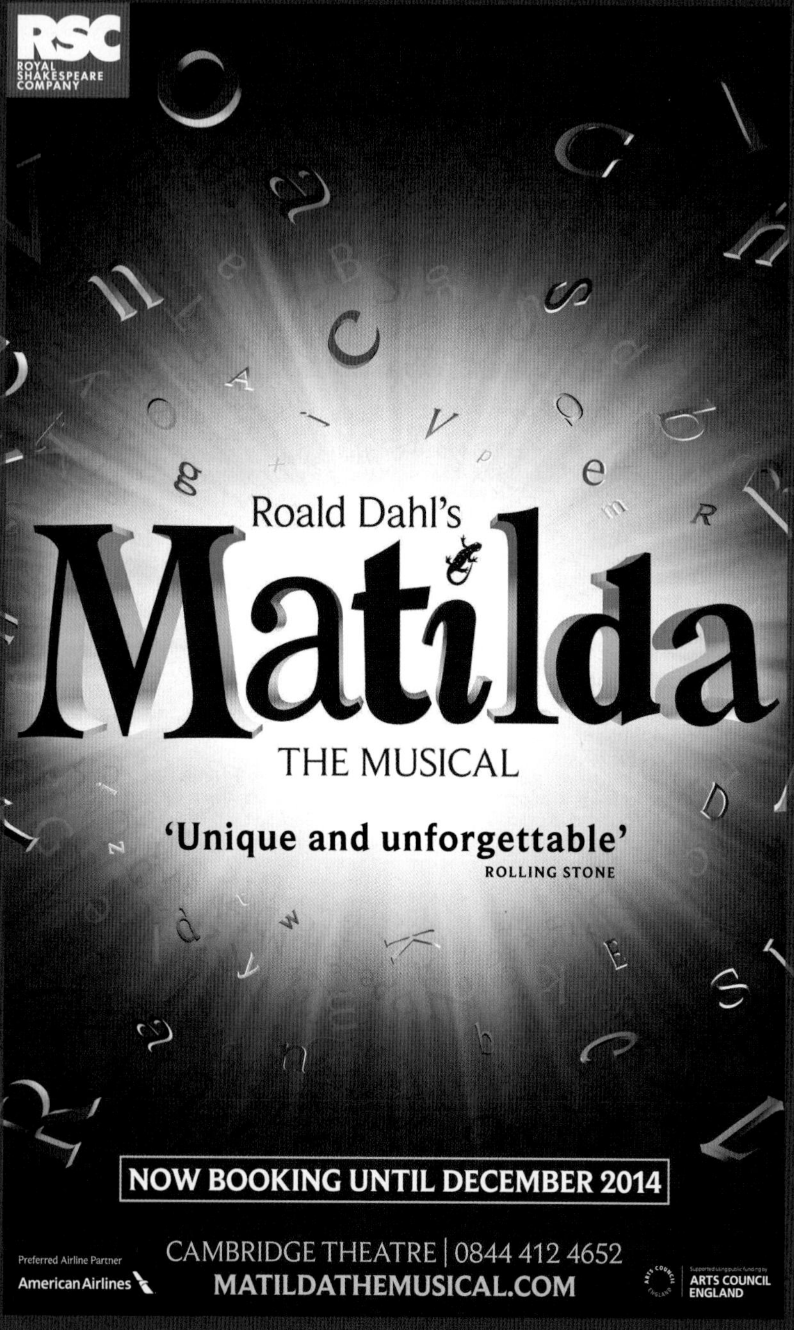
RSC
ROYAL SHAKESPEARE COMPANY
Roald Dahl's
Matilda
THE MUSICAL
'Unique and unforgettable'
ROLLING STONE
NOW BOOKING UNTIL DECEMBER 2014
Preferred Airline Partner
American Airlines
CAMBRIDGE THEATRE | 0844 412 4652
MATILDATHEMUSICAL.COM
Supported using public funding by
ARTS COUNCIL ENGLAND

Somerset House welcomes an array of big and generally pretty mainstream acts for roughly ten days of open-air shows.

BBC Proms

Royal Albert Hall, Kensington Gore, South Kensington, SW7 2AP (0845 401 5040, www.bbc.co.uk/proms). **Date** mid July-mid Sept.
The Proms overshadow all other classical music festivals in the city, with around 70 concerts, covering everything from early music recitals to orchestral world premières, and from boundary-pushing debut performances to reverent career retrospectives. BBC Radio 3 plays recordings of the concerts. *Photo p35.*

Camden Fringe

Various venues (www.camdenfringe.org).
Date late July-Aug.
An eclectic bunch of new, experimental and short shows, staged by everyone from experienced performers to newcomers.

Prudential RideLondon

7902 0212, www.prudentialridelondon.com.
Date early Aug.
This cycling festival encourages around 50,000 people to don branded fluorescent vests and ride an eight-mile traffic-free circuit from Buckingham Palace to the Tower. Competitive races also form part of the weekend's festivities.

Carnaval del Pueblo

Burgess Park, Southwark, SE5 7QH (www.carnavaldelpueblo.co.uk). Elephant & Castle tube/rail. **Date** early Aug.
This vibrant outdoor parade and festival is more than just a loud-and-proud day out for South American Londoners: it attracts people from all walks of life (as many as 60,000, most years) looking to inject a little Latin spirit into the weekend.

London Mela

Gunnersbury Park, Ealing, W3 (7387 1203, www.londonmela.org). Acton Town or South Ealing tube. **Date** late Aug.
Thousands flock to this exuberant celebration of Asian culture, dubbed the Asian Glastonbury. You'll find urban, classical and experimental music, circus, dance, comedy, children's events, and food.

IN THE KNOW
CHEAP WITH NO SEATS

You can buy tickets for the **Proms** (*see above*) in advance, but many prefer to queue on the day for the £5 'promenade' tickets after which the festival is named. These allow entry to the standing-room stalls or gallery at the top of the auditorium.

Pride London. *See p35.*

★ Notting Hill Carnival

Notting Hill, W10, W11 (www.thenottinghillcarnival.com). Ladbroke Grove, Notting Hill Gate or Westbourne Park tube. **Date** end Aug.
Two million people stream into Notting Hill to Europe's largest street party, full of the aromas, colours and music of the Caribbean. Massive mobile sound systems dominate the streets with whatever bass-heavy party music is currently hip, but there's plenty of tradition from the West Indies too: calypso music and a spectacular costumed parade. *Photo p30.*

Tetley's Challenge Cup Final

Wembley Stadium, Stadium Way, Middx HA9 0WS (www.thechallengecup.com). Wembley Park tube or Wembley Stadium rail. **Date** late Aug.
Rugby league is mainly played in the north of the country, but for the Challenge Cup Final the north heads south, bringing boisterous, convivial crowds to Wembley Stadium for some hard-tackling action.

Autumn

London African Music Festival

Various venues (7328 9613, www.joyfulnoise.co.uk). **Date** Sept.
A wonderfully eclectic affair, held over a fortnight in September. Recent performers have included Osibisa (from Ghana), Modou Toure (Senegal) and Hanisha Solomon (Ethiopia).

Mayor's Thames Festival

Between Westminster Bridge & Tower Bridge (7928 8998, www.thamesfestival.org). Blackfriars or Waterloo tube/rail. **Date** Sept.

Chelsea Physic Garden
FOUNDED 1673
London's Oldest Botanic Garden
Guided & Audio Tours • Café • Gift Shop
Sloane Square / South Kensington
www.chelseaphysicgarden.co.uk

THE ROALD DAHL MUSEUM AND STORY CENTRE
Discover the stories behind the stories...
...and let your imagination run wild
www.roalddahlmuseum.org
Just 45 minutes by train from London Marylebone

FREUD MUSEUM LONDON
The final home of Sigmund Freud, father of psychoanalysis
freud.org.uk

FREE
400 years of English homes
THE GEFFRYE
MUSEUM OF THE HOME
www.geffrye-museum.org.uk
Hoxton 136 Kingsland Road, London E2 8EA 020 7739 9893

A giant party along the Thames, this month of events is London's largest free arts festival. It's a family-friendly mix of carnival, pyrotechnics, art installations, river events and live music alongside craft and food stalls. The highlight is the last-night lantern procession and firework finale.

Tour of Britain

www.thetour.co.uk. **Date** mid Sept.
Join spectators on the streets of the capital for a stage of British cycling's biggest outdoor event.

★ Open-House London

3006 7008, www.open-city.org.uk. **Date** mid Sept.
An opportunity to snoop round other people's property, for one weekend only. Taking part are more than 500 palaces, private homes, corporate skyscrapers, pumping stations and bomb-proof bunkers, many of which are normally closed to the public.

London Literature Festival

Southbank Centre, Belvedere Road, South Bank, SE1 8XX (7960 4200, www.southbankcentre.co.uk). Waterloo tube/rail. **Date** mid Sept-mid Oct.
The London Literature Festival combines superstar writers with stars from other fields: architects, comedians, sculptors and cultural theorists examining anything from queer literature to migration.

Great River Race

River Thames, from Millwall Docks, Docklands, E14, to Ham House, Richmond, Surrey TW10 (8398 8141, www.greatriverrace.co.uk). **Date** late Sept.
Much more interesting than the Boat Race (*see p33*), the Great River Race sees an exotic array of around 300 traditional rowing boats (including skiffs, canoes, dragon boats and Cornish gigs) from around the globe racing in the 'river marathon'. Hungerford Bridge, the Millennium Bridge and Tower Bridge are all good viewpoints.

American Football: NFL

Wembley Stadium, Stadium Way, Middx HA9 0WS (www.nfluk.com). Wembley Park tube or Wembley Stadium rail. **Date** late Sept-early Nov.
The NFL took a regular-season fixture out of North America for the first time in 2007 – it was a huge success, and immediately became an annual fixture. In 2012, the Jacksonville Jaguars announced they would play a home game here for four seasons from 2013 through to 2016.

London Film Festival

Various venues (www.bfi.org.uk/lff). **Date** Oct.
The most prestigious of the capital's film fests – in fact, the key film festival in the country. Nearly 200 new British and international features are screened each year, mainly at the BFI Southbank and Leicester Square's Vue West End, and there's always a smattering of red-carpet events for the celebrity-crazed. For more film festivals, *see p253.*

Big Draw

8351 1719, www.campaignfordrawing.org. **Date** Oct.
Engage with your inner artist at the month-long Big Draw, using anything from pencils to vapour trails.

Dance Umbrella

Various venues (7407 1200, www.danceumbrella.co.uk). **Date** Oct.
A leading international dance festival, featuring a range of events (many free) in unusual spaces.

Diwali

Trafalgar Square, WC2 (7983 4100, www.london.gov.uk). Charing Cross tube/rail. **Date** Oct/Nov.
A celebration of the annual Festival of Light by Hindu, Jain and Sikh communities.

Winter

London to Brighton Veteran Car Run

Departs Serpentine Road, Hyde Park, W2 2UH (01483 524433, www.veterancarrun.com). Hyde Park Corner tube. **Date** early Nov.

BE A SPORT

Key upcoming events in London.

Tour de France

The Mall, *see p80* *(www.letour.2014stage3.com).* **Date** 7 July 2014.
Stage 3 runs from Cambridge to the Mall.

Venture Offshore Cup

Tower Bridge, *see p186* *(www.ventureoffshorecup.com).* **Date** 7 June 2014.
Start of a powerboat race to Monte Carlo.

Royal Greenwich Tall Ships Regatta

Greenwich Pier, *see p214.* **Date** 5-9 Sept 2014.

Cricket internationals

www.ecb.co.uk
England play home Test matches (the classic five-day format) and One-Day Internationals (50 overs) each year: India's visit is a highlight, with Tests at Lord's (17-21 July 2014) and the Oval (15-19 Aug 2014).

Rugby World Cup 2015

Twickenham Stadium & Olympic Stadium (www.rugbyworldcup.com). **Date** 18 Sept-31 Oct 2015.

The London to Brighton is not so much a race as a sedate procession southwards by around 500 pre-1905 cars. The first pair trundles off at sunrise (around 7-8.30am), but you can catch them a little later crossing Westminster Bridge, or view them on a closed-off Regent's Street the day before the event (11am-3pm).

★ Bonfire Night
Date 5 Nov & around.
Britain's best-loved excuse for setting off fireworks: the celebration of Guy Fawkes's failure to blow up the Houses of Parliament in 1605. Check the dedicated page at www.timeout.com for a list of public displays – several put on for free, and many charging only a nominal entry fee.

★ Lord Mayor's Show
Through the City (7332 3456, www.lordmayorsshow.org). **Date** early Nov.
This big show marks the traditional presentation of the new Lord Mayor for approval by the monarch's justices. The Lord Mayor leaves Mansion House in a fabulous gold coach at 11am, along with a colourful procession of floats and marchers. At 5pm, there's a fireworks display on the river.
▶ *The Lord Mayor is a City officer, elected each year by the livery companies and with no real power outside the City of London; don't confuse him with the Mayor of London, currently Boris Johnson (see pp18-23* **London Today***).*

Remembrance Sunday Ceremony
Cenotaph, Whitehall, Westminster, SW1. Charing Cross tube/rail. **Date** early Nov.
Held on the Sunday nearest to 11 November – the day World War I ended – this solemn commemoration honours those who died fighting in the World Wars and later conflicts; 2014 marks the centenary of the start of the Great War. The Queen, the prime minister and other dignitaries lay poppy wreaths at the Cenotaph. A two-minute silence at 11am is followed by a service of remembrance.

★ London Jazz Festival
Various veues (7324 1880, www.londonjazzfestival.org.uk). **Date** mid Nov.
Covering most bases, from trad to free improv, this is the biggest London jazz festival of the year, lasting the best part of a fortnight.

Christmas Celebrations
Covent Garden (0870 780 5001, www.coventgardenlondonuk.com); Bond Street (www.bondstreetassociation.com); St Christopher's Place (www.stchristophersplace.com); Marylebone High Street (7580 3163, www.marylebonevillage.com); Trafalgar Square (www.london.gov.uk). **Date** Nov-Dec.
Of the big stores, Fortnum & Mason (*see p83*) still creates enchantingly old-fashioned Christmas windows. Otherwise, though, skip the commercialised lights on Oxford and Regent's streets and head, instead, for smaller shopping areas such as St Christopher's Place, Bond Street, Marylebone High Street and Covent Garden. It's traditional to sing carols beneath a giant Christmas tree in Trafalgar Square (*see p68*) – an annual gift from Norway in gratitude for Britain's support during World War II – but you can also join in a mammoth singalong at the Royal Albert Hall (*see p281*), enjoy the starry choral Christmas Festival at St John Smith Square (*see p282*) or an evocative carol service at one of London's historic churches. London's major cathedrals all, naturally, celebrate Christmas with splendid liturgies and music.

Chinese New Year Festival; Lord Mayor's Show

Spitalfields Music Winter Festival
Date Dec.
See p33 **Spitalfields Music Summer Festival**.

New Year's Eve Celebrations

Date 31 Dec.

The focus of London's public celebrations has officially moved from overcrowded Trafalgar Square to the full-on fireworks display launched from the London Eye and rafts on the Thames. You have to get there early for a good view. Those with stamina can take in the New Year's Day Parade in central London the next day (www.londonparade.co.uk).

London International Mime Festival

Various venues (www.mimefest.co.uk). **Date** Jan.

Theatrical magic in many forms, from haunting visual theatre to puppetry for adults.

★ Chinese New Year Festival

Around Gerrard Street, Chinatown, W1, Leicester Square, WC2, & Trafalgar Square, WC2 (7851 6686, www.thelondonchinatown.org.uk). Leicester Square or Piccadilly Circus tube. **Date** Feb.

Launch the Years of the Sheep (19 Feb 2015) and Monkey (8 Feb 2016) in style at celebrations that engulf Chinatown and Leicester Square. Lion dancers gyrate alongside a host of acts in the grand parade to Trafalgar Square, while the restaurants of Chinatown get even more packed than usual.

Six Nations Tournament

Twickenham Stadium, Rugby Road, Middx TW1 1DZ (8892 2000, www.rfu.com). **Dates** Feb-Mar.

This major rugby union tournament for the northern hemisphere teams sees England take on Wales, Scotland, Ireland, France and Italy, with some fixtures played at home in the code's headquarters at Twickenham.

STUNNING CEREMONIALS

London is a past master when it comes to military pomp.

On alternate days from 10.45am (www.royal.gov.uk/RoyalEventsandCeremonies/ChangingtheGuard/Overview.aspx has the details), one of the five Foot Guards regiments lines up in scarlet coats and tall bearskin hats in the forecourt of Wellington Barracks; at exactly 11.27am, the soldiers start to march to **Buckingham Palace**, joined by their regimental band, to relieve the sentries there in a 45-minute ceremony for the **Changing of the Guard**.

Not far away, at **Horse Guards Parade** in Whitehall, the Household Cavalry mounts the guard daily at 11am (10am on Sunday). Although this ceremony isn't as famous as the one at Buckingham Palace, it's more visitor-friendly: the crowds aren't as thick as they are at the palace, and spectators aren't held far back from the action by railings. After the old and new guard have stared each other out in the centre of the parade ground, you can nip through to the Whitehall side to catch the departing old guard perform their hilarious dismount choreography, a synchronised, firm slap of approbation to the neck of each horse before the gloved troopers all swing off.

As well as these near-daily ceremonies, London sees other, less frequent parades on a far grander scale. The most famous is **Trooping the Colour**, staged to mark the Queen's official birthday on 13 June (her real birthday is in April). At 10.45am, the Queen rides in a carriage from Buckingham Palace to Horse Guards Parade to watch the soldiers, before heading back to Buckingham Palace for a midday RAF flypast and the impressive gun salute from Green Park.

Also at Horse Guards, on 3-4 June, a pageant of military music and precision marching begins at 7pm when the Queen (or another royal) takes the salute of the 300-strong drummers, pipers and musicians of the Massed Bands of the Household Division. This is known as **Beating the Retreat** (7414 2271, tickets 7839 5323).

London's Best

Check off the essentials with our list of hand-picked highlights.

London Eye.

Sightseeing

BEST VIEWS

Emirates Air Line p241
London Eye p51
The Monument p185
Parliament Hill (on Hampstead Heath) p228
The Shard p63
Westminster Cathedral p78

HISTORY

British Library p156
British Museum p150
Tour the Houses of Parliament p75
Imperial War Museum p55
Museum of London p179
National Maritime Museum p215
Tower of London p186
V&A p90

ART

Courtauld Gallery p146
Dulwich Picture Gallery p238
Kenwood House p229
National Gallery p68
Photographers' Gallery p132
Serpentine & Serpentine Sackler Galleries p94
Tate Britain p77
Tate Modern p56
Wallace Collection p110
Whitechapel Gallery p204
White Cube Bermondsey p62

QUIRKY

Geffrye Museum p205
Grant Museum p154
Horniman Museum p238
Leighton House p225
Old Operating Theatre p60
Sir John Soane's Museum p165

Berners Tavern.

Two Temple Place p174
Wellcome Collection p154
William Morris Gallery p233

OUTDOORS
Chelsea Physic Garden p97
Granary Square p157
Queen Elizabeth Olympic Park p237
Regent's Park p195
Royal Botanic Gardens, Kew p299
St James's Park p80
WWT Wetland Centre p250

IMPRESSIVE ARCHITECTURE
30 St Mary Axe p184
Lloyd's of London p183
Old Royal Naval College p214
St Bride's Church p173
St Paul's Cathedral p176
Westminster Abbey p76

DEAD FAMOUS
Hendrix at the Handel House Museum p117
Highgate Cemetery p230
Keats House p229

CHILDREN
Cutty Sark p212
Diana, Princess of Wales Memorial Playground p251
Front seats on the Dockland Light Railway p240
London Transport Museum p138
Natural History Museum p87
Neon-lit fountains in Granary Square p157
Science Museum p90
Warner Bros Studio Tour p301
WWT Wetland Centre p250
ZSL London Zoo p195

NATURAL WORLD
Pelicans in St James's Park p80
Natural History Museum p87
Science Museum p90
ZSL London Zoo p195

DAYS OUT
Brighton p301
Cambridge p302
Hampton Court Palace p299
Jerwood Gallery, Hastings p304
Whitstable p307
Windsor p309

Eating & drinking

ALL-DAY EATING
Balthazar p141
Caravan King's Cross p158
Delaunay p147
Dishoom p141
Hoi Polloi p206
Kopapa p142
Wolseley p82

MODERN BRITISH
Great Queen Street p141
Hereford Road p220
St John p170

TREAT EATS
Berners Tavern p159
Le Café Anglais p94
Dabbous p160
J Sheekey p142
Ledbury p222
Moro p170
Zuma p95

FOOD WITH A VIEW
Hutong p64
Paramount p142
Skylon p54
Sushisamba p187

PRIME CUTS
Hawksmoor Seven Dials p141
Meat Liquor p110
Pitt Cue Co p133

GASTROPUBS
Anchor & Hope p56
Bull & Last p229
Eagle p169
Lady Ottoline p154

Regency Café.

BUDGET EATS
Brick Lane Beigel Bake p202
E Pellicci p210
Hummus Bros p129
M Manze p64
Regency Café p78
Towpath p235
Tayyabs p205

GLOBAL
Gymkhana p118
Heron p110
Lima London p161
Sông Quê p206
Trullo p232

COCKTAILS
69 Colebrooke Row p232
Coburg Bar p119
Oskar's Bar p161
Purl p111
White Lyan p207
Worship Street Whistling Shop p207

PUBS
Cock Tavern p235
French House p129
Wenlock Arms p207
Ye Olde Mitre p165

WINE BARS
Gordon's Wine Bar p147
Terroirs p143
Vinoteca p170

Shopping

DEPARTMENT STORES & ARCADES
Burlington Arcade p121
Fortnum & Mason p83
Liberty p115
Selfridge's p107

CONCEPT
Dover Street Market p120
LN-CC p236
Shop at Bluebird p99

GORGEOUS INTERIORS
House of Hackney p208
Liberty p115

VINTAGE
Blitz p203
Vintage Emporium p203

HIGH-STREET
Topshop p107

FOOD & DRINK
Algerian Coffee Stores p129
Brixton Village p243
Maltby Street p65
Neal's Yard Dairy p146

GIFTS & SOUVENIRS
Fortnum & Mason p83
James Smith & Sons p145
Labour & Wait p208

BOOKS & MUSIC
Cecil Court p135
Daunt Books p111
Fopp p145
Foyles p126
Rough Trade East p203

MARKETS
Broadway Market p236
Camden Market p194
Columbia Road Market p210
Portobello Road Market p223
Spitalfields Market p198

Nightlife

CLUBS
Corsica Studios p268
Dalston Superstore p260
Fabric p265
Oslo p267
XOYO p268

Burlington Arcade.

Lord Mayor's Show.

CLASSICAL MUSIC
Barbican p280
Kings Place p281
Royal Festival Hall at the Southbank Centre p282
Royal Opera House p284
Wigmore Hall p282

ALTERNATIVE & CABARET
Bethnal Green Working Men's Club p277
RVT p259

ROCK & POP MUSIC
Koko p270
Lexington p275
02 Academy Brixton p271
02 Arena p271
Roundhouse p271

JAZZ
Charlie Wright's International Bar p276
Ronnie Scott's p276

DIVE VENUES
12 Bar Club p272
100 Club p272
Nest p275
Shacklewell Arms p275
Windmill p275

FOLK & COUNTRY
Borderline p274
Cecil Sharp House p274
Union Chapel p275

EXPERIMENTAL EDGE
Café Oto p276
Vortex p277

COMEDY
Comedy Store p279
Leicester Square Theatre p279

Arts & culture

FESTIVALS
Chinese New Year Festival p41
Greenwich & Docklands International Festival p35
London Film Festival p39
London Jazz Festival p40
Lord Mayor's Show p40
Notting Hill Carnival p37
Open House London p39

SPORT
Epsom Derby p33
Virgin London Marathon p33
Wimbledon Tennis Championships p35

PLAYS
Donmar Warehouse p289
National Theatre p285
Open Air Theatre p286
Royal Court Theatre p286
Shakespeare's Globe p286

ATMOSPHERIC THEATRICALS
Sam Wanamaker Playhouse p287
Wilton's Music Hall p292

LONG-RUNNING SHOWS
Billy Elliot the Musical p288
Matilda the Musical p288
War Horse p289

FILM
BFI Southbank p255
Phoenix p255
Prince Charles Cinema p256

OPERA & BALLET
English National Opera p282
The Place p292
Sadler's Wells p293
Royal Opera House p284

Explore

The South Bank & Bankside

An estimated 14 million people come this way each year, and it's easy to see why. Between the London Eye and Tower Bridge, the south bank of the Thames offers a two-mile procession of diverting, largely state-funded arts and entertainment venues and events.

The area's modern-day life began in 1951 with the Festival of Britain, staged to boost morale in the wake of World War II. The Royal Festival Hall stands testament to the inclusive spirit of the project; it was later expanded into the Southbank Centre, alongside BFI Southbank and the concrete ziggurat of the National Theatre. But the riverside really took off in the new millennium, with the arrival of the London Eye, Tate Modern, the Millennium Bridge and the expansion of Borough Market.

The Shard.

Don't Miss

1 The Shard A whole new angle on the city (p63).

2 Tate Modern Power station turned artistic powerhouse (p56).

3 Southbank Centre 1950s architecture for the arts (p50).

4 Borough Market Gourmet goodies (p62).

5 Imperial War Museum Conflict histories (p55).

EAT.

Hayward Gallery.

THE SOUTH BANK

Embankment or Westminster tube, or Waterloo tube/rail.

Thanks to the sharp turn the Thames makes around Waterloo, **Lambeth Bridge** lands you east of the river, not south, opposite the Tudor gatehouse of **Lambeth Palace**. Since the 12th century, it's been the official residence of the Archbishops of Canterbury. The palace is not normally open to the public, except on holidays. The church next door, St Mary at Lambeth, is now the **Garden Museum** (*see p51*).

The benches along the river here are great for viewing the Houses of Parliament opposite, before things get crowded after **Westminster Bridge**, where London's major riverside tourist zone begins. Next to the bridge is **County Hall**, once the seat of London government, currently home to the **Sea Life London Aquarium** (*see p54*) and the **London Dungeon** (*see p51*). In front of these attractions, in full view of the lovely **Jubilee Gardens**, the wheel of the **London Eye** (*see p51*) rotates serenely.

When the **Southbank Centre** (*see p282*) was built in the 1950s, the big concrete boxes that together contain the Royal Festival Hall (RFH), the Queen Elizabeth Hall (QEH) and the Purcell Room were hailed as a daring statement of modern architecture. Along with the Royal National Theatre and the Hayward, they comprise one of the largest and most popular arts centres in the world.

The centrepiece is Sir Leslie Martin's handsome **Royal Festival Hall** (1951), given a £91m overhaul in 2007. The main auditorium has had its acoustics enhanced and seating refurbished; the upper floors include an improved Poetry Library, and event rooms in which readings are delivered against the backdrop of the Eye and, on the far side of the river, Big Ben. Behind the hall, **Southbank Centre Square** hosts a food market every weekend, and there are cafés and chain restaurants all around.

Next door to the Royal Festival Hall, just across from the building housing the QEH and the Purcell Room, the **Hayward Gallery** (*see p51*) is a landmark of Brutalist architecture – all three venues are set to benefit from a proposed multi-million pound refurbishment. Tucked under Waterloo Bridge is **BFI Southbank** (*see p255*); the UK's premier arthouse cinema, it's run by the British Film Institute. At the front is a second-hand book market – fun, but not brilliant for real finds. Due to its relative height and location just where the Thames bends from north–south to east–west, **Waterloo Bridge** provides some of the finest views of London, especially at dusk. It was designed by Sir Giles Gilbert Scott, the man behind Tate Modern (*see p56*), in 1942.

East of the bridge is Denys Lasdun's terraced **National Theatre** (*see p285*), another Brutalist concrete structure, and one that still divides opinion like few other London buildings. Shaded by trees dotted with blue LEDs, the river path leads past a rare sandy patch of riverbed, busy with sand sculptors in warm weather, to **Gabriel's Wharf**, a collection of eateries, and small independent shops that range from stylish to kitsch.

Next door, the deco tower of **Oxo Tower Wharf** was designed to circumvent advertising regulations for the stock-cube company that used to own the building. Saved by local action group Coin Street Community Builders, it now provides affordable housing, interesting designer shops and galleries, and restaurants (including a rooftop restaurant and bistro with more wonderful views). Behind, **Bernie Spain Gardens** is great for a break from the crowds.

Sights & museums

Florence Nightingale Museum

St Thomas's Hospital, 2 Lambeth Palace Road, SE1 7EW (7620 0374, www.florence-nightingale.co.uk). Westminster tube or Waterloo tube/rail. **Open** 10am-5pm daily. **Admission** £5.80; £4.80 reductions; £16 family; free under-5s. **Map** p52 A4 ❶

The nursing skills and campaigning zeal that made Nightingale a Victorian legend are honoured here. Reopened after refurbishment for the centenary of her death in 2010, the museum is a chronological tour through a remarkable life under three key themes: family life, the Crimean War, health reformer. Among the period mementoes – clothing, furniture, books, letters and portraits – are Nightingale's lantern and stuffed pet owl, Athena.

Garden Museum

Lambeth Palace Road, SE1 7LB (7401 8865, www.gardenmuseum.org.uk). Lambeth North tube or Waterloo tube/rail. **Open** 10.30am-5pm Mon-Fri; 10.30am-4pm Sat. **Admission** £7.50; £3-£6.50 reductions; free under-16s. **Map** p52 A5 ❷

The world's first horticulture museum fits neatly into the old church of St Mary's. A 'belvedere' gallery (built from eco-friendly Eurban wood sheeting) contains the permanent collection of artworks, antique gardening tools and horticultural memorabilia, while the ground floor is used for interesting temporary exhibitions. In the small back garden, the replica of a 17th-century knot garden was created in honour of John Tradescant, intrepid plant hunter and gardener to Charles I; Tradescant is buried here. A stone sarcophagus contains the remains of William Bligh, the captain of the mutinous HMS *Bounty*.

London Eye.

Hayward Gallery

Southbank Centre, Belvedere Road, SE1 8XX, (0844 875 0073, www.southbankcentre.co.uk). Embankment tube or Waterloo tube/rail. **Open** noon-6pm Mon-Wed, Sat, Sun; 10am-8pm Thur, Fri. **Admission** varies; check website for details. **Map** p52 B2 ❸

This versatile gallery has no permanent collection, but runs a good programme of temporary exhibitions, with a particular taste for participatory installations: Antony Gormley's fog-filled chamber for 'Blind Light', a rooftop rowing boat for group show 'Psycho Buildings', a kind of informal university for the arts at the 'Wide Open School', even an exhibition that contained no art. Visitors can hang out in the industrial-look café downstairs (it's a bar at night), before visiting free contemporary exhibitions at the inspired Hayward Project Space; take the stairs to the first floor from the glass foyer extension, an elliptical pavilion designed in collaboration with light artist Dan Graham.

London Dungeon

County Hall, Westminster Bridge Road, SE1 7PB (0871 423 2240, www.thedungeons.com). Westminster tube or Waterloo tube/rail. **Open** *Term-time* 10am-5pm Mon-Wed, Fri; 11am-5pm Thur; 10am-6pm Sat, Sun. *School holidays* 10am-7pm Mon-Wed, Sat, Sun; 11am-7pm Thur. **Admission** £18.50-£25.20; £16.95-£19.80 reductions. **Map** p52 A3 ❹

This jokey celebration of torture, death and disease (book your tickets online to keep prices down) has reopened near the London Eye, having moved west along the river from Tooley Street. The attraction itself is much the same, with visitors led through a dry-ice fog past gravestones and hideously rotting corpses to experience the nastiest sides of the last 1,000 years of London history. Expect an actor-led medley of boils, projectile vomiting, worm-filled skulls and scuttling rats for the Black Death, gory skulduggery from the likes of Guy Fawkes and Jack the Ripper, and any number of unspeakable royals doing unspeakable things – Henry VIII prominent among them.

London Eye

Jubilee Gardens, SE1 7PB (0870 500 0600, www.londoneye.com). Westminster tube or Waterloo tube/rail. **Open** times vary; check website for details. **Admission** £19.95; £12.60-£17.96 reductions; free under-4s. **Map** p52 A3 ❺

Here only since 2000, the Eye is already up there with Tower Bridge and 'Big Ben' as one of the capital's most postcard-friendly tourist assets. Assuming you choose a clear day, a 30-minute circuit on the Eye

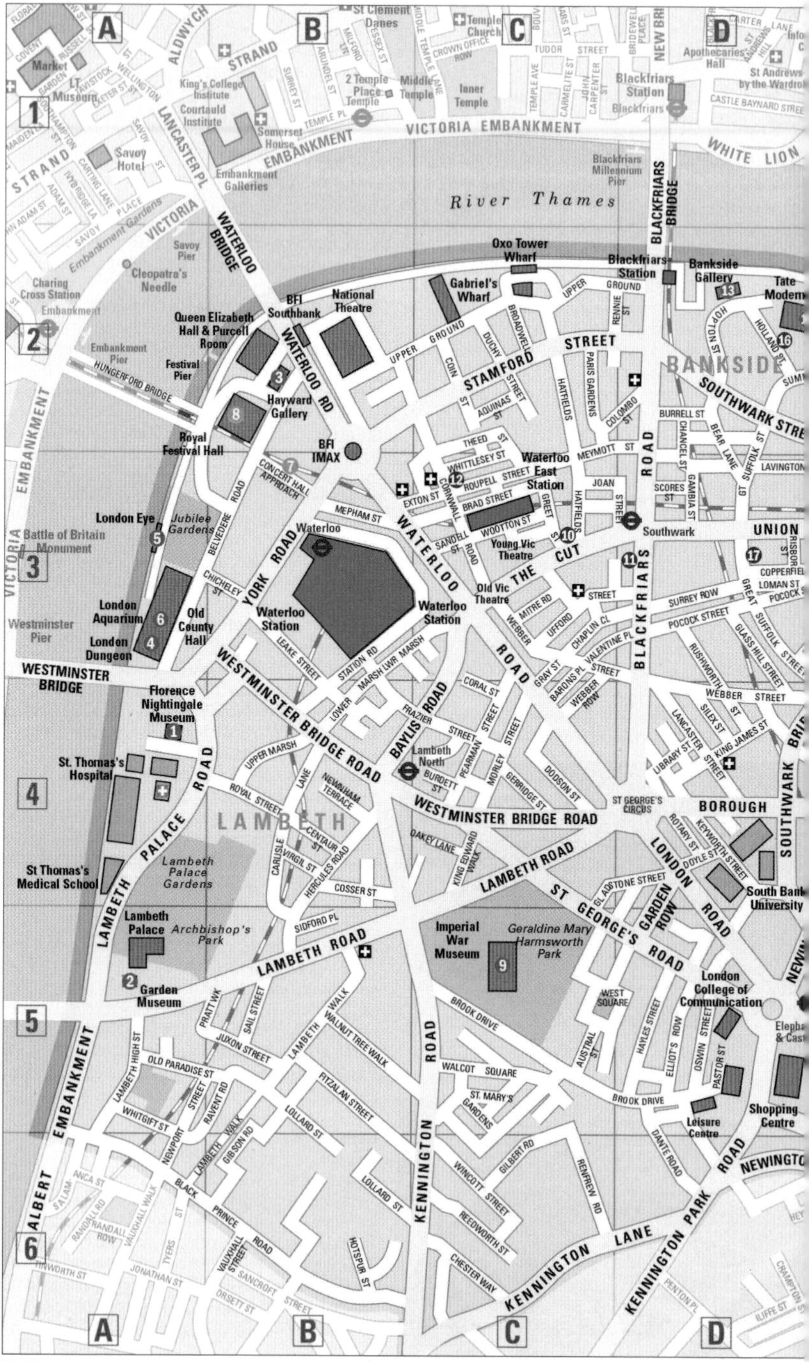
A
B
C
D
1
2
3
4
5
6
St Clement Danes
Temple Church
Apothecaries' Hall
St Andrews by the Wardrobe
Market
LT Museum
King's College Institute
Courtauld Institute
Somerset House
2 Temple Place
Middle Temple
Inner Temple
Blackfriars Station
Blackfriars
Savoy Hotel
Embankment Galleries
Blackfriars Millennium Pier
River Thames
Savoy Pier
Cleopatra's Needle
Charing Cross Station
Embankment
Embankment Pier
Oxo Tower Wharf
Gabriel's Wharf
Bankside Gallery
Tate Modern
BFI Southbank
National Theatre
Queen Elizabeth Hall & Purcell Room
Festival Pier
Hayward Gallery
Royal Festival Hall
BFI IMAX
BANKSIDE
Waterloo East Station
Southwark
London Eye
Jubilee Gardens
Battle of Britain Monument
Waterloo
Young Vic Theatre
Old Vic Theatre
London Aquarium
Old County Hall
Waterloo Station
Westminster Pier
London Dungeon
WESTMINSTER BRIDGE
Florence Nightingale Museum
St. Thomas's Hospital
Lambeth North
LAMBETH
BOROUGH
St Thomas's Medical School
Lambeth Palace Gardens
South Bank University
Lambeth Palace
Archbishop's Park
Imperial War Museum
Geraldine Mary Harmsworth Park
Garden Museum
London College of Communication
WEST SQUARE
Leisure Centre
Shopping Centre
STRAND
ALDWYCH
LANCASTER PL
WATERLOO BRIDGE
VICTORIA EMBANKMENT
BLACKFRIARS BRIDGE
UPPER GROUND
STAMFORD STREET
SOUTHWARK STREET
WATERLOO RD
YORK ROAD
BELVEDERE ROAD
THE CUT
BLACKFRIARS ROAD
UNION ST
WESTMINSTER BRIDGE ROAD
BAYLIS ROAD
LAMBETH PALACE ROAD
LAMBETH ROAD
ST GEORGE'S ROAD
LONDON ROAD
KENNINGTON ROAD
KENNINGTON LANE
KENNINGTON PARK ROAD
ALBERT EMBANKMENT
BLACK PRINCE ROAD
NEWINGTON

EXPLORE

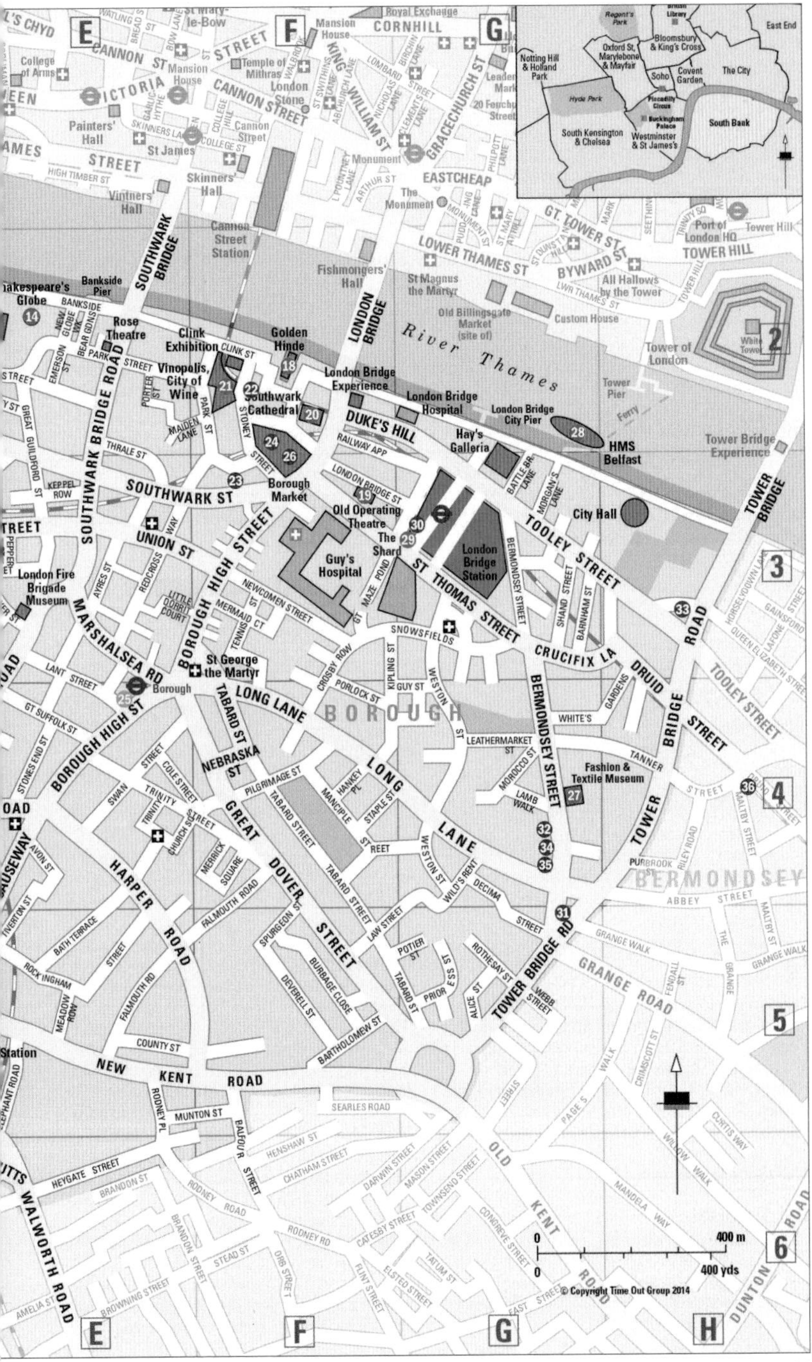

Royal Exchange
Mansion House
CORNHILL
CANNON ST
CANNON STREET
Temple of Mithras
London Stone
College of Arms
Painters' Hall
St James
Skinners' Hall
Vintners' Hall
Cannon Street Station
Cannon Street
HIGH TIMBER ST
KING WILLIAM ST
GRACECHURCH ST
Monument
EASTCHEAP
The Monument
LOWER THAMES ST
St Magnus the Martyr
Fishmongers' Hall
Old Billingsgate Market (site of)
Custom House
All Hallows by the Tower
BYWARD ST
GT. TOWER ST
Port of London HQ
Tower Hill
TOWER HILL
Tower of London
Tower Pier
Ferry
River Thames
SOUTHWARK BRIDGE
LONDON BRIDGE
Shakespeare's Globe
Bankside Pier
BANKSIDE
Rose Theatre
Clink Exhibition
CLINK ST
Golden Hinde
Vinopolis, City of Wine
Southwark Cathedral
London Bridge Experience
London Bridge Hospital
London Bridge City Pier
HMS Belfast
Hay's Galleria
DUKE'S HILL
RAILWAY APP
LONDON BRIDGE ST
Borough Market
Old Operating Theatre
The Shard
Guy's Hospital
London Bridge Station
City Hall
TOOLEY STREET
TOWER BRIDGE
Tower Bridge Experience
SOUTHWARK BRIDGE ROAD
SOUTHWARK ST
UNION ST
BOROUGH HIGH STREET
London Fire Brigade Museum
MARSHALSEA RD
St George the Martyr
Borough
ST THOMAS STREET
SNOWSFIELDS
CRUCIFIX LA
BERMONDSEY STREET
DRUID STREET
TOWER BRIDGE ROAD
LONG LANE
BOROUGH
TABARD ST
NEBRASKA ST
GREAT DOVER STREET
HARPER ROAD
Fashion & Textile Museum
LEATHERMARKET ST
TANNER STREET
BERMONDSEY
ABBEY STREET
GRANGE WALK
GRANGE ROAD
NEW KENT ROAD
Station
OLD KENT ROAD
WALWORTH ROAD
HEYGATE STREET
RODNEY ROAD
MANDELA WAY
Notting Hill & Holland Park
Oxford St, Marylebone & Mayfair
Bloomsbury & King's Cross
The City
East End
Soho
Covent Garden
South Kensington & Chelsea
Westminster & St James's
South Bank
Hyde Park
Regent's Park
0
400 m
400 yds
© Copyright Time Out Group 2014
E
F
G
H
2
3
4
5
6

EXPLORE

affords predictably great views of the city. Take a few snaps from the comfort of your pod and your sightseeing's done.

The London Eye was the vision of husband-and-wife architect team Julia Barfield and David Marks, who entered a 1992 competition to design a structure for the millennium. The Marks' giant wheel idea came second in the contest; the winning entry is conspicuous by its absence. The Eye was planned as a temporary structure but its removal now seems unthinkable. Indeed, the wheel's popularity is such that owner Merlin Entertainments has seen fit to future-proof its investment with a three-year, £12.5m renovation programme. Much of the work concerned reducing the Eye's carbon footprint, but each of the wheel's 32 pods (one for every London borough) now has a touchscreen to guide you around the vista.

Sea Life London Aquarium

County Hall, Westminster Bridge Road, SE1 7PB (0871 663 1678, tours 7967 8007, www.sealife.co.uk). Westminster tube or Waterloo tube/rail. **Open** *term time* 10am-7pm daily; *school holidays* 10am-8pm daily. **Admission** £21.60; £15.90 reductions; £75 family; free under-3s. **Map** p52 A3 ❻

This is one of Europe's largest aquariums and a huge hit with kids. The inhabitants are grouped by geographical origin, beginning with the Atlantic, where blacktail bream swim alongside the Thames Embankment. The 'Rainforests of the World' exhibit has introduced poison arrow frogs, crocodiles and piranhas. The Ray Lagoon is still popular, though touching the friendly flatfish is no longer allowed (it's bad for their health). Starfish, crabs and anenomes can be handled in special open rock pools instead, and the clown fish still draw crowds. There's a mesmerising Seahorse Temple, a tank full of turtles and enchanting Gentoo peguins. The centrepieces, though, are the massive Pacific and Indian Ocean tanks, with menacing sharks quietly circling fallen Easter Island statues.

Restaurants

Around the Royal Festival Hall you'll find plenty of chain restaurants (including Canteen, Feng Sushi, Giraffe, Pizza Express, Wahaca and Wagamama), as well as crêpe and pizza restaurants in Gabriel's Wharf along the bank to the east. **Skylon** (*see right*) has a grill and restaurant serving smart, seasonal British food.

Pubs & bars

Bar Topolski

150-152 Hungerford Arches, Concert Hall Approach, SE1 8XU (7620 0627, www.bartopolski.co.uk). Waterloo tube/rail. **Open** 11am-11pm Mon-Wed; 11am-midnight Thur; 11am-1am Fri, Sat. **Map** p52 B3 ❼

The former Topolski Century, an extensive mural by Polish-born artist Feliks Topolski depicting an extraordinary procession of 20th-century events and faces, has been turned into a bar-café. Occupying two capacious brick arches beneath Hungerford Bridge (some of Topolski's artworks are incorporated into the design), it serves cured meat, fish and cheese and other snacks, both savoury and sweet. There are assorted musical entertainments too.

Skylon

Royal Festival Hall, Belvedere Road, SE1 8XX (7654 7800, www.skylon-restaurant.co.uk). Waterloo tube/rail. **Open** noon-1am Mon-Sat; noon-10.30pm Sun. *Food served* noon-11pm Mon-Sat; noon-10.30pm Sun. **Map** p52 B2 ❽

There can't be many better river views in town – certainly for transport geeks. Sit at the cocktail bar (between the two restaurant areas), and gaze at trains trundling out of Charing Cross, cars and buses whizzing across Waterloo Bridge, and boats and cruisers pootling along the Thames. Drinks aren't cheap, but they're well made, and you're nicely insulated from the madness of the riverbank crowds.

WATERLOO & LAMBETH

Waterloo tube/rail or Lambeth North tube.

Surprisingly, perhaps, there's plenty of interest around the stone-meets-glass rail terminus of London Waterloo. The most obvious attraction is the massive **BFI IMAX** (*see p256*), located in the middle of a roundabout at the southern end of Waterloo Bridge. The £20m cinema makes imaginative use of a desolate space that, in the 1990s, was notorious for its 'Cardboard City' population of homeless residents.

South, on the corner of Waterloo Road and the Cut, is the restored Victorian façade of the **Old Vic** theatre (*see p286*), which will continue to be overseen by Kevin Spacey until 2015. Further down the Cut is the renovated home of the **Young Vic** (*see p292*), a hotbed of theatrical talent with a stylish balcony bar. Both bring a touch of West End glamour across the river. To the north of the Cut, off Cornwall Road, are a number of atmospheric terraces made up of mid 19th-century artisans' houses.

Further south, into Lambeth, is the impressive – and steadily revamped – **Imperial War Museum** (*see p55*). The imposing premises were built in 1814 as a lunatic asylum (the Bethlehem Royal Hospital, aka Bedlam). After »the inmates were moved out in 1930, the central block became the war museum, only to be damaged by World War II air raids. Today, it provides a compelling, frequently hard-hitting history of armed conflict since World War I, as well as many excellent, long-running temporary exhibitions that are suitable for children.

Imperial War Museum.

Sights & museums

★ FREE Imperial War Museum

Lambeth Road, SE1 6HZ (7416 5000, www.iwm.org.uk). Lambeth North tube or Elephant & Castle tube/rail. **Open** 10am-6pm daily. **Admission** free. *Special exhibitions* prices vary. **Map** p52 C5 ❾

Another of London's great museums, IWM London has decided on a major refit – by Foster & Partners architects – in time for the 2014 centenary of World War I. When it reopens, in July 2014, the Central Hall will still be the attention-grabbing repository of major artefacts: guns, tanks and aircraft hung from the ceiling (not least a Harrier GR9 that saw action in Afghanistan). Terraced galleries will allow this section of the museum also to show a Snatch Land Rover from Iraq and an Argentine operating table from the Falklands. The already extensive World War I gallery will be expanded, then you head into the original displays for World War II.

The museum's tone darkens as you ascend. On the third floor, the Holocaust Exhibition (not recommended for under-14s) traces the history of European anti-Semitism and its nadir in the concentration camps. Upstairs, Crimes Against Humanity (unsuitable for under-16s) is a minimalist space in which a film exploring contemporary genocide and ethnic violence rolls relentlessly. At the top will be a new gallery exploring contemporary conflicts.

Restaurants

Anchor & Hope

36 The Cut, SE1 8LP (7928 9898). Southwark tube or Waterloo tube/rail. **Open** 5-11pm Mon; 11am-11pm Tue-Sat; 12.30-5pm Sun. *Food served* 6-10.30pm Mon; noon-2.30pm, 6-10.30pm Tue-Sat. **Main courses** £12-£22. **Map** p52 C3 ❿ **Gastropub**

Open for more than a decade, the Anchor & Hope is still a leading exponent of head-to-tail ingredients in simple but artful combinations, served in a relaxed setting. Bookings aren't taken, so most evenings you join the waiting list for a table (45 minutes midweek is typical) and hover at the crammed bar enjoying a glass of wine or a pint. The food is terrific: beautifully textured venison kofte, say, served on perkily dressed little gem lettuce leaves, or rabbit served savagely red, with salty jus, fat chips and a big pot of béarnaise.

Baltic

74 Blackfriars Road, SE1 8HA (7928 1111, www.balticrestaurant.co.uk). Southwark tube. **Open** 5.30-11.15pm Mon; noon-3pm, 5.30-11.15pm Tue-Sat; noon-4.30pm, 5.30-10pm Sun. **Main courses** £9-£18.50. **Map** p52 D3 ⓫ **Eastern European**

A modern take on Polish/central European classics is served in surroundings of understated glamour, with pared-down monochrome decor punctuated by a supersized chandelier dripping shards of golden amber. You'll struggle to find elsewhere such enjoyable buckwheat blinis topped with smoked salmon or tender herring. Home-style pleasures abound, such as rabbit braised in a fragrant broth flavoured with sweet prune and smoky bacon, served with little knobbly spaetzle dumplings. Start with a classy clear vodka like Zytnia (rye), then move on to one of Baltic's own tasty ginger or spicy orange varieties.

Shops & services

Konditor & Cook

22 Cornwall Road, Waterloo, SE1 8TW (7633 3333, www.konditorandcook.com). Waterloo tube/rail. **Open** 7.30am-6.30pm Mon-Wed; 7.30am-7pm Thur, Fri; 8.30am-7pm Sat; 10am-4.30pm Sun. **Map** p52 C3 ⓬ **Food & drink**

Gerhard Jenne caused a stir when he opened this bakery on a South Bank side street in 1993, selling gingerbread people for grown-ups and lavender-flavoured cakes. Success lay in lively ideas such as cakes that spell the recipient's name in a series of individually decorated squares. Quality pre-packed salads and sandwiches are also sold.
Other locations throughout the city.

BANKSIDE

Borough or Southwark tube, or Blackfriars or London Bridge tube/rail.

In Shakespeare's day, the area known as Bankside was the centre of bawdy Southwark, neatly located just beyond the jurisdiction of the City fathers. As well as playhouses such as the Globe and the Rose, there were the famous 'stewes' (brothels) presided over by the Bishops of Winchester, who made a tidy income from the fines they levied on the area's 'Winchester Geese' (or, in common parlance, prostitutes). There's less drinking, carousing and mischief-making here these days, but the area's cultural heritage remains alive thanks to the reconstructed **Shakespeare's Globe** and, pretty much next door to it, **Tate Modern** (for both, *see below*), a former power station that's now a gallery.

Spanning the river in front of the Tate, the **Millennium Bridge** for pedestrians opened in 2000, when it became the first new Thames crossing in London since Tower Bridge (1894). Its early days were fraught with troubles; after just two days, the bridge was closed because of a pronounced wobble, and didn't reopen until 2002. Its troubles long behind it, the bridge is an elegant structure; a 'ribbon of steel' in the words of its conceptualists, architect Lord Foster and sculptor Anthony Caro. Cross it and you're at the foot of the stairs leading up to St Paul's Cathedral (*see p176*); to its left, the massively refurbished Blackfriars rail station not only has a brand-new entrance on the south bank of the river, but runs train platforms right across the river on the podiums of an earlier, incomplete version of **Blackfriars Bridge** (*see p173* **In the Know**).

Sights & museums

FREE Bankside Gallery

48 Hopton Street, SE1 9JH (7928 7521, www.banksidegallery.com). Blackfriars tube/rail or Southwark tube. **Open** 11am-6pm daily (during exhibitions). **Admission** free; donations appreciated. **Map** p52 D2 ⑬

In the shadow of Tate Modern, this tiny gallery is the home of the Royal Watercolour Society and the Royal Society of Painter-Printmakers. The gallery runs a frequently changing programme of delightful print and watercolour exhibitions throughout the year; many of the works on show are for sale. Both societies hold frequent events here, including talks and demonstrations.

★ Shakespeare's Globe

21 New Globe Walk, SE1 9DT (7401 9919, www.shakespearesglobe.com). Blackfriars tube/rail or Southwark tube. **Open** *Exhibition* Feb-Oct 9am-5.30pm daily; Nov-Jan 10am-5.30pm daily. *Globe Theatre tours* daily, *Rose Theatre tours* Mar-Oct, check website for details. **Admission** £13.50; £8-£12 reductions; £36 family; free under-5s. **Map** p53 E2 ⑭

The original Globe Theatre, where many of William Shakespeare's plays were first staged and which he co-owned, burned to the ground in 1613 during a performance of *Henry VIII*. Nearly 400 years later, it was rebuilt not far from its original site, using construction methods and materials as close to the originals as possible, and it is now open to the public for tours throughout the year (allow 90 minutes for the visit). During matinées, the tours go to the site of the Rose (21 New Globe Walk, SE1 9DT, 7261 9565, www.rosetheatre.org.uk), built by Philip Henslowe in 1587 as the first theatre on Bankside; red lights show the position of the original theatre. Funds are being sought to continue excavations and preserve the site.

Under the adventurous artistic directorship of Dominic Dromgoole, the Globe is also a fully operational theatre. From 23 April, conventionally regarded as the bard's birthday, into early October, Shakespeare's plays and the odd new drama are performed in the open air. Year-round performances can also be seen in the new 350-seater indoor theatre, the Sam Wanamaker Playhouse (*see p287* **Theatre by Candlelight**), which opened in January 2014.

▶ *We've also included a Shakespeare-themed walk, see p58.*

★ FREE Tate Modern

Bankside, SE1 9TG (7887 8888, www.tate.org.uk). Blackfriars tube/rail or Southwark tube. **Open** 10am-6pm Mon-Thur, Sun; 10am-10pm Fri, Sat. *Tours* 11am, noon, 2pm, 3pm daily. **Admission** free. *Temporary exhibitions* vary. **Map** p52 D2 ⑮

Thanks to its industrial architecture, this powerhouse of modern art is awe-inspiring even before you enter. Built after World War II as Bankside Power Station, it was designed by Sir Giles Gilbert Scott, architect of Battersea Power Station. The power station shut in 1981; nearly 20 years later, it opened as an art museum, and has enjoyed spectacular popularity ever since. The gallery attracts five million visitors a year to a building intended for half that number; the first

Tate Modern.

Shakespeare's Globe.

fruits of work on the immensely ambitious, £215m TM2 extension opened in 2012: the Tanks, so-called because they occupy vast, subterranean former oil tanks, stage performance and film art. As for the rest of the extension, a huge new origami structure, designed by Herzog & de Meuron (who were behind the original conversion), will gradually unfold above the Tanks until perhaps 2016, but the work won't interrupt normal service in the main galleries.

In the main galleries themselves, the original cavernous turbine hall will be used to jaw-dropping effect once again from 2015, when another series of sponsored installations begins. Beyond, the permanent collection draws from the Tate's collections of modern art (international works from 1900) and features heavy hitters such as Matisse, Rothko and Beuys – a genuinely world-class collection, expertly curated. There are vertiginous views down inside the building from outside the galleries, which group artworks according to movement (Surrealism, Minimalism, Post-war abstraction) rather than by theme.

► *The polka-dotted Tate-to-Tate boat zooms to Tate Britain (see p77) every 40 minutes, with a stop-off at the London Eye (see p51). Tickets are available at both Tates, on board, online or by phone (7887 8888; £6.50, £2.15-£5.85 reductions).*

Restaurants

There are some handy chain restaurants (Pizza Express, The Real Greek, Tas Pide) on the river near the Globe Theatre, plus more (Tsuru, Leon) behind Tate Modern on Canvey Street. **Tate Modern Café**: **Level 2** (*see p249*) is good for those with children.

Albion Neo Bankside

Pavilion B, Holland Street, SE1 9FU (7827 4343, www.albioncafes.com). Southwark tube. **Open** 8am-11pm Mon-Sat; 9am-10.30pm Sun. **Main courses** £5.50-£13.50. **Map** p52 D2 ⑯ **British**

This glass-walled eaterie just behind Tate Modern is the second of Terence Conran's poshed-up British cafés. A secluded outdoor terrace overlooks a beautifully landscaped garden of mature silver birches – perfect for summer dining. Breakfast runs from toast and Marmite to a full English or kedgeree. Later on, the menu expands to include fish and chips, pies, bread and butter pudding and afternoon teas. *Photo p60.*

Union Street Café

47-51 Great Suffolk Street, SE1 0BS (7592 7977, www.gordonramsay.com). Southwark tube. **Open** *Restaurant* noon-3pm, 6-11pm Mon-Fri; noon-4pm, 6-10.30pm Sat, Sun. *Bar* 5pm-midnight Mon-Thur, Sat; 5pm-2am Fri; 5-10.30pm Sun. **Main courses** £11-£21. **Map** p52 D3 ⑰ **Italian**

A mish-mash of styles, with exposed ducts and wiring, but also parquet flooring and leather seats, greets diners at this addition to the Gordon Ramsey empire. The intentionally casual, smiling service and Italian style of the daily-changing menu can be undermined by meagre portion sizes: a 'secondi' octopus dish of two meaty tentacles perched on braised borlotti beans, or a soup bowl-sized seafood stew. Highlights might include a chocolate and peanut butter cake topped with vanilla ice-cream, with espresso poured over.

BOROUGH

Borough or Southwark tube, or London Bridge tube/rail.

On the east side of Blackfriars Bridge, you'll find the **Anchor Bankside** pub (34 Park Street, SE1 9EF, 7407 1577). Built in 1775 on the site of an even older inn, the Anchor has, at various points, been a brothel, a chapel and a ship's chandlers. The outside terrace, across the pathway, offers fine river views – a fact lost on no one each summer, when it's invariably crammed with people.

All that's left of the Palace of Winchester, home of successive bishops, is the ruined rose window of the Great Hall on Clink Street. It stands next to the site of the bishops' former Clink prison, where thieves, prostitutes and debtors all served their

WALK SHAKESPEARE'S LONDON

Follow in Will's footsteps.

The world's most famous playwright arrived in London in the 1580s – settling as a young jobbing actor in the rough but exciting new theatreland that was growing up east of the City – but he made his name as a playwright among the bearpits and prostitutes of the South Bank. These days, standing at London Bridge station in the shadow of the **Shard** (*see p63*), the towering emblem of modern London, it is hard to imagine the Elizabethan city, but traces do remain. Start towards the river, and imagine London Bridge was the only Thames crossing. Lined on both sides with shops and houses, it was then claustrophobically narrow and so traffic-choked that getting across could take over an hour.

Head over, and on reaching Monument tube station, turn left down Cannon Street. Behind an iron grate, in the wall of the WH Smith store, is the **London Stone** (*see p181*). The stone's symbolic importance was immortalised in *Henry VI, part II,* with Jack Cade proclaiming himself Lord Mayor while sat upon it.

Head north along St Swithin's Lane, passing the statue of Wellington atop his horse at Bank, and on to Threadneedle Street. Just off Bishopsgate (and next to the building site from which another London skyscraper, the Pinnacle, is due to emerge after numerous financial woes in 2017) is **St Helen's Bishopsgate** (*see p185*), the rather lovely church where Shakespeare would have worshipped.

Walk west along the busy London Wall, a road that traces the line of the City's former defences. Passing Moorgate turn left on to peaceful Coleman Street. Head west along Basinghall Avenue, becoming Aldermanbury. This will lead you to a bust of the Bard, in a small park, an eccentric monument that honours the publishers of the First Folio in 1623 – the first important collection of Shakespeare's plays. Follow the aptly named Love Lane, where prostitutes once plied their trade, and head back towards London Wall. Turn left. On your way to the Museum of London, you'll pass the site of St Olave's, the church which stood opposite Shakespeare's house in the shadow of the city wall.

The **Museum of London** (*see p179*) holds the sign for the Boar's Head, the pub in which Prince Hal and Falstaff caroused under the watchful eye of Mistress Quickly, and is a wonderful social history of the city. Walking south from the museum down St Martin-le-Grand will lead you to **St Paul's Cathedral** (*see p176*). It isn't Wren's masterpiece that is of interest to us now – that wasn't completed until 1708, with a medieval cathedral of monstrous proportions (despite its fallen spire) on the site in Shakespeare's time. Instead, we're here to visit the courtyard, where London booksellers peddled the First Folio, an event commemorated by a small plaque.

Head down to the Thames. Just after the City Information Centre, venture a little way down Carter Lane. An inconspicuous plaque dated 1899 acknowledges the pub from which the only surviving letter to Shakespeare was written, by a certain Richard Quinney. The weighty matter at hand? A loan of 30 quid.

Return to the main path, head down to the river and cross Millennium Bridge. From the middle, look back and try to imagine the Old St Paul's as the major landmark of a low-rise city, then attempt the same historical trick with the river: gone is Blackfriars Bridge to the west; gone too are Southwark Bridge, the Cannon Street rail bridge and Tower Bridge.

On the far bank, turn left along the river to pass the modern **Globe** (*see p56*), a wonderful reconstruction of the famous theatre. Shortly after the Globe, set into the wall of the Real Greek restaurant, is the only surviving ferryman's seat, the perch of Tudor cabbies who paddled punters across the river to enjoy the entertainments of the South Bank. Turn into Bear Gardens, noting the name: this was the site of one of many popular bear-baiting arenas.

Turn left along Park Street and just a few steps will bring you to the site of the Globe's direct competitor, the **Rose Theatre** (tours 10am-5pm Sat). A little further along, the walls of the original Globe are marked in tiles along the floors, while informative boards help to reconstruct a picture of the scene. Heading east to the end of the street, veer left to go under the bridge and along Clink Street. Shakespeare was never an inmate of this prison, but is said to have visited an unhappy actor friend who had ended up 'in the clink'.

Following the walkway along past the beautiful reconstruction of the *Golden Hinde*, you emerge finally at **Southwark Cathedral** (*see p60*), the final resting place of Shakespeare's brother. Play pictionary at the stained-glass window depicting an impressive number of the plays, beneath which the bard reclines in an oddly come-hither fashion, quill in hand.

From here, head straight to London Bridge station. Or, if you're of Sir Toby Belch's cast of mind in *Twelfth Night* ('Dost thou think, because thou are virtuous, there shall be no more cakes and ale?'), turn right down Borough High Street to the **George Inn** (77 Borough High Street, SE1 1NH, 7407 2056) for a tankard. Shakespeare would likely have frequented this ancient establishment (many other actors did), and although the current building post-dates him, it is a fine example of a galleried coaching inn – the only one to remain in London.

Albion Neo Bankside. *See p57.*

sentences; it's now the **Clink Prison Museum** (1 Clink Street, SE1 9DG, 7403 0900, www.clink.co.uk). Around the corner is the entrance to the wine showcase **Vinopolis** (*see right*). At the other end of Clink Street, St Mary Overie's dock contains a terrific full-scale replica of Sir Francis Drake's ship, the **Golden Hinde** (*see right*).

The main landmark here is the Anglican **Southwark Cathedral** (*see right*), formerly St Saviour's and before that the monastic church of St Mary Overie. Shakespeare's brother Edmund was buried in the graveyard; there's a monument to the playwright inside. Just south of the cathedral is **Borough Market** (*see p62*), a busy covered food market dating from the 13th century, although with its new glass-fronted premises you'd hardly think so. There's still plenty of Victorian ironwork to enjoy. The market is wholesale only for most of the week, but hosts London's foodiest public food market on Thursdays, Fridays and Saturdays (when it gets very crowded). It's surrounded by good places to eat and drink. Not far away, the quaint **George** (77 Borough High Street, 7407 2056) is London's last surviving galleried coaching inn.

Fans of gore should head to the interesting and grisly **Old Operating Theatre, Museum & Herb Garret** (*see right*), with its body parts and surgical implements.

Sights & museums

Golden Hinde

Pickfords Wharf, Clink Street, SE1 9DG (7403 0123, www.goldenhinde.com). London Bridge tube/rail. **Open** 10am-5.30pm daily. **Admission** £6; £4.50 reductions; £18 family; free under-3s. **Map** p53 F2 18

This meticulous replica of Sir Francis Drake's 16th-century flagship is thoroughly seaworthy: the ship has even reprised the privateer's circumnavigatory voyage. You can visit by means of a self-guided tour, but if you've got kids it's much more fun to join in on a 'living history' experience (some overnight): participants dress in period clothes, eat Tudor fare and learn the skills of the Elizabethan seafarer; book well in advance. At weekends, the ship swarms with children dressed up as pirates for birthday dos.

★ Old Operating Theatre, Museum & Herb Garret

9A St Thomas's Street, SE1 9RY (7188 2679, www.thegarret.org.uk). London Bridge tube/rail. **Open** 10.30am-5pm daily. **Admission** £6.50; £3.50-£5 reductions; £13.90 family; free under-6s. **No credit cards. Map** p53 F3 19

The tower that houses this reminder of the surgical practices of the past used to be part of the chapel of St Thomas's Hospital. Before moving there, operations took place in the wards. Visitors enter via a vertiginous spiral staircase to inspect a pre-anaesthetic operating theatre dating from 1822, with tiered viewing seats for students. The operating tools look more like torture implements.

FREE Southwark Cathedral

London Bridge, SE1 9DA (7367 6700, www.cathedral.southwark.anglican.org). London Bridge tube/rail. **Open** 10am-5pm daily (closing times vary on religious holidays). *Services* 8am, 8.15am, 12.30pm, 12.45pm, 5.30pm Mon-Fri; 9am, 9.15am, 4pm Sat; 8.45am, 9am, 11am, 3pm, 6.30pm Sun. **Admission** free; suggested donation £4. **Map** p53 F2 20

The oldest bits of this building date back more than 800 years. The retro-choir was the setting for several Protestant martyr trials during the reign of Mary Tudor. Inside, there are memorials to Shakespeare, John Harvard (benefactor of the American university) and Sam Wanamaker (the force behind the reconstruction of the Globe); Chaucer features in the stained glass. There are displays throughout the cathedral explaining its history. The courtyard is one of the area's prettiest places for a rest; there's also a café.

Vinopolis

1 Bank End, SE1 9BU (7940 8300, www.vinopolis.co.uk). London Bridge tube/rail. **Open** 6-9.30pm Wed; 2-10pm Thur, Fri; noon-9.30pm Sat; 1-6pm Sun. **Admission** £27-£38. **Map** p53 F2 21

Glossy Vinopolis is more of an introduction to wine-tasting than a resource for cognoscenti, but you do need to have some prior interest to get a kick out of it. Participants are introduced to systematic wine tasting and then given a wine glass. Exhibits are organised by 'taste profile', with opportunities to taste wine or champagne from different regions in each category. Gin crashes the party courtesy of a Bombay Sapphire cocktail, and you can also sample Caribbean rum, whisky and beer.

Restaurants

Borough Market (*see p62*), full of stalls selling all kinds of wonderful food, is a good forage for gourmet snackers.

Elliot's

12 Stoney Street, SE1 9AD (7403 7436, www.elliotscafe.com). London Bridge tube/rail. **Open** 8am-10pm Mon-Sat. **Main courses** £12-£23. **Map** p53 F2 ㉒ **Brasserie**

Light and airy, with stripped brick walls and a contemporary feel, Elliot's is a busy little spot. Sit out front and watch the world go by, perch at the bar or take a seat in the bright back area. The seasonal menu is small but innovative, and carefully sourced. Smaller plates such as crab on toast or buffalo mozzarella and polenta are listed alongside larger plates such as lemon sole, wild garlic and fino. Drinks include a selection of natural wines (orange wines are listed alongside the expected white, red and rosé). *Photo p62.*

Gelateria 3bis

4 Park Street, SE1 9AB (7378 1977, www.gelateria3bis.it). London Bridge tube/rail. **Open** *Summer* 8am-10pm Mon-Sat; 10am-6pm Sun. *Winter* 8am-8pm Mon-Sat; 11am-6pm Sun. **Map** p53 F3 ㉓ **Ice-cream**

The menu at one of our favourite gelaterias encompasses frozen yoghurt, ice-cream cakes, brioches and crêpes, plus speciality coffees – but the real star is the gelato. It's made on the premises and the repertoire includes Italian classics as well as creative English innovations (eton mess, anyone?). Behind a green frontage, the bright, spacious dining room has full-length windows opening on to the pavement in summer.

Roast

Floral Hall, Borough Market, Stoney Street, SE1 1TL (3641 7958, www.roast-restaurant.com). London Bridge tube/rail. **Open** 7-11am, noon-3.45pm, 5.30-10.45pm Mon-Fri; 8.30-11.30am, noon-3.45pm, 5.30-10.45pm Sat; 11.30am-6.30pm Sun. **Main courses** £10-£37. **Map** p53 F2 ㉔ **British**

This formal operation (pianist, precise service, gleaming tableware on white cloths) contrasts with the jolly mayhem of Borough Market below. It's a very pleasant place for a long lunch or luxurious breakfast, and the roasts themselves are among the city's best. Free-range pork belly with apple sauce, Goosnargh chicken with bread sauce, or Blackface lamb with mint relish all appear. These are bracketed by sophisticated starters and grown-up versions of British puds.

Old Operating Theatre, Museum & Herb Garret.

Elliot's. *See p61.*

Pubs & bars

If top-quality beer is your priority when choosing a pub, then you're in luck: there's a superb range at the tiny **Rake** (14A Winchester Walk, SE1 9AG, 7407 0557), while the unflashy **Royal Oak** (44 Tabard Street, SE1 4JU, 7357 7173) is the only London pub run by estimable Sussex brewer Harveys.

Gladstone Arms

64 Lant Street, SE1 1QN (7407 3962, www.thegladpub.com). Borough tube. **Open** noon-11pm Mon-Thur; noon-midnight Fri; 1pm-midnight Sat; 1-10.30pm Sun. *Food served* noon-10pm Mon-Fri; 1-9pm Sat, Sun. **Map** p53 E4 25

While the Victorian prime minister glares from the massive mural on the outer wall, inside is funky, freaky and candlelit. Gigs (blues, folk, acoustic, five nights a week) take place at one end of a cosy space; opposite is the bar. Pies provide sustenance. Retro touches include an old-fashioned 'On Air' studio sign and a communist-style railway clock.

Shops & services

★ Borough Market

Southwark Street, SE1 (7407 1002, www.boroughmarket.org.uk). London Bridge tube/rail. **Open** 10am-5pm Wed, Thur; 10am-6pm Fri; 8am-5pm Sat. **No credit cards. Map** p53 F3 26 **Market**

The food hound's favourite market is also London's oldest, dating back to the 13th century. It's the busiest, too, occupying a sprawling site near London Bridge. Gourmet goodies run the gamut, from fresh loaves and rare-breed meats, via fish, game, fruit and veg, to cakes and all manner of preserves, oils and teas; head out hungry to take advantage of the numerous free samples. A rail viaduct, vigorously campaigned against, is now in place, which means restored historic features have been returned and works disruption should now be at an end. As if to celebrate, a new Market Hall, facing on to Borough High Street, has been opened: it acts as a kind of greenhouse for growing plants (including hops), as well as hosting workshops, tastings and foodie demonstrations. You can also nip in with your snack if the weather's poor.

► *Although the market's open on Monday and Tuesday, those days are mainly for tradespeople, with fewer stalls open. Given that weekends are usually mobbed, Wednesday and Thursday are usually the best days to visit.*

LONDON BRIDGE TO TOWER BRIDGE

Bermondsey tube or London Bridge tube/rail.

Nothing can compete with the colossal, 1,016-foot **Shard** development at London Bridge station (*see p63*) – it dominates the immediate area, and the London skyline for miles. Next to the Thames is **Hay's Galleria**. Once an enclosed dock, it's now dominated by a peculiar kinetic sculpture called *The Navigators*. Exiting on the riverside, you can walk east past the great grey hulk of **HMS Belfast** (*see p63*) to Tower Bridge. Beyond the battleship you pass the pristine environs of the **More London** complex – sold off to Kuwaiti investors in a £1.7bn property deal – part of which is **City Hall**, home of London's current government. There's a pleasant outside area called the Scoop, used for outdoor events, and a handful of chain cafés.

South of here, many of the historic houses on Bermondsey Street now host hip design studios or funky shops. This is also where you'll find the **Fashion & Textile Museum** (*see p63*), as well as the largest and newest of Jay Jopling's **White Cube** art galleries (nos.144-152, 7930 5373, www.whitecube.com; closed Mon). At the street's furthest end, the redevelopment of Bermondsey Square created an arthouse cinema and the Bermondsey Square Hotel, alongside a charming cemetery park, but old-timers linger on: the classic

IN THE KNOW ABOVE IT ALL

The **Rooftop Café** (The Exchange, 28 London Bridge Street, SE1 9SG, 3102 3770, www.theexchange.so/rooftop) is a friendly modern café with Mediterranean-slanted food and great views.

eel and pie shop **M Manze** and a Friday antique market (6am-2pm) – great for browsing, but get there early if you want to find a bargain.

If the Borough Market (*see p62*) crowds are too much on a Saturday, there is a winning cluster of food stalls around **Maltby Street** (*see p65*), **Druid Street** and nearby **Spa Terminus** and on the redeveloped **Ropewalk**.

Back on the riverfront, a board announces when **Tower Bridge** is next due to be raised. The bridge is one of the lowest to span the Thames, hence its twin lifting sections or bascules. The original steam-driven machinery can be seen at the **Tower Bridge Exhibition** (*see p186*). Further east, the former warehouses of **Butler's Wharf** are now mainly given over to expensive riverside dining; one of them currently houses the **Design Museum** (Shad Thames, SE1 2YD, 7403 6933, www.designmuseum.org; £12.40, free-£9.30 reductions), which will move to grand premises in Kensington in 2015 (*see p224* **Designs on Kensington**).

Sights & museums

Fashion & Textile Museum

83 Bermondsey Street, SE1 3XF (7407 8664, www.ftmlondon.org). London Bridge tube/rail. **Open** 11am-6pm Tue-Sat. **Admission** £8.80; £4.40-£6.60 reductions; free under-12s. **Map** p53 G4 27

As flamboyant as its founder, fashion designer Zandra Rhodes, this pink and orange museum holds 3,000 of Rhodes's garments and her archive of paper designs, sketchbooks, silk screens and show videos. Temporary shows explore the work of trend-setters or themes such as the development of underwear. A quirky shop sells ware by new designers.

HMS Belfast

Morgan's Lane, Tooley Street, SE1 2JH (7940 6300, www.iwm.org.uk). London Bridge tube/rail. **Open** *Mar-Oct* 10am-6pm daily. *Nov-Feb* 10am-5pm daily. **Admission** £15.50; £12.40 reductions; free under-16s (must be accompanied by an adult). **Map** p53 G2 28

This 11,500-ton 'Edinburgh' class large light cruiser is the last surviving big-gun World War II warship in Europe. It's also a floating branch of the Imperial War Museum, and is a popular if unlikely playground for children, who tear around its complex of gun turrets, bridge, decks and engine room. The *Belfast* was built in 1938, ran convoys to Russia, supported the Normandy Landings and helped UN forces in Korea before being decommissioned in 1965.

★ Shard

32 London Bridge Street, SE1 9SS (0844 499 7111, www.theviewfromtheshard.com). London Bridge tube/rail. **Open** 10am-8.30pm daily. **Admission** £24.95; £18.95 reductions; free under-4s. **Map** p53 G3 29

You can't miss the Shard – which is, after all, the point of the structure. It shoots into the sky 'like a shard of glass' – to use the words of its architect, Renzo Piano. Already by 2010, when the building was still a skeleton, it had overtaken One Canada Square ('Canary Wharf', *see p240*) as London's tallest building. And it kept going: in 2011, it became the tallest building in the EU, but even then

City Hall & Shard.

had still to reach its full height. Finally, in 2012, when its 217-foot, 500-tonne spire was winched into place, it topped out at 1,016 feet. As is the fate of skyscrapers, the Shard's claims to be the tallest are relative: it's beaten in Moscow, the Arab Emirates and across South-east Asia. But this slim, slightly irregular pyramid is the centrepiece of views from right across London – except, ironically, from in those Victorian alleys at its foot, where the monstrous building plays peek-a-boo with visitors as they scurry around looking for a good snapshot. High-speed lifts whisk passengers up to stunning 360-degree, 40-mile views, but the real joy of a visit is looking down: even seasoned London-watchers find peering down on the likes of the Tower of London (*see p186*) from this height oddly revelatory.

► *There are no toilets or refreshments on the viewing platforms – if you plan to take your time up there, be prepared.*

Restaurants

Hutong

Level 33, The Shard, 31 St Thomas Street, SE1 9RY (7478 0540, www.hutong.co.uk). London Bridge tube/rail. **Open** noon-3pm, 6-11pm daily. **Dishes** £8-£58. **Map** p53 G3 ㉚ **Chinese**

The original Hutong in Hong Kong is a glitzy restaurant with magnificent views. This branch, halfway up the Shard, is exactly the same. The same Sichuanese and northern Chinese menu, the same mix of plate glass and ersatz Old Beijing decor. Prices are high: but then this is the Shard, not Chinatown. A great place to impress a date.

M Manze

87 Tower Bridge Road, SE1 4TW (7407 2985, www.manze.co.uk). Bus 1, 42, 188. **Open** 11am-2pm Mon; 10.30am-2pm Tue-Thur;

MARKET UP

Faced by an upstart neighbour, Borough spruces itself up.

Back in the noughties, when TV chef Jamie Oliver was zooming around it on his scooter, Borough Market (*see p62*) became a destination. The arrival of stalls of carefully sourced produce and lovingly made snacks, frequently sold by their producers – knowledgeable, enthusiastic and generous with the tasting samples – meant that the ancient market was suddenly quite the thing. Word spread, and it was soon a fixture on the tourist route. But, within a few years, there were growing complaints (not without reason) about crowds and rising prices. Then some wholesalers in the arches around Maltby Street (*see p65*) started selling to the public, which encouraged other producers to join them from Borough, and suddenly all the cachet had shifted a few blocks east.

Borough wasn't standing still, however. In summer 2013, its trading hours were significantly increased. There was also a fancy new bit of frontage, the Market Hall – the opening of which was also a neat full-stop to the disruption that had been caused to the market by Thameslink. But, in truth, the recent history of the market has been one of constant change: that Victorian portico, for instance, that looks so at home beside Roast? It came from the Floral Hall of Covent Garden Market in 2004. So it's evolution, not revolution here – and that includes extending a welcome to Maltby Street. After all, two foodie destinations are surely better than one.

EXPLORE

10am-2.30pm Fri; 10am-2.45pm Sat. **Main courses** £2.75-£5.20. **Map** p53 G5 ㉛ **Pie & mash**
One of the few remaining purveyors of the dirt-cheap traditional foodstuff of London's working classes. It's the oldest pie shop in town, established in 1902, with tiles, marble-topped tables and wooden benches – and is almost as beautiful as L Manze's on Walthamstow High Street, now Grade II listed. Orders are simple: minced beef pies or, for braver souls, stewed eels with mashed potato and liquor (a thin parsley sauce).

Pizarro
194 Bermondsey Street, SE1 3TQ (7378 9455, www.pizarrorestaurant.com). Borough tube or London Bridge tube/rail. **Open** noon-3pm, 6-11pm Mon-Fri; noon-11pm Sat; 10am-10pm Sun. **Main courses** £12-£18. **Map** p53 G4 ㉜ **Spanish**
José Pizarro's restaurant continues in the style set in his tapas bar, José, up the street (no.104, SE1 3UB, 7403 4902, http://joserestaurant.co.uk). Menus are more extensive than at the tapas-only José, a selection of mostly traditional dishes prepared with care and skill, and fine ingredients, including an expertly slow-braised beef stew. The space artfully combines old-Spanish touches – tiles, warm wood, exposed brick – with a stripped-down New Bermondsey look.

Restaurant Story
201 Tooley Street, SE1 2UE (7183 2117, www.restaurantstory.co.uk). London Bridge tube/rail. **Open** noon-2pm, 6.30-9.30pm Tue-Sat. **Set meal** £55 6 courses, £75 10 courses. **Map** p53 H3 ㉝ **British**
Story, from starry young chef Tom Sellers, continues this area's rise to foodie haven, securing a Michelin star within months of opening. It's set in a sparse room – all the better to emphasise the view of the Shard through floor-to-ceiling windows, and, of course, the food: an enjoyable procession of modernist dishes layered with culinary puns (bread and dripping, for instance, features a lit candle made from dripping) and tastebud challenges (mackerel versus green strawberries). Fruit appears in many guises throughout the meal, and savoury notes characterise the puddings.
► *As with many of London's coolest restaurants, you'll need to book far ahead: a month's notice at time of writing.*

Zucca
184 Bermondsey Street, SE1 3TQ (7378 6809, www.zuccalondon.com). Bermondsey tube or London Bridge tube/rail. **Open** noon-3pm, 6-10pm Tue-Fri; noon-3.30pm, 6-10pm Sat; noon-4pm Sun. **Main courses** £14-£18. **Map** p53 G4 ㉞ **Italian**
The sleek interior and light streaming in through the floor-to-ceiling windows lend a sophisticated Sydney vibe to Zucca. Own-made breads might be followed by burrata with broad beans in a garlicky dressing, or spider crab served prettily in its shell. The own-made pasta is superb, served with sauces such as a sweetly earthy combination of lentils, walnuts and basil.

Maltby Street.

Pubs & bars

There's a branch of gastropub **Draft House** (206-208 Tower Bridge Road, SE1 2UP, 7924 1814, www.drafthouse.co.uk), at the south side of Tower Bridge.

Shops & services

Bermondsey Square Antiques Market
Corner of Bermondsey Street & Long Lane, SE1. Borough tube or London Bridge tube/rail. **Open** 4am-1pm Fri. **No credit cards. Map** p53 G4 ㉟ **Market**
Following the redevelopment of Bermondsey Square, the antiques market – which started in 1855 in north London – continues in an expanded space that now accommodates 200 stalls. Traditionally good for china and silverware, as well as furniture and glassware, there are now also food, fashion and crafts stalls. It's famous for being the spot where, back in the day, thieves could sell their goods with impunity: it's half car boot sale, half chic Parisian fleamarket. Get there early – lunchtime arrivals will be disappoingted to find grouchy antiques sellers (well, they did start work at 4am) packing up.

Maltby Street
Maltby Street, Druid Street, Spa Terminus, Ropewalk, SE1 (www.maltby.st). Bermondsey or Southwark tube. **Map** p53 H4 ㊱ **Food & drink**
Borough Market's trade has been challenged by former stallholders who have set up camp under the railway arches around Maltby Street and further south. Head here for delicious raclette from Kappacasein (Arch 1), craft beer from Kernel Brewery (Arch 12) and the city's finest custard doughnuts, courtesy of St John Bakery (Arch 72). Most producers are open on Saturday mornings (9am-2pm), some on Sundays too – the website www.spa-terminus.co.uk has a useful map showing locations and opening hours.

EXPLORE

Westminster & St James's

England is ruled from Westminster. The monarchy has been in residence here since the 11th century, when Edward the Confessor moved west from the City, and the government of the day also calls it home. It's a key destination for visitors as well, with the most significant area designated a UNESCO World Heritage Site back in 1987.

As well as being home to some of London's most impressive buildings, it's also an area packed with culture: Tate Britain, the National Gallery and the National Portrait Gallery are all here. For such an important part of London, it's surprisingly spacious. St James's Park is one of London's finest green spaces, Trafalgar Square is a tourist hotspot, and the Mall offers a properly regal route to Buckingham Palace.

St James's Park.

Don't Miss

1 St James's Park Central London's prettiest park, with great birdlife (p80).

2 National Gallery One masterpiece after another (p68).

3 Westminster Abbey Magnificent, sacred and packed with history (p76).

4 Tate Britain The original Tate, revamped (p77).

5 Fortnum & Mason The ultimate for traditional foodie souvenirs (p83).

TRAFALGAR SQUARE

Leicester Square tube or Charing Cross tube/rail.

Laid out in the 1820s by John Nash, Trafalgar Square is the heart of modern London. Tourists come in their thousands to pose for photographs in front of **Nelson's Column**. It was erected in 1840 to honour Vice Admiral Horatio Nelson, who died at the point of victory at the Battle of Trafalgar in 1805. The statue atop the 150-foot Corinthian column is foreshortened to appear in perfect proportion from the ground. The granite fountains were added in 1845; Sir Edwin Landseer's bronze lions joined them in 1867.

Once surrounded on all sides by busy roads, the square was improved markedly by pedestrianisation in 2003 of the North Terrace, right in front of the **National Gallery**. A ban on feeding pigeons was another positive step. The square feels more like public space now, and is a focus for performance and celebration.

Around the perimeter are three plinths bearing statues of George IV and two Victorian military heroes, Henry Havelock and Sir Charles James Napier. The long-empty fourth plinth, which never received its planned martial statue, has been used since 1998 to display temporary, contemporary art. Until spring 2015, Katharina Fritsch's *Hahn/Cock*, a larger-than-life cockerel in ultramarine blue, will stand there, to be replaced by an equine skeleton – *Gift Horse* by Hans Haacke – and then David Shrigley's huge thumbs-up *Really Good*. Other points of interest around the square include an equestrian statue of Charles I dating from the 1630s, with a plaque behind it that marks the original site of Edward I's Eleanor Cross, the official centre of London. (A recently renovated Victorian replica of the cross stands outside Charing Cross Station.) At the square's north-east corner is the refurbished **St Martin-in-the-Fields** (*see p69*).

Trafalgar Square.

IN THE KNOW
STAY OFF THE LIONS!

A scholarly report has found that 150 years of people climbing on their backs is wearing away the lions in **Trafalgar Square**. Bronze on the beasts' flanks and backs, which was originally 15mm thick, is now down to just 3mm in some areas. To make matters worse, deep gashes have been made by people gouging the statues with coins and keys.

★ FREE National Gallery

Trafalgar Square, WC2N 5DN (7747 2885, www.nationalgallery.org.uk). Charing Cross tube/rail. **Open** 10am-6pm Mon-Thur, Sat, Sun; 10am-9pm Fri. *Tours* 11.30am, 2.30pm Mon-Thur, Sat, Sun; 11.30am, 2.30pm, 7pm Fri. **Admission** free. *Special exhibitions* vary. **Map** p71 B5 ❶

Founded in 1824 to display 36 paintings, the National Gallery is now one of the world's great repositories for art. There are masterpieces from virtually every European school of art, from austere 13th-century religious paintings to the sensual delights of Caravaggio and Van Gogh.

Furthest to the left of the main entrance, the modern Sainsbury Wing extension contains the gallery's earliest works: Italian paintings by masters such as Giotto and Piero della Francesca, as well as the *Wilton Diptych*, the finest medieval English picture in the collection, showing Richard II with the Virgin and Child.

In the West Wing (left of the main entrance) are Italian Renaissance masterpieces by Correggio, Titian and Raphael. Straight ahead on entry, in the North Wing, are 17th-century Dutch, Flemish, Italian and Spanish Old Masters, including works such as Rembrandt's *A Woman Bathing in a Stream* and Caravaggio's *Supper at Emmaus*. Velázquez's *Rokeby Venus* is one of the artist's most famous paintings. Also in this wing are works by the great landscape artists Claude and Poussin. Turner insisted that his *Dido Building Carthage* and *Sun Rising through Vapour* should hang alongside two Claudes here that particularly inspired him.

In the East Wing are some of the gallery's most popular paintings: you'll find works by the French

National Gallery.

Impressionists and Post-Impressionists, including Monet's *Water-Lilies*, one of Van Gogh's *Sunflowers* and Seurat's *Bathers at Asnières*. Don't miss Renoir's astonishingly lovely *Les Parapluies*. You shouldn't plan to see everything in one visit, but free guided tours, audio guides and the superb Art Start computer (which allows you to tailor and map your own itinerary of must-sees) help you make the best of your time.

★ FREE National Portrait Gallery

St Martin's Place, WC2H 0HE (7306 0055, www.npg.org.uk). Leicester Square tube or Charing Cross tube/rail. **Open** 10am-6pm Mon-Wed, Sat, Sun; 10am-9pm Thur, Fri. **Admission** free. *Special exhibitions* vary. **Map** p71 A5 ❷
Portraits don't have to be stuffy. The excellent National Portrait Gallery has everything from oil paintings of stiff-backed royals to photographs of soccer stars and gloriously unflattering political caricatures. The portraits of musicians, scientists, artists, philanthropists and celebrities are arranged in chronological order from top to bottom.

At the top of the escalator up from the main foyer, on the second floor, are the earliest works, portraits of Tudor and Stuart royals and notables, including Holbein's 'cartoon' of Henry VIII and the 'Ditchley Portrait' of his daughter, Elizabeth I, her pearly slippers placed firmly on a colourful map of England. On the same floor, the 18th-century collection features Georgian writers and artists, with one room devoted to the influential Kit-Cat Club of bewigged Whig (leftish) intellectuals, Congreve and Dryden among them. More famous names include Wren and Swift. The second floor also shows Regency greats, military men such as Wellington and Nelson, plus Byron, Wordsworth and other Romantics. The first floor is devoted to the Victorians (Dickens, Brunel, Darwin) and to 20th-century luminaries, such as TS Eliot and Ian McKellen.

FREE St Martin-in-the-Fields

Trafalgar Square, WC2N 4JJ (7766 1100, www.smitf.org). Leicester Square tube or Charing Cross tube/rail. **Open** 8.30am-1pm, 2-6pm Mon, Tue, Thur, Fri; 8.30am-1pm, 2-5pm Wed; 9.30am-6pm Sat; 3.30-5pm Sun. *Brass Rubbing Centre* 10am-6pm Mon-Wed; 10am-8pm Thur-Sat; 11.30am-5pm Sun. **Admission** free. *Brass rubbing* £4.50. **Map** p71 B6 ❸
There's been a church 'in the fields' between Westminster and the City since the 13th century, but the current one was built in 1726 by James Gibbs, using a fusion of neoclassical and Baroque styles. The parish church for Buckingham Palace (note the royal box to the left of the gallery), St Martin's bright interior was fully restored a few years back, with Victorian furbelows removed and the addition of a brilliant altar window that shows the Cross, stylised as if rippling on water. Downstairs in the crypt are a fine café and the London Brass Rubbing Centre. *Photo p73.*
► *For details of the lunchtime and evening concerts here, see p282.*

IN THE KNOW GO FOR BUS

Trundling these streets since the 1950s, the Routemaster, London's original hop-on, hop-off double-decker bus, was finally retired in 2005. However, you can still experience the joy of the old on a 'heritage route'. Refurbished buses from the 1960-64 Routemaster fleet run on route 15 (from Trafalgar Square to Tower Hill, with glimpses of the Strand, Fleet Street and St Paul's Cathedral); head to stop F, to the east of Trafalgar Square. Buses run every 15 minutes from around 9.30am; fares match ordinary buses, but you must buy a ticket before boarding (*see p367*).

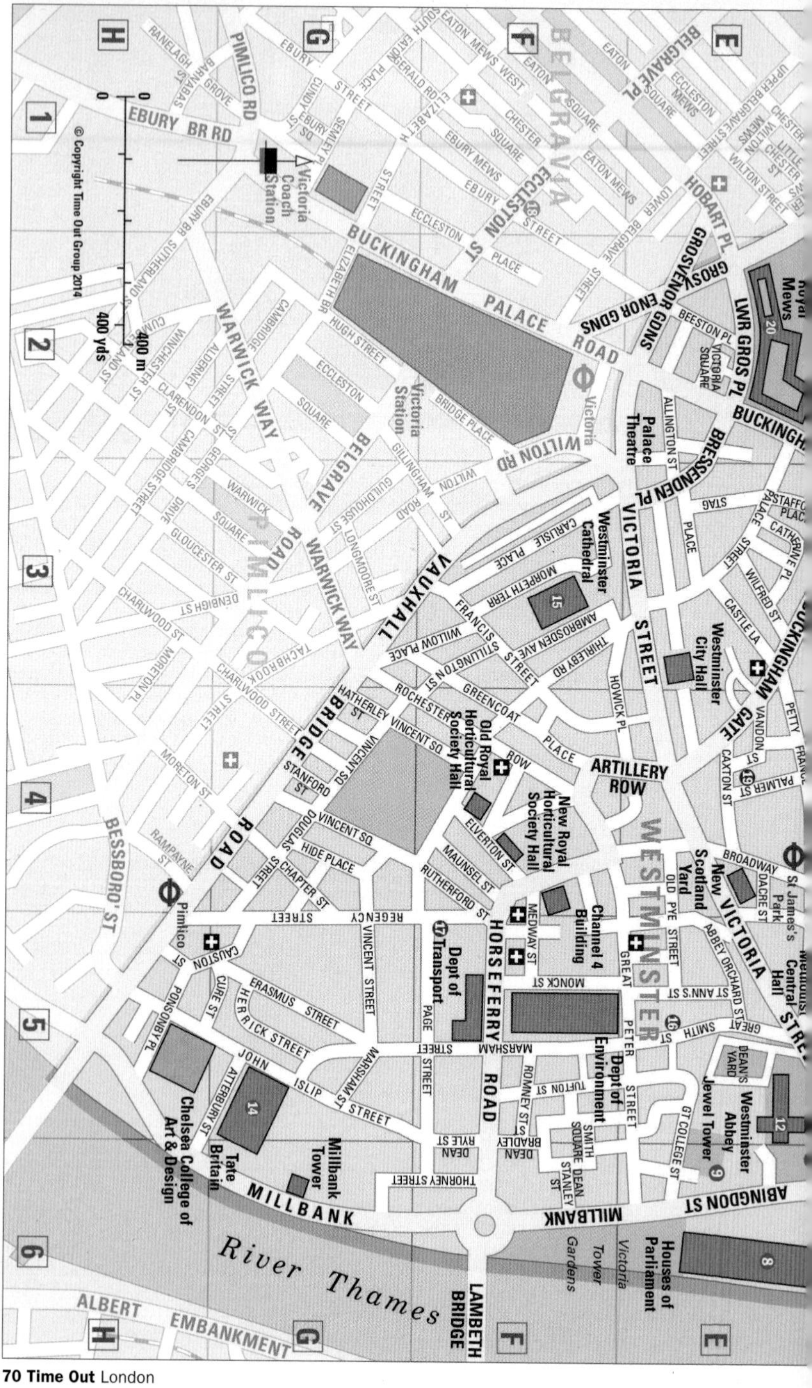
BELGRAVIA
PIMLICO
WESTMINSTER
River Thames
Victoria Coach Station
Victoria Station
Victoria
Pimlico
St James's Park
Westminster Cathedral
Westminster City Hall
Palace Theatre
Royal Mews
Old Royal Horticultural Society Hall
New Royal Horticultural Society Hall
New Scotland Yard
Methodist Central Hall
Channel 4 Building
Dept of Transport
Dept of Environment
Westminster Abbey
Jewel Tower
Houses of Parliament
Victoria Tower Gardens
Millbank Tower
Tate Britain
Chelsea College of Art & Design
LAMBETH BRIDGE
ALBERT EMBANKMENT
MILLBANK
BUCKINGHAM PALACE ROAD
VAUXHALL BRIDGE ROAD
VICTORIA STREET
HORSEFERRY ROAD
WARWICK WAY
BELGRAVE ROAD
ARTILLERY ROW
BUCKINGHAM GATE
EBURY BR RD
PIMLICO RD
WILTON RD
BRESSENDEN PL
ECCLESTON ST
GROSVENOR GDNS
LWR GROS PL
BESSBORO' ST
ABINGDON ST
400 m
400 yds
© Copyright Time Out Group 2014

EXPLORE

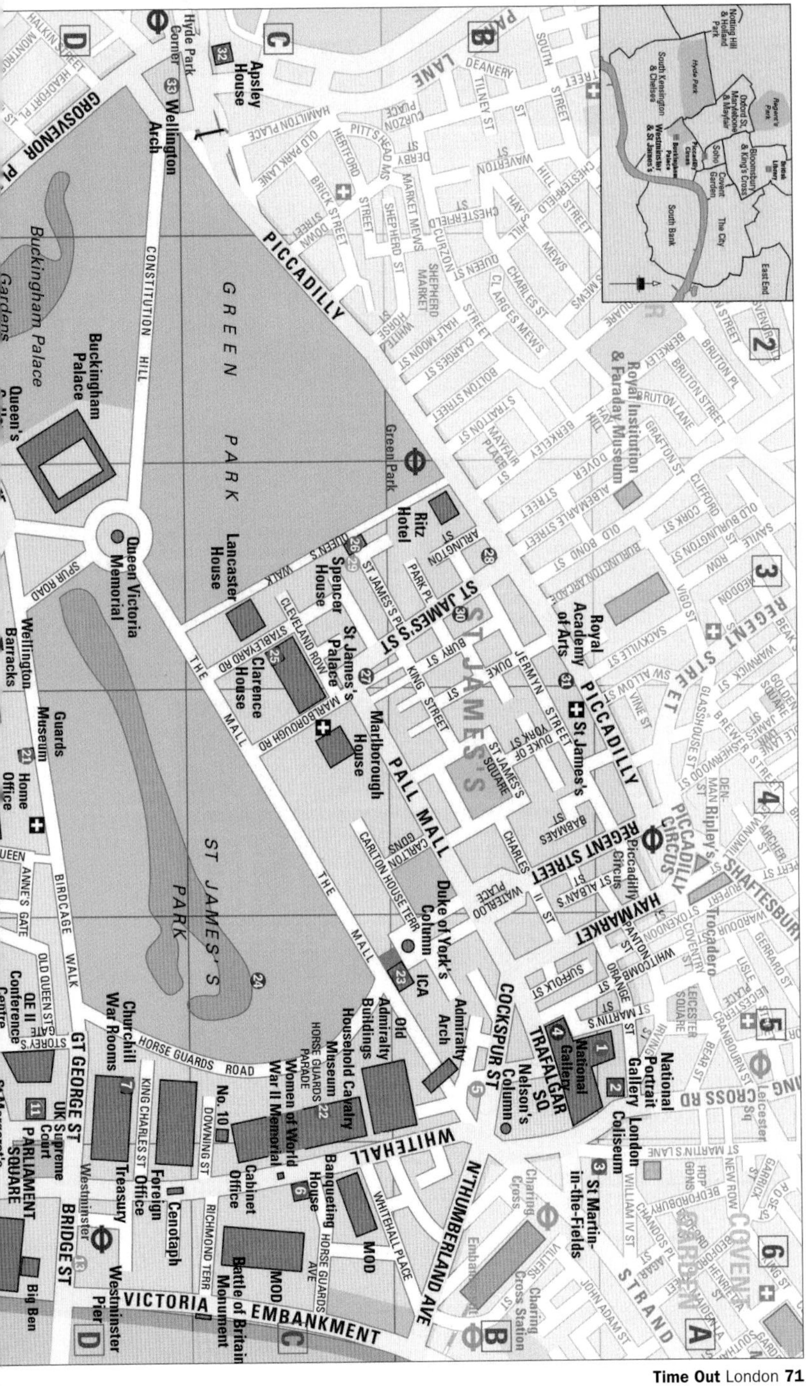
Hyde Park Corner
Apsley House
Wellington Arch
Grosvenor Pl
Piccadilly
Green Park
Constitution Hill
Buckingham Palace
Buckingham Palace Gardens
Queen Victoria Memorial
Lancaster House
Clarence House
St James's Palace
Spencer House
Ritz Hotel
Marlborough House
St James's St
Pall Mall
The Mall
St James's Park
Birdcage Walk
Wellington Barracks
Guards Museum
Home Office
Churchill War Rooms
Horse Guards Road
Treasury
Foreign Office
Cenotaph
No. 10
Downing St
Cabinet Office
Banqueting House
Whitehall
Household Cavalry Museum
Horse Guards Parade
Women of World War II Memorial
Old Admiralty Buildings
Admiralty Arch
ICA
Duke of York's Column
Trafalgar Sq
Nelson's Column
National Gallery
National Portrait Gallery
London Coliseum
St Martin-in-the-Fields
Charing Cross
Charing Cross Station
N'thumberland Ave
Victoria Embankment
Westminster Pier
Big Ben
Parliament Square
UK Supreme Court
Westminster
Bridge St
Gt George St
QE II Conference Centre
Battle of Britain Monument
MOD
Strand
Covent Garden
Leicester Square
Trocadero
Shaftesbury
Haymarket
Regent Street
Piccadilly Circus
Ripley's
St James's
Royal Academy of Arts
Royal Institution & Faraday Museum
Jermyn Street
St James's Square
Cockspur St
Park Lane
Notting Hill & Holland Park
Hyde Park
Regent's Park
South Kensington & Chelsea
Oxford St, Marylebone & Mayfair
Bloomsbury & King's Cross
British Library
Soho
Covent Garden
Piccadilly Circus
Buckingham Palace
Westminster & St James's
South Bank
The City
East End

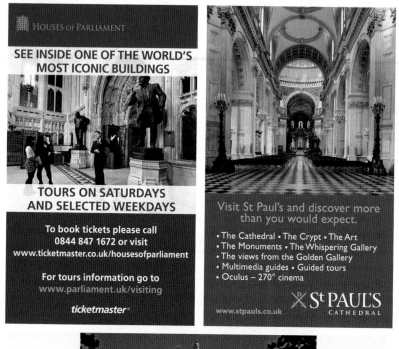

Restaurants

The multifarious dining options in nearby **Soho** can be found on *pp122-135*.

National Dining Rooms

Sainsbury Wing, National Gallery, Trafalgar Square, WC2N 5DN (7747 2525, www.peytonandbyrne.co.uk). Charing Cross tube/rail. **Open** *Bakery* 10am-5pm Mon-Thur, Sat, Sun; 10am-8pm Fri. *Restaurant* noon-3pm Mon-Thur, Sat, Sun; noon-3pm, 5-7.30pm Fri. **Main courses** *Bakery* £6.50-£11.50. *Restaurant* £16.50-£32.50. **Map** p71 B5 ❹ **British**

Ascend the stairs to Oliver Peyton's first-floor dining room – in the quieter Sainsbury Wing of the National Gallery – and enter a professionally run and peaceful place, where the views (over the Square in one direction, of a vast Paula Rego mural in the other) are matched by the superb food. Dishes are light, artfully presented and with clever additions. They also make the most of in-season ingredients: an early spring vegetable salad featured delicately braised chunks of squash, golden beetroot and carrot, a line of vivid beetroot 'dust' and horseradish popcorn. The bakery side of the operation ably fulfils the cakes-and-a-cuppa role of the traditional museum café.

► *The handsome National Café, on the east side of the gallery, has good food and a continental brasserie atmosphere.*

Pubs & bars

Albannach

66 Trafalgar Square, WC2N 5DS (7930 0066, www.albannach.co.uk). Charing Cross tube/rail. **Open** noon-1am Mon-Sat. *Food served* noon-4pm, 5-10.30pm Mon-Sat. **Map** p71 B5 ❺

Right on Trafalgar Square, Albannach (as opposed to 'sassanach') specialises in Scotch whiskies and cocktails thereof. A map in the menu details the origins of these Highland and Island malts, the pages brimming with 17-year-old Glengoyne, 12-year-old Cragganmore and 29-year-old Auchentoshan. But location is the main appeal: kilted staff and loud office groups tend to detract from the quality on offer.

WHITEHALL TO PARLIAMENT SQUARE

Westminster tube or Charing Cross tube/rail.

The offices of the British government are lined along **Whitehall**, itself named after Henry VIII's magnificent palace, which burned to the ground in 1698. Walking south from Trafalgar Square, you pass the old **Admiralty Offices** and **War Office**, the **Ministry of Defence**, the **Foreign Office** and the **Treasury**, as well as the **Banqueting House** (*see p75*), one of the few buildings to survive the blaze. Also here is

St Martin-in-the-Fields café. *See p69.*

Horse Guards, headquarters of the Household Cavalry, the elite army unit that protects the Queen.

Either side of **Downing Street** – home to the prime minister (no.10) and chancellor (no.11), but closed to the public after IRA attacks in the 1980s – are significant war memorials. The millions who died in the service of the nation in World Wars I and II are commemorated by Sir Edwin Lutyens's dignified **Cenotaph**, focal point of Remembrance Day (*see p40*), while a separate memorial to the women of World War II, by sculptor John Mills, recalls the seven million women who contributed to the war effort. Just past the Cenotaph and hidden beneath government offices at the St James's Park end of King Charles Street, the claustrophobic **Churchill War Rooms** (*see p75*) are where Britain's wartime PM planned his campaigns and delivered his fiery speeches.

The broad sweep of Whitehall is an apt introduction to the monuments of **Parliament Square**. Laid out in 1868, this tiny green space is flanked by the extravagant **Houses of Parliament** (*see p75*), the neo-Gothic Middlesex Guildhall (now the **Supreme Court**; *see p76*) and the twin, square spires of **Westminster Abbey** (*see p76*). Parliament Square can seem little more than a glorified traffic island, despite all the statues of British politicians (Disraeli, Churchill) and foreign dignitaries (Lincoln, Mandela), but its symbolic value has been brought back into focus in recent years through court battles over its suitability as a site for different kinds of political protest.

Parliament itself simply dazzles. An outrageous neo-Gothic fantasy, the seat of the British government is still formally known as the Palace of Westminster, though the only remaining parts of the medieval palace are **Westminster Hall** and the **Jewel Tower** (*see p75*). At the

"an ESSENTIAL
part of the London summer
Sunday Times
REGENT'S PARK
OPEN AIR THEATRE
THE ROYAL PARKS
2014 Season | 15 May - 13 Sept
openairtheatre.com

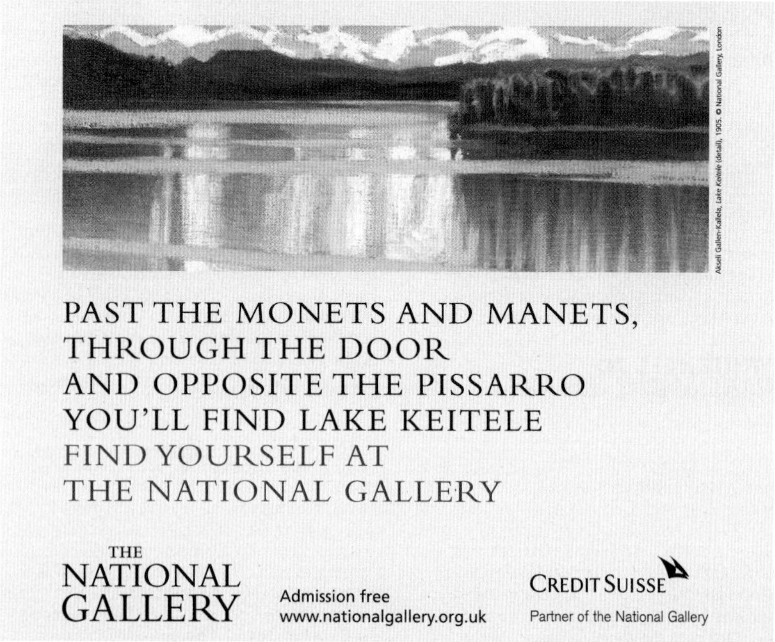
Akseli Gallen-Kallela, Lake Keitele (detail), 1905. © National Gallery, London
PAST THE MONETS AND MANETS,
THROUGH THE DOOR
AND OPPOSITE THE PISSARRO
YOU'LL FIND LAKE KEITELE
FIND YOURSELF AT
THE NATIONAL GALLERY
THE NATIONAL GALLERY
Admission free
www.nationalgallery.org.uk
CREDIT SUISSE
Partner of the National Gallery

north end of the palace is the clocktower housing the huge **'Big Ben'** bell that gives the clocktower its popular name; more than seven feet tall, the bell (itself formally known as the 'Great Bell') weighs over 13 tons. The tower was, in fact, renamed in 2012: rather than bowing to common usage, it became the Elizabeth Tower – in honour of the Queen's Diamond Jubilee.

Banqueting House

Whitehall, SW1A 2ER (0844 482 7777, www.hrp.org.uk). Westminster tube. **Open** 10am-5pm Mon-Sat. **Admission** £6; £5 reductions; free under-16s. **Map** p71 C6 ❻

This handsome Italianate mansion, which was designed by Inigo Jones and constructed in 1620, was the first true Renaissance building in London. The sole surviving part of the Tudor and Stuart kings' Whitehall Palace, the Banqueting House features a lavish painted ceiling by Rubens, glorifying James I, 'the wisest fool in Christendom'. Regrettably, James's successor, Charles I, did not rule so wisely. After losing the English Civil War to Cromwell's Roundheads, he was executed in front of Banqueting House in 1649 – subject of a new set of displays here. The event is still marked by a dogged bunch of royalists every 31 January at the equestrian statue of Charles I on a traffic island just south of Trafalgar Square.

Churchill War Rooms

Clive Steps, King Charles Street, SW1A 2AQ (7930 6961, www.iwm.org.uk). St James's Park or Westminster tube. **Open** 9.30am-6pm daily. **Admission** £17.50; £14 reductions; free under-16s. **Map** p71 D5 ❼

Out of harm's way beneath Whitehall, this cramped and spartan bunker was where Winston Churchill planned the Allied victory in World War II, and the rooms powerfully bring to life the reality of a nation at war. The cabinet rooms were sealed on 16 August 1945, keeping the complex in a state of suspended animation: every pin stuck into the vast charts was placed there in the final days of the conflict. The humble quarters occupied by Churchill and his deputies give a tangible sense of wartime hardship, an effect reinforced by the wailing sirens and wartime speeches on the audio guide (free with admission).

Houses of Parliament

Parliament Square, SW1A 0AA (Commons information 7219 4272, Lords information 7219 3107, www.parliament.uk). Westminster tube. **Open** (when in session) *House of Commons Visitors' Gallery* 2.30-10.30pm Mon; 11.30am-7.30pm Tue, Wed; 9.30am-5.30pm Thur; 9.30am-3pm Fri. *House of Lords Visitors' Gallery* 2.30-10pm Mon, Tue; 3-10pm Wed; 11am-7.30pm Thur; from 10am Fri. *Tours* 9.15am-4.30pm Sat & summer recess; check website for details. **Admission** *Visitors' Galleries* free. *Tours* £16.50; £7-£14 reductions; free under-15s with adult. **Map** p70 E6 ❽

The British parliament has an extremely long history, with the first parliamentary session held in St Stephen's Chapel in 1275. The Palace of Westminster, however, only became the permanent seat of Parliament in 1532, when Henry VIII moved to a new des-res in Whitehall. The current Palace is a wonderful mish-mash of styles, dominated by Gothic buttresses, towers and arches. It looks much older than it is: the Parliament buildings were designed in 1860 by Charles Barry (ably assisted by Augustus Pugin) to replace the original building, which had been destroyed by fire in 1834. Now the compound contains 1,000 rooms, 11 courtyards, eight bars and six restaurants, plus a small cafeteria for visitors. Of the original palace, only the Jewel Tower (*see below*) and the ancient Westminster Hall remain.

Visitors are welcome (subject to stringent security checks at St Stephen's Gate, the only public access point into Parliament) to observe the political debates in the House of Lords and House of Commons, but tickets must be arranged in advance through your embassy or MP, who can also arrange tours – even free trips up the 334 spiral steps of the Elizabeth Tower to hear 'Big Ben'. The experience of listening in on the Houses of Parliament in session is often soporific, but Prime Minister's Question Time at noon on Wednesday is usually fun: the PM has alternately to rebuff a barrage of hostile questions from the opposition (and occasionally their own rebellious backbenchers) and massage value out of soft questions from loyal backbenchers eager to present the government in a good light.

► *The best way to see these historic buildings is to book on one of the revealing 75min guided tours (0844 847 1672, www.ticketmaster.co.uk) on Saturday or during summer recess. Tours take in both Houses, Westminster Hall, the Queen's Robing Room and the Royal Gallery.*

Jewel Tower

Abingdon Street, SW1P 3JY (7222 2219, www.english-heritage.org.uk). Westminster tube. **Open** *Apr-Oct* 10am-5pm daily. *Nov-Mar* 10am-4pm Sat, Sun. **Admission** £3.90; £2.30-£3.50 reductions; free under-5s. **Map** p70 E6 ❾

This easy-to-overlook little stone tower opposite Parliament was built in 1365 to house Edward III's treasure. It is, with Westminster Hall, all that remains of the medieval Palace of Westminster. It contains a small exhibition on Parliament's history.

► *Nowadays, the Crown Jewels are on display in the Tower of London;* *see p186.*

FREE St Margaret's Church

Parliament Square, SW1P 3PA (7654 4840, www.westminster-abbey.org). St James's Park or Westminster tube. **Open** 9.30am-3.30pm Mon-Fri; 9.30am-1.30pm Sat; 2-4.30pm Sun (times vary due to services). *Services* times vary; check website for details. **Admission** free. **Map** p70 E6 ❿

EXPLORE

Tucked in under the grandeur of Westminster Abbey, this little church was founded in the 12th century; since 1614, it's served as the official church of the House of Commons. The interior features some of the most impressive pre-Reformation stained glass in London. The east window (1509) commemorates the marriage of Henry VIII and Catherine of Aragon; others celebrate Britain's first printer, William Caxton (buried here in 1491), explorer Sir Walter Raleigh (executed in Old Palace Yard in 1618) and writer John Milton (1608-74), who married his second wife here in 1656.

FREE Supreme Court

Parliament Square, SW1P 3BD (7960 1900, www.supremecourt.gov.uk). St James's Park or Westminster tube. **Open** 9.30am-4pm Mon-Fri. *Tours* 11am, 2pm, 3pm Fri. **Admission** free. *Tours* £5; £3.50 reductions. **Map** p71 D5 ⑪

In 2005, Parliament made a momentous decision – not that anyone noticed. The right to adjudicate final appeals was taken from the House of Lords and given to a new, independent Supreme Court, which was duly opened by the Queen in 2009, directly opposite Parliament. Part of the notion was to open up higher processes of law to the public – in plain English, you can visit any time you like (through airport-style security gates) to see lawyers debate 'points of law of general public importance' in front of the country's most senior judges. Recent cases have included whether an MP can be tried in a magistrate's court for alleged criminal misconduct within Parliament, and how binding a prenuptial agreement should be. You can also look around the lovely Grade II*-listed, neo-Gothic premises, built for Middlesex County Council in 1913. There's even a café and souvenirs on sale.

▶ *Although you're welcome to visit on a Friday, the Supreme Court doesn't sit that day.*

★ Westminster Abbey

20 Dean's Yard, SW1P 3PA (7222 5152 information, 7654 4834 tours, www.westminster-abbey.org). St James's Park or Westminster tube. **Open** *May-August* 9.30am-3.30pm Mon, Tue, Thur-Sat; 9.30am-6pm Wed. *Sep-Apr* 9.30am-3.30pm Mon, Tue, Thur, Fri; 9.30am-6pm Wed; 9.30am-1.30pm Sat. *Abbey Museum, Chapter House & College Gardens* Times vary, phone for details. *Tours* May-Aug 10am, 10.30am, 11am, 2pm, 2.30pm Mon-Fri; 10am, 10.30am, 11am Sat. Sep-Apr 10.30am, 11am, 2pm, 2.30pm Mon-Fri; 10.30am, 11pm Sat. **Admission** £18; £8-£15 reductions; £44 family; free under-10s with adult. *Tours* £3. **Map** p70 E5 ⑫

The cultural, historic and religious significance of Westminster Abbey is impossible to overstate, but also hard to remember as you're shepherded around, forced to elbow fellow tourists out of the way to read a plaque or see a tomb – even more so after the 2012 Royal Wedding 'twixt Prince William and Kate Middleton, which resulted in a mighty impressive 36% boost in visitor numbers. The best plan is to get here as early in the day as you can. Edward the Confessor commissioned a church to St Peter on the site of a seventh-century version, but it was only consecrated on 28 December 1065, eight days before he died. William the Conqueror subsequently had himself crowned here on Christmas Day 1066 and, with just two exceptions, every English coronation since has taken place in the abbey.

Many royal, military and cultural notables are interred here. The most haunting memorial is the Grave of the Unknown Warrior, in the nave. Elaborate resting places in side chapels are taken up by the tombs of Elizabeth I and Mary Queen of Scots. In Innocents Corner lie the remains of two lads believed to be Edward V and his brother Richard (their bodies were found at the Tower of London), as well as two of James I's children. Poets' Corner is the final resting place of Chaucer, the first to be buried here. Few of the other writers who have stones here are buried in the abbey, but the remains of Dryden, Johnson, Browning and Tennyson are all present. Henry James, TS Eliot and Dylan Thomas have dedications – on the floor, fittingly for Thomas.

In the vaulted area under the former monks' dormitory, one of the abbey's oldest parts, the Abbey Museum celebrated its centenary in 2008. You'll find effigies and waxworks of British monarchs, among them Edward II and Henry VII, wearing the robes they donned in life. The 900-year-old College Garden

Westminster Abbey.

is one of the oldest cultivated spaces in Britain and a useful place to escape the crowds. For snacks, a new refectory-style restaurant – the Cellarium Café & Terrace (www.cellariumcafe.com) – opened in autumn 2012.

Pubs & bars

St Stephen's Tavern

10 Bridge Street, SW1A 2JR (7925 2286, www.hall-woodhouse.co.uk). Westminster tube. **Open** 10am-11.30pm Mon-Thur, Sat; 10am-midnight Fri; 10.30am-10.30pm Sun. *Food served* 10am-10pm daily. **Map** p71 D6 ⑬

Done out with dark woods, etched mirrors and Arts and Crafts-style wallpaper, this is a lovely old pub. The food is reasonably priced and the ales are excellent, but drinks can be expensive. Opposite Big Ben, its location is terrific, yet it's neither too touristy nor too busy. If the downstairs bars are full, head upstairs and look for a seat on the mezzanine.

▶ *St Stephen's nearest rival is the Red Lion (48 Parliament Street, SW1A 2NH, 7930 5826), by tradition the politicians' favourite.*

MILLBANK

Pimlico or Westminster tube.

Running south from Parliament along the river, Millbank leads eventually to **Tate Britain** (*see right*), built on the site of an extraordinary pentagonal prison that held criminals destined for transportation to Botany Bay. If you're walking south from the Palace of Westminster, look out on the left for **Victoria Tower Gardens**, which contain a statue of suffragette leader Emmeline Pankhurst and the rather colourful Buxton Drinking Fountain, which commemorates the emancipation of slaves. There's also a version of Rodin's sombre *Burghers of Calais*.

On the other side of the road, Dean Stanley Street leads to Smith Square, home to the architecturally striking **St John's Smith Square** (*see p282*), built as a church in grand Baroque style and now a popular venue for classical music. **Lord North Street**, the elegant row of Georgian terraces running north from the square, has long been a favourite address of politicians; note, too, the directions on the wall for wartime bomb shelters.

Across the river from Millbank is **Vauxhall Cross**, the oddly conspicuous HQ of the Secret Intelligence Service (SIS), commonly referred to by its old name MI6. In case any enemies of the state were unaware of its location, the cream and green block appeared as itself in the 1999 James Bond film *The World is Not Enough* – reprising the role (and suffering serious bomb damage along the way) in 2012's *Skyfall*.

> **IN THE KNOW**
> **LONDON BY GASLIGHT**
>
> Most of London's street lights are now electric, but there are still an astonishing 1,600 gas-powered lamps dotted around the capital. Casting a softer glow than their modern-day counterparts, examples can be seen outside Buckingham Palace and Westminster Abbey, and along the Mall and Pall Mall, where a 200th anniversary plaque commemorates the lighting of the world's first public streetlamp in 1807. A less salubrious variant can also be found: the gas lamp on Carting Lane, beside the Savoy (*see p348*), is powered by the fumes from sewage.

★ FREE Tate Britain

Millbank, SW1P 4RG (7887 8888, www.tate.org.uk). Pimlico tube. **Open** 10am-6pm daily. *Tours* 11am, noon, 2pm, 3pm daily. **Admission** free. *Special exhibitions* vary. **Map** p70 G5 ⑭

Tate Modern (*see p56*) gets the attention, but the original Tate Gallery, founded by sugar magnate Sir Henry Tate, has a broader brief. Housed in a stately building on the riverside, Tate Britain is second only to the National Gallery (*see p68*) when it comes to British art. It's also looking to steal back a bit of the limelight from its starrier sibling with a 20-year redevelopment plan called the Millbank Project: conserving the building's original features, upgrading the galleries, opening new spaces to the public and adding a new café (*see p79* **The Original and the Best**). The art here is exceptional. The historical collection includes work by Hogarth, Gainsborough, Reynolds, Constable (who gets three rooms) and Turner (in the superb Clore Gallery). Many contemporary works were shifted to the other Tate when it opened, but Stanley Spencer, Lucian Freud and Francis Bacon are well represented, and Art Now installations showcase up-and-coming Britsh artists. Temporary exhibitions include headline-hungry blockbusters and the annual controversy-courting Turner Prize exhibition (Oct-Jan). The gallery has a good restaurant and an exemplary gift shop.

▶ *The handy Tate-to-Tate boat (see p57) zips along the river to Tate Modern every 40mins.*

VICTORIA

Pimlico tube or Victoria tube/rail.

As you might expect from London's main backpacker hangout, Victoria is colourful and chaotic. Victoria rail station is a major hub for trains to southern seaside resorts and ferry terminals, while the nearby coach station is served by buses from all over Europe. The theatres dotted around Victoria form a western outpost of the West End's Theatreland.

Not to be confused with Westminster Abbey (*see p76*), **Westminster Cathedral** is the headquarters of the Roman Catholic Church in England. South and east of Victoria Station are the Georgian terraces of **Pimlico** and **Belgravia**. Antique stores and restaurants line Pimlico Road; the intriguing independent shops of Tachbrook Street are worth a look.

North of Victoria Street towards Parliament Square is **Christchurch Gardens**, burial site of Thomas ('Colonel') Blood, who stole the Crown Jewels in 1671. He was apprehended making his getaway but, amazingly, managed to talk his way into a full pardon. Also in the area are **New Scotland Yard**, with its famous revolving sign, and the art deco headquarters of **London Underground** at 55 Broadway. Public outrage about Jacob Epstein's graphic nudes on the façade almost led to the resignation of the managing director in 1929.

FREE Westminster Cathedral

42 Francis Street, SW1P 1QW (7798 9055, www.westminstercathedral.org.uk). Victoria tube/rail. **Open** 7am-7pm Mon-Fri; 8am-8pm Sat, Sun. *Exhibition & Bell tower* 9.30am-4.45pm Mon-Sat; 9.30am-5.30pm Sun. **Admission** free; donations appreciated. *Exhibition* £5; free-£2.50 reductions; £11 family. *Bell tower & exhibition* £8; free-£4 reductions; £17.50 family. **Map** p70 F3 ⑮

With its domes, arches and soaring tower, the most important Catholic church in England looks surprisingly Byzantine. There's a reason: architect John Francis Bentley, who built it between 1895 and 1903, was heavily influenced by Hagia Sophia in Istanbul. Compared to the candy-cane exterior, the interior is surprisingly restrained (in fact, it's unfinished), but there are still some impressive marble columns and mosaics. Eric Gill's sculptures of the Stations of the Cross (1914-18) were dismissed as 'Babylonian' when they were first installed, but worshippers have come to love them. An upper gallery holds the 'Treasures of the Cathedral' exhibition, where you can see an impressive Arts and Crafts coronet, a Tudor chalice, holy relics and Bentley's amazing architectural model of his cathedral, complete with tiny hawks.

► *There are great views from the bell tower's viewing gallery – as well as a lift to help you climb the 210 feet to get up there.*

Restaurants

Cinnamon Club

Old Westminster Library, 30-32 Great Smith Street, SW1P 3BU (7222 2555, www.cinnamonclub.com). St James's Park or Westminster tube. **Open** 7.30-10am, noon-2.45pm, 6-10.45pm Mon-Fri; noon-2.45pm, 6-10.45pm Sat. **Main courses** £16-£34. **Map** p70 E5 ⑯ **Indian**

There's a gentlemen's club feel to this grand, Grade II-listed Victorian building (once a library). It's an established haunt of sharp-suited power brokers and Westminster politicians who enjoy a fine-dining menu of updated rustic and regal pan-Indian dishes, like sliced veal escalope with its toasted coriander seasoning – an innovative complement to creamy tomato-cumin sauce. The kitchen excels in seafood preparations, such as whiting fillet with a marvellous, rich coconut cream infused with ginger and turmeric.
Other locations Cinnamon Kitchen, 9 Devonshire Square, the City, EC2M 4WY (7626 5000); Cinnamon Soho, 5 Kingly Street, Soho, W1B 5PF (7437 1664).

Regency Café

17-19 Regency Street, SW1P 4BY (7821 6596). St James's Park tube or Victoria tube/rail. **Meals served** 7am-2.30pm, 4-7.15pm Mon-Fri; 7am-noon Sat. **Main courses** £2.70-£6.55. **Map** p70 F5 ⑰ **Café**

Behind its black-tiled art deco exterior, this classic caff has been here since 1946. Customers sit on brown plastic chairs at Formica-topped tables, watched over by muscular boxers and Spurs stars of yore, whose photos hang on the tiled walls. Lasagne, omelettes, salads, every conceivable cooked breakfast and mugs of tannin-rich tea are meat and drink to the Regency. Stodgetastic own-made specials include steak pie. Still hungry? The improbably gigantic cinnamon-flavoured bread and butter pud will see you right for the rest of the week.

Pubs & bars

Boisdale of Belgravia

13-15 Eccleston Street, SW1W 9LX (7730 6922, www.boisdale.co.uk). Victoria tube/rail. **Open/ food served** noon-1am Mon-Fri; 6pm-1am Sat. **Admission** free before 10pm, then £12. **Map** p70 F1 ⑱

There's nowhere quite like this posh, Scottish-themed enterprise, and that includes its sister branches in the City and Canary Wharf. If you're here to drink, you'll be drinking single malts from a terrific range. That said, the outstanding wine list is surprisingly affordable, with house selections starting at under £20. Additional appeal comes from live jazz (six nights a week) and a heated cigar terrace.
Other locations Swedeland Court, 202 Bishopsgate, the City, EC2M 4NR (7283 1763); Cabot Place, Canary Wharf, E14 4QT (7715 5818).

Shops & services

Run & Become

42 Palmer Street, Victoria, SW1H 0PH (7222 1314, www.runandbecome.com). St James's Park tube. **Open** 9am-6pm Mon-Wed, Sat; 9am-8pm Thur; 9am-7pm Fri. **Map** p70 E4 ⑲ **Health & beauty**

THE ORIGINAL AND THE BEST

The first Tate gallery stakes a serious claim for a bit more love.

One of London's more remarkable cultural success stories has been **Tate Modern** (*see p56*), which opened in a disused power station in May 2000 to throngs of people. It now enjoys three times as many visitors as 'the original Tate' (**Tate Britain**, *see p77*), which opened in 1897 with a display of 245 British paintings.

It is perhaps with that in mind that Tate Britain has undertaken major renovations – so major, in fact, that the complete programme is anticipated to take two decades. In that context, the first move seems modest: in May 2013, a comprehensive rehang of the collections was revealed. Covering British art from Holbein in the 1540s up to the present, Tate Britain major holdings are now shown largely in chronological order – allowing you to trace the development of British art through history – and with a minimum of hectoring curatorial captions. A few key artists are given more substantial treatment: the Turners remain together in their own galleries, and works by Henry Moore and William Blake are grouped rather than being separated by date.

Caruso St John architects have also improved the fabric of the oldest part of the building as part of this initial £45m tranche of improvements. Sturdier floors mean more sculpture has been displayed, and the amount of natural light allowed in has been increased. At the Millbank entrance, there's now a stained-glass window by Turner Prize-winner Richard Wright; inside, you'll find a spiral staircase; and downstairs in the restaurant, a new ceiling mural has been designed by Alan Johnston to complement the restored 1926-27 Rex Whistler wall mural *Pursuit of Rare Meats*.

There is also a space for temporary exhibitions, including an exploration of the site's fascinating early history as the ill-fated Millbank prison, unwanted home to convicts prior to deportation.

Now we're delighted that Tate Britain has a new chance to shine, but we can't entirely wish it well. Why not? Well, since the crowds descended on Tate Modern, we've come to enjoy seeing the Blakes, Turners and our favourite Epstein here in comparative tranquillity...

The experienced staff here, most of them enthusiastic runners, will find the right pair of shoes for your physique and running style. The gamut of running kit, from clothing to speed monitors, is available.

AROUND ST JAMES'S PARK

St James's Park tube.

Handsome **St James's Park** was founded as a deer park for the royal occupants of St James's Palace, and remodelled by John Nash on the orders of George IV. The central lake is home to various species of wildfowl; pelicans have been kept here since the 17th century, when the Russian ambassador donated several of the bag-jawed birds to Charles II. The pelicans are fed between 2.30pm and 3pm daily. Lots of humans picnic here, too, notably around the bandstand during the summer weekend concerts. The bridge over the lake offers good views of Buckingham Palace. Head that way and you'll see Green Park, the beginning of a relaxing stroll that will take you under trees as far as Hyde Park Corner (for both, *see p83*).

Along the north side of the park, the Mall connects Buckingham Palace with Trafalgar Square. It looks like a classic processional route, but the Mall was actually laid out as a pitch for Charles II to play 'pallemaille' (an early version of croquet imported from France) after the pitch at Pall Mall became too crowded. On the south side of the park, Wellington Barracks contains the **Guards Museum** (*see right*); to the east, Horse Guards contains the **Household Cavalry Museum** (*see right*).

Carlton House Terrace, on the north flank of the Mall, was the last project completed by John Nash before his death in 1835. Part of the terrace now houses the **ICA** (*see p81*). Just behind is the **Duke of York column**, commemorating Prince Frederick, Duke of York, who led the British Army against the French. He's the nursery rhyme's 'Grand old Duke of York', who marched his 10,000 men neither up nor down Cassel hill in Flanders.

Buckingham Palace & Royal Mews

The Mall, SW1A 1AA (Palace 7766 7300, Royal Mews 7766 7302, Queen's Gallery 7766 7301, www.royalcollection.org.uk). Green Park tube or Victoria tube/rail. **Open & admission** times & prices vary; check website for details. **Map** p70 E2 ⑳

Although nearby St James's Palace (*see p81*) remains the official seat of the British court, every monarch since Victoria has used Buckingham Palace as their primary home. Originally known as Buckingham House, the present home of the British royals was constructed as a private house for the Duke of Buckingham in 1703, but George III liked it so much he purchased it for his German bride Charlotte in 1761. George IV decided to occupy the mansion himself after taking the throne in 1820 and John Nash was hired to convert it into a palace befitting a king. Construction was beset with problems, and Nash – whose expensive plans had always been disliked by Parliament – was dismissed in 1830. When Victoria came to the throne in 1837, the building was barely habitable. The job of finishing the palace fell to the reliable but unimaginative Edward Blore ('Blore the Bore'). The neoclassical frontage now in place was the work of Aston Webb in 1913.

As the home of the Queen, the palace is usually closed to visitors, but you can view the interior for a brief period each year while the Windsors are away on their holidays; you'll be able to see the State Rooms, still used to entertain dignitaries and guests of state, and part of the garden. There's even a café – paper cups, sadly, but coloured a pretty blue-green and clearly marked with the palace crest for souvenir-hunters. At any time of year, you can visit the Queen's Gallery to see her personal collection of treasures, including paintings by Rubens and Rembrandt, Sèvres porcelain and the Diamond Diadem crown. Further along Buckingham Palace Road, the Royal Mews is a grand garage for the royal fleet of Rolls-Royces and home to the splendid royal carriages and the horses, individually named by the Queen, that pull them.

Guards Museum

Wellington Barracks, Birdcage Walk, SW1E 6HQ (7414 3428, www.theguardsmuseum.com). St James's Park tube. **Open** 10am-4pm daily. **Admission** £5; £1-£2.50 reductions; free under-16s. **Map** p71 D4 ㉑

Just down the road from Horse Guards, this small museum tells the 350-year story of the Foot Guards, using flamboyant uniforms, period paintings, medals and intriguing memorabilia, such as the stuffed body of Jacob the Goose, the Guard's Victorian mascot, who was regrettably run over by a van in barracks. Appropriately, the shop is well stocked with toy soldiers of the British regiments.

► *The Guards assemble on the parade ground here before marching to the palace for the Changing of the Guard; see p41* **Stunning Ceremonials**.

Household Cavalry Museum

Horse Guards, Whitehall, SW1A 2AX (7930 3070, www.householdcavalrymuseum.co.uk). Westminster tube or Charing Cross tube/rail. **Open** *Mar-Sept* 10am-6pm daily. *Oct-Feb* 10am-5pm daily. **Admission** £7; £5 reductions; £18 family ticket; free under-5s. **Map** p71 C5 ㉒

Household Cavalry is a fairly workaday name for the military peacocks who make up the Queen's official guard. They tell their stories through video diaries at this small but entertaining museum, which also offers the chance to see medals, uniforms and shiny cuirasses (breastplates) up close. You also get a peek – and sniff – of the magnificent horses that

Buckingham Palace.

parade just outside every day: the stables are separated from the main museum by no more than a screen of glass.

▶ *The entrance to the museum is from the parade ground where the cavalry assemble for their Changing the Guard;* *see p41* **Stunning Ceremonials**.

FREE ICA (Institute of Contemporary Arts)

The Mall, SW1Y 5AH (7930 0493 information, 7930 3647 tickets, www.ica.org.uk). Piccadilly Circus tube or Charing Cross tube/rail. **Open** *Galleries* (during exhibitions) 11am-6pm Tue, Wed, Fri-Sun; 11am-9pm Thur. **Admission** free. **Map** p71 B5 ㉓

Founded in 1947 by a collective of poets, artists and critics, the ICA has recently found itself somewhat adrift. The institute moved to the Mall in 1968 and set itself up as a venue for arthouse cinema, performance art, philosophical debates, exhibitions, art-themed club nights and anything else that might challenge convention – but 'convention' is much harder to challenge now, when everyone's doing it. New director Gregor Muir has some interesting ideas, including a redesigned interior and Friday lunchtime talks from top contemporary artists.

Restaurants

Inn the Park

St James's Park, SW1A 2BJ (7451 9999, www.innthepark.com). St James's Park tube. **Open** *Summer* 8am-10pm Mon-Fri, 9am-10pm Sat, Sun. *Winter* 8am-5pm Mon-Fri; 9am-5pm Sat, Sun. **Main courses** £14-£23.50. **Map** p71 C5 ㉔ **British**

It's all about the location at this beautifully appointed and designed café-restaurant. The seasonal British cooking isn't always up to expectations, especially given the prices, but there is plenty on the plus side: staff are lovely, and the setting (overlooking the duck lake, with trees all around and the London Eye in the distance) is really wonderful.

ST JAMES'S

Green Park or Piccadilly Circus tube.

One of London's most refined residential areas, St James's was laid out in the 1660s for royal and aristocratic families, some of whom still live here. It's a rewarding district, a sedate bustle of intriguing mews and grand squares. Bordered by Piccadilly, Haymarket, the Mall and Green Park, the district is centred on **St James's Square**. Just south of the square, **Pall Mall** is lined with members-only gentlemen's clubs (in the old-fashioned sense of the word). Polished nameplates reveal such prestigious establishments as the **Institute of Directors** (no.116) and the **Reform Club** (nos.104-105), site of Phileas Fogg's famous bet in *Around the World in Eighty Days*. Around the corner on St James's Street, the **Carlton Club** (no.69) is the official club of the Conservative Party; Lady Thatcher remains the only woman to be granted full membership. The world's oldest fine art auctioneers, **Christie's** (7839 9060, www.christies.com), is on King Street.

At the south end of St James's Street, **St James's Palace** was built for Henry VIII in the 1530s. Extensively remodelled over the centuries, the red-brick palace is still the official address of the Royal Court, even though every monarch since 1837 has lived at Buckingham Palace. Here, Mary Tudor surrendered Calais, Elizabeth I led the campaign against the Spanish Armada, and Charles I was confined before his 1649 execution. The palace is home to the Princess Royal (the title given to the monarch's eldest daughter, currently Princess Anne); it's closed to the public, but you can attend Sunday services at its historic **Chapel Royal** (1st Sun of mth, Oct-Easter Sunday; 8.30am, 11.15am).

Adjacent to St James's Palace is **Clarence House**, former residence of the Queen Mother; a few streets north, delightful **Spencer House** (for both, *see p82*) is the ancestral home of the family of the late Princess Diana. Across

Marlborough Road lies the pocket-sized **Queen's Chapel**, designed by Inigo Jones in the 1620s for Charles I's Catholic queen Henrietta Maria, at a time when Catholic places of worship were officially banned. The Queen's Chapel can only be visited for Sunday services (Easter-July; 8.30am, 11.15am).

Clarence House

The Mall, SW1A 1AA (7766 7303, www.royalcollection.org.uk). Green Park tube. **Open** *Aug* 10am-4pm Mon-Fri; 10am-5.30pm Sat, Sun. Advance bookings only. **Admission** £9.50; £5.50 reductions; free under-5s. *Tours* pre-booked tickets only. **Map** p71 C3 ㉕

Currently the official residence of Prince Charles and the Duchess of Cornwall, this austere royal mansion was built between 1825 and 1827 for Prince William Henry, Duke of Clarence, who stayed on in the house after his coronation as King William IV. Designed by John Nash, the house has been much altered. Five receiving rooms and the late Queen Mother's British art collection are open to the public in summer.

Spencer House

27 St James's Place, SW1A 1NR (7499 8620, www.spencerhouse.co.uk). Green Park tube. **Open** *Feb-July, Sept-Dec* 10.30am-5.45pm Sun. Last tour 4.45pm. **Admission** £12; £10 reductions. Under-10s not allowed. **Map** p71 C3 ㉖

One of the last surviving private residences in St James's, this handsome mansion was designed for John Spencer by John Vardy, but was completed in 1766 by Hellenophile architect James Stuart, hence the mock Greek flourishes. Lady Georgiana, the 18th-century socialite and beauty – played by Keira Knightley in 2008's *The Duchess* – lived here, but the Spencers left generations before their most famous scion, Diana, married into the Windsors. The palatial building has painstakingly restored interiors, and a wonderful garden, sometimes open to the public (although it will remain closed through 2014).

Restaurants

Boulestin

5 St James's Street, SW1A 1EF (7930 2030, www.boulestin.com). Green Park tube. **Open** 7am-3pm, 5-11pm Mon-Wed; 7am-3pm, 5-11.30pm Thur, Fri; 11.30am-4pm, 5-11.30pm Sat. **Main courses** £12.50-£37. *Set dinner* (5.30-6.45pm) £19.50 2 courses; £24.50 3 courses. **Map** p71 C3 ㉗ **French**

Named after Marcel Boulestin – a pioneer of pre-war London cooking – this new Boulestin is no relation, though it does pay homage to the era of the great chef. The menu lists oeufs en gelée – a dish which, much like old-school St James's, is preserved in aspic. Classic French cooking at its best shines in dishes such as daube of beef or boudin noir. A few dishes seem almost daringly modern with their rocket and

Dukes Bar.

preserved lemons; but for the most part, this menu is as classic, French and retro as the grand setting.

► *The all-day Café Marcel at the same address is cheaper and less formal, and serves good value pre- and post-theatre menus.*

★ Wolseley

160 Piccadilly, W1J 9EB (7499 6996, www.thewolseley.com). Green Park tube. **Open** 7am-midnight Mon-Fri; 8am-midnight Sat; 8am-11pm Sun. **Main courses** £11.25-£34.75. *Cover* £2. **Map** p71 B3 ㉘ **Brasserie**

A self-proclaimed 'café-restaurant in the grand European tradition', the Wolseley combines London heritage and Viennese grandeur. The kitchen is much-celebrated for its breakfasts, and the scope of the main menu is admirable. From oysters, steak tartare or soufflé suisse, via wiener schnitzel or grilled halibut with wilted spinach and béarnaise, to tarte au citron or apple strudel, there's something for everyone. On Sunday afternoons, three-tiered afternoon tea stands are in abundance.

► *Owners Chris Corbin and Jeremy King now run a number of London's favourite restaurants, including the Delaunay (see p147) and Brasserie Zédel (see p114), and plan to open their first hotel, the Beaumont (www.thebeaumont.com) in 2014.*

Pubs & bars

★ Dukes Bar

Dukes Hotel, 35 St James's Place, SW1A 1NY (7491 4840, www.dukeshotel.com). Green Park tube. **Open** 2-11pm Mon-Sat; 4-10.30pm Sun. **Map** p71 C3 ㉙

If you want to go out for a single cocktail, strong and expensive and very well made, go to Dukes. It's in a luxury hotel, but everyone gets the warmest of

EXPLORE

welcomes. There are three small rooms, all decorated in discreetly opulent style; you feel cocooned. The bar is famous for the theatre of its martini making – at the table, from a trolley, using vermouth made exclusively for them at the Sacred distillery in Highgate – but other drinks are just as good.

Shops & services

DR Harris

29 St James's Street, SW1A 1HB (7930 3915, www.drharris.co.uk). Green Park or Piccadilly Circus tube. **Open** 8.30am-6pm Mon-Fri; 10am-5pm Sat. **Map** p71 B3 ㉚ **Health & beauty**

Founded in 1790, this venerable chemist has a royal warrant. Wood-and-glass cabinets are full of bottles, jars and old-fashioned shaving brushes.

► *DR Harris is at 34 Bury Street while the St James's Street premises get a refurb. They are due to move back in mid 2015.*

Fortnum & Mason

181 Piccadilly, W1A 1ER (7734 8040, www.fortnumandmason.co.uk). Green Park or Piccadilly Circus tube. **Open** 10am-8pm Mon-Sat; noon-6pm Sun. **Map** p71 B3 ㉛ **Department store**

In business for over 300 years, Fortnum & Mason is as historic as it is inspiring. A sweeping spiral staircase soars through the four-storey building, while light floods down from a central glass dome. The iconic eau de nil blue and gold colour scheme with flashes of rose pink abound on both the store design and the packaging of the fabulous ground-floor treats, such as chocolates, biscuits, teas and preserves. A food hall in the basement has a good range of fresh produce; Fortnum's Bees honey comes from beehives on top of the building. There are various eateries, including an ice-cream parlour. The famous hampers start from £40 – though they rise to a whopping £5,000 for the most luxurious.

GREEN PARK & HYDE PARK CORNER

Green Park or Hyde Park tube.

The flat green expanse just beyond the Ritz on Picadilly is **Green Park**; it's rather dull in itself, but makes a very pleasant middle section of walk through three Royal Parks, connecting St James's Park (*see p80*) to Hyde Park (*see p92*).

Work your way along Piccadilly, following the northern edge of Green Park past the queue outside the Hard Rock Café (where the Vault's displays of memorabilia are free to visit and open every day; www.hardrock.com) to the Duke of Wellington's old home, **Apsley House**, opposite **Wellington Arch**. This is hectic **Hyde Park Corner**; Buckingham Palace (*see p80*) is just a short walk south-east, while Hyde Park and the upper-crust enclave of Belgravia are to the west, but it also has a collection of memorials that are worth lingering over. The newest is the Bomber Command Memorial. Unveiled in 2012, it recognises the sacrifice of the 55,573 men of Bomber Command, killed between 1939 and 1945 as they pulverised Nazi-held Europe into submission. But we find Charles Sargeant Jagger's thoughtful tribute to the 49,076 men of the Royal Regiment of Artillery, slain between 1914 and 1919, to be more deeply moving. It's both vast – a huge Portland stone slab with giant gunners on three sides – and strangely muted, with a dead soldier lying on the monument's north side.

Apsley House

149 Piccadilly, W1J 7NT (7499 5676, www.english-heritage.org.uk). Hyde Park Corner tube. **Open** *Nov-Mar* 10am-4pm Sat, Sun. *Apr-Oct* 11am-5pm Wed-Sun. *Tours* by arrangement. **Admission** £6.90; £4.10-£6.20 reductions; free under-5s. *Tours* phone in advance. *Joint ticket with Wellington Arch* £8.90; £5.30-£8 reductions; £23.10 family. **Map** p71 C1 ㉜

Called No.1 London because it was the first London building encountered on the road to the city from the village of Kensington, Apsley House was built by Robert Adam in the 1770s. The Duke of Wellington kept it as his London home for 35 years. Although his descendants still live here, several rooms are open to the public, providing a superb feel for the man and his era. Admire the extravagant porcelain dinnerware and plates or ask for a demonstration of the crafty mirrors in the scarlet and gilt picture gallery, where a fine Velázquez and a Correggio hang near Goya's portrait of the Iron Duke after he defeated the French in 1812. This was a last-minute edit: X-rays have revealed that Wellington's head was painted over that of Joseph Bonaparte, Napoleon's brother.

► *Atmospheric twilight tours are held in winter.*

Wellington Arch

Hyde Park Corner, W1J 7JZ (7930 2726, www.english-heritage.org.uk). Hyde Park Corner tube. **Open** *Apr-Oct* 10am-5pm daily. *Nov-Mar* 10am-4pm daily. **Admission** £4.20; £2.50-£3.80 reductions; free under-5s. *Joint ticket with Apsley House* £8.90; £5.30-£8 reductions; £23.10 family. **Map** p71 D1 ㉝

Built in the late 1820s to mark Britain's triumph over Napoleonic France, Decimus Burton's Wellington Arch was initially topped by an out-of-proportion equestrian statue of Wellington. However, Captain Adrian Jones's 38-ton bronze *Peace Descending on the Quadriga of War* has finished it with a flourish since 1912. The Arch has three floors, with a bookshop and various displays, covering the history of the arch and the Blue Plaques scheme, and in the Quadriga Gallery providing space for excellent temporary exhibitions. There are great views from the balcony in winter (leafy trees obscure the sightlines in spring and summer).

South Kensington & Chelsea

There can be few cities in the world with a square mile so crammed with cultural highlights as you'll find in South Kensington: three of the world's greatest museums, some extraordinary colleges, a grand concert hall and an expansive park. Neighbouring Knightsbridge, on the other hand, has no cultural pretensions: a certain type of Londoner comes here to spend, spend, spend. Or, at least, to hang around with the non-doms and hyperwealthy incomers who are spend, spend, spending in the designer shops and world-famous department stores. Underlying them both, Chelsea's raffish youth is long behind it – but there are pleasures to be found amid its red-brick gentility.

Serpentine Gallery.

Don't Miss

1 **Science Museum** How the world works (p90).

2 **Harrods** Legendary department store (p95).

3 **Victoria & Albert Museum** Applied arts from around the world (p90).

4 **Serpentine Gallery** Art in the park (p94).

5 **Natural History Museum** Life on earth from prehistory to today (p87).

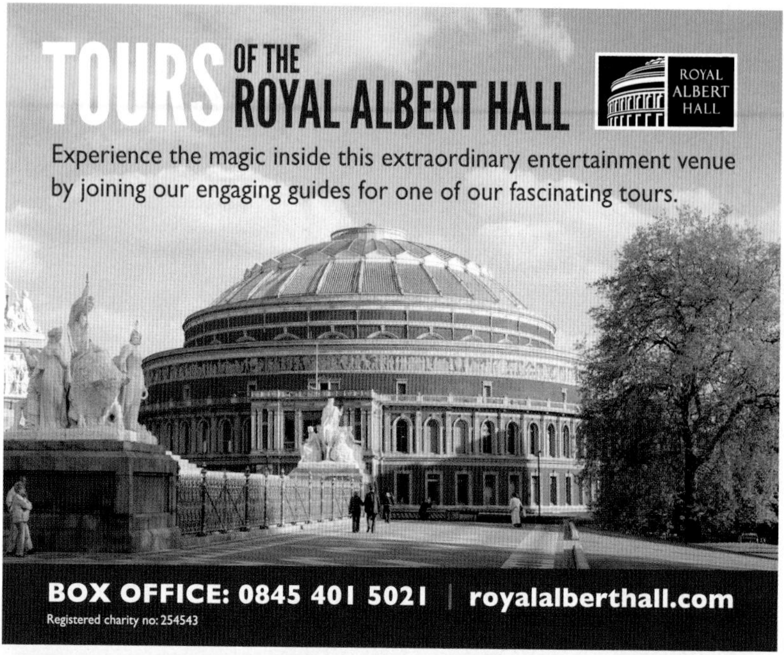
TOURS OF THE ROYAL ALBERT HALL
ROYAL ALBERT HALL
Experience the magic inside this extraordinary entertainment venue by joining our engaging guides for one of our fascinating tours.
BOX OFFICE: 0845 401 5021 | royalalberthall.com
Registered charity no: 254543

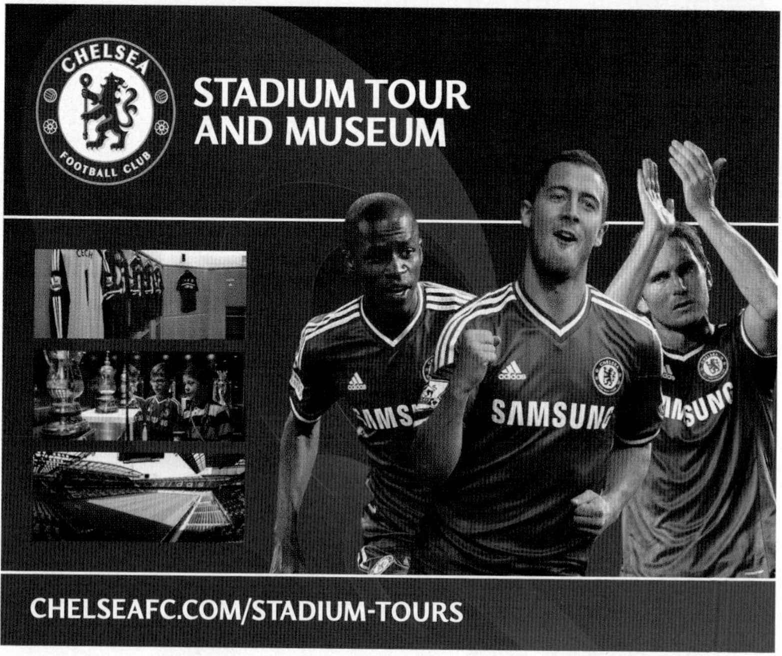
CHELSEA FOOTBALL CLUB
STADIUM TOUR AND MUSEUM
CHELSEAFC.COM/STADIUM-TOURS

SOUTH KENSINGTON

Gloucester Road or South Kensington tube.

As far as cultural and academic institutions are concerned, this is the land of plenty. It was Prince Albert who oversaw the inception of its world-class museums, colleges and concert hall, using the profits of the 1851 Great Exhibition; the area was nicknamed 'Albertopolis' in his honour. You'll find the **Natural History Museum**, the **Science Museum** and the **Victoria & Albert Museum**, **Imperial College**, the **Royal College of Art** and the **Royal College of Music** (Prince Consort Road, 7589 3643; call for details of the musical instrument museum), which forms a unity with the **Royal Albert Hall** (*see p281*), open since 1871 and variously used for boxing, motor shows, marathons, table tennis tournaments, fascist rallies and rock concerts. Opposite is the **Albert Memorial**.

Sights & museums

FREE Albert Memorial

Kensington Gardens (7936 2568, www.tourguides.co.uk). South Kensington tube. **Tours** *Mar-Dec* 2pm, 3pm 1st Sun of mth. **Admission** *Tours* £7; £6 reductions. **Map** p88 B2 ❶

'I would rather not be made the prominent feature of such a monument,' was Prince Albert's reported response when the subject of his commemoration arose. Hard, then, to imagine what he would have made of this extraordinary thing, unveiled 15 years after his death. Created by Sir George Gilbert Scott, it centres on a gilded Albert holding a catalogue of the 1851 Great Exhibition, guarded on four corners by the continents of Africa, America, Asia and Europe. The pillars are crowned with bronze statues of the sciences, and the frieze at the base depicts major artists, architects and musicians. It's one of London's most dramatic monuments.

★ FREE Natural History Museum

Cromwell Road, SW7 5BD (7942 5000, www.nhm.ac.uk). South Kensington tube. **Open** 10am-5.50pm daily. **Admission** free; charges apply for special exhibitions. *Tours* free. **Map** p88 C4 ❷

Both a research institution and a fabulous museum, the NHM opened in Alfred Waterhouse's purpose-built, Romanesque palazzo on the Cromwell Road in 1881. Now joined by the splendid Darwin Centre extension, the original building still looks quite magnificent. The pale blue and terracotta façade just about prepares you for the natural wonders within.

Taking up the full length of the vast entrance hall is the cast of a *Diplodocus* skeleton. A left turn leads into the west wing or Blue Zone, where long queues form to see animatronic dinosaurs – especially the endlessly popular *T rex*. A display on biology features an illuminated, man-sized model of a foetus in the womb along with graphic diagrams of how it might have got there.

A right turn from the central hall leads past the 'Creepy Crawlies' exhibition to the Green Zone. Stars include a cross-section through a Giant Sequoia tree and an amazing array of stuffed birds, including the chance to compare the egg of a hummingbird, smaller than a little finger nail, with that of an elephant bird (now extinct), almost football-sized. Beyond is the Red Zone. 'Earth's Treasury' is a mine of information on a variety of precious metals, gems and crystals; 'From the Beginning' is a brave attempt to give the expanse of geological time a human perspective. Outside, the delightful Wildlife Garden (Apr-Oct only) showcases a range of British lowland habitats, including a 'Bee Tree', a hollow tree trunk that opens to reveal a busy hive.

Many of the museum's 22 million insect and plant specimens are housed in the new Darwin Centre, where they take up nearly 17 miles of shelving. With its eight-storey Cocoon, this is also home to the museum's research scientists, who can be watched at work. But a great deal of this amazing institution is hidden from public view, given over to labs and specialised storage.

▶ *Dino Snores – massively popular children's sleepover events at the museum – have been extended to adults. Check the website for details.*

Science Museum. *See p90.*

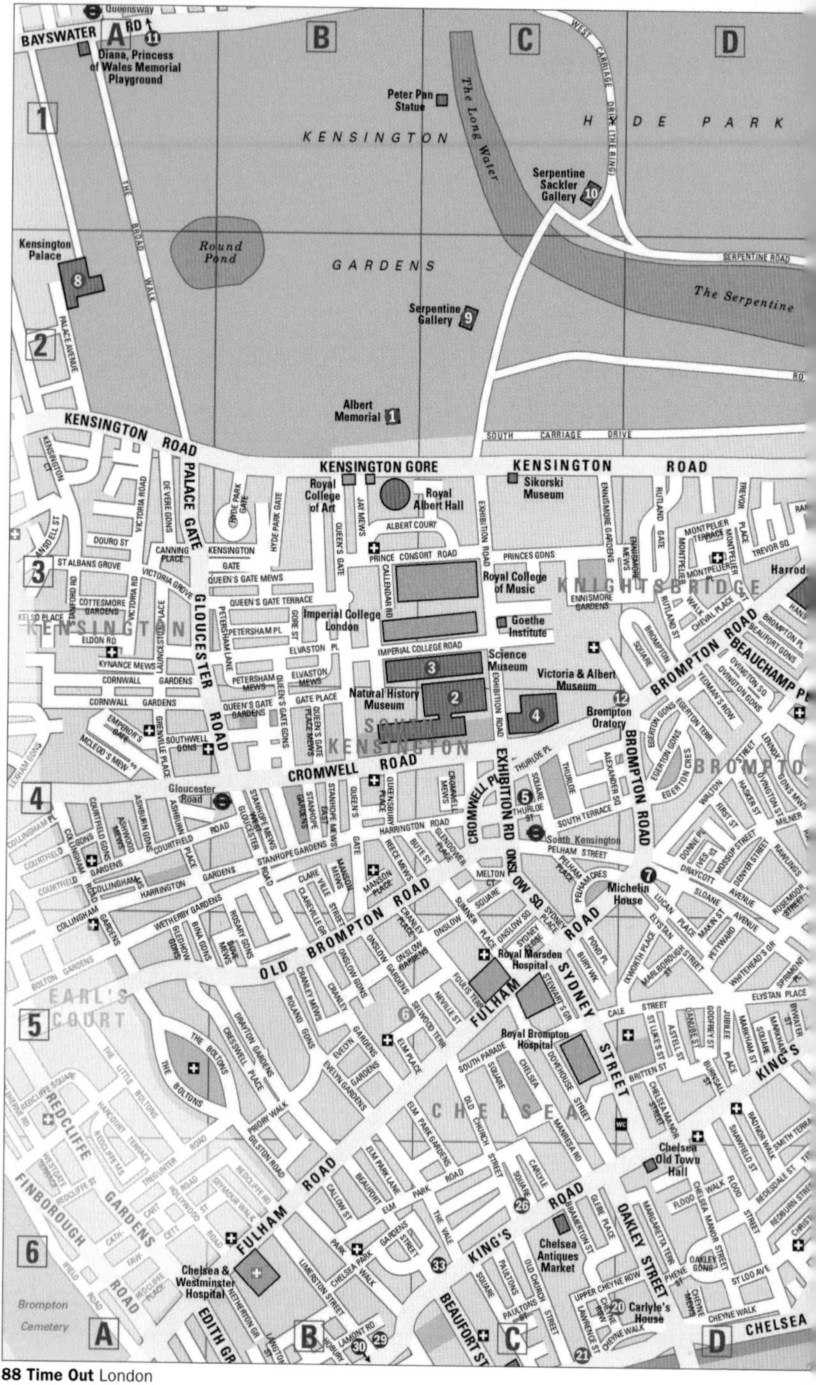

Queensway
BAYSWATER RD
Diana, Princess of Wales Memorial Playground
Peter Pan Statue
KENSINGTON GARDENS
The Long Water
HYDE PARK
WEST CARRIAGE DRIVE (THE RING)
Serpentine Sackler Gallery
Kensington Palace
Round Pond
THE BROAD WALK
SERPENTINE ROAD
The Serpentine
Serpentine Gallery
PALACE AVENUE
Albert Memorial
SOUTH CARRIAGE DRIVE
KENSINGTON ROAD
KENSINGTON GORE
Royal College of Art
Royal Albert Hall
Sikorski Museum
PALACE GATE
HYDE PARK GATE
VICTORIA ROAD
DE VERE GDNS
JAY MEWS
QUEEN'S GATE
ALBERT COURT
EXHIBITION ROAD
ENNISMORE GARDENS
RUTLAND GATE
TREVOR PLACE
MONTPELIER TERRACE
TREVOR SQ
Harrods
DOURO ST
CANNING PLACE
KENSINGTON GATE
PRINCE CONSORT ROAD
PRINCES GDNS
ST ALBANS GROVE
QUEEN'S GATE MEWS
Royal College of Music
KNIGHTSBRIDGE
COTTESMORE GARDENS
QUEEN'S GATE TERRACE
Imperial College London
Goethe Institute
KENSINGTON
PETERSHAM PL
ELDON RD
ELVASTON PL
IMPERIAL COLLEGE ROAD
Science Museum
Victoria & Albert Museum
KYNANCE MEWS
CORNWALL GARDENS
GLOUCESTER ROAD
Natural History Museum
Brompton Oratory
BROMPTON ROAD
BEAUCHAMP PL
EMPEROR'S GATE
SOUTHWELL GDNS
SOUTH KENSINGTON
CROMWELL ROAD
THURLOE PL
BROMPTON
Gloucester Road
HARRINGTON ROAD
South Kensington
PELHAM STREET
ONSLOW SQ
Michelin House
SLOANE AVENUE
COLLINGHAM GARDENS
OLD BROMPTON ROAD
SYDNEY STREET
Royal Marsden Hospital
FULHAM ROAD
EARL'S COURT
ELYSTAN PLACE
THE BOLTONS
Royal Brompton Hospital
KING'S ROAD
CHELSEA
REDCLIFFE GARDENS
Chelsea Old Town Hall
FINBOROUGH ROAD
Chelsea & Westminster Hospital
Chelsea Antiques Market
OAKLEY STREET
Carlyle's House
CHEYNE WALK
Brompton Cemetery
BEAUFORT ST
EDITH GR
CHELSEA
A B C D
1 2 3 4 5 6

EXPLORE

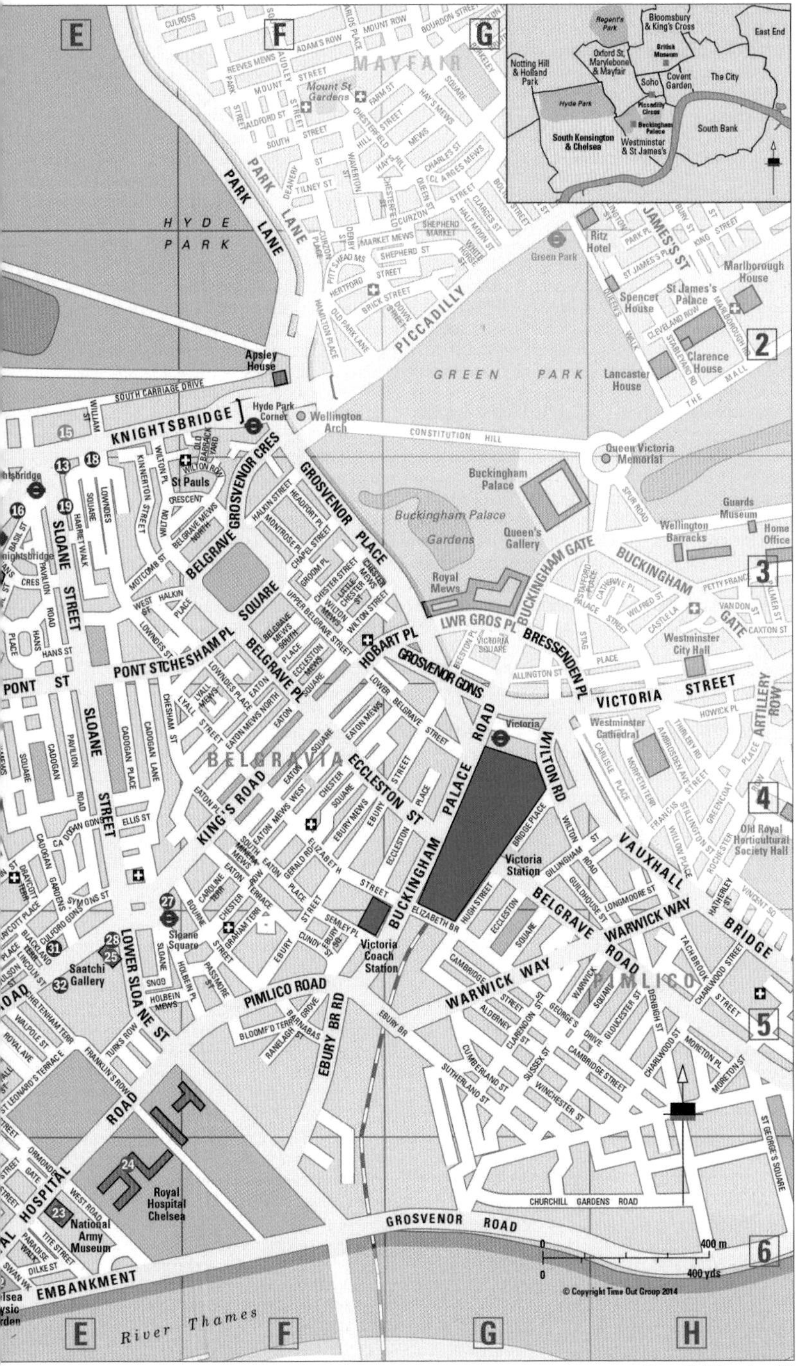

E
F
G
H
2
3
4
5
6
MAYFAIR
Mount St Gardens
HYDE PARK
PARK LANE
Regent's Park
Bloomsbury & King's Cross
East End
Notting Hill & Holland Park
Oxford St, Marylebone & Mayfair
Soho
Covent Garden
The City
Hyde Park
Piccadilly Circus
Buckingham Palace
South Kensington & Chelsea
Westminster & St James's
South Bank
Ritz Hotel
Green Park
Marlborough House
St James's Palace
Spencer House
Clarence House
Lancaster House
PICCADILLY
GREEN PARK
Apsley House
SOUTH CARRIAGE DRIVE
Hyde Park Corner
Wellington Arch
KNIGHTSBRIDGE
CONSTITUTION HILL
Queen Victoria Memorial
Buckingham Palace
Buckingham Palace Gardens
Queen's Gallery
Royal Mews
Guards Museum
Wellington Barracks
Home Office
St Pauls
GROSVENOR PLACE
GROSVENOR CRES
BELGRAVE SQUARE
BUCKINGHAM GATE
LWR GROS PL
BRESSENDEN PL
Westminster City Hall
VICTORIA STREET
ARTILLERY ROW
SLOANE STREET
PONT ST
CHESHAM PL
HOBART PL
GROSVENOR GDNS
Victoria
Westminster Cathedral
BELGRAVIA
BELGRAVE PL
ECCLESTON ST
BUCKINGHAM PALACE ROAD
WILTON RD
Old Royal Horticultural Society Hall
KING'S ROAD
Victoria Station
VAUXHALL BRIDGE
Victoria Coach Station
BELGRAVE ROAD
WARWICK WAY
PIMLICO
Sloane Square
Saatchi Gallery
LOWER SLOANE ST
PIMLICO ROAD
EBURY BR RD
CHURCHILL GARDENS ROAD
GROSVENOR ROAD
ROYAL HOSPITAL ROAD
Royal Hospital Chelsea
National Army Museum
EMBANKMENT
River Thames
400 m
400 yds
© Copyright Time Out Group 2014

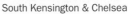

EXPLORE

EXPLORE

★ FREE Science Museum

Exhibition Road, SW7 2DD (switchboard 7942 4000, information 0870 870 4868, www.sciencemuseum.org.uk). South Kensington tube. **Open** 10am-6pm daily. **Admission** free; charges apply for special exhibitions. **Map** p88 C3 ❸

The Science Museum is a celebration of the wonders of technology in the service of our daily lives. On the ground floor, the shop – selling brilliant toys, not least because you can pretend they're educational – is part of the 'Energy Hall', which introduces the museum's collections with impressive 18th-century steam engines. In 'Exploring Space', rocket science and the lunar landings are illustrated by dramatically lit mock-ups and models, before the museum gears up for its core collection in 'Making the Modern World'. Introduced by Puffing Billy, the world's oldest steam locomotive (built in 1815), the gallery also contains Stephenson's Rocket. Also here are the Apollo 10 command module, classic cars and an absorbing collection of everyday technological marvels from 1750 right up to the present.

In the main body of the museum, the second floor holds displays on computing, marine engineering and mathematics; the third floor is dedicated to flight, among other things, including the hands-on Launchpad gallery, which has levers, pulleys, explosions and all manner of experiments for children (and their associated grown-ups). On the fifth floor, you'll find an old-fashioned but intriguing display on the science and art of medicine.

Beyond 'Making the Modern World', bathed in an eerie blue light, the three floors of the Wellcome Wing are where the museum makes sure it stays on the cutting edge of science. On the ground floor, 'Antenna' is a web-savvy look at breaking science stories, displaying video interviews and Q&As with real research scientists alongside the weird new objects they've been working on. Upstairs is the enjoyable and troubling 'Who Am I?' gallery. A dozen silver pods surround brightly lit cases of objects with engaging interactive displays – from a cartoon of ethical dilemmas that introduces you to your dorsolateral prefrontal cortex to a chance to find out what gender your brain is. Compelling objects include a jellyfish that's 'technically immortal', the statistically average British man (he's called Jose) and a pound of human fat, displayed alongside a gastric band. There's also the new Media Space on the second floor, for exhibitions drawn from the museum's impressive photographic archive. *Photo p87.*

► *There are plenty of other scientific and medical museums in London: the Wellcome Collection (see p154), the Hunterian (see p164) and the Royal Observatory (see p216) are all also recommended.*

★ FREE Victoria & Albert Museum

Cromwell Road, SW7 2RL (7942 2000, www.vam.ac.uk). South Kensington tube. **Open** 10am-5.45pm Mon-Thur, Sat, Sun; 10am-10pm Fri. *Tours* 10.30am, 12.30am, 1.30pm, 3.30pm daily. **Admission** free; charges for special exhibitions. **Map** p88 C4 ❹

The V&A is one of the world's – let alone London's – most magnificent museums, its foundation stone laid on this site by Queen Victoria in her last official public engagement in 1899. It is a superb showcase for applied arts from around the world, appreciably calmer than its tearaway cousins on the other side of Exhibition Road. Some 150 grand galleries on seven floors contain countless pieces of furniture, ceramics, sculpture, paintings, posters, jewellery, metalwork, glass, textiles and dress, spanning several centuries. Items are grouped by theme, origin or age: for advice, tap the patient staff, who field a formidable combination of leaflets, floorplans, general knowledge and polite concern.

Highlights include the seven Raphael Cartoons painted in 1515 as tapestry designs for the Sistine Chapel; the finest collection of Italian Renaissance sculpture outside Italy; the Ardabil carpet, the world's oldest and arguably most splendid floor covering, in the Jameel Gallery of Islamic Art; and the Luck of Edenhall, a thirteenth-century glass beaker from Syria. The Fashion galleries run from eighteenth-century court dress right up to contemporary chiffon numbers; the Architecture gallery has videos, models, plans and descriptions of various styles; and the famous Photography collection holds over 500,000 images.

Over more than a decade, the V&A's ongoing FuturePlan transformation has been a revelation. The completely refurbished Medieval & Renaissance Galleries are stunning, but there are many other eye-catching new or redisplayed exhibits: they were preceded by the restored mosaic floors and beautiful stained glass of the 14th- to 17th-century sculpture rooms, just off the central John Madejski Garden, and followed by the Furniture Galleries – an immediate hit on opening in late 2012. On a smaller scale, the Gilbert Collection of silver, gold and gemmed ornaments arrived from Somerset House; the Ceramics Galleries have been renovated and supplemented with an eye-catching bridge; there's lovely Buddhist sculpture in the Robert HN Ho Family Foundation Galleries; and the Theatre & Performance Galleries took over where Covent Garden's defunct Theatre Museum left off.

There's more to come. In December 2014, the latest grand opening will be the ambitious Europe 1600-1800 galleries, which cost £12.5m. A stunning 13ft-long table fountain – is due to form the centrepiece of seven new galleries, taking a chronological and thematic approach to European clothes, furnishings and other artefacts. We're also looking forward to seeing what's been done with the magnificent Cast Courts – the public should be allowed back to ogle the 18ft-high plaster David and other monumental sculptures in these double-height Victorian galleries in November 2014. *See also p91* **Improving the Classics**.

IMPROVING THE CLASSICS

The V&A's ongoing renovation programme is a thing of joy and wonder.

What's the best museum in London? The most recent figures (2012) say the British Museum is most popular, with 5.5m visits – ahead of a cluster of other attractions each with more than 5m: Tate Modern, the National Gallery, the Natural History Museum. The V&A is next, with 3.2m visitors – but that was a stunning increase of 16 per cent on last year.

What has been behind this increase? Over the last decade, the V&A has been undergoing major improvements, with the opening of the lovely Medieval and Renaissance Galleries in 2009 the culmination of phase I of what the museum calls its FuturePlan – some 43 projects, spread over a massive 26,500sq ft of gallery space. The next phase is dominated by the development of entirely new gallery spaces and a new entrance to the museum from Exhibition Road, and will take years, but the first phase II opening, the new Dr Susan Weber Gallery, was another beauty: six centuries of furniture-making explored with 200 pieces from Britain, Europe and Asia. In December 2014, it will be joined by the ambitious Europe 1600-1800 galleries, which cost £12.5m. A stunning 13ft-long table fountain – which had to be painstakingly reconstructed from tiny 18th-century fragments – is due to form the centrepiece of seven new galleries, taking a chronological and thematic approach to European clothes, furnishings and other artefacts.

However, we're most excited by the prospect of being able to wander in the double-height Victorian Cast Courts again. Established in 1873, the Courts contain full-scale casts of Classical monuments – 46A has a perfect copy of Trajan's Column (it can be viewed from Room 111 while work is ongoing), while 46B is a compendium of European sculpture that includes an 18ft cast of Michelangelo's *David*. Both Courts are being restored to their original Victorian splendour, and are due to reopen to the public in November 2014.

EXPLORE

Restaurants

Daquise

20 Thurloe Street, SW7 2LT (7589 6117, www.daquise.co.uk). South Kensington tube. **Open** noon-11pm daily. **Main courses** £15-£22. *Set lunch (noon-4pm Mon-Fri)* £9 2 courses. **Map** p88 C4 ❺ **Polish**

In May 2013 regulars were distressed at news that this much-loved grande dame of London Polish restaurants (established 1947) was to close – but staff and the restaurant's previous owners rallied round to save it. In the shabby-chic, light and airy interior, enlivened with fresh flowers, robust, flavourful, no-nonsense traditional dishes are served with great charm. Classic cold starters of meltingly tender herring with cream, apple, onion and flax oil, or beetroot with subtly warming horse-radish, are ladled directly from capacious earthenware bowls, while mains are assembled directly at the table from well-worn saucepans, borne by the chefs who lovingly prepared the dishes.

Pubs & bars

Anglesea Arms

15 Selwood Terrace, SW7 3QG (7373 7960, www.capitalpubcompany.com). South Kensington tube. **Open** 11am-11pm Mon-Sat; 11am-10.30pm Sun. *Food served* noon-3pm, 6-10pm Mon-Fri; noon-5pm, 6-10pm Sat; noon-5pm, 6-9.30pm Sun. **Map** p88 B5 ❻

The local of both Charles Dickens and DH Lawrence, this old boozer is packed on summer evenings, the front terrace and main bar filled with professional blokes chugging ale, and their female equivalents putting bottles of Sancerre on expenses. But the Anglesea has always had more aura than the average South Kensington hostelry; perhaps it's the link with the Great Train Robbery, reputedly planned here.

Shops & services

Conran Shop

Michelin House, 81 Fulham Road, South Kensington, SW3 6RD (7589 7401, www.conranshop.co.uk). South Kensington tube. **Open** 10am-6pm Mon, Tue, Fri; 10am-7pm Wed, Thur; 10am-6.30pm Sat; noon-6pm Sun. **Map** p88 D4 ❼ **Homewares**

Sir Terence Conran's flagship store in the Fulham Road's beautiful 1909 Michelin Building showcases furniture and design for every room in the house as well as the garden. As well as design classics, such as the Eames DAR chair, there are plenty of portable accessories, gadgets, books, stationery and toiletries that make great gifts or souvenirs.

Other location 55 Marylebone High Street, Marylebone, W1U 5HS (7723 2223).

HYDE PARK & KENSINGTON GARDENS

Hyde Park Corner, Knightsbridge, Lancaster Gate or Queensway tube.

At one and a half miles long and about a mile wide, **Hyde Park** (7298 2000, www.royalparks.gov.uk) is one of the largest of London's Royal Parks. The land was appropriated in 1536 from the monks of Westminster Abbey by Henry VIII for hunting deer. Although opened to the public in the early 1600s, the parks were favoured only by the upper echelons of society.

Serpentine, Hyde Park.

EXPLORE

Serpentine Sackler Gallery. *See p94.*

At the end of the 17th century, William III, averse to the dank air of Whitehall Palace, relocated to **Kensington Palace** (*see right*). A corner of Hyde Park was sectioned off to make grounds for the palace and closed to the public, until King George II opened it on Sundays to those wearing formal dress. Nowadays, **Kensington Gardens** is delineated from Hyde Park only by the line of the Serpentine and the Long Water. Beside the Long Water is a bronze statue of **Peter Pan**, erected in 1912: it was in Kensington Gardens beside the Round Pond eight years earlier that playwright JM Barrie met Jack Llewelyn Davies, the boy who was the inspiration for Peter. The **Diana, Princess of Wales Memorial Playground** (*see p251*) is a kids' favourite, as is Kathryn Gustafson's ring-shaped **Princess Diana Memorial Fountain**. Near the fountain, Simon Gudgeon's giant bird *Isis* was in 2009 the first sculpture added to the park for half a century. There are changing exhibitions of contemporary art at the **Serpentine Gallery**, which has opened a brand-new – Zaha Hadid-designed – counterpart just across the bridge.

The **Serpentine** itself is London's oldest boating lake, home to ducks, coots, swans, tufty-headed grebes and, every summer, gently perspiring blokes rowing their children or lovers about. The lake is at the bottom of **Hyde Park**, which isn't a beautiful park, but is of historic interest. The legalisation of public assembly in the park led to the establishment of **Speakers' Corner** in 1872 (close to Marble Arch tube), where political and religious ranters – sane and otherwise – still have the floor every Sunday afternoon. Marx, Lenin, Orwell and the Pankhursts all spoke here. It has made the park a traditional destination for protest marches: notably the million opponents of the Iraq War in 2003, more recently trades union protests against government austerity measures in 2012. There is also an interesting memorial in the south-east corner of the park. On 7 July 2005, 52 people were killed by suicide bombers as they made their way to work. Their commemoration, set between the Lovers' Walk and busy Park Lane, consists of 52 10ft-tall, square steel columns, one for each fatality, each marked with the date, time and location of that person's death.

The park perimeter is popular with skaters, as well as with bike- and horse-riders. If you're exploring on foot and the vast expanses defeat you, look out for the **Liberty Drives** (May-Oct). Driven by volunteers, these electric buggies, each with space for a wheelchair, pick up groups of sightseers and ferry them around; there's no fare, but offer a donation if you can.

Sights & museums

Kensington Palace

Kensington Gardens, W8 4PX (information 0844 482 7777, reservations 0844 482 7799, www.hrp.org.uk). High Street Kensington or Queensway tube. **Open** *Apr-Oct* 10am-6pm daily. *Nov-Mar* 10am-5pm daily. **Admission** £16.50; £13.75 reductions; free under-16s. **Map** p88 A2 ❽

Sir Christopher Wren extended this Jacobean mansion to palatial proportions on the instructions of William III, initiating the palace's long love affair with royalty – which culminated with the floral memorials for one particular resident, Princess Diana, at the palace's gate after her fatal accident in 1997. Wren's work too was adapted, under George I, with the addition of

IN THE KNOW GIDDY-UP!

Watch members of the Household Cavalry emerge from their South Carriage Drive barracks in **Hyde Park** at 10.30am daily (9.30am Sunday). They then ride to Horse Guards Parade for the **Changing the Guard** (*see p41* **Stunning Ceremonials**).

EXPLORE

intricate trompe l'oeil ceilings and staircases. Visitors can now follow a whimsical trail focused on four 'stories' of former residents – Diana, of course; William and Mary, and Mary's sister Queen Anne; Georges I and II; Queen Victoria – unearthing the facts through handily placed 'newspapers'. Artefacts include paintings by the likes of Tintoretto, contemporary art and fashion installations, and even Victoria's (tiny) wedding dress.

★ FREE Serpentine & Serpentine Sackler Galleries

Kensington Gardens, nr Albert Memorial, W2 3XA (7402 6075, www.serpentinegalleries.org). Lancaster Gate or South Kensington tube. **Open** 10am-6pm daily. **Admission** free; donations appreciated. **Map** p88 C2 ❾ & p88 C1 ❿

The secluded location south-west of the Long Water and Serpentine makes this small 1930s tea house an attractive destination for lovers of contemporary art. The rolling two-monthly programme of exhibitions features a mix of up-to-the-minute artists and edgy career retrospectives. Every spring, a renowned architect, who's never before built in the UK, is commissioned to build a new pavilion. It then opens to the public, with a packed programme of cultural events, from June to September.

In 2013, the gallery underwent a massive expansion – by dint of opening a second location, the Serpentine Sackler, just across the bridge. Devoted to emerging art in all forms, the Sackler is a Grade II-listed, Palladian former gunpowder store, over the restaurant area of which starchitect Zaha Hadid has cast a billowing white cape of roof. *Photo p93.*

► *Hadid designed the first Serpentine Pavilion back in 2000, and now has both Sackler and the Olympic Aquatics Centre (see p237) as London representatives of her singular architectural vision.*

Restaurants

★ Le Café Anglais

8 Porchester Gardens, W2 4DB (7221 1415, www.lecafeanglais.co.uk). Bayswater tube. **Open** noon-3.30pm, 6.30-10.30pm Mon-Thur; noon-3.30pm, 6.30-11pm Fri; 11am-3.30pm, 6.30-11pm Sat; noon-3.30pm, 6.30-10pm Sun. **Main courses** £9.50-£27.50. **Map** p88 A1 ⓫ **Modern European**

Rowley Leigh's celebrated brasserie looks as good as when it opened in 2008, with its art deco lines, tall leaded windows and graceful grey-green banquettes. At one end, beneath a stunning chandelier, is the café/oyster bar; at the other, the open kitchen. The appealing menu is nicely varied, from raw, cured and smoked seafood and meat (oysters, pickled herrings, rabbit rillettes) via assorted appetisers (the famous parmesan custard with anchovy toast) to straightforward bistro fare (omelette, burger, fish pie) and dishes such as roast chicken leg with oregano and skordalia.

KNIGHTSBRIDGE

Knightsbridge tube.

Knightsbridge in the 11th century was a village celebrated for its taverns, highwaymen and the legend that two knights once fought to the death on the bridge spanning the Westbourne River (later dammed to form Hyde Park's Serpentine lake). In modern Knightsbridge, urban princesses would be too busy unsheathing the credit card to notice such a farrago. Voguish **Harvey Nichols** holds court at the top of **Sloane Street**, which leads down to Sloane Square. Expensive brands – Gucci, Prada, Chanel – dominate. East of Sloane Street is **Belgravia**, characterised by a cluster of embassies around **Belgrave Square**. Hidden behind the stucco-clad parades fronting the square are numerous mews, worth exploring for the pubs they conceal, notably the **Nag's Head** (53 Kinnerton Street, 7235 1135).

For many tourists, Knightsbridge means one thing: **Harrods** (*see p95*). From its olive green awning to its green-coated doormen, it's an instantly recognisable retail legend. Further along is the imposing **Brompton Oratory**.

Sights & museums

FREE Brompton Oratory

Thurloe Place, Brompton Road, SW7 2RP (7808 0900, www.bromptonoratory.com). South Kensington tube. **Open** 6.30am-8pm daily. **Admission** free; donations appreciated. **Map** p88 D4 ⓬

The second-biggest Catholic church in the country (after Westminster Cathedral; *see p78*) is formally the Church of the Immaculate Heart of Mary, but almost universally known as the Brompton Oratory. Completed in 1884, it feels older, partly because of the Baroque Italianate style but also because much of the decoration pre-dates the structure: Mazzuoli's 17th-century apostle statues, for example, are from Siena cathedral. The 11am Solemn Mass sung in Latin on Sundays is enchanting, as are Vespers, at 3.30pm; the website has details.

► *During the Cold War, KGB agents used the church as a dead-letter box.*

Restaurants

There's a branch of the popular – and self-explanatory – minichain **Burger & Lobster** (*see p127*) in **Harvey Nichols** (*see p96*).

★ Bar Boulud

Mandarin Oriental Hyde Park, 66 Knightsbridge, SW1X 7LA (7201 3899, www.barboulud.com). Knightsbridge tube. **Open** noon-11pm Mon-Sat; noon-10pm Sun. **Main courses** £13-£32. **Map** p89 E3 ⓭ **French**

Overseen by renowned chef Daniel Boulud, the restaurant has an eye-catching view of the open-plan kitchen where chefs work in zen-like calm. Charcuterie from Gilles Verot is a big draw, as are the elegant French brasserie options and finger-licking American staples. We've had burgers here and loved every bite – try a beef patty topped with pulled pork and green chilli mayonnaise. On our latest visit, we enjoyed such culinary gems as a robust french onion soup, resplendent with caramelised onions and topped with molten gruyère.

★ Zuma

5 Raphael Street, SW7 1DL (7584 1010, www.zumarestaurant.com). Knightsbridge tube. **Open** *Restaurant* noon-2.45pm, 6-10.45pm Mon-Fri; 12.30-3.15pm, 6-10.45pm Sat, Sun. *Bar* noon-11pm Mon-Fri; 12.30-11pm Sat, Sun. **Main courses** £14.80-£70. **Map** p89 E3 ⓮ **Japanese**

Out of simplicity can come excellence, and the food at Zuma is a case in point. The venue may be swish but when it comes to the food, much of the wow factor is down to high-class ingredients that haven't been messed around with too much. Own-made silken tofu, presented in a cedar saké cup, is rich, creamy and light. More indulgent dishes like spicy miso with lobster have a clarity of flavour. Give the saké list a proper look too: there are more than 40 to choose from.

Zuma.

Pubs & bars

Mandarin Bar

Mandarin Oriental Hyde Park, 66 Knightsbridge, SW1X 7LA (7235 2000, www.mandarinoriental.com/london). Knightsbridge tube. **Open** 10.30am-1.30am Mon-Sat; 10.30am-12.30am Sun. **Map** p89 E2 ⓯

The Mandarin Oriental is in part famous as the location of Heston Blumenthal's Dinner, so some customers at the bar are praying for a walk-in space in the restaurant. If you're going to choose a waiting room, you can't do much better than this. The room is dazzling, with a central bar and an array of glass, wood and marble. The drinks are done expertly. House cocktails are devised with good sense, and classics are well handled – and with serving sizes to match the high prices. They're matched with polished service and good bar snacks.

Shops & services

Cutler & Gross

16 Knightsbridge Green, Knightsbridge, SW1X 7QL (7581 2250, www.cutlerandgross.com). Knightsbridge tube. **Open** 9.30am-7pm Mon-Sat; noon-5pm Sun. **Map** p89 E3 ⓰ **Accessories**

C&G celebrated its 40th anniversary in 2009, and its stock of handmade frames is still at the cutting edge of optical style. Stock runs from Andy Warhol-inspired glasses to naturally light buffalo-horn frames, and recent collaborations have included frames with trend-leaders Comme des Garçons.

Other location 7 Knightsbridge Green, Knightsbridge, SW1X 7QL (7590 9995).

► *For cool vintage frames and sunglasses, check out Covent Garden's Opera Opera (98 Long Acre, WC2E 9NR, 7836 9246, www.operaopera.net), which has operated from the same corner site for over three decades.*

Harrods

87-135 Brompton Road, Knightsbridge, SW1X 7XL (7730 1234, www.harrods.com). Knightsbridge tube. **Open** 10am-8pm Mon-Sat; noon-6pm Sun (browsing from 11.30am). **Map** p89 E3 ⓱ **Department store**

All the glitz and marble can be a bit much, but in the store that boasts of selling everything, it's hard not to leave with at least one thing. In fact, it even sold itself in 2010: former owner Mohammed Al Fayed received a reported £1.5bn from Qatar Holdings for the place. It's on the fashion floors that Harrods really comes into its own, with a 10,000sq ft Designer Studio on the first floor, featuring well-edited collections from the heavyweights, including a revamped Chanel boutique. There's also an excellent lingerie section and a top-notch sport section. The legendary food halls and restaurants range even have a branch of 18th-century Venetian coffee bar Caffè Florian. *Photo p96.*

Harrods. *See p95.*

Harvey Nichols

109-125 Knightsbridge, SW1X 7RJ (7235 5000, www.harveynichols.com), Knightsbridge tube.
Open 10am-8pm Mon-Sat; noon-6pm Sun.
Map p89 E3 ⓲ **Department store**
Harvey Nicks is coasting a little these days, but you'll still find a worthy clutch of unique fashion brands over the eight floors of beauty, fashion, food and homeware. The fashion floors showcase emerging British talent, new designers and established favourites. The fifth floor has the well-stocked food market and a branch of the Burger & Lobster minichain (*see p127*).

Tom Ford

201-202 Sloane Street, SW1X 9QX (3141 7800, www.tomford.com). Knightsbridge tube.
Open 10am-6pm Mon-Sat; 10am-7pm Sun.
Map p89 E3 ⓳ **Fashion**
Just when Sloane Street's reputation for boutiques that are expensive but hardly classy seemed secure, up rocks the coolest man in fashion. No one who knows Ford's suave tailoring will be surprised that his first stand-alone store in Britain is stunning, with an eye-catchingly sci-fi spiral staircase the centrepiece of an impressive 8,000sq ft of retail space. Expect big lapels for gents, hip-hugging skirts and dresses for ladies – and consummate good taste.

IN THE KNOW
CHIHULY ARE YOU?

The extraordinary sculptural blown-glass of American artist Dale Chihuly has enlivened the foyer of the **V&A** (*see p90*) since his 30m-long chandelier was hung over the information desk in 2001. Now **Harrods** (*see p95*) is getting in on the act: with a 1,500-piece Chihuly commission installed at the start of 2014.

CHELSEA

Sloane Square tube then various buses.

Chelsea is where London's wealthy classes play in cultural and geographical isolation. Originally a fishing hamlet, the area was a 'village of palaces' by the 16th century, home to the likes of Henry VIII's ill-fated advisor Sir Thomas More. Artists and poets (Whistler, Carlyle, Wilde) followed from the 1880s, before the fashionistas arrived with the opening of Mary Quant's Bazaar in 1955. Soon after, Chelsea had acquired a raffish reputation and was at the forefront of successive youth culture revolutions. Synonymous with the Swinging Sixties and immortalised by punk, the dissipated phase of the **King's Road** is now a matter for historians as the street teems with pricey fashion houses and air-conditioned poodle parlours. Yet on a sunny day, it does make a vivid stroll. For one thing, you don't have to take yourself as seriously as the locals. And for another, the area is figuratively rich in historical associations, and literally so with the expensive red-brick houses that slumber down leafy mews and charming, cobbled sidestreets.

At the top (east end) of the King's Road is **Sloane Square**. It's named after Sir Hans Sloane, who provided the land for the Chelsea Physic Garden (*see p97*), invented milk chocolate in the early 18th century and was instrumental in the founding of the British Museum (which was set up to hold his collections when he died). The shaded benches in the middle of the square provide a lovely counterpoint to the looming façades of Tiffany & Co and the enormous Peter Jones department store, in a 1930s building with excellent views from its top-floor café. A certain edginess is lent to proceedings by the **Royal Court Theatre** (*see p286*), which shocked the nation with its 1956 première of John Osborne's *Look Back in Anger*.

To escape the bustle and fumes, head to the **Duke of York Square**, a pedestrianised enclave of boutiques and restaurants presided over by a statue of Sir Hans. In the summer, the cooling fountains attract hordes of children, their parents sitting to watch from the outdoor café tables or taking advantage of the Saturday food market. The square is also home to the mercilessly modern art of the **Saatchi Gallery** (*see p98*), housed in former military barracks.

The once-adventurous shops on the King's Road are now a mix of trendier-than-thou fashion houses and high-street chains, but there are still a few gems around: **Shop at Bluebird** (*see p99*) and London's second branch of **Anthropologie** (*see p115*) suggest future directions. Wander Cale Street for some pleasing boutiques, or head for the **Chelsea Farmers' Market** on adjoining Sydney Street to find a clutter of artfully distressed rustic sheds housing restaurants and shops selling everything from cigars to garden products. Sydney Street leads to **St Luke's Church**, where Charles Dickens married Catherine Hogarth in 1836.

Towards the western end of the King's Road is **Bluebird**, a dramatic art deco former motor garage housing a café, a restaurant and the hip shop mentioned above. A little further up the road, the **World's End** store (no.430) occupies what was once Vivienne Westwood's notorious leather- and fetishwear boutique Sex; a green-haired Johnny Rotten auditioned for the Sex Pistols here in 1975 by singing along to an Alice Cooper record on the shop's jukebox.

Running parallel to the King's Road, Chelsea's riverside has long been noted for its nurseries and gardens, lending a village air that befits a place of retirement for the former British soldiers living in the **Royal Hospital Chelsea** (*see p98*). In summer, the Chelsea Pensioners, as they're known, regularly don red coats and tricorn hats when venturing beyond the gates. The Royal Hospital's lovely gardens host the **Chelsea Flower Show** (*see p33*) each spring. Next door is the **National Army Museum** (*see p98*).

West from the river end of Royal Hospital Road is **Cheyne Walk**. Its river-view benches remain good spots for a sit-down, but the tranquillity of the **Chelsea Physic Garden** (*see right*) is the real treat.

Further west on Cheyne Walk, the park benches of **Chelsea Embankment Gardens** face Albert Bridge, where signs still order troops to 'Break step when marching over this bridge'. In the small gardens, you'll find a statue of the great historian Thomas Carlyle – the 'sage of Chelsea', whose home is preserved (*see right* **Carlyle's House**). Nearby, a gold-faced statue of Sir Thomas More looks out over the river from the garden of **Chelsea Old Church** (*see below*), where he once sang in the choir and may well be (partially) buried. Follow Old Church Street north and you'll find the **Chelsea Arts Club** (no.143), founded in 1871 by Whistler and now host to occasional public events, including classical recitals.

North of the western extremity of Cheyne Walk are Brompton Cemetery (suffragette Emmeline Pankhurst is buried here) and the home ground of London's first Champions League winners: Chelsea FC. Tickets for league games are hard to come by, but **Stamford Bridge** (Fulham Road, SW6 1HS, 0871 984 1905, www.chelseafc.com) does have the excellent **Chelsea Centenary Museum** (10.30am-4.30pm daily, £11, £9-£10 reductions), surely the only museum in England to display a photograph of Raquel Welch in football strip – making a valiant attempt to side-foot the ball.

Sights & museums

Carlyle's House

24 Cheyne Row, SW3 5HL (7352 7087, www.nationaltrust.org.uk). Sloane Square tube or bus 11, 19, 22, 49, 170, 211, 319. **Open** *Mar-Oct* 11am-4.30pm Wed-Sun. **Admission** £5.10; £2.60 children; £12.80 family. **No credit cards. Map** p88 D6 ⑳

Thomas Carlyle and his wife Jane moved to this four-storey, Queen Anne house in 1834. The house was inaugurated as a museum in 1896, 15 years after Carlyle's death, offering an intriguing snapshot of Victorian life. The writer's quest for quiet (details of his valiant attempts to soundproof the attic) strikes a chord today: he was plagued by the sound of revelry from Cremorne Pleasure Gardens.

FREE Chelsea Old Church

Old Church Street, SW3 5DQ (7795 1019, www.chelseaoldchurch.org.uk). Sloane Square tube or bus 11, 19, 22, 49, 319. **Open** 2-4pm Tue-Thur; 1.30-5pm Sun. *Services* 8am, 10am, 11am, 12.15pm Sun. *Evensong* 6pm Sun. **Admission** free; donations appreciated. **Map** p88 C6 ㉑

Legend has it that the Thomas More Chapel, which remains on the south side, contains More's headless body buried somewhere under the walls (his head, after being spiked on London Bridge, was 'rescued' and buried in a family vault in St Dunstan's church, Canterbury). There's a striking statue of More outside the church. Guides are on hand on Sundays.

★ Chelsea Physic Garden

66 Royal Hospital Road, SW3 4HS (7352 5646, www.chelseaphysicgarden.co.uk). Sloane Square tube or bus 11, 19, 22. **Open** *Apr-June, Oct* 11am-6pm Tue-Fri, Sun. *July, Aug* 11am-6pm Mon, Tue, Thur, Fri, Sun; 11am-10pm Wed. *Tours* times vary; phone to check. **Admission** £9.90; £6.60 reductions; free under-5s. *Tours* free. **Map** p89 E6 ㉒

EXPLORE

The capacious grounds of this gorgeous botanic garden are filled with healing herbs and vegetables, rare trees and dye plants. It was founded in 1673 by Sir Hans Sloane with the purpose of cultivating and studying plants for medical purposes. The first specimens were brought to England and planted in 1676, with the famous Cedars of Lebanon arriving a little later. The garden opened to the public in 1893.

FREE National Army Museum

Royal Hospital Road, SW3 4HT (7730 0717, www.nam.ac.uk). Sloane Square tube or bus 11, 137, 170. **Open** 10am-5.30pm daily. **Admission** free. **Map** p89 E6 ㉓

This museum dedicated to the history of the British Army runs chronologically, from the wars of Empire ('Changing the World, 1784-1904'), through the two World Wars and into contemporary conflicts including Northern Ireland, the Falklands, and Afghanistan ('Conflicts of Interest, 1969-present'). Key artefacts include a French eagle standard from the Napoleonic Wars and a model of Waterloo with 70,000 soldiers. There's also a gallery of military art since the early 17th century, including paintings of boozing soldiers and bloody battles and a bust of Florence Nightingale.

FREE Royal Hospital Chelsea

Royal Hospital Road, SW3 4HT (7881 5200, www.chelsea-pensioners.org.uk). Sloane Square tube or bus 11, 19, 22, 137, 170. **Open** 10am-4pm Mon-Sat; 10am-2pm Sun. **Admission** free. **Map** p89 E6 ㉔

Around 350 Chelsea Pensioners (retired soldiers) live at the Royal Hospital, founded in 1682 by Charles II and designed by Sir Christopher Wren (with adjustments by Robert Adam and Sir John Soane). Retired soldiers are still eligible to apply for a final posting here if they're over 65 and in receipt of an Army or War Disability Pension for Army Service. The pensioners have their own club room, bowling green and gardens, and get tickets to Chelsea FC home games. The museum (same times) has more about their lives.

FREE Saatchi Gallery

Duke of York's HQ, King's Road, SW3 4SQ (7811 3070, www.saatchigallery.com). Sloane Square tube. **Open** 10am-6pm daily. **Admission** free. **Map** p89 E5 ㉕

Charles Saatchi's gallery offers 50,000sq ft of space for temporary exhibitions. Given his fame as a promoter in the 1990s of what became known as the Young British Artists – Damien Hirst, Tracey Emin, Gavin Turk, Sarah Lucas et al – it will surprise many that the opening exhibition a few years back was devoted to new Chinese art. More recent shows have continued the international feel.

Restaurants

★ Cadogan Arms

298 King's Road, SW3 5UG (7352 6500, www.thecadoganarmschelsea.com). Sloane Square tube then bus 19, 22, 319. **Open** 11am-11pm Mon-Sat; 11am-10pm Sun. *Food served* noon-3.30pm, 6-10.30pm Mon-Fri; noon-10.30pm Sat; noon-9pm Sun. **Main courses** £14-£24. **Map** p88 C6 ㉖ **Gastropub**

In 2009, this 19th-century Chelsea pub was given a major rebuild by its new owners, the Martin brothers. It now has a countrified look, complete with stuffed animals and fly-fishing displays, and remains a proper boozer, with top-quality real ales, notwithstanding the snug and smoothly run dining area, where great food is on offer.

▶ *On Sloane Square, the Martin brothers' Botanist (no.7, 7730 0077) provides a similar mix of fine booze and hearty food.*

Colbert

51 Sloane Square, SW1W 8AX (7730 2804, www.colbertchelsea.com). Sloane Square tube. **Open** 8am-11pm Mon-Thur; 8am-11.30pm Fri, Sat; 8am-10.30pm Sun. **Main courses** £6.95-£30. **Map** p89 E4 ㉗ **Brasserie**

Paying homage to Continental grand cafés with marble, linen napkins and mirrors aplenty, Colbert feels more casual and local than its siblings – the Wolseley (*see p82*), the Delaunay (*see p147*) and Brasserie Zédel (*see p114*) – and the posters in the booth-lined bar area advertising performances by Olivier and Vivien Leigh next door at the Royal Court Theatre (*see p286*) lend a sense of history. It also trumps the others with pavement tables from which to admire the beautiful people of SW3. More importantly, it serves the best lunch in the area: perhaps a deliciously decadent smoked haddock florentine served on spinach, under a perfectly poached egg, in a buttery cream sauce, or

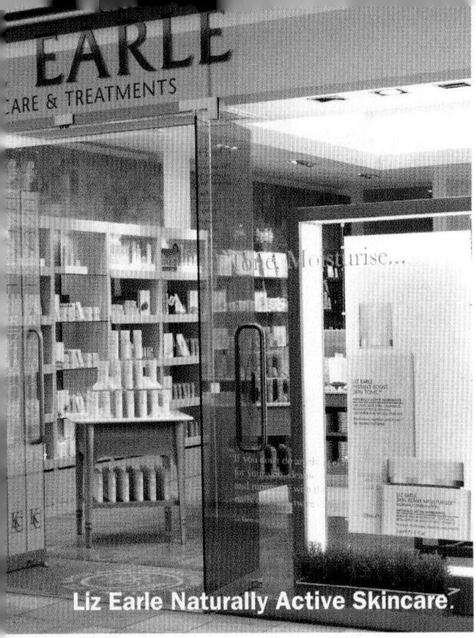

Liz Earle Naturally Active Skincare.

a croque grand'mère – perfectly fried brioche filled with melted comté cheese, bayonne ham and béchamel sauce, topped with a fried egg.

Gallery Mess

Saatchi Gallery, Duke of York's HQ, King's Road, SW3 4LY (7730 8135, www.saatchigallery.com/gallerymess). Sloane Square tube. **Open** *Bar* 10am-11pm Mon-Sat; 10am-7pm Sun. *Restaurant* noon-9.30pm Mon-Sat; noon-6.30pm Sun. **Main courses** £13.50-£22. **Map** p89 E5 (28) **Brasserie**

As befits its Chelsea location, this welcoming brasserie at the Saatchi art gallery is smarter than most, with white linen tablecloths, exposed brickwork and impressive bar all somewhat in thrall to the vaulted ceiling and expansive curtain of floor-to-ceiling arched windows. There's also a large outdoor terrace. Service is disarmingly friendly and mains offer comforting flavours and proportions. So you'll find cod and chips, steak sandwich, charcuterie and smoked fish platters, caesar salad and afternoon tea.

Medlar

438 King's Road, SW10 0LJ (7349 1900, www.medlarrestaurant.co.uk). Fulham Broadway tube or bus 11, 22. **Open** noon-3pm, 6.30-10.30pm daily. **Set lunch** (Mon-Fri) £27 3 courses; (Sat) £30 3 courses; (Sun) £35 3 courses. **Set dinner** (Mon-Sat) £45 3 courses; (Sun) £35 3 courses. **Map** p88 B6 (29) **Modern European**

The decor here is understated: soothing grey-green colour scheme and unobtrusive artwork. The real artistry arrives on the plates, dishes of astounding excellence. Assemblies are complex and have lengthy names: crisp calf's brain with smoked duck breast, aïoli, pink fir potatoes and tardivo (raddichio), for example. But every ingredient justifies its place in entirely natural-seeming juxtapositions of flavour, texture and colour. And the execution is nearly flawless. Save room for wonderful (and relatively simple) puddings, such as cardamom custard with saffron oranges, pomegranate and langues de chat.

Mona Lisa

417 King's Road, SW10 0LR (7376 5447). Fulham Broadway tube or bus 11, 22. **Meals served** 6.30am-11pm Mon-Sat; 8.30am-5.30pm Sun. **Main courses** £6-£18.95. **Map** p88 B6 (30) **Italian/café**

Not much to look at, either inside or out, the Mona Lisa is hidden away at the 'wrong' end of the King's Road, just beyond World's End. But the bonhomie is infectious, and if you order the right thing, such as the meltingly tender calf's liver alla salvia (with butter and sage), served with old-school potatoes and veg, you won't care about the homely decor. The menu ranges across breakfasts, sandwiches, burgers, omelettes, jacket potatoes and pastas to three-course blow-outs (at lunch, the latter is just £8.95).

Shops & services

John Sandoe

10 Blacklands Terrace, SW3 2SR (7589 9473, www.johnsandoe.com). Sloane Square tube. **Open** 9.30am-6.30pm Mon-Sat; 11am-5pm Sun. **Map** p89 E5 (31) **Books & music**

Tucked away on a side street, this 50-year-old independent always looked just as a bookshop should, with stock literally packed to the rafters – they used to say that of the 25,000 books here, 24,000 were a single copy, which is some serious breadth of stock. The shop was undergoing refurbishment in early 2014, but the enthusiasm and knowledge of the staff can be taken as, forgive us, read.

Liz Earle Naturally Active Skincare

38-39 Duke of York Square, SW3 4LY (7881 7750, http://uk.lizearle.com). Sloane Square tube. **Open** 10am-7pm Mon, Wed-Sat; 10.30am-7pm Tue; 11am-5pm Sun. **Map** p89 E5 (32) **Health & beauty**

The London flagship of Liz Earle's botanical skincare range is housed in a large, light, fresh space, and stocks the full range of pleasingly gimmick-free and affordable products based on a regime of cleansing, toning and moisturising. Highlights among the products include the Instant Boost Skin Tonic and Superskin Moisturiser. 'Minis' and essentials packs are a great introduction (£14.75 for a starter kit).

Shop at Bluebird

350 King's Road, SW3 5UU (7351 3873, www.theshopatbluebird.com). Sloane Square tube. **Open** 10am-7pm Mon-Sat; noon-6pm Sun. **Map** p88 C6 (33) **Fashion & homewares**

Part lifestyle boutique and part design gallery, the Shop at Bluebird offers a shifting showcase of clothing for men, women and children, accessories, furniture, books and gadgets. The shop has a retro feel, with vintage furniture and hand-printed fabrics. The menswear range is particularly strong.

Oxford Street, Marylebone & Mayfair

Oxford Street is working hard to stay top of London's shopping destinations, with a revamped roundabout at Marble Arch, wider pavements, the innovative pedestrian crossings at Oxford Circus, and an all-new 'eastern gateway' development near the fabulous new Tottenham Court Road superstation for Crossrail (due for completion in 2018).

North are the luxury cafés and boutiques of Marylebone, bounded to the north by Regent's Park and to the west by the Arab shisha cafés and juice bars of the Edgware Road. South of Oxford Street, Mayfair oozes wealth, while to the south-east, neon-lit Piccadilly Circus is a bit of town every Londoner does their best to avoid.

La Fromagerie.

Don't Miss

1 Royal Academy of Arts Impressive home to blockbuster shows (p121).

2 Liberty As charming as shopping gets (p115).

3 Gymkhana Riding high as London's favourite posh Indian (p118).

4 La Fromagerie Cheese nirvana (p110).

5 Selfridges London's leading department store (p107).

THE WALLACE COLLECTION
A serene oasis just minutes from Oxford Street
Free & Open Daily 10am – 5pm
www.wallacecollection.org
The Swinging 1760s
Romantic Rococo Revelations
Experience wonderful art from around the worl
in one beautiful, central London setting
19 September – Re-opening of the refurbished Great Gallery
The Wallace Collection, Manchester Square, London W1U 3BN (nearest tube Bond Street)
A Family Collection | A National Museum | An International Treasure Hous

OXFORD STREET

Bond Street, Marble Arch, Oxford Circus or Tottenham Court Road tube.

Official estimates put the annual footfall at somewhere near 200 million people per year, but few Londoners love **Oxford Street**. A shopping district since the 19th century, it's unmanageably busy on weekends and in the run-up to Christmas. Even outside these times, it's rarely pretty, lined as it is with over-familiar chain stores and choked with bus traffic. The New West End Company (www.newwestend.com) has been charged with changing all that, and Oxford Circus, Marble Arch and Regent Street are beginning to feel the benefits.

The street gets smarter as you walk from east to west. The eastern end around Tottenham Court Road station is under major redevelopment for Crossrail, but its lack of destination shops was solved a couple of years ago by the opening of teen-magnet fashion flagship **Primark** (*see p106*). The string of classy department stores – **John Lewis** (nos.278-306, 7629 7711), **Debenhams** (nos.334-348, 0844 561 6161) and **Selfridges** (no.400; *see p107*) – begins west of chaotic **Oxford Circus**, where there are more Crossrail works at Bond Street station. Apart from the art deco splendour of Selfridges, architectural interest along Oxford Street is largely limited to Oxford Circus's four identical convex corners, constructed between 1913 and 1928. The crowds and rush of traffic hamper investigations, a problem the council addressed by widening pavements, removing street clutter and creating Tokyo Shibuya-style diagonal crossings, which actually work rather well.

Oxford Street gained notoriety as the route by which condemned men were conveyed from Newgate Prison to the old Tyburn gallows, stopping only for a last pint at the **Angel** (61-62 St Giles High Street, 7240 2876), in the shadow of Centre Point. For over six centuries, crowds would gather to watch executions at the west end of the street, at Tyburn; held in 1783, the final execution to be carried out here is marked by an X on a traffic island at the junction of the Edgware and Bayswater roads.

Close by, also at the western end of Oxford Street, stands **Marble Arch**, with its Carrara marble cladding and sculptures celebrating Nelson and Wellington. It was designed by John Nash in 1827 as the entrance to a rebuilt Buckingham Palace, but the arch was moved here in 1851, after – it is said – a fuming Queen Victoria found it to be too narrow for her coach. Now given a £2m revamp, it's been joined by renovated water fountains and gardens that contain an ongoing series of large-scale public sculpture commissions.

North of Oxford Circus

Great Portland Street, Oxford Circus or Regent's Park tube.

North of Oxford Circus runs **Langham Place**, notable for the Bath stone façade of John Nash's **All Souls Church** (Langham Place, 2 All Souls Place, 7580 3522, www.allsouls.org). Its bold combination of a Gothic spire and classical rotunda wasn't popular: in 1824, a year after it opened, the church was condemned in Parliament as 'deplorable and horrible'.

Tucked to one side of the church you'll find the BBC's **Broadcasting House** (*see below*), an oddly asymmetrical art deco building, much extended by recent redevelopment. Over the road is the **Langham Hotel**, which opened in 1865 as Britain's first grand hotel and has been home at various points to Mark Twain, Napoleon III and Oscar Wilde; for its swanky bar **Artesian**, *see p106*.

North, Langham Place turns into **Portland Place**, designed by Robert and James Adam as the glory of 18th-century London. Its Georgian terraced houses are now mostly occupied by embassies and swanky offices. At no.66 is the **Royal Institute of British Architects** (RIBA; *see p333*). Parallel to Portland Place are **Harley Street**, famous for its high-cost dentists and doctors, and **Wimpole Street**, erstwhile home to the poet Elizabeth Barrett Browning (no.50), Sir Paul McCartney (no.57) and Sir Arthur Conan Doyle (2 Upper Wimpole Street).

Sights & museums

BBC Broadcasting House

Portland Place, Upper Regent Street, W1A 1AA (0370 901 1227, www.bbc.co.uk/showsandtours/tours). Oxford Circus tube. **Open** *Pre-booked tours only* from 10am daily. **Admission** £13.50; £9-£11.25 reductions. No under-9s. **Map** p104 C5 ❶

Completed in 1932, this was Britain's first purpose-built broadcast centre; in 2013, it acquired a swanky neighbour, New Broadcasting House. There are daily tours of the BBC's HQ, but you'll need to book ahead on the website – and under-9s are not admitted. Tours take in the studios, including those used for television and radio news, and you'll be able to read the news and weather on an interactive set. The guides also explain the history of the BBC and the original building. Prominent among the carvings is a 10ft-tall statue of Prospero and Ariel, the spirit of the air – or, in this case, the airwaves – from Shakespeare's *The Tempest*. The statue caused controversy when it was unveiled due to the flattering size of the airy sprite's manhood; artist Eric Gill was recalled and asked to make it more modest.

EXPLORE

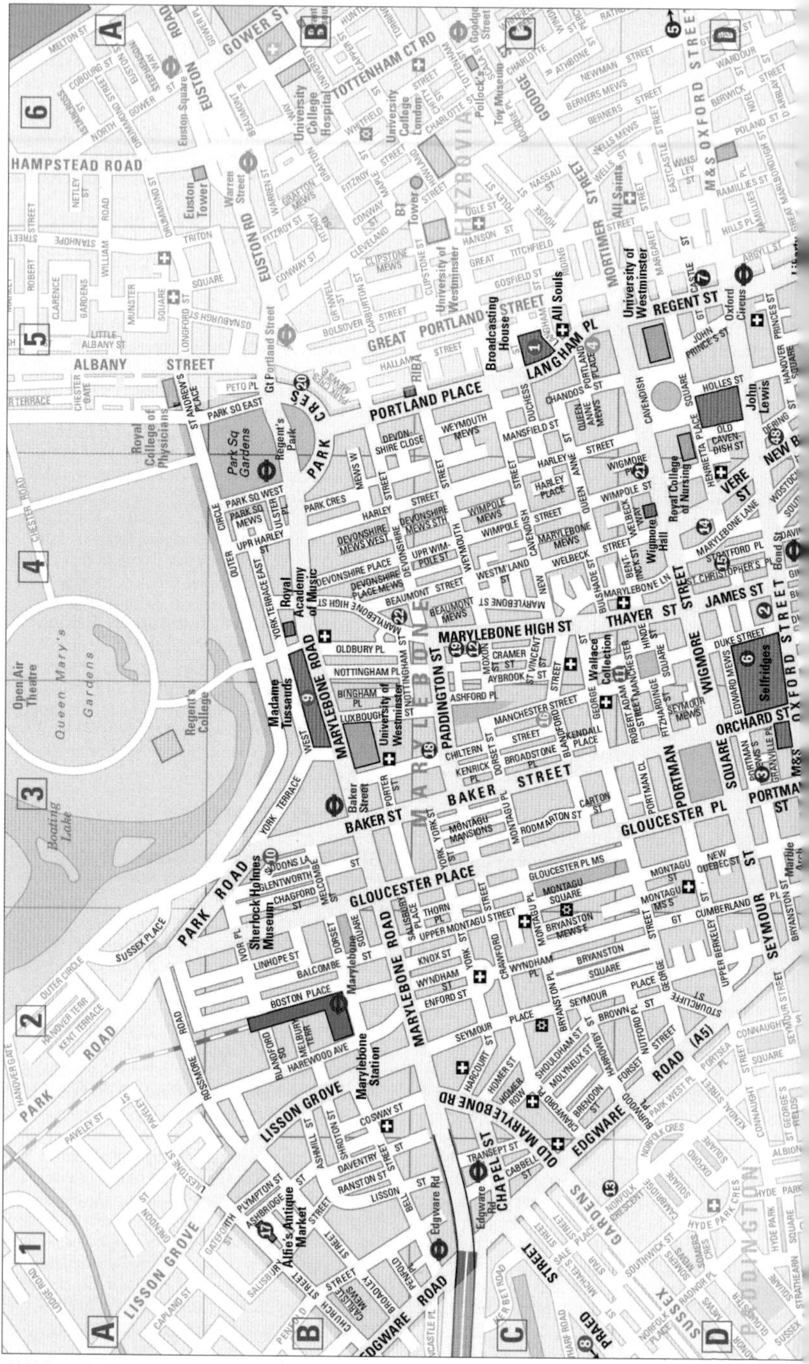
HAMPSTEAD ROAD
EUSTON RD
Euston Square
Euston Tower
Warren Street
TOTTENHAM CT RD
University College Hospital
University College London
BT Tower
FITZROVIA
Goodge Street
GOODGE ST
Pollock's Toy Museum
OXFORD STREET
Oxford Circus
REGENT ST
All Souls
Broadcasting House
GREAT PORTLAND STREET
Gt Portland Street
ALBANY STREET
PARK SQ EAST
Park Sq Gardens
Regent's Park
Royal College of Physicians
PORTLAND PLACE
LANGHAM PL
CAVENDISH SQUARE
John Lewis
Royal College of Nursing
Wigmore Hall
WIGMORE ST
MARYLEBONE HIGH ST
MARYLEBONE LN
THAYER ST
JAMES ST
Bond St
Selfridges
ORCHARD ST
Wallace Collection
MANCHESTER SQUARE
PORTMAN SQUARE
GLOUCESTER PL
BAKER STREET
Baker Street
Madame Tussauds
Royal Academy of Music
MARYLEBONE ROAD
University of Westminster
Open Air Theatre
Queen Mary's Gardens
Regent's College
Boating Lake
PARK ROAD
Sherlock Holmes Museum
GLOUCESTER PLACE
Marylebone
Marylebone Station
MONTAGU SQUARE
BRYANSTON SQUARE
LISSON GROVE
Alfie's Antique Market
Edgware Rd
EDGWARE ROAD
OLD MARYLEBONE RD
CHAPEL ST
SUSSEX GARDENS
PRAED STREET
PADDINGTON
Marble Arch
PORTMAN ST
SEYMOUR PL

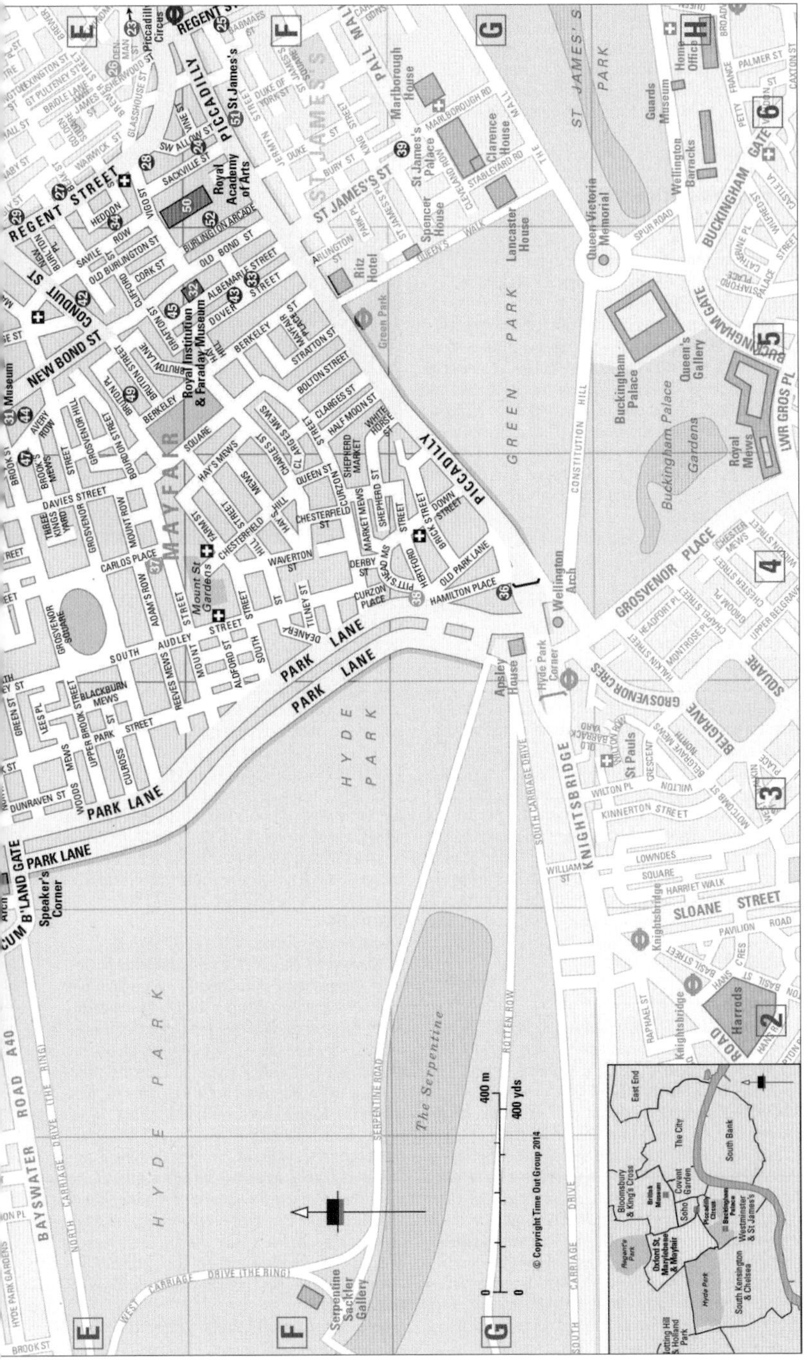
E
F
G
H
2
3
4
5
6
REGENT STREET
PICCADILLY
Piccadilly Circus
St James's
Royal Academy of Arts
Royal Institution & Faraday Museum
BURLINGTON ARCADE
OLD BOND ST
NEW BOND ST
CONDUIT ST
ALBEMARLE STREET
DOVER ST
BERKELEY SQUARE
MAYFAIR
Mount St Gardens
GROSVENOR SQUARE
DAVIES STREET
SOUTH AUDLEY STREET
PARK LANE
CURZON ST
SHEPHERD MARKET
HALF MOON ST
CLARGES ST
BOLTON STREET
STRATTON ST
HAMILTON PLACE
OLD PARK LANE
ST JAMES'S ST
ST JAMES'S SQUARE
PALL MALL
JERMYN STREET
Marlborough House
St James's Palace
Clarence House
Spencer House
Lancaster House
Ritz Hotel
Green Park
GREEN PARK
ST JAMES'S PARK
THE MALL
Queen Victoria Memorial
Buckingham Palace
Buckingham Palace Gardens
Queen's Gallery
Royal Mews
BUCKINGHAM GATE
BUCKINGHAM PALACE RD
Wellington Barracks
Guards Museum
Home Office
CONSTITUTION HILL
Wellington Arch
Apsley House
Hyde Park Corner
GROSVENOR PLACE
GROSVENOR CRES
BELGRAVE SQUARE
KNIGHTSBRIDGE
WILTON PL
KINNERTON STREET
LOWNDES SQUARE
SLOANE STREET
Knightsbridge
Harrods
HYDE PARK
The Serpentine
SERPENTINE ROAD
ROTTEN ROW
SOUTH CARRIAGE DRIVE
NORTH CARRIAGE DRIVE (THE RING)
WEST CARRIAGE DRIVE (THE RING)
Serpentine Sackler Gallery
Speaker's Corner
CUM B'LAND GATE
BAYSWATER ROAD A40
400 m
400 yds
© Copyright Time Out Group 2014
East End
The City
South Bank
Bloomsbury & King's Cross
British Museum
Covent Garden
Soho
Piccadilly Circus
Buckingham Palace
Westminster & St James's
Regent's Park
Oxford St, Marylebone & Mayfair
Hyde Park
South Kensington & Chelsea
Notting Hill & Holland Park

EXPLORE

► *The original Broadcasting House contains the Radio Theatre, where the public can join the audience for shows. For tickets for radio and TV shows, visit www.bbc.co.uk/showsandtours.*

Restaurants

★ Busaba Eathai

8-13 Bird Street, W1U 1BU (7518 8080, www.busaba.com). Bond Street tube. **Open** noon-11pm Mon-Thur; noon-11.30pm Fri, Sat; noon-10pm Sun. **Main courses** £7.30-£12.50. **Map** p104 D4 ❷ **Thai**

Busaba is a ten-strong chain – but it's not your average Thai joint. The dark, handsome interior combines dark wood, incense and dimly lit lanterns. With spacious shared tables, no reservations and brisk service, it remains a great spot for a casual meal with friends. Among the Thai classics you'll find a few dishes that aren't often seen in London, such as sen chan pad thai (a pimped pad thai with crab originating from the Chanthaburi province of eastern Thailand).

Other locations throughout the city.

Roti Chai

3-4 Portman Mews South, W1H 6HS (7408 0101, www.rotichai.com). Marble Arch tube. **Meals served** noon-10.30pm Mon-Sat; 12.30-9pm Sun. **Main courses** £4.80-£8.50. **Map** p104 D3 ❸ **Pan-Indian**

The ground-floor 'street kitchen', with its utilitarian furniture and canteen vibe, is ideal for a swift midday feed – and the alert young staff keep things pacy. The menu is modelled on those of urban India's snack shacks, so you'll find bhel pooris, samosas and moist, light Gujarati dhokra sponge, topped with two relishes: tangy tamarind and spicy coconut. Larger dishes include 'railway lamb curry' (tender meat and potato in a rich gravy spiced with star anise and cinnamon bark). In the basement, the evening-only 'dining room' is a darker, sexier (and pricier) space.

Pubs & bars

Artesian

Langham Hotel, 1C Portland Place, W1B 1JA (7636 1000, www.artesian-bar.co.uk). Oxford Circus tube. **Open** 11am-2am Mon-Sat; noon-midnight Sun. **Map** p104 C5 ❹

The Artesian is very nearly a very great bar. Its elegant space on the ground floor of the Langham Hilton is lovely. Tables are well spaced. Service is friendly and ultra-efficient even when – as so often happens – it's packed out. A free plate of tasty canapés may arrive unbidden. Their own cocktails are well conceived, and the classics are flawlessly rendered and generously poured. One downer: piping in incredibly loud Euro-pop, which is completely at odds with the room – and with the pricing of the drinks, which are among London's most expensive.

Artesian.

Shops & services

Popular department store **John Lewis** (www.johnlewis.com) has its flagship branch at 300 Oxford Street, while **Marks & Spencer** (www.marksandspencer.com), high-street favourite for undies, sandwiches and ready meals, but also offering several reliable fashion ranges, has two huge branches here. **Urban Outfitters** (200 Oxford Street, W1D 1NU, 7907 0800, www.urbanoutfitters.co.uk) sells a great range of boutique labels, and **Clarks** (260 Oxford Street, W1C 1LD, 0844 499 9032, www.clarks.co.uk) has shed its school-shoe image to be fêted as the inventor of Wallabees.

Primark

14-28 Oxford Street, W1 1BJ (7580 5510, www.primark.co.uk). Tottenham Court Road tube. **Open** 8am-10pm Mon-Fri; 8am-9pm Sat; 11.30am-6pm Sun. **Map** p104 D6 ❺ **Fashion**

With more than 80,000sq ft over four floors, this branch of Primark is even bigger than its sister branch near Marble Arch (and is in the process of getting even bigger). Stock changes rapidly, and prices are low. Many would argue that the concept of throwaway fashion is increasingly wrong and outmoded, but the value of Primark clothing is precisely that – it trades in trend-led pieces that'll get you through a weekend, a party or a summer holiday, all for a few quid. Primark has even flipped a finger at allegations – proven false – about its overseas production by signing up to the Ethical Trading Initiative. The other big London branch is at 499-517 Oxford Street.

Other locations throughout the city.

EXPLORE

★ Selfridges

400 Oxford Street, Marylebone, W1A 1AB (0800 123400, www.selfridges.com). Bond Street or Marble Arch tube. **Open** 9.30am-8pm Mon-Wed, Fri, Sat; 9.30am-9pm Thur; noon-6.15pm Sun (browsing from 11.30am). **Map** p104 D4 ❻ **Department store**

With its plethora of concession boutiques, store-wide themed events and collections from all the hottest brands, Selfridges is as dynamic as a department store could be. Although the store layout changes regularly, the useful floor plans make navigating the place easy-peasy. While the basement is chock-full of hip home accessories and stylish kitchen equipment, it's Selfridges' fashion floors that really get hearts racing. With a winning combination of new talent, hip and edgy labels, high-street brands and luxury high-end designers, the store stays ahead of the pack. Highlights include the huge denim section, and the extensive Shoe Galleries, the world's biggest women's footwear department. Level 4 hosts the Toy Shop. There are always new draws in the food hall, ranging from great deli and bakery produce to classy packaged goods. Regularly changing pop-ups and special events keep customers on their toes.

★ Topshop

36-38 Great Castle Street, W1W 8LG (0844 848 7487, www.topshop.com). Oxford Circus tube. **Open** 9am-9pm Mon-Sat; 11.30am-6pm Sun. **Map** p104 D5 ❼ **Fashion**

Topshop has been the queen of the British high street for the past decade, and walking into the busy Oxford Street flagship, it's easy to see why. Spanning three huge floors, the place lays claim to being the world's largest fashion shop, and is always buzzing with fashion-forward teens and twentysomethings keen to get their hands on the next big trends. The store covers a huge range of styles and sizes, and includes free personal shoppers, boutique label concessions, capsule collections, a Metalmorphosis tattoo parlour, a Daniel Hersheson Blow Dry Bar, a café and sweet shop. Topman is as on-the-ball and innovative as its big sister, stocking niche menswear labels such as Garbstore, and housing a trainer boutique, a suit section, and a new personal shopping suite, featuring consultation rooms, Xbox 360s and an exhibition space. Both shops are even more of a hive of activity than normal during London Fashion Week, when a series of special events are held.

Other locations throughout the city.

MARYLEBONE & BAKER STREET

Baker Street, Bond Street, Marble Arch, Oxford Circus or Regent's Park tube.

North of Oxford Street, the fashionable district known to its boosters as 'Marylebone Village' has become a magnet for moneyed Londoners. However, most visitors to the area head directly for the waxworks of **Madame Tussauds** (*see p109*); there's also a small and oft-overlooked museum at the neighbouring **Royal Academy of Music** (7873 7300, www.ram.ac.uk), while the northern end of **Baker Street** is unsurprisingly heavy on nods of respect to the world's favourite freelance detective: the **Sherlock Holmes Museum** (*see p110*), but studious fans may find more of interest among the books and photos of the **Sherlock Holmes Collection** at Marylebone Library (7641 1206, by appointment only). The Beatles painted 94 Baker Street with a psychedelic mural before opening it in December 1967 as the Apple Boutique, a clothing store run on such whimsical hippie principles that it had to close within six months due to financial losses. Fab Four pilgrims head to the **London Beatles Store** (no.231, 7935 4464, www.beatles-storelondon.co.uk), where the ground-floor shop offers a predictable array of Beatles-branded accessories alongside genuine collectibles.

IN THE KNOW
BOOZE WITH A VIEW

The **St George's Hotel** (4-15 Langham Place, Regent Street, W1B 2QS, 7580 0111, www.saintgeorgeshotel.com) doesn't look entirely welcoming, but take one of the lifts to the top-floor bar and you'll be rewarded with surprisingly good views of town.

Selfridges.

EXPLORE

Rainforest Cafe
A WILD PLACE TO SHOP AND EAT ®
HOW ABOUT A WILD DAY OUT?
Located in Piccadilly Circus, Rainforest Cafe is a unique and vibrant restaurant and bar bringing together the sights and sounds of the jungle.
15% DISCOUNT
off your final food bill*
PERFECT FOR KIDS & BIG KIDS
GREAT FOR GROUPS & BIRTHDAY CELEBRATIONS
Book online: www.therainforestcafe.co.uk
Tel: 020 7434 3111
Email: sales@therainforestcafe.co.uk
*Offer valid seven days a week. Maximum party size of 6. Please present to your safari guide when seated. Cannot be used in conjunction with any other offer.

For Londoners, the area's beating heart is **Marylebone High Street**, teeming with interesting shops. The name of the neighbourhood is a contraction of the church's earlier name, St Mary by the Bourne; the 'bourne' in question, Tyburn stream, still filters into the Thames near Pimlico, but its entire length is now covered. **St Marylebone Church** stands in its fourth incarnation at the northern end of the street. The church's garden hosts designer clothing and artisan food stalls at the **Cabbages & Frocks** market on Saturdays (www.cabbagesandfrocks.co.uk).

Lovely boutiques can be found on winding **Marylebone Lane**, along with the **Golden Eagle** (no.59, 7935 3228), which hosts regular singalongs around its piano. There's fine food here, too, with smart, often upmarket eateries snuggling alongside delicatessens such as **La Fromagerie** (*see p110*) and century-old lunchroom **Paul Rothe & Son** (35 Marylebone Lane, 7935 6783). **Marylebone Farmers' Market** takes place in the Cramer Street car park every Sunday.

Further south, the soaring neo-Gothic interior of the 19th-century **St James's Roman Catholic Church** (22 George Street, 7935 0943) is lit dramatically by stained-glass windows; Vivien Leigh (née Hartley) married barrister Herbert Leigh Hunt here in 1932. Other cultural diversions include the **Wallace Collection** (*see p110*) and the **Wigmore Hall** (*see p282*).

Part of the Romans' Watling Street from Dover to Wales, **Edgware Road** rules a definite north–south line marking the western edge of the West End. It's now the heart of the city's Middle East end: if you want to pick up your copy of *Al Hayat*, cash a cheque at the Bank of Kuwait or catch Egyptian football, head here. The fact that the name Paddington has been immortalised by a certain small, ursine Peruvian émigré is appropriate, given that the area has long been home to refugees and immigrants. It was a country village until an arm of the Grand Union Canal arrived in 1801, linking London to the Midlands, followed in the 1830s by the railway. **Paddington Station**, with its fine triple roof of iron and glass, was built in 1851 to the specifications of the great engineer Isambard Kingdom Brunel. Paddington's proximity to central London eventually drew in developers. To the east of the station, gleaming **Paddington Central** now provides a million square feet of office space, canalside apartments and restaurants. In St Mary's Hospital, the old-fashioned **Alexander Fleming Laboratory Museum** (*see right*) gives a sense of what the district used to be like.

Sights & museums

Alexander Fleming Laboratory Museum

St Mary's Hospital, Praed Street, W2 1NY (7886 6528, www.medicalmuseums.org). Paddington tube/rail. **Open** 10am-1pm Mon-Thur. *By appointment* 2-5pm Mon-Thur; 10am-5pm Fri. **Admission** £4; £2 reductions; free under-5s. **No credit cards. Map** p104 C1 ❽

Buzz in at the entrance on your left as you enter the hospital and head up the stairs to find this tiny, dusty, instrument-cluttered lab. Enthusiastic guides conjure up the professor who, in 1928, noticed that mould contamination had destroyed some staphylococcus bacteria on a set-aside culture plate: he had discovered penicillin. The keen entrepreneurs across the street immediately began to advertise their pub's healthful properties, claiming the miracle fungus had blown into the lab from them. The video room has a documentary on Fleming's life and discovery.

Madame Tussauds

Marylebone Road, NW1 5LR (0870 400 3000, www.madametussauds.com/london). Baker Street tube. **Open** times vary; check website for details. **Admission** £30; £25.80 reductions; £111.60 family; free under-4s. **Map** p104 B3 ❾

Streams of humanity jostle excitedly here for the chance to take pictures of one another planting a smacker on the waxen visage of fame and fortune. Madame Tussaud brought her show to London in 1802, 32 years after it was founded in Paris, and it's been expanding ever since, on these very premises since 1884. There are now some 300 figures in the collection: current movie A-listers who require no more than a first name (Brad, Keira, Arnie), as well as their illustrious forebears for whom the surname seems more fitting (Monroe, Chaplin); a bevy of Royals (not least Wills and Kate), and sundry sports stars – not just Nadal, Tendulkar, Muhammad Ali and Messi, but an Athletes' Village of 2012 Olympians, among them Jessica Ennis and Usain Bolt. Rihanna can be found hanging out among the Music Megastars, while Dickens and Einstein kick back together in the Culture section, and even French president François Hollande has sat for the modellers. If you're not already overheating, your palms will be sweating by the time you descend to the Chamber of Horrors in 'Scream', where only teens claim to enjoy the floor drops and scary special effects. Much more pleasant is the kitsch 'Spirit of London' ride, whisking you through 400 years of London life in a taxi pod.

Tussauds also hosts Marvel Super Heroes 4D. Interactives and waxworks of Iron Man, Spiderman and an 18ft Hulk provide further photo ops, but the highlight is the nine-minute film in '4D' (as well as 3D projections, there are 'real' effects such as a shaking floor and smoke in the auditorium).

► *Get here before 10am to avoid the enormous queues, and book online in advance to make the steep admission price more palatable.*

Sherlock Holmes Museum

221B Baker Street, NW1 6XE (7224 3688, www.sherlock-holmes.co.uk). Baker Street tube. **Open** 9.30am-6pm daily. **Admission** £8, £5 under-16s. **Map** p104 B3 ⑩

Founded in 1989 at what used to be no.239, the museum fought long and hard for the right to claim the address 221B Baker Street as its own. When you visit you are likely to be greeted by an august person wearing a bowler hat and whiskers; this, you will deduce, is Dr Watson. And every lovingly recreated detail – murder weapons, Victoriana, waxwork tableaux of key scenes from Conan Doyle's stories – conspires to persuade visitors to suspend their disbelief and feel themselves travelling back in time to a preserved fragment of historical reality. Perhaps most interesting is a folder of letters upstairs in Mrs Hudson's room: they were all actually sent to Holmes by fans from all over the world, asking for help or offering their assistance as wannabe sleuths.

★ FREE Wallace Collection

Hertford House, Manchester Square, W1U 3BN (7935 0687, www.wallacecollection.org). Bond Street tube. **Open** 10am-5pm daily. **Admission** free. **Map** p104 D4 ⑪

Built in 1776 and tucked away on a quiet square, this handsome house contains an exceptional collection of 18th-century French furniture, painting and objets d'art, as well as an amazing array of medieval armour and weaponry. It all belonged to Sir Richard Wallace, who, as the illegitimate offspring of the fourth Marquess of Hertford, inherited in 1870 the treasures his father had amassed in the last 30 years of his life. Room after grand room contains Louis XIV and XV furnishings and Sèvres porcelain; the galleries are hung with paintings by Titian, Gainsborough and Reynolds, as well as Fragonard's *The Swing*. The refurbished West Galleries display 19th-century and Venetian works, including paintings by Canaletto; the East Galleries, reopened in 2012, are dedicated to Dutch paintings; and the collections of miniatures and gold boxes are on show in the Boudoir Cabinet. To see the Wallace at its best, though, you'll have to wait until work on the Great Gallery is complete in late 2014. Following painstaking improvements to lighting and decor, there you'll see Franz Hals's *Laughing Cavalier* (neither laughing nor a cavalier), Nicolas Poussin's *A Dance to the Music of Time*, Velázquez's *The Lady with a Fan* and Rubens' *The Rainbow Landscape* in their full glory.

► *The museum restaurant is beautifully set in a glass-roofed courtyard and makes a good – if pricey – choice for a shopping-day lunch.*

Restaurants

La Fromagerie

2-6 Moxon Street, W1U 4EW (7935 0341, www.lafromagerie.co.uk). Baker Street or Bond Street tube. **Open** 8am-7.30pm Mon-Fri; 9am-7pm Sat; 10am-6pm Sun. **Main courses** £6.95-£18.50. **Map** p104 C4 ⑫ **Café**

There are cheeseboards and then there are La Fromagerie cheeseboards. We'd like to live in a world in which we were only ever served the latter – carefully sourced, themed by nation (with suggested wines to match) and prettily arranged on a wooden slab at the back of an enticing deli and cheese shop. The café doesn't take bookings, so time your visit with care – a late-afternoon table (the cakes are also delicious) offers prime people-watching potential.

★ Heron

Basement karaoke room of the Heron pub, 1 Norfolk Crescent, W2 2DN (7706 9567). Edgware Road or Marble Arch tube. **Open** 1-11pm daily. **Main courses** £7.50-£20. **Map** p104 C1 ⑬ **Thai**

Located in a shabby boozer round the back of the Edgware Road, the Heron is certainly a rough diamond. Yet look beyond the slightly dingy interior and you'll discover some of the most authentic Thai food to be found in London. Blaring Thai pop signals the way to the diminutive basement dining room. The kitchen specialises in north-eastern (Esarn) cooking, offering an impressive range of spicy salads, sour curries, stir-fries and much more besides. Expect things to get lively after 9pm, as the dining room doubles as a karaoke lounge. Service couldn't be friendlier.

Meat Liquor

74 Welbeck Street, W1G 0BA (7224 4239, www.meatliquor.com). Bond Street tube. **Meals served** noon-4pm, 6-10.30pm Mon-Sat; noon-4pm, 6-8.30pm Sun. **Main courses** £6.50-£8.50. **Map** p104 D4 ⑭ **North American**

Inside, this cult destination is dark and loud: more hell-raising nightclub than restaurant. Signs point out the rules ('No suits', 'No ballet pumps'). The graffiti murals are occult-themed, and the staff heavily tattooed. The Deep South cooking is gutsy stuff, with the likes of crunchy-coated 'bingo wings' served not only with a terrific Louisiana-style hot sauce but also a feisty blue cheese dip. There are cheese steaks and dogs, though the real show-stoppers are the burgers. Staff make a mean cocktail.

Patty & Bun

54 James Street, W1U 1HE (7487 3188, www.pattyandbun.co.uk). Bond Street tube. **Open** noon-10.15pm Tue-Sat; noon-9.15pm Sun. **Main courses** £7.50-£8.50. **Map** p104 D4 ⑮ **Burgers**

P&B has carved out a reputation for serving some of London's finest burgers. All-day queues are testament to the fact that it's tiny (with space for only 30 diners) and that the amiable staff have the format spot-on. The signature Ari Gold burger is a generous patty slathered in ketchup and smoky mayo, inside a glazed brioche bun. More original is the Lambshank

Wallace Collection.

Redemption, a firm lamb burger strongly flavoured with coriander, chilli and cumin aïoli. Don't miss the skin-on rosemary salt chips.

Pubs & bars

★ Purl

50 Blandford Street, W1U 7HX (7935 0835, www.purl-london.com). Bond Street tube.
Open 5-11.30pm Mon-Thur; 5pm-midnight Fri, Sat. **Map** p104 C3 16

Purl, one of London's first speakeasy-type bars, is popular, which means that booking is advisable – though walk-ins will be seated if there's space. The layout of the bar, over a number of smallish spaces in a vaulted basement, gives the opportunity for genuine seclusion, if that's what you're looking for. And if you're interested in cutting-edge cocktail making, you're also in luck. Novel methods and unusual ingredients are used in many of the unique drinks, but the classics are always sound too. And the music is chosen by someone who has very good taste in jazz.

Shops & services

Marylebone has a **farmers' market** (Cramer Street car park, corner of Moxton Street; 10am-2pm Sun), while **Church Street** is a major area for vintage homewares, including those at **Alfie's Antique Market**.

Alfie's Antique Market

13-25 Church Street, NW8 8DT (7723 6066, www.alfiesantiques.com). Edgware Road tube or Marylebone tube/rail. **Open** 10am-6pm Tue-Sat. **No credit cards. Map** p104 B1 17 **Homewares**

For more than three decades, Alfie's three floors and basement have hosted a hundred dealers in vintage furniture and fashion, art, books, maps and the like. There's a pleasant rooftop café.

Cadenhead's Whisky Shop & Tasting Room

26 Chiltern Street, W1U 7QF (7935 6999, www.whiskytastingroom.com). Baker Street tube. **Open** 10.30am-6.30pm Mon-Fri; 10.30am-6pm Sat. **Map** p104 C3 18 **Food & drink**

Cadenhead's is a survivor of a rare breed: the independent whisky bottler. And its shop is one of a kind, at least in London. Cadenhead's selects barrels from distilleries all over Scotland and bottles them without filtration or any other intervention.

► *For a wider range of spirits – the widest to be found in London, according to the staff – head to Soho and Gerry's (74 Old Compton Street, W1D 4UW, 7734 4215, www.gerrys.uk.com). Another whisky specialist, Milroy's (3 Greek Street, W1D 4NX, 7437 2385, www.milroys.co.uk), is close by.*

★ Daunt Books

83-84 Marylebone High Street, W1U 4QW (7224 2295, www.dauntbooks.co.uk). Baker Street tube.
Open 9am-7.30pm Mon-Sat; 11am-6pm Sun.
Map p104 C4 19 **Books & music**

This beautiful Edwardian shop's elegant three-level back room – complete with oak balconies, viridian-green walls and stained-glass window – houses a much-praised travel section featuring guidebooks, maps, language reference, travelogues and related fiction. Travel aside, Daunt is also a first-rate stop for literary fiction, biography, gardening and more. **Other locations** throughout the city.

WALK THE SIDESTREET SHUFFLE

Avoid Oxford Street's clogged pavements with a backstreet trail.

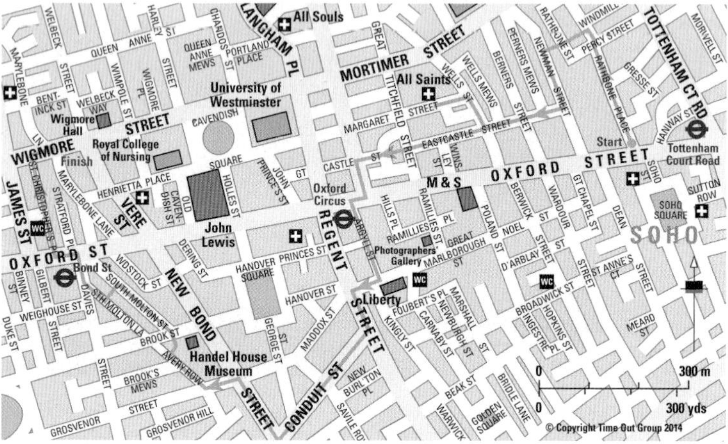

This hour-long walk follows the hinterlands of Oxford Street, which offer not only useful routes parallel to the main drag but also a backstreet take on retail and London life.

Rathbone Place marks the lower reaches of Fitzrovia, where the worlds of media and design collide with the rag trade. The fun begins at **Hobgoblin** (no.24, 7323 9040), a folk music store where musicians test-drive zithers, banjos and ukuleles. Keep north up restaurant-lined Charlotte Street, then turn left beside the suave **Charlotte Street Hotel** (*see p343*) through Percy Passage. Cross the dog-leg of Rathbone Street, and head on via Dickensian Newman Passage to emerge in Newman Street. Pause for a snap of the **BT Tower** (right), then go left and right on to Eastcastle Street. Detour up Margaret Street to **All Saints** church (*see p159*).

All along Eastcastle Street is a startling proliferation of galleries. Our favourites are art spaces **Art First** (no.21, 7734 0386, www.artfirst.co.uk), **Carroll/Fletcher** (nos.56-57, 7323 6111, www.carrollfletcher.com), **Pilar Corrias** (no.54, *see p159*), along with **Getty Images Gallery** (no.46, 7291 5380, www.gettyimagesgallery.com), which holds great photography exhibitions. On the same stretch of road, **Fever** (nos.52-53, 7636 6326, www.feverdesigns.co.uk) mixes cute retro-inspired clothing and accessories with vintage. Market Place opens ahead, a collection of sidewalk cafés. Head across Oxford Street down Argyll Street, aiming for **Liberty** (*see p115*).

Next, cross Regent Street towards Conduit Street, where a visit to **Vivienne Westwood**'s flamboyant flagship store (no.44, 7439 1109, www.viviennewestwood.com) provides a taste of punky London couture. Continue to New Bond Street into Grosvenor Street, then right up Avery Row. This is the land of Victorian London's great aristocratic estates, where narrow service alleys brought tradesmen to the rear entrances of the grand residences. The alleys still offer services to the gentry, but they're now exclusive little boutiques and restaurants. On Avery Row, check out the **Paul Smith Sale Shop** (*see p120*).

Adjoining Lancashire Court is home to restaurants and the **Handel House Museum** (*see p117*), which faces Brook Street and, close by, Italian design legend **Alessi** (22 Brook Street, 7518 9090, www.alessi.com). Move on to pedestrianised South Molton Street and its mix of stores, among them glittery **Butler & Wilson** (no.20, 7409 2955, www.butlerandwilson.co.uk). Take the passage to the left of fashion queen **Browns** (*see p119*) and pop out by **Grays Antique Market** (*see p120*).

Cross Oxford Street again, battling your way to the freestanding clock signposting the narrow entrance to St Christopher's Place. This warren of little streets houses a traffic-free complex of cafés and shops, including Finnish designer **Marimekko** (nos.16-17, 7486 6454, www.marimekko.com). There's also a fountain and a flower-decked Victorian WC. Need a rest? Head north to Wigmore Street for one last stop at **Robert Clergerie Shoes** (no.67, 7935 3601, www.robertclergerie.com), before heading a couple of doors down to **Comptoir Libanais** (no.65, 7935 1110, www.lecomptoir.co.uk). This colourful and inviting Lebanese eaterie is the perfect place to mull over your purchases.

Handel House Museum.

Hale Clinic

7 Park Crescent, W1B 1PF (7631 0156, www.haleclinic.com). Great Portland Street or Regent's Park tube. **Open** 8.30am-9pm Mon-Fri; 9am-5pm Sat. **Map** p104 B5 (20) **Health & beauty**

Around 100 practitioners are affiliated to the Hale Clinic, which was founded with the aim of integrating complementary and conventional medicine. The treatment list is an A-Z of alternative therapies; the shop stocks supplements, skincare products and books.

Margaret Howell

34 Wigmore Street, W1U 2RS (7009 9009, www.margarethowell.co.uk). Bond Street tube. **Open** 10am-6pm Mon-Wed, Fri, Sat; 10am-7pm Thur; noon-5pm Sun. **Map** p104 D4 (21) **Fashion**

Margaret Howell's wearable clothes are made in Britain with an old-fashioned attitude to quality. These principles combine with her elegant designs to make for the best 'simple' clothes for sale in London. Her pared-down approach means prices seem steep, but these are clothes that last and seem only to get better with time. Some homewares are also sold here.

Other locations 111 Fulham Road, Chelsea, SW3 6RL (7591 2255); 7-8 Duke Street, Richmond, TW9 1HP (8948 5005); MHL Shop, 19 Nichol Street, Shoreditch, E2 7HR (7033 9494); MHL Shop, 22 New Cavendish Street, Marylebone, W1G 8TT (7487 3803).

La Pâtisserie des Rêves

43 Marylebone High Street, W1U 4QD (3603 7333, www.lapatisseriedesreves.com/uk). Baker Street or Regent's Park tube. **Open** 8.30am-7.30pm Mon-Sat; 8.30am-6.30pm Sun. **Map** p104 B4 (22) **Food & drink**

Imported from Paris in 2014, this cake shop is all about exquisite versions of the classics – both French and English – by chef-pâtissier Philippe Conticini. Whether you choose an éclair, tarte au citron, rhubarb tart or humble croissant, you are unlikely to better the version sold here.

PICCADILLY CIRCUS & REGENT STREET

Oxford Circus or Piccadilly Circus tube.

Busy **Piccadilly Circus** is an uneasy mix of the tawdry and the grand, a mix with little to do with the vision of its architect. John Nash's 1820s design for the intersection of Regent Street and Piccadilly, two of the West End's most elegant streets, was a harmonious circle of curved frontages. But 60 years later, Shaftesbury Avenue muscled in. A revamp of the traffic junction (by the same design consultants who successfully remodelled Oxford Circus) is now complete, with a mile of railings ripped out.

Alfred Gilbert's memorial fountain in honour of child-labour abolitionist Earl Shaftesbury was erected in 1893. It's properly known as the **Shaftesbury Memorial**, with the statue on top intended to show the Angel of Christian Charity, but critics and public alike recognised the likeness of **Eros** and their judgement has stuck. The illuminated advertising panels around the intersection appeared late in the 19th century and have been present ever since: a Coca-Cola ad has been here since 1955, making it the world's longest-running advertisement. Running Sky News broadcasts indicate the likely media-saturated future for the illuminations.

Opposite the memorial, the **Trocadero Centre** (www.londontrocadero.com) has seen several ventures come and go, driven out by high rents and low footfall in a prime but tired location, although **Ripley's Believe It or Not!** (*see below*) seems well established.

Connecting Piccadilly Circus to Oxford Circus to the north and Pall Mall to the south, the broad curve of **Regent Street** was designed by Nash in the early 1800s with the aims of improving access to Regent's Park and bumping up property values in Haymarket and Pall Mall. Much of Nash's architecture was destroyed in the early 20th century, but the grandeur of the street remains impressive.

Sights & museums

Ripley's Believe It or Not!

1 Piccadilly Circus, W1J 0DA (3238 0022, www.ripleyslondon.com). Piccadilly Circus tube. **Open** 10am-midnight daily (last entry 10.30pm). **Admission** £26.95; £21.95-£24.95 reductions; £87.95 family; free under-4s. **Map** p105 E6 ㉓

This 'odditorium' follows a formula more or less unchanged since Robert Ripley opened his first display at the Chicago World Fair in 1933: an assortment of 800 curiosities is displayed, ranging from the world's smallest road-safe car to da Vinci's *Last Supper* painted on a grain of rice – via the company's signature shrunken heads.

Restaurants

Set in a grand art deco basement just off Piccadilly Circus, **Brasserie Zédel** is a huge, all-day French eaterie run by the team behind the Wolseley (*see p82*); good on its own terms, it's also home to **Bar Américain** (*see right*).

Bentley's Oyster Bar & Grill

11-15 Swallow Street, W1B 4DG (7734 4756, www.bentleys.org). Piccadilly Circus tube. **Open** *Oyster Bar* noon-midnight Mon-Sat; noon-10pm Sun. *Restaurant* noon-3pm, 5.30-10.45pm Mon-Fri; 5.30-10.45pm Sat. **Main courses** *Oyster Bar* £12.50-£50. *Restaurant* £19-£50. **Map** p105 F6 ㉔ **Fish & seafood**

Richard Corrigan first overhauled this grande dame of the capital's restaurant scene (established 1916) in 2005. The interior remains as polished as ever, with art deco windows, the original marble oyster bar and wood panelling. Week-nights in the more formal first-floor Grill restaurant have a restrained business-dinner vibe, but the downstairs oyster bar is pleasingly laid-back. Theatrics at the gleaming marble counter (part staff speedily shucking, part competitive knocking 'em back) provide entertaining distraction as you decide between menu classics and imaginative daily specials.

▶ *Corrigan also runs the estimable Corrigan's Mayfair (28 Upper Grosvenor Street, W1K 7EH, 7499 9943), which serves high-class British food.*

Shoryu Ramen

9 Regent Street, SW1Y 4LR (no phone, www.shoryuramen.com). Piccadilly Circus tube. **Open** 11am-3.30pm, 5-11.30pm Mon-Sat; 11am-3.30pm, 5-10.30pm Sun. **Main courses** £9-£12.50. **Map** p105 F6 ㉕ **Japanese**

Shoryu pips its West End tonkotsu rivals when it comes to the texture and stock of its broth. As well as Hakata-style ramen (noodles in a rich, boiled-down, pork-bone broth), the other notable feature is speed. Both help to ease the hassle of no-bookings dining. Dracula tonkotsu – with caramelised garlic oil, balsamic vinegar and garlic chips – packs a flavoursome punch. Extra toppings such as bamboo shoots and boiled egg are to be expected, but kaedama (plain refill noodles) are a godsend for anyone sharing soup stock between small children. There's a varied choice of sides, sakés and sweets. **Other location** 3 Denman Street, Soho, W1D 7HA.

Pubs & bars

Bar Américain

Brasserie Zédel, 20 Sherwood Street, W1F 7ED (7734 4888, www.brasseriezedel.com). Piccadilly Circus tube. **Open** 4.30pm-midnight Mon-Sat; 4.30pm-11pm Sun. **Map** p105 E6 ㉖

We love the simplicity of the cocktail list here: around 20 drinks and most of them tried and tested classics. Martinis, manhattans and daiquiris are all expertly rendered, and you can get the true Vesper, James Bond's own-recipe martini made with gin, vodka and Lillet Blanc. For a quiet drink in the West End, in a beautiful art deco interior with widely spaced tables, and without paying ultra-high prices, you can't do much better than the Américain.

Shops & services

Behind the grand façades of Regent Street, there are many fashion chains, including branches of **Banana Republic** (no.224, W1B 3BR, 7758 3550, www.bananarepublic.co.uk) and H&M's upmarket sibling **COS** (no.222, W1B 5BD, 7478 0400, www.cosstores.com), as well as a big **Apple Store** (235 Regent Street, W1B 2 EL, 7153 9000, www.apple.com) that offers all the services you'd expect, including the trademark 'Genius Bar' for technical support.

Anthropologie

158 Regent Street, W1B 5SW (7529 9800, www.anthropologie.co.uk). Piccadilly Circus tube.
Open 10am-7pm Mon-Wed, Fri, Sat; 10am-8pm Thur; noon-6pm Sun. **Map** p105 E6 ㉗ **Fashion**
Anthropologie, the romantically inclined elder sister to fellow US brand Urban Outfitters, opened the doors of its first European store here in 2009. Stock is of a feminine bent, with delicate necklaces and soft-knit cardies, while the store's signature large-scale window displays and 1,500sq ft living wall of plants are worth the trip alone.
Other location 131-141 King's Road, Chelsea, SW3 4PW (7349 3110).

Burberry

121 Regent Street, W1B 4TB (7806 8904, www.burberry.com). Piccadilly Circus tube.
Open 10am-9pm Mon-Sat; 12.30-7pm Sun.
Map p105 E6 ㉘ **Fashion**
The flagship store of the Burberry brand melds together the building's near-200 years of history with the attributes of hyper-modern retailing, but the gracious surroundings and an emphasis on natural light create a welcoming atmosphere. There's a beauty room here, as well as fashion and accessories.
Other locations throughout the city.

Hamleys

188-196 Regent Street, W1B 5BT (0871 704 1977, www.hamleys.com). Oxford Circus tube.
Open 10am-8pm Mon-Fri; 9am-8pm Sat; noon-6pm Sun. **Map** p105 E6 ㉙ **Children**
Visiting Hamleys is certainly an experience – whether a good one or not will depend on your tolerance for noisy, over-excited children, especially during school holidays and the run-up to Christmas, when the store runs special kids' events. As you doubtless know, Hamleys is a ginormous toy shop, perhaps *the* ginormous toy shop, with attractive displays of all that season's must-have toys across five crazed floors, and perky demonstrators ramping up the temptation levels.

★ Liberty

Regent Street, W1B 5AH (7734 1234, www.liberty.co.uk). Oxford Circus tube.
Open 10am-8pm Mon-Sat; noon-6pm Sun.
Map p104 D5 ㉚ **Department store**
Charmingly idiosyncratic, Liberty is housed in a 1920s mock Tudor structure. The store was given a major revamp in early 2009, and was given a further boost as the subject of a TV documentary series in 2013.

The expanded beauty hall on the ground floor goes from strength to strength, with a perfumerie selling scents from cult brands such as Le Labo and Byredo, and skincare from the much-celebrated Egyptian Magic; the basement holds a Margaret Dabbs Sole Spa, for pedicures, polishing and shaping. At the main entrance to the store is Wild at Heart's exuberant floral concession, and just off from here you'll find yourself in a room devoted to

Liberty

the store's own label. Fashion brands focus on high-end British designers, such as Vivienne Westwood and Christopher Kane. But despite being up with the latest fashions, Liberty still respects its dress-making heritage with a range of cottons in the third-floor haberdashery department. Stationery also pays homage to the traditional, with beautiful Liberty of London notebooks, address books and diaries embossed with the art nouveau 'Ianthe' print, while the interiors departments showcase new furniture designs alongside a dazzling collection of 20th-century classics. Artful and arresting window displays, exciting new collections and luxe labels make it an experience to savour.

MAYFAIR

Bond Street or Green Park tube.

The gaiety suggested by the name of Mayfair, derived from a long-gone spring celebration, isn't matched by its latter-day atmosphere today. Even on Mayfair's busy shopping streets, you may feel out of place without the reassuring heft of a platinum card. Nonetheless, there are many pleasures to enjoy if you fancy a stroll, not least the rapidly changing roster of blue-chip commercial art galleries.

The Grosvenor and Berkeley families bought the rolling green fields that would become Mayfair in the middle of the 17th century. In the 1700s, they developed the pastures into a posh new neighbourhood, focused on a series of landmark squares. The most famous of these, **Grosvenor Square** (1725-31), is dominated by the supremely inelegant US Embassy, due to close in 2017 for its move to Vauxhall. The embassy's only decorative touches are a fierce eagle and a mass of post-9/11 protective barricades. Out front, pride of place is taken by a statue of President Dwight Eisenhower, who stayed in nearby **Claridge's** (*see p253*) when in London; Roosevelt is in the park nearby.

Brook Street has impressive musical credentials: GF Handel lived and died at no.25, and Jimi Hendrix roomed briefly next door at no.23, adjacent buildings that have been combined into the **Handel House Museum** (*see p117*). For most visitors, however, this part of town is all about shopping. Connecting Brook Street with Oxford Street to the north, **South Molton Street** is home to the fabulous boutique-emporium **Browns** (*see p119*) and the excellent **Grays Antique Market** (*see p120*), while **New Bond Street** is an A-Z of top-end, mainstream fashion houses.

EXPLORE

THE BEST IN ALL DEPARTMENTS

Blame Gordon 'Mile-a-Minute' Selfridge – London is in love.

Whenever we ask people for a list of favourite shops, one name recurs to the point where we have to reword our question: 'Apart from **Selfridges** (*see p107*), what is the best shop in London?'. The store even stars in a TV period drama focusing on founder Gordon Selfridge (author of *The Romance of Commerce*), whose pithy one-liner 'Selfridges is for everyone' sums things up.

Alongside designer labels and luxurious services, it has clip-in hair extensions, cheapo nail bars and a ground floor of fashion well within the reach of a teenager's purse. And Mr Selfridge's passion for the theatre of shopping has survived – in 2012, a giant confectionery golf course was built on the roof by Bompas and Parr; in 2013, a whole floor was taken over by Hong Kong fashion giant IT. There is always something happening, whether a shoe-tattooing service or the world's best make-up artist doing your lippy for free.

Stunts aside, if you can't find something to buy in Selfridges, you just aren't looking. In summer 2013 alone, it unveiled the

capital's best denim department and boosted the paltry toy offering to add a messy Play-Doh station, a car-racing track and a regular programme of events such as a bear-fixing hospital and Makies 3D printing. But should this talk of egalitarian shopping leave the luxe customer yearning for a little exclusivity, take heart: Louis Vuitton recently unveiled a three-storey townhouse within the store – a London first.

IN THE KNOW LOST RIVER

The water feature in the basement of **Grays Antique Market** (*see p120*) is formed from the Tyburn Brook. One of London's several buried rivers, it runs underground from Hampstead to Westminster.

Beyond New Bond Street, **Hanover Square** is another of the area's big squares, now a busy traffic chicane. Just to the south is **St George's Church**, built in the 1720s and once everyone's favourite place to be seen and to get married. Handel, who married nobody, attended services here. South of St George's, salubrious **Conduit Street** is where fashion shocker Vivienne Westwood (no.44) faces staid Rigby & Peller (no.22A), corsetière to the Queen.

Running south off Conduit Street is the most famous Mayfair shopping street of all, **Savile Row**. Gieves & Hawkes (no.1) is a must-visit for anyone interested in the history of British menswear; at no.15, the estimable Henry Poole & Co has cut suits for clients including Napoleon III, Charles Dickens and 'Buffalo' Bill Cody. No.3 was the home of the Beatles' Apple Records and their rooftop farewell concert.

Two streets west, **Cork Street** was long the heart of the West End art scene – but Eastcastle Street is mounting a pretty serious challenge (*see p112* **Walk**). **Flowers Central** (no.21, 7439 7766, www.flowersgalleries.com) is one of the notable small galleries that remain in the face of heavy competition elsewhere in Mayfair from major US art dealers: notably the 10,000sq ft **David Zwirner** gallery (24 Grafton Street, 3538 3165, www.davidzwirner.com). **Pace** (3206 7600, www.pacegallery.com), which shares the Royal Academy's premises at 6 Burlington Gardens (*see p121*), has also staged some arresting shows. A couple of streets over is Albemarle Street, where you'll find the troubled **Royal Institution**, home to the **Faraday Museum**.

Just west of Albemarle Street, **44 Berkeley Square** is one of the original houses in this grand square. Built in the 1740s, it was described by architectural historian Nikolaus Pevsner as 'the finest terrace house of London'. Curzon Street, which runs off the south-west corner of Berkeley Square, was home to MI5, Britain's secret service, from 1945 until the '90s. It's also the northern boundary of **Shepherd Market**, named after a food market set up here by architect Edward Shepherd in the early 18th century and now a curious little enclave in the heart of this exclusive area.

From 1686, this was where the raucous May Fair was held, until it was shut down in the late 18th century due to 'drunkenness, fornication, gaming and lewdness'. You'll still manage the drunkenness easily enough at a couple of good pubs (such as **Ye Grapes**, at 16 Shepherd Market). The cobbler on adjoining White Horse Street ('Don't throw away old shoes, they can be restored!') and the ironmongers on Shepherd Street keep things from becoming too genteel.

Sights & museums

★ Handel House Museum

25 Brook Street, W1K 4HB (7399 1953, www.handelhouse.org). Bond Street tube. **Open** 10am-6pm Tue, Wed, Fri, Sat; 10am-8pm Thur; noon-6pm Sun. **Admission** £6.50; £2-£5.50 reductions; free under-5s. **Map** p105 E5 ㉛

Handel moved to Britain from his native Germany aged 25 and settled in this house 12 years later, remaining here until his death in 1759. It has been beautifully restored with original and recreated furnishings, paintings and a welter of the composer's scores. The programme of events includes Thursday recitals on the museum's period instruments.

As recorded by a blue plaque outside, Jimi Hendrix lived with his girlfriend in an upstairs flat next door at no.23 in 1968 – so impressed was he by his illustrious former neighbour that he bought the *Messiah* and *Water Music* on vinyl. The flat is now museum offices, but plans are afoot to refurbish the room as it was in Hendrix's day; depending on funding, it could reopen permanently to the public in autumn 2015.

► *Admission is waived for under-17s at the weekend.*

FREE Royal Institution & Faraday Museum

21 Albemarle Street, W1S 4BS (7409 2992, www.rigb.org). Green Park tube. **Open** 9am-6pm Mon-Fri. Closes for events; phone ahead. **Admission** free. *Multimedia tours* £3. **Map** p105 F5 ㉜

The Royal Institution was founded in 1799 for 'diffusing the knowledge… and application of science to the common purposes of life'; from behind its neoclassical façade, it's been at the forefront of London's scientific achievements ever since. In 2008, Sir Terry Farrell completed a £22m rebuild, hoping to improve accessibility and lure people in with more open frontage, a licensed café and spruced-up events. Instead, the Ri found itself in a recession and saddled with major debt – after reports in early 2013 that the premises would have to be sold, illustrious benefactors stepped in to help.

The Michael Faraday Laboratory, a replica of the great scientist's former workspace, is in the basement, alongside a working laboratory in which Ri scientists can be observed researching their current projects. Some 1,000 of the Ri's 7,000-odd scientific objects are on display, including the world's first electric transformer, a prototype Davy lamp and, from 1858, a print of the first transatlantic telegraph signal.

► *The Ri holds a terrific rolling programme of talks and demonstrations in its lecture theatre.*

EXPLORE

Theo Randall at the InterContinental.

Restaurants

★ Gymkhana

42 Albemarle Street, W1S 4JH (3011 5900, www.gymkhanalondon.com). Green Park tube. **Open** noon-2.45pm, 5.30-10.30pm Mon-Sat. **Main courses** £7.50-£40. **Map** p105 F5 33 **Indian**

Much-lauded Gymkhana looks and feels like an Indian colonial club, with its retro ceiling fans, marble-topped tables and yesteryear photos of polo and cricket team triumphs. It serves a splendid spread of modern Indian dishes based on regional masalas and marinades: a starter of South Indian fried chicken wings, steeped in chilli batter, perhaps, followed by Goan pork vindaloo – slow-cooked chunks of suckling pig cheek, with a vinegary red chilli and garlic masala, spiced with sweet cinnamon and pounded coriander.

Momo

25 Heddon Street, W1B 4BH (7434 4040, www.momoresto.com). Piccadilly Circus tube. **Open** *Restauraunt* noon-2.15pm, 6.30pm-1am Mon-Sat; 6.30pm-midnight Sun. *Café/Bar* noon-1am Mon-Sat; noon-midnight Sun. **Main courses** £13-£28. **Meze** *Café/bar only* £4.50-£9.75. **Map** p105 E6 34 **North African**

Always fun and glamorous, the kasbah-like Momo rocks. Though serious enough about its food not to be a themed restaurant, the staff's end-of-evening ululating and dancing to Maghrebi beats can send confusing signals. Seductive lighting, plush seating, and heavy crystal glasses indicate the kind of bill to expect, but it's worth splashing out for a heady experience and cooking that mostly justifies the prices. Meze are pastries and dips of the highest calibre; tagines, such as lamb tagine with whole almonds in a rich sauce with prune and pear, have a good balance of flavours. Tables on the street terrace for shisha smoking add to the authenticity.

Pollen Street Social

8 Pollen Street, W1S 1NQ (7290 7600, www.pollenstreetsocial.com). Oxford Circus tube. **Open** *Bar* noon-midnight Mon-Sat. *Restaurant* noon-2.30pm, 6-10.30pm Mon-Sat. **Main courses** £29.50-£38. **Map** p105 E5 35 **Modern European**

Pollen Street Social's philosophy is 'deformalised fine dining', and to this end the decor is smart but approachable – white-walled, linen-draped and wood-panelled. Dishes are grounded in French and English tradition and embellished with occasionally esoteric side notes of texture and taste. The delicious subtlety and artistry of Cornish sea bass and red mullet with bouillabaisse sauce, fennel, cuttlefish and saffron potato (self-served from the pan) revealed real skill in the kitchen, as did a masterly strawberry and basil eton mess.

★ Theo Randall at the InterContinental

1 Hamilton Place, Park Lane, W1J 7QY (7409 3131, www.theorandall.com). Hyde Park Corner tube. **Open** noon-3pm, 5.45-11pm Mon-Fri; 5.45-11pm Sat. **Main courses** £30-£50. **Map** p105 G4 36 **Italian**

This colourful, spacious dining room is high on comfort, if a little corporate, service is caring and warm-hearted and the cooking is joyous. The carte is not cheap, but the lunchtime and off-peak hours set menu (around £30) provides more than a glimpse of the kitchen's quality output. Starters might include a subtle combination of smoked eel, golden and red beetroots, and horseradish. This could be followed by a wood-roasted guinea fowl, stuffed with parma ham and mascarpone, and served with porcini and portobello mushrooms.

Pubs & bars

★ Coburg Bar

The Connaught, Carlos Place, W1K 2AL (7499 7070, www.the-connaught.co.uk). Bond Street or Green Park tube. **Open** 8am-11pm Mon, Sun; 8am-1am Tue-Sat. **Map** p105 E4 ㊲

The Connaught has always had the most country house-like feeling of London's great hotels, and the effect reaches perfection in the Coburg. It seems effortlessly beautiful, from the deep patterned carpet to the moulded ceiling; the wing chairs, a long-time fixture, can induce torpor even if you're drinking a double espresso. Great champagnes and cognacs feature prominently on the drinks menu, and the cocktail list focuses on classics. Execution is flawless. Bowls of crisps and olives, both outstanding in quality, are replaced when empty.

▶ *If the Coburg isn't 'scene' enough for you, try the hotel's other, noisier and busier bar, the Connaught.*

Galvin at Windows

London Hilton, Park Lane, W1K 1BE (7208 4021). Hyde Park Corner tube. **Open** 11am-1am Mon-Wed; 11am-2.30am Thur, Fri; 3pm-2.30am Sat; 11am-10.30pm Sun. *Food served* noon-midnight Mon-Fri; 3pm-2.30am Sat; noon-10.30pm Sun. **Map** p105 G4 ㊳

There's suddenly no shortage of rooftop venues in London, but the location of Windows is still superb. It offers remarkable panoramic views from the 28th floor of the Park Lane Hilton. Add a sleek interior that mixes art deco glamour with a hint of 1970s petrodollar kitsch, and you can't go wrong. The wine and cocktails don't come cheap, but the drinks are assembled with care, and the service is attentive without being obsequious.

Shops & services

This is a focal area for British designer showcases. The key locations are **Vivienne Westwood** (44 Conduit Street, W1S 2YL, 7439 1109, www.viviennewestwood.com), **Stella McCartney** (30 Bruton Street, W1J 6QR, 7518 3100, www.stellamccartney.com) and **Alexander McQueen** (4-5 Old Bond Street, W1S 4PD, 7355 0088, www.alexandermcqueen.com), plus the diffusion line, **McQ** (14 Dover Street, W1S 4LW, 7318 2220). Those after some Parisian style have the luxurious **Louis Vuitton Maison** flagship (17-20 New Bond Street, W1S 2UE, 3214 9200, www.louisvuitton.com), or the more pared-down but equally fashion-forward **Vanessa Bruno** boutique (1A Grafton Street, W1S 4EB, 7499 7838, www.vanessabruno.com), the designer's first London store. Also in Mayfair are royal corsetière **Rigby & Peller** (22A Conduit Street, W1S 2XT, 0845 076 5545, www.rigbyandpeller.com) and shoe specialist **Russell & Bromley** (24-25 New Bond Street, W1S 2PS, 7629 6903, www.russellandbromley.co.uk).

Berry Bros & Rudd

3 St James's Street, SW1A 1EG (7396 9600, www.bbr.com). Green Park tube. **Open** 10am-6pm Mon-Fri; 10am-5pm Sat. **Map** p105 G6 ㊴
Food & drink

Britain's oldest wine merchant has been trading on the same premises since 1698, and its heritage is reflected in its panelled sales and tasting rooms. Burgundy- and claret-lovers will drool at the hundreds of wines, but there are also decent selections from elsewhere in Europe and the New World.

Bosideng

28 South Molton Street, W1K 5RF (7290 3170, www.bosidenglondon.com). Bond Street tube. **Open** 10am-8pm Mon-Sat; noon-6pm Sun. **Map** p104 D4 ㊵ **Fashion**

Set over three floors, Bosideng's first overseas flagship store and honorary European headquarters is looking as plush as its 500-piece collection (and with a £10,000 origami sculpture and a £30 million renovation we'd expect no less). This menswear label is Asia's largest manufacturer of down apparel – every feather is a by-product we might add – jetting straight in from China where it has a whopping 10,000 outlets. Every item in the collection is sourced from the UK and Europe (apart from the down) and rendered in posh fabrics: pure cashmere cardies, wool-blend tweed blazers and Egyptian-cotton tops. The space itself is ultra-glossy and airy.

Browns

24-27 South Molton Street, W1K 5RD (7514 0016, www.brownsfashion.com). Bond Street tube. **Open** 10am-6.30pm Mon-Wed, Fri, Sat; 10am-7pm Thur. **Map** p104 D4 ㊶ **Fashion**

Browns has been on the fashion cutting-edge for more than four decades. Among the 100-odd designers jostling for attention in Joan Burstein's five interconnecting shops (menswear is at no.23) are Chloé, Christopher Kane and Balenciaga, with plenty of fashion exclusives. No.24 now also houses Shop 24, selling 'staple items you can't live without'. Browns Focus is younger and more casual; Labels for Less is loaded with last season's leftovers.

Other location 160 Sloane Street, Chelsea, SW1X 9BT (7514 0040).

Daniel Hersheson

45 Conduit Street, W1F 2YN (7434 1747, www.danielhersheson.com). Oxford Circus tube. **Open** 9am-7pm Mon, Sat; 9am-6.30pm Tue, Wed; 9am-8pm Thur, Fri. **Map** p105 E5 ㊷
Health & beauty

EXPLORE

Despite its location in the heart of upmarket Mayfair, this modern two-storey salon isn't at all snooty. Prices start at £60 (£40 for men), though you'll pay £300 for a cut with Daniel (£150 for men). There's also a menu of therapies; the swish Harvey Nichols branch has a dedicated spa. Hersheson's Blow Dry Bars are located at Topshop (*see p107*; 7927 7888 to book), Westfield London (8743 0868) and One New Change (*see p177*; 7248 6225).

★ Dover Street Market

17-18 Dover Street, W1S 4LT (7518 0680, www.doverstreetmarket.com). Green Park tube. **Open** 11am-6.30pm Mon-Wed; 11am-7pm Thur-Sat; noon-5pm Sun. **Map** p105 F5 ㊸ **Fashion**

Comme des Garçons designer Rei Kawakubo's ground-breaking six-storey space combines the edgy energy of London's indoor markets – concrete floors, tills inside corrugated iron shacks, Portaloo dressing rooms – with a fine range of rarefied labels. All 14 of the Comme des Garçons collections are here, alongside exclusive lines from such designers as Lanvin and Azzedine Alaïa.

Elemis Day Spa

2-3 Lancashire Court, W1S 1EX (7499 4995, www.elemis.com). Bond Street tube. **Open** 10.30am-9pm Mon-Fri; 9am-9pm Sat; 10am-6pm Sun. **Map** p105 E5 ㊹ **Health & beauty**

This leading British spa brand's exotic, unisex retreat is tucked away down a cobbled lane off Bond Street. Treatments, from wraps to facials, take place in elegantly ethnic treatment rooms.

Garrard

24 Albemarle Street, W1S 4HT (0870 871 8888, www.garrard.com). Bond Street or Green Park tube. **Open** 10am-6pm Mon-Fri; 10am-5pm Sat. **Map** p105 E5 ㊺ **Accessories**

The Crown Jeweller's diamond-studded designs have appealed to a new generation of bling-seekers since the brand was modernised by Jade Jagger. It's now in the hands of London-based jeweller Stephen Webster, who took over as creative director in 2009.

Grays Antique Market & Grays in the Mews

58 Davies Street, W1K 5LP & 1-7 Davies Mews, W1K 5AB (7629 7034, www.graysantiques.com). Bond Street tube. **Open** 10am-6pm Mon-Fri; 11am-5pm Sat. **Map** p104 D4 ㊻ **Homewares**

Sibling of Alfie's (*see p111*), Grays gathers more than 200 dealers in a smart covered market building. They sell everything from antique furniture and rare books to vintage fashion and jewellery.

Paul Smith Sale Shop

23 Avery Row, W1X 9HB (7493 1287, www.paulsmith.co.uk). Bond Street tube. **Open** 10.30am-6.30pm Mon-Wed, Fri, Sat; 10.30am-7pm Thur; noon-6pm Sun. **Map** p105 E4 ㊼ **Fashion**

Samples and previous season's stock are sold at a 30-50% discount at this sale shop. The varied stock includes clothes for men, women and children, as well as a range of accessories.

★ Postcard Teas

9 Dering Street, W1S 1AG (7629 3654, www.postcardteas.com). Bond Street or Oxford Circus tube. **Open** 10.30am-6.30pm Mon-Sat. **Map** p104 D5 ㊽ **Food & drink**

The range in Timothy d'Offay's exquisite little shop is not huge, but it is selected with great care, and all teas are sourced from small co-operatives. There's a central table for those who want to try a pot; or book in for one of the tasting sessions held on Saturdays between 10am and 11am. Tea-ware and accessories are also sold.

Timothy Everest

35 Bruton Place, W1J 6NS (7629 6236, www.timothyeverest.co.uk). Bond Street tube. **Open** 10am-6pm Mon-Fri; 11am-5pm Sat. **Map** p105 E5 ㊾ **Fashion**

One-time apprentice to the legendary Tommy Nutter, Everest is a star among the new generation of London tailors, with an international reputation for his relaxed 21st-century definition of style.

PICCADILLY

Green Park, Hyde Park Corner or Piccadilly Circus tube.

Piccadilly's name is derived from the 'picadil', a type of suit collar that was in vogue during the 18th century. The first of the area's main buildings was built by tailor Robert Baker and, indicating the source of his wealth, nicknamed 'Piccadilly Hall'. A stroll through the handful of Regency shopping arcades confirms that the rag trade is still flourishing mere minutes away from Savile Row and Jermyn Street. At the renovated **Burlington Arcade** (*see p121*), the oldest and most famous of these arcades, top-hatted security staff known as 'beadles' ensure there's no singing, whistling or hurrying in the arcade: such uncouth behaviour is prohibited by archaic bylaws. Formerly Burlington House (1665), the **Royal Academy of Arts** (*see p121*) is next door to the arcade's entrance. It hosts several lavish, crowd-pleasing exhibitions each year.

On Piccadilly are further representatives of high-end retail. **Fortnum & Mason** (*see p83*), London's most prestigious food store, was founded in 1707 by a former footman to Queen Anne. Look for the fine clock: a 1964 articulated effort, it features 18th-century effigies of Mr Fortnum and Mr Mason, who bow to each other on the hour. The plain church at no.197 is **St James's Piccadilly** (*see p121*), where William Blake was baptised.

EXPLORE

To the west along Piccadilly, smartly uniformed doormen mark former car showroom turned restaurant, the **Wolseley** (*see p82*), and the expensive, exclusive **Ritz** (*see p355*).

Sights & museums

FREE Royal Academy of Arts

Burlington House, W1J 0BD (7300 8000, www.royalacademy.org.uk). Green Park or Piccadilly Circus tube. **Open** 10am-6pm Mon-Thur, Sat, Sun; 10am-10pm Fri. **Admission** free. *Exhibitions* vary. **Map** p105 F6 50

Britain's first art school was founded in 1768 and moved to the extravagantly Palladian Burlington House a century later, but it's now best known not for education but for exhibitions. Ticketed blockbusters are generally held in the Sackler Wing or the main galleries; shows in the John Madejski Fine Rooms are drawn from the RA's holdings, which range from Constable to Hockney, and are free. The biggest event here is the annual Summer Exhibition, which for more than two centuries has drawn from works entered by the public. Towards the end of 2013, the RA opened a decent Peyton & Byrne restaurant, the Keeper's House, with a little courtyard 'garden'.

The RA has also expanded into a nearby 19th-century building: 6 Burlington Gardens. Coveniently located directly behind the main location, it has been exhibiting unabashedly contemporary art, from Tracey Emin and David Hockney to lightworks by Mariko Mori. There's a Peyton & Byrne café here, and the Studio Shop.

▶ *The red phonebox outside the RA is a 1924 wooden prototype of the classic Giles Gilbert Scott design, its roof modelled on Sir John Soane's mausoleum at Old St Pancras church (see p158).*

Burlington Arcade

FREE St James's Piccadilly

197 Piccadilly, W1J 9LL (7734 4511, www.st-james-piccadilly.org). Piccadilly Circus tube. **Open** 8am-6.30pm daily. *Evening events* times vary. **Admission** free. **Map** p105 F6 51

Consecrated in 1684, St James's is the only church Sir Christopher Wren built on an entirely new site. A calming building with few architectural airs or graces, it was almost destroyed in World War II, but painstakingly reconstructed. Grinling Gibbons's delicate limewood garlanding around the sanctuary survived and is one of the few real frills. Beneath a new tiled roof, the church stages regular classical concerts, provides a home for the William Blake Society and hosts markets in the churchyard: food on Monday, antiques on Tuesday, and arts and crafts from Wednesday to Saturday. There's also a handy café in the basement with plenty of tables.

Restaurants

Just across Piccadilly in St James's is one of the grandest brasseries in London: the **Wolseley** (*see p82*).

Shops & services

The **Royal Arcades** in the vicinity of Piccadilly are a throwback to shopping past – the Burlington Arcade (*see below*) is both the largest and grandest, but the **Piccadilly Arcade**, opposite it, and the **Royal Arcade**, at 28 Old Bond Street, are also worth a visit.

A bibliophile could happily waste hours in the **Waterstones** flagship (203-206 Piccadilly, SW1Y 6WW, 7851 2400, www.waterstones.co.uk), which has several floors of books, a refurbished bar-café and a Trailfinders travel agency concession.

★ Burlington Arcade

Piccadilly, W1 (7355 8317, www.burlington-arcade.co.uk). Green Park tube. **Open** 9am-8pm Mon-Sat; 11am-6pm Sun. **Map** p105 F6 52 **Mall**

In 1819, Lord Cavendish commissioned Britain's very first shopping arcade. Nearly two centuries later, the Burlington is still one of London's most prestigious shopping 'streets', patrolled by 'beadles' decked out in top hats and tailcoats. Highlights include collections of classic watches at David Duggan, established British fragrance house Penhaligon's, the British luxury luggage brand Globe-Trotter and Sermoneta, selling Italian leather gloves in a range of bright colours. High-end food shops come in the form of Luponde Tea and Ladurée; head to the latter for exquisite Parisian macaroons. Burlington also houses a proper shoe-shine boy working with waxes and creams for just £4.

▶ *Looking for luggage that's a solution rather than an investment? Marks & Spencer (www.marksandspencer.co.uk) does reliable basics.*

EXPLORE

Soho & Leicester Square

For more than two centuries, poseurs, spivs, tarts, whores, toffs, drunks and divas have gathered in Soho to ply their trades. Many of the area's music, film and advertising businesses have moved on, but the gay scene still thrives. Soho is packed with a huge range of bars, clubs, restaurants and shops, sharing the streets with a sizeable residential community. There are more chains than there used to be, but independents – and an independent frame of mind – still dominate.

Just to the south of Soho, beyond London's bustling little Chinatown, Leicester Square – mainly known for cinemas and, for many years, drunk and disappointed out-of-towners – is beginning to build a classier reputation.

Algerian Coffee Stores.

Don't Miss

1 Algerian Coffee Stores An aromatic piece of Soho history (p129).

2 Photographers' Gallery Explore the handsome new premises (p132).

3 Mark's Bar Classy cocktail joint (p133).

4 Foyles London's biggest independent bookshop (p126, p131).

5 Carnaby Street Back in fashion as a shopping hotspot (p132).

TROCADERO

SOHO SQUARE & AROUND

Tottenham Court Road tube.

Forming the area's northern gateway, **Soho Square** was laid out in 1681. It was initially called King's Square; a weather-beaten statue of Charles II stands just north of the centre. One of the square's benches is dedicated to singer Kirsty MacColl, in honour of her song named after the square.

Two classic Soho streets run south from the square. **Greek Street**, its name a nod to a church that once stood here, is lined with restaurants and bars, among them 50-year-old Hungarian eaterie the **Gay Hussar** (no.2, 7437 0973, http://gayhussar.co.uk) and the nearby **Pillars of Hercules** pub (no.7, 7437 1179), where the literati once enjoyed long liquid lunches. Just by the Pillars, an arch leads to Manette Street and Charing Cross Road, where you'll find **Foyles** (*see p131* **'Foyled Again?'**). Back on Greek Street, no.49 was once Les Cousins, a folk venue (note the mosaic featuring a musical note); Casanova lived briefly at no.46.

Parallel to Greek Street is **Frith Street**, once home to Mozart (1764-65, no.20) and painter John Constable (1810-11, no.49). Humanist essayist William Hazlitt died in 1830 at no.6, now a discreet hotel named in his memory (*see p349* **Hazlitt's**). Further down the street are **Ronnie Scott's** (*see p276*), Britain's best-known jazz club, and, across from Ronnie's, the similarly mythologised 24-hour coffee haunt **Bar Italia** (no.22, 7437 4520).

EXPLORE

Restaurants

★ 10 Greek Street

10 Greek Street, W1D 4DH (7734 4677, www.10greekstreet.com). Tottenham Court Road tube. **Open** noon-2.30pm, 5.30pm-10.45pm Mon-Sat. **Main courses** £12-£19. **Map** p125 D3 ❶ **Modern European**

This small, unshowy restaurant has made a name for itself with a short but perfectly formed menu and an easy-going conviviality. Dishes are seasonal and the kitchen produces lots of interesting but ungimmicky combinations – like a special of halibut fillet with yellow beans, chilli and garlic, on a vivid romesco sauce. It's good value, too. Tables are closely packed, and in the evening it can get noisy; bookings are taken for lunch but not dinner. *Photo p126.*

★ Arbutus

63-64 Frith Street, W1D 3JW (7734 4545, www.arbutusrestaurant.co.uk). Tottenham Court Road tube. **Open** noon-2.30pm, 5-11pm Mon-Thur; noon-2.30pm, 5-11.30pm Fri, Sat; noon-3pm, 5.30-10.30pm Sun. **Main courses** £8-£19. **Map** p125 C3 ❷ **Modern European**

This smart modern eaterie is successfully creative with unusual and less-used ingredients: saddle of rabbit, prettily presented with small root vegetables and stuffed with liver, accompanied by shepherd's pie, for example. We like the good-value set lunch and pre-theatre menus, the posh but proper puds and the fact that every wine is available by 250ml carafe.

▶ *Also try sister restaurant Wild Honey (12 St George Street, Mayfair, W1S 2FB, 7758 9160, www.wildhoneyrestaurant.co.uk).*

Barrafina

54 Frith Street, W1D 4SL (7813 8010, www.barrafina.co.uk). Leicester Square or Tottenham Court Road tube. **Open** noon-3pm, 5-11pm Mon-Sat; 1-3.30pm, 5.30-10.30pm Sun. **Tapas** £4-£18.50. **Map** p125 C3 ❸ **Spanish**

If proof is needed that tapas is fashionable, the queues at Barrafina are it. (Bookings aren't taken for the 20 or so stools around the L-shaped bar.) Nibbles and drinks are served as you wait – service is excellent. Meanwhile, chefs shout out orders, grill, fry and plate up their creations. Barrafina's menu is studded with Mallorcan and Catalan tapas dishes, such as juicy, crisp-skinned grilled chicken thighs served with exemplary romesco sauce.

▶ *For a more formal – and bookable – Spanish experience, try sibling restaurant Fino (33 Charlotte Street, entrance on Rathbone Street, Fitzrovia, W1T 1RR, 7813 8010).*

Ceviche

17 Frith Street, W1D 4RG (7292 2040, www.cevicheuk.com). Leicester Square tube. **Open** noon-11.30pm Mon-Sat; noon-10.15pm Sun. **Tapas** £4.50-£11. **Map** p125 C3 ❹ **Peruvian**

Ceviche showcases the country's most sexy and metropolitan export: ceviche. Here, citrus-cured fish is available in half a dozen different forms, though the menu also includes everything from terrific chargrilled meat and fish skewers (anticuchos) to a simple but perfectly executed corn cake. Factor in the seating options (trendy at the steel counter-bar, more comfortable in the rear dining area), the charismatic, attentive staff and the party atmosphere, and it's no wonder this place has been such a huge hit.

Koya

49 Frith Street, W1D 4SG (7434 4463, www.koya.co.uk). Tottenham Court Road tube. **Open** noon-3pm; 5.30-10.30pm Mon-Sat; 5.30-10pm Sun. **Main courses** £6.90-£14.90. **Map** p125 C3 ❺ **Japanese**

With blond-wood sharing tables, white walls and a generally fresh-faced crowd of diners, the venue feels more like a friendly caff than a slick West End eaterie. The handmade udon noodles produced here are top notch, which explains why expectant diners often queue out of the door (no bookings are taken). Service is snappy, so you won't have to wait too long.

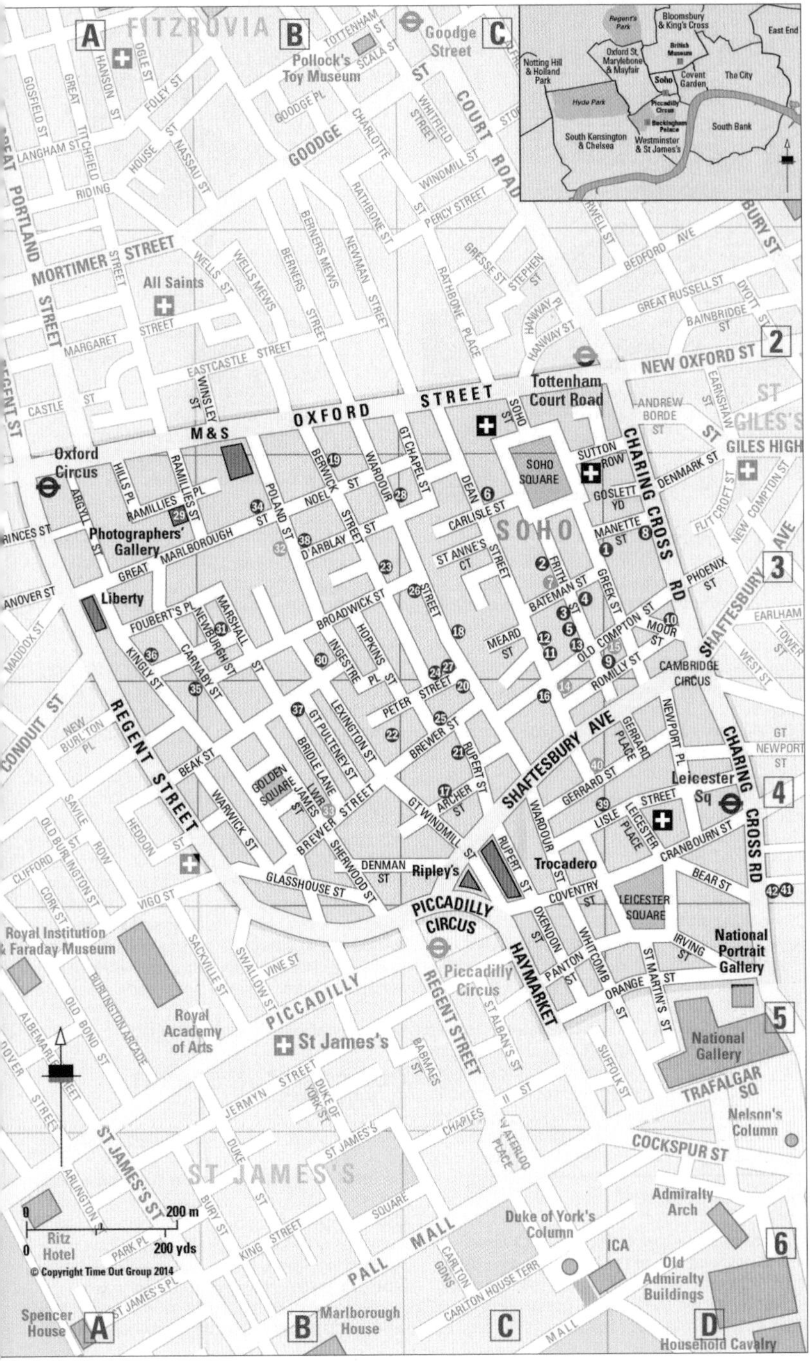
FITZROVIA
A
B
C
D
1
2
3
4
5
6
Regent's Park
Bloomsbury & King's Cross
East End
Notting Hill & Holland Park
Oxford St, Marylebone & Mayfair
British Museum
Soho
Covent Garden
The City
Hyde Park
Piccadilly Circus
Buckingham Palace
South Kensington & Chelsea
Westminster & St James's
South Bank
Pollock's Toy Museum
Goodge Street
TOTTENHAM ST
SCALA ST
GOODGE ST
GOODGE PL
CHARLOTTE
WHITFIELD STREET
COURT ROAD
WINDMILL ST
PERCY STREET
RATHBONE ST
HANSON ST
OGLE ST
FOLEY ST
GOSFIELD ST
GREAT TITCHFIELD
LANGHAM ST
HOUSE
NASSAU ST
RIDING
GREAT PORTLAND
MORTIMER STREET
All Saints
WELLS ST
WELLS MEWS
BERNERS ST
BERNERS MEWS
NEWMAN STREET
RATHBONE PLACE
GRESSE ST
STEPHEN ST
HANWAY PL
HANWAY ST
BEDFORD AVE
GREAT RUSSELL ST
DYOTT ST
BAINBRIDGE ST
NEW OXFORD ST
MARGARET STREET
EASTCASTLE STREET
WINSLEY ST
CASTLE ST
REGENT ST
OXFORD STREET
Tottenham Court Road
ANDREW BORDE ST
EARNSHAW ST
ST GILES'S
GILES HIGH
M & S
Oxford Circus
HILLS PL
RAMILLIES PL
RAMILLIES ST
BERWICK
WARDOUR
GT CHAPEL ST
SOHO ST
DEAN ST
SOHO SQUARE
SUTTON ROW
CHARING CROSS RD
DENMARK ST
FLITCROFT ST
NEW COMPTON ST
ARGYLL ST
PRINCES ST
Photographers' Gallery
GREAT MARLBOROUGH ST
POLAND ST
NOEL ST
D'ARBLAY ST
CARLISLE ST
SOHO
GOSLETT YD
MANETTE ST
ST ANNE'S CT
FRITH
BATEMAN ST
GREEK ST
PHOENIX ST
SHAFTESBURY AVE
Liberty
HANOVER ST
FOUBERT'S PL
MARSHALL
NEWBURGH ST
BROADWICK ST
STREET
MEARD ST
OLD COMPTON ST
MOOR ST
EARLHAM
TOWER ST
WEST ST
MADDOX ST
KINGLY ST
CARNABY ST
INGESTRE PL
HOPKINS ST
ROMILLY ST
CAMBRIDGE CIRCUS
PETER STREET
CONDUIT ST
NEW BURLINGTON PL
REGENT STREET
GT PULTENEY ST
LEXINGTON ST
BREWER ST
RUPERT ST
GERRARD PLACE
NEWPORT PL
GT NEWPORT ST
BEAK ST
GOLDEN SQUARE
BRIDLE LANE
LWR JAMES ST
ARCHER ST
GERRARD ST
Leicester Sq
WARWICK ST
SAVILE ROW
BREWER STREET
GT WINDMILL ST
WARDOUR ST
LISLE STREET
LEICESTER PLACE
LEICESTER ST
CRANBOURN ST
CROSS RD
OLD BURLINGTON ST
HEDDON ST
SHERWOOD ST
DENMAN ST
Ripley's
RUPERT ST
Trocadero
CLIFFORD ST
GLASSHOUSE ST
COVENTRY ST
BEAR ST
CORK ST
VIGO ST
PICCADILLY CIRCUS
LEICESTER SQUARE
Royal Institution & Faraday Museum
SACKVILLE ST
SWALLOW ST
VINE ST
HAYMARKET
OXENDON ST
WHITCOMB ST
PANTON ST
IRVING ST
National Portrait Gallery
Piccadilly Circus
ORANGE ST
ST MARTIN'S ST
BURLINGTON ARCADE
Royal Academy of Arts
PICCADILLY
REGENT STREET
ST ALBAN'S ST
National Gallery
ALBEMARLE STREET
OLD BOND ST
St James's
BABMAES ST
SUFFOLK ST
TRAFALGAR SQ
DOVER STREET
JERMYN STREET
DUKE OF YORK ST
CHARLES II ST
WATERLOO PLACE
Nelson's Column
ST JAMES'S ST
DUKE ST
ST JAMES'S
ST JAMES'S SQUARE
COCKSPUR ST
ARLINGTON ST
BURY ST
Admiralty Arch
0 200 m
0 200 yds
Ritz Hotel
PARK PL
KING STREET
PALL MALL
CARLTON GDNS
Duke of York's Column
ICA
Old Admiralty Buildings
© Copyright Time Out Group 2014
ST JAMES'S PL
CARLTON HOUSE TERR
Spencer House
Marlborough House
MALL
Household Cavalry

EXPLORE

10 Greek Street. *See p124.*

Pizza Pilgrims

11 Dean Street, W1D 3RP (7287 8964, http://pizzapilgrims.co.uk). Tottenham Court Road tube. **Meals served** noon-10.30pm daily. **Main courses** £7-£11. **Map** p125 C3 6 **Pizza**

The main basement dining area is intimate, with wipe-clean green checked tablecloths and 1960s Italian film posters helping to create the feel of a retro Soho trattoria. The friendly, slightly trendy mood is helped by an alcove for table football. Pizzas are chewy and soft in the Neapolitan style, the appealing, thick bases layered with on-trend toppings: 'nduja, a spicy Calabrian sausage, is paired well with a simple marinara sauce, for example. No bookings.

Pubs & bars

Dog & Duck

18 Bateman Street, W1D 3AJ (7494 0697, www.nicholsonspubs.co.uk). Tottenham Court Road tube. **Open** noon-11pm daily. *Food served* 10am-10pm daily. **Map** p125 C3 7

This Soho landmark pub is best known for its literary heritage, but the vintage interior (etched mirrors, carved mahogany) and ever-changing selection of good ales – from the familiar London Pride to an altogether rarer range of beers from the Newman Brewery – also appeal. Sausages also feature. The George Orwell room upstairs, where the writer sometimes drank, offers more space.

Shops & services

Off the Charing Cross Road, Denmark Street was in the 1960s the site of the legendary recording studio Regent Sounds; it is now a hub for music shops, especially those selling guitars. For recorded music, though, head across the road to Foyles, which is also home to **Ray's Jazz**. Ray's offers a predominantly CD-based stock that covers blues, avant-garde, gospel, folk and world, but is strongest in modern jazz.

Foyles

113-119 Charing Cross Road, WC2H 0EB (7437 5660, www.foyles.co.uk). Tottenham Court Road tube. **Open** 9.30am-9pm Mon-Sat; noon-6pm Sun (browsing from 11.30am). **Map** p125 D3 8 **Books & music**

Probably the single most impressive independent bookshop in London: 56 specialist subjects are covered in the flagship store, with the music, gay interest, foreign fiction, law and philosophy sections especially strong. The shop's five storeys accommodate several concessions, too, including the Grant & Cutler foreign-language bookstore, and, on the third floor, Ray's Jazz. The popular first-floor café hosts readings, as well as occasional gigs and other events. And things promise to get even better when the store moves into larger premises next door at no.107; *see p131* **'Foyled Again?'**.

Other locations throughout the city.

OLD COMPTON STREET & AROUND

Leicester Square or Tottenham Court Road tube.

Linking Charing Cross Road to Wardour Street and crossed by Greek, Frith and Dean streets, **Old Compton Street** is London's gay catwalk. Tight T-shirts congregate around **Balans** (*see p258*), **Compton's** (nos.51-53) and the **Admiral Duncan** (no.54). However, the street has an interesting history that dates back long before rainbow flags were hung above its doors: no.59

was formerly the 2i's Coffee Bar, the skiffle venue where stars and svengalis mingled in the late 1950s and early '60s.

Visit Old Compton Street in the morning for a sense of the mostly vanished immigrant Soho of old. Cheeses and cooked meats from **Camisa** (no.61, 7437 7610, www.camisa.co.uk) and roasting beans from the **Algerian Coffee Stores** (*see p129*) scent the air, as **Pâtisserie Valerie** (no.44, 7437 3466, www.patisserie-valerie.co.uk), first of a now significant national chain, does a brisk trade in croissants and cakes.

Valerie's traditional rival is the older **Maison Bertaux** (7437 6007, www.maisonbertaux.com), an atmospheric holdover from the 19th century that sits near the southern end of Greek Street. At the corner of Greek and Romilly streets is the **Coach & Horses** (no.29, 7437 5920, www.coachandhorsessoho.co.uk), where irascible Soho flâneur Jeffrey Bernard held court for decades. It's almost opposite the members' club **Soho House** (no.40, 7734 5188), where media types and wannabes hope to channel the same vibe. Two streets along, Dean Street holds the **French House** (*see p129*); formerly the York Minster pub, it was de Gaulle's London base for French resistance in World War II and in later years became a favourite of painters Francis Bacon and Lucian Freud.

North of Old Compton Street on Dean Street sits the **Groucho Club** (no.45), a members-only media hangout that was founded in the mid 1980s and named in honour of the familiar Groucho Marx quote about not wanting to join any club that would have him as a member. A few doors along, at no.28, the other famous Marx lived in a garret from 1850 to 1856; he would probably not have approved of the high-class, high-cost dinners served there now – at **Quo Vadis** (nos.26-29). To the north is the **Soho Theatre** (*see p289*), which programmes comedy shows and new plays.

Restaurants

Barshu

28 Frith Street, W1D 5LF (7287 6688, www.bar-shu.co.uk). Leicester Square tube. **Open** noon-11pm Mon-Thur, Sun; noon-11.30pm Fri, Sat. **Main courses** £9.90-£30.90. **Map** p125 D3 ❾ **Chinese**

Barshu is distinct from Chinatown's mostly Cantonese restaurants in looks and pricing, as well as its Sichuanese cuisine. The dark wooden ground floor is brightened by red lanterns and partitioned by a beautifully carved screen; upstairs is similarly woody. Sichuan cooking is characterised by fiery, sour flavours, and the menu holds much interest, listing the likes of pea jelly, prairie tripe, and stir-fried chicken gizzards with pickled chilli. Many dishes are hot and oily, so order steamed rice and plain vegetables for balance.

▶ *For more unusual (and cheap) Chinese food in Soho, try Barshu's siblings Ba Shan (24 Romilly Street, W1D 5AH, 7287 3266) and Baozi Inn (25 Newport Court, WC2H 7JS, 7287 6877).*

La Bodega Negra

16 Moor Street, W1D 5NH (7758 4100, www.labodeganegra.com). Leicester Square tube. **Open** *Café* noon-midnight Mon-Wed; noon-1am Thur-Sat; noon-11pm Sun. *Restaurant* 6pm-1am Mon-Sat; 6-midnight Sun. **Main courses** £12-£26. **Map** p125 D3 ❿ **Mexican**

It's so dark and loud in this nightclub-like basement restaurant that you'll need a moment to adjust. The cooking is perhaps the least thrilling aspect of the place, though effort is put into presentation. Soft flour tacos with a tender beef filling are beautifully arranged on a wooden board. Factor-in the small portions and two-hour table limits and you might wonder what the fuss is all about. But that would be missing the point. You come here to see and be seen, and for a thrilling atmosphere and exceptionally friendly service.

Burger & Lobster

36 Dean Street, W1D 4PS (7432 4800, www.burgerandlobster.com). Leicester Square tube. **Open** noon-10.30pm Mon-Sat; noon-10pm Sun. **Main courses** £20. **Map** p125 C3 ⓫ **American**

With its no-nonsense choice of, you've guessed it, burger or lobster, this place has been a runaway hit. Food costs £20, an all-in price that includes a huge carton of thin-cut fries and a side salad: you won't go hungry here. The burger is good, but for ultimate value, choose the lobster (boiled, grilled or in a brioche roll with mayonnaise).

Other locations throughout the city.

Cây Tre

42-43 Dean Street, W1D 4PZ (7317 9118, www.caytresoho.co.uk). Leicester Square tube. **Open** noon-11pm Mon-Thur; noon-11.30pm Fri, Sat; noon-10pm Sun. **Main courses** £8-£13. **Map** p125 C3 ⓬ **Vietnamese**

Cây Tre is chic, with minimal decor, impeccably smart and efficient black-clad staff, and beautifully served food. The chain prides itself on using fresh ingredients with impeccable provenance – witness the barbecued Somerset ribs with lemongrass, Sriracha chilli sauce and galangal. Counters with stools have been provided by the entrance, facing the street, for those in a hurry or singletons.

Other location 301 Old Street, Shoreditch, EC1V 9LA (7729 8662).

Herman Ze German

33 Old Compton Street, W1D 5JU (no phone, www.herman-ze-german.co.uk). Leicester Square tube. **Open** 11am-11.30pm Mon-Thur; 11am-midnight Fri, Sat; 11am-10.30pm Sun. **Main courses** £4.45-£9.95. **Map** p125 C3 ⓭ **German**

THEATRELAND'S VERY OWN TICKET BOOTH
TKTS
EST 1980
tkts
Great choice, genuine deals and friendly advice. Come and see us at
The Clocktower, Leicester Square
www.TKTS.co.uk

London BeatlesStore
231/233 BAKER STREET
LONDON NW16XE
TEL: 020 7935 4464
www.beatlesstorelondon.co.uk
IT'S ONLY ROCK 'N' ROLL
230 BAKER ST
LONDON NW1 5RT
TEL: 020 7224 0277
www.itsonlyrocknrolllondon.co.uk
OPEN DAILY 10am - 6:30pm
If you love The Beatles, The Rolling Stones, Led Zeppelin, The Who, Pink Floyd, Elvis, Jimi Hendrix, David Bowie, Queen, The Doors, Ramones, Sex Pistols, Clash, AC/DC, Iron Maiden, Metallica, Green Day, Nirvana, Oasis etc. this is the place for you!
From t-shirts to autographs, we sell a large range of new and original merchandise.
Just 1 minute north of Baker Street Station
BAKER STREET
IT'S ONLY ROCK'N'ROLL
LONDON BEATLES STORE
BAKER STREET STATION
MARYLEBONE ROAD

Going shopping?
Find a parking space in central London with no hassle
ParkRight
Less time parking, more time shopping!
Download the FREE ParkRight app and you can plan your parking before you leave home, and find an available space with real-time information.
Find out more at westminster.gov.uk/baysensorparking or download the app now from the Apple, Windows or Google stores.
Available on the App Store
Google play
Download from Windows Store
City of Westminster

Herman Ze German is a purveyor of German sausages. with a playfully utilitarian interior. The sausages are imported from the Schwarzwald (the Black Forest), and are *sehr gut*: high-quality pork; juicy, springy middles; and a proper 'knack' when you bite. More bonus points for serving them in chewy baguettes.
Other location 19 Villiers Street, Charing Cross, WC2N 6NE (no phone).

Pubs & bars

★ French House

49 Dean Street, W1D 5BG (7437 2799, www.frenchhousesoho.com). Leicester Square tube. **Open** noon-11pm Mon-Sat; noon-10.30pm Sun. *Food served* noon-4pm daily. **Map** p125 C4 ⓮
Through the door of this venerable establishment have passed many titanic drinkers of the pre- and post-war era. The venue's French heritage also enticed de Gaulle to run a Resistance operation from upstairs – it's now a tiny restaurant. De Gaulle's image survives behind the bar, where beer is served in half-pints and litre bottles of Breton cider are still plonked on the famed back alcove table.

LAB

12 Old Compton Street, W1D 4TQ (7437 7820, www.labbaruk.com). Leicester Square tube. **Open** 4pm-midnight Mon-Sat; 4-10.30pm Sun. **Map** p125 D3 ⓯
LAB was created in 1999, which makes it a granddaddy in London's cool bar scene. But it shows no signs of decline. Most cocktails on the long (90-plus) list are grounded in LAB's core principle: understanding and perfecting cocktail fundamentals. Tables are bookable.

Shops & services

★ Algerian Coffee Stores

52 Old Compton Street, W1V 6PB (7437 2480, www.algcoffee.co.uk). **Open** 9am-7pm Mon-Wed; 9am-9pm Thur, Fri; 9am-8pm Sat. **Map** p125 C4 ⓰ **Food & drink**
For over 125 years, this unassuming little shop has been trading over the same wooden counter. The range of coffees is broad, with house blends sold alongside single-origin beans, and some serious teas and brewing hardware are also available.
▶ *Passing? Take away a single or double espresso for £1, or a cappuccino or a latte for £1.20.*

WARDOUR STREET & AROUND

Leicester Square or Tottenham Court Road tube.

Parallel to Dean Street, **Wardour Street** provides offices for film and TV production companies, but is also known for its rock history. No.100 was, for nearly three decades, the Marquee, where Led Zeppelin played their first London gig and Hendrix appeared four times. The latter's favourite Soho haunt was the nearby **Ship** pub (no.116), still with a sprinkling of music-themed knick-knacks. There's more music history at Trident Studios on nearby **St Anne's Court**: Lou Reed recorded *Transformer* here, and David Bowie cut both *Hunky Dory* and *The Rise and Fall of Ziggy Stardust* on the site.

Back when he was still known as David Jones, Bowie played a gig at the Jack of Clubs on Brewer Street, now **Madame JoJo's** (*see p277*). But this corner of Soho is most famous not for music but for its position at the heart of Soho's dwindling but still notorious sex trade. The Raymond Revuebar opened on the neon alleyway of Walker's Court in 1958, swiftly becoming London's most famous strip club. It closed in 2004, became a series of short-lived gay clubs, then reopened as edgy, celebrity-loved, exclusive alt-cabaret club the **Box** (www.theboxsoho.com), the London branch of a New York original.

North of here, **Berwick Street** is a lovely mix of old-school London raffishness and new-Soho style. The former comes courtesy of the fruit and veg market (support it: more custom needed), and the egalitarian, old-fashioned and unceasingly popular **Blue Posts** pub (no.22, 7437 5008), where builders, post-production editors, restaurateurs and market traders gabble and glug as one beneath a portrait of Berwick Street-born star of stage and radio Jessie Matthews (1907-81). It's quite a contrast with the **Endurance** (no.90, 7437 2944, www.theendurance.co.uk), the street's gastropub, and **Flat White** (no.17, 7734 0370, www.flatwhitecafe.com) coffee bar.

Restaurants

Bocca di Lupo

12 Archer Street, W1D 7BB (7734 2223, www.boccadilupo.com). Piccadilly Circus tube. **Open** 12.15-2.45pm, 5.15-11pm Mon-Sat; 12.15-3.15pm, 5.15-11pm Sun. **Dishes** £6-£26.50. **Map** p125 C4 ⓱ **Italian**
The buzz is as important as the food at this popular restaurant. The menu is a slightly confusing mix of small and large plates to share: buttery brown shrimp on soft, silky white polenta, say, and a deep-fried mix of calamari, soft-shell crab and lemon. The radish, celeriac, pomegranate and pecorino salad with truffle dressing is a much-imitated Bocca di Lupo signature.
▶ *The same team runs the fine gelateria, Gelupo, at no.7 (7287 5555, www.gelupo.com).*

★ Hummus Bros

88 Wardour Street, W1F 0TH (7734 1311, www.hbros.co.uk). Oxford Circus or Tottenham Court Road tube. **Open** noon-10pm Mon-Wed;

EXPLORE

noon-11pm Thur-Sat; noon-4pm Sun. **Dishes** £3.20-£8.45. **Map** p125 C3 ⓲ **Café**
The humble chickpea paste is elevated to something altogether more delicious in the hands of Hummus Bros. Though the wraps aren't bad, go for the bowls of silky-smooth houmous sprinkled with paprika and olive oil. Mashed, cumin-scented fava beans is a good choice of topping, but our favourite is the chunky slow-cooked beef. Side dishes are heartily recommended, with deliciously smoky barbecued aubergine and zingy tabouleh particular highlights. Service is quick and casual.
Other locations 62 Exmouth Market, Clerkenwell, EC1R 4QE (7812 1177); 37-63 Southampton Row, Bloomsbury, WC1B 4DA (7404 7079); 128 Cheapside, the City, EC2V 6BT (7726 8011).

Polpetto

11 Berwick Street, W1F 0PL (7439 8627, www.polpo.co.uk). Oxford Circus tube.
Open noon-11pm Mon-Sat; noon-4pm Sun.
Map p125 B3 ⓳ **Italian**
Following on from the success of Polpetto at its former residence above the French House (*see p129*), chef Florence Knight has found a new Soho home. Expect the same mix of Venetian-style small plates. *See p144* **Russell Up Some Eats**.
Other locations 6 Maiden Lane, WC2E 7NA (7836 8448); 41 Beak Street, W1F 9SB (7734 4479); 3 Cowcross Street, EC1M 6DR (7250 0034).

Princi

135 Wardour Street, W1F 0UF (7478 8888, www.princi.co.uk). Leicester Square or Tottenham Court Road tube. **Open** 8am-midnight Mon-Sat; 8.30am-10pm Sun. **Main courses** £7.50-£12.50. **Map** p125 C4 ⓴ **Bakery-café**
This smart outpost of a Milanese bakery chain remains a popular all-day option. It's an airy, good-looking room, and the food is varied: as well as cakes, pastries and breads, there's a choice of filled focaccia (parma ham, say, or mortadella), hot dishes (lasagne, aubergine parmigiana), slices of pizza and lots of attractive salads. It's all quality, seasonal stuff. Finding a seat at the communal counters can be something of a trial. Opt out by dining in the pizzeria, which offers table service and a calmer atmosphere in which to enjoy a short but classy range of pizzas.

★ Spuntino

61 Rupert Street, W1D 7PW (no phone, www.spuntino.co.uk). Piccadilly Circus tube.
Open noon-midnight Mon-Wed; noon-1am Thur-Sat; noon-11pm Sun. **Main courses** £5-£10. **Map** p125 C4 ㉑ **North American**
A challenge to find (look for 'number 61'), the venue is laid out as a bar – and a tiny one at that, with a smattering of fixed, backless seats allowing diners to perch along the counter. This is no wholesome 1950s-style diner, but a dark, grungy space where dim lights dangle in cages, the walls are cracked and battered, and the staff sport daring tattoos under flimsy vests (and that's just the girls). The menu is Italian-American with plenty of 'additude', featuring big bold flavours packed into tiny portions. No bookings are accepted.
▶ *Owner Russell Norman also runs the excellent Polpo mini-chain (www.polpo.co.uk); see p144* **Russell Up Some Eats**.

Yalla Yalla

1 Green's Court, W1F 0HA (7287 7663, www.yalla-yalla.co.uk). Piccadilly Circus tube.
Open 10am-11pm daily. **Main courses** £9.75-£14.50. **Map** p125 B4 ㉒ **Lebanese**
The 'Beirut street food' resonates with the upbeat informality of these dinky Soho premises. Diners cram on to faux-rustic tables, while others nip in for takeaway wraps – filled with everything from falafel to spicy sujuk sausage – from the prepared selection behind the counter. A concise list of classic meze dishes includes a chunky, smoky baba ganoush and a flavour-packed fattoush salad. There's also a selection of grills. Cocktails are served in the evening.
Other location 12 Winsley Street, Marylebone, W1W 8HQ (7637 4748).

Shops & services

Berwick Street (www.berwickstreetlondon.co.uk) is really the heart of Soho, with its breezy street market (9am-6pm Mon-Sat), one of London's oldest, in an area better known for its lurid, neon-lit trades. Dating back to 1778, it's still great for seasonal produce and cheap fabric. The indie record shops that used to cluster here have taken a pasting over the last few years, but **Revival Records** (no.30) is full of vinyl beans – as is **Sounds of the Universe** (*see p131*), round the corner. **Agent Provocateur** is now a glossy chain, but the original outpost of the shop that went on to popularise high-class kink around the world is still in Soho (6 Broadwick Street, W1F 8HL, 7439 0229, www.agentprovocateur.com). Just next door is a big branch of beauty chain **Space NK** (8-10 Broadwick Street, W1F 8HW, 7734 3734, www.spacenk.com).

Chris Kerr

31 Berwick Street, W1F 8RJ (7437 3727, www.eddiekerr.co.uk). Oxford Circus tube.
Open 8.30am-5.30pm Mon-Fri; 9am-1pm Sat.
Map p125 B3 ㉓ **Fashion**
Chris Kerr, son of legendary 1960s tailor Eddie Kerr, is the man to visit if Savile Row's prices or attitude aren't to your liking. The versatile Kerr has no house style; instead, he makes every suit to each client's exact specifications, and those clients include Johnny Depp and David Walliams. A good place to get started with British tailoring.

Gosh!

1 Berwick Street, W1F 0DR (7636 1011, www.goshlondon.com). Oxford Circus tube. **Open** 10.30am-7pm daily. **Map** p125 C3 24 **Books & music**

There's nowhere better to bolster your comics collection. There's a huge selection of Manga, but graphic novels take centre stage, from early classics such as *Krazy Kat* to Alan Moore's erotic Peter Pan adaptation *Lost Girls*. Classic children's books, of the *This is London* vein, are another strong point.

Lina Stores

18 Brewer Street, W1F 0SH (7437 6482, www.linastores.co.uk). Leicester Square tube. **Open** 8.30am-7.30pm Mon, Tue, Sat; 8.30am-8pm Wed-Fri; 11am-5pm Sun. **Map** p125 C4 25 **Food & drink**

Behind the 1950s green ceramic Soho frontage is an iconic family-run Italian deli that's been in business for over half a century. A recent modernisation has taken away some of the old-school character, but a new coffee machine goes some way to making up for it. Besides dried pastas, there's a deli counter chock-full of cured meats, hams, salamis, olives, pesto, cheeses, marinated artichokes and fresh pastas. It's also one of the best places to buy truffles in season.

Sounds of the Universe

7 Broadwick Street, W1F 0DA (7734 3430, www.soundsoftheuniverse.com). Tottenham Court Road tube. **Open** 11am-7.30pm Mon-Sat; 11.30am-5.30pm Sun. **Map** p125 C3 26 **Books & music**

SOTU's affiliation with reissue kings Soul Jazz records means its remit is broad. This is especially true on the ground floor (new vinyl and CDs), where

'FOYLED AGAIN?'

The second coming of London's greatest bookshop.

In the mid-1980s, **Foyles** (*see p126*) wasn't just the worst bookshop in London – it was probably the worst in the world. Founded in 1903, the shop was run from 1945 by charming but thoroughly autocratic Christina Foyle, daughter of the founder.

She would sack anyone who'd worked at the shop for six months, lest they acquire an improved contract. She would move staff from their areas of specialist knowledge, so they'd be less tempted to browse at work. Notoriously, to prevent too many staff having access to cash, she introduced a quasi-Stalinist double queuing system – you took your book to a desk, swapped it for a ticket, paid the ticket at a second desk, then collected your purchase from a third. Foyles had massive stock, but few staff knew where books were – they were shelved by publisher, not author or subject. No wonder a competitor felt able to run a series of posters saying: 'Foyled again? Try Dillons'.

Still, she kept Foyles in operation until her death in 1999 – the year, incidentally, that Dillons folded. 'In her 80s,' her *Guardian* obituary noted, 'she was still reading at least a book a day, drinking only champagne and declining even to try to cook.'

But the most surprising twist was yet to come. After a decade of shrewd management, Foyles became the most impressive independent bookshop in London, winning awards for range of stock and clued-in, friendly customer service.

And now it's time to change again. With Central St Martins art school having decamped to Granary Square (*see p157*), bigger premises suddenly became available in the art deco building next door at 107-109 Charing Cross Road. Huge picture windows either side of the new building's entrance used to house installations by the students; now they will be where Foyles' Art and Design Department is situated. There is a wonderful central atrium, and the stage of the former Assembly Hall (once graced – perhaps disgraced – by the Sex Pistols) will be the Children's section. Fiction will be on what was a ballroom floor, peered down upon from Cookery, Travel and Lifestyle on a mezzanine above. And a gallery, café and events space will crown the building either side of the atrium.

One thing has remained certain: at the centre of the shop will be, as there always were, shelves of thousands of wonderful books.

Photographers' Gallery.

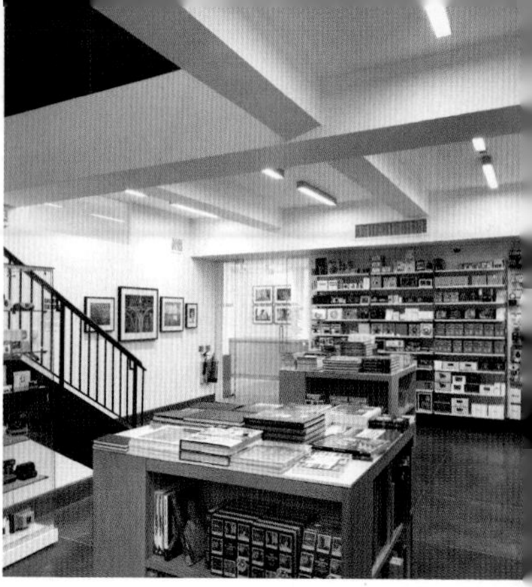

grime and dubstep 12-inches jostle for space alongside new wave cosmic disco, electro-indie re-rubs and Nigerian compilations. The second-hand vinyl basement is big on soul, jazz, Brazilian and alt-rock.

Supreme

2-3 Peter Street, W1F 0AA (7437 0493, www.supremenewyork.com). Oxford Circus or Piccadilly Circus tube. **Open** 11am-7pm Mon-Sat; noon-6pm Sun. **Map** p125 C3 27 **Fashion**

Europe's first Supreme store opened in 2011 to much excitement among the city's skaters and streetwear fans. The standalone Soho store stocks the entire collection of the cool New York brand's clothing, footwear and boards.

Yamaha Music London

152-160 Wardour Street, W1F 8YA (7432 4400, www.yamahamusiclondon.com). Tottenham Court Road tube. **Open** 9.30am-6pm Mon-Fri; 10am-5.30pm Sat. **Map** p125 B3 28 **Books & music**

This vast three-storied space (previously Chappell of Bond Street) is now the leading Yamaha stockist in the UK, but more portable purchases can be found in the collection of sheet music (classical, pop and jazz), reputedly the largest in Europe.

WEST SOHO

Piccadilly Circus tube.

The area west of Berwick Street was rebranded 'West Soho' in a misplaced bid to give it some kind of upmarket identity. **Brewer Street** does have some interesting places; among them is the **Vintage Magazine Store** (nos.39-43, 7439 8525), offering everything from retro robots to pre-war issues of *Vogue*. Star restaurant **Hix** with its hip downstairs bar (*see p133,* **Mark's Bar**) is also here. On Great Windmill Street is the **Windmill Theatre** (nos.17-19), which gained fame in the 1930s and '40s for its 'revuedeville' shows with erotic 'tableaux' – naked women who remained stationary in order to stay within the law. The place is now a lap-dancing joint. North of Brewer Street is **Golden Square**. Developed in the 1670s, it became the political and ambassadorial district of the late 17th and early 18th centuries, and remains home to some of the area's grandest buildings (many now bases for media firms) and a purveyor of cinnamon buns: the **Nordic Bakery** (no.14A, 3230 1077, www.nordicbakery.com).

Just north of Golden Square is **Carnaby Street**, which became a fashion mecca shortly after John Stephen opened His Clothes here in 1956; Stephen, who went on to own more than a dozen fashion shops on the street, is now commemorated with a plaque at the corner with Beak Street. After thriving during the Swinging Sixties, Carnaby Street became a rather seamy commercialised backwater. However, along with nearby **Newburgh Street** and **Kingly Court** (*see p133*), it's undergone a revival, with the tourist traps and chain stores joined by a wealth of independent stores.

A little further north, just short of Oxford Street, is the new **Photographers' Gallery**.

Sights & museums

FREE Photographers' Gallery

16-18 Ramillies Street, W1F 7LW (0845 262 1618, www.thephotographersgallery.org.uk). Oxford Circus tube. **Open** 10am-6pm Mon-Wed, Fri, Sat; 10am-8pm Thur; 11.30am-6pm Sun. **Admission** free. *Temporary exhibitions* vary. **Map** p125 A3 29

Given a handsome refit by Irish architects O'Donnell+Tuomey, this old brick corner building reopened in 2012 as the new home for London's only gallery dedicated solely to the photographic arts. The upper floors have two airy new exhibition spaces, while a bookshop, print sales room and café (open the same hours as the gallery) are tucked into the ground floor and basement. The exhibitions are varied, and enhanced by quirky details such as the camera obscura in the third-floor Eranda Studio and a projection wall in the café.

Restaurants

Andrew Edmunds

46 Lexington Street, W1F 0LW (7437 5708, www.andrewedmunds.com). Oxford Circus tube. **Open** noon-3.30pm, 5.30-10.45pm Mon-Fri; 12.30-3.30pm, 5.30-10.45pm Sat; 1-4pm, 6-10.30pm Sun. **Main courses** £11-£20. **Map** p125 B3 ㉚ **Bistro**

A Soho stalwart that seems not to have changed for nearly three decades. With unfussy starters (daily changing salad, welsh rarebit, smoked salmon plate or dressed crab are typical) and no-nonsense, well-portioned mains, such as roast lamb with butter beans and broccoli, eating here is like the best sort of dinner party (if your hosts had a great wine cellar). Set on two small, slightly cramped floors, the place looks wine bar-shabby and the atmosphere is cosy; service is brisk but friendly.

Pitt Cue Co

1 Newburgh Street, W1F 7RB (www.pittcue.co.uk). Oxford Circus tube. **Open** noon-3pm, 6-10.30pm Mon-Sat; noon-4pm Sun. **Main courses** £9.50-£16. **Map** p125 B3 ㉛ **North American**

Come to this trailblazing 30-seater rib joint on a Friday or Saturday night and there's one certainty: a painfully long queue. For rib-lovers, it'll be worth it. The Pitt Cue-ers's cooking rarely misses a beat. The gargantuan signature ribs arrive with blistered, blackened skin, revealing ruby fall-off-the bone meat that is both smoky and dangerously rich. A fine 'slaw, with two kinds of cabbage, coriander seeds and a zingy vinaigrette, cuts through the cholesterol.

Pubs & bars

Lucky Voice

52 Poland Street, W1F 7LR (7439 3660, www.luckyvoice.co.uk). Oxford Circus tube. **Open** 5.30pm-1am Mon-Wed; 5.30pm-3am Thur, Fri; 3pm-3am Sat; 3-10.30pm Sun. **Map** p125 B3 ㉜

There are nine rooms at this karaoke venue, each with space for between four and 12 singers; some come with props such as hats, wigs and inflatable electric guitars. A drinks menu includes cocktails (£7.90), saké and spirits, brought to your room when you press the 'thirsty' button; food is pizza and snacks. The place to discover your inner Beyoncé. **Other location** 173-174 Upper Street, Islington, N1 1RG (7354 6280).

★ Mark's Bar

Hix, 66-70 Brewer Street, W1F 9UP (7292 3518, www.marksbar.co.uk). Piccadilly Circus tube. **Open** noon-1am Mon-Sat; noon-midnight Sun. **Map** p125 B4 ㉝

The basement cocktail bar at Mark Hix's restaurant is first-rate. The historical drinks are both interesting and good, especially those in the Cocktail Explorer's Club list. Rum drinkers should make a beeline for the Royal Bermuda Yacht Club: Mount Gay Barbados rum with orange curaçao, Mark's own falernum and lime juice. The selection of scotch would take several months to drink through. The bar 'snax' are terrific, and the place looks great, with its big smoked mirrors.

Shops & services

As famous as the King's Road back when the Sixties swung, **Carnaby Street** was, until a few years ago, more likely to sell you a postcard of the Queen snogging a punk rocker than a fishtail parka. But the noughties have been kind and Carnaby is cool again. **Kingly Court** (*see below*) is the highlight, but classy chains (Lush, Muji) and boutiques have appeared in the nearby alleys, and branches of **Size?** (nos.33-34, 7287 4016, www.size.co.uk) and **Puma** (nos.52-55, 7439 0221, www.puma.com) make this a good place to stalk some rare sneakers.

Harold Moores Records

2 Great Marlborough Street, W1F 7HQ (7437 1576, www.hmrecords.co.uk). Oxford Circus tube. **Open** 10am-6.30pm Mon-Sat; noon-6pm Sun. **Map** p125 B3 ㉞ **Books & music**

Harold Moores is not your stereotypical classical music store: young, open-minded staff and an expansive stock of new and second-hand music bolster its credentials. This collection sees some great stuff from old masters complemented by a range of eclectic contemporary music. There's a basement dedicated to second-hand classical vinyl, including an excellent selection of jazz music.

Kingly Court

Carnaby Street, opposite Broadwick Street, W1B 5PW (7333 8118, www.carnaby.co.uk). Oxford Circus tube. **Open** 11am-7pm Mon-Sat; noon-6pm Sun. **Map** p125 B4 ㉟ **Mall**

If you want to shop modern Carnaby Street, Kingly Court is the place to start – in fact, it's also the place that started the area's revival as a cool shopping destination. It's a three-tiered complex that contains a funky mix of established chains, independents, vintage and vintage-style boutiques, with courtyard cafés in the centre.

OTHER/shop

21 Kingly Street, W1B 5QA (7734 6846, www.other-shop.com). Oxford Circus tube. **Open** 10.30am-6.30pm Mon-Sat; noon-5pm Sun. **Map** p125 A3 ㊱ **Fashion**

The Other shop opened in 2012, but founders Matthew Murphy and Kirk Beattie have more than a decade's experience in running another successful indie boutique – b Store. Other occupies the same site

EXPLORE

as its (now defunct) predecessor, sells similar stock, even a continuation of the excellent b Clothing brand – now called Other – that the store had become famous for. A sun-lit basement stocks Other's edit of brands such as Peter Jensen, Our Legacy and Sophie Hulme. The store often houses installations and exhibitions by artists, and also stocks a range of mags and coffee-table books.

Tommy Guns

65 Beak Street, W1F 9SN (7439 0777, www.tommyguns.com). Oxford Circus or Piccadilly Circus tube. **Open** 10am-8pm Mon-Fri; 10am-6pm Sat. **Map** p125 B4 ㊲ **Health & beauty**

Now over a decade old, Tommy Guns remains a very cool prospect indeed. This original Soho space, complete with retro fittings, is filled with youthful colourists and cutters and there's a friendly, relaxed buzz to the place most days. Men's cuts start from £39.95, and women's cuts can be had from £49.95. Billy and Bo (65 Brewer Street, Soho, W1F 9TQ, 7287 0011, www.billyandbo.com) is part of the group.

Other location 49 Charlotte Road, Shoreditch, EC2A 3QT (7739 2244).

YMC

11 Poland Street, W1F 8QA (7494 1619, www.youmustcreate.com). Oxford Circus tube. **Open** 11am-7pm Mon-Sat. **Map** p125 B3 ㊳ **Fashion**

Impeccably designed staples are the forte of this London label, which opened its first store in 2010. It's the place to head to for simple vest tops and T-shirts, stylish macs, tasteful knits and chino-style trousers, for both men and women.

Other location 23 Hanbury Street, Spitalfieds, E1 6QR (3432 3010).

CHINATOWN & LEICESTER SQUARE

Leicester Square tube.

Shaftesbury Avenue is the very heart of Theatreland. The Victorians built seven grand theatres here, six of which still stand. The most impressive is the gorgeous **Palace Theatre** on Cambridge Circus, which opened in 1891 as the Royal English Opera House; when grand opera flopped, the theatre reopened as a music hall two years later. Appropriately, it's most famous for the musicals it has staged: *The Sound of Music* (1961) and *Jesus Christ Superstar* (1972) had their London premières here, and *Les Misérables* racked up 7,602 performances between 1985 and 2004.

Marks & Co, the shop that was made famous by Helene Hanff's book *84 Charing Cross Road*, used to stand just opposite the Palace Theatre, on a road that was once a byword for bookselling. Sadly, just a few second-hand bookshops remain on **Charing Cross Road**; bibliophiles should head towards Leicester Square, where **Cecil Court** (*see p135*) continues to fight the good fight for readers. West of Charing Cross Road and south of Shaftesbury Avenue, and officially just outside Soho, is the city's **Chinatown**.

The Chinese are relative latecomers to this part of town. London's original Chinatown was set around Limehouse in east London, but hysteria about Chinese opium dens and criminality led to 'slum clearances' in 1934 (interestingly, the surrounding slums were deemed to be in less urgent need of clearance). It wasn't until the 1950s that the Chinese put down roots here, attracted by the cheap rents along Gerrard and Lisle streets.

The ersatz oriental gates, stone lions and pagoda-topped phone boxes around Gerrard Street suggest a Chinese theme park, but this remains a close-knit residential and working enclave, a genuine focal point for London's Chinese community. The area is crammed with restaurants, Asian grocery stores, great bakeries and a host of small shops selling iced-grass jelly, speciality teas and cheap air tickets to Beijing.

South of Chinatown, **Leicester Square** was one of London's most exclusive addresses in the 17th century; in the 18th, it became home to the royal court of Prince George (later George II). Satirical painter William Hogarth had a studio here (1733-64), as did 18th-century artist Sir Joshua Reynolds – busts of both once resided in the small gardens at the heart of the square, along with a now vanished statue of Charlie Chaplin. They've been swept away in the fine refurbishment of the square, which has left just a statue of a wistful Shakespeare presiding over modish white 'ribbon' seating and the cut-price theatre tickets booth **tkts** (*see p285*).

For many years locals left the square to the unimaginative tourists and drunk suburban kids who were its only denizens. But the arrival in 2011 of a couple of high-class hotels (**W**, *see p348*; **One Leicester Street**, *see p349*) and the reopening in 2012 of the Frank Matcham-designed, castle-like, red-brick Hippodrome on the corner of Cranbourn Street and Charing Cross Road as a high-rolling casino gave the area a bit of pull. Not all memories of the square's cheerfully tacky phase have gone,

IN THE KNOW THE ART OF CONTEMPLATION

Just north of Leicester Square, the Lady Chapel of **Notre Dame de France** (5 Leicester Place, 7437 9363, www.ndfchurch.org) contains a series of Jean Cocteau murals from 1959.

EXPLORE

Chinatown.

however: the Swiss Glockenspiel has returned, with its 27 bells and mechanical mountain farmers chiming out the time on behalf of Switzerland Tourism.

Film premières are still regularly held in the monolithic **Odeon Leicester Square** (*see p255*), which once boasted the UK's largest screen and probably still has the UK's highest ticket prices; this is where the **London Film Festival** (*see p253*) kicks off every year. Its 1930s counterpart, the **Odeon West End**, is currently under threat of redevelopment into 10 storeys of chain hotel-cum-cinema – a move excoriated by many heritage groups. Get a price-conscious cinema fix just north of the square on Leicester Place, at the excellent **Prince Charles** rep cinema (*see p256*).

Restaurants

Chinatown stalwarts such as **Mr Kong** (21 Lisle Street, 7437 7341) and **Wong Kei** (41-43 Wardour Street, 7437 8408) still ply their reliable Anglo-Cantonese trade, but there's more gastronomic excitement offered by newcomers such as **Barshu** (*see p127*).

Imperial China

White Bear Yard, 25A Lisle Street, WC2H 7BA (7734 3388, www.imperialchina-london.com). Leicester Square tube. **Open** noon-midnight Mon-Sat; 11.30am-10.30pm Sun. **Main courses** £7.50-£26.50. **Dim sum** £3.20-£4.50. **Minimum** £10. **Map** p125 C4 (39) **Chinese**

A small wooden bridge spanning an ornamental fish pond, wood panelling, kind lighting and a second floor offering a view of the dining room below set this Cantonese stalwart apart. Yet in every other respect, it's indistinguishable. Dishes are delivered quickly, and food is reliable and of decent quality, though portions can be rather miserly.

Pubs & bars

★ Experimental Cocktail Club

13A Gerrard Street, W1D 5PS (7434 3559, www.chinatownecc.com). Leicester Square tube. **Open** 6pm-3am Mon-Sat; 6pm-midnight Sun. **Admission** £5 after 11pm. **Map** p125 C4 (40)

ECC is hard to find, but once inside all is elegant opulence, arranged over three floors of an old townhouse. Booking isn't essential (half of the capacity is kept for walk-ins), but is recommended (email only, between noon and 5pm). The cocktails are among London's best: sophisticated, complex and strong – try the Havana (cigar-infused bourbon, marsala wine, Bruichladdich Octomore single malt 'wash').

Shops & services

★ Cecil Court

Between Charing Cross Road & St Martin's Lane, WC2N (www.cecilcourt.co.uk). Leicester Square tube. **Map** p125 D4 (41) **Books & music**

Quaint Cecil Court is known for its antiquarian book, map and print dealers, housed in premises that haven't changed in a hundred years. Notable residents include children's specialist Marchpane (no.16, 7836 8661), 40-year veteran David Drummond of Pleasures of Past Times (no.11, 7836 1142) with his playbills and Victoriana, and the mystical, spiritual and occult specialist Watkins (nos.19-21, 7836 2182).

Lipman & Sons

22 Charing Cross Road, WC2H 0HR (7240 2310, www.lipmanandsons.co.uk). Leicester Square tube. **Open** 9am-6pm Mon-Wed, Fri, Sat; 9am-8pm Thur. **Map** p125 D4 (42) **Fashion**

A reliable formalwear firm, that can tailor and/or rent out a morning coat or lounge suit.

Other locations 44 Fleet Street, the City EC4Y 1BN (7353 1731); 4 Staples Inn, Holborn, WC1V 7QH (7404 5080).

Covent Garden & the Strand

EXPLORE

Covent Garden has always been an index of the extremes of London life: on one hand, it had a previous existence as the capital's wholesale fruit and veg market; on the other, it has been home since the 1700s to the Royal Opera House, purveyor of the most refined of all the arts. The masses now descend daily on the restored 19th-century market and its cobbled 'piazza' to peruse the increasingly high-end shops and gawp at the street entertainment, with even the most crowd-averse Londoner finding some aspects appealing: grudgingly the buskers, eagerly the London Transport Museum. Down towards the river on the grubbily historic Strand, the Courtauld Gallery and vast courtyard of Somerset House are further attractions.

Royal Opera House.

Don't Miss

1 London Transport Museum Fun for all the family (p138).

2 Covent Garden Piazza A pedestrian-friendly gem (p138).

3 J Sheekey Fish-based star restaurant (p142)

4 Royal Opera House Great wow factor, whatever's on (p138).

5 Somerset House Reinvented cultural hub (p147).

Ag
PYLONES
COVENT GARDEN

COVENT GARDEN

Covent Garden (exit only until Nov 2014) or Leicester Square tube.

Covent Garden was once the property of the medieval Abbey ('convent') of Westminster. When Henry VIII dissolved the monasteries, it passed to John Russell, first Earl of Bedford, in 1552; his family still owns land hereabouts. During the 16th and 17th centuries, they developed the area: the fourth Earl employed Inigo Jones to create the Italianate open square that remains the area's centrepiece.

A market was first documented here in 1640 and grew into London's pre-eminent fruit and vegetable wholesaler, employing over 1,000 porters; its success led to the opening of coffee-houses, theatres, gambling dens and brothels. A flower market was added (where the London Transport Museum now stands).

In the second half of the 20th century, it became obvious that the congested streets of central London were unsuitable for such market traffic and the decision was taken to move the traders out. In 1974, with the market gone, the threat of property development loomed for the empty stalls and offices. It was only through demonstrations that the area was saved. It's now a pleasant place for a stroll, especially if you catch it early on a fine morning before the crowds descend.

Covent Garden Piazza

Centred on Covent Garden Piazza, the area now offers a combination of gentrified shops, restaurants and cafés, supplemented by street artists and busking musicians in the lower court-yard. The majority of the entertainment takes place under the portico of **St Paul's Covent Garden** (*see p140*). Tourists favour the 180-year-old **covered market**, which combines upmarket chain stores with a collection of small, sometimes quirky but often rather twee independent shops. Its handsome architecture is best viewed from the Amphitheatre Café Bar's terrace loggia at the **Royal Opera House**.

Since 2006, property investor Capco has consumed great chunks of prime real estate in Covent Garden, scooping up property on the Piazza, King Street, James Street, Long Acre and beyond – £780m of it, to be exact. As a result, a slew of ho-hum shops have been replaced by high-street heavyweights and luxury brands. Fred Perry, Whistles, L'Artisan Parfumier, Kurt Geiger, Ralph Lauren's Rugby brand and Burberry Brit have all appeared. The world's largest **Apple Store** (*see p143*) set up shop. Perhaps most tellingly, the West Cornwall Pasty Co became a Ladurée café, with waistcoated staff dispensing dainty orange-blossom macaroons where once they trowelled out pastries. Classy restaurateurs have also been lured in: Russell Norman's **Polpo Covent Garden** (6 Maiden Lane, WC2E 7NA, 7836 8448, www.polpo.co.uk; *see p144* **Russell Up Some Eats**), **Terroirs** (*see p143*) and **Delauney** (*see p147*) are all near. There's also been an improvement in the sightseeing, with the always excellent **London Transport Museum** (*see below*) joined by the **London Film Museum** (*see below*).

Change is barely evident elsewhere. The **Apple Market**, in the North Hall, still has arts and crafts stalls from Tuesday to Sunday, and antiques on Monday. Across the road, the tackier **Jubilee Market** deals mostly in novelty T-shirts and other tat.

Sights & museums

London Film Museum

45 Wellington Street, WC2E 7BN (7202 7043, www.londonfilmmuseum.com). Covent Garden tube. **Open** 10am-6pm Mon-Fri, Sun; 10am-7pm Sat. **Admission** £14.50; £9.50 5-15s, reductions; £38 family. **Map** p139 C4 ❶

Having left its former home on the South Bank, the LFM relaunched its collection of Brit film memorabilia in spring 2014 with 'Bond in Motion' – a display of 50 of 007's most covetable high-end motors.

★ London Transport Museum

Covent Garden Piazza, WC2E 7BB (7379 6344, www.ltmuseum.co.uk). Covent Garden tube. **Open** 10am-6pm Mon-Thur, Sat, Sun; 11am-6pm Fri. **Admission** £15; £11.50 reductions; free under-17s. **Map** p139 C4 ❷

The London Transport Museum traces the city's transport history from the horse age to the present day. It does so in an engaging and inspiring fashion, with a focus on social history and design, illustrated by a superb array of preserved buses, trams and trains, and backed up by some brilliant temporary exhibitions. The collections are in broadly chronological order, beginning with the Victorian gallery, where a replica of Shillibeer's first horse-drawn bus service in 1829 takes pride of place. Another gallery is dedicated to the museum's truly impressive collection of poster art. Under the leadership of Frank Pick, in the early 20th century London Transport developed one of the most coherent brand identities in the world. The new museum also raises some interesting and important questions about the future of public transport in the city, with a display on ideas that are 'coming soon' (Faster, Smarter, Easier), and Future Journey, Future City, a fanciful imagining of London's travel network in the years ahead.

FREE Royal Opera House

Bow Street, WC2E 9DD (7304 4000, www.roh.org.uk). Covent Garden tube. **Open** 10am-3.30pm Mon-Sat. **Admission** free.

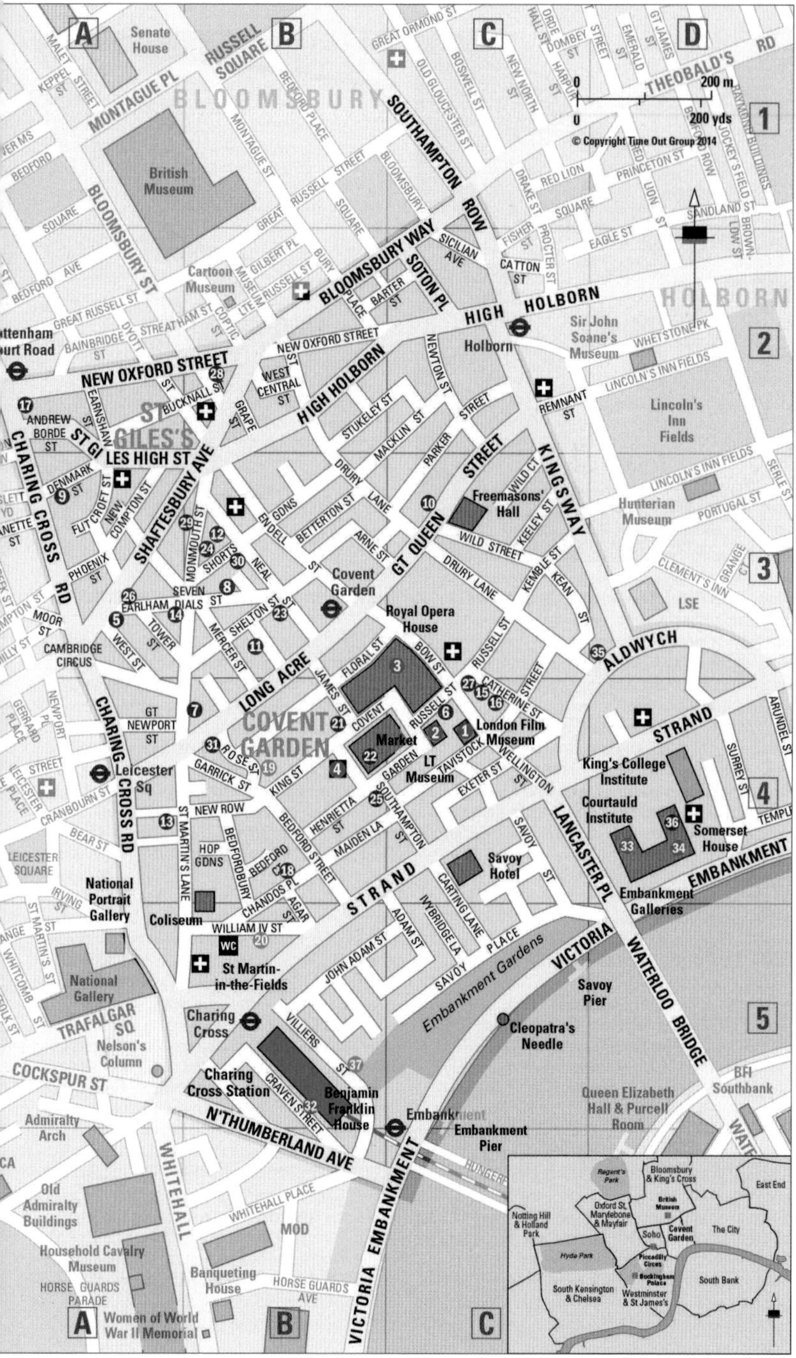
A
B
C
D
1
2
3
4
5
BLOOMSBURY
HOLBORN
ST GILES'S
COVENT GARDEN
British Museum
Senate House
Cartoon Museum
Sir John Soane's Museum
Lincoln's Inn Fields
Hunterian Museum
LSE
Freemasons' Hall
Royal Opera House
Market
LT Museum
London Film Museum
King's College Institute
Courtauld Institute
Somerset House
Embankment Galleries
Savoy Hotel
Savoy Pier
Cleopatra's Needle
National Portrait Gallery
Coliseum
St Martin-in-the-Fields
National Gallery
TRAFALGAR SQ
Nelson's Column
Charing Cross
Charing Cross Station
Benjamin Franklin House
Embankment
Embankment Pier
Queen Elizabeth Hall & Purcell Room
BFI Southbank
Admiralty Arch
Old Admiralty Buildings
Household Cavalry Museum
Banqueting House
MOD
Women of World War II Memorial
Leicester Sq
Tottenham Court Road
Holborn
Covent Garden
© Copyright Time Out Group 2014
0
200 m
200 yds
STRAND
ALDWYCH
KINGSWAY
HIGH HOLBORN
NEW OXFORD STREET
SHAFTESBURY AVE
CHARING CROSS RD
LONG ACRE
DRURY LANE
VICTORIA EMBANKMENT
WATERLOO BRIDGE
N'THUMBERLAND AVE
WHITEHALL
COCKSPUR ST
SOUTHAMPTON ROW
BLOOMSBURY WAY
Regent's Park
Bloomsbury & King's Cross
East End
Notting Hill & Holland Park
Oxford St, Marylebone & Mayfair
British Museum
Soho
Covent Garden
The City
Hyde Park
Piccadilly Circus
Buckingham Palace
South Kensington & Chelsea
Westminster & St James's
South Bank

EXPLORE

Dishoom.

Stage tours (Mon, Tue, Thur, Sat) £12; £9-£11 reductions. **Map** p139 C3 ❸

The Royal Opera House was founded in 1732 by John Rich on the profits of his production of John Gay's *Beggar's Opera*; the current building, constructed roughly 150 years ago but extensively remodelled since, is the third on the site. Visitors can explore the massive eight-floor building as part of an organised tour, including the main auditorium, the costume workshops and sometimes even a rehearsal. Certain parts of the building are also open to the general public, including the glass-roofed Paul Hamlyn Hall, the Crush Bar (so named because in Victorian times the only thing served during intermissions was orange and lemon crush) and the Amphitheatre Café Bar.

▶ *For music at the Opera House, see p284.*

FREE St Paul's Covent Garden

Bedford Street, WC2E 9ED (7836 5221, www.actorschurch.org). Covent Garden tube.
Open 8.30am-5pm Mon-Fri; 9am-1pm Sun. Times vary Sat; phone for details. *Services* 1.10pm Tue, Wed; 11am Sun. *Choral Evensong* 4pm 2nd Sun of mth. **Admission** free; donations appreciated. **Map** p139 B4 ❹

Known as the Actors' Church for its long association with Covent Garden's theatres, this pleasingly spare building was designed by Inigo Jones in 1631. A lovely limewood wreath by the 17th-century master carver Grinling Gibbons hangs inside the front door as a reminder that he and his wife are interred in the crypt. But most visitors come to see the memorial plaques: many thespians are commemorated here, among them Vivien Leigh, Charlie Chaplin and Hattie Jacques of *Carry On* fame.

Elsewhere in Covent Garden

Outside Covent Garden Piazza, the area offers a mixed bag of entertainment, eateries and shops. Nearest the markets, most of the more unusual shops have been superseded by a homogeneous mass of cafés, while big fashion chains – and the **St Martin's Courtyard** mall (www.stmartins courtyard.co.uk) – have all but domesticated Long Acre. There are more interesting stores north of here on Neal Street and Monmouth Street; Earlham Street is also home to the **Donmar Warehouse** (*see p289*), a former banana-ripening depot that's now an intimate and groundbreaking theatre. On tiny Shorts Gardens next door is the **Neal's Yard Dairy** (*see p145*), purveyor of exceptional UK cheeses; down a passageway one door along is **Neal's Yard** itself, a pleasant courtyard with communal seating, and a welcome remnant of a less corporate Covent Garden.

South of Long Acre and east of the Piazza, historical depravity is called to account at the former **Bow Street Magistrates Court**. Once home to the Bow Street Runners, the precursors of the Metropolitan Police, this was also where Oscar Wilde entered his plea when arrested for 'indecent acts' in 1895. Plans to convert it into a hotel have not yet come to fruition. To the south, Wellington and Catherine streets mix restaurants and theatres, including the grand **Theatre Royal**. Other diversions in and around Covent Garden include the museum at **Freemasons' Hall** (7395 9257, www.freemasonry.london.museum; call for details of tours), the eye-catchingly bombastic white stone building where Long Acre becomes Great Queen Street; and the **Coliseum** (*see p282*), home of the English National Opera.

Restaurants

Ape & Bird

142 Shaftesbury Avenue, WC2H 8HJ (7836 3119, www.apeandbird.com). Leicester Square or Tottenham Court Road tube. **Open** 10am-11.30pm Mon-Sat; noon-10.30pm Sun. **Main courses** £9-£20. **Map** p139 A3 ❺ **Gastropub**

We were thrilled to hear Russell Norman (*see p144* **Russell Up Some Eats**) was not only opening a gastropub, but one bang in the centre of town. But… we prefer his intimate Venetian Polpos to this whopping space. It's well fitted out – with ceilings of tin tiles, green banquettes, and industrial light fittings that work in harmony with the grand Victorian proportions – but the food isn't cheap, and rarely excels. Still, the location is good for a pre-theatre meet, and the ground-floor 'pub' (already a big hit with the post-work boozy crowd) and much cooler 'dive bar' below serve craft beers and well-chosen wines.

Balthazar

4-6 Russell Street, WC2E 7BN (3301 1155, www.balthazarlondon.com). Covent Garden tube. **Open** 7.30am-midnight Mon-Fri; 10am-midnight Sat; 10am-11pm Sun. **Main courses** £13-£37. **Map** p139 C4 ❻ **Brasserie**

NYC import Balthazar presents a Manhattan interpretation of a French brasserie, with signature dishes such as the onion soup (grilled gruyère lid on thick country bread, immersed in a rich and sweet chicken stock); duck shepherd's pie is another powerfully flavoured treat. Bread, from master baker Jon Rolfe, is a must-try – and is sold at the Boulangerie next door. Balthazar London mimics the New York original perfectly, with red awnings, red leather banquettes, giant antique-mirrored walls and mosaic floors.

Dishoom

12 Upper St Martin's Lane, WC2H 9FB (7420 9320, www.dishoom.com). Covent Garden or Leicester Square tube. **Open** 8am-11pm Mon-Thur; 8am-midnight Fri; 9am-midnight Sat; 9am-10pm Sun. **Main courses** £5.50-£16.50. **Map** p139 B4 ❼ **Pan-Indian**

A swish, self-styled 'Bombay café', Dishoom is filled with retro features: whirring ceiling fans, low-level lighting and vintage Bollywood posters. The place is crowded all day, from breakfast (for sausage naan rolls with chilli jam) to dinner (for the usual curries and tandoori grills). Quality can vary: vada pau (potato croquettes with sharp chutney in a fluffy Portuguese-style bun) and bhel (crunchy puffed rice with tangy tamarind chutney) are tasty; kebabs and curries are fairly standard renditions. Bookings are only taken for groups at dinner.

Flesh & Buns

41 Earlham Street, WC2H 9LX (7632 9500, www.fleshandbuns.com). Covent Garden tube. **Open** noon-3pm, 5-10.30pm Mon, Tue; noon-3pm, 5-11.30pm Wed-Fri; noon-11.30pm Sat; noon-9.30pm Sun. **Main courses** £13.50-£19.50. **Map** p139 B3 ❽ **Japanese**

Flesh & Buns is hidden in a capacious basement, with industrial-chic decor and young, pierced and tattooed staff setting the tone. It serves hirata buns – a US take on Taiwanese street food – with a side order of rock music. Sweet, fluffy dough is folded, then steamed and brought to table. Diners then stuff these pockets with their choice of 'flesh'. Mustard miso and a few slices of subtly pickled apple make a foil for tender pulled pork; crisp-skinned grilled sea bass is served with fresh tomato salsa.

La Giaconda

9 Denmark Street, WC2H 8LS (7240 3334, www.giacondadining.com). Tottenham Court Road tube. **Open** 8am-10pm Mon-Fri; 9am-6pm Sat. **Main courses** £10.50-£32. **Cover** £1.50. **Map** p139 A3 ❾ **Modern European**

Here the front café area covers breakfast fry-ups, porridge, and toasted banana bread at very fair prices, while lunch might be takeaway sandwiches or a dish of the day or two: maybe polenta with chicken leg and a red pepper ragout. But slip through to the more formal rear dining room, and you have a very different menu to choose from, with starters from around £7 and mains at £17. Game, veal and offal always feature, showcasing Paul Merrony's elegantly butch cooking style. The owners' Australian heritage gets a nod on the idiosyncratic wine list.

Great Queen Street

32 Great Queen Street, WC2B 5AA (7242 0622). Covent Garden or Holborn tube. **Open** *Bar* 5.30-11.30pm Tue-Sat. *Restaurant* noon-2.30pm, 6-10.30pm Mon-Sat; 1-3pm Sun. **Main courses** £10.80-£22. **Map** p139 C3 ❿ **British**

The excellent location, mere steps away from central Covent Garden, ensures Great Queen Street's perennial popularity. The outdoor tables are almost never vacant, but walk-ins may find space at the bar, where the full menu is served. The menu changes daily. There's minimal fussing with ingredients; for example, a plump piece of bone-in smoked mackerel is served with a dollop each of cooked gooseberries and horseradish. Pork is slow-cooked before having a generous quantity of cockles added to the stew.

★ Hawksmoor Seven Dials

11 Langley Street, WC2H 9JJ (7856 2154, www.thehawksmoor.co.uk). Covent Garden tube. **Open** noon-3pm, 5-10.30pm Mon-Thur; noon-3pm, 5-11pm Fri, Sat; noon-9.30pm Sun. **Main courses** £14.50-£49.50. **Map** p139 B3 ⓫ **Steakhouse**

The short main menu centres on steak (ribeye, T-bone, porterhouse, fillet, sirloin and more), at

EXPLORE

serious prices, plus the likes of grilled chicken, lobster with garlic butter, monkfish grilled over charcoal, and a meat-free choice for the odd misplaced vegetarian. If you're not on expenses, pay heed to the 'express menu', where the delectably charred ribeye comes in a 250g size (more than enough for most people's appetites, especially when paired with the triple-cooked chips). A good kick-off is one of Hawksmoor's renowned cocktails.
Other locations 157 Commercial Street, Shoreditch, E1 6BJ (7247 7392); 10 Basinghall Street, the City, EC2V 5BQ (7397 8120); 5 Air Street, Piccadilly Circus, W1J 0AD.

Homeslice

13 Neal's Yard, WC2H 9DP (7836 4604, www.homeslicepizza.co.uk). Covent Garden or Leicester Square tube. **Open** noon-10.30pm Mon-Sat; noon-8pm Sun. **Pizza** £4 slice, £20 whole pizza. **Map** p139 B3 ⓬ **Pizza**

Served fresh from the wood-fired oven, most of the thin-crust pizzas at this Neal's Yard joint are available by the slice. Or you can order a 20-incher: enough to feed you and two pals. A well-constructed margherita can be a little slice of heaven – there are a couple of ingredient combos that wouldn't get the green light in Naples, but taste pretty good. On one, slivers of bone marrow are melted over the tomato base, imparting a meaty savouriness, then it's scattered with watercress and roasted spring onions. Service is attentive and chummy. To drink, there are craft beers and even prosecco on tap.

EXPLORE

★ J Sheekey

28-32 St Martin's Court, Leicester Square, WC2N 4AL (7240 2565, www.j-sheekey.co.uk). Leicester Square tube. **Open** noon-3pm, 5.30pm-midnight Mon-Sat; noon-3.30pm, 6-11pm Sun. **Main courses** £13.50-£48.50. **Map** p139 A4 ⓭ **Fish & seafood**

After well over a century of service, Sheekey's status as a West End institution is assured. With its monochrome photos of stars of stage and screen, wooden panelling and cream crackle walls, and array of silver dishes atop thick white tablecloths, it oozes old-fashioned glamour. The menu runs from super-fresh oysters and shellfish via old-fashioned snacks (herring roe on toast) to upmarket classics (dover sole, lobster thermidor). The fish pie – a rich, comforting treat – is deservedly acclaimed, but we feel the shrimp and scallop burger merits similar status.

► *The adjoining J Sheekey Oyster Bar (nos.33-35, WC2N 4AL) serves a similar menu to customers sitting casually at the counter, and with an expanded choice of oysters.*

Kopapa

32-34 Monmouth Street, WC2H 9HA (7240 6076, www.kopapa.co.uk). Covent Garden or Leicester Square tube. **Open** 8.30-11am, noon-11pm Mon-Fri; 9.30am-4pm, 4.30-11pm Sat; 9.30am-4pm, 4.30-9.45pm Sun. **Main courses** £18-£23. **Map** p139 A3 ⓮ **Fusion**

The exciting and well-executed menu at this handily located all-dayer includes Turkish eggs (poached eggs with yoghurt, hot chilli butter and flatbread) for breakfast and brunch. Lunch features weighty sandwiches (steak on focaccia with caramelised onion, mustard cream cheese, roast tomatoes and pickles) and burgers (soft-shell crab burger with Asian salad, spicy peanut mayonnaise and avocado), alongside salads and a selection of more inventive dishes, many of which also appear on the evening menu. Quality produce, imaginatively teamed, served by smiling, clued-up staff.

Mishkin's

25 Catherine Street, WC2B 5JS (7240 2078, www.mishkins.co.uk). Covent Garden tube. **Open** noon-11.30pm Mon-Sat; noon-10.30pm Sun. **Main courses** £6-£12. **Map** p139 C4 ⓯ **American**

Mishkin's calls itself 'a kind-of Jewish deli with cocktails', which is a pretty good description. We're partial to the reuben (pastrami, sauerkraut, swiss cheese and russian dressing on toasted rye bread), though it's no bargain at £11. Sides such as chips, fried onion rings and coleslaw are hard to resist too. The menu is an attractive selection, mixing tradition (chicken matzo ball soup) and innovation (cod cheek popcorn), sometimes in the same dish (smoked mackerel latkes). The small, shabby-chic, NYC-style interior is low-lit, and staff mix a mean cocktail.

Opera Tavern

23 Catherine Street, WC2B 5JS (7836 3680, www.operatavern.co.uk). Covent Garden tube. **Open** noon-3pm, 5-11.30pm Mon-Fri; noon-11.30pm Sat; noon-5pm Sun. **Tapas** £3.75-£12. **Map** p139 C4 ⓰ **Spanish/Italian tapas**

The Opera Tavern, split into an upstairs restaurant and a cosy, mirror-backed bar, remains one of London's top tapas restaurants. The signature burger of juicy ibérico pork and foie gras remains deservedly popular, though more inventive combinations better showcase the kitchen's delicate touch and careful sourcing of ingredients. Chargrilled venison, for example, is enlivened by jerusalem artichoke, pickled walnuts and truffle, while the natural sweetness of scallops (served in the shell) was balanced by a feather-light pea, fennel and mint purée.

Paramount

32nd floor, Centre Point, 101-103 New Oxford Street, WC1A 1DD (7420 2900, www.paramount.uk.net). Tottenham Court Road tube. **Open** *Bar* 8am-1.30am Mon-Wed; 8am-2.30am Thur, Fri; noon-2.30am Sat; noon-10pm Sun. *Restaurant* 8-10.30am, noon-2.45pm, 3-5pm (tea), 5.30-11pm Mon-Fri; noon-2.45pm, 3-5pm (tea), 5.30-11pm Sat; noon-2.45pm, 3-5pm (tea), 5-945pm Sun. **Main courses** £10.50-£28. **Map** p139 A2 ⓱ **Modern European**

On the 33rd floor of the Centre Point building, with spectacular views on every side across central London, Paramount bar and restaurant is a glam spot, especially by night. Cooking is competent, though some dishes – like a tasty double-baked cheese starter – seem rather dated. Most à la carte dishes only prove the rule that the higher the elevation of a restaurant, the more vertiginous the pricing, but there are also set meals that offer better value. Afternoon tea is popular too.

▶ *If dinner prices are too vertiginous, check out the surprisingly reasonable breakfast menu.*

Wahaca

66 Chandos Place, WC2N 4HG (7240 1883, www.wahaca.co.uk). Covent Garden or Leicester Square tube. **Open** noon-11pm Mon-Sat; noon-10.30pm Sun. **Main courses** £5-£14.45. **Map** p139 B4 ⓲ **Mexican**

Thomasina Miers's Mexican 'market food' concept is a successful mini-chain, with a dozen branches across London. The restaurants share a cheery vibe, with young, efficient staff buzzing round bright interiors. Tortillas loom large – in soft, crisp, toasted and chip variations, and in flour and corn versions – though there are also a few grills (fish, steak or chicken served with green rice). Favourites include the steak burrito (which comes with a zingy chipotle salsa).

Other locations throughout the city.

Terroirs.

Pubs & bars

Lamb & Flag

33 Rose Street, WC2E 9EB (7497 9504, www.lambandflagcoventgarden.co.uk). Covent Garden tube. **Open** 11am-11pm Mon-Thur; 11am-11.30pm Fri, Sat; noon-10.30pm Sun. *Food served* noon-8pm Mon-Thur, Sun; noon-5pm Sat, Sun. **Main courses** £5.95-£12.95. **Map** p139 B4 ⓳

This dog-leg alleyway used to be a pit of prostitution and bare-knuckle bashes, the latter hosted at this historic, low-ceilinged Covent Garden tavern back when it was called the Bucket of Blood; poet John Dryden was beaten up here in 1679. The place is popular and space is always at a premium. Two centuries of mounted cuttings and caricatures amplify the sense of character.

▶ *If it's too busy, try the Benelux-themed beer-café Lowlander (36 Drury Lane, WC2B 5RR, 7379 7446, www.lowlander.com).*

★ Terroirs

5 William IV Street, WC2N 4DW (7036 0660, www.terroirswinebar.com). Charing Cross tube/rail. **Open** noon-3pm, 5.30-11pm Mon-Sat. **Main courses** £8.50-£32.50. **Map** p139 B5 ⓴

Terroirs – a wine bar with excellent food – is really two places under one roof. The always crowded ground floor has a casual wine bar feel and a menu to match, focused on small plates for sharing. You can sample some of the same dishes in the atmospheric and surprisingly roomy basement, although the menu here, with a focus on rustic French dishes, seems designed to guide diners more towards a starter-main-dessert tradition. The wine list is an encyclopaedia of organic and biodynamic bottles; if you're a first-timer, order by the glass to give yourself a sense of the astonishing variety offered.

Shops & services

Eco pioneer **Neal's Yard Remedies** (15 Neal's Yard, WC2H 9DP, 7379 7222, www.nealsyardremedies.com) offers organic products and a herbal dispensary. It has several central branches, but this is the most charming.

Apple Store

1-7 The Piazza, WC2E 8HA (7447 1400, www.apple.com). Covent Garden tube. **Open** 9am-9pm Mon-Sat; noon-6pm Sun. **Map** p139 B4 ㉑ **Electronics & photography**

A temple to geekery, this is the world's biggest Apple Store, with separate rooms – set out over three storeys – devoted to each product line. The exposed brickwork, big old oak tables and stone floors make it an inviting place, and it's also the world's first Apple Store with a Start Up Room, where staff will help to set up your new iPad, iPhone, iPod or Mac, or transfer files from your old computer to your new one – all for free.

EXPLORE

RUSSELL UP SOME EATS

The secrets of success for TV's Restaurant Man.

Spuntino.

What makes a successful restaurant? A great concept, surely. Certainly Russell Norman – owner of an extraordinary sequence of triumphant London restaurants, and now troubleshooter in chief for debutant restaurateurs in BBC2's *The Restaurant Man* – had that when he opened his first venue, Polpo, in Soho in autumn 2009. *Cicchetti* were the inspiration – Venetian bar snacks that combined all the sociability of sharing tapas, which was at that time having something of a moment across the city, but with a new twist of rarity that would appeal to London's gastro-savvy and self-consciously cosmopolitan diners. Simple. Except that isn't the way Norman tells it. In an early episode of *The Restaurant Man*, he attributes his own success to two things: a tape measure and hanging out on a street corner.

The tape measure had been Norman's constant companion, so that any time he sat at a bar that he liked, he could record its dimensions – height of bartop, height of stool, relationship between the two – until he was confident he knew the perfect combination. And the street corner? Outside what became Polpo: before he took the lease, Norman stood for 45 minutes counting and analysing the passersby. When he got to a thousand, he says, he knew he would get enough passing trade to make his debut restaurant a success. And what a success it's been.

Of course, both of these are aspects of the same attribute: attention to detail, specifically the details of the customer experience. And that's what unites what has become a disparate portfolio of restaurants – four Venetian *bacari*, NYC Jewish **Mishkin's** (*see p142*) and the speakeasy/diner **Spuntino** (*see p130*) – the focus on diners having a good time.

But a note of caution: Norman's first foray into gastropubs at **Ape & Bird** (*see p141*) was also the first of his restaurants not to impress us. It wasn't a matter of measurements, nor customer experience as such, but the failure of attention to detail in the cooking – which may be resolved – and the layout – which may not.

So we suggest adding a third thing to the list: picking the right team. When Florence Knight became chef of the Polpetto pop-up restaurant above the French House (*see p129*), Norman discovered a new culinary star. She's now at Soho's new **Polpetto** (*see p130*). Go experience it when you can.

Benjamin Pollock's Toy Shop

44 The Market, WC2E 8RF (7379 7866, www.pollocks-coventgarden.co.uk). Covent Garden tube. **Open** 10.30am-6pm Mon-Sat; 11am-4pm Sun. **Map** p139 B4 ㉒ **Children**

Best known for its toy theatres, Pollock's is also superb for traditional toys, such as knitted animals, china tea sets, masks, glove puppets, cards, spinning tops and fortune-telling fish.

Camper

34 Shelton Street, WC2H 9HP (7836 7973, www.camper.com). Covent Garden tube. **Open** 10am-7pm Mon-Wed; 10am-8pm Thur-Sat; noon-6pm Sun. **Map** p139 B3 ㉓ **Fashion**

The successful Spanish eco footwear brand – one of Mallorca's best exports – has become more sophisticated in recent seasons, moving away from its funky but sensible image towards a more fashion-oriented aesthetic. However, most of its styles are still distinctively recognisable, with the classic, round-toed and clod-heeled models still featuring.

Other locations throughout the city.

★ Coco de Mer

23 Monmouth Street, WC2H 9DD (7836 8882, www.coco-de-mer.com). Covent Garden tube. **Open** 11am-7pm Mon-Wed, Fri, Sat; 11am-8pm Thur; noon-6pm Sun. **Map** p139 B3 ㉔ **Accessories**

London's most glamorous erotic emporium sells a variety of tasteful books, toys and lingerie, from glass dildos that double as objets d'art to a Marie Antoinette costume of crotchless culottes and corset. Trying on items can be fun as well: the peepshow-style velvet changing rooms allow your lover to peer through and watch you undress from a 'confession box' next door.

Ellis Brigham

Tower House, 3-11 Southampton Street, WC2E 7HA (7395 1010, www.ellis-brigham.com). Covent Garden tube. **Open** 9am-8pm Mon-Fri; 9.30am-6.30pm Sat; 11.30am-5.30pm Sun. **Map** p139 B4 ㉕ **Travel**

This is the largest of a clutch of mountain sports and camping equipment shops in the area, so big, in fact, that it is also able to house the city's only ice-climbing wall, a grand 8m (26ft) high.

Other locations throughout the city.

Fopp

1 Earlham Street, WC2H 9LL (7845 9770, www.fopp.com). Leicester Square tube. **Open** 10am-10pm Mon-Wed; 10am-11pm Thur-Sat; noon-6pm Sun. **Map** p139 A3 ㉖ **Books & music**

Three floors of new releases and back-catalogue surprises, plus good selections of books and DVDs, all at competitive prices, make this a great place for bargains. Look out for world cinema, arthouse masterpieces and anime – plus '80s teen classic DVDs on the ground floor and basement, with Fopp's full music selection upstairs.

Other location 82 Gower Street, Bloomsbury, WC1E 6EQ (7636 871).

Hope & Greenwood

1 Russell Street, WC2B 5JD (7240 3314, www.hopeandgreenwood.co.uk). Covent Garden tube. **Open** 11am-7.30pm Mon-Fri; 10.30am-7.30pm Sat; noon-6pm Sun. **Map** p139 C4 ㉗ **Food & drink**

Everything from chocolate gooseberries to sweetheart candies is prettily displayed in plastic beakers, cellophane bags, glass jars, illustrated boxes, porcelain bowls and cake tins. Indulge in a bag of sherbert Flying Saucers or gobstoppers. Gift possibilities include retro gumball machines.

Other location 20 Northcross Road, East Dulwich, SE22 9EU (8613 1777).

James Smith & Sons

53 New Oxford Street, WC1A 1BL (7836 4731, www.james-smith.co.uk). Holborn or Tottenham Court Road tube. **Open** 10am-6pm Mon-Sat. **Map** p139 B2 ㉘ **Accessories**

More than 175 years after it was established, this charming shop, with Victorian fittings still intact, is holding its own in the niche market of umbrellas and walking sticks. The stock here isn't the throwaway type of brolly that breaks at the first sign of a bit of wind. Lovingly crafted 'brellas, such as a classic City umbrella with a Malacca Cane handle at £120, are built to last. A repair service is also offered.

Miller Harris

14 Monmouth Street, WC2H 9HB (7836 9378, www.millerharris.com). Covent Garden tube. **Open** 10.30am-6.30pm Mon-Sat. **Map** p139 B3 ㉙ **Health & beauty**

Grasse-trained British perfumer Lyn Harris's scents, in lovely floral packaging, are made with natural extracts and oils. Noix de Tubéreuse, a lighter and more palatable tuberose scent than many on the market, is a perennial favourite, while Fleurs de Bois evokes a traditional English garden. This flagship branch has recently been refurbished.

Other locations 21 Bruton Street, Mayfair, W1J 6QD (7629 7750); 14 Needham Road, Notting Hill, W11 2RP (7221 1545); Unit 16, The Market, Covent Garden, WC2E 8RB (7836 0837).

★ Neal's Yard Dairy

17 Shorts Gardens, WC2H 9AT (7240 5700, www.nealsyarddairy.co.uk). Covent Garden tube. **Open** 10am-7pm Mon-Sat. **Map** p139 B3 ㉚ **Food & drink**

Neal's Yard buys from small farms and creameries and matures the cheeses in its own cellars until they're ready to sell in peak condition. Names such as Stinking Bishop and Lincolnshire Poacher are as evocative as the aromas in the shop. It's best to walk in and ask what's good today: you'll be given tasters

by the well-trained staff. There's a shop in Borough Market too (6 Park Street, SE1 9AB, 7367 0799).
▶ *For more great cheese, try La Fromagerie (see p110) and Paxton & Whitfield (93 Jermyn Street, SW1Y 6JE, 7930 0259).*

Stanfords

12-14 Long Acre, WC2E 9LP (7836 1321, www.stanfords.co.uk). Covent Garden or Leicester Square tube. **Open** 9am-8pm Mon-Fri; 10am-8pm Sat; noon-6pm Sun. **Map** p139 B4 ㉛ **Travel**
Three floors of travel guides, travel literature, maps, language guides, atlases and magazines. The basement houses the full range of British Ordnance Survey maps; there's a café too.

THE STRAND, EMBANKMENT & THE ALDWYCH

Embankment or Temple tube or Charing Cross tube/rail.

Until as recently as the 1860s, the Strand ran beside the Thames; indeed, it was originally the river's bridlepath. In the 14th century, it was lined with grand residences with gardens that ran down to the water. It wasn't until the 1870s that the Thames was pushed back with the creation of the Embankment and its adjacent gardens. By the time George Newnes's famed *Strand* magazine was introducing its readership to Sherlock Holmes (1891), the street boasted the Cecil Hotel (long since demolished), **Simpson's**, **King's College** and **Somerset House** (*see p147*). Prime Minister Benjamin Disraeli described it as 'perhaps the finest street in Europe'. Nobody would make such a claim today but there's still plenty to interest visitors.

In 1292, the body of Eleanor of Castile, consort to King Edward I, completed its funerary procession from Lincoln to the small hamlet of Charing, at the western end of what is now the Strand. The occasion was marked by the erection of the last of 12 elaborate crosses. A replica of the Eleanor Cross (originally set just south of nearby Trafalgar Square; *see pp68-73*) was placed in 1865 on the forecourt of **Charing Cross Station**; it remains there today, looking like the spire of a sunken cathedral. Across the road, behind **St Martin-in-the-Fields** (*see p69*), is Maggi Hambling's weird memorial to a more recent queen, *A Conversation with Oscar Wilde*.

The Embankment itself can be reached down Villiers Street. Pass through the tube station to the point at which boat tours with on-board entertainment depart. Just to the east stands **Cleopatra's Needle**, an obelisk presented to the British nation by the viceroy of Egypt, Mohammed Ali, in 1820 but not set in place by the river for a further 59 years. The obelisk was originally erected around 1500 BC by the pharaoh Tuthmosis III at a site near modern-day Cairo, before being moved to Alexandria, Cleopatra's capital, in 10 BC. By this time, however, the great queen was 20 years dead.

Back on the Strand, the majestic **Savoy** hotel (*see p348*) was first opened in 1889, financed by profits from Richard D'Oyly Carte's productions of Gilbert and Sullivan's light operas at the neighbouring **Savoy Theatre**. The theatre, which pre-dates the hotel by eight years, was the first to use electric lights. Two grand hotels guard the Aldwych, at the eastern end of the Strand: **One Aldwych** and, directly opposite, **ME by Meliá London** (for both, *see p347*). This grand crescent dates only from 1905, but the name 'ald wic' (old settlement or market) has its origins in the 14th century. To the south is **Somerset House** (*see p147*). Almost in front of it is **St Mary-le-Strand** (7836 3126, www.stmarylestrand.org, open 11am-4pm Tue-Thur, 10am-1pm Sun), James Gibbs's first public building, completed in 1717. On Strand Lane, reached via Surrey Street, is the so-called **'Roman' bath** where Dickens took the waters – you have to peer through a dusty window.

On a traffic island just east of the Aldwych is **St Clement Danes** (7242 2380, www.raf.mod.uk/stclementdanes). It's believed that a church was first built here by the Danish in the ninth century, but the current building is mainly Wren's handiwork. It's the principal church of the RAF. Just beyond the church are the Royal Courts of Justice (*see p173*) and the original site of Temple Bar (*see p174*).

Sights & museums

Benjamin Franklin House

36 Craven Street, the Strand, WC2N 5NF (7925 1405, www.benjaminfranklinhouse.org). Charing Cross tube/rail. **Open** noon-5pm Mon, Wed-Sun. *Tours* noon, 1pm, 2pm, 3.15pm and 4.15pm. **Admission** £7; £5 reductions; free under-16s. **Map** p139 B5 ㉜
This is the house where Franklin – scientist, diplomat, philosopher, inventor and Founding Father of the US – lived between 1757 and 1775. It isn't a museum in the conventional sense, but can be explored on 'experiences' lasting 45 minutes (Wed-Sun, booking advised). The tours are led by an actress playing Franklin's landlady's daughter Polly Stevenson, using projections and sound to conjure up the world in which Franklin lived. From noon on Mondays, there are more straightforward architectural tours (20 mins, £3.50).

★ Courtauld Gallery

The Strand, WC2R 1LA (7848 2526, www.courtauld.ac.uk/gallery). Temple tube. **Open** 10am-6pm daily. *Tours* phone for details. **Admission** £6; £5 reductions; students & under-18s free; £3 Mon. **Map** p139 D4 ㉝

EXPLORE

Somerset House.

Located for the last two decades in the north wing of Somerset House (*see below*), the Courtauld has one of Britain's greatest collections of paintings, and contains several works of world importance. Although there are some outstanding early works (Cranach's *Adam & Eve*, for one), the collection's strongest suit is in Impressionist and Post-Impressionist paintings. Popular masterpieces include Manet's *A Bar at the Folies-Bergère*, alongside plenty of superb Monets and Cézannes, important Gauguins, and some Van Goghs and Seurats. On the top floor, there's a selection of gorgeous Fauvist works, a lovely room of Kandinskys and plenty more besides. Hidden downstairs, the little gallery café is delightful.

FREE Somerset House & the Embankment Galleries

The Strand, WC2R 1LA (7845 4600, www.somersethouse.org.uk). Temple tube or Charing Cross tube/rail. **Open** 10am-6pm daily (last entry to galleries 5pm). *Tours* phone for details. **Admission** *Courtyard & terrace* free. *Embankment Galleries* prices vary; check website for details. *Tours* phone for details. **Map** p139 D4 34

The original Somerset House was a Tudor palace commissioned by the Duke of Somerset. In 1775, it was demolished to make way for the first purpose-built office block in the world. Architect Sir William Chambers spent the last 20 years of his life working on the neoclassical edifice overlooking the Thames, built to accommodate learned societies such as the Royal Academy and government departments.

The taxmen are still here, but the rest of the building is open to the public. Attractions include the Courtauld (*see p146*), the handsome fountain court, and a terrace café and a classy restaurant. The Embankment Galleries house temporary exhibitions, and at Christmas usually host a market. In summer, children never tire of running through the choreographed fountains while parents watch from café tables; in winter, an ice rink takes over the courtyard.

Restaurants

Delaunay

55 Aldwych, WC2B 4BB (7499 8558, www.thedelaunay.com). Covent Garden or Temple tube. **Open** 7am-midnight Mon-Fri; 8am-midnight Sat; 9am-11pm Sun. **Main courses** £6.50-£27.50. **Cover** £2. **Map** p139 D3 35 **Brasserie**

European grand cafés are the inspiration here, resulting in a striking interior of green leather banquette seating, dark wood, antique mirrors and a black and white marble floor. The menu runs from breakfast to dinner, taking in afternoon tea (try the Austrian-biased cakes, all made in-house). There's a dish of the day (goulash, say, or chicken curry), soups, sandwiches, salads and egg dishes, plus savouries (welsh and buck rarebits) and crustacea. In short, there's something for everyone.

▶ *If the Delaunay is full, try their no-bookings Counter café next door for cakes and light meals.*

Fernandez & Wells

East Wing, Somerset House, the Strand, WC2R 1LA (7420 9408, www.fernandezandwells.com). Temple tube. **Open** 10am-10pm Mon-Sat; 10am-8pm Sun. **Sharing plates** £4.50-£15. **Map** p139 D4 36 **Café**

Four impressive rooms in the east wing of Somerset House, set up for all-day grazing. Meat is central: the 'ham room' is set up for carving slices of lomito ibérico, jamón de lampiño, or wild fennel Tuscan salami. Breakfasts are simple but good, and feature dishes such as fried eggs sprinkled with za'atar, miniature morcilla sausages and toasted sourdough. **Other locations** throughout the city.

Pubs & bars

★ Gordon's Wine Bar

47 Villiers Street, Strand, WC2N 6NE (7930 1408, www.gordonswinebar.com). Embankment tube or Charing Cross tube/rail. **Open** 11am-11pm Mon-Sat; noon-10pm Sun. **Map** p139 B5 37

Gordon's was established in its present form as long ago as 1890, but the exposed brickwork and flickering candlelight make this basement feel older still. Although this is the definitive old-school wine bar, it gets packed with a young and lively crowd. The wine list is surprisingly modern; still, in such surroundings, it seems a shame not to drink the fortified wines, which are drawn directly from casks behind the bar.

EXPLORE

Bloomsbury, King's Cross & Fitzrovia

London's neighbourhoods north of Oxford Street are bookish and bohemian. Bloomsbury is best known as the home of the British Museum. The unofficial heart of the area is the redeveloped Brunswick Centre and the buzzing network of surrounding streets.

To the west, Fitzrovia is a favourite source of stories for London nostalgists, but the days of postwar spivs and drunken poets have given way to an era of new media offices. At least they keep the pubs lively and the restaurant quality high.

To the north of Bloomsbury, the legendarily seedy King's Cross has gone the way of formerly raffish Fitzrovia, with the arrival of the British Library and the rebirth of St Pancras Station as an international rail hub.

Wellcome Collection.

Don't Miss

1 British Museum A treasure trove (p150).

2 Wellcome Collection Science made scintillating (p154).

3 Berners Tavern Jason Atherton's hit (p159).

4 Foundling Museum Top tearjerker (p151).

5 London Review Bookshop Be inspired (p155).

COSTA

British Museum.

BLOOMSBURY

Euston Square, Holborn, Russell Square or Tottenham Court Road tube.

Bloomsbury's florid name is, prosaically, taken from 'Blemondisberi' – the manor ('bury') of William Blemond, who acquired the area in the 13th century. It remained rural until the 1660s, when the fourth Earl of Southampton built Bloomsbury Square around his house. The Southamptons intermarried with the Russells, the Dukes of Bedford; together, they developed the area as one of London's first planned suburbs.

Over the next two centuries, the group built a series of grand squares. **Bedford Square** (1775-80) is London's only complete Georgian square (regrettably, its central garden is usually closed to the public); huge **Russell Square** has been restored as a public park with a popular café. To the east, the cantilevered postwar **Brunswick Centre** is full of shops, flats, restaurants and a cinema. The nearby streets, particularly **Marchmont Street**, are some of the more characterful in the West End.

Bloomsbury's charm is the sum of its parts, best experienced on a meander through its bookshops (many on **Great Russell Street**) and pubs. The blue plaques are a *Who's Who* of literary modernists – TS Eliot, Virginia Woolf, WB Yeats – with a few interlopers from more distant history: Edgar Allan Poe (83 Southampton Row), Anthony Trollope (6 Store Street) and, of course, Dickens (48 Doughty Street; *see p151* **Charles Dickens Museum**).

On Bloomsbury's western border, Malet Street, Gordon Street and Gower Street are dominated by the **University of London**. The most notable building is Gower Street's University College, founded in 1826. Inside is the 'autoicon' of utilitarian philosopher and founder of the university Jeremy Bentham: his preserved cadaver, fully clothed, sits in a glass-fronted cabinet. The university's main library is housed in towering **Senate House** on Malet Street, one of the city's most imposing examples of monumental art deco. It was the model for Orwell's Ministry of Truth in *1984* – but don't be scared to step inside: the lower floors and little café are open to the public.

South of the university sprawls the **British Museum** (*see below*), the must-see of all London must-sees. Running off Great Russell Street, where you'll find the museum's main entrance, are three attractive parallel streets (Coptic, Museum and Bury) and, nearby, the **Cartoon Museum** (*see p151*); also close by, Bloomsbury Way is home to Hawksmoor's restored **St George's Bloomsbury** (*see p154*). Across from here, **Sicilian Avenue** is an Italianate, pedestrian precinct of colonnaded shops – take it in over a fine ale and beer fodder at the Holborn Whippet (3137 9937, www.holbornwhippet.com).

North-east of the British Museum, **Lamb's Conduit Street** is a convivial neighbourhood lined with interesting shops. At the north end of the street is **Coram's Fields** (*see p251*), a delightful children's park on the grounds of the former Thomas Coram's Foundling Hospital. Coram's legacy is commemorated in the beautiful **Foundling Museum** (*see p151*).

Sights & museums

★ FREE British Museum

Great Russell Street, WC1B 3DG (7323 8299, www.britishmuseum.org). Russell Square or Tottenham Court Road tube. **Open** *Galleries* 10am-5.30pm Mon-Thur, Sat, Sun; 10am-8.30pm Fri. *Great Court* 9am-6pm Mon-Thur, Sat; Sun;

9am-8.30pm Fri. *Multimedia guides* 10am-4.30pm Thur, Sat, Sun; 10am-7.30pm Fri. *Eye Opener tours* (40mins) phone for details. **Admission** free; donations appreciated. *Temporary exhibitions* prices vary. *Multimedia guides* £5; £3.50-£4.50 reductions. *Eye Opener tours* free. **Map** p153 G4 ❶

Officially the country's most popular tourist attraction, the British Museum opened to the public in 1759 in Montagu House, which then occupied this site. The current building is a neoclassical marvel built in 1847 by Robert Smirke, one of the pioneers of the Greek Revival style. In 2000, Lord Foster added a glass roof to the Great Court, now claimed to be 'the largest covered public square in Europe' and a popular public space ever since. This £100m landmark surrounds the domed Reading Room (used by the British Library, *see p156,* until its move to King's Cross), where Marx, Lenin, Dickens, Darwin, Hardy and Yeats once worked. In 2014, the museum added a brand-new building to the east of the original premises, containing research and conservation labs, and the Sainsbury Exhibitions Gallery, which will host more of the fabulous, sell-out blockbuster shows (China's Terracotta Army, Pompeii, Ice Age art and now the Vikings) that have propelled the museum to the top of the visitor-number charts.

In the museum proper, star exhibits include ancient Egyptian artefacts – the Rosetta Stone on the ground floor (with a barely noticed, perfect replica in the King's Library), mummies upstairs – and Greek antiquities, including the marble friezes from the Parthenon known as the Elgin Marbles. Room 41 has just reopened, with a display of early medieval artefacts, including the famous Sutton Hoo treasure. Also upstairs, the Celts gallery has Lindow Man, killed in 300 BC and so well preserved in peat you can see his beard, while the ground-floor Wellcome Gallery of Ethnography holds an Easter Island statue and regalia collected during Captain Cook's travels. The King's Library provides a calming home to a permanent exhibition that is entitled 'Enlightenment: Discovering the World in the 18th Century', a 5,000-piece collection devoted to the extraordinary formative period of the museum. The remit covers archaeology, science and the natural world; the objects displayed range from Indonesian puppets to a beautiful orrery.

IN THE KNOW POOR CHARLES

The **Charles Dickens Museum** (*see right*) was long thought to be his only residence to survive in London, but a plaque on Cleveland Street tells a different story: his childhood home was at no.22, a few doors from the partially listed **Cleveland Street Workhouse** (http://clevelandstreetworkhouse.org).

You won't be able to see everything in one day, so buy a souvenir guide and pick out the showstoppers, or plan several visits. Highlights tours focus on specific aspects of the huge collection; Eye Opener tours offer specific introductions to world cultures.

► *A fine range of cask beer makes historic Museum Tavern (49 Great Russell Street, 7242 8987), by the front gate, no mere tourist trap.*

Cartoon Museum

35 Little Russell Street, WC1A 2HH (7580 8155, www.cartoonmuseum.org). Tottenham Court Road tube. **Open** 10.30am-5.30pm Mon-Sat; noon-5.30pm Sun. **Admission** £7; free-£5 reductions. **Map** p153 G4 ❷

The best of British cartoon art is displayed on the ground floor of this former dairy. The displays start in the early 18th century, when high-society types back from the Grand Tour introduced the Italian practice of *caricatura* to polite company. From Hogarth, it moves through Britain's cartooning 'golden age' (1770-1830) to examples of wartime cartoons, ending up with modern satirists such as Gerald Scarfe and the wonderfully loopy Ralph Steadman. Upstairs is a celebration of UK comic art, with original 1921 *Rupert the Bear* artwork by Mary Tourtel, Frank Hampson's Dan Dare, Leo Baxendale's Bash Street Kids and a painted *Asterix* cover by that well-known Briton, Albert Uderzo.

Charles Dickens Museum

48 Doughty Street, WC1N 2LX (7405 2127, www.dickensmuseum.com). Chancery Lane or Russell Square tube. **Open** 10am-5pm daily. *Tours* by arrangement. **Admission** £8; £4-£6 reductions; free under-6s. **Map** p153 F6 ❸

London is scattered with plaques marking addresses where Dickens lived, but this is the only one to have been preserved as a museum. He lived here from 1837 to 1840, writing *Nicholas Nickleby* and *Oliver Twist* while in residence. Ring the doorbell to gain access to four floors of Dickensiana, collected over the years from various former residences. Some rooms are arranged as they might have been when he lived here; others deal with different aspects of his life, from struggling hack to famous performer. Recent refurbishment has created a pleasant downstairs café.

Foundling Museum

40 Brunswick Square, WC1N 1AZ (7841 3600, www.foundlingmuseum.org.uk). Russell Square tube. **Open** 10am-5pm Tue-Sat; 11am-5pm Sun. **Admission** £8.25; £5.50 reductions; free under-16s. **Map** p153 E5 ❹

The Foundling Museum recalls the social history of the Foundling Hospital, set up in 1739 by shipwright and sailor Thomas Coram. Returning to England from America in 1720, Coram was appalled by the number of abandoned children he saw. Securing royal patronage, he persuaded Hogarth and Handel to become governors; it was Hogarth who made the

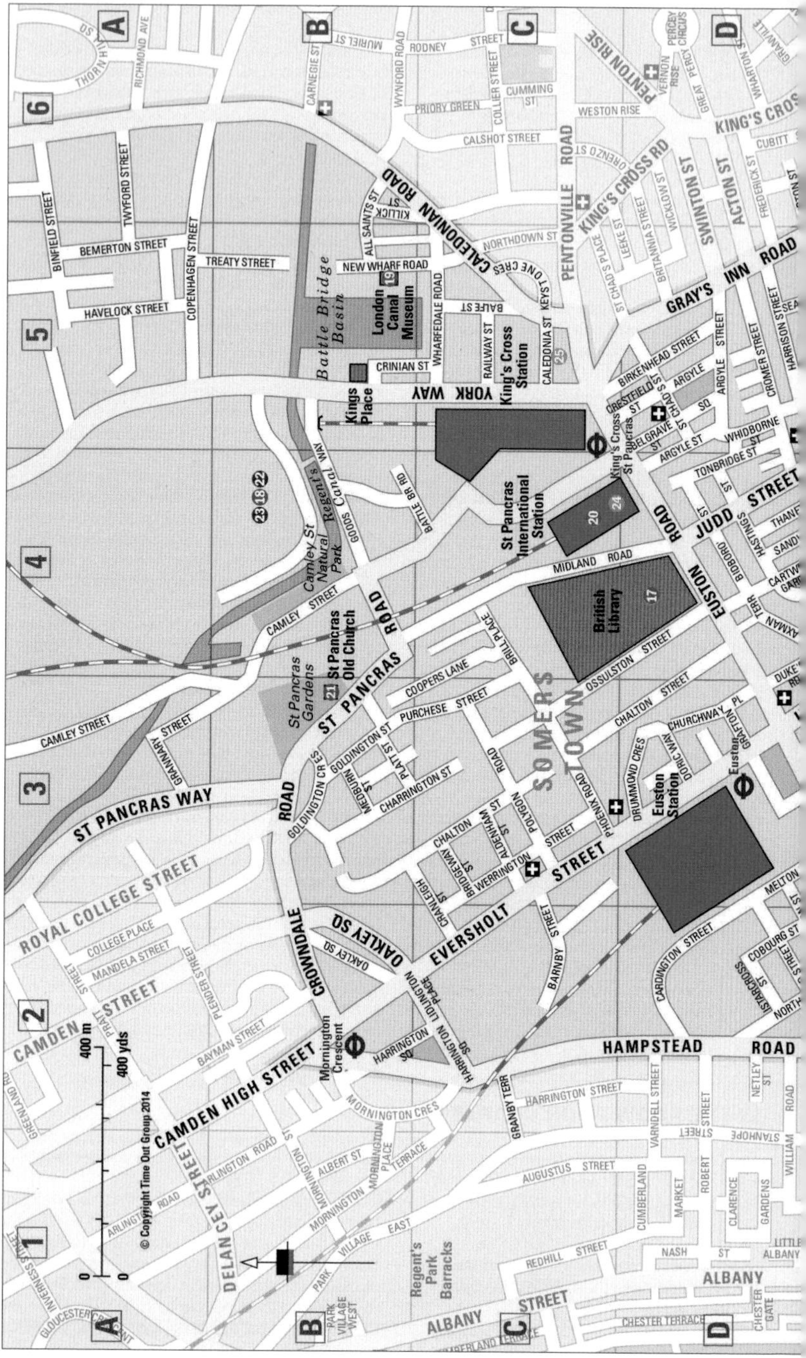
Battle Bridge Basin
London Canal Museum
Kings Place
King's Cross Station
St Pancras International Station
British Library
Camley St Natural Park
Regent's Canal
St Pancras Gardens
St Pancras Old Church
SOMERS TOWN
Euston Station
Mornington Crescent
Regent's Park Barracks
CALEDONIAN ROAD
YORK WAY
PENTONVILLE ROAD
KING'S CROSS RD
GRAY'S INN ROAD
EUSTON ROAD
MIDLAND ROAD
ST PANCRAS ROAD
ST PANCRAS WAY
CAMLEY STREET
ROYAL COLLEGE STREET
CAMDEN STREET
CAMDEN HIGH STREET
CROWNDALE ROAD
EVERSHOLT STREET
OAKLEY SQ
HAMPSTEAD ROAD
AUGUSTUS STREET
ALBANY STREET
CHESTER TERRACE
OSSULSTON STREET
CHALTON STREET
JUDD STREET
BEMERTON STREET
COPENHAGEN STREET
TREATY STREET
HAVELOCK STREET
NEW WHARF ROAD
GOODS WAY
ARGYLE ST
DELANCEY STREET
400 m
400 yds
© Copyright Time Out Group 2014

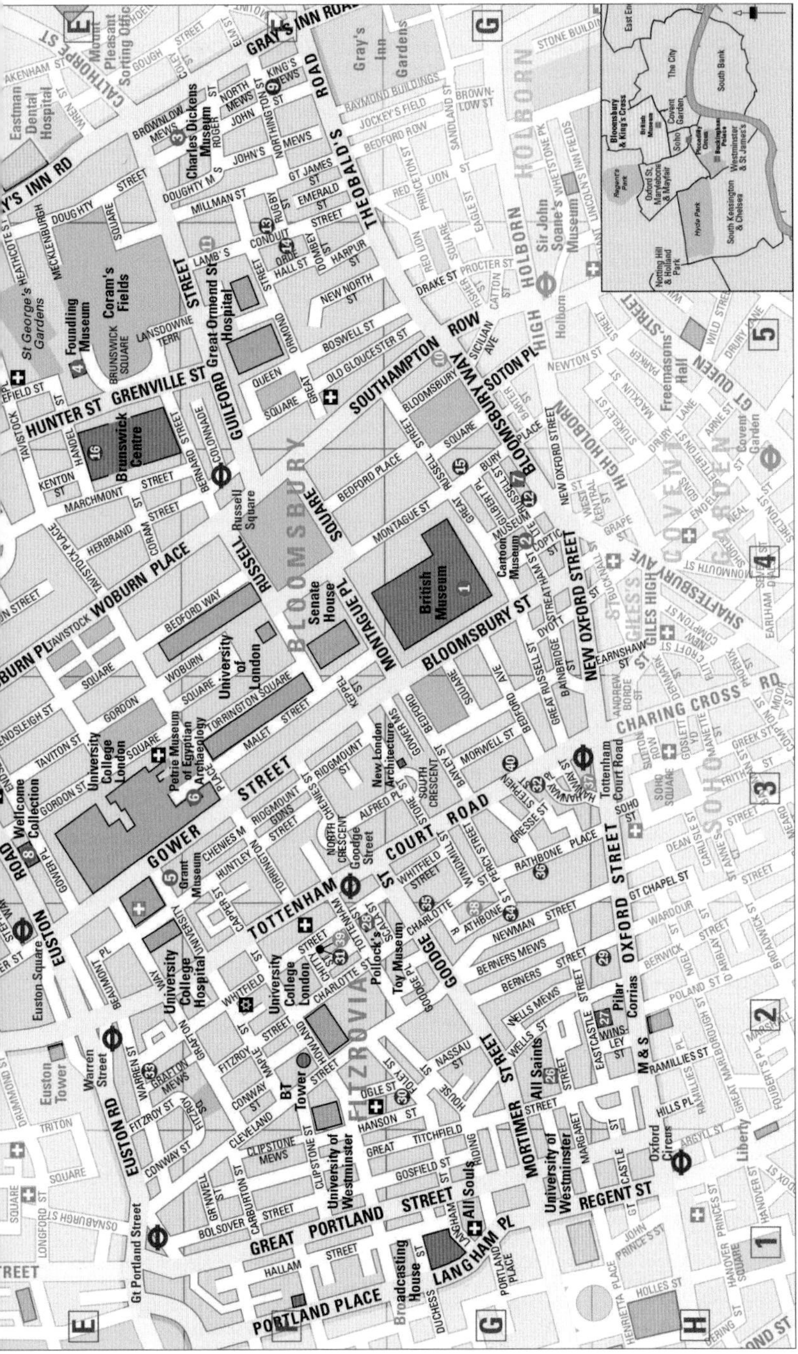
Gray's Inn Road
Gray's Inn Gardens
Eastman Dental Hospital
Mount Pleasant Sorting Office
Calthorpe St
Charles Dickens Museum
Theobald's Road
Doughty St
Mecklenburgh Square
Coram's Fields
St George's Gardens
Foundling Museum
Brunswick Square
Great Ormond St Hospital
Guilford Street
Lamb's Conduit St
Grenville St
Hunter St
Brunswick Centre
Marchmont Street
Russell Square
Southampton Row
Holborn
Sir John Soane's Museum
Lincoln's Inn Fields
High Holborn
Freemasons Hall
Drury Lane
Covent Garden
Bloomsbury Square
Bloomsbury Way
Bloomsbury
Woburn Place
Tavistock Square
Gordon Square
Senate House
Montague Pl
British Museum
Bloomsbury St
Cartoon Museum
Great Russell St
New Oxford Street
St Giles High St
Shaftesbury Ave
Charing Cross Rd
Soho Square
Soho
University of London
Torrington Square
Malet Street
Petrie Museum of Egyptian Archaeology
University College London
Gower Street
Wellcome Collection
Euston Road
Euston Square
Grant Museum
Tottenham Court Road
Goodge Street
New London Architecture
Charlotte St
Pollock's Toy Museum
Fitzrovia
BT Tower
University College Hospital
Warren Street
Euston Tower
Fitzroy Square
Cleveland St
Great Portland Street
University of Westminster
All Souls
Langham Pl
Broadcasting House
Portland Place
Mortimer Street
All Saints
Oxford Street
Oxford Circus
Regent St
Pilar Corrias
M & S
Liberty
Carnaby St
Hanover Square
Great Marlborough St
Gt Portland Street

EXPLORE

building Britain's first public art gallery; works by artists as notable as Gainsborough and Reynolds are on display. The most heart-rending display is a tiny case of mementoes that were all mothers could leave the children they abandoned here. Work was under way on a new introductory gallery and café as we went to press.

★ FREE Grant Museum
Rockefeller Building, 21 University Street, WC1E 6JJ (3108 2052, www.ucl.ac.uk/museums/zoology). Goodge Street tube. **Open** 1-5pm Mon-Sat. **Admission** free. **Map** p153 E3 ❺
Now rehoused in a former Edwardian library in the University College complex, the Grant Museum retains the air of an avid Victorian collector's house. Its 67,000 specimens include the remains of many rare and extinct creatures, including skeletons of the dodo and the zebra-like quagga (hunted out of existence in the 1880s). Visitors are engaged in dialogue about the distant evolutionary past via the most modern means available, including iPads and smartphones. The Micrarium – a kind of booth walled with illuminated microscope slides – is a lovely addition.
► *If the grisliness of body parts in jars appeals, check out the Hunterian as well; see p164.*

FREE Petrie Museum of Egyptian Archaeology
University College London, Malet Place, WC1E 6BT (7679 2884, www.petrie.ucl.ac.uk). Warren Street tube. **Open** 1-5pm Tue-Sat. **Admission** free; donations appreciated. **Map** p153 F3 ❻
Set up in 1892 by eccentric traveller and diarist Amelia Edwards, the refurbished museum is named after Flinders Petrie, tireless excavator of ancient Egypt. Where the British Museum's Egyptology collection is strong on the big stuff, the Petrie is dim case after dim case of minutiae: pottery shards, grooming accessories, beads. Highlights include artefacts from the heretic pharaoh Akhenaten's capital Tell el Amarna. Wind-up torches illuminate gloomy corners and computers offer 3D views of select objects.

FREE St George's Bloomsbury
Bloomsbury Way, WC1A 2HR (7242 1979, www.stgeorgesbloomsbury.org.uk). Holborn or Tottenham Court Road tube. **Open** times vary; phone for details. *Services* 9am Tue, Thur; 9am, 1.10pm Wed, Fri; 10.30am Sun. **Admission** free. **Map** p153 G4 ❼
Consecrated in 1730, St George's is a grand and disturbing Nicholas Hawksmoor church, with an offset, stepped spire that was inspired by Pliny the Elder's account of the Mausoleum at Halicarnassus. Highlights of its renovation include the mahogany reredos and the sculptures of lions and unicorns clawing at the base of the steeple. The opening hours are erratic, but on Sundays, the church always remains open for visitors after the regular service. Check online for details of concerts.

★ FREE Wellcome Collection
183 Euston Road, NW1 2BE (7611 2222, www.wellcomecollection.org). Euston Square tube or Euston tube/rail. **Open** 10am-6pm Tue, Wed, Fri, Sat; 10am-10pm Thur; 11am-6pm Sun. *Library* 10am-6pm Mon-Wed, Fri; 10am-8pm Thur; 10am-4pm Sat. **Admission** free. **Map** p153 E3 ❽
Sir Henry Wellcome, a pioneering 19th-century pharmacist, amassed a vast and idiosyncratic collection of implements and curios relating to the medical trade, now displayed here. In addition to these fascinating and often grisly items – ivory carvings of pregnant women, used guillotine blades, Napoleon's toothbrush – there are several serious works of modern art, most on display in a smaller room to one side of the main chamber of curiosities. The temporary exhibitions are often brilliant and come with all manner of associated events, from talks to walks. The Wellcome remains open while undergoing a £17.5 million development project, which will open up even more areas of the building to the public: in autumn 2014, it should reopen fully with a new second gallery and the 'Reading Room', which will be a combination of library, gallery and event space.

Restaurants

Lady Ottoline
11A Northington Street, WC1N 2JF (7831 0008, www.theladyottoline.com). Chancery Lane or Russell Square tube. **Open** *Pub* noon-11pm Mon-Sat; noon-9pm Sun. *Food served* noon-3pm, 6.30-10pm Mon-Fri; noon-4pm, 6.30-10pm Sat; noon-8pm Sun. **Main courses** £10.95-£19.50. **Map** p153 F6 ❾ **Gastropub**
One of a group of upmarket gastropubs, all of which have a commitment to drink as well as food, with space for drinkers and a selection that runs from cocktails and real ales to a thoughtful wine list. Food is served in the ground-floor bar at the Lady Ottoline, but for a more sedate meal, it's best to dine in the pleasant first-floor room. The menu is a bit more adventurous than at most gastropubs – witness creamy rabbit pie with chicory and pomegranate salad.
Other locations Princess of Shoreditch, 76-78 Paul Street, Shoreditch, EC2A 4NE (7729 9270); Pig & Butcher, 80 Liverpool Road, Islington, N1 0QD (7226 8304).

Pubs & bars

All Star Lanes
Victoria House, Bloomsbury Place, WC1B 4DA (7025 2676, www.allstarlanes.co.uk). Holborn tube. **Open** 4-11.30pm Mon-Wed; 4pm-midnight Thur; noon-2am Fri; 11am-2am Sat; 11am-11pm Sun. *Food served* 5-10pm Mon-Thur; noon-10pm Fri-Sun. *Bowling* £6.95-£8.95/person per game. **Map** p153 G5 ❿
Of Bloomsbury's two subterranean bowling dens, this is the one with aspirations. Walk past the lanes

EXPLORE

and smart, diner-style seating, and you'll find yourself in a comfortable, subdued side bar with chilled glasses, classy red furnishings, an unusual mix of bottled lagers and some impressive cocktails. There's an American menu and, at weekends, DJs. **Other locations** Whiteleys, 6 Porchester Gardens, Bayswater, W2 4DB (7313 8363); Old Truman Brewery, 95 Brick Lane, Spitalfields, E1 6QL (7426 9200). Westfield Stratford City, Stratford, E20 1ET (3167 2434).

► *Nearby, Bloomsbury Bowling Lanes (Bedford Way, 7183 1979, WC1H 9EU, www.bloomsburybowling.com) offers a pints-and-worn-carpets take on the game – and private karaoke booths.*

Lamb

94 Lamb's Conduit Street, WC1N 3LZ (7405 0713, www.youngs.co.uk). Holborn or Russell Square tube. **Open** noon-11pm Mon-Wed; noon-midnight Thur-Sat; noon-10.30pm Sun. *Food served* noon-9pm daily. **Map** p153 F5 ⓫

The standard range of Young's beers is dispensed from a central horseshoe bar in this 280-year-old pub, around which are ringed original etched-glass snob screens, used to prevent Victorian gentlemen from being seen when liaising with 'women of dubious distinction'. A sunken back area gives access to a convenient square of summer patio.

Shops & services

The Brunswick Centre (www.brunswick.co.uk) has a variety of chain shopping and eating options. For a more ethical type of shopping, head to Lamb's Conduit Street for the **People's Supermarket** (nos.72-78, WC1N 3LP, 7430 1827, www.thepeoplessupermarket.org), a co-operative that focuses on locally sourced produce. The street has become known for its fashion outlets (*see below*) and the tiny but delightful **Persephone Books** (no.59, WC1N 3NB, 7242 9292, www.persephonebooks.co.uk).

Darkroom.

Aperture Photographic

44 Museum Street, WC1A 1LY (7242 8681, www.apertureuk.com). Holborn or Tottenham Court Road tube. **Open** 11am-7pm Mon-Fri; noon-7pm Sat. **Map** p153 G4 ⓬ **Electronics & photography**

This camera shop-cum-café has a great atmosphere. The photographic side centres on an excellent selection of new and vintage, manual and autofocus Nikons, Leicas, Canons and Hasselblads, along with a sprinkling of other makes, at reasonable prices. The café is frequented by paparazzi and camera enthusiasts. Staff are happy to answer questions. **Other location** 27 Rathbone Place, Bloomsbury (7436 1015).

Darkroom

52 Lamb's Conduit Street, WC1N 3LL (7831 7244, www.darkroomlondon.com). Holborn tube. **Open** 11am-7pm Mon-Fri; 11am-6pm Sat; noon-5pm Sun. **Map** p153 F5 ⓭ **Fashion**

This shop is quite literally dark (with black walls and lampshades), creating a striking backdrop for the carefully chosen selection of unisex fashion, accessories and interiors items for sale. The space doubles up as a gallery, with art displays intermingling with a range of sculptural jewellery.

Folk

53 Lamb's Conduit Street, WC1N 3NG (8616 4191, www.folkclothing.com). Holborn or Russell Square tube. **Open** 11am-7pm Mon-Sat; noon-5pm Sun. **Map** p153 F5 ⓮ **Fashion**

While the menswear store at no.49 (7404 6458) concentrates on the stylish own-label (albeit with additional pieces from Scandinavian brands Our Legacy and Han Kjøbenhavn), this branch of Folk is a godsend for women, with Scandinavian labels such as Acne, as well as boutique faves Humanoid and Sessùn. Bags from Ally Capellino provide the finishing touch. **Other locations** 12-14 Shepherd Street, Mayfair, W1J 7JS (7499 8598); 11 Dray Walk, Spitalfields, E1 6QL (7375 2844).

London Review Bookshop

14 Bury Place, WC1A 2JL (7269 9030, www.lrbshop.co.uk). Holborn or Tottenham Court Road tube. **Open** 10am-6.30pm Mon-Sat; noon-6pm Sun. **Map** p153 G4 ⓯ **Books & music**

From the inviting presentation to the sheer quality of the books selected, this is an inspiring bookshop – no wonder it was able to celebrate its tenth anniversary in 2014. Politics, current affairs and history are well represented on the ground floor; downstairs, audio books lead on to exciting poetry and philosophy sections, everything you'd expect from a shop owned by the *London Review of Books*. Browse through your purchases in the sweet little adjoining café, and check the website for stimulating events.

Skoob

Unit 66, The Brunswick, WC1N 1AE (7278 8760, www.skoob.com). Russell Square tube. **Open** 10.30am-8pm Mon-Sat; 10.30am-6pm Sun. **Map** p153 E5 ⓰ **Books & music**

A back-to-basics basement beloved of students from the nearby University of London, Skoob showcases some 50,000 titles covering virtually every subject, from philosophy and biography to politics and the occult. Prices are very reasonable.

KING'S CROSS & ST PANCRAS

King's Cross tube/rail.

North-east of Bloomsbury, King's Cross is becoming a major European transport hub, thanks to a £500m makeover of the area. The renovated and restored **St Pancras International** (*see right*) was the key arrival, but neighbouring King's Cross station has now benefitted with an expanded station concourse, a snazzy new cascading roof and much-improved restaurants and cafés; 2013 saw the completion, in front of the original 1851 façade, of a new public square. What were once badlands to the north have been transformed into a mixed-use nucleus called **King's Cross Central**, with the University of the Arts London the most important new resident (*see p157* **Hip to Be a Square**). There were, however, already several places to explore: the **London Canal Museum** (*see right*), the **Kings Place** arts complex (*see p281*) and **St Pancras Old Church** (*see p158*).

Sights & museums

★ FREE British Library

96 Euston Road, NW1 2DB (01937 546060, www.bl.uk). Euston or King's Cross St Pancras tube/rail. **Open** 9.30am-6pm Mon, Wed-Fri; 9.30am-8pm Tue; 9.30am-5pm Sat; 11am-5pm Sun. **Admission** free; donations appreciated. **Map** p152 D4 ⓱

'One of the ugliest buildings in the world,' opined a Parliamentary committee on the opening of the new British Library in 1997. But don't judge a book by its cover: the interior is a model of cool, spacious functionality, the collection is unmatched (150 million items and counting), and the reading rooms (open only to cardholders) are so popular that regular users complain that they can't find a seat. The focal point of the building is the King's Library, a six-storey glass-walled tower housing George III's collection, but the library's main treasures are on permanent display in the John Ritblat Gallery: Magna Carta, the Lindisfarne Gospels, original Beatles lyrics. There is also a great programme of temporary exhibitions and associated events: the Folio Society Gallery is free and hosts focused little shows based around key artefacts, while the engaging blockbuster shows are ticketed but cover meaty themes such as sci-fi, the Mughal Empire and the English language itself.

IN THE KNOW HAWK EYES

If a distant movement from above catches your eye in **St Pancras International** (*see right*), you might just have spotted Comet or Electra, the two Harris hawks employed, with their handler, to ensure the great shed stays pigeon-free.

FREE House of Illustration

2 Granary Square, N1C 4BH (www.houseofillustration.org.uk). King's Cross St Pancras tube/rail. **Open** check website for details. **Admission** free. **Map** p152 B4 ⓲

The world's first gallery dedicated to the art of illustration will open on Granary Square in summer 2014. There will be demonstrations, talks, debates and hands-on workshops covering all aspects of illustration from children's books and scabrous cartoons to advertising and animation, as well as a regular programme of exhibitions.

London Canal Museum

12-13 New Wharf Road, off Wharfdale Road, N1 9RT (7713 0836, www.canalmuseum.org.uk). King's Cross St Pancras tube/rail. **Open** 10am-4.30pm Tue-Sun; 10am-7.30pm 1st Thur of mth. **Admission** £4; £2-£3 reductions; free under-5s. **Map** p152 B5 ⓳

Housed on two floors of a former 19th-century ice warehouse, the London Canal Museum has a barge cabin to sit in and models of boats, but the displays (photos and videos about ice-importer Carlo Gatti) on the history of the ice trade are perhaps the most interesting. The canalside walk (download a free MP3 audio tour from the museum website) from Camden Town to the museum is lovely.

► *In summer, don't miss the dank exploration of the Islington Tunnel, organised by the museum.*

FREE St Pancras International

Pancras Road, N1C 4QP (7843 7688, www.stpancras.com). King's Cross St Pancras tube/rail. **Open** 24hrs daily. **Admission** free. **Map** p152 C4 ⓴

The redeveloped St Pancras station has become a destination in more ways than the obvious, now containing large sculptures, the self-proclaimed 'longest champagne bar in Europe', high-end boutiques –

HIP TO BE A SQUARE

Granary Square makes a good impression.

What's the new fashion in London? Having your own postcode. That chunk of real estate out east, the Olympic something-or-other, is now E20, and here – north of the station – is King's Cross Central, N1C to the postman. To earn such an accolade, you're looking at serious redevelopment. The stats alone for King's Cross Central are impressive: 67 acres, 20 'historic structures' being refurbed, 'up to 2,000 homes and serviced apartments', 'up to 500,000sq ft of retail space', 20 new streets, three new bridges, ten new parks and squares, and 400 trees planted.

The concept behind the numbers is interesting. The developers are trying to create from scratch a 'mixed-use' development – one with the virtues of multiplicity and resilience normally found in communities that have grown up over time. To this end, they are paying careful attention to the area's industrial heritage, to attracting the right mix of residents, and to the kind of events that might draw in visitors. No doubt the Olympic Park's London Legacy Develoment Corporation is paying close attention.

How's it shaping up? Nicely, in fact. Heading north-east from the station, **King's Boulevard** – a lively changing collection of street-food stalls organised by Petra Barran's KERB (www.kerbfood.com; noon-2.30pm Tue-Fri) – leads directly to the superb **Granary Square**. Filled with choreographed fountains (1,080 water spouts, operating 8am-8pm daily, and lit in many colours at night), the square's terracing down to the canal is already populated most sunny days. No wonder: there's a ready supply of students from St Martins College of Art, which in 2011 moved into the building behind – a sensitively and impressively converted, Grade II-listed 1850s industrial building. From the summer of 2014, the square should also be home to a new attraction: the **House of Illustration** (*see p156*).

A little further along the canal, the Filling Station houses **Shrimpy's** restaurant (8880 6111, www.shrimpys.co.uk) until it's eventually redeveloped. From there, as you look one way to once-stranded **Kings Place** (*see p281*), another to the station and the square, you might think it's all starting to make sense.

For more, visit the **King's Cross Visitor Centre** (Western Transit Shed, 11 Stable Street, N1C 4AB, 3479 1795, www.kingscross.co.uk; open 10am-5pm Mon, Thur, Fri; noon-5pm Tue, Wed; 10am-4pm Sat).

even a gastropub and farmers' market. But the new additions are mere window-dressing for the stunning original structures: famously George Gilbert Scott's grandiloquent red-brick exterior (much of which is now the St Pancras Renaissance hotel, *see p344*), but perhaps more impressively William Barlow's gorgeous Victorian glass-and-iron roof to the train shed, a single span that is airy and light, as though some kind of cathedral to 19th-century industry.

FREE St Pancras Old Church & St Pancras Gardens

St Pancras Road, NW1 1UL (7974 1693, www.camden.gov.uk). Mornington Crescent tube or King's Cross tube/rail. **Open** *Gardens* during daylight hours daily. *Services* times vary; check website (www.posp.co.uk/old-st-pancras) for details. **Admission** free.
Map p152 B3 ㉑

St Pancras Old Church has been ruined and rebuilt many times. The current structure is handsome, but it's the churchyard that delights. Among those buried here are writer William Godwin and his wife, Mary Wollstonecraft; over their grave, their daughter Mary Godwin (author of *Frankenstein*) declared her love for poet Percy Bysshe Shelley. Also here is the last resting place of Sir John Soane, one of only two Grade I-listed tombs (the other is that of Karl Marx, in Highgate Cemetery; *see p230*). Designed for his wife, the tomb's dome influenced Gilbert Scott's design for the red British phone box.

Restaurants

The new area behind King's Cross station is shaping up to be a gastro-destination, with an excellent set of restaurants and a healthy street food scene (*see p157* **Hip to Be a Square**).

★ Caravan King's Cross

Granary Building, 1 Granary Square, N1C 4AA (7101 7661, www.caravankingscross.co.uk). King's Cross St Pancras tube/rail. **Meals served** 8am-10.30pm Mon-Fri; 10am-10.30pm Sat; 10am-4pm Sun. **Main courses** £7-£15.50.
Map p152 B4 ㉒ **Global**

This offshoot of Caravan is an altogether bigger, more urbane operation than the original in Exmouth Market. The ethos is the same in both branches: welcoming staff and a menu of what they call 'well-travelled food'. Most are small plates – deep-fried duck egg with baba ganoush, chorizo oil and crispy shallots, say, or grits, collard greens and brown shrimp butter – plus a few large plates and (at King's Cross only) a handful of first-class pizzas. Recent favourites include a naughty-but-nice crispy fried chicken with jerk mayo and pawpaw salsa. The setting, overlooking the fountains of Granary Square, is another plus.

Other location 11-13 Exmouth Market, Clerkenwell, EC1R 4QD (7833 8115).

Caravan King's Cross.

Grain Store

Granary Square, 1-3 Stable Street, N1C 4AB (7324 4466, www.grainstore.com). King's Cross St Pancras tube/rail. **Open** noon-2.30pm, 6-10.30pm Mon-Fri; 11am-3pm, 6-10.30pm Sat; 11am-4pm Sun. **Main courses** £9.50-£16. **Set dinner** £35 5 courses. **Map** p152 B4 ㉓ **Modern European**

Grain Store occupies just one part of a vast former Victorian warehouse, next to Caravan (*see left*). Most of the rest of the building has been imaginatively transformed into Central Saint Martins arts college. The restaurant is run by Bruno Loubet, the man behind Bistrot Bruno Loubet (86-88 Clerkenwell Road, EC1M 5RJ, 7324 4455). His cooking is grounded in the classical traditions of south-west France, but not bound by them. The menu is a pick 'n' mix of ingredients and cuisines: a dish such as sticky pork belly with a corn and quinoa tamale is typical.

Pubs & bars

Booking Office

St Pancras Renaissance London Hotel, NW1 2AR (7841 3566, www.bookingofficerestaurant.com). King's Cross St Pancras tube/rail. **Open** 6.30am-1am Mon-Wed, Sun; 6.30am-3am Thur-Sat.
Map p152 C4 ㉔

Sit indoors at this smart cocktail bar and you gaze at Sir George Gilbert Scott's lofty interior, a stirring example of the Victorian architect's interpretation of Gothic revival. Outside, under spacious canopies, you have a nearly ceiling-level view of St Pancras International station. The cocktail list gives a prominent place to traditional punches, served in mugs, but the list is a long one. Martinis are well made, and the gin fix (a variant on gin fizz using fresh berries) is a wonderful and refreshing potion. Warning: the free bar snacks – coated peanuts – are dangerously addictive.

EXPLORE

VOC

2 Varnishers Yard, Regents Quarter, N1 9AW (7713 8229, www.voc-london.co.uk). King's Cross St Pancras tube/rail. **Open** 5pm-midnight Mon-Thur; 5pm-12.30am Fri, Sat. **Map** p152 C5 ㉕

VOC bar occupies a smallish, cosy space in one of north London's most restaurant-intensive precincts. The name derives from the Dutch East India Company, and there's a nautical and historical theme to the drinks list. Punches based on old recipes figure large, though modern technology brings them right up to date. Playing it safe with the classics is by no means the inferior option, however, as textbook martinis and caipirinhas prove. But on our visit, more people were drinking beer or wine than cocktails.

FITZROVIA

Goodge Street or Tottenham Court Road tube.

Squeezed in between Tottenham Court Road, Oxford Street, Great Portland Street and Euston Road, Fitzrovia isn't as famous as Bloomsbury, but its history is just as rich. The origins of the name are hazy: some believe it comes from **Fitzroy Square**, named after Henry Fitzroy (son of Charles II); others insist it's due to the famous **Fitzroy Tavern** (16 Charlotte Street, 7580 3714), focal venue for London bohemia of the 1930s and '40s and a favourite with the likes of Dylan Thomas and George Orwell. Fitzrovia also had its share of artists: James McNeill Whistler lived at 8 Fitzroy Square, later taken over by British Impressionist Walter Sickert, while Roger Fry's Omega Workshops, blurring the distinction between fine and decorative arts, had its studio at no.33. Fitzrovia's raffish image is largely a thing of the past (media offices are in the ascendance these days) but the steady arrival of new galleries – notably **Pilar Corrias** (*see right*) – has given the district back some of its artiness, even if local rents means it will never again be home to the dissolute.

The district's icon is the **BT Tower**, completed in 1964 as the Post Office Tower. Its revolving restaurant and observation deck featured in any film that wanted to prove how much London was swinging (*Bedazzled* is just one example). The restaurant is now reserved for corporate functions, but **Charlotte Street** and neighbouring byways have plenty of good options for food and drink.

Sights & museums

FREE All Saints

7 Margaret Street, W1W 8JG (7636 1788, www.allsaintsmargaretstreet.org.uk). Oxford Circus tube. **Open** 7am-7pm daily. *Services* 7.30am, 8am, 1.10pm, 6pm, 6.30pm Mon-Fri; 7.30am, 8am, 6pm, 6.30pm Sat; 8am, 10am, 11am, 5.15pm, 6pm Sun. **Admission** free. **Map** p153 G2 ㉖

Respite from the tumult of Oxford Street, this 1850s church was designed by William Butterfield, one of the great Gothic Revivalists. The church looks as if it has been lowered into its tiny site, so tight is the fit; its lofty spire is the second-highest in London. Behind the polychromatic brick façade, the lavish interior is one of the capital's finest ecclesiastical triumphs, with luxurious marble, flamboyant tile work and glittering stones built into its pillars.

FREE Pilar Corrias

54 Eastcastle Street, W1W 8EF (7323 7000, www.pilarcorrias.com). Oxford Circus tube. **Open** 10am-6pm Mon-Fri; 11am-6pm Sat. **Admission** free. **Map** p153 H2 ㉗

Formerly a director at the pioneering Lisson and Haunch of Venison galleries, Corrias opened this 3,800sq ft, Rem Koolhaas-designed gallery in 2008 with a giant aluminium Christmas tree by Philippe Parreno. It was one of the first of an influx of private galleries to the area – several from the art-infested East End. *See also p160* **In the Know**.

Pollock's Toy Museum

1 Scala Street, W1T 2HL (7636 3452, www.pollockstoymuseum.com). Goodge Street tube. **Open** 10am-5pm Mon-Sat. **Admission** £6; £3-£5 reductions; free under-3s. **Map** p153 F2 ㉘

Named after Victorian toy theatre printer Benjamin Pollock, this place is in turns beguiling and creepy, a nostalgia-fest of old board games, tin trains, porcelain dolls and gollies – fascinating for adults but less so for children; describing a pile of painted woodblocks in a cardboard box as a 'Build a skyscraper' kit may make them feel lucky to be going home to their Wii.

► *The attached shop is great for stocking fillers.*

Restaurants

★ Berners Tavern

10 Berners Street, W1T 3NP (7908 7979, www.bernerstavern.com). Oxford Circus or Tottenham Court Road tube. **Open** *Bar* 11am-11pm daily. *Restaurant* 7-10.30am, noon-2.30pm, 6-10.30pm Mon-Fri; 7-10.30am, 11am-4pm, 6-10.30pm Sat, Sun. **Main courses** £15-£26. **Map** p153 H2 ㉙ **Modern European**

The huge lobby bar of the London Edition hotel (*see p344*) looks fabulous, but the vast dining room, with its ornate plasterwork ceiling and lively bar area, looks even better. Food is playful and appealing: tender pork belly with capers, golden raisins and apple coleslaw, and cod with fennel and cider sauce, are sublime. Any caveats? Sometimes dizzy service; frequent upselling of extras; and lighting so low it's hard to read the menu. But Berners Tavern is glamtastic. Wear your best threads, and book ahead for a preliminary cocktail in the adjoining Punch Room bar to steel yourself for the bill. *Photo p161.*

EXPLORE

★ Bonnie Gull

21A Foley Street, W1W 6DS (7436 0921, www.bonniegull.com). Goodge Street tube. **Open** noon-2.45pm, 6-9.45pm Mon-Fri; noon-3.45pm, 6-9.45pm Sat; noon-3.45pm, 6.30-8.45pm Sun. **Main courses** £13-£23. **Map** p153 G2 ㉚ **Fish**

After starting as a pop-up in Hackney in 2011, Bonnie Gull landed in Fitzrovia in 2012. The premises do a good job of evoking a seaside shack. The menu changes daily, but super-fresh crab, with the brown meat mixed with mayo in the shell and the white meat ready to be cracked out, is often featured. More complex dishes are beautifully presented, and equally good. Hake with courgette purée, beer-battered courgette flower and courgette ribbons is an assured plateful.

★ Dabbous

39 Whitfield Street, W1T 2SF (7323 1544, www.dabbous.co.uk). Goodge Street or Warren Street tube. **Open** noon-2.30pm, 6.30-9.30pm Tue-Fri; 6.15-9.30pm Sat. **Set lunch** £28 4 courses. **Set dinner** £45 4 courses. **Tasting menu** £59 7 courses. **Map** p153 F2 ㉛ **International**

The hype surrounding Dabbous' 2012 opening has not entirely diminished and securing a booking can be tricky, so it's a pleasure to arrive and find a relaxed, friendly restaurant. Even at £59 per person for seven dishes the tasting menu is great value. The international wine list is an enticing read, and several varieties offered by glass and carafe underscore the amenable attitude. The kitchen majors in plant foods, setting a light, contemporary culinary tone concisely expressed in dishes such as mixed alliums with chilled pine infusion. Meats are skilfully cooked too; we love the barbecued ibérico pork with almond praline. There's a great bar, Oskar's (*see p161*), in the basement. No wonder this place is popular.

Hakkasan

8 Hanway Place, W1T 1HD (7927 7000, www.hakkasan.com). Tottenham Court Road tube. **Open** *Restaurant* noon-3pm, 6-11pm Mon-Wed; noon-3pm, 5.45-11.45pm Thur, Fri; noon-4pm, 5.45-11.45pm Sat; noon-5.45pm, 6-11pm Sun. **Main courses** £17-£61. **Set lunch** £28 2 courses; £58 dim sum (Sun). **Map** p153 G3 ㉜ **Chinese**

More than a decade after it started wowing London's big spenders with its classy Cantonese cooking, this Michelin-starred trendsetter remains a benchmark against which high-end Chinese restaurants should be judged. The basement's stylish interior (all dark wood lattice screens and moody lighting) still attracts beautiful people, who come for signature dishes such as silver cod roasted in champagne, and jasmine tea-smoked organic pork ribs. Drinks run from cocktails via high-priced wines to specialist teas.

Other location 17 Bruton Street, Mayfair, W1J 6QB (7907 1888).

IN THE KNOW FITZROVIA LATES

Fancy a bit of wine and some cutting-edge art? For **Fitzrovia Lates** (www.fitzrovialates.co.uk), on the last Thursday of each month, more than two dozen galleries between Euston Road, Tottenham Court Road, Oxford Street and Portland Place open until 9pm – a great way to sample the area's new creative self-confidence.

Honey & Co

25A Warren Street, W1T 5LZ (7388 6175, www.honeyandco.co.uk). Warren Street tube. **Open** 8am-10.30pm Mon-Fri; 9.30am-10.30pm Sat. **Main courses** £8.50-£12.50. **Set dinner** (Mon-Sat) £26.50 2 courses; £29.50 3 courses. **Map** p153 E2 ㉝ **Middle Eastern**

A bijou delight, with small tables and chairs packed closely together. The kitchen is run by an accomplished Israeli husband-and-wife team. This pedigree shines in a daily-changing menu that draws influences from across the Middle East. The meze selection includes fabulously spongy, oily bread, sumac-spiked tahini, smoky taramasalata, crisp courgette croquettes with labneh, pan-fried feta and a bright salad with lemon and radishes. A main might be a whole baby chicken with lemon and a chilli and walnut muhamara paste. It's imaginative home-style cooking, and service is charming.

Koba

11 Rathbone Street, W1T 1NA (7580 8825). Goodge Street or Tottenham Court Road tube. **Lunch served** noon-2.30pm, 6-10.30pm Mon-Sat; 6-10.30pm Sun. **Main courses** £8.50-£12. **Set lunch** £6.50-£11.50. **Set meal** £25-£35. **Map** p153 G2 ㉞ **Korean**

Koba is one of the strongest players on the West End Korean scene. Barbecue meats such as beef kalbi or bulgogi are well marinated, and grilled at the table by efficient staff. Barbecued squid is fresh as a daisy, with just the right amount of tongue-tingling heat in the vibrant red sauce. Stews make a sound choice too, with umami-rich stocks and accompanying bowls of pearly rice. Service is polished but not too formal, and the dark, modern-East-Asian-meets-industrial interior is slick. Drinks include Korean beers, soju and a short wine list.

Lantana

13 Charlotte Place, W1T 1SN (7637 3347, www.lantanacafe.co.uk). Goodge Street tube. **Meals served** 8-11.30am, noon-3pm Mon-Fri; 9am-3pm Sat, Sun. **Main courses** £5.50-£11.50. **Map** p153 G2 ㉟ **Café**

Lantana is a lively spot. Its look – wooden tables, mismatched chairs, small pieces of art on white walls – is now commonplace, but the staff pride themselves

Berners Tavern. *See p159.*

on their coffee-making and baking skills, and rightly so. The flat whites are super-smooth and go well with a moist raspberry friand or an Aussie 'cherry ripe' cake slice. The breakfast and brunch menu includes the likes of maple french toast with streaky bacon, grilled banana and candied pecans. Savoury dishes can be ordered with a glass of wine. The kiosk next door sells some dishes as takeaways.
Other location Salvation Jane, 1 Oliver's Yard, 55 City Road, Shoreditch, EC1Y 1HQ (7253 5273).

★ Lima London
31 Rathbone Place, W1T 1JH (3002 2640, www.limalondon.com). Tottenham Court Road tube. **Open** noon-2.30pm, 5.30-10.30pm Mon-Sat. **Main courses** £16-£29. **Set meal** noon-2.30pm, 5.30-6pm Mon-Fri £20 2 courses, £23 3 courses. **Map** p153 G3 36 **Peruvian**
Part of the 'Peruvian wave' of restaurants to hit the capital in 2012, Lima London pitched itself squarely at the high end. The modish rear dining room mixes the hum of low-level beats with polite chatter; only the occasional Inca-patterned cushion adds colour. Well-drilled staff bring out a medley of carefully crafted small plates, the likes of sea bream ceviche flecked with hot aji limo chilli and pieces of roasted corn, and thick wedges of suckling pig – part dense meat, part salty, crispy crackling, matched by a rough corn mash spiked with two kinds of peppers.

Pubs & bars

Bradley's Spanish Bar
42-44 Hanway Street, W1T 1UT (7636 0359, www.bradleysspanishbar.co.uk). Tottenham Court Road tube. **Open** noon-11.30pm Mon-Thur; noon-midnight Fri, Sat; 3-10.30pm Sun. **Map** p153 G3 37
There's something of the Barcelona dive bar about the place, and San Miguel or Cruzcampo on draught, but Bradley's isn't really very Spanish. A hotchpotch of local workers, shoppers and foreign exchange students fill the cramped two-floor space, unperturbed by the routinely unpleasant toilets. After all, there's a good jukebox and a good atmosphere – what more could anyone want?

Newman Arms
23 Rathbone Street, W1T 1NG (7636 1127, www.newmanarms.co.uk). Goodge Street tube. **Open** noon-midnight Mon-Fri. *Food served* noon-3pm, 6-10pm Mon-Fri. **Map** p153 G2 38
There's been a business at this gateway to a cobbled alleyway since 1730 – see the red sign outside and etched writing over the bar – but as a pub it had its heyday in the mid 20th century, when George Orwell was a regular and Michael Powell filmed scenes from *Peeping Tom* outside. Today, this is the lunchtime and post-work haunt of undemanding chaps laying into decent beer, perhaps accompanying a cheese-and-ham toastie or prefacing a shift upstairs from the tiny and often packed street-level bar to the pie room.

★ Oskar's Bar
Dabbous, 39 Whitfield Street, W1T 2SF (7323 1544, www.dabbous.co.uk). Goodge Street tube. **Open** noon-3pm, 5.30-11pm Tue-Fri; 6.15-11pm Sat. **Map** p153 F2 39
Dabbous (*see p160*) astonishes with its cutting-edge cooking, and its downstairs cocktail bar sets out to do the same. There are plenty of unorthodox ingredients: the Giddy Up contains tequila, bramley and gage slider (traditional sloe-infused cider from Devon), elderflower cordial, lemon juice and camomile-infused acacia honey topped with Sierra Nevada IPA. (Other drinks stay closer to classicism.) The bar has the same stripped-back industrial decor as the restaurant, so it can be noisy. Service is sweet and solicitous, and bar snacks are a cut above.

Shops & services

There are lots of electronics shops at the southern end of **Tottenham Court Road**, with several offering laptop repairs, while toward the north is a clutch of homeware and furniture stores, the most notable of which is **Heals** (196 Tottenham Court Road, W1T 7LQ, 7636 1666, www.heals.co.uk). And of course, you're only minutes from **Oxford Street** (*see pp103-107*).

Ask
248 Tottenham Court Road, Fitzrovia, W1T 7QZ (7637 0353, www.askdirect.co.uk). Tottenham Court Road tube. **Open** 10am-7pm Mon-Sat; noon-6pm Sun. **Map** p153 G3 40 **Electronics & photography**
Four capacious, well-organised floors, with plenty of space to browse. Stock, spanning digital cameras, MP3 players, laptops, hi-fis and TVs, concentrates on the major consumer brands. Prices are competitive.

The City

The City's current fame merely as the financial heart of London does no justice to its 2,000-year history. Here – on top of a much more ancient ritual landscape – the Romans founded the city they called Londinium, building a bridge to the west of today's London Bridge. Here were a forum-basilica, an amphitheatre, public baths and the defensive wall that still defines what we now call the Square Mile (an area, in fact, of 1.21 square miles).

Although the City has just over 9,000 residents, 330,000 people arrive each weekday to work as bankers, lawyers and traders, taking over 85 million square feet of office space. Tourists come, too, to see St Paul's Cathedral and the Tower of London, but there's much else besides. No area of London offers quite so much in so small a space. Roman ruins? Medieval? Iconic 21st-century offices? You're in the right place.

Museum of London.

Don't Miss

1 **St Paul's Cathedral** Sir Christopher Wren's masterpiece (p176).

2 **Sir John Soane's Museum** Former home packed with art, furniture and ornamentation (p165).

3 **Tower of London** Crown Jewels, Beefeaters, armour: a historic attraction par excellence (p186).

4 **Sushisamba** Stunning views from this Heron Tower restaurant (p187).

5 **Museum of London** Life in the city from 1666 to the present (p179).

To understand the City properly, visit on a weekday when the great economic machine is running at full tilt and the commuter is king. Despite efforts by the City authorities to improve the district's prospects as a weekend leisure destination, many of the streets still fall eerily quiet. If you do visit at the weekend, try the Cheapside shops and the street's anchor mall, the rather antiseptic One New Change; drop in on the always wonderful Museum of London; or just do as a discerning minority of locals do – potter about enjoying the place's odd nooks and crannies in relative tranquillity.

Also in this chapter, we've included rather more lived-in adjuncts to the City proper: Holborn, where London-connoisseurs can wander some of the city's finest small museums, and Clerkenwell, where you'll find some of the best places to eat anywhere in London. They are underscored by historic Fleet Street, famous for its now-absent newspaper industry, to the south of which you can ponder powdered wigs and legal quiddities in the calm surrounds of Temple and the Inns of Court.

Lincoln's Inn Fields.

HOLBORN

Holborn tube.

A sharp left turn out of Holborn tube and then another left leads into the unexpectedly lovely **Lincoln's Inn Fields**. Surely London's largest square (indeed, it's more of a park), it's blessed with gnarled oaks casting dappled shade over a tired bandstand. On the south side of the square, the neoclassical façade of the Royal College of Surgeons hides the **Hunterian Museum** (*see right*); facing it from the north is the magical **Sir John Soane's Museum** (*see p165*).

East of the square lies **Lincoln's Inn** (7405 1393, www.lincolnsinn.org.uk), one of the city's four Inns of Court. Its grounds are open to the public, ogling an odd mix of Gothic, Tudor and Palladian buildings. On nearby Portsmouth Street lies the **Old Curiosity Shop** (nos.13-14, WC2A 2ES, 7405 9891), its timbers apparently known to Charles Dickens, but now selling Daita Kimura's decidedly modern shoes. Nearby, Gray's Inn Road runs north alongside the second Inn of Court. The sculpted gardens at **Gray's Inn** (7458 7800, www.graysinn.org.uk), dating to 1606, are open on weekdays, noon-2.30pm.

Opened in 1876 on Chancery Lane as a series of strongrooms in which the upper classes could secure their valuables, the **London Silver Vaults** (7242 3844, www.thesilvervaults.com) are now a hive of dealers buying, selling and repairing silverware. There are also glittering displays on **Hatton Garden**, the city's jewellery and diamond centre. It's no distance to walk but a million miles in nature from the Cockney fruit stalls and sock merchants of the market on **Leather Lane** (10am-2pm Mon-Fri).

Further on is **Ely Place**, its postcode absent from the street sign as a result of it technically falling under the jurisdiction of Cambridgeshire. The church garden of ancient **St Etheldreda** (*see below*) produced strawberries so delicious that they made the pages of Shakespeare's *Richard III*; a celebratory Strawberrie Fayre is still held on the street each June. The 16th-century **Ye Olde Mitre** (*see p165*) is one of the city's most atmospheric pubs, hidden down a barely marked alley.

Sights & museums

FREE Hunterian Museum

Royal College of Surgeons, 35-43 Lincoln's Inn Fields, WC2A 3PE (7869 6560, www.rcseng.ac.uk/museums). Holborn tube. **Open** 10am-5pm Tue-Sat. **Admission** free. **Map** p166 A4 ❶

The collection of medical specimens once held by John Hunter (1728-93), physician to King George III, can be viewed in this museum. The sparkling glass cabinets of the main room offset the goriness of the exhibits, which include Charles Babbage's brain and Winston Churchill's dentures, as well as shelf after shelf of diligently classified pickled body parts. The upper floor holds a brutal account of surgical techniques. Notably interesting kids' activities have included demonstrations by a 'barber surgeon'. The museum also runs lunchtime lectures (on the first Tuesday of the month, £4).

FREE St Etheldreda

14 Ely Place, EC1N 6RY (7405 1061, www.stetheldreda.com). Chancery Lane tube. **Open** 8am-5pm Mon-Sat; 8am-12.30pm Sun. **Admission** free; donations appreciated. **Map** p166 C3 ❷

Dedicated to the saintly seventh-century Queen of Northumbria, this is Britain's oldest Catholic church and London's only surviving example of 13th-century Gothic architecture; it was saved from the Great Fire by a change in the wind. The crypt is darkly atmospheric, untouched by traffic noise, and the stained glass (actually from the 1960s) is stunning.

★ FREE Sir John Soane's Museum

13 Lincoln's Inn Fields, WC2A 3BP (7405 2107, www.soane.org). Holborn tube. **Open** 10am-5pm Tue-Sat; 10am-5pm, 6-9pm 1st Tue of mth. *Tours* 11am Sat. **Admission** free; donations appreciated. *Tours* £5; free reductions. **Map** p166 A4 ❸

When he wasn't designing notable buildings (among them the original Bank of England), Sir John Soane (1753-1837) obsessively collected art, furniture and architectural ornamentation. In the 19th century, he turned his house into a museum to which, he said, 'amateurs and students' should have access. The result is this perfectly amazing place.

Much of the museum's appeal derives from the domestic setting. The modest rooms were modified by Soane with ingenious devices to channel and direct daylight, and to expand space, including walls that open out like cabinets to display some of his many paintings (Canaletto, Turner, Hogarth). The Breakfast Room has a beautiful domed ceiling, inset with convex mirrors. The extraordinary Monument Court contains a sarcophagus of alabaster, so fine that it's almost translucent, that was carved for the pharaoh Seti I (1291-78 BC) and discovered in his tomb in Egypt's Valley of the Kings. There are also numerous examples of Soane's eccentricity, not least the cell for his imaginary monk 'Padre Giovanni'. *See p168* **The Known Unknown**.

Restaurants

Leather Lane (*see p164*) is a good place to grab a bite, as it's lined with street food stalls (during market hours), caffs and two of the best coffee bars in London, **Department of Coffee & Social Affairs** (nos.14-16, EC1N 7SU, no phone, www.departmentofcoffee.co.uk) and **Prufrock Coffee** (nos.23-25 EC1N 7TE, 7242 0467, www.prufrockcoffee.com).

Pubs & bars

28°-50° Wine Workshop & Kitchen

140 Fetter Lane, EC4A 1BT (7242 8877, www.2850.co.uk). Farringdon tube/rail. **Open** noon-11pm Mon-Fri. *Food served* noon-2.30pm, 6-9.30pm Mon-Fri. **Map** p166 B4 ❹

The Fetter Lane branch of 28°-50°, in a basement with a French country-kitchen vibe, has a French-inspired menu and a bright, on-the-ball attitude. The wine list is a thing of joy, offering upwards of 30 varied and delicious wines, many of them from small producers, plus a changing themed selection. It's well worth exploring: order 75ml glasses and follow the young staff's enthusiastic advice.

Other locations 17-19 Maddox Street, Mayfair, W1S 2QH (7495 1505); 15-17 Marylebone Lane, Marylebone, W1U 2NE (7486 7922).

Ye Olde Mitre

1 Ely Court, EC1N 6SJ (7405 4751, www.yeoldemitreholborn.co.uk). Farringdon tube/rail. **Open/Food served** 11am-11pm Mon-Fri. **Map** p166 C3 ❺

Largely due to its location – down a barely marked alley between Hatton Garden's jewellers and Ely Place – this little traditional pub, the foundation of which dates to 1546, is a favourite of secret London lists. There's always a good range of ales on offer at the tiny central bar, but people come for the atmosphere: lots of cosy dark wood and some overlooked curiosities, such as the tree in the front bar. It's a cherry tree that Good Queen Bess is said to have danced around, but now supports a corner of the front bar.

Shops & services

Kate Kanzier

67-69 Leather Lane, EC1N 7TJ (7242 7232, www.katekanzier.com). Chancery Lane tube or Farringdon tube/rail. **Open** 9.30am-6.30pm Mon-Fri; 11am-4pm Sat. **Map** p166 C3 ❻ **Fashion**

Adored for great-value directional footwear for women, Kate Kanzier is the place to visit for brogues, ballerinas, sandals and leather boots in a huge range of colours. Sexy high-heeled pumps in patent, suede, leather and animal prints are characterised by vintage designs. Handbags and clutches are also stocked in the spacious shop.

CLERKENWELL

Farringdon tube/rail.

Few places encapsulate London's capacity for reinvention quite like Clerkenwell, an erstwhile religious centre that takes its name from the parish clerks who once performed Biblical mystery plays on its streets. The most lasting holy legacy is that of the 11th-century knights of the **Order of St John**; the remains of their priory can still be seen at St John's Gate, a crenellated gatehouse that dates from 1504 and is home to the **Museum of the Order of St John** (*see p169*). For a little peace and quiet, stroll by the **Charterhouse** in Charterhouse Square. This Carthusian monastery, founded in 1370, is now Anglican almshouses that retain the original 14th-century chapel and a 17th-century library. It's opening to the public for the first time in 2016 – curated by the Museum of London. Until then, there are occasional guided tours (£10; check the museum's website for details). It's right beside the **Malmaison** hotel (*see p341*).

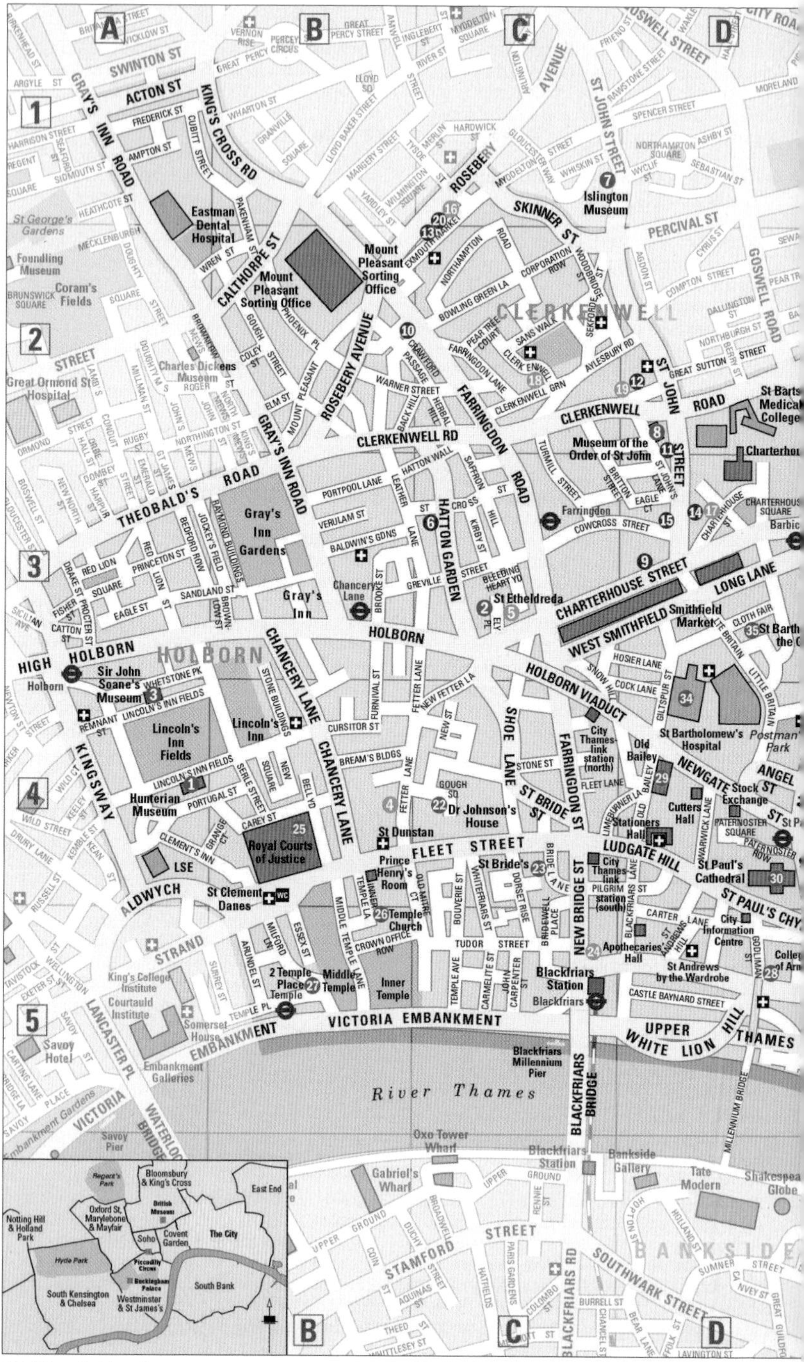
A
B
C
D
1
2
3
4
5
SWINTON ST
ACTON ST
GRAY'S INN ROAD
KING'S CROSS RD
FREDERICK ST
AMPTON ST
Eastman Dental Hospital
Mount Pleasant Sorting Office
CALTHORPE ST
ROSEBERY AVENUE
ROSEBERY
SKINNER ST
Islington Museum
ST JOHN STREET
GOSWELL ROAD
PERCIVAL ST
CLERKENWELL
St George's Gardens
Foundling Museum
Coram's Fields
Great Ormond St Hospital
Charles Dickens Museum
THEOBALD'S ROAD
CLERKENWELL RD
CLERKENWELL ROAD
FARRINGDON ROAD
Museum of the Order of St John
St Barts Medical College
Charterhouse
Gray's Inn Gardens
Gray's Inn
HATTON GARDEN
Farringdon
COWCROSS STREET
CHARTERHOUSE STREET
LONG LANE
Smithfield Market
WEST SMITHFIELD
St Etheldreda
Chancery Lane
HOLBORN
HIGH HOLBORN
Holborn
Sir John Soane's Museum
Lincoln's Inn Fields
Lincoln's Inn
CHANCERY LANE
HOLBORN VIADUCT
SHOE LANE
FARRINGDON ST
City Thameslink station (north)
Old Bailey
St Bartholomew's Hospital
Postman's Park
NEWGATE ST
ANGEL ST
Stock Exchange
KINGSWAY
Hunterian Museum
Royal Courts of Justice
LSE
Dr Johnson's House
St Dunstan
FLEET STREET
St Bride's
ST BRIDE ST
NEW BRIDGE ST
LUDGATE HILL
Stationers Hall
Cutlers Hall
St Paul's Cathedral
ST PAUL'S CHY
City Thameslink PILGRIM station (south)
City Information Centre
Apothecaries' Hall
St Andrews by the Wardrobe
ALDWYCH
St Clement Danes
Prince Henry's Room
Temple Church
Middle Temple
Inner Temple
2 Temple Place
Temple
STRAND
King's College Institute
Courtauld Institute
Somerset House
EMBANKMENT
VICTORIA EMBANKMENT
Blackfriars Station
Blackfriars
CASTLE BAYNARD STREET
UPPER THAMES
WHITE LION HILL
Savoy Hotel
Embankment Galleries
LANCASTER PL
WATERLOO BRIDGE
Blackfriars Millennium Pier
River Thames
BLACKFRIARS BRIDGE
MILLENNIUM BRIDGE
Savoy Pier
Oxo Tower Wharf
Gabriel's Wharf
Blackfriars Station
Bankside Gallery
Tate Modern
Shakespeare's Globe
BANKSIDE
UPPER GROUND
STAMFORD STREET
BLACKFRIARS RD
SOUTHWARK STREET
Regent's Park
Bloomsbury & King's Cross
British Museum
East End
Notting Hill & Holland Park
Oxford St, Marylebone & Mayfair
Soho
Covent Garden
The City
Hyde Park
Piccadilly Circus
Buckingham Palace
South Kensington & Chelsea
Westminster & St James's
South Bank

EXPLORE

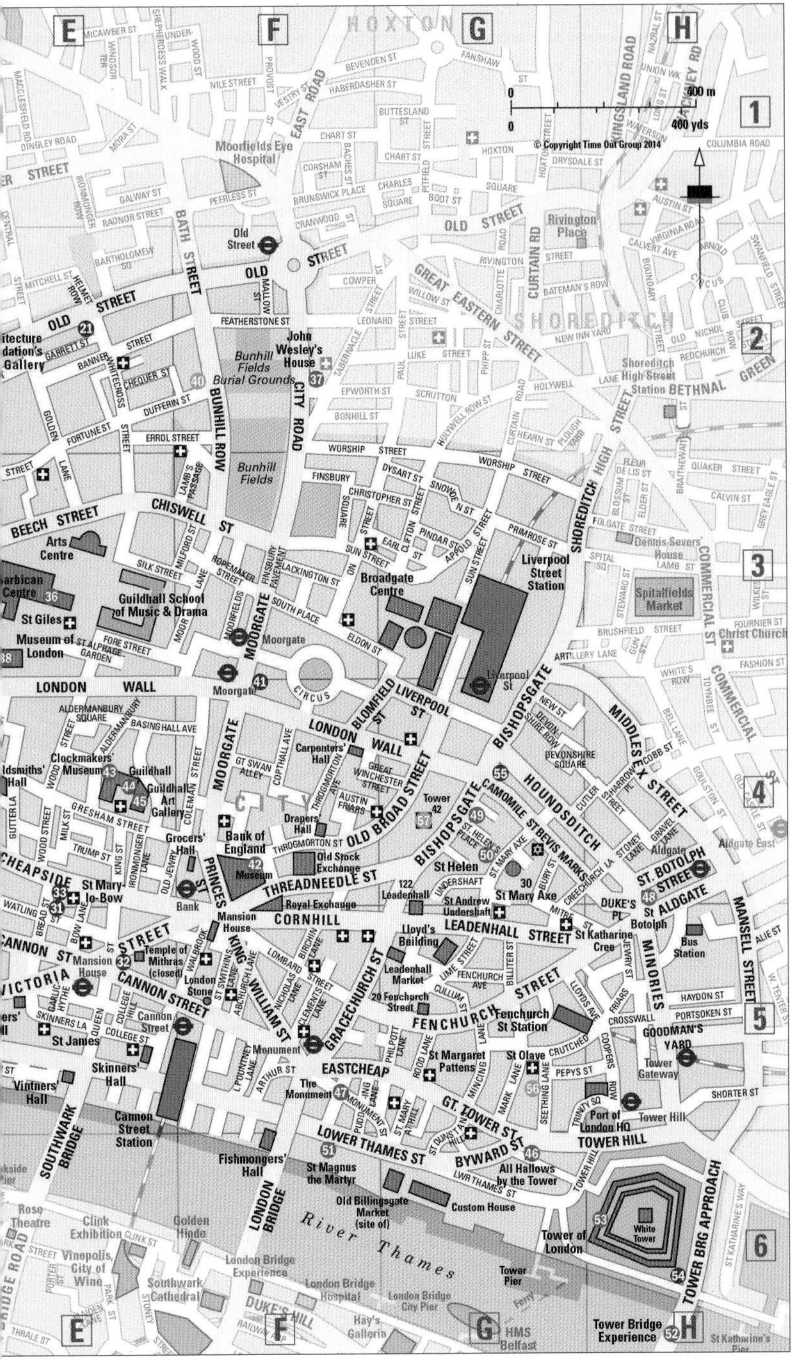
HOXTON
SHOREDITCH
CITY
River Thames
0
400 m
0
400 yds
© Copyright Time Out Group 2014
E
F
G
H
1
2
3
4
5
6
Moorfields Eye Hospital
Old Street
John Wesley's House
Bunhill Fields Burial Grounds
Bunhill Fields
Arts Centre
Barbican Centre
Guildhall School of Music & Drama
St Giles
Museum of London
Broadgate Centre
Liverpool Street Station
Liverpool St
Moorgate
Dennis Severs' House
Spitalfields Market
Christ Church
Shoreditch High Street Station
Rivington Place
Clockmakers' Museum
Guildhall
Guildhall Art Gallery
Carpenters' Hall
Drapers' Hall
Tower 42
Bank of England Museum
Old Stock Exchange
Royal Exchange
Grocers' Hall
St Mary-le-Bow
Bank
Mansion House
Temple of Mithras (closed)
London Stone
St Helen
St Andrew Undershaft
30 St Mary Axe
122 Leadenhall
Lloyd's Building
Leadenhall Market
20 Fenchurch Street
St Katharine Cree
St Botolph Aldgate
Aldgate
Aldgate East
Bus Station
Fenchurch St Station
Cannon Street
St James
Skinners' Hall
Vintners' Hall
Cannon Street Station
Monument
The Monument
St Margaret Pattens
St Olave
Port of London HQ
Tower Hill
Tower Gateway
Fishmongers' Hall
St Magnus the Martyr
All Hallows by the Tower
Custom House
Old Billingsgate Market (site of)
Tower of London
White Tower
Tower Pier
Ferry
Rose Theatre
Clink Exhibition
Golden Hinde
Vinopolis, City of Wine
Southwark Cathedral
London Bridge Experience
London Bridge Hospital
London Bridge City Pier
Hay's Galleria
HMS Belfast
Tower Bridge Experience
St Katharine's Pier
OLD STREET
CITY ROAD
EAST ROAD
GREAT EASTERN STREET
KINGSLAND ROAD
HACKNEY RD
SHOREDITCH HIGH STREET
COMMERCIAL ST
BETHNAL GREEN
WORSHIP STREET
CHISWELL ST
BEECH STREET
BUNHILL ROW
MOORGATE
LONDON WALL
BISHOPSGATE
HOUNDSDITCH
MIDDLESEX STREET
LIVERPOOL ST
OLD BROAD STREET
THREADNEEDLE ST
CORNHILL
LEADENHALL STREET
FENCHURCH STREET
CHEAPSIDE
CANNON STREET
QUEEN VICTORIA
KING WILLIAM ST
GRACECHURCH ST
EASTCHEAP
GT. TOWER ST
LOWER THAMES ST
BYWARD ST
TOWER HILL
MINORIES
MANSELL STREET
TOWER BRG APPROACH
LONDON BRIDGE
SOUTHWARK BRIDGE
DUKE'S HILL
CLINK ST

EXPLORE

THE KNOWN UNKNOWN

Once 'undiscovered', the Soane has grown to meet demand.

Formerly a staple of 'unknown London' lists, the **Sir John Soane's Museum** (*see p165*) has gone from being a treasured secret to something approaching a must-visit. These days you can expect queues at this eccentric house of curiosities – more than 93,000 people visit each year. And slowly the museum has been changing to meet its growing fame. The process started in 1996, with the purchase of 14 Lincoln's Inn Fields, which allowed the research library to move from no.12, which could be connected to the original house: no.13. Now the stage was set for an ambitious £7m restoration project.

For the 200th anniversary of the building of the house in 2012, the Tivoli Recess – the city's first gallery of contemporary sculpture, with a stained-glass window and skylights with plaster sunbursts – was returned to its original function after years as a staff lavatory. Further stained glass illuminated the Shakespeare Recess, with William's likeness from his Stratford-upon-Avon tomb set there. The old entrance to the house – a narrow corridor where all those visitors had to sign in, buy their house guidebooks and postcards, and leave coats and bags with the volunteers – was far too cramped, so a cloakroom was established in no.12. Now, once you've toured the treasures, seen the ingenious fold-out walls of paintings and admired the clever lighting effects and archaeological oddments, you exit through no.12, past a new shop full of one-off gifts and commissions. There's also an Exhibition Room, and room for more details on Soane and the objects you've just seen (Soane wasn't much given to labelling and the museum is obliged, by the 1833 Act of Parliament that set up the museum, to follow his lead).

Since his arrival from the V&A, new director Abraham Thomas seems to have brought a new liveliness to the Soane: for a Christmas shopping evening in 2013 there were bespoke cocktails from food-theatre experts Bompas & Parr, and early 2014 saw a pop-up exhibition on the architects who had just won the 2013 Stirling Prize. And under Thomas's watchful gaze, the improvements continue: the entire second floor will open to the public – including private rooms not seen since Soane's death in 1837. Most excitingly, from late 2014, you'll be able to visit the Model Room for the first time since 1850: this holds Britain's largest collection of historical architectural models.

EXPLORE

By the 17th century, Clerkenwell was a fashionable locale, but the Industrial Revolution soon buried it under warehouses and factories. Printing houses were established, and the district gained a reputation as a safe haven for radicals, from 16th-century Lollards to 19th-century Chartists. In 1903, Lenin is believed to have met Stalin for a drink in what is now the **Crown Tavern** (43 Clerkenwell Green, 7253 4973, www.thecrowntavernec1.co.uk), one year after moving the publication of the newspaper *Iskra* to no.37A (now the **Marx Memorial Library**; 7253 1485, www.marx-memorial-library.org).

Industrial dereliction and decay were the theme until property development in the 1980s and '90s turned Clerkenwell into a desirable area. The process was aided by a slew of artfully distressed gastropubs (following the lead of the **Eagle**; *see right*), and the food stalls, fashion boutiques, restaurants and bars along the colourful strip of **Exmouth Market**. Now the area is one of London's dining powerhouses, with **St John** (*see p170*) the acknowledged pioneer of the new British cuisine – reviving the taste for unfavoured cuts of meat and offal under the catchy motto of 'nose-to-tail eating'.

Sights & museums

FREE Islington Museum

245 St John Street, EC1V 4NB (7527 3235, www.islington.gov.uk). Angel tube. **Open** 10am-5pm Mon, Tue, Thur-Sat. **Admission** free. **Map** p166 C1 ❼

The Islington Museum covers local history and the political and ethical credentials of the borough, exemplified by local residents such as reformist preacher John Wesley, playwright Joe Orton and eminent feminist Mary Wollstonecraft.

FREE Museum of the Order of St John

St John's Gate, St John's Lane, EC1M 4DA (7324 4005, www.museumstjohn.org.uk). Farringdon tube/rail. **Open** 10am-5pm Mon-Sat. *Tours* 11am, 2.30pm Tue, Fri, Sat. **Admission** free. *Tours* free. Suggested donation £5; £4 reductions. **Map** p166 D2 ❽

Now best known for its ambulance service, the Order of St John's roots lie in Christian medical practices from the Crusades of the 11th to 13th centuries. Artefacts related to the Order of Hospitaller Knights, from Jerusalem, Malta and the Ottoman Empire, are displayed; there's a separate collection relating to the ambulance service. A major refurbishment has reorganised the galleries in the Tudor gatehouse and, across St John's Square, opened the Priory Church (11am-4pm Mon-Sat), its secluded garden, and the pleasingly gloomy 12th-century crypt to the public.

▶ *One of Caravaggio's masterpieces,* The Cardsharps, *was unveiled here last year. It is on long-term loan to the museum.*

Restaurants

Comptoir Gascon

61-63 Charterhouse Street, EC1M 6HJ (7608 0851, www.comptoirgascon.com). Farringdon tube/rail. **Open** noon-2.30pm, 6-10pm Tue-Sat. **Main courses** £9-£14.50. **Map** p166 D3 ❾ **French**

This bistro/deli specialises in the cuisine of Gascony: richer than Depardieu and earthier than Gainsbourg. Pork and duck appear in various dishes – grilled duck hearts, crackling with duck egg, duck confit – while starters include the must-order 'piggy treats', a charcuterie board with saucisson, pâté, rillettes and slivers of cured tongue. Rustic, yes, but sophisticated too, and every dish comes with a bold whack of flavour. The oddly shaped space is stripped back to brick in that typical Farringdon way, but manages to be cosy and welcoming.

▶ *The smarter, similarly excellent Club Gascon (57 West Smithfield, EC1A 9DS, 7600 6144, www.clubgascon.com) is across the meat market.*

Eagle

159 Farringdon Road, EC1R 3AL (7837 1353). Farringdon tube/rail. **Open** noon-11pm Mon-Sat; noon-5pm Sun. **Food served** noon-3pm, 6.30-10.30pm Mon-Fri; 12.30-3.30pm, 6.30-10.30pm Sat; 12.30-4pm Sun. **Main courses** £5-£15. **Map** p166 B2 ❿ **Gastropub**

Widely credited with launching the food-in-pubs revolution when it opened in its current form in 1991, the Eagle has long since passed into both legend and middle age. But this high-ceilinged corner room remains a cut above the competition. Globetrotting mains are chalked twice daily above the bar/open kitchen. You can just drink but few do, aware they're missing the big-flavoured likes of moreish tomato and bread soup; daisy-fresh scallops, pan-fried and served on toast with chorizo; and succulent leg of lamb with jansson's temptation (a potato gratin-style Swedish dish).

Foxlow

69-73 St John Street, EC1M 4AN (7014 8070, www.foxlow.co.uk). Farringdon tube/rail. **Open** noon-3pm, 5.30-10.30pm Mon-Sat; noon-5.30pm Sun. **Main courses** £10-£19.50. **Map** p166 D2 ⓫ **International**

Will Beckett and Huw Gott, the duo behind the very popular Hawksmoor steakhouses, have scored again with this newcomer. It has a cosily masculine vibe (warm woods, low lighting and comfy retro-themed furniture) and a compact menu of meaty dishes to comfort and soothe, plus impeccably sourced steaks. 'Smokehouse rillettes' sees a smoky mound of beef, turkey, pork and lardo knocked into shape by a tart jumble of cucumber, pickles and capers. The youthful staff are a marvel, with bags of personality, beaming smiles and a nothing-too-much-trouble attitude.

Modern Pantry

47-48 St John's Square, EC1V 4JJ (7250 0833, www.themodernpantry.co.uk). Farringdon tube/rail. **Open** *Café* 8am-10pm Mon; 8am-10.30pm Tue-Fri; 9am-4pm, 6-10.30pm Sat; 10am-4pm, 6-10pm Sun. *Restaurant* noon-3pm, 6-11pm Tue-Fri; 9am-5pm, 6-11pm Sat; 10am-4pm Sun. **Main courses** £8.50-£20.50. **Map** p166 D2 ⓬ **International**

Chef Anna Hansen creates enticing fusion dishes that make the most of unusual ingredients sourced from around the globe. Antipodean and Asian flavours (yuzu, tamarind) pop up frequently, alongside plenty of seasonal British fare (wild garlic, purple sprouting broccoli); the combinations can seem bewildering on the page, but rarely falter in execution, and the signature dish of sugar-cured prawn omelette with chilli, coriander and spring onion is still a winner. The stylish ground-floor café is quite feminine in feel, with soothing white and grey paintwork, white furniture and burnished copper light fittings; there's a more formal restaurant upstairs.

★ Moro

34-36 Exmouth Market, EC1R 4QE (7833 8336, www.moro.co.uk). Farringdon tube/rail or bus 19, 38, 341. **Open** *Bar* noon-10.30pm Mon-Sat; 12.30-2.45pm Sun. *Restaurant* noon-2.30pm, 6-10.30pm Mon-Sat; 12.30-2.45pm Sun. **Main courses** £18.50-£21. *Tapas* £3.50-£14.50. **Map** p166 C2 ⓭ **North African/Spanish**

Sam(antha) and Sam Clark's Exmouth Market restaurant and cookbooks set the benchmark for a distinctly British style of Iberian-with-a-North-African-twist Mediterranean cooking, and they're still in the front rank 17 years later. Moro provides a spectacular showcase of modern Spanish and Portuguese wines, and vibrantly fresh food that throws out surprising and pleasurable flavours at every turn, such as wood-roasted pork offset by a hazelnut picada (like a nut pesto), and chargrilled trout that's cleverly balanced by lemon, capers and a bitter note from hispi cabbage.

► *Next door, Morito (no.32, EC1R 4QE, 7278 7007, closed Sun) is a fine no-booking tapas bar offshoot.*

★ St John

26 St John Street, EC1M 4AY (7251 0848, www.stjohnrestaurant.com). Barbican tube or Farringdon tube/rail. **Open** noon-2.45pm, 6-10.45pm Mon-Fri; 6-10.45pm Sat; 1-2.30pm Sun. **Main courses** £13.50-£23.80. **Map** p166 D3 ⓮ **British**

Fergus Henderson and Trevor Gulliver's restaurant has been praised to the skies for reacquainting the British with the full possibilities of native produce, and especially anything gutsy and offal-ish. Perhaps as influential, however, has been its almost defiantly casual style. The mezzanine dining room in the former Smithfield smokehouse has bare white walls, battered floorboards and tables lined up canteen-style. St John's cooking is famously full-on, but also sophisticated, concocting flavours that are delicate as well as rich, as in black cuttlefish and onions, with a deep-flavoured ink-based sauce with a hint of mint. The airy bar here is a great place for a drink and a no-fuss snack.

Other location St John Bread & Wine, 94-96 Commercial Street, Spitalfields, E1 6LZ (7251 0848).

Vinoteca

7 St John Street, EC1M 4AA (7253 8786, www.vinoteca.co.uk). Barbican tube or Farringdon tube/rail. **Open** noon-11pm Mon-Sat. *Food served* noon-2.45pm, 5.45-10pm Mon-Fri; noon-4pm, 5.45-10pm Sat. **Main courses** £10-£21. **Map** p166 D3 ⓯ **Wine bar**

Charmingly but sparingly decorated, and with delightfully friendly staff, this bijou spot is the original branch in the small chain. Serious about its commitment to the grape, Vinoteca offers 25 wines by the glass, 300 by the bottle, all available to take away. But even without the fabulous wines, it would still be a great restaurant. Dishes such as mussels, clams and john dory with chorizo, or barnsley chop with greens, are excellent combinations of light, bright flavours – and go perfectly with the recommended wines.

Other locations 55 Beak Street, Soho, W1F 9SH (3544 7411); 18 Devonshire Road, Chiswick, W4 2HD (3701 8822); 15 Seymour Place, Marylebone, W1H 5BD (7724 7288).

Zetter Townhouse.

EXPLORE

Pubs & bars

Clerkenwell has a compelling claim to being the birthplace of the now ubiquitous gastropub: the **Eagle** (*see p169*) kicked things off. **St John** and **Vinoteca** (for both, *see p170*) are both good options for a relaxed glass of wine.

Café Kick

43 Exmouth Market, EC1R 4QL (7837 8077, www.cafekick.co.uk). Angel tube or Farringdon tube/rail. **Open** 11am-11pm Mon-Thur; 11am-midnight Fri, Sat; noon-10.30pm Sun. *Food served* noon-3pm Mon-Fri; noon-10pm Sat, Sun. **Map** p166 C1 ⑯

Clerkenwell's most likeable bar is this table football-themed gem. The soccer paraphernalia is authentic, retro-cool and mainly Latin (you'll find a Zenit St Petersburg scarf amid the St Etienne and Lusitanian gear); bar staff, beers and bites give the impression you could be in Lisbon. A modest open kitchen ('we don't microwave or deep-fry') dishes out tapas, sandwiches and charcuterie platters.

Other location Bar Kick, 127 Shoreditch High Street, Shoreditch, E1 6JE (7739 8700).

★ Fox & Anchor

115 Charterhouse Street, EC1M 6AA (7250 1300, www.foxandanchor.com). Barbican tube or Farringdon tube/rail. **Open** 7am-11pm Mon-Fri; 8.30am-11am Sat; 8.30am-10pm Sun. *Food served* 7am-9.30pm Mon-Fri; 8.30am-9.30pm Sat; 8.30am-8.30pm Sun. **Map** p166 D3 ⑰

Pristine mosaic tiling, etched glass and a dark wood front bar lined with pewter tankards help make this refurbished old pub a local treasure. To the back is the Fox's Den, a series of intimate rooms used for both drinking and dining. Local sourcing is a priority and a pleasure: in addition to the own-label ale, cask beers might include Red Poll and Old Growler from Suffolk's fine Nethergate brewery. There are plenty more delights among the bottles.

Three Kings of Clerkenwell

7 Clerkenwell Close, EC1R 0DY (7253 0483). Farringdon tube/rail. **Open** noon-11pm Mon-Fri; 5.30-11pm Sat. *Food served* noon-3pm, 6-10pm Mon-Fri. **Map** p166 C2 ⑱

Rhinoceros heads, Egyptian felines and photos of Dennis Bergkamp provide the decorative backdrop at this great little boozer. Glug Scrumpy Jack, Beck's Vier, Old Speckled Hen or London Pride, and tap the well-worn tables to the Cramps and other gems from an outstanding jukebox that is crammed with fabulous old platters.

★ Zetter Townhouse

49-50 St John's Square, EC1V 4JJ (7324 4545, www.thezettertownhouse.com). Farringdon tube/rail. **Open** 7am-midnight Mon-Wed, Sun; 7am-1am Thur-Sat. **Map** p166 D2 ⑲

Hula Nails.

The decor at Townhouse embodies a 'more is more' philosophy: every square inch of surface area is occupied by something lovely. The result: one of the most beautiful bars in London. The cocktail list is of fittingly high quality and is devised by Tony Conigliaro. Even though Conigliaro is known as a techno-wizard, the original drinks here are fairly simple and restrained. And wonderful. Among the house cocktails, check out the Köln martini, the Somerset sour, and the jasmine tea gimlet. Service is friendly and helpful.

Shops & services

ec one

41 Exmouth Market, EC1R 4QL (7713 6185, www.econe.co.uk). Farringdon tube/rail. **Open** 10am-6pm Mon-Wed, Fri; 11am-7pm Thur; 10.30am-6pm Sat. **Map** p166 C1 ⑳ **Accessories**

Husband-and-wife team Jos and Alison Skeates have a magpie's eye for good design, which makes for delightfully varied browsing at this stylish shop. Over 50 designers are showcased: the choice runs from serious pieces to tempting trinkets such as colourful lucite bangles and sweet little heart necklaces.

Hula Nails

203-205 Whitecross Street, EC1Y 8QP (7253 4453, www.hulanails.com). Old Street tube/rail. **Open** 10.30am-7.30pm Mon,Tue, Thur, Fri; 10.30am-9pm Wed; 11am-6pm Sat. **Map** p167 E2 ㉑ **Health & beauty**

EXPLORE

Georgiana Amador worked at Mac for many years, in contrast, Hula's boudoir-style beauty rooms are gloriously decked out in Hawaiian wallcoverings, with plush velvet sofas and burlesque flourishes. The salon specialises in luxurious grooming – come for a vintage style pit-stop, with victory rolls and retro make-up all on offer. Nail treatments take place in the window of the parlour, so you can sip on a free grated ginger tea and have a gossip as you watch the media types go by (waxes and spray tans are in cosily decked-out backrooms).

FLEET STREET

Temple tube or Blackfriars rail.

Without Fleet Street, the daily newspaper might never have been invented. Named after the vanished River Fleet, Fleet Street was a major artery for the delivery of goods into the City, including the first printing press, which was installed behind **St Bride's Church** (*see p173*) in 1500 by William Caxton's assistant, Wynkyn de Worde, who also set up a bookstall in the churchyard of St Paul's. London's first daily newspaper, the *Daily Courant*, rolled off the presses in 1702; in 1712, Fleet Street saw the first of innumerable libel cases when the *Courant* leaked the details of a private parliamentary debate.

By the end of World War II, half a dozen offices were churning out scoops and scandals between the Strand and Farringdon Road. Most of the newspapers moved away after Rupert Murdoch won his war with the print unions in the 1980s; the last of the news agencies, Reuters, finally followed suit in 2005. Until recently, the only periodical published on Fleet Street was a comic, the much-loved *Beano*. However, in 2009, left-wing weekly the *New Statesman* moved into offices around the corner from Fleet Street on Carmelite Street. Relics from the media days remain: the Portland-stone **Reuters building** (no.85), the Egyptian-influenced **Daily Telegraph building** (no.135) and the sleek, black **Daily Express building** (nos.121-128), designed by Owen Williams in the 1930s and arguably the finest art deco building in London. Tucked away on an alley behind St Bride's Church is the **St Bride Foundation**, (7353 4660, www.stbride.org; open 11am-6pm Wed), dedicated to printing and typography. There are events, a library and temporary exhibitions showing off its collections, which include rare works by Eric Gill and maquettes for Kinnear and Calvert's distinctive road signs.

At the top of Fleet Street itself is the church of **St Dunstan-in-the-West** (7405 1929, www.stdunstaninthewest.org; closed Sat & Sun, except for services), where the poet John Donne was rector in the 17th century. The church was rebuilt in the 1830s, but the eye-catching clock dates from 1671. The clock's chimes are beaten by clockwork giants who are said to represent Gog and Magog, tutelary spirits of the City. Next door, no.186 is the house where Sweeney Todd, the 'demon barber of Fleet Street', reputedly murdered his customers before selling their bodies to a local pie shop. The legend, sadly, is a porky pie: Todd was invented by the editors of a Victorian penny dreadful in 1846 and propelled to fame rather later by a stage play.

St Bride's Church

Fleet Street was always known for its pubs; half the newspaper editorials in London were composed over liquid lunches, but there were also more literary imbibers. If you walk down Fleet Street, you'll see **Ye Olde Cheshire Cheese** (no.145, 7353 6170), a favourite of Dickens and Yeats. In its heyday, it hosted the bibulous literary salons of Dr Samuel Johnson, who lived nearby at 17 Gough Square (*see p173* **Dr Johnson's House**). It also had a famous drinking parrot, the death of which prompted hundreds of newspaper obituaries. At no.66, the **Tipperary** (7583 6470) is the oldest Irish pub outside Ireland: it sold the first pint of Guinness on the British mainland in the 1700s. Just south of Fleet Street, near Blackfriars station, is the **Black Friar** (*see p173*), a lovely art nouveau meets Arts and Crafts pub.

EXPLORE

Sights & museums

Dr Johnson's House

17 Gough Square, off Fleet Street, EC4A 3DE (7353 3745, www.drjohnsonshouse.org). Chancery Lane tube or Blackfriars tube/rail. **Open** *May-Sept* 11am-5.30pm Mon-Sat. *Oct-Apr* 11am-5pm Mon-Sat. *Tours* by arrangement, groups of 10 or more only. **Admission** £4.50; £1.50-£3.50 reductions; £10 family; free under-5s. *Tours* £3.50. **No credit cards**. **Map** p166 C4 22

Famed as the author of one of the first – as well as the most significant and unquestionably the wittiest – dictionaries of the English language, Dr Samuel Johnson (1709-84) also wrote poems, a novel and an early travelogue, an acerbic account of a tour of the Western Isles with his biographer James Boswell. You can tour the stately Georgian townhouse where he came up with his inspired definitions – 'to make dictionaries is dull work,' was his definition of the word 'dull'.

▶ *A neat statue of Johnson's cat Hodge sits contentedly in the square outside.*

FREE St Bride's Church

Fleet Street, EC4Y 8AU (7427 0133, www.stbrides.com). Temple tube. **Open** 9am-6pm Mon-Fri; 10am-6.30pm Sun. Times vary Sat, so phone ahead to check. **Admission** free. **Map** p166 C4 23

Hidden down an alley south of Fleet Street, St Bride's is known as the journalists' church: in the north aisle, a shrine is dedicated to hacks killed in action. Down in the crypt a surprisingly interesting little museum displays fragments of the churches that have existed on this site since the sixth century.

▶ *An 18th-century Fleet Street pâtissier, William Rich, was famous for tiered bride cakes modelled on the church's lovely Wren-designed spire.*

IN THE KNOW
RIVER CROSSING

Blackfriars Bridge is certainly worth exploring, and not just for its splendid red-and-white painted Victorian ironwork (designed by Thomas Cubitt and dating from 1869). It also gives a great view of a rather interesting initiative to the east: London's first cross-river railway station. Needing extended platforms to accommodate longer trains, the designers simply ran them across the Thames. Now commuters can peer out along the river from inside the station – which is pretty cool in itself – safe in the knowledge they're generating green energy at the same time. At least, the station roof is: it supports the capital's largest array of solar panels, supplying half of the station's energy.

Pubs & bars

Black Friar

174 Queen Victoria Street, EC4V 4EG (7236 5474, www.nicholsonpubs.co.uk). Blackfriars tube/rail or Mansion House tube. **Open** 10am-11pm Mon-Thur, Sat; 10am-11.30pm Fri; noon-10.30pm Sun. **Map** p166 C5 24

Built in 1875 on the site of a medieval Dominican friary, the Black Friar had its interior completely remodelled in the Arts and Crafts style. It is now a Nicholson's (they run most of the trad pubs in the City: serving moderate food, but decent real ales), but the bright panes, intricate friezes and carved slogans ('Industry is Ale', 'Haste is Slow') of the main saloon make it a stunning work of art. Admittedly, there's a far more prosaic bar adjoining it but this remains one of London's most stunning pub interiors.

TEMPLE & THE INNS OF COURT

Temple tube.

At its western end, the arterial Strand (*see p146*) becomes Fleet Street at **Temple Bar**, the City's ancient western boundary and once the site of Wren's great gateway (now in Paternoster Square beside St Paul's; *see p176*). A newer, narrower, but still impressive wyvern-topped monument marks the original spot. The area has long been linked to the law, and here stands the splendid neo-Gothic **Royal Courts of Justice** (*see below*). On the other side of the road, stretching almost to the Thames, are the several courtyards that make up **Middle Temple** (7427 4800, www.middletemple.org.uk) and **Inner Temple** (7797 8250, www.innertemple.org.uk), two of the Inns of Court that provided training and lodging for London's medieval lawyers. Anybody may visit the grounds, but access to the grand, collegiate buildings is for lawyers and barristers only.

The site was formerly the headquarters of the Knights Templar, a religious warrior order founded in the 12th century to protect pilgrims to the Holy Land. The Templars built the original **Temple Church** (*see p174*) in 1185, but fell foul of Catholic orthodoxy during the Crusades and their order was disbanded.

Almost due south of Temple Bar, alongside Middle Temple, is the virtually unknown and fabulous **Two Temple Place** (*see p174*).

Sights & museums

FREE Royal Courts of Justice

Strand, WC2A 2LL (7947 6000, tours 7947 7684, www.hmcourts-service.gov.uk). Temple tube. **Open** 9am-4.30pm Mon-Fri. **Admission** free. *Tours* £10. **Map** p166 B4 25

EXPLORE

Two of the highest civil courts in the land sit in these imposing buildings: the High Court and the Appeals Court, justice at its most bewigged and ermine-robed. Visitors are welcome to observe the process of law in any of the 88 courtrooms, but very little happens in August and September. There are also two-hour tours (11am or 2pm; pre-book on 7947 7684 or rcjtours@talktalk.net). Cameras and children under 14 are not allowed on the premises.

Temple Church

Fleet Street, EC4Y 7HL (7353 8559, www.templechurch.com). Chancery Lane or Temple tube. **Open** times vary; check website for details. **Admission** £4; free reductions. **Map** p166 B5 ㉖

Inspired by Jerusalem's Church of the Holy Sepulchre, the Temple Church was the chapel of the Knights Templar. The rounded apse contains the worn gravestones of several Crusader knights, but the church was refurbished by Wren and the Victorians, and was damaged in the Blitz. Not that it puts off the wild speculations of fans of Dan Brown's *Da Vinci Code*. There are organ recitals most Wednesdays at 1.15pm.

FREE Two Temple Place

2 Temple Place, WC2R 3BD (7836 3715, www.twotempleplace.org). Temple tube. **Open** *Late Jan-mid Apr* 10am-4.30pm Mon, Thur-Sat; 10am-9pm Wed; 11am-4.30pm Sun. **Admission** free. *Tours* free. **Map** p166 B5 ㉗

The pale Portland stone exterior and oriel windows here are handsome – but the interior is extraordinary. You get a hint about what's to come before you open the door: look right and there's a cherub holding an old-fashioned telephone to his ear. Built as an estate office in 1895 to the close specifications of William Waldorf Astor, Two Temple Place now opens to the public three months a year with exhibitions of 'publicly-owned art from around the UK', arranged by an up-and-coming curator. Ring the bell and you're warmly welcomed by volunteers into a house with decor that combines sublime, extravagant craftsmanship with a thorough lack of interest in coherence: above porphyry tiles, the Three Musketeers adorn the banisters of a staircase; intricately carved literary characters crowd the first floor, mixing Shakespeare with Hawthorne and Fenimore Cooper; the medieval-style Great Hall, with lovely stained glass, crams together 54 random busts: Voltaire and Marlborough, Anne Boleyn enjoying the company of Mary Queen of Scots.

ST PAUL'S & AROUND

St Paul's tube.

The towering dome of **St Paul's Cathedral** (*see p176*) is, excluding the 'Big Ben' clocktower, probably the definitive symbol of traditional London. It was also an architectural two fingers to the Great Fire and, later, the Nazi bombers that pounded the city in 1940 and 1941. North of the cathedral is the redeveloped **Paternoster Square**, a modern plaza incorporating a sundial that rarely tells the time. The name harks back to the days when priests from St Paul's walked the streets chanting the Lord's Prayer (*Pater noster*, Latin for 'Our Father').

Also of interest is Wren's statue-covered **Temple Bar**. It once stood at the intersection of Fleet Street and the Strand, marking the boundary between the City of London and neighbouring Westminster; during the Middle Ages, the monarch was allowed to pass through the Temple Bar into the City only with the approval of the Lord Mayor of London. The archway was dismantled as part of a Victorian road-widening programme in 1878 and became a garden ornament for a country estate in Hertfordshire, before being installed in its current location, as the gateway between St Paul's and Paternoster Square, in 2004. The gold-topped pillar in the centre of the square looks as if it commemorates something important, but it's just an air vent for the Underground.

South of St Paul's, steps cascade down to the **Millennium Bridge**, which spans the river to Tate Modern (*see p56*) and now offers the main gateway to the City for tourists. The grand **St Lawrence Jewry Memorial Fountain** is another peripatetic monument: kept in storage since the 1970s after it was removed from the church (*see p182*), it was placed here in 2011. The structure dates to 1866. The stairs take you close to the 17th-century **College of Arms** (*see p175*), official seat of British heraldry.

East of the cathedral is the huge **One New Change** shopping mall and office development (*see p177*). Designed by French starchitect Jean Nouvel, its most interesting aspects are a gash that gives views straight through the building to St Paul's and, for a fine roof-level panorama, the sixth-floor public terrace and bar-restaurant. Meekly hidden among the alleys behind it, you'll find narrow Bow Lane. At one end sits **St Mary-le-Bow** (7248 5139, www.stmarylebow.co.uk; open 7am-6pm Mon-Thur; 7am-4pm Fri), built by Wren between 1671 and 1680. The church bell's peals once defined anyone born within earshot as a true Cockney. At the other end of Bow Lane is **St Mary Aldermary** (7248 9902, www.moot.uk.net; open 9am-6pm Mon-Fri). With a pin-straight spire designed by Wren's office, this was the only Gothic church by him to survive World War II. Inside, there's a fabulous moulded plaster ceiling and original wooden sword rest (London parishioners carried arms until the late 19th century).

There are more Wren creations south of St Paul's. On Garlick Hill, named for the medieval

EXPLORE

garlic market, is **St James Garlickhythe** (7236 1719, www.stjamesgarlickhythe.org.uk; open 10.30am-4pm Thur). The official church of London's vintners and joiners, it was built by Wren in 1682. Hidden in the tower are the naturally mummified remains of a young man, nicknamed Jimmy Garlick, discovered in the vaults in 1855. The church was hit by bombs in both World Wars, and partly ruined by a falling crane in 1991, but the interior has been convincingly restored. Off Victoria Street, **St Nicholas Cole Abbey** was the first church rebuilt after the Great Fire.

Built on the site of the infamous Newgate prison to the north-west of the cathedral is the **Old Bailey** (*see right*). A remnant of the prison's east wall can be seen in Amen Corner.

Sights & museums

FREE College of Arms

130 Queen Victoria Street, EC4V 4BT (7248 2762, www.college-of-arms.gov.uk). St Paul's tube or Blackfriars tube/rail. **Open** 10am-4pm Mon-Fri. *Tours* by arrangement. **Admission** free. **Map** p166 D5 ㉘

Originally created to identify competing knights at medieval jousting tournaments, coats of arms soon became an integral part of family identity for the landed gentry of Britain. Scriveners still work here to create beautiful heraldic certificates. Only the Earl Marshal's Court is open to the general public, but visitors can book for evening tours (groups of ten or more only, Mon-Fri) around the historic interior, led by a herald who will usually be able to show you documents from the archive.

IN THE KNOW
FACTS AND FIGURES

Perfectly located on the river side of St Paul's Cathedral (*see p176*), the spiky-roofed **City of London Information Centre** (7332 1456, www.cityoflondon.gov.uk) opens 9.30am-5.30pm Mon-Sat and 10am-4pm Sun. It has information and brochures on sights, events, walks and talks, as well as offering tours with specialist guides.

FREE Old Bailey (Central Criminal Court)

Corner of Newgate Street & Old Bailey, EC4M 7EH (7248 3277, www.cityoflondon.gov.uk). St Paul's tube. **Open** *Public gallery* 10am-1pm, 2-4.45pm Mon-Fri. **Admission** free. No under-14s; 14-16s only if accompanied by adults. **Map** p166 D4 ㉙

A gilded statue of blind (meaning impartial) justice stands atop London's most famous criminal court. The current building was completed in 1907; the site itself has hosted some of the most famous trials in British history, including that of Oscar Wilde. Anyone is welcome to attend a trial, but bags,

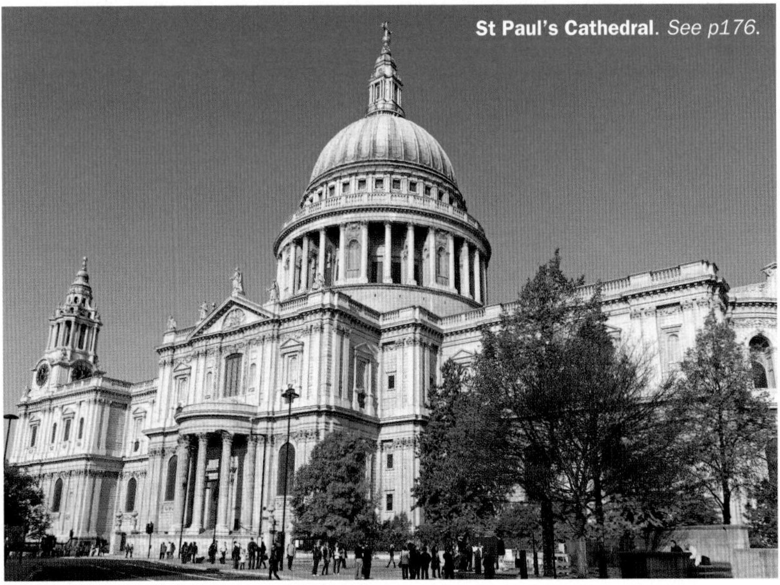

St Paul's Cathedral. *See p176.*

IN THE KNOW LIVERY IT UP

The City is dotted with halls belonging to the powerful livery companies, originally established as guilds but now largely charitable institutions. One of the most striking is the **Cutlers' Hall** on Warwick Lane, with a fine frieze of cutlers at work.

cameras, dictaphones, mobile phones and food are banned (and no storage facilities are provided).
▶ *A blocked-up door in St Sepulchre Without is the visible remains of a priest tunnel into the court; the Newgate Execution Bell is also there.*

★ St Paul's Cathedral

Ludgate Hill, EC4M 8AD (7236 4128, www.stpauls.co.uk). St Paul's tube. **Open** 8.30am-4pm Mon-Sat. *Galleries, crypt & ambulatory* 9.30am-4.15pm Mon-Sat. Special events may cause closure; check before visiting. *Tours of cathedral & crypt* 10am, 11am, 1pm, 2pm Mon-Sat. **Admission** *Cathedral, crypt & gallery* (incl tour) £16; £7-£14 reductions; £39 family; free under-6s. **Map** p166 D4 ㉚

The first cathedral to St Paul was built on this site in 604, but fell to Viking marauders. Its Norman replacement, a magnificent Gothic structure with a 490ft spire (taller than any London building until the 1960s), burned in the Great Fire. The current church was commissioned in 1673 from Sir Christopher Wren as the centrepiece of London's resurgence from the ashes. Modern buildings now encroach on the cathedral from all sides, but the passing of three centuries has done nothing to diminish the appeal of London's most famous cathedral.

A £40m restoration project has removed most of the Victorian grime from the outside walls and the extravagant main façade looks as brilliant today as it must have when the last stone was placed in 1708. On the cathedral's south side, an austere park has been laid out, tracing the outline of the medieval chapter house whose remains lie 4ft under it.

The vast open spaces of the interior contain memorials to national heroes such as Wellington and Lawrence of Arabia. The statue of John Donne, metaphysical poet and former Dean of St Paul's, is often overlooked, but it's the only monument to have been saved from Old St Paul's. There are also more modern works, including a Henry Moore sculpture and temporary Arts Project displays of contemporary art. The Whispering Gallery, inside the dome, is reached by 259 steps from the main hall; the acoustics here are so good that a whisper can be bounced clearly to the other side of the dome. Steps continue up to first the Stone Gallery (119 tighter, steeper steps), with its high external balustrades, then outside to the Golden Gallery (152 steps), with its giddying views.

Before leaving St Paul's, head down to the maze-like crypt (through a door whose frame is decorated with skull and crossbones), which contains a shop and café and memorials to such dignitaries as Alexander Fleming, William Blake and Admiral Lord Nelson, whose grand tomb (purloined from Wolsey by Henry VIII but never used by him) is right beneath the centre of the dome. To one side is the small, plain tombstone of Christopher Wren himself, inscribed by his son with the epitaph, 'Reader, if you seek a monument, look around you'; at their request, Millais and Turner were buried near him.

Bread Street Kitchen.

EXPLORE

One New Change.

As well as tours of the main cathedral and self-guided audio tours (which are free), you can join special tours of the Triforium, visiting the library and Wren's 'Great Model', at 11.30am and 2pm Monday and Tuesday and at 2pm on Friday (pre-book on 7246 8357, £22 incl admission). *Photo p175.*

Restaurants

Bread Street Kitchen

One New Change, 10 Bread Street, EC4M 9AB (3030 4050, www.breadstreetkitchen.com). St Paul's tube. **Open** 7am-11pm Mon-Fri; 11.30am-11pm Sat; 11am-8pm Sun. **Main courses** £12.50-£35. **Map** p167 E5 ㉛ **Brasserie**

Part of the Gordon Ramsay Holdings stable, Bread Street Kitchen is set in the glitzy One New Change shopping centre, on the doorstep of St Paul's Cathedral. The space is vast – you can barely see from one end to the other – with floor-to-ceiling windows on one side, and a long open kitchen on the other. The menu is pretty huge too, with influences from Britain, Italy, the States and beyond. It's a fun place to eat, with friendly and focused staff, and mostly excellent cooking.

Sweetings

39 Queen Victoria Street, EC4N 4SA (7248 3062, www.sweetingsrestaurant.com). Mansion House tube. **Open** 11.30am-3pm Mon-Fri. **Main courses** £12.50-£35. **Map** p167 E5 ㉜ **Fish & seafood**

Things don't change much at this enduring City classic, and that's the way everyone likes it. The walls remain covered with photos of old sports teams, and many of the staff have been here for years. Lobster and crab bisques preface a choice of fish and seafood dishes that read and taste like upmarket versions of a pub-side stall – smoked fish, whitebait, smoked trout and so forth. Top-quality fish are then served fried, grilled or poached to order. The handful of more elaborate dishes includes a fish pie that bears witness to its well-practised makers.

Shops & services

One New Change

New Change Road, EC4M 9AF (7002 8900, www.onenewchange.com). Mansion House or St Paul's tube or Bank tube/DLR. **Open** varies; check website for opening hours of individual shops. **Map** p167 E4 ㉝ **Mall**

This sprawling Jean Nouvel-designed development is opposite the east end of St Paul's Cathedral, and features a warren of high-street retailers, office buildings and restaurants (Jamie Oliver's Barbecoa, Wahaca and Bread Street Kitchen – *see left* – among the latter). Nicknamed the 'stealth building' due to the structure's resemblance to a stealth bomber, the place is unsurprisingly popular with City workers on their lunchbreaks or on post-work spending sprees, but the cut-above chain stores are less of a pull than the unusual mid-height view of the cathedral and the Thames from the top floor.

NORTH TO SMITHFIELD

Barbican or St Paul's tube.

North of St Paul's Cathedral on Foster Lane is **St Vedast-alias-Foster** (7606 3998; open 8am-5.30pm Mon-Fri; 11am-4pm Sat), another finely proportioned Wren church, restored after World War II using spare trim from other churches in the area. Off nearby Aldersgate Street, peaceful **Postman's Park** contains the Watts Memorial to Heroic Sacrifice: a wall of ceramic plaques, each of which commemorates a heroic but doomed act of bravery. Most date to Victorian times – pantomime artiste Sarah Smith, for example, who received 'terrible injuries when attempting in her inflammable dress to extinguish the flames which had engulfed her companion (1863)' – but the first new plaque for 70 years was added in 2009. It was dedicated to 30-year-old Leigh Pitt, who died while saving a child from drowning.

Further west on Little Britain (named after the Duke of Brittany) is **St Bartholomew-the-Great** (*see p178*), founded along with **St Bartholomew's Hospital** in the 12th century. Popularly known as Bart's, the hospital treated air-raid casualties throughout World War II; shrapnel damage from German bombs is still visible on the exterior walls. Scottish nationalists now come here to lay flowers at the monument to William Wallace, executed in front of the church on the orders of Edward I in 1305.

Just beyond Bart's is the fine ironwork of **Smithfield Market**. The market – under almost constant threat of redevelopment, usually with associated promises to maintain historic façades – provides a colourful, not to say visceral, link to an age when the quality of British beef was a symbol of national virility and good humour. Meat has been traded here for a millennium; the current market, designed by Horace Jones, opened in 1868, though it's since been altered (in part out of necessity, thanks to World War II bombs). For now, the meat trucks start arriving around 11pm; early risers will find traders setting up stalls at first light.

The meat traders are joined at night these days by revellers settling in for dinner at vast **Smiths of Smithfield** (67-77 Charterhouse Street, EC1M 6HJ, 7251 7950, www.smithsof smithfield.co.uk) or taking to the dancefloor at the indefatigable superclub **Fabric** (*see p265*).

Sights & museums

FREE Museum of St Bartholomew's Hospital

St Bartholomew's Hospital, North Wing, West Smithfield, EC1A 7BE (3465 5798, www.barts health.nhs.uk). Barbican tube or Farringdon tube/rail. **Open** 10am-4pm Tue-Fri. **Admission** free; donations welcome. **Map** p166 D4 34

Be glad you're living in the 21st century. Many of the displays in this small museum inside St Bart's Hospital relate to the days before anaesthetics, when surgery and carpentry were kindred occupations. Every Friday at 2pm, visitors can take a guided tour of the museum that takes in the Hogarth paintings in the Great Hall, the little church of St Bartholomew-the-Less, neighbouring St Bartholomew-the-Great and Smithfield.

St Bartholomew-the-Great

West Smithfield, EC1A 9DS (7600 0440, www.greatstbarts.com). Barbican tube or Farringdon tube/rail. **Open** 8.30am-5pm Mon-Fri (until 4pm Nov-Feb); 10.30am-4pm Sat; 8.30am-8pm Sun. **Admission** £4; £3 reductions; £10 family; free under-7s. **Map** p166 D3 35

This atmospheric medieval church was built over the remains of the 12th-century priory hospital of St Bartholomew, founded by Prior Rahere, a former courtier of Henry I. The church was chopped about during Henry VIII's reign and the interior is now firmly Elizabethan, although it also contains donated works of modern art. You may recognise the main hall from *Shakespeare in Love* or *Four Weddings and a Funeral.*

► *If you need refreshment, the church has a bar-café in the 15th-century cloister, serving coffee, monastery beers and home-made weekday lunches.*

MUSEUM OF LONDON & THE BARBICAN

Barbican tube or Moorgate tube/rail.

From Bart's, the road known as London Wall runs east to Bishopsgate, following the approximate route of the old Roman walls. Tower blocks have sprung up here like daisies, but the odd lump of weathered stonework can still be seen poking up between the office blocks, marking the path of the old City wall. You can patrol the remaining stretches of the wall, with panels (some barely legible) pointing out highlights on a route of two miles. The walk starts near the brilliant **Museum of London** (*see p179*) and runs to the Tower of London.

The area north of London Wall was reduced to rubble by German bombs in World War II. In 1958, the City of London and London County Council clubbed together to buy the land for the construction of 'a genuine residential neighbourhood, with schools, shops, open spaces and amenities'. What Londoners got was the **Barbican**, a vast concrete estate of 2,000 flats that feels a bit like a university campus after the students have gone home. Casual visitors may get the eerie feeling they have been miniaturised and transported into a giant architect's model, but design enthusiasts will recognise the Barbican – with its landmark saw-toothed towers – as a prime example of 1970s Brutalism, softened a little by time and rectangular ponds of friendly resident ducks. Learn to love the place by taking one of the regular, 90-minute architectural tours of the complex (www.barbican.org.uk/education) – which will also help you to navigate its famously confusing layout.

Barbican.

Museum of London.

The main attraction here is the Barbican arts complex, with its library, cinema, theatre and concert hall – each reviewed in the appropriate chapters – plus an art gallery (*see below*) and the **Barbican Conservatory** (open 11am-5pm Sun), a steamy greenhouse full of tropical plants, exotic fish and twittering birds. Marooned amid the towers is the only pre-war building in the vicinity: the restored 16th-century church of **St Giles Cripplegate** (7638 1997, www.stgilescripplegate.com; open 11am-4pm Mon-Fri), where Oliver Cromwell was married and John Milton buried.

North-east of the Barbican on City Road are **John Wesley's House** (*see below*) and **Bunhill Fields**, the nonconformist cemetery where William Blake, the preacher John Bunyan and novelist Daniel Defoe are buried.

Sights & museums

Barbican Art Gallery

Barbican Centre, Silk Street, EC2Y 8DS (7638 8891, www.barbican.org.uk). Barbican tube or Moorgate tube/rail. **Open** 10am-6pm Mon-Wed, Sat; 10am-9pm Thur, Fri. **Admission** varies; check website for details. **Map** p167 E3 36

The art gallery on the third floor at the Barbican Centre isn't quite as 'out there' as it would like you to think, but the exhibitions on architecture, fashion, design and pop culture are usually pretty diverting, and accompanied by interesting events.

▶ *On the ground floor, the Curve is a long, thin gallery (yes, it's curved) that commissions free large-scale installations. They're often superb.*

FREE John Wesley's House & the Museum of Methodism

Wesley's Chapel, 49 City Road, EC1Y 1AU (7253 2262, www.wesleyschapel.org.uk). Moorgate or Old Street tube/rail. **Open** 10am-4pm Mon-Sat; after the service until 1.45pm Sun. *Tours* arrangements on arrival; groups of 6 or more phone ahead. **Admission** free; donations welcome. **Map** p167 F2 37

John Wesley (1703-91), the founder of Methodism, was a man of legendary self-discipline. You can see the minister's nightcap, preaching gown and personal experimental electric-shock machine on a tour of his austere home on City Road. The adjacent chapel has a small museum on the history of Methodism and fine memorials of dour, sideburn-sporting preachers. Downstairs (to the right) are some of the finest public toilets in London, built in 1899 with original fittings by Sir Thomas Crapper.

★ FREE Museum of London

150 London Wall, EC2Y 5HN (7001 9844, www.museumoflondon.org.uk). Barbican or St Paul's tube. **Open** 10am-6pm daily. **Admission** free; suggested donation £5. **Map Map** p167 E3 38

A five-year, £20m refurbishment came to completion in 2010 with the unveiling of a thrilling lower-ground-floor gallery that covers the city from 1666 to the present day. The new space features everything from an unexploded World War II bomb, suspended in a room where the understated and very moving testimony of ordinary Blitz survivors is screened, to clothes by the late Alexander McQueen. There are displays and brilliant interactives on poverty (an actual debtor's cell has been reconstructed, complete with graffiti), finance, shopping and 20th-century fashion, including a recreated Georgian pleasure garden, with mannequins that sport Philip Treacy masks and hats. Some displays are grand flourishes – the suspended installation that chatters London-related web trivia in the Sackler Hall, a printing press gushing changing news-sheets – others ingeniously solve problems: games to engage the kids, glass cases in the floors to maximise display space. The museum's biggest obstacle had always been its location: the entrance is two floors above street level, and hidden behind a dark and rather featureless brick wall. To solve this, a new space was created on the ground floor, allowing one key exhibit – the Lord Mayor's gold coach – to be seen from outside.

Upstairs, the social history of London is told in chronological displays that begin with 'London Before London', where artefacts include flint axes from 300,000 BC, found near Piccadilly, and the bones of an aurochs. 'Roman London' includes an impressive reconstructed dining room complete with mosaic floor. Windows overlook a sizeable fragment of the City wall, whose Roman foundations have clearly been built upon many times over the centuries. Sound effects and audio-visual displays illustrate the medieval, Elizabethan and Jacobean city, with particular focus on the plague and the Great Fire.

► *The museum has issued a number of excellent free apps, including Streetmuseum and Streetmuseum Londinium. They offer archive images and information about historic sites, geolocated to where you're standing.*

Restaurants

Dining options in the **Barbican** aren't inspiring, although the café-bar in the new Beech Street screens (*see p252*) is appealing. Otherwise, the **Chiswell Street Dining Rooms** (56 Chiswell Street, EC1Y 4SA, 7614 0177, www.chiswellstreetdining.com) is an upscale alternative nearby, or there are some cheap-and-cheerful places up Whitecross Street.

Fish Central

149-155 Central Street, EC1V 8AP (7253 4970, www.fishcentral.co.uk). Old Street tube/rail or bus 55. **Open** 11.30am-2.30pm, 5-10.30pm Mon-Thur; 11.30am-2.30pm, 5-11pm Fri; noon-10pm Sat. **Main courses** £5.95-£19.95. **Map** p167 E1 ㊴
Fish & chips

This long-standing, family-run restaurant still has fish and chips at its centre – despite serving treats such as oysters and lobster at smartly clothed tables in a bright, modern room. The quality is outstanding. Fish Central is slightly off the beaten track, in a shopping precinct, but it's handy not only for the Barbican but also LSO St Luke's (*see p281*).

Pubs & bars

Artillery Arms

102 Bunhill Row, EC1Y 8ND (7253 4683, www.artillery-arms.co.uk). Moorgate or Old Street tube/rail. **Open** noon-11pm Mon-Sat; noon-10.30pm Sun. *Food served* noon-3pm, 5-9pm Mon-Fri; noon-7pm Sat, Sun. **Map** p167 F2 ㊵

Close to the Barbican and opposite Bunhill Fields, this small tucked-away pub has an agreeably local feel, as post-work City folk mix easily with neighbourhood stalwarts at the bar. It has a slightly austere feel, but is an easy place to lose track of time, aided by the local vibe and the predictably fine Fuller's beers: easygoing Chiswick, toothsome London Pride and potent ESB.

Shops & services

★ F Flittner

86 Moorgate, EC2M 6SE (7606 4750, www.fflittner.com). Moorgate tube/rail. **Open** 8am-6pm Mon-Wed, Fri; 8am-6.30pm Thur. **Map** p167 F4 ㊶
Health & beauty

F Flittner.

In business since 1904, Flittner seems not to have noticed that the 21st century has begun. Hidden behind beautifully frosted doors (marked 'Saloon') is a simple, handsome room, done out with an array of classic barber's furniture that's older than your gran. Within these hushed confines, up to six black coat-clad barbers deliver straightforward haircuts (dry cuts £18-£20, wet cuts £25-£30) and shaves (£24 with hot towels).

BANK & AROUND

Mansion House tube or Bank tube/DLR.

Above Bank station, seven streets come together to mark the symbolic heart of the Square Mile, ringed by some of the most important buildings in the City. Constructed from Portland stone, the Bank of England, the Royal Exchange and Mansion House form a stirring monument to the power of money: most decisions about the British economy are still made within this small precinct. Few places in London have quite the same sense of pomp and circumstance.

Easily the most dramatic building is the **Bank of England**, founded in 1694 to fund William III's war against the French. It's a fortress, with no accessible windows and just one public entrance (leading to the **Bank of England Museum**; *see p182*). The outer walls were designed in 1788 by Sir John Soane, whose own museum can be seen in Holborn (*see p168* **Sir John Soane's Museum**). Millions have been stolen from its depots elsewhere in London, but the bank itself has never been robbed. Today, it's responsible for printing the nation's banknotes and setting the base interest rate. On the south side of the junction is the Lord Mayor of London's official residence, **Mansion House** (7626 2500, www.cityoflondon.gov.uk; tours run 2pm Tue, £7), an imposing neoclassical building constructed by George Dance in 1753. It's the only private residence in the country to have its own court and prison cells for unruly guests. Just behind Mansion House is the superbly elegant church of **St Stephen Walbrook** (7626 9000, www.ststephen walbrook.net; open 10am-4pm Mon-Fri), built by Wren in 1672. Its gleaming domed, coffered ceiling was borrowed from Wren's original design for St Paul's; other features include an incongruous modernist altar, sculpted by Sir Henry Moore and cruelly dubbed 'the camembert'. The Samaritans were founded here in the 1950s.

To the east of Mansion House is the **Royal Exchange**. It's the Parthenon-like former home of the London Stock Exchange, founded back in 1565 to facilitate the newly invented trade in stocks and shares with Antwerp. In 1972, the exchange shifted to offices on

Bank of England.

Threadneedle Street, thence to Paternoster Square in 2004; today, the Royal Exchange houses a posh champagne bar and some expensive fashion and gift shops. Flanking the Royal Exchange are statues of James Henry Greathead, who invented the machine that cut the tunnels for the London Underground, and Paul Reuter, who founded the Reuters news agency here in 1851.

The period grandeur is undermined by the monstrosity on the west side of the square, **No.1 Poultry**. The name fits: it's a turkey. A short walk down Queen Victoria Street is the most recent site of the Roman **Temple of Mithras** – discovered by accident in the 1950s, the little temple was a media sensation. Duly opened to the public, just a few scrubby courses of old brick remained, and no longer on the original site. Things have moved on since then: Museum of London Archaeology have been excavating the site, and a better restoration of the Temple will reopen in due course – back where it was found (for details, *see p317* **London under London**).

Further south, turn left on to Cannon Street, where – set into a wall behind a slightly fancy grille at no.111 – you can see the **London Stone**. Possibly a Roman milestone, mentioned by Shakespeare and William Blake, this rather boring lump of rock was first written of in 1188. One of its many legends insists that, should it be moved, the City will founder. In fact, it has already moved twice (1742, 1798), and was in 1962 put back in place when the current office replaced Blitz-damaged St Swithin's church.

Near Cannon Street Station, roughly opposite the London Stone, is the late Wren church of **St Michael Paternoster Royal** (7248 5202; open 9am-5pm Mon-Fri), the final resting place of Richard 'Dick' Whittington. Later transformed into a rags-to-riches pantomime hero, the real Dick Whittington was a wealthy merchant elected Lord Mayor of London four times between 1397 and 1420. The role of Dick Whittington's cat is less clear – many now believe that 'cat' was actually slang for a ship – but an excavation to find Whittington's tomb in 1949 did uncover a mummified medieval moggy. The happy pair are shown in the stained-glass windows.

Returning to Bank, stroll north along Prince's Street, beside the Bank of England's blind wall. Look right along Lothbury to find **St Margaret Lothbury** (7726 4878, www.stml.org.uk; open 7am-5.15pm Mon-Fri). The grand screen dividing the choir from the nave was designed by Wren himself; other works here by his favourite woodcarver, Grinling Gibbons, were recovered from various churches damaged in World War II. Lothbury also features a beautiful neo-Venetian building, now apartments, built by 19th-century architect Augustus Pugin, who worked with Charles Barry on the Houses of Parliament.

South-east of Bank on Lombard Street is Hawksmoor's striking, twin-spired church of **St Mary Woolnoth** (7626 9701; open 9.30am-4.30pm Mon-Fri), squeezed in between what were 17th-century banking houses. Only their gilded signboards now remain, a hanging heritage artfully maintained by the City's planners. The gilded grasshopper at 68 Lombard Street is the heraldic emblem of Sir Thomas Gresham, who founded the Royal Exchange and **Gresham College**.

Further east on Lombard Street is Wren's **St Edmund the King** (7621 1391, www.spiritualitycentre.org; open 10am-4pm Mon-Fri), which now houses a centre for modern spirituality. Other significant churches in the area include Wren's handsome red-brick **St Mary Abchurch**, off Abchurch Lane, and **St Clement**, on Clement's Lane, immortalised in the nursery rhyme 'Oranges and Lemons'. Over on Cornhill are two more Wren churches: **St Peter-upon-Cornhill**, mentioned by Dickens in *Our Mutual Friend*, and **St Michael Cornhill**, which contains a bizarre statue of a pelican feeding its young with pieces of its own body – a medieval symbol for the Eucharist, it was sculpted by someone who had plainly never seen a pelican.

North-west of the Bank of England is the **Guildhall**, the City of London headquarters. 'Guildhall' can either describe the original banqueting hall or the cluster of buildings around it, of which the **Guildhall Art Gallery**, the **Clockmakers' Museum & Library** (for all three, *see below*) and the church of **St Lawrence Jewry** (7600 9478, www.stlawrencejewry.org.uk; open 8am-5pm Mon-Fri), opposite the hall, are also open to the public. St Lawrence is another restored Wren, with an impressive gilt ceiling. Within, you can hear the renowned Klais organ at lunchtime organ recitals (usually from 1pm Tue).

Glance north along Wood Street to see the isolated tower of **St Alban**, built by Wren in 1685 but ruined in World War II and now an eccentric private home. At the end of the street is **St Anne & St Agnes**, laid out in the form of a Greek cross, and now home to a music charity.

Sights & museums

FREE Bank of England Museum

Entrance on Bartholomew Lane, EC2R 8AH (7601 5545, www.bankofengland.co.uk/museum). Bank tube/DLR. **Open** 10am-5pm Mon-Fri. **Admission** free. **Map** p167 F4 42

Housed inside the former Stock Offices of the Bank of England (there's a full-size recreation of Sir John Soane's Bank Stock Office from 1693), this surprisingly lively museum explores the history of the national bank. As well as ancient coins and original artwork for British banknotes, the museum offers a rare chance to lift nearly 30lbs of gold bar (you reach into a secure box, closely monitored by CCTV). After a three-month refurb in early 2014, the museum emerged with a new display of curious objects gathered from the vaults.

FREE Clockmakers' Museum & Guildhall Library

Aldermanbury, EC2V 7HH (Guildhall Library 7332 1868, www.clockmakers.org). St Paul's tube or Bank tube/DLR. **Open** 9.30am-4.45pm Mon-Sat. **Admission** free. **Map** p167 E4 43

Hundreds of clocks and watches are displayed in this single-room museum, from the egg-sized Elizabethan pocket watches to marine chronometers via a 'fuse for a nuclear device'. Highlights include Marine Chronometer H5, built by John Harrison (1693-1776) to solve the problem of longitude, and the plain Smith's Imperial wristwatch worn by Sir Edmund Hillary on the first (Rolex-sponsored) ascent of Everest. Just down the corridor, the library has books, manuscripts and prints relating to the history of London – original historic works can be requested for browsing (bring ID), but much of the archive is now at the London Metropolitan Archives in Clerkenwell (www.cityoflondon.gov.uk/lma).

FREE Guildhall

Gresham Street, EC2P 2EJ (7606 3030, www.guildhall.cityoflondon.gov.uk). St Paul's tube or Bank tube/DLR. **Open** *May-Sept* 10am-5pm

EXPLORE

Guildhall Art Gallery.

daily. *Oct-Apr* 10am-4.30pm Mon-Sat. Closes for functions; phone ahead. **Admission** free. **Map** p167 E4 44

The City of London and its progenitors have been holding grand ceremonial dinners in this hall for eight centuries. Memorials to national heroes line the walls, shields of the 100 livery companies grace the ceiling, and every Lord Mayor since 1189 gets a namecheck on the windows. Many famous trials have taken place here, including the treason trial of 16-year-old Lady Jane Grey, 'the nine days' queen', in 1553. Above the entrance to the Guildhall are statues of Gog and Magog. Born of the union of demons and exiled Roman princesses, these two mythical giants are said to protect the City. The current statues replaced 18th-century forebears that were destroyed in the Blitz.

★ FREE Guildhall Art Gallery

Guildhall Yard, off Gresham Street, EC2P 2EJ (7332 3700, www.guildhall-art-gallery.org.uk). St Paul's tube or Bank tube/DLR. **Open** 10am-5pm Mon-Sat; noon-4pm Sun. **Admission** free. *Temporary exhibitions* £5; £3 reductions; free under-16s. **Map** p167 E4 45

The City of London's gallery contains numerous dull portraits of royalty and long-gone mayors, but also some wonderful surprises, including a brilliant Constable, some suberbly camp Pre-Raphaelite works (Clytemnestra looks mighty riled) and a number of absorbing paintings of London, from moving depictions of war and melancholy working streets to the likes of the grandiloquent (and never-enacted) George Dance plan for a new London Bridge. The collection's centrepiece is the massive *Siege of Gibraltar* by John Copley, which spans two entire storeys of the purpose-built gallery. A sub-basement contains the scant remains of London's 6,000-seater Roman amphitheatre, built around AD 70; *Tron*-like figures and crowd sound effects give a quaint inkling of scale.

MONUMENT & THE TOWER OF LONDON

Aldgate, Monument or Tower Hill tube, Liverpool Street tube/rail, or Tower Gateway DLR.

From Bank, King William Street runs south-east towards London Bridge, passing the small square containing the **Monument** (*see p185*). South on Lower Thames Street is the moody-looking church of **St Magnus the Martyr** (*see p186*); nearby are several relics from the days when this area was a busy port, including the old Customs House and **Billingsgate Market**, London's main fish market until 1982 (when it was relocated to east London).

North of the Monument along Gracechurch Street is the atmospheric **Leadenhall Market**, constructed in 1881 by Horace Jones (who also built the market at Smithfield; *see p178*). The vaulted roof was restored to its original Victorian finery in 1991 and City workers come here in droves to lunch at the pubs, cafés and restaurants, including the historic Lamb Tavern. Fantasy fans may recognise the market as Diagon Alley in *Harry Potter & the Philosopher's Stone*.

Behind the market is Lord Rogers's high-tech **Lloyd's of London** building, constructed in 1986, with all its ducts, vents, stairwells and lift shafts on the outside, like an oil rig dumped in the heart of the City. Rogers has a new building – 122 Leadenhall (the **Cheesegrater**) – taking shape directly opposite, perhaps reaching completion in 2014. The original Lloyd's Register of Shipping, decorated with evocative bas-reliefs of sea monsters and nautical scenes, is on Fenchurch Street, where the next in the sequence of distinctive new City

IN THE KNOW
THE WRITE STUFF

In the shadow of the Gherkin, **St Andrew Undershaft** has a statue of John Stow, who wrote London's first guidebook, the *Survey of London* in 1598. In a ceremony every 5 April, the Lord Mayor places a new quill in the statue's hand; the old quill is given to the child who has written the best essay on London.

skyscrapers has emerged: Rafael Viñoly's 20 Fenchurch Street (www.20fenchurchstreet.co.uk), nicknamed the **Walkie Talkie** due to its distinctive top-heavy shape. South of Fenchurch Street, on Eastcheap (derived from the Old English *ceap* meaning 'barter'), is Wren's **St Margaret Pattens**, with an original 17th-century interior.

Several more of the City's tallest buildings are nearby. To the north, the ugly and rather dated **Tower 42** (25 Old Broad Street) was the tallest building in Britain until the construction of One Canada Square in Docklands in 1990. And topped out at 755 feet (including a radio mast), **Heron Tower** (110 Bishopsgate, www.herontower.com) became the City's tallest building at the end of 2009. Its 46 storeys include bar-restaurants, complete with outdoor terraces, and reached by an external, glass-sided lift. A rival, 945-foot monster called the **Pinnacle** has been begun on Bishopsgate – but is currently stalled. Also on Bishopsgate, behind Tower 42, is **Gibson Hall**, ostentatious former offices of the National Provincial Bank of England.

A block south, St Mary Axe is an insignificant street named after a vanished church that is said to have contained an axe used by Attila the Hun to behead English virgins. It is now known for Lord Foster's **30 St Mary Axe**, arguably London's finest modern building. The building is known as 'the Gherkin', for reasons that are obvious. On curved stone benches either side of 30 St Mary Axe are inscribed the 20 lines of Scottish poet Ian Hamilton Finlay's 'Arcadian Dream Garden', a curious counterpart to Lord Foster's building. Nearby are two medieval churches that survived the Great Fire: **St Helen's Bishopsgate** (*see p185*) and **St Andrew Undershaft** (*see above* **In the Know**).

The north end of St Mary Axe intersects with two interesting streets. The more northerly, Houndsditch, is where Londoners threw dead dogs and other rubbish in medieval times – the ditch ran outside the London Wall, dividing the City from the East End. The southerly one is Bevis Marks, home to the superbly preserved **Bevis Marks Synagogue** (7626 1274; open 10.30am-2pm Mon, Wed, Thur; 10.30am-1pm Tue, Fri; 10.30am-12.30pm Sun), founded in 1701 by Sephardic Jews fleeing the Spanish Inquisition. Services are still held in Portuguese as well as Hebrew. There's a kosher restaurant here too – Restaurant 1701 (7621 1701, www.restaurant1701.co.uk).

South along Bevis Marks are **St Botolph's-without-Aldgate** (*see p185*) and the tiny stone church of **St Katharine Cree** (7488 4318; open 9am-5pm Mon-Fri) on Leadenhall Street, one of only eight churches to survive the Great Fire. Inside is a memorial to Sir Nicholas Throckmorton, Queen Elizabeth I's ambassador to France, who was imprisoned for treason on numerous occasions, despite – or perhaps because of – his friendship with the temperamental queen.

Further south, towards the Tower of London, streets and alleys have evocative names: Crutched Friars, Savage Gardens, Pepys Street and the like. The famous diarist lived in nearby Seething Lane and observed the Great Fire of London from **All Hallows by the Tower** (*see p185*). Pepys is buried in the church of **St Olave** (www.sanctuaryinthecity.net) on Hart Street, nicknamed 'St Ghastly Grim' by Dickens due to the skulls above the entrance.

Monument.

Marking the eastern edge of the City, the **Tower of London** (*see p186*) was the palace of the medieval kings and queens of England. Home to the Crown Jewels and the Royal Armoury, it's one of Britain's best-loved tourist attractions and, accordingly, is mobbed by visitors seven days a week. Overlooking the Tower from the north, beside the tube station, **Trinity Square Gardens** are a humbling memorial to the tens of thousands of merchant seamen killed in the two World Wars, and across the road is a small square in which London's druids celebrate each spring equinox with an elaborate ceremony. Just beyond is one of the City's finest Edwardian buildings: the former **Port of London HQ** at 10 Trinity Square, with a huge neoclassical façade and gigantic statues symbolising Commerce, Navigation, Export, Produce and Father Thames. Work is underway to turn this into a luxury hotel. Next door is **Trinity House**, the home of the General Lighthouse Authority, founded by Henry VIII for the upkeep of shipping beacons along the river.

At the south-east corner of the Tower is **Tower Bridge** (*see p187*), built in 1894 and still London's most distinctive bridge. Used as a navigation aid by German bombers, it escaped the firestorm of the Blitz. East across Bridge Approach is **St Katharine Docks**, the first London docks to be formally closed. The restaurants around the marina, slightly hidden behind modern office blocks, offer more dignified dining than those around the Tower.

Sights & museums

FREE All Hallows by the Tower

Byward Street, EC3R 5BJ (7481 2928, www.ahbtt.org.uk). Tower Hill tube or Tower Gateway DLR. **Open** 9am-5pm Mon-Fri; 10am-5pm Sat, Sun. *Tours* phone for details; donation requested. **Admission** free; donations appreciated. **Map** p167 G6 46

Often described as London's oldest church, All Hallows is built on the foundations of a seventh-century Saxon church. Much of what survives today was reconstructed after World War II, but several Saxon details can be seen in the main hall, where the Knights Templar were tried by Edward II in 1314. The undercroft contains a museum with Roman and Saxon relics and a Crusader altar. William Penn, the founder of Pennsylvania, was baptised here in 1644.

★ Monument

Monument Street, EC3R 8AH (7626 2717, www.themonument.info). Monument tube. **Open** *Oct-Mar* 9.30am-5pm daily. *Apr-Sept* 9.30am-5.30pm daily. **Admission** £3; £1.50-£2 reductions; free under-5s. **Map** p167 F5 47

One of 17th-century London's most important landmarks, the Monument is a magnificent Portland stone column, topped by a landmark golden orb with more than 30,000 fiery leaves of gold – it looks decidedly like the head of a thistle. The Monument was designed by Sir Christopher Wren and his (often overlooked) associate Robert Hooke as a memorial to the Great Fire. The world's tallest free-standing stone column, it measures 202ft from the ground to the tip of its golden flames, exactly the distance east to Farriner's bakery in Pudding Lane, where the fire is supposed to have begun on 2 September 1666. The viewing platform is surrounded by a lightweight mesh cage, but the views are great – you have to walk 311 steps up the internal spiral staircase to enjoy them, though. At least everyone who makes it to the top gets a certificate.

FREE St Botolph's-without-Aldgate

Aldgate High Street, EC3N 1AB (7283 1670, www.stbotolphs.org.uk). Aldgate tube. **Open** 9am-3pm Mon-Fri. *Eucharist* 1.05pm Tue, Thur; 10.30am Sun. **Admission** free; donations appreciated. **Map** p167 H4 48

The oldest of three churches of St Botolph in the City, this handsome monument was built at the gates of Roman London as a homage to the patron saint of travellers. The building was reconstructed by George Dance in 1744 and a beautiful ornamental ceiling was added in the 19th century by John Francis Bentley, who also created Westminster Cathedral.

FREE St Ethelburga Centre for Reconciliation & Peace

78 Bishopsgate, EC2N 4AG (7496 1610, www.stethelburgas.org). Bank tube/DLR or Liverpool Street tube/rail. **Open** 11am-3pm Wed, Fri. **Admission** free; donations appreciated. **Map** p167 G4 49

Built around 1390, the tiny church of St Ethelburga was reduced to rubble by an IRA bomb in 1993 and rebuilt as a centre for peace and reconciliation. Behind the chapel is a Bedouin tent where events are held to promote dialogue between the faiths (phone or check the website for details), an increasingly heated issue in modern Britain.

FREE St Helen's Bishopsgate

Great St Helen's, off Bishopsgate, EC3A 6AT (7283 2231, www.st-helens.org.uk). Liverpool Street tube/rail or Bank tube/DLR. **Open** 9.30am-12.30pm Mon-Fri, afternoons by appointment only. **Admission** free. **Map** p167 G4 50

Founded in 1210, St Helen's Bishopsgate is actually two churches knocked into one, which explains its unusual shape. The church survived the Great Fire and the Blitz, but was partly wrecked by IRA bombs in 1992 and 1993. The hugely impressive 16th- and 17th-century memorials inside include the grave of Thomas Gresham, founder of the Royal Exchange (*see p181*).

FREE St Magnus the Martyr

Lower Thames Street, EC3R 6DN (7626 4481, www.stmagnusmartyr.org.uk). Monument tube. **Open** 10am-4pm Tue-Fri; 10am-1pm Sun. *Mass* 12.30pm Tue-Fri; 11am Sun. **Admission** free; donations appreciated. **Map** p167 F6 51

Downhill from the Monument, this looming Wren church marked the entrance to the original London Bridge. There's a scale model of the old bridge inside the church, and the porch has a timber from the original version. There's also a statue of axe-wielding St Magnus, the 12th-century Earl of Orkney. The church is mentioned at one of the climaxes of TS Eliot's *The Waste Land*: 'Where the walls/Of Magnus Martyr hold/Inexplicable splendour of Ionian white and gold.'

► *St Mary Woolnoth (see p182) is another star of* The Waste Land*: keeping 'the hours/With a dead sound on the final stroke of nine'.*

Tower Bridge Exhibition

Tower Bridge, SE1 2UP (7403 3761, www.towerbridge.org.uk). Tower Hill tube or Tower Gateway DLR. **Open** *Apr-Sept* 10am-6pm daily. *Oct-Mar* 9.30am-5.30pm daily. **Admission** £8; £3.40-£5.60 reductions; £12.50-£18 family; free under-5s. **Map** p167 H6 52

Opened in 1894, this is the 'London Bridge' that wasn't sold to America. Originally powered by steam, the drawbridge is now opened by electric rams when big ships need to venture upstream (check when the bridge is next due to be raised on the bridge's website or follow the Twitter feed). The bridge looks resplendent after a three-year restoration was completed in 2011. An entertaining exhibition on its history is displayed in the old steamrooms and the west walkway, which provides a crow's-nest view along the Thames.

★ Tower of London

Tower Hill, EC3N 4AB (0844 482 7777, www.hrp.org.uk). Tower Hill tube or Tower Gateway DLR. **Open** *Mar-Oct* 10am-5.30pm Mon, Sun; 9am-5.30pm Tue-Sat. *Nov-Feb* 10am-4.30pm Mon, Sun; 9am-4.30pm Tue-Sat. **Admission** £21.45; £10.75-£18.15; £57.20 family; free under-5s. **Map** p167 H6 53

If you haven't been to the Tower of London before, you should go now. Despite the exhausting crowds and long climbs up barely accessible, narrow stairways, this is one of Britain's finest historical attractions. Who would not be fascinated by a close-up look at the crown of Queen Victoria or the armour (and prodigious codpiece) of King Henry VIII? The buildings of the Tower span 900 years of – mostly violent – history, and the bastions and battlements house a series of interactive displays on the lives of British monarchs, and the often excruciatingly painful deaths of traitors. There's easily enough to do here to fill a whole day, which makes the steep entry price pretty good value, and it's worth joining one of the highly recommended and entertaining free tours led by the Yeoman Warders (or Beefeaters).

Make the Crown Jewels your first stop, and as early in the day as you possibly can: if you wait until you've pottered around a few other things the queues are usually immense. Beyond satisfyingly solid vault doors, you get to glide along a set of travelators (each branded with the Queen's official 'EIIR' badge) past such treasures of state as the Monarch's Sceptre, mounted with the Cullinan I diamond, and the Imperial State Crown, which is worn by the Queen each year for the opening of Parliament.

The other big draw is the Royal Armoury in the central White Tower, with its swords, armour, poleaxes, morning stars (spiky maces) and other gruesome tools for separating human beings from their body parts. Kids are entertained by swordsmanship games, coin-minting activities and even a child-sized longbow. The garderobes (medieval toilets) also seem to appeal.

Back outside, Tower Green – where executions of prisoners of noble birth were carried out (the last execution, of World War II German spy Joseph Jakobs, was in 1941) – is marked by a poem and a stiff glass

Tower of London.

EXPLORE

Sushisamba.

pillow, sculpted by poet and artist Brian Catling. Overlooking the green, Beauchamp Tower, dating from 1280, has an upper floor full of intriguing graffiti by the prisoners who were held here. The Tower only ceased functioning as a prison in 1952 and over the years counted figures as diverse as Anne Boleyn, Rudolf Hess and the Krays among its inmates.

Towards the entrance, the 13th-century Bloody Tower is another must-see that gets overwhelmed by numbers later in the day. The ground floor is a reconstruction of Sir Walter Raleigh's study, the upper floor details the fate of the Princes in the Tower. In the riverside wall is the unexpectedly beautiful Medieval Palace, with its reconstructed bedroom and throne room, and spectacularly complex stained glass in the private chapel. The whole palace is deliciously cool if you've been struggling round on a hot summer's day.

Restaurants

Perkin Reveller

The Wharf at the Tower of London, EC3N 4AB (3166 6949, www.perkinreveller.co.uk). Tower Hill tube or Tower Gateway tube/DLR. **Open** 10am-11pm Tue-Sat; 10am-5pm Sun. **Main courses** £13.50-£28. **Map** p167 H6 ⓹⓸ **Brasserie**

This white, minimal dining room is named after the cook's apprentice in Chaucer's *Canterbury Tales*, who preferred revelry to hard work. The reason? The location, on Tower Wharf, had its construction overseen by Chaucer. Food is a seasonal mix of classic British and Modern European dishes, plus breakfast and afternoon tea.

Sushisamba

Floors 38 & 39, Heron Tower, 110 Bishopsgate, EC2N 4AY (3640 7330, www.sushisamba.com). Liverpool Street tube/rail. **Open** 11.30am-midnight Mon-Fri; 11.30am-11pm Sunday. **Dishes** £8-£42. **Map** p167 G4 ⓹⓹ **Japanese/Brazilian/Peruvian**

Japan, Brazil and Peru come together here. That's not an eye-opener these days, but the entrance to this expensive New York import is. Take the glass elevator that clings to the side of Heron Tower, shoot up 38 floors in a few stomach-flipping seconds, then walk into a bar (close views of the Gherkin) and through to the double-height glasshouse of a restaurant. Here your table will likely face north across Spitalfields towards Alexandra Palace or east over Stepney and out to Essex. It's tough visual competition for the food, but the sushi does its damnedest to catch the eye with cloaks of red or green yuba (soybean curd skin).

▶ *On the 40th floor is Duck & Waffle (3640 7310, www.duckandwaffle.com), serving a menu of small plates. It's open 24 hours, every day.*

Pubs & bars

Draft House

14-15 Seething Lane, EC3N 4AX (7626 3360, www.drafthouse.co.uk). Tower Hill tube or Tower Gateway tube/DLR. **Open** 11am-11pm Mon-Wed; 11am-midnight Thur, Fri; 10am-midnight Sat. **Map** p167 G5 ⓹⓺

Pretty much the archetypal 'beer bars', the Draft House minichain focuses on serving a brilliant range of superb beers, simple but relaxed surroundings, and eats that don't travel far from the sausage/burger/ hot dog booze fodder axis. In addition to its handy location, this branch has a big screen for sporting events – which it shows with considerable verve. **Other central locations** 206-208 Tower Bridge Road, Borough, SE1 2UP (7378 9995); 43 Goodge Street, Fitzrovia, W1T 1TA (7323 9361).

Vertigo 42

Tower 42, 25 Old Broad Street, EC2N 1HQ (7877 7842, www.vertigo42.co.uk). Bank tube/DLR or Liverpool Street tube/rail. **Open** noon-4.30pm, 5-11pm Mon-Fri; 5-11pm Sat. **Map** p167 G4 ⓹⓻

Stretching out across the City, the views from this 42nd-floor bar are breathtaking. So, too, are the prices (house wine, £9.20 a glass). Food is tapas and small plates, while seating is arranged so everyone can enjoy the 360° panorama; for the privilege, you must book ahead, promise a minimum £10 spend and then undergo airport-style security.

IN THE KNOW
PRIVATE PROPERTY

If you'd like to see inside the City's most interesting buildings but are keen to avoid the queues at September's **Open House London** weekend (*see p39*), try the **City of London Festival** (*see p35*). There are special tours at Mansion House, Bank and St Paul's Cathedral.

EXPLORE

Camden

Some parts of London loom large in legend: Camden is one such. Everybody under a certain age who's spent any time in this city will have been to Camden Market – a crazy melée of more than 700 shops and stalls, with the Regent's Canal cutting through it. Despite the East End's recent dominance of art, fashion and culture, Camden clings on to some residual cool. Perhaps this is in part due to the late Amy Winehouse, presiding over the place like a tutelary deity; certainly plenty of energy is brought here by the legion of never-will-be bands that troop up looking for some rock'n'roll magic to rub off on them. Whatever the reasons, the ramshackle is still ahead of the gentrified by a short head. In contrast, to the west, is chichi and celeb-heavy Primrose Hill, where life seems slower and smarter amid the chic cafés and gastropubs. And in the northern reaches of Regent's Park is one of London's top attractions – London Zoo.

ZSL London Zoo.

Don't Miss

1 Camden Market Crazy clothes, music, crafts and much more (p194).

2 Jewish Museum Britain's Jewish heritage explored (p191).

3 ZSL London Zoo More than 600 species and a new Tiger Territory (p195).

4 Roundhouse Railway turntable shed turned performance venue (p190).

5 Regent's Park Acres of green, rose gardens and an open-air theatre (p195).

NEW ROCK
DARK SIDE
245

Regent's Canal.

CAMDEN TOWN

Camden Town tube or Camden Road rail.

Despite the pressures of gentrification, Camden refuses to leave behind its grungy history as the cradle of British rock music. Against a backdrop of social deprivation in Thatcher's Britain, venues such as the **Electric Ballroom** (184 Camden High Street – but seemingly always under threat of redevelopment) and **Dingwalls** (Middle Yard, Camden Lock, 7428 5929, www.dingwalls.com) provided a platform for musical rebels. By the 1990s, the Creation label was based in nearby Primrose Hill (*see p194*), unleashing My Bloody Valentine and the Jesus & Mary Chain on the world, before making it big with Oasis. The Gallagher brothers were often seen trading insults with Blur at the **Good Mixer** (30 Inverness Street, 7916 7929). The music still plays at Camden icon the **Roundhouse** (*see p271*) in the north, **Koko** (*see p270*) to the south, and any number of pubs and clubs between.

Before the Victorian expansion of London, this was no more than a watering stop on the highway to Hampstead, with two notorious taverns – the Mother Black Cap and Mother Red Cap (now the **World's End**, right opposite Camden Town tube) – frequented by highwaymen and brigands. After the gaps were filled in with terraced houses, the borough became a magnet for Irish and Greek railway workers, many of them working in the engine turning-house that is now the Roundhouse. The area's squalor had a powerful negative influence on the young Charles Dickens, who lived briefly on Bayham Street – you can see a blue plaque that commemorates his residence there.

From the 1960s, things started to pick up, helped by an influx of students, lured by low rents and the growing arts scene that nurtured punk, then indie, then Britpop – and now any number of short-lived indie-electro and alt-folk hybrids, whose young protagonists will all tell you with great fervour about the Camden they knew before it went upmarket.

Parts of Camden still have a rough quality, but the hardcore rebellion of the rock 'n' roll years has been replaced by a more laid-back carnival vibe, as young shoppers join the international parade of counterculture costumes. Tourists travel here in their thousands for the sprawling mayhem of **Camden Market** (*see p194*), which stretches north from the tube along boutique-lined Camden High Street and Chalk Farm Road.

But there are unmistakeable signs of gentrification: not least **Shaka Zulu** (Stables Market, Chalk Farm Road, 3376 9911, www.shaka-zulu.com), a hugely over-the-top Zulu-themed bar-restaurant, right beneath **Gilgamesh** (7428 4922, www.gilgameshbar.com), a hugely over-the-top Sumerian-themed bar-restaurant. Drop in to **Proud** (*see p267*) if you want to reset your cultural compass.

Cutting through the market is **Regent's Canal**, which opened in 1820 to provide a link between east and west London for horse-drawn narrowboats loaded with coal. Today, the canal is used by the jolly tour boats of the London Waterbus Company (7482 2660, www.londonwaterbus.com) and Walker's Quay (7485 4433, www.walkersquay.com), which run between Camden Lock and **Little Venice** in the warmer months. The canal towpath is a convenient walking route west to **Regent's Park** (*see p195*) and **ZSL London Zoo** (*see p195*), or east to Islington.

Camden's single avowed 'sight' is west of Camden Town – the excellent **Jewish Museum** (*see p191*) – but this remains a good bit of town for rough-and-ready gigs. As well as Koko and the Roundhouse, there are plenty of pub stages where this year's hopefuls try to get spotted: try the **Barfly** (*see p272*), **Underworld** (*see p275*) and the **Dublin Castle** (94 Parkway, 7485

1773), where Madness and, later, Blur were launched. The **Jazz Café** (*see p275*) and the **Blues Kitchen** (*see p274*) offer a different vibe.

Sights & museums

Jewish Museum

Raymond Burton House, 129-131 Albert Street, NW1 7NB (7284 7384, www.jewishmuseum.org.uk). Camden Town tube. **Open** 10am-5pm Mon-Thur, Sun; 10am-2pm Fri (10am-9pm Thur during temporary exhibitions). **Admission** £7.50; £3.50-£6.50 reductions; free under-5s. **Map** p191 C3 ❶

This museum is a brilliant exploration of Jewish life in Britain since 1066, combining fun interactives – you can wield the iron in a tailor's sweatshop, sniff chicken soup, pose for a wedding photo or take part in some Yiddish theatre – with serious history. There's a powerful Holocaust section, using the testimony of a single survivor, Leon Greenman, to bring tight focus to the unimaginable horror of it all. Opposite, a beautiful room of religious artefacts, including a 17th-century synagogue ark and centrepiece chandelier of Hanukkah lamps, does an elegant job of introducing Jewish ritual. Access is free to the downstairs café, located beside an ancient ritual bath, and to the shop.

Restaurants

Haché

24 Inverness Street, NW1 7HJ (7485 9100, www.hacheburgers.com). Camden Town tube. **Open** noon-10.30pm Mon-Wed; noon-11pm Thur-Sat; noon-10pm Sun. **Main courses** £6.95-£17.95. **Map** p191 B2 ❷ **Burgers**

If you can imagine a girly burger joint, Haché would be it. It's full of feminine French touches: from pretty vintage chandeliers to the creamy walls with ornate, oversized mirrors. In the open kitchen at the back, classic 'man food' is prettied up wherever possible. Thick-cut slices of onions are encased in huge balloons of batter, while frites are thin-cut, seasoned and skinny – and the upmarket burgers are decent too. If you want to be really metrosexual, ditch the bun entirely: staff will happily replace it with a green salad. Who said burger joints have to be butch?

Other locations 329 Fulham Road, Chelsea, SW10 9QL (7823 3515); 153 Clapham High Street, Clapham, SW4 7SS (7738 8760); 147 Curtain Road, Shoreditch, EC2A 3QE (7739 8396).

Made in Camden

Roundhouse, Chalk Farm Road, NW1 8EH (7424 8495, www.madeincamden.com). Chalk Farm tube. **Open** noon-2.30pm, 6-10.30pm

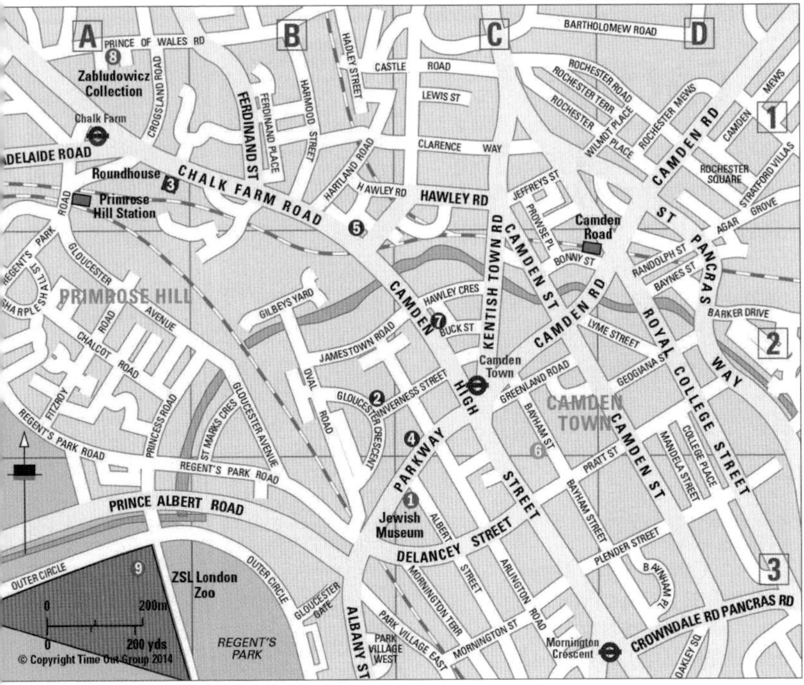

BrewDog.

Mon-Fri; 10.30am-3pm, 6-10.30pm Sat; 10.30am-3pm Sun. **Main courses** £8-£16.50. **Set lunch** (noon-3pm Tue-Sun) £11.95 3 courses. **Map** p191 A1 ❸ **Brasserie**
This bar and restaurant in the Roundhouse concert venue has won much applause. The kitchen is capable of excellent fusion cooking, with memorable plates such as fennel with feta, pistachios, salted caramel, lemon zest and dill. Once the concert-goers have taken their seats, noise diminishes and the red and wood-toned room transforms into a chilled spot well worth considering as an alternative to stand-alone restaurants.

Market

43 Parkway, NW1 7PN (7267 9700, www.marketrestaurant.co.uk). Camden Town tube. **Open** noon-2.30pm, 6-10.30pm Mon-Sat; 11am-3pm Sun. **Main courses** £13-£17. **Set lunch** (Mon-Sat) £10 2 courses. **Set dinner** (6-7pm) £17.50 2 courses. **Map** p191 C2 ❹ **British**
One of the best venues to eat in the area. 'Simple things, done well' is a phrase that could apply to the whole operation. The narrow space has been denuded back to its structural brick; specials are chalked on a blackboard. The proudly British and mainly meaty food is straightforward and effective too, like a spring starter of golden and mauve beetroot adorned simply with goat's cheese and pickled walnuts. You might move on to a signature pie – chicken and leek, say – or the 'modern British' modish standard of onglet and chips.

Porky's

18 Chalk Farm Road, NW1 8AG (7428 0998, www.porkys.co.uk). Camden Town tube. **Open** 5-10pm Mon-Thur; noon-11pm Fri; 9am-11pm Sat; 9am-10pm Sun. **Main courses** £5.95-£9.80. **Map** p191 B1 ❺ **Brasserie**
From Carolina 'cue' joints to rough-and-ready pop-ups, southern barbecue is all over London now. The vibe here is low-key and the service friendly, providing massive, full-flavoured portions at reasonable prices. Hog is the main attraction: tender, perfectly seasoned, 18-hour slow-cooked pulled pork, and plump, juicy wet ribs are the most popular dishes, but you'll also find spit-roast barbecue chicken, fried catfish and quinoa chilli, a polite nod to vegetarians. The corn and cheese hush puppies were the most sublime we've encountered outside the US, and the British and American craft beer menu is extensive.

Pubs & bars

The **Lock Tavern** and **Proud** (for both, *see p267*) are excellent Camden DJ bars, while the **Blues Kitchen** (*see p274*) and scuzzy indie-den the **Dublin Castle** (94 Parkway, NW1 7AN, 7485 1773) supply live music.

BrewDog

113 Bayham Street, Camden, NW1 0AG (7284 4626, www.brewdog.com). Camden Town tube or Camden Road rail. **Open** noon-11.30pm Mon-Thur; noon-midnight Fri, Sat; noon-10.30pm Sun. **Map** p191 C2 ❻
The Scottish craft brewery's Camden outpost is an initiation into the exciting and groundbreaking world of craft beer, but never feels intimidating. The list features BrewDog's beers on keg draught (with occasional guests). Fridges hold a selection from other microbreweries, mainly from the US.

EXPLORE

Camden Market.

Other locations 51-55 Bethnal Green Road, Shoreditch, E1 6LA (7729 8476); 15-19 Goldhawk Road, Shepherd's Bush, W12 8QQ (8749 8094).

Shops & services

Camden Market

Camden Lock *Camden Lock Place, off Chalk Farm Road, NW1 8AF (7485 7963, www.camdenlockmarket.com).* **Open** 10am-6pm daily. Note: there are fewer stalls Mon-Fri.
Camden Lock Village *east of Chalk Farm Road, NW1 (www.camdenlock.net).* **Open** 10am-6pm daily.
Camden Market *Camden High Street, at Buck Street, NW1 (www.camdenmarkets.org).* **Open** 10am-5.30pm Thur-Sun.
Inverness Street Market *Inverness Street, NW1 (www.camdenlock.net/inverness).* **Open** 8.30am-5pm daily.
Stables Market *off Chalk Farm Road, opposite Hartland Road, NW1 8AH (7485 5511, www.stablesmarket.com).* **Open** 10.30am-6pm Mon-Fri (reduced stalls); 10am-6pm Sat, Sun.
All *Camden Town or Chalk Farm tube.*
Map p191 C2 ❼ **Market**

Camden Market actually refers to the microcosm of markets that make up the northern Camden Town area – more than 700 shops and stalls in all. The Camden Market is the place for neon sunglasses and pseudo-witty slogan garments. Almost next door, and perennially threatened by proposed tube station expansions, is the listed building the Electric Ballroom, which sells vinyl and CDs on weekends and is also a music venue. The Inverness Street Market opposite sells similar garb to the Camden Market as well as a diminishing supply of fruit and veg. North, next to the railway bridge, is Camden Lock, with stalls selling crafts, home furnishings, jewellery, toys and gifts – head into the West Yard for global food. There are further crafty doodahs, fashion and nibbles in the Camden Lock Village, which runs along the towpath.
► *From Camden Lock Village, it's a pleasant half-hour walk east then south on the Regent's Canal to Granary Square (see p157), passing the sweet little Camley Street Natural Park (www.wildlondon.org.uk) on the opposite bank.*

AROUND CAMDEN

Primrose Hill, to the west of Camden, is just as attractive as the celebrities who frequent the gastropubs and quaint cafés along **Regent's Park Road** and **Gloucester Avenue**. It's all rather spacious and slow-moving after the crowds in Camden proper. Favourite hangouts on Regent's Park Road include the long-established **Primrose Pâtisserie** (no.136, 7722 7848) and upmarket Greek bistro **Lemonia** (no.89, 7586 7454). For a gastropub feed, head to Gloucester Avenue: both the **Engineer** (no.65, 7483 1890) and **Lansdowne** (no.90, 7483 0409) are here. On a clear day, the walk up the hill is a delight.

Sights & museums

FREE Zabludowicz Collection

176 Prince of Wales Road, Chalk Farm, NW5 3PT (7428 8940, www.zabludowiczcollection.com). Chalk Farm tube or Kentish Town West rail.
Open noon-6pm Thur-Sun. **Admission** free.
Map p191 A1 ❽

This former Methodist chapel – a remarkable neo-classical building that makes a superb setting for art exhibitions – holds three shows a year, enabling artists to create experimental new work and curators to build exhibitions around the Collection's global emerging art in all media.

REGENT'S PARK

Baker Street or Regent's Park tube.

Regent's Park (open 5am-dusk daily) is one of London's most delightful open spaces. Originally a hunting ground for Henry VIII, it remained a royals-only retreat long after it was formally designed by John Nash in 1811; only in 1845 did it open to the public. Attractions run from the animal noises and odours of **ZSL London Zoo** (*see below*) to the enchanting **Open Air Theatre** (*see p286*); rowing boat hire, beautiful rose gardens, ice-cream stands and the **Garden Café** (7935 5729, www.companyofcooks.com) complete the postcard-pretty picture. West of Regent's Park rises the golden dome of the **London Central Mosque** (www.iccuk.org); exit to the south and you're in Marylebone (*see p107*).

IN THE KNOW
CROWD CONTROL

Camden Market's crowds can be awful at the weekends – which, since you're coming for atmosphere, means it's also the best time to visit. So recuperate after the madness by slipping out of the markets sideways on to the canal, then strolling five minutes west into sedate **Primrose Hill** (*see p194*), the perfect place to reassess your purchases – with wonderful views south over London.

Sights & museums

★ ZSL London Zoo
Regent's Park, NW1 4RY (0844 225 1826, www.zsl.org/london-zoo). Baker Street or Camden Town tube then bus 274, C2. **Open** times vary; check website for details. **Admission** £21-£26; £15.50-£23.40 reductions; free under-3s. **Map** p191 A3 ❾

London Zoo has been open in one form or another since 1826. Spread over 36 acres and containing more than 600 species, it cares for many of the endangered variety – part of the entry price (pretty steep at £26 in peak season) goes towards the ZSL's projects around the world. Regular events include 'animals in action' and keeper talks. Exhibits are entertaining: look out, for example, for the re-creation of a kitchen overrun with large cockroaches. The latest big attraction (opened in 2013) is Tiger Territory, where Sumatran tigers can be watched through floor-to-ceiling windows. The relaunched 'Rainforest Life' biodome and the 'Meet the Monkeys' attractions allow visitors to walk through enclosures that recreate the natural habitat of, respectively, tree anteaters and sloths, and black-capped Bolivian squirrel monkeys, while personal encounters of the avian kind can be had in the Victorian Blackburn Pavilion – as well as at Penguin Beach, where you can watch the black-and-white favourites swim underwater. 'Gorilla Kingdom' is another highlight, as are the snakes and crocs in the reptile house. Bring a picnic and you could easily spend the day here.

Regent's Park.

East End

Read the fashion blogs, and it's hard to believe how recently the East End was notorious for its slums and cursed with the smelliest and most unpleasant industries. Jack the Ripper stalked through Whitechapel; the presence of the docks – the sanitised remains of which can be enjoyably explored at Wapping and Limehouse – later attracted some of the most brutal bombing during the Blitz. How things change. The East End now comprises much of what is most vibrant about London: Spitalfields and Brick Lane, Shoreditch and Hoxton are all now must-visits.

A word about geography: the boundaries of the East End are notoriously difficult to pin down. One neat definition would include everything east of the City from the Thames in the south, north all the way through Hackney, and everything east as far as the River Lea. For ease of navigation, we've gathered just the focal areas in this chapter. For more of east London (including Dalston), *see pp234-242*.

White Lyan.

Don't Miss

1 Geffrye Museum Charming domestic interiors museum, celebrating a double centenary in 2014 (p205).

2 House of Hackney Fashion-forward Shoreditch store (p208).

3 Broadway Market Shop and people-watch in the heart of Hackney (p210).

4 White Lyan Cocktail pioneer (p207).

5 Columbia Road Market Sunday flower power (p210).

WHISTLES
A.GOLD.
A.GOL
Traditional Foods of Britain

Spitalfields Market.

SPITALFIELDS

Aldgate East tube or Liverpool Street tube/rail.

Approach this area from Liverpool Street Station, up Brushfield Street, and you'll know you're on the right track when the magnificent spiky spire of **Christ Church Spitalfields** (*see right*) comes into view. The area's other signature sight, **Spitalfields Market**, has emerged from redevelopment and the market stalls have moved back underneath the vaulted Victorian roof of the original building.

Outside, along Brushfield Street, the shops might look as if they're from Dickens's day, but most are recent inventions: the charming grocery shop **A Gold** (no.42, 7247 2487) was lovingly restored in the noughties; the owners of the **English Restaurant** (nos.50-52, 7247 4110) put reclaimed wood panelling and creaky furniture into an empty shell; and the deli **Verde & Co** (no.40, 7247 1924) was opened by its owner, author Jeanette Winterson, inspired by the local food shops she found in – whisper it – France. This tendency will, after Mayor Boris Johnson overruled the council's objections, be made literal by the redevelopment of the **Fruit & Wool Exchange**, built in 1920 – only the façade will remain of a building that sheltered as many as 10,000 East Enders from the Blitz, and still bears graffiti from those days. Settle any anxieties about gentrification by heading a few streets south: on Sundays, the salt-of-the-earth **Petticoat Lane Market** hawks knickers and cheap electronics around Middlesex Street.

A block north of Spitalfields Market is **Dennis Severs' House** (*see right*), while across from the market, on the east side of Commercial Street and in the shadow of Christ Church, the **Ten Bells** (84 Commercial Street, 0753 049 2986) is where one of Jack the Ripper's victims drank her last gin. On the next corner, Sandra Esqulant's **Golden Heart** pub (no.110, 7247 2158) has hosted every Young British Artist of note, ever since the day Gilbert & George decided to pop in on their new local. The streets between here and Brick Lane to the east are dourly impressive, lined with tall, shuttered Huguenot houses; **19 Princelet Street** (www.19princeletstreet.org.uk) is open to the public a few times a year. This unrestored 18th-century house was home first to French silk merchants and later to Polish Jews who built a synagogue in the garden.

Sights & museums

FREE Christ Church Spitalfields

Commercial Street, E1 6QE (7859 3035, www.christchurchspitalfields.org). Liverpool Street tube/rail or Shoreditch High Street rail. **Open** 10am-4pm Tue; 1-4pm Sun. **Admission** free. **Map** p200 C4 ❶

Built in 1729 by architect Nicholas Hawksmoor, this splendid church has in recent years been restored to its original state (tasteless alterations had been made to the building following a lightning strike in the 19th century). Most tourists get no further than cowering before the wonderfully overbearing spire, but the revived interior is impressive too, its pristine whiteness in marked contrast to its architect's dark reputation. The formidable 1735 Richard Bridge organ is almost as old as the church. Regular concerts are held here, notably during the two annual Spitalfields festivals (*see p33*).

★ Dennis Severs' House

18 Folgate Street, E1 6BX (7247 4013, www.dennissevershouse.co.uk). Liverpool Street tube/rail or Shoreditch High Street rail. **Open** 6-9pm Mon, Wed; noon-4pm Sun; noon-2pm 1st & 3rd Mon of the mth. **Admission** £10 Sun; £7 noon-2pm Mon; £14 Mon evenings. **Map** p200 C4 ❷

The ten rooms of this original Huguenot house have been decked out to recreate vivid snapshots of daily life in Spitalfields between 1724 and 1914. A tour through the compelling 'still-life drama', as American creator Dennis Severs dubbed it, takes you through the cellar, kitchen, dining room, smoking room and upstairs to the bedrooms. With hearth and candles burning, smells lingering and objects scattered apparently haphazardly, it feels as though the inhabitants have deserted the building only moments before you arrived.

Restaurants

Poppies

6-8 Hanbury Street, E1 6QR (7247 0892, www.poppiesfishandchips.co.uk). Liverpool Street tube/rail or Shoreditch High Street rail.

Meals served 11am-11pm Mon-Sat; 11am-10.30pm Sun. **Main courses** £10.90-£15.90. **Map** p200 D4 ❸ **Fish & chips**

Poppies' pick and mix assortment of shiny British kitsch – including a jukebox, mini red telephone box and a monochrome photo of heart-throb Cliff Richard – makes it look like a simulation of a fish and chip shop. The food on the plate is also better than the real thing, and offered grilled as well as fried. Extending beyond the staples of cod and haddock, the menu encompasses mackerel, seafood platters and jellied eels. The bill, however, gives the game away – Poppies is a cut above. It's spawned a second branch in Camden: not suprising, since this is as good as fish and chips gets.

Other location 30 Hawley Crescent, Camden, NW1 8NP (7267 0440).

Rosa's

12 Hanbury Street, E1 6QR (7247 1093, www.rosaslondon.com). Liverpool Street tube/rail. **Meals served** noon-10.30pm Mon-Thur, Sun; noon-11pm Fri, Sat. **Main courses** £7.50-£16.50. **Map** p200 C4 ❹ **Thai**

The original branch of Rosa's plays host to a vibrant young crowd of visiting tourists and local hipsters. The dining room is clean and contemporary, and the usual Thai repertoire is executed well: stir-fried slices of European aubergine coated in a sweet, salty soya and yellow bean sauce, and laced with plenty of ginger and black pepper, or a salad of chargrilled beef strips in chilli dressing. Service is mostly quick and efficient.

Other locations 48 Dean Street, Soho, W1D 5BF (7494 1638); 23 Ganton Street, Soho, W1F 9BW (7287 9617); 1st floor, Westfield Stratford City, E15 1AA.

Pubs & bars

Commercial Tavern

142 Commercial Street, E1 6NU (7247 1888). Liverpool Street tube/rail or Shoreditch High Street rail. **Open** 5-11pm Mon-Thur; 2-11pm Fri; noon-11pm Sat, Sun. **Map** p200 C4 ❺

The inspired chaos of retro-eccentric decor and warm, inclusive atmosphere make this landmark flat-iron corner pub very likeable. It seems to have escaped the attentions of the necking-it-after-work masses, perhaps because of the absence of wall-to-wall lager pumps in favour of some proper real ale. The bar is made up of colourful art deco tiles, and there's a decorative playfulness throughout; it's a great example of how a historic pub can be lit up with new life.

▶ *Just down the street, the fabulous, ever-busy Golden Heart (no.110, E1 6LZ, 7247 2158) is a famous nursery for East End artists.*

Mayor of Scaredy Cat Town

12-16 Artillery Lane, E1 7LS (7078 9639, www.themayorofscaredycattown.com). Liverpool Street tube/rail or Shoreditch High Street rail. **Open** 5pm-midnight Mon-Thur; noon-midnight Fri, Sat; noon-10.30pm Sun. **Map** p200 C4 ❻

Part of the trend for 'secret' speakeasies, this one is a basement bar beneath Breakfast Club. The entrance

Rosa's.

EXPLORE

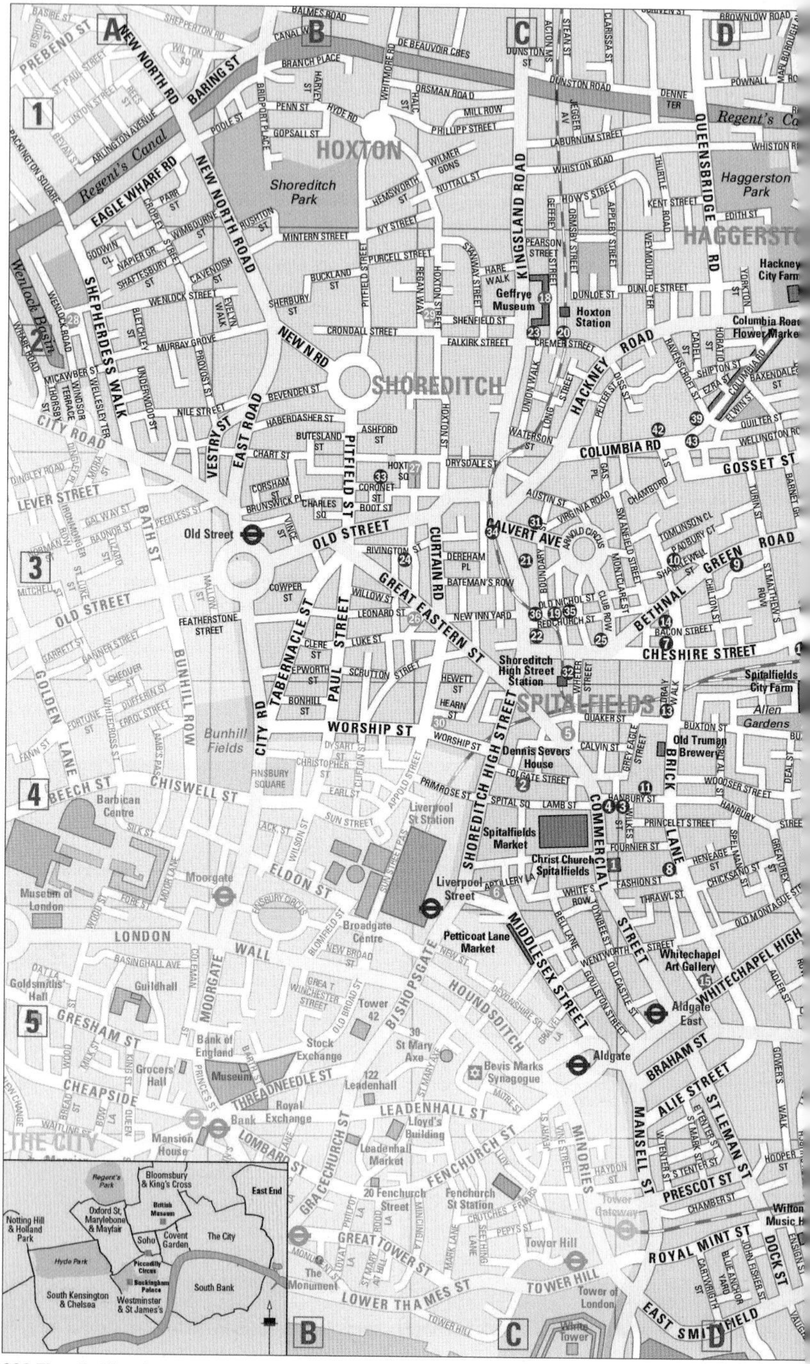

A
B
C
D
1
2
3
4
5
HOXTON
SHOREDITCH
HAGGERSTON
SPITALFIELDS
THE CITY
Regent's Canal
Wenlock Basin
Shoreditch Park
Haggerston Park
Hackney City Farm
Columbia Road Flower Market
Geffrye Museum
Hoxton Station
Old Street
Shoreditch High Street Station
Spitalfields City Farm
Allen Gardens
Old Truman Brewery
Dennis Severs' House
Spitalfields Market
Christ Church Spitalfields
Liverpool St Station
Liverpool Street
Petticoat Lane Market
Whitechapel Art Gallery
Aldgate East
Aldgate
Bevis Marks Synagogue
30 St Mary Axe
Tower 42
Broadgate Centre
Bunhill Fields
Barbican Centre
Museum of London
Moorgate
Guildhall
Goldsmiths' Hall
Bank of England
Museum
Stock Exchange
Grocers' Hall
Royal Exchange
Bank
Mansion House
122 Leadenhall
Lloyd's Building
Leadenhall Market
20 Fenchurch Street
Fenchurch St Station
Tower Gateway
Tower Hill
Tower of London
White Tower
The Monument
Monument
Wilton's Music Hall
NEW NORTH RD
NEW NORTH ROAD
BARING ST
KINGSLAND ROAD
QUEENSBRIDGE RD
HACKNEY ROAD
COLUMBIA RD
GOSSET ST
OLD STREET
CITY ROAD
CITY RD
EAST ROAD
VESTRY ST
PITFIELD ST
CURTAIN RD
GREAT EASTERN ST
SHOREDITCH HIGH STREET
BETHNAL GREEN ROAD
CHESHIRE STREET
BRICK LANE
COMMERCIAL STREET
WORSHIP ST
TABERNACLE ST
PAUL STREET
BUNHILL ROW
CHISWELL ST
BEECH ST
GOLDEN LANE
LONDON WALL
MOORGATE
GRESHAM ST
CHEAPSIDE
THREADNEEDLE ST
LEADENHALL ST
LOMBARD ST
GRACECHURCH ST
FENCHURCH ST
BISHOPSGATE
HOUNDSDITCH
MIDDLESEX STREET
MINORIES
MANSELL ST
ALIE STREET
ST LEMAN ST
PRESCOT ST
ROYAL MINT ST
DOCK ST
EAST SMITHFIELD
TOWER HILL
LOWER THAMES ST
GREAT TOWER ST
WHITECHAPEL HIGH ST
BRAHAM ST
SHEPHERDESS WALK
EAGLE WHARF RD
Regent's Park
Bloomsbury & King's Cross
East End
Oxford St, Marylebone & Mayfair
British Museum
Notting Hill & Holland Park
Soho
Covent Garden
The City
Hyde Park
Piccadilly Circus
Buckingham Palace
South Bank
South Kensington & Chelsea
Westminster & St James's

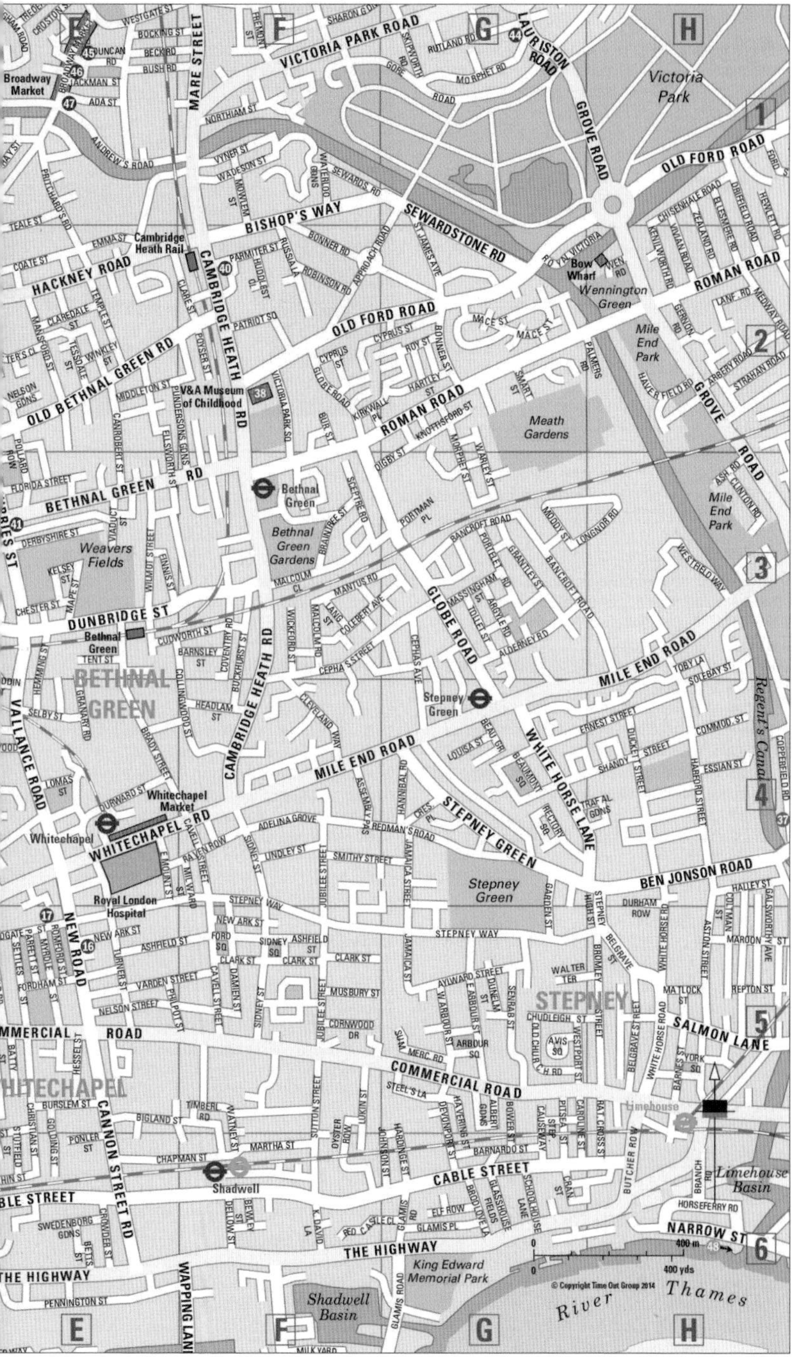

E
F
G
H
1
2
3
4
5
6
Victoria Park
Broadway Market
Cambridge Heath Rail
Bow Wharf
Wennington Green
Mile End Park
Meath Gardens
V&A Museum of Childhood
Bethnal Green
Bethnal Green Gardens
Weavers Fields
BETHNAL GREEN
Whitechapel Market
Whitechapel
Royal London Hospital
Stepney Green
STEPNEY
WHITECHAPEL
Shadwell
Limehouse
Limehouse Basin
King Edward Memorial Park
Shadwell Basin
River Thames
Regent's Canal
VICTORIA PARK ROAD
LAURISTON ROAD
GROVE ROAD
OLD FORD ROAD
MARE STREET
BISHOP'S WAY
SEWARDSTONE RD
HACKNEY ROAD
CAMBRIDGE HEATH RD
OLD BETHNAL GREEN RD
ROMAN ROAD
BETHNAL GREEN RD
DUNBRIDGE ST
GLOBE ROAD
MILE END ROAD
VALLANCE ROAD
WHITECHAPEL RD
STEPNEY GREEN
WHITE HORSE LANE
BEN JONSON ROAD
NEW ROAD
COMMERCIAL ROAD
SALMON LANE
CANNON STREET RD
CABLE STREET
THE HIGHWAY
NARROW ST
WAPPING LANE
STEPNEY WAY
400 m
400 yds
© Copyright Time Out Group 2014

EXPLORE

is the one that looks like a big Smeg fridge door. Venture inside and you'll find a quirky, dimly lit cocktail bar clad in exposed brick and wood: it's all a bit like a cabin from *Twin Peaks*. The drinks menu makes an amusing mockery of more self-conscious 'underground' venues. The cocktails, consisting of classics and house specials, are well crafted on the whole.

BRICK LANE

Aldgate East tube.

Join the crowds flowing east from Spitalfields Market along Hanbury Street at the weekend, and the direction you turn at the end determines which Brick Lane you see. Turn right and you'll know you're in 'Banglatown', the name adopted by the ward back in 2002: until you hit the bland modern offices beside the kitsch Banglatown arch, it's almost all Bangladeshi cafés, curry houses, grocery stores, money transfer services and sari shops – plus the **Pride of Spitalfields** (3 Heneage Street, 7247 8933), an old-style East End boozer serving ale to all-comers.

Despite the street's global reputation for Indian food, most of the food on offer in the street is disappointing, but nearby there are some good restaurants: try **Needoo Grill** or **Tayyabs** (for both, *see p205*). Alternatively, opt for Bengali sweets from the **Madhubon Sweet Centre** at no.42.

Between Fournier Street and Princelet Street, **Jamme Masjid Mosque** is a key symbol of Brick Lane's hybridity. It began as a Huguenot chapel, became a synagogue and was converted, in 1976, into a mosque – in other words, immigrant communities have been layering their experiences on this street at least since 1572, when the St Bartholomew's Day Massacre forced many French Huguenots into exile.

The newest layer is boho gentrification. On Sunday, there's the lively street market, complemented by the trendier UpMarket and Backyard Market (for arts and crafts), both held in the **Old Truman Brewery** (nos.91-95). Pedestrianised Dray Walk, full of hip independent businesses, is crowded every day. Heading north on Brick Lane, you'll find bars, cafés and vintage fashion shops.

Restaurants

★ Brick Lane Beigel Bake

159 Brick Lane, E1 6SB (7729 0616). Shoreditch High Street rail. **Open** 24hrs daily. **Bagels** £1.95-£5.95. **No credit cards.** **Map** p200 D3 ❼ **Jewish**

This little East End institution rolls out perfect bagels (egg, cream cheese, salt beef, at seriously low prices), good bread and moreish cakes. Even at 3am, fresh-baked goods are pulled from the ovens at the back; no wonder the queue for bagels trails out the door when the local bars and clubs close. Note that it's essentially a takeaway operation.

Brick Lane Beigel Bake.

Chez Elles

45 Brick Lane, E1 6PU (7247 9699, www.chezellesbistroquet.co.uk). Aldgate East tube or Shoreditch High Street rail. **Open** 6.30-10.30pm Tue; noon-3pm, 6.30-10.30pm Wed-Sat; 11am-5pm Sun. **Main courses** £12.50-£16.50. **Map** p200 D4 ❽ **Bistro**

Chez Elles narrowly misses being a parody of itself, saved by fantastic cooking and an unexpected location – somehow, the cutesy Parisian hipster vibe grates far less on Brick Lane than it would elsewhere. There's coffee and own-made cakes at a counter propping up (French) regulars, and a disarming, heavily accented welcome. The menu is beyond reproach: smoky, spicy, peppery charcuterie with lots of bread; soft, nutty snails swimming in garlic butter; and a seriously good, tearingly tender bavette steak with triple-fried chips.

Lady Dinah's Cat Emporium

152-154 Bethnal Green Road, E2 6DG (7729 0953, http://ladydinahs.com). Shoreditch High Street rail. **Open/main courses** check website for details. **Map** p201 E3 ❾ **Café**

A Taiwanese concept popularised in Tokyo, the cat café is finally arriving in London. Moggy-lover Lauren Pears crowdfunded £108,000 through IndieGoGo to provide urbanites with cats to pet while they enjoy tea and cakes, simultaneously giving lonely pussies a loving, comfortable home.

Shops & services

Bernstock Speirs

234 Brick Lane, E2 7EB (7739 7385, www.bernstockspeirs.com). Shoreditch High Street rail. **Open** 10am-6pm Mon-Fri; 11am-5pm Sat, Sun. **Map** p200 D3 ❿ **Accessories**

EXPLORE

Paul Bernstock and Thelma Speirs's unconventional hats for men and women have a loyal following, being both wearable and fashion-forward. Past ranges have included collaborations with Peter Jensen and Emma Cook.

Blitz

55-59 Hanbury Street, E1 5JP (7377 0730, www.blitzlondon.co.uk). Shoreditch High Street rail. **Open** 11am-7pm Mon-Wed; 11am-8pm Thur-Sat; 11am-7pm Sun. **Map** p200 D4 ⓫ **Fashion**

Blitz puts the other vintage shops in the capital to shame. This is a vintage department store, covering all floors of a glorious old furniture factory. The building itself is jaw-dropping, and has been renovated beautifully by the Blitz team. There's a furniture selection from Broadway Market's the Dog & Wardrobe, an accessories floor, a book collection and rails and rails of neatly presented fashion. Buyers Jan Skinners and John Howlin look to nearby Brick Lane for inspiration, which means the selection is all killer and no filler – and cleaned, steamed and folded before it hits the shop floor.

► *Although overshadowed by Blitz, Beyond Retro (112 Cheshire Street, E2 6EJ, 7613 3636, www.beyondretro.com) is worth a rummage. It's off the north end of Brick Lane.*

Comfort Station

22 Cheshire Street, E2 6EH (7033 9099, www.comfortstation.co.uk). Liverpool Street tube/rail or Shoreditch High Street rail. **Open** 11am-6pm Tue-Sun. **Map** p200 D3 ⓬ **Accessories**

Fine art graduate and designer Amy Anderson is the creative talent behind this ladylike Cheshire Street boutique. Offbeat touches, such as birds painted on the door and a piano-turned-display cabinet, provide the ideal environment to showcase her handmade accessories. Alongside the beautiful, ethically made bags and bone-china crockery covered in wonderfully weird collaged prints is her jewellery line. The collection changes each season, with classically elegant but original designs in gold, silver, cord, wood and onyx. Favourites include 'Sliced Poetry' range (delicate leaf-shaped 'books' that fan open to reveal pages of Victorian poetry), and Anderson's 'Globe' pendants – moveable silver rings that form a clever 3D sphere.

★ Rough Trade East

Dray Walk, Old Truman Brewery, 91 Brick Lane, E1 6QL (7392 7788, www.roughtrade.com). Shoreditch High Street rail. **Open** 8am-9pm Mon-Thur; 8am-8pm Fri; 10am-8pm Sat; 11am-7pm Sun. **Map** p200 D4 ⓭ **Books & music**

Indie music label Rough Trade's 5,000sq ft record store, café and gig space offers a dizzying range of vinyl and CDs, spanning punk, indie, dub, soul, electronica and more. With 16 listening posts and a stage for live sets, this is close to musical nirvana. **Other location** 130 Talbot Road, Notting Hill, W11 1JA (7229 8541).

Vintage Emporium

14 Bacon Street, E1 6LF (7739 0799, www.vintageemporiumcafe.com). Shoreditch High Street rail. **Open** *Shop* 11am-7pm Mon-Fri; 10am-7pm Sat, Sun. *Café* 11am-10pm Mon-Fri; 10am-10pm Sat, Sun. **Map** p200 D3 ⓮ **Fashion**

With a well-edited range of clothing (in the basement) from the Victorian era to the 1950s, this café-shop's vintage time frame is somewhat tighter than that of its nearby rivals, but maybe all the better for it. Beautiful lace blouses, 1950s dresses, a great selection of hats, and top-notch accessories are all for sale, and, considering the age of most of the items, prices are high – but reasonable.

WHITECHAPEL

Aldgate East or Whitechapel tube.

Not one of London's prettier thoroughfares, busy but anonymous Whitechapel Road sets the tone for this area. One bright spot is **Whitechapel Gallery** (*see p204*), west from the foot of Brick Lane, while a little to the east, the **Whitechapel Bell Foundry** (nos.32 & 34, 7247 2599, www.whitechapelbellfoundry.co.uk) continues to manufacture bells, as it has since 1420. It famously produced Philadelphia's Liberty Bell and 'Big Ben'. To join one of the fascinating Saturday tours you'll have to reserve a place (usually well in advance).

At Whitechapel's foremost place of worship, it isn't bells but a muezzin that summons the faithful each Friday: the **East London**

Vintage Emporium.

Mosque, founded elsewhere in 1910 and now the focal point for the largest Muslim community in Britain, can accommodate 10,000 worshippers. Behind is Fieldgate Street and the dark mass of **Tower House**, a former doss house whose 700 rooms have, inevitably, been redeveloped into flats. This 'sought after converted warehouse building' was a dismal – but decidedly cheaper – proposition when Joseph Stalin and George Orwell (researching his book *Down and Out in Paris and London*) kipped here for pennies. The red-brick alleys give a flavour of what Victorian Whitechapel must have been like.

East again is the frontage of the Royal London Hospital – the hospital itself is now in that monstrous blue towerblock – and behind it, in a small crypt on Newark Street, the **Royal London Hospital Archives & Museum** (7377 7608, closed Mon, Sat & Sun). Inside are reproduction letters from Jack the Ripper (including the notorious missive 'From Hell', delivered with an enclosed portion of human kidney) and information on Joseph Merrick, the 'Elephant Man', rescued by Royal London surgeon Sir Frederick Treves. Behind the hospital is the high-tech **Centre of the Cell** (4 Newark Street, 7882 2562, www.centreofthecell.org, term time only), which gives visitors a lively, interactive insight into cell biology in a purpose-built pod, suspended over labs investigating cancer and tuberculosis.

Sights & museums

★ FREE Whitechapel Gallery

77-82 Whitechapel High Street, E1 7QX (7522 7888, www.whitechapelgallery.org). Aldgate East tube. **Open** 11am-6pm Tue-Sun. **Admission** free. *Temporary exhibitions* vary. **Map** p200 D5 ⑮

This East End stalwart reopened in 2009, following a major redesign that saw the Grade II-listed building expand into the similarly historic former library next door – rather brilliantly, the architects left the two buildings stylistically distinct rather than trying to smooth out their differences. As well as nearly tripling its exhibition space, the Whitechapel gave itself a research centre and archives, plus a café/bar. It looks set to improve a stellar reputation as a contemporary art pioneer built on shows of Picasso – *Guernica* was shown here in 1939 – Jackson Pollock, Mark Rothko and Frida Kahlo. With no permanent collection, there's a rolling programme of temporary shows, but an increasing number of artists have contributed permanently to the fabric of the building: most recently Rachel Whiteread added a lovely frieze with gold vine leaves to a space on the front of the gallery.

Tayyabs.

Restaurants

Needoo Grill

87 New Road, E1 1HH (7247 0648, www.needoo grill.co.uk). Whitechapel tube. **Open** noon-11.30pm daily. **Main courses** £5-£14. **Map** p201 E5 ⑯ **Pakistani**

This squashed space doesn't suffer from the same problem of endless queues as its rival Tayyabs (*see below*), though you will usually have a wait, but it is just as gaudy. Bright red walls, leather benches and blaring flatscreen TVs are the order of the day, yet with curries this good, the decor just fades into the background. What you get are succulent karahi dishes and specials that include nihari (lamb on the bone) and a very passable biriani. Service is swift and friendly, and it's hard to argue with the appeal of BYOB and curries of such high standard.

Tayyabs

83 Fieldgate Street, E1 1JU (7247 9543, www.tayyabs.co.uk). Aldgate East or Whitechapel tube. **Open** noon-11.30pm daily. **Main courses** £5-£13. **Map** p201 E5 ⑰ **Pakistani**

Tayyabs is a full-on, hectic, loud, in-and-out sort of place, and if you come here without booking, expect to wait up to an hour for a table. But we recommend this Punjabi stalwart because of the cheapness and unreserved boldness of the food. Fiery grilled lamb chops are a must. The rest of the menu is all about rich dals and masala channa; unctuous, slow-cooked lamb curries; and good versions of North Indian staples – spice-rubbed tikka, hot, buttery breads and juicy kebabs. The corkage-free BYO policy doesn't do its popularity any harm either.

SHOREDITCH & HOXTON

Old Street tube/rail, or Hoxton or Shoreditch High Street rail.

The story is familiar: in the 1980s, impecunious artists moved into the derelict warehouses in the triangle formed by Old Street, Shoreditch High Street and Great Eastern Street, and quickly turned it into the place to be. Rising rents have since driven many of the artists further east, but they've been replaced by the tech-hip denizens of 'silicon roundabout'. The area around Old Street roundabout has become a focus for digital start-ups, the beginning of Prime Minister David Cameron's **East London Tech City** (www.techcityuk.com).

Nightlife permeates the area (linking conveniently to Brick Lane), with centres on Curtain Road, the lower end of Kingsland Road and around Hoxton Square. But the nature of the scene has changed dramatically: growing up in some people's eyes, losing its edge for others. New hotels and smart shops are opening, and there's commercial culture of a different type to come, following the discovery of the remains of the Curtain Theatre behind a pub on Plough Yard, south of Great Eastern Street. The Curtain, which opened in 1577, is intimately connected to Shakespeare's early career, probably hosting the première of *Romeo and Juliet*. Plans for the site – a 250-seat outdoor auditorium (managed by the people at the Globe) and a Shakespeare museum – are under way.

At present, apart from seemingly countless galleries – Wharf Road neighbours (**Parasol Unit**, no.14, N1 7RW, 7490 7373, www.parasol-unit.org; **Victoria Miro**, no.16, N1 7RW, 7336 8109, www.victoria-miro.com) and not-for-profit pioneer **Raven Row** (56 Artillery Lane, E1 7LS, 7377 4300, www.ravenrow.org) are notable – the area's sole bona fide tourist attraction is the exquisite **Geffrye Museum** (*see below*), a short walk north up Kingsland Road. The surrounding area is dense with good, cheap Vietnamese restaurants (try **Sông Quê**; *see p206*).

To the east, it's a short walk to **Columbia Road flower market** (*see p210*).

Sights & museums

★ FREE Geffrye Museum

136 Kingsland Road, E2 8EA (7739 9893, www.geffrye-museum.org.uk). Hoxton rail. **Open** 10am-5pm Tue-Sun. *Almshouse tours* 1st Sat, 1st & 3rd Tue, Wed of mth. **Admission** free; donations appreciated. *Almshouse tours* £2.50; free under-16s. **Map** p200 C2 ⑱

Housed in a set of 18th-century almshouses, the Geffrye Museum offers a vivid physical history of the English interior. Displaying original furniture, paintings, textiles and decorative arts, the museum recreates a sequence of typical middle-class living rooms from 1600 to the present. It's an oddly interesting way to take in domestic history, with any number of intriguing details to catch your eye – from a bell jar of stuffed birds to a particular decorative flourish on a chair. There's an airy restaurant overlooking the lovely gardens, which include a walled plot for herbs and a chronological series in different historical styles. *Photo p206.*

IN THE KNOW DOUBLE BUBBLY

In 2014 the **Geffrye** (*see above*) celebrates a special anniversary – or rather two. It is 300 years since these charming brick buildings were founded as almshouses, and 100 years since those almshouses reopened as a museum. Celebratory events will run all year: www.geffrye-museum.org.uk/whatson/centenary-celebrations.

EXPLORE

Restaurants

Albion

2-4 Boundary Street, E2 7DD (7729 1051, www.albioncaff.co.uk). Shoreditch High Street rail. **Open** 8am-11pm Mon-Sat; 8am-10pm Sun. **Main courses** £8-£14. **Map** p200 C3 ⓳ **British**

Albion may describe itself as a 'caff', but no greasy spoon in London was ever designed and owned by Terence Conran. But in spirit, at least, it is something approaching a café for 21st-century Shoreditch – a place where locals can drop in for a casual breakfast, lunch or dinner, or a cup of tea and a slice of cake. Menu descriptions suggest dishes wouldn't seem out of place in your average caff too – ham and mustard sandwich, devilled kidneys, sausage and mash, fish and chips. They're all prepared with top-quality ingredients, great care and an eye for presentation. A new branch, Albion NEO (*see p57*), has opened near Tate Modern, and there's a swanky hotel upstairs (*see p361* **Boundary**).

Beagle

397-400 Geffrye Street, E2 8HZ (7613 2967, www.beaglelondon.co.uk). Hoxton rail. **Open** *Bar* 4pm-midnight Mon, Tue; noon-midnight Wed-Fri; 11am-midnight Sat; 11am-10.30pm Sun. *Restaurant* 6-10pm Tue; noon-3pm, 6-10pm Wed-Fri; 11am-3pm, 6-10pm Sat; 11am-5pm Sun. **Main courses** £13.50-£18. **Map** p200 C2 ⓴ **British**

Beagle is a smart café, bar and restaurant in the railway arches below Hoxton station.There's a bar, serving sophisticated cocktails, leading into a dining area with open kitchen. A back-to-basics British ethos governs the food. Grilled cuttlefish comes with new potatoes and a salsa-like coriander pesto. Pigeon terrine, made in-house, is well textured and has a slightly gamey flavour. Beagle deserves success for making E2 a culinary destination beyond the area's famous budget Vietnamese cafés.

★ Hoi Polloi

Ace Hotel, 100 Shoreditch High Street, E1 6JQ (8880 6100, www.hoi-polloi.co.uk). Shoreditch High Street rail. **Open** 7am-midnight Mon-Wed, Sun; 7am-1am Thur-Sat. **Main courses** £14-£18. **Map** p200 C3 ㉑ **Brasserie**

You enter this restaurant via the tiny flower shop of the Ace Hotel (*see p361*), to find yourself amid retro and contemporary styling that wouldn't look out of place on a 1950s Scandinavian cruise ship. The casual and sneaker-clad service is notably smooth and well informed. The music (a mix of retro '80s pop and US alt electronic) isn't too loud, allowing attention to focus on conversation – and the food. Covering breakfast, lunch, snacks, cocktails and dinner, the dishes are British, seasonal and juxtapose flavours in modern but not outlandish ways that leave you craving more. The small bar is a destination in itself, with cocktails that bear silly names but appealing combinations of modish spirits.

Geffrye Museum. *See p205.*

Pizza East

56 Shoreditch High Street, E1 6JJ (7729 1888, www.pizzaeast.com). Shoreditch High Street rail. **Open** noon-midnight Mon-Wed; noon-1am Thur; noon-2am Fri; 10am-2am Sat; 10am-midnight Sun. **Main courses** £8-£17. **Map** p200 C3 ㉒ **Pizza**

The huge warehouse space features sharing benches, industrial decor and more bare brick and concrete than your average multistorey car park. It's busy, noisy and dark. The regularly changing menu, however, remains inventive and original. Pizza bases are crusty around the outside and thin and gorgeously saturated in the middle, and toppings employ fresh, quality ingredients. Antipasti and salads are also good.

Other locations 310 Portobello Road, Ladbroke Grove, W10 5TA (8969 4500); 53-79 Highgate Road, Kentish Town, NW5 1TL (3310 2000).

Sông Quê

134 Kingsland Road, E2 8DY (7613 3222). Hoxton rail. **Open** noon-3pm, 5.30-11pm Mon-Fri; noon-11pm Sat; noon-10.30pm Sun. **Main courses** £4.80-£14.80. **Map** p200 C2 ㉓ **Vietnamese**

This is still the undoubted star of the Kingsland Road Vietnamese scene. Big, light, buzzy (if slightly resembling a school canteen), Sông Quê is constantly packed with customers including many families and a good showing of Vietnamese locals. Flavours are full and true, and textures perfect, bringing the best out of each dish. Fans claim the kitchen makes the best pho in London. It's very handy for the Geffrye Museum (*see p205*).

EXPLORE

Tramshed

32 Rivington Street, EC2A 3LX (7749 0478, www.chickenandsteak.co.uk). Old Street tube/rail or Shoreditch High Street rail. **Open** 11.30am-11pm Mon-Tue; 11.30am-midnight Wed-Sat; 11.30am-9.30pm Sun. **Main courses** £13.50-£32.50. **Map** p200 B3 ㉔ **British**

Mark Hix's chicken and steak restaurant serves steaks, roast chicken for one or to share (it can stretch to three, especially if accompanied by seasonal sides such as wild garlic mushrooms), along with chicken salad and steak salad. All this happens in a turn-of-the-century Grade II-listed industrial building, a vast room with a soaring ceiling. In pride of place is a work by Damien Hirst: a formaldehyde-filled tank containing a bullock and a rooster.

► *The Cock and Bull Gallery downstairs exhibits work by emerging young artists (1-6.30pm daily).*

Les Trois Garçons

1 Club Row, E1 6JX (7613 1924, www.lestroisgarcons.com). Shoreditch High Street rail. **Open** 6-9.30pm Mon-Wed; noon-2.30pm, 6-9.30pm Thur; noon-2.30pm, 6-10.30pm Fri; 6-10.30pm Sat. **Main courses** £15-£32.50. **Map** p200 C3 ㉕ **French**

London's most OTT restaurant interior gives the eye no idea where to settle. Inside this former pub is an entire zoo of stuffed, ceramic and other animals, cascading glass, dangling handbags, giant, unearthly purple flowers and more – all to sustain the mood of ironic, decadent opulence. Les Trois Garçons buzzes at night, when hip crowds come to enjoy inventive modern French cuisine. The 3G mini-empire also includes the equally louche Loungelover Bar next door and, most recently, Maison Trois Garçons 'lifestyle café' (*see p208*) in nearby Redchurch Street.

Pubs & bars

Late-night **Charlie Wright's International Bar** (*see p276*) is as much about drinking as it is about music, and there's music, food and booze at Concrete, beneath **Pizza East** (*see p206*).

Book Club

100-106 Leonard Street, EC2A 4RH (7684 8618, www.wearetbc.com). Old Street tube/rail or Shoreditch High Street rail. **Open** 8am-midnight Mon-Wed; 8am-2am Thur, Fri; 10am-2am Sat; 10am-midnight Sun. **Admission** *Club* free-£12. **Map** p200 B3 ㉖

Behind the sedate name is one of the most consistently creative cocktail bars in London. You could visit for the drinks alone: cocktails come with names like Don't Go To Dalston. Or – and this is what sets Book Club apart – you could visit for the packed timetable of events, which includes bands, DJs, ping-pong tournaments, life drawing and classic video-game nights. The young and laid-back crowd that packs into the spacious artwork-dotted space are here for a bit of everything.

Happiness Forgets

8-9 Hoxton Square, N1 6NU (7613 0325, www.happinessforgets.com). Old Street tube/rail or Shoreditch High Street rail. **Open** 5.30-11pm Mon-Sat; 6pm-11pm Sun. **Map** p200 B3 ㉗

From the moment you walk in, staff here know how to make you happy. The short list of original cocktails is unfailingly good: lots of nice twists on classic ideas but never departing from the essential cocktail principles of balance, harmony and drinkability. Star turns: Mr McRae, Perfect Storm and Tokyo Collins. But the classics are brilliantly handled too, and the food is fabulous, as is the service. This very special place is not very large and plenty of people know about it, so booking is a good idea.

★ Wenlock Arms

26 Wenlock Road, N1 7TA (7608 3406, www.wenlockarms.com). Old Street tube/rail. **Open** noon-midnight Mon-Thur, Sun; noon-1am Fri, Sat. **Map** p200 A2 ㉘

On an unremarkable backstreet, this old pub was the tap for a nearby brewery, and poured its first pint in 1836; it closed with its parent brewery in the 1960s, then reopened in 1994, whereupon it won awards for the quality of its real ale and plaudits for the toastiness of its real fire. In 2010 threats of redevelopment began, but a sympathetic Hackney Council included it in a conservation area and in 2011 new owners stepped in: cue quality paintjob, new furniture and even more beer fonts. Now the Wenlock is again the quintessence of all that is good about pubs – minimal decor, minimal food (salt beef sandwiches, own-made scratchings) and a great range of ace beer.

★ White Lyan

153 Hoxton Street, N1 6PJ (3011 1153, www.whitelyan.com). Hoxton rail. **Open** 6pm-1am Mon-Wed, Sun; 6pm-2am Thur; 6am-3am Fri, Sat. **Map** p200 C2 ㉙

Comparing White Lyan to your local boozer is like comparing Heston Blumenthal's Fat Duck to a greasy spoon. This former pub doesn't give much away from the outside, but it's a genuine pioneer in a new cocktail movement. It doesn't use ice, nor citrus, sugar, fruit or other perishables, and next to no branded products. You can't order off menu, and there's only one of each colour of wine and one lager. Big fridges hold the pre-made products of hours of labour by cocktailian Ryan Chetiyawardana and his team. Spirits are especially made to order, or refined and 'rebuilt' using filtered water and distillations. All this, unsurprisingly, results in unusual – and amazing – cocktails.

Worship Street Whistling Shop

63 Worship Street, EC2A 2DU (7247 0015, www.whistlingshop.com). Old Street tube/rail. **Open** 5pm-midnight Mon-Wed; 5pm-1am Thur; 5pm-2am Fri, Sat. **Map** p200 C4 ㉚

This cellar cocktail bar is decked out in what seems to be a speakeasy/Victorian mash-up (dark wood and lots of eccentric decorative touches). It makes much of its experimental techniques; if your curiosity is tickled by the sound of 'enzymes, acids, proteins and hydrocolloids', you're all set. The list is mercifully short, and classics are well handled. There's an extensive selection of spirits, including their own barrel-aged ones. Staff are skilled, friendly and eager to please.

Shops & services

Once a shabby cut-through, **Redchurch Street** has become a strong contender for London's most interesting shopping street, starting with Aesop and Sunspel (*see right*) at one end, then a parade including Hostem, Maison Trois Garçons and Labour & Wait (*see right*).

Ally Capellino

9 Calvert Avenue, E2 7JP (7033 7843, www.allycapellino.co.uk). Shoreditch High Street rail. **Open** 11am-6pm Tue-Sat; 11am-5pm Sun. **Map** p200 C3 ㉛ **Accessories**

This shop stocks the full range of Ally Capellino's stylishly understated unisex leather and waxed cotton bags, satchels, wallets, purses and laptop cases. Prices start at around £40 for a cute leather coin purse, rising to over £600 for larger, more structured models. There's a second branch in Notting Hill (312 Portobello Road, W10 5RU, 8964 1022).

▶ *While you're on Calvert Avenue, check out the homewares and accessories by the collective of young artisans at Luna & Curious (nos.24-26, 3222 0034, www.lunaandcurious.com).*

Boxpark

2-4 Bethnal Green Road, E1 6GY (7033 9441, www.boxpark.co.uk). Shoreditch High Street rail. **Open** 11am-7pm Mon-Wed, Fri, Sat; 11am-8pm Thur; noon-6pm Sun. **Map** p200 C3 ㉜ **Mall**

Refitted shipping containers plonked underneath the elevated Shoreditch High Street Overground station make up this contemporary 'shopping mall'. Installed in 2011, the units of Boxpark are full of high-street labels (Puma, Nike), but also contain an impressive array of independents, cafés and pop-ups.

▶ *Food stalls here open from 8am (10am Sun).*

IN THE KNOW HEAR HERE

Victoria Park (*see p210*) is a real East London asset, and it has an extraordinary history. Did you know, for instance, there are chunks of the 1831 London Bridge lying in the park? All is revealed on a free audio tour, put together by an oral historian; it can be downloaded from www.memoryscape.org.uk.

Other Memoryscape tours cover the Royal Docks, Greenwich and Hampton Court Palace.

Goodhood Store

41 Coronet Street, N1 6HD (7729 3600, www.goodhood.co.uk). Old Street tube/rail. **Open** 11am-6.30pm Mon-Sat; noon-5pm Sun. **Map** p200 B3 ㉝ **Fashion**

A first stop for East End trendies, Goodhood is owned by streetwear obsessives Kyle and Jo. Japanese independent labels are well represented, while other covetable brands include Pendleton, Norse Projects and Wood Wood.

★ House of Hackney

131 Shoreditch High Street, E1 6JE (7739 3901, www.houseofhackney.com). Old Street tube/rail or Shoreditch High Street rail. **Open** 10am-7.30pm Mon-Sat; 11am-5pm Sun. **Map** p200 C3 ㉞ **Homewares**

House of Hackney has the makings of a new Liberty: buy your future design classics now, we say. This is one of the most gorgeous retail establishments to land in London in years – bedecked in the deliberately over-the-top juxtapositions of print-on-print-on-print that have made the brand's name, and with the entrance full of flowers. Upstairs you'll find rolls of gorgeous paper, fabric, trays, mugs, fashion and collaborative designs with brands like Puma; downstairs are generously proportioned sofas and plump armchairs in more-is-more combinations of print and texture.

★ Labour & Wait

85 Redchurch Street, E2 7DJ (7729 6253, www.labourandwait.co.uk). Shoreditch High Street rail. **Open** 11am-6pm Tue-Sun. **Map** p200 C3 ㉟ **Homewares**

This retro-stylish store, on London's ultra-trendy Redchurch Street, sells the sort of things everybody would have had in their kitchen or pantry 60 years ago: functional domestic goods that have a timeless style. For the kitchen there are some great simple classics such as enamel milk pans in retro pastels, and lovely 1950s-inspired Japanese teapots, and you can garden beautifully with ash-handled trowels. Vintage Welsh wool blankets, classic toiletries, and some great old-fashioned gifts, such as a pinhole camera kit and a lovely range of handmade notebooks from Portugal, make it hard to leave empty-handed. Labour & Wait also has a space at concept store Dover Street Market (*see p120*).

Sunspel

7 Redchurch Street, E2 7DJ (7739 9729, www.sunspel.com). Shoreditch High Street rail. **Open** 11am-7pm Mon-Sat; noon-5pm Sun. **Map** p200 C3 ㊱ **Fashion**

EXPLORE

Labour & Wait.

It may look like a trendy east London newcomer, but Sunspel is actually a classic British label, which has been producing quality menswear for over 150 years. It even claims to have introduced boxer shorts to the UK. This corner space showcases the range of underwear, T-shirts, merino wool knitwear and polo shirts, as well as the smaller line of equally pared-down womenswear.
Other locations 13-15 Chiltern Street, Marylebone, W1U 7PG (7009 0650); 21 Jermyn Street, St James's, SW1Y 6HP (7434 0974); 40 Old Compton Street, Soho, W1D 4TU (7734 4491).

BETHNAL GREEN

Bethnal Green tube/rail, Cambridge Heath rail, or Mile End tube.

Once a gracious suburb of spacious townhouses, by the mid 19th century Bethnal Green was one of the city's poorest neighbourhoods. As in neighbouring Hoxton, a recent upturn in fortunes has in part been occasioned by Bethnal Green's adoption as home by a new generation of artists, attracted by the low rents resulting from the area's long-standing misfortunes. The **Maureen Paley** gallery in Herald Street (no.21) remains the key venue, but the new Bethnal Green is typified by places such as **Herald Street** (no.2), just down the road, and the arrival of the ambitious **Town Hall Hotel** (*see p361*) and its restaurants, Viajante and **Corner Room** (*see p210*). Take a seat at **E Pellicci** (*see p210*), the exemplary traditional London caff, for a taste of the old Bethnal Green.

The **V&A Museum of Childhood** (*see right*) is close to Bethnal Green tube station, but the area's other main attraction is a bit of a walk away (almost in Shoreditch). Nonetheless, a visit to the weekly **Columbia Road flower market** (*see p210*) is a lovely way to fritter away a Sunday morning. A microcosmic retail community has grown up around the market: **Treacle** (nos.110-112, 7729 0538) for groovy crockery and cupcakes; **Angela Flanders** (no.96, 7739 7555) for perfume; **Marcos & Trump** (no.146, 7739 9008) for vintage fashion.

Sights & museums

FREE Ragged School Museum

46-50 Copperfield Road, E3 4RR (8980 6405, www.raggedschoolmuseum.org.uk). Mile End tube. **Open** 10am-5pm Wed, Thur; 2-5pm 1st Sun of mth. *Tours* by arrangement. **Admission** free; donations appreciated. **Map** p201 H4 37
Ragged schools were an early experiment in public education: they provided tuition, food and clothes for destitute children. This one was the largest in London, and Dr Barnardo himself taught here. It's now a sweet local museum that contains complete mock-ups of a ragged classroom and Edwardian kitchen, with displays on vanished local history.

★ FREE V&A Museum of Childhood

Cambridge Heath Road, E2 9PA (8983 5235, www.museumofchildhood.org.uk). Bethnal Green tube/rail or Cambridge Heath rail. **Open** 10am-5.45pm daily. **Admission** free; donations appreciated. **Map** p201 F2 38
Home to one of the world's finest collections of children's toys, dolls' houses, games and costumes, the Museum of Childhood shines brighter than ever after extensive refurbishment, which has given it an impressive entrance. Part of the Victoria & Albert Museum (*see p90*), the museum has been amassing childhood-related objects since 1872 and continues

to do so, with *Incredibles* figures complementing bonkers 1970s puppets, Barbie Dolls and Victorian praxinoscopes. The museum has lots of hands-on stuff for kids dotted about the many cases of historic artefacts. Regular exhibitions are held upstairs, while the café helps to revive flagging grown-ups.

Restaurants

★ Brawn

49 Columbia Road, E2 7RG (7729 5692, www.brawn.co). Hoxton rail or bus 26, 48, 55. **Open** 6-10.30pm Mon; noon-3pm, 6-10.30pm Tue-Thur; noon-3pm, 6-11pm Fri, Sat; noon-3pm Sun. **Dishes** £6-£16. **Map** p200 D2 ㊴ **Modern European**

With its lack of airs and graces and bare-brick decor, Brawn may look unassuming, but the cooking is quietly ambitious, precise and, above all, delicious. The meat dishes that run through the menu might have peasant origins, but they're executed with top-drawer flair, including offal dishes such as the seldom-found tête de veau with sauce ravigote, or pork cheek and trotter pie. Fish, shellfish and vegetable dishes show the same judgement.

Corner Room

Town Hall Hotel, Patriot Square, E2 9NF (7871 0460, www.townhallhotel.com/corner_room). Bethnal Green tube. **Open** 7-10am, noon-4pm, 6-10.30pm Mon-Fri; 7.30-10.30am Sat, Sun. **Main courses** £10-£16. **Map** p201 F2 ㊵ **Modern European**

In its role as the less formal of the two restaurants in the Town Hall Hotel, the Corner Room strikes a happy medium between impressive and approachable. The food – inspired by globetrotting culinary adventurer Nuno Mendez, who departed in 2014 but left his team in place – is consistently excellent. The short menu is a terse list of ingredients that barely hints at the complexities on the plate. 'Sprouting broccoli and garlic tea, stracciatella', for example, comes with beer-pickled onions, the near-sour dressing a teasing foil for the stracciatella (creamy mozzarella). Good food at any price; terrific at these prices.

▶ *The hotel's other restaurant, Viajante, serves no-choice set menus of six or nine courses (with an option of 12 in the evening). Expect a roll call of exquisitely presented morsels.*

★ E Pellicci

332 Bethnal Green Road, E2 0AG (7739 4873). Bethnal Green tube/rail or bus 8. **Open** 7am-4pm Mon-Sat. **Main courses** £5.50-£8.20. **No credit cards. Map** p201 E3 ㊶ **Café**

You go to Pellicci's as much for the atmosphere as for the food. Opened in 1900, and still in the hands of the same family, this Bethnal Green landmark has chrome and Vitrolite outside, wood panelling with deco marquetry, Formica tabletops and stained glass within – it earned the café a Grade II listing in 2005. Fry-ups are first rate, and the fish and chips, daily grills and Italian specials aren't half bad either.

Shops & services

★ Columbia Road Market

Columbia Road, Hoxton, E2 (www.columbiaroad.info). Hoxton rail or bus 26, 48, 55. **Open** 8am-3pm Sun. **Map** p200 D2 ㊷ **Market**

On Sunday mornings, this unassuming East End street is transformed into a swathe of fabulous plant life and the air is fragrant with blooms and the shouts of old-school Cockney stallholders (most offering deals for 'a fiver'). But a visit here isn't only about flowers and pot plants: alongside the market is a growing number of shops selling everything from pottery and arty prints to cupcakes and perfume; don't miss Ryantown's delicate paper cut-outs at no.126 (7613 1510). Refuel at Jones Dairy (23 Ezra Street, 7739 5372, www.jonesdairy.co.uk) or at Brawn (*see left*).

Two Columbia Road

2 Columbia Road, E2 7NN (7729 9933, www.twocolumbiaroad.com). Hoxton or Shoreditch High Street rail. **Open** noon-7pm Wed-Fri; noon-6pm Sat; 10am-4pm Sun. **Map** p200 D2 ㊸ **Homewares**

Well-selected 20th-century pieces are the order of the day here, whether it's 1970s chrome pendant lights, Danish 1960s rosewood desks, or Charles Eames wooden chairs. The corner site is owned by Tommy Roberts and run by his son Keith. Expect to find well-known names such as Arne Jacobsen and Willy Rizzo among the stock as well as more affordable pieces.

NORTH OF REGENT'S CANAL

The area of London Fields, just over the canal, demonstrates Hackney's changing demographics. Once a failing fruit and veg market, **Broadway Market** is now brimming – sometimes choking – with young urbanites and trendy families. The food and vintage garb market on Saturdays has been joined by two eclectic food and collectibles markets on Westgate Street; the street is lined with browsable boutiques, curiosity shops and modish boho eating and drinking venues. Even venerable pie-and-mash shop **F Cooke** (*see p211*) recently hosted a pop-up.

From the south end of Broadway Market, you can walk east along the Regent's Canal to **Victoria Park**. Opened in 1845 to give the impoverished working classes access to green space, this sprawling, 290-acre oasis was designed by Sir James Pennethorne, a pupil of John Nash; its elegant landscaping (with rose garden and waterfowl lake) is reminiscent of Nash's Regent's Park (*see p195*). There's also a terrific lakeside café. For a new way to enjoy the park, *see p208* **In the Know**. At the eastern end of the park, across a nasty dual carriageway, is the mish-mash of artist-colonised post-industrial buildings that makes up **Hackney Wick**.

Restaurants

If your tastes extend to the old East End, dig into some eels at **F Cooke** (9 Broadway Market, 7254 6458), a pie and mash place that's been in operation since the early 1900s.

Empress

130 Lauriston Road, E9 7LH (8533 5123, www.empresse9.co.uk). Mile End tube then bus 277, 425. **Open** noon-3.30pm, 6-10.15pm Mon-Fri; 10am-midnight Sat; noon-9.30pm Sun. **Main courses** £12-£25. **Map** p201 G1 44 **Gastropub**

Everything about this gloriously updated former pub is bang on, from the linen napkins and red leather banquettes to the food, which packs sensational combinations of flavours. You might find gorgeous guinea fowl on puy lentils with salsa verde; or trout with watercress, slivers of apple celeriac and an English mustard sauce; or perhaps half a hollowed-out bone filled with snails, bone marrow, caramelised onions and pork. Very impressive.

Stories

30 Broadway Market, E8 4QJ (7254 6898, www.storiesonbroadway.com). London Fields rail. **Open** 10am-midnight daily. **Main courses** £6-£9. **Map** p201 E1 45 **Café**

From the people behind Book Club (*see p207*), Stories is a handsome all-rounder – and heaving at weekends. Large, sail-like lights are adjusted by complex pulleys across the ceiling; on the walls hang local artworks. The comestibles are as cool, from an innovative cocktail list via brunch to beer fodder (beef and chorizo burger with manchego and triple-cooked chips) and bar food – risotto balls, polenta chips with rosemary and parmesan.

Shops & services

For a fashion show and farmers' market in one, head to Hackney's **Broadway Market** on Saturday – all the hipsters, wannabe hipsters and people who like to gawp at both descend.

Artwords

20-22 Broadway Market, E8 4QJ (7923 7507, www.artwords.co.uk). London Fields rail. **Open** 10.30am-6.30pm Mon-Fri; 10am-6pm Sat; noon-6pm Sun. **Map** p201 E1 46 **Books & music**

Artwords has its finger firmly on the pulse when it comes to contemporary visual arts publications. Stock relating to contemporary fine art dominates, but there are also plenty of architecture, photography, graphic design, fashion, advertising and film titles on display, plus an excellent range of industry and creative magazines.

Other location 69 Rivington Street, Shoreditch, EC2A 3QQ (7729 2000).

Black Truffle

4 Broadway Market, E8 4QJ (7923 9450, www.blacktruffle.co.uk). London Fields rail or bus 394. **Open** 11am-6pm Tue-Fri; 10am-6pm Sat; noon-6pm Sun. **Map** p201 E1 47 **Fashion**

Quirky, stylish yet wearable footwear for women, men and children. Look out in particular for shoes by Melissa and Falke.

WAPPING & LIMEHOUSE

Just a few stops from where the DLR starts at Bank station is Shadwell, south of which is **Wapping**. In 1598, John Stowe described Wapping High Street as 'a filthy strait passage, with alleys of small tenements or cottages, inhabited by sailors' 'victuallers'. This can still just about be imagined as you walk along it now, flanked by tall Victorian warehouses. The historic **Town of Ramsgate** pub (no.62, 7481 8000), dating from 1545, helps. Here 'hanging judge' George Jeffreys was captured in 1688, trying to escape to Europe in disguise as a woman. Privateer Captain William Kidd was executed in 1701 at Execution Dock, near Wapping New Stairs; the bodies of pirates were hanged from a gibbet until seven tides had washed over them. Further east, the more touristy **Prospect of Whitby** (57 Wapping Wall, 7481 1095) dates from 1520 and counted Pepys and Dickens among its regulars. It has good riverside terraces and a fine pewter bar counter.

Pubs & bars

Grapes

76 Narrow Street, E14 8BP (7987 4396, www.thegrapes.co.uk). Westferry DLR. **Open** noon-3.30pm, 5.30-11pm Mon-Wed; noon-11.30pm Thur-Sat; noon-10.30pm Sun. *Food served* noon-2.30pm, 6.30-9.30pm Mon-Fri; noon-9.30pm Sat; noon-3.30pm Sun. **Map** p201 H6 48

If you're trying to evoke the feel of the Thames docks before their Disneyfication into Docklands, these narrow, ivy-covered and etched-glass 1720 riverside premises in Limehouse are a good place to start: the downstairs is all wood panels and nautical jetsam; upstairs is plainer, but it's easier to find seats for Sunday lunch. Expect good ales and a half-dozen wines of each colour by glass and bottle, plus jugs of kir royale or strawberry fizz for summer and port for winter. There's a tiny terrace too.

► *Nearby, Gordon Ramsay's gastropub, the Narrow (44 Narrow Street, E14 8DQ, 7592 7950, www.gordonramsay.com), serves great bar snacks.*

Greenwich

Riverside Greenwich is an irresistible mixture of maritime, royal and horological history, a combination that earned it recognition as a UNESCO World Heritage Site, and in 2012 it was elevated to the status of a Royal Borough as part of the Queen's Jubilee celebrations.

After many years under wraps, the beautiful tea clipper *Cutty Sark* is open again to the public, and the new galleries at the National Maritime Museum have brought this wonderful attraction back to prominence. Together with the *Cutty Sark*, the NMM is now one of a proud cluster of venues collectively known as the Royal Museums Greenwich.

Also here is glorious Greenwich Park, home to the Royal Observatory & Planetarium, as well as the charming Queen's House. The views from the top of the hill are splendid and far-reaching.

Discover Greenwich.

Don't Miss

1 National Maritime Museum Now bigger and better than ever (p215).

2 Cutty Sark See the newly restored tea clipper from all angles (p214).

3 02 Arena Have fun at this giant multi-entertainment centre. (p217).

4 Royal Observatory & Planetarium Two marvels on one site (p216).

5 Thames Clipper Arrive in style – by boat from central London (p214).

ROYAL GREENWICH

Cutty Sark for Maritime Greenwich DLR or Greenwich rail.
Royalty has stalked this area since 1300, when Edward I stayed here. Henry VIII was born in Greenwich Palace; the palace was built on land that later contained Wren's Royal Naval Hospital, now the **Old Royal Naval College** (*see below*). The College is now a very handy first port of call. Its Pepys Building not only contains the **Greenwich Tourist Information Centre** (0870 608 2000, www.greenwich.gov.uk), but is also the home of **Discover Greenwich** (*see below*), which provides a great overview of the area's numerous attractions. Just opposite, shoppers swarm to **Greenwich Market** (*see p217*), a handsome 19th-century building sheltering a mixture of shops and stalls.

Near the DLR stop is Greenwich Pier; every 15 minutes (peak times), the popular and speedy **Thames Clipper** boats (0870 781 5049, www.thamesclippers.com) shuttle passengers to and from central London. This is where you'll find the *Cutty Sark*, as well as a domed structure that is the entrance to a Victorian **pedestrian tunnel** that emerges on the far side of the Thames in Island Gardens. The tunnel is rather dingy, due to incomplete repair work, but it's still fun to walk beneath the river.

At the north end of Greenwich Park are the **Queen's House** and **National Maritime Museum**, beyond which it's a ten-minute walk (or shorter shuttle-bus trip) up the steep slopes of Greenwich Park to the **Royal Observatory**. The building looks even more stunning at night, when the bright green Meridian Line Laser illuminates the path of the Prime Meridian across the London sky.

IN THE KNOW FANS OF TEA

The **Fan Museum** (*see p215*) has a small tearoom, the Orangery. English cream teas are served here on Tuesdays and Sundays (2.15pm and 3.45pm, booking essential). The room overlooks a pretty garden, replete with Japanese themed plantings and fan-shaped flowerbeds.

Sights & museums

Cutty Sark

King William Walk, SE10 9HT (8858 2698, www.cuttysark.org.uk). Cutty Sark DLR. **Open** 10am-6pm daily. **Admission** £13.50; £7-£11.50 reductions; £24-£35 family; free under-5s. **Map** p215 B2 ❶

Built in Scotland in 1869, this tea clipper was the quickest in the business when she was launched in 1870 – renovation after the *Cutty Sark* went up in flames in 2007 was rather slower. But you can visit her once more (by timed tickets) in her permanent berth in a purpose-built dry dock beside the Thames. The ship is now raised three metres off the ground and surrounded by a dramatic glass 'skirt', which allows visitors to admire the hull from underneath for the first time – while sipping a cup of tea from the museum café, should they desire. Critics have objected that the glazed canopy obscures the elegant lines of the *Cutty Sark*'s hull – as well as raising fears about the stresses that are being put on the elderly ship – but the visitor experience is much improved, with interactives giving context to a story of reckless, high-speed trade in tea, wine, spirits, beer, coal, jute, wool and castor oil. The sailing clippers were gradually put out of business by steamships: by 1922, the *Cutty Sark* was the last of her breed afloat. The space beneath the ship displays another lost tradition: a display of more than 80 figureheads, including Florence Nightingale, William Wilberforce, Hiawatha and Sir Lancelot.

► *In a move not likely to win over the critics, the Cutty Sark Studio Theatre was launched in early 2014; see p278* **Laugh on the Open Waves**.

★ FREE Discover Greenwich & the Old Royal Naval College

2 Cutty Sark Gardens, SE10 9LW (8269 4799, www.ornc.org). Cutty Sark DLR or Greenwich DLR/rail. **Open** 10am-5pm daily. *Tours* noon daily; other times by arrangement. **Admission** free. *Tours* £5. **Map** p215 B1 ❷

The block of the Old Royal Naval College nearest to the *Cutty Sark* is now the excellent Discover Greenwich. It's full of focused, informative exhibits on architecture and building techniques of the surrounding buildings, the life of Greenwich pensioners, Tudor royalty and so forth, delivered with a real sense of fun: while grown-ups read about coade stone or scagliola (popular fake stone building materials), for example, children can build their own chapel with soft bricks or try on a knight's helmet. There's also a well-stocked shop and a Tourist Information Centre.

It's a perfect introduction to the superb collection of buildings that make up the Naval College. Designed by Wren in 1694, with Hawksmoor and Vanbrugh helping to complete the project, it was originally a hospital for the relief and support of seamen and their dependants, with pensioners living here from 1705 to 1869, when the complex became the Royal Naval College. The Navy left in 1998, and the neoclassical buildings now house part of the University of Greenwich and Trinity College of Music. The public are allowed into the impressive rococo chapel, where there are free organ recitals, and Painted Hall, a tribute to William and Mary that took Sir James Thornhill 19 years to complete. Nelson lay in state in the Painted Hall for three days in 1806, before being taken to St Paul's Cathedral for his funeral.

There's a lively events programme in the grounds, ranging from comedy shows and early music to weekend appearances from historic figures – costumed actors – ranging from Pepys and Sir James to the 'pirate queen' Grace O'Malley and Joe Brown, veteran of the Battle of Trafalgar.

Fan Museum

12 Crooms Hill, SE10 8ER (8305 1441, www.fan-museum.org). Cutty Sark DLR or Greenwich DLR/rail. **Open** 11am-5pm Tue-Sat; noon-5pm Sun. **Admission** £4; £3 reductions; £10 family; free under-7s. **Map** p215 B2 ❸

The world's most important collection of hand-held fans is displayed in a pair of Georgian townhouses. There are about 3,500 fans, including some beauties in the Hélène Alexander collection, but not all are on display at any one time. For details of fan-making workshops and temporary exhibitions, see the website. *See also p214,* **In the Know**.

★ FREE National Maritime Museum

Romney Road, SE10 9NF (8858 4422, information 8312 6565, www.nmm.ac.uk). Cutty Sark DLR or Greenwich DLR/rail.

Open 10am-5pm Mon-Wed, Fri-Sun; 10am-8pm Thur. *Tours* phone for details. **Admission** free; donations appreciated. *Temporary exhibitions* vary; check website for details. **Map** p215 B2 ❹

The world's largest maritime museum contains a huge store of creatively organised maritime art, cartography, models, interactives and regalia – and is even bigger since the impressive expansion in 2011 into the new Sammy Ofer Wing. Centred on Voyagers: Britons and the Sea – a collection of 200 artefacts, accompanied by an impressive audio-visual installation called the Wave – this extension also has the Compass Lounge (with free Wi-Fi), where you can explore the collection using computers, and a brasserie, café and shop. Downstairs, the temporary gallery is building a reputation for

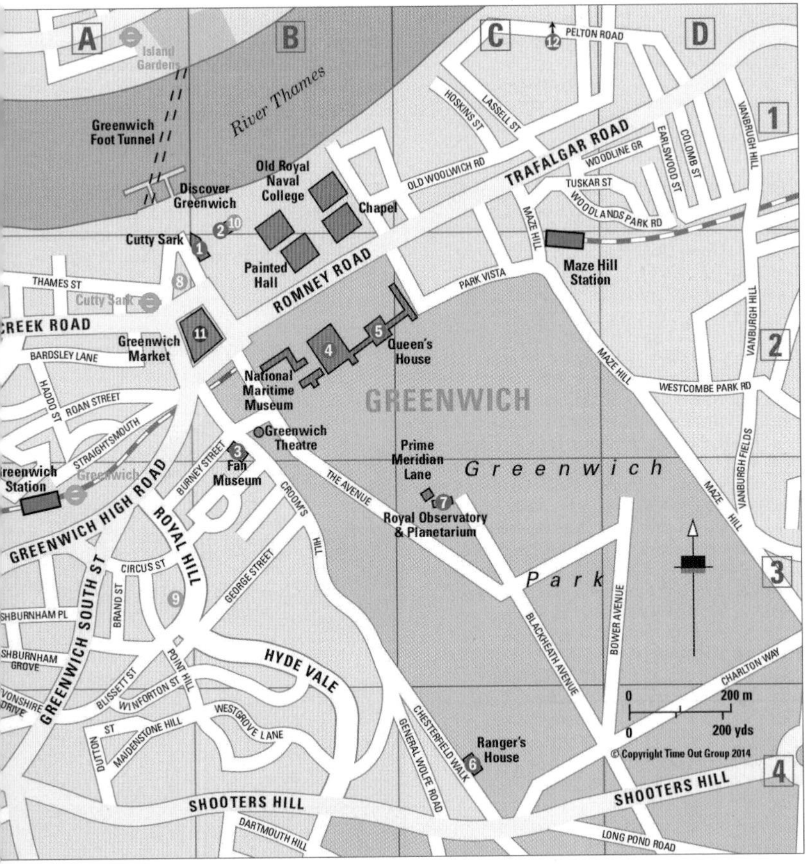

compelling – and varied – exhibitions of historic art (Ansel Adams and Turner have both appeared here).

Ground-level galleries include Explorers, which covers great sea expeditions back to medieval times, and Maritime London, which concentrates on the city as a port. Upstairs is the Environment Gallery, which reveals our dependence on the health of the world's oceans. Level two holds the interactives: the Bridge has a ship simulator, and All Hands lets children load cargo, and you can even try your hand as a ship's gunner. The Ship of War is the museum's superb collection of models, dating from 1660 to 1815, and the Atlantic: Slavery, Trade, Empires gallery looks at the transport of goods between Britain, Africa and the Americas during the 17th to 19th centuries.

More recent additions are the Great Map, a large interactive floor map of the oceans, and a Nelson, Navy, Nation gallery, which recalls the sea-borne battles of the 18th century, and the glamour and gore of life as a Naval Officer at the time. Here you'll find Nelson's Trafalgar uniform, blood-stained and with fatal bullet-hole, as well as a 3D reconstruction of him, as if laid in a coffin.

► *The main entrance (from Greenwich Park) is now overlooked by Yinka Shonibare's playful* Nelson's Ship in a Bottle, *formerly on show on the Fourth Plinth in Trafalgar Square; see* *p68.*

FREE Queen's House

Romney Road, SE10 9NF (8312 6565, www.nmm.ac.uk). Cutty Sark DLR or Greenwich DLR/rail. **Open** 10am-5pm daily. **Admission** free. **Map** p215 B2 ❺

The art collection of the National Maritime Museum (*p215*) is displayed in what was formerly the summer villa of Charles I's queen, Henrietta Maria. Completed in 1638 by Inigo Jones, the house has an interior as impressive as the paintings on the walls. As well as the stunning 1635 marble floor, look for Britain's first centrally unsupported spiral stair, fine painted woodwork and ceilings, and the proportions of the Great Hall – it is a perfect cube. The collection includes portraits of famous maritime figures and works by Hogarth and Gainsborough, as well as some arresting wartime art from the 20th century.

► *Among all the pictures of bluff seamen and naval cannonades, check out the exotic paintings from Captain Cook's explorations – mysterious creatures lurk in the depths.*

Ranger's House

Chesterfield Walk, SE10 8QX (8853 0035, www.english-heritage.org.uk). Blackheath rail, Cutty Sark DLR or bus 53. **Open** *Apr-Sept* guided tours only. *Tours* 11.30am, 2.30pm Mon-Wed, Sun. Closed Oct-Mar. **Admission** £6.70; £4-£6 reductions; free under-5s. **Map** p215 C4 ❻

The house of the 'Ranger of Greenwich Park' (a post held by George III's niece, Princess Sophia Matilda, from 1815) now contains the treasure – medieval and Renaissance art, jewellery, bronzes, tapestries, furniture, porcelain, paintings – amassed by Julius Wernher, a German who made his considerable fortune trading in South African diamonds. His booty is displayed through a dozen lovely rooms in this red-brick Georgian villa, the back garden of which is the fragrant Greenwich Park rose collection.

★ FREE Royal Observatory & Planetarium

Greenwich Park, SE10 9NF (8312 6565, www.rmg.co.uk/royal-observatory). Cutty Sark DLR or Greenwich DLR/rail. **Open** 10am-5pm daily. *Tours* phone for details. **Admission** free-prices vary; check website for details. **Map** p215 C3 ❼

The northern section of this two-halved attraction chronicles Greenwich's horological connection. Flamsteed House, the observatory built in 1675 on the orders of Charles II, contains the apartments of Sir John Flamsteed and other Astronomers Royal, as well as the instruments used in timekeeping since the 14th century. John Harrison's four timekeepers, used to crack the problem of longitude, are here, while the onion dome houses the country's largest (28-inch) refracting telescope – it was completed in 1893. The courtyard is where tourists gather for their Prime Meridian Line photo-opportunity.

The south site houses the Astronomy Centre, home to the Peter Harrison Planetarium and the Astronomy & Time Galleries. The 120-seater planetarium's architecture cleverly reflects its astrological position: the semi-submerged cone tilts at 51.5 degrees, the latitude of Greenwich, pointing to the

Royal Observatory & Planetarium.

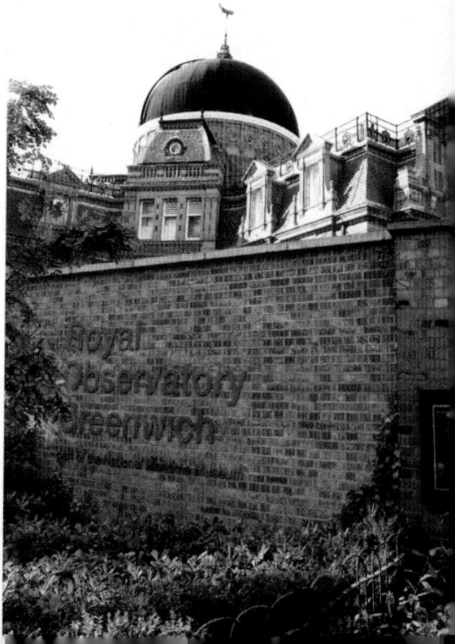

north star, and its reflective disc is aligned with the celestial equator. Daily and weekend shows include 'Sky Tonight Live'.

Pubs & bars

Gipsy Moth

60 Greenwich Church Street, SE10 9BL (8858 0786, www.thegipsymothgreenwich.co.uk). Cutty Sark DLR. **Open/meals served** 10am-11pm Mon-Thur; 10am-midnight Fri, Sat; 10am-10.30pm Sun. **Map** p215 A2 ⑧

The split-level garden and roomy interior at this moderately funky pub are ideal for a sit-down after roaming around Greenwich. The pub offers an impressive number of beers (Früli, Budvar, Paulaner and at least six others), well-priced wines and pretty decent food, from bar snacks to full meals (including breakfasts).

► *In good weather, the riverside seats of Cutty Sark Tavern (4-6 Ballast Quay, SE10 9PD, 8858 3146, www.cuttysarktavern.co.uk) are popular.*

Greenwich Union

56 Royal Hill, SE10 8RT (8692 6258, www.greenwichunion.com). Greenwich rail/DLR. **Open** noon-11pm Mon-Fri; 11am-11pm Sat; 11.30am-10.30pm Sun. *Food served* noon-4pm, 5.30-10pm Mon-Fri; 11am-10pm Sat; noon-9pm Sun. **Map** p215 A3 ⑨

Decorated with framed covers of the *Picture Post*, this is the spiritual home of Alistair Hook's mission to bring his Meantime Brewery's German-style beers to the British public. Six tap options complement a couple of dozen bottled international beers; food runs from bacon butties to steaks. Coffee, tea and a small terrace make it a decent option for non-drinkers.

Old Brewery

Pepys Building, Old Royal Naval College, SE10 9LW (3327 1280, www.oldbrewerygreenwich.com). Cutty Sark DLR. **Open** 11am-11pm Mon-Sat; 10am-10.30pm Sun. **Main courses** £8.50-£24.50. **Map** p215 B1 ⑩

Meantime Brewery's flagship: by day, it's a café; by night, a restaurant. There's a small bar, with tables outside in a large walled courtyard – a lovely spot in which to test the 50-strong beer list – but most of the action is in the vast, high-ceilinged main space. Dishes, such as smoked barbecue pork ribs with chips and spicy coleslaw, come with matching beers.

Shops & services

Greenwich Market

King William Walk, SE10 9HZ (8269 5090, www.greenwichmarketlondon.com). Cutty Sark DLR. **Open** 10am-5.30pm Tue-Sun. **Map** p215 B2 ⑪ **Market**

Reprieved in late 2012 from the long-running threat of redevelopment, Greenwich Market can trace its origins to 1737 – although the current covered building dates only to the 19th century. Tuesdays, Thursdays and Fridays up to 120 stalls are dominated by antiques (including classic 20th-century pieces); Tuesdays, Wednesdays and weekends are for the craftier end of things. There is also a cluster of shops dedicated to art, fashion and jewellery – even a stall run by Alex Pittas, 'the Urban Magician'. If you're flagging, there is plenty of street food.

GREENWICH PENINSULA

The riverside Thames Path leads north from the main attractions of Greenwich, past rusting piers and boarded-up factories, on to the **Greenwich Peninsula**, now dominated by the **O2 Arena** (*see p271*). Designed by the Richard Rogers Partnership as the Millennium Dome, this once-maligned structure's fortunes have improved considerably since its change of use. Alongside the concerts and sporting events in the huge auditorium, and movies in the cineplex, attractions include chain restaurants, big temporary exhibitions and the glossy, permanent **British Music Experience** – you can now even book **Up at the O2** tickets (www.theo2.co.uk/upattheo2) to walk right over the top of the Dome, safely attached to a security line. A rather elegant (but, for public transport purposes, almost entirely useless) cable car, the **Emirates Air Line** (*see p249* **In the Know**), runs from the east flank of the peninsula right across the Thames to the ExCeL conference centre on the far side.

The Dome and its environs are all something of a contrast with the **Greenwich Peninsula Ecology Park** (www.tcv.org.uk), and with the nearby riverside walks that afford broad, flat, bracing views and works of art; you could hardly miss *Slice of Reality*, a rusting ship cut in half by Richard Wilson, and Antony Gormley's 100-foot *Quantum Cloud*, which consists of a seemingly random cloud of steel sections, but look into it from a distance and you'll see a denser area at the centre in the shape of a human body.

Sights & museums

British Music Experience

O2 Bubble, Millennium Way, SE10 0BB (8463 2000, www.britishmusicexperience.com). North Greenwich tube. **Open** 11am-7.30pm daily. **Admission** £13; £6.50-£8 reductions; free under-5s. **Map** p215 C1 ⑫

The memorabilia on show on the top floor of the O2 Arena includes David Bowie's Ziggy Stardust costume and Noel Gallagher's Union Jack guitar. The main focus, though, is on interactive exhibits: downloading archive music, trying your hand at guitar tutorials and similar activities. Workshops, lectures and concerts are also part of the experience.

Notting Hill & Holland Park

For a cadre of right-wing politicians and certain celebs, Notting Hill is the coolest address in London, with Portobello Market surrounded by some of the most desirable addresses in west London – as well as the inimitable Museum of Brands, Packaging & Advertising. As in so many parts of London, any patina of funkiness is down to previous generations of resident – poor working class and immigrants mostly – who made the place in their own image. The huge Notting Hill Carnival (*see p37*) gives the best flavour of this community. More high-end, elegant housing is found to the south in Holland Park and Kensington, where there are more millionaires per square mile than in any other part of Europe. Apart from rubbernecking the rich, visitors will soon be able to enjoy the opening of ambitious new premises for the Design Museum.

Portobello Road Market.

Don't Miss

1 Portobello Road Market Antiques and fruit and veg (p223).

2 Leighton House Art and oriental decor (p225).

3 Design Museum New premises destined to be a design classic (p224).

4 Clarke's Seasonal and local ingredients pioneer restaurant (p225).

5 Museum of Brands, Packaging & Advertising Stuff we throw away (p220).

THE GOLD
ANTIQUE CLOCKS & REPAIRS
SCOTTISH CASHMERE
Gallery GUESTHOUSE
OYSTER
RARE BOOKS

NOTTING HILL

Notting Hill Gate, Ladbroke Grove or Westbourne Park tube.

Head north up Queensway from Kensington Gardens and turn west along **Westbourne Grove**. The road starts humble but gets posher the further west you go; cross Chepstow Road and you're in upmarket **Notting Hill**. A host of fashionable restaurants and bars exploit the lingering street cred of the fast-disappearing black and working-class communities; posh shops are a better reflection of the area's current character. **Notting Hill Gate** isn't a pretty street, but the leafy avenues to the south are; so is **Pembridge Road**, to the north, leading to the boutique-filled streets of Westbourne Grove and Ledbury Road, and to **Portobello Road** and its renowned market (*see p223*).

Halfway down, **Blenheim Crescent** boasts a couple of independent booksellers, but the Travel Bookshop (nos.13-15), the store on which Hugh Grant's bookshop was based in the movie *Notting Hill*, has now closed down. Under the Westway, that elevated section of the M40 motorway linking London with Oxford, is the small but busy **Portobello Green Market**.

North of the Westway, Portobello's vitality fizzles out. It sparks back to life at **Golborne Road**, the heartland of London's North African community. Here, too, is a fine Portuguese café-deli, the **Lisboa Pâtisserie** (no.57, 8968 5242). At the north-eastern end of the road stands **Trellick Tower**, an architecturally significant, like-it-or-loathe-it piece of Ernö Goldfinger modernism. At its western end, Golborne Road connects with Ladbroke Grove, which can be followed north to **Kensal Green Cemetery**.

EXPLORE

Sights & museums

FREE Kensal Green Cemetery

Harrow Road, Kensal Green, W10 4RA (8969 0152, www.kensalgreen.co.uk). Kensal Green tube. **Open** *Apr-Sept* 9am-6pm Mon-Sat; 10am-6pm Sun. *Oct-Mar* 9am-5pm Mon-Sat; 10am-5pm Sun. **Tours** *Mar-Oct* 2pm Sun. *Nov-Feb* 2pm 1st & 3rd Sun of mth. **Admission** free. *Tours* £5 (£4 reductions) donation. **No credit cards. Map** p221 C1 ❶

Behind a neoclassical gate is a green oasis of the dead. It's the resting place of both the Duke of Sussex, sixth son of George III, and his sister, Princess Sophia; also buried here are Wilkie Collins, Anthony Trollope and William Makepeace Thackeray.

Museum of Brands, Packaging & Advertising

Colville Mews, Lonsdale Road, W11 2AR (7908 0880, www.museumofbrands.com). Notting Hill Gate tube. **Open** 10am-6pm Tue-Sat; 11am-5pm Sun. **Admission** £6.50; £2.25-£4 reductions; £15 family; free under-7s. **Map** p221 B2 ❷

Robert Opie began collecting the things others throw away when he was 16. His collection now includes anything from milk bottles to vacuum cleaners and cereal packets. The emphasis is on the last century of British consumerism, design and domestic life, but there are older items, such as an ancient Egyptian doll.

> **IN THE KNOW MARKET FINDS**
>
> **Portobello Green Market** has the area's best vintage fashion stalls. Look out for the excellent second-hand boot and shoe stall and brilliant vintage handbag stall (usually outside Falafel King), along with vintage clothing stall Sage Femme, often outside the Antique Clothing Shop.

Restaurants

Assaggi

1st floor, 39 Chepstow Place, W2 4TS (7792 5501). Bayswater, Notting Hill Gate or Queensway tube. **Open** 12.30-2.30pm, 7.30-11pm Mon-Fri; 1-2.30pm, 7.30-11pm Sat. **Main courses** £19.80-£29.99. **Map** p221 D3 ❸ **Italian**

The look is low-key and the style is relaxed and informal, but there's nothing frivolous about the cooking at Assaggi: the likes of chargrilled cuttlefish and artichoke salad with a dressing of squid ink, or soft gnocchi served with an intensely flavoured venison and tomato ragù. Don't miss the classic Assaggi dessert, a fluffy baverese (vanilla cream) doused with espresso.

Electric Diner

191 Portobello Road, W11 2ED (7908 9696, www.electricdiner.com). Ladbroke Grove tube. **Open** 8am-11pm Mon-Wed; 8am-midnight Thur-Sat; 8am-10pm Sun. **Main courses** £7-£19. **Map** p221 B2 ❹ **Americas**

The unfinished brick and concrete walls, low lighting, french grey-painted plank ceiling, red leather banquettes and lively open kitchen evoke a sort of chic US railway car diner. The hip vibe extends to the menu, which features artery-unfriendly American classics: cheeseburgers; hot dogs; milkshakes. Each dish is well-thought-out and composed of good ingredients: french fries are thin and crispy, and even a simple bibb lettuce and avocado salad was enlivened with finely chopped chives and tarragon. *Photo p222.*

★ Hereford Road

3 Hereford Road, W2 4AB (7727 1144, www.herefordroad.org). Bayswater tube. **Open** noon-3pm, 6-10.30pm Mon-Sat; noon-4pm, 6-10pm Sun. **Main courses** £10-£16.50. **Map** p221 D2 ❺ **British**

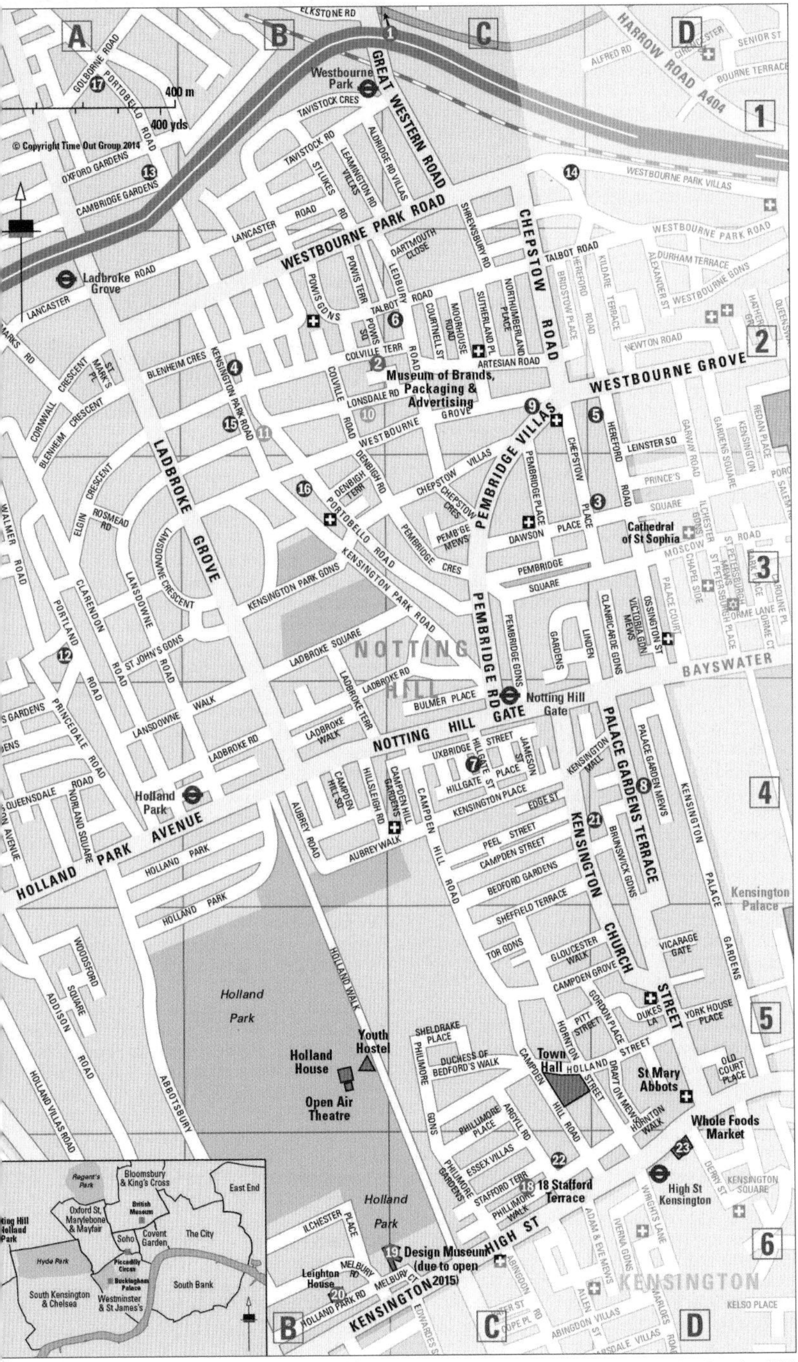

A
B
C
D
1
2
3
4
5
6
400 m
400 yds
© Copyright Time Out Group 2014
ELKSTONE RD
HARROW ROAD A404
ALFRED RD
SENIOR ST
BOURNE TERRACE
GOLBORNE ROAD
PORTOBELLO ROAD
Westbourne Park
GREAT WESTERN ROAD
TAVISTOCK CRES
TAVISTOCK RD
OXFORD GARDENS
CAMBRIDGE GARDENS
ST LUKES RD
LEAMINGTON RD VILLAS
ALDRIDGE RD VILLAS
WESTBOURNE PARK VILLAS
WESTBOURNE PARK ROAD
LANCASTER ROAD
Ladbroke Grove
SHREWSBURY RD
CHEPSTOW ROAD
TALBOT ROAD
HEREFORD ROAD
BRIDSTOW PLACE
KILDARE TERRACE
ALEXANDER ST
DURHAM TERRACE
WESTBOURNE GDNS
DARTMOUTH CLOSE
POWIS GDNS
POWIS TERR
LEDBURY ROAD
POWIS SQ
COURTNELL ST
MOORHOUSE ROAD
SUTHERLAND PL
NORTHUMBERLAND PLACE
ARTESIAN ROAD
NEWTON ROAD
COLVILLE TERR
Museum of Brands, Packaging & Advertising
WESTBOURNE GROVE
BLENHEIM CRES
KENSINGTON PARK ROAD
ST MARK'S PL
CORNWALL CRESCENT
BLENHEIM CRESCENT
LONSDALE RD
COLVILLE ROAD
PEMBRIDGE VILLAS
CHEPSTOW PLACE
LEINSTER SQ
PRINCE'S SQUARE
GARWAY ROAD
GARDENS SQUARE
KENSINGTON
REDAN PLACE
LADBROKE GROVE
ELGIN CRESCENT
ROSMEAD RD
DENBIGH RD
DENBIGH TERR
CHEPSTOW VILLAS
CHEPSTOW CRES
PEMB'GE MEWS
PEMBRIDGE PLACE
DAWSON PLACE
Cathedral of St Sophia
MOSCOW ROAD
ILCHESTER GDNS
CHAPEL SIDE
ST PETERSBURGH MEWS
ST PETERSBURGH PLACE
ORME LANE
ORME CT
CAROLINE PL
WALMER ROAD
PORTLAND ROAD
CLARENDON ROAD
LANSDOWNE ROAD
LANSDOWNE CRESCENT
KENSINGTON PARK GDNS
PEMBRIDGE CRES
PEMBRIDGE SQUARE
PEMBRIDGE RD
PEMBRIDGE GDNS
CLANRICARDE GDNS
VICTORIA GDN MEWS
OSSINGTON ST
PALACE COURT
LINDEN GARDENS
BAYSWATER
NOTTING HILL
ST JOHN'S GDNS
LADBROKE SQUARE
LADBROKE RD
LADBROKE TERR
BULMER PLACE
Notting Hill Gate
NOTTING HILL GATE
LANSDOWNE WALK
LADBROKE WALK
LADBROKE RD
PRINCEDALE ROAD
QUEENSDALE ROAD
NORLAND SQUARE
Holland Park
HOLLAND PARK AVENUE
UXBRIDGE STREET
HILLGATE ST
HILLGATE PLACE
JAMESON ST
KENSINGTON MALL
PALACE GARDENS TERRACE
PALACE GARDEN MEWS
CAMPDEN HILL SQ
HILLSLEIGH RD
CAMPDEN HILL GARDENS
CAMPDEN HILL ROAD
AUBREY ROAD
AUBREY WALK
KENSINGTON PLACE
EDGE ST
PEEL STREET
CAMPDEN STREET
BEDFORD GARDENS
SHEFFIELD TERRACE
KENSINGTON CHURCH STREET
BRUNSWICK GDNS
KENSINGTON PALACE GARDENS
Kensington Palace
HOLLAND PARK
WOODSFORD SQUARE
ADDISON ROAD
HOLLAND VILLAS ROAD
ABBOTSBURY ROAD
HOLLAND WALK
Holland Park
Holland House
Youth Hostel
Open Air Theatre
TOR GDNS
GLOUCESTER WALK
CAMPDEN GROVE
VICARAGE GATE
GORDON PLACE
PITT STREET
DUKES LA
YORK HOUSE PLACE
SHELDRAKE PLACE
PHILLIMORE GDNS
DUCHESS OF BEDFORD'S WALK
Town Hall
HORNTON STREET
HOLLAND STREET
CAMPDEN HILL ROAD
DRAYTON MEWS
HORNTON WALK
St Mary Abbots
OLD COURT PLACE
Whole Foods Market
PHILLIMORE PLACE
ARGYLL RD
ESSEX VILLAS
PHILLIMORE GARDENS
STAFFORD TERR
PHILLIMORE WALK
18 Stafford Terrace
High St Kensington
DERRY ST
KENSINGTON SQUARE
WRIGHTS LANE
ADAM & EVE MEWS
IVERNA GDNS
ILCHESTER PLACE
Design Museum (due to open 2015)
HIGH ST
KENSINGTON
MELBURY RD
MELBURY CT
Leighton House
HOLLAND PARK RD
KENSINGTON HIGH ST
EDWARDES SQ
ABINGDON RD
ALLEN ST
ABINGDON VILLAS
MARLOES ROAD
KELSO PLACE
Regent's Park
Bloomsbury & King's Cross
East End
Oxford St, Marylebone & Mayfair
British Museum
Notting Hill & Holland Park
Soho
Covent Garden
The City
Hyde Park
Piccadilly Circus
Buckingham Palace
South Bank
South Kensington & Chelsea
Westminster & St James's

This restaurant makes its intentions clear: the first thing you see upon entering the long, narrow space is the kitchen; if it were any more open you'd be eating off the chefs' laps. Sit and wonder how the restaurant can manage to serve two marvellous courses for £13 at lunch as you tuck into hearty dishes such as devilled duck livers with shallots, brill with roasted cauliflower, or onglet and chips. The slightly fancier à la carte menu includes the likes of lamb rump with purple sprouting broccoli.

★ Ledbury

127 Ledbury Road, W11 2AQ (7792 9090, www.theledbury.com). Westbourne Park tube. **Open** 6.30-10.15pm Mon; noon-2.15pm, 6.30-10.15pm Tue-Sat; noon-2.30pm, 7-10pm Sun. **Main courses** (lunch) £32-£34. **Set dinner** £90 4 courses. **Map** p221 C2 ❻ **French**

Few haute establishments have the hospitable hum of the Ledbury; this former pub remains top-tier for gustatory good times. British ingredients – smoked eel, Cumbrian lamb – line up alongside delicacies such as Tokyo turnips, Bresse chicken and black truffle, but it's chef Brett Graham's clever contemporary treatment of them that sets the place apart. Ledbury signatures are consistently thrilling – particularly the flame-grilled mackerel with pickled cucumber, celtic mustard and shiso; and, well, all the desserts.

Mazi

12-14 Hillgate Street, W8 7SR (7229 3794, www.mazi.co.uk). Notting Hill tube. **Open** 6.30-10.30pm Mon, Tue; noon-3pm, 6.30-10.30pm Wed-Sat; noon-3pm, 6.30-10pm Sun. **Main courses** £8-£28. **Map** p221 C4 ❼ **Greek**

Purists might be troubled by the progressive presentation – mezédes are served in Kilner jars – but the Greek flavours are reassuringly authentic. A jar of creamy white taramá hits just the right note of tangy, savoury deliciousness; another of fava (spilt-pea purée), accompanied by tender octopus, is so light it could have been whipped. Hot dishes are better still: slabs of feta encased in black-sesame tempura with punchy lemon marmalade might well consign the humble saganáki to history.

★ Shed

122 Palace Gardens Terrace, W8 4RT (7229 4024, www.theshed-restaurant.com). Notting Hill Gate tube. **Open** 6-10pm Mon; noon-3pm, 6-11pm Tue-Fri; noon-4pm, 6-11pm Sat. **Dishes** £4-£9.50. **Map** p221 D4 ❽ **British**

From a distance, with its white wooden cladding and high pitched roof, this restaurant does look suspiciously like a shed. Close up, it's as much barnyard as back-garden, with piggy portraits, bits of tractor, and charming staff in check shirts. Plates are small, meant for sharing. Many ingredients are sourced from in or around the family farm in Nutbourne, West Sussex. From the meaty goodness of the Nutbourne banger with own-made mustard to hake

Electric Diner. *See p220.*

with samphire, capers and a slick of red pepper sauce, it's all delicious, and inventive without being tricksy.

Taqueria

139-143 Westbourne Grove, W11 2RS (7229 4734, www.taqueria.co.uk). Notting Hill Gate tube. **Open** noon-11pm Mon-Thur; noon-11.30pm Fri; 10am-11.30pm Sat; noon-10.30pm Sun. **Main courses** £5-£8.20. **Map** p221 C2 ❾ **Mexican**

The word 'taquería' is traditionally associated with street stands churning out endless tacos. They do that here too, but in rather more salubrious surroundings. It's a charming, independent-feeling little place of two rooms, with dark wood floors and pristine white walls decorated with a few Mexican film posters. The food is equally unfussy: a dozen or so tacos (using corn tortillas made in-house daily), a handful of tostadas and a few monthly changing specials.

Pubs & bars

★ Lonsdale

48 Lonsdale Road, W11 2DE (7727 4080, www.thelonsdale.co.uk). Ladbroke Grove or Notting Hill Gate tube. **Open** 6pm-midnight Tue-Thur; 6pm-1am Fri, Sat. **Map** p221 B2 ❿

The scholarliness of the cocktail list here breeds confidence. Nearly every drink is given a time and place of creation and, in most cases, the bartender responsible is named. This makes for informative, sometimes amusing reading, and anything you order will be first rate. Classics like martinis are always very proper. Sitting at the incredibly long and atmospherically lit bar, and watching the bartenders work is entertainment in itself. There's a restaurant too, specialising in top-quality meat.

Portobello Star

171 Portobello Road, W11 2DY (7229 8016, www.portobellostarbar.co.uk). Ladbroke Grove or Notting Hill Gate tube. **Open** 11am-11.30pm Mon-Thur, Sun; 11am-12.30am Fri, Sat. **Map** p221 B2 ⓫

This 'cocktail tavern' deftly blends discerning bar and traditional boozer. The well-stocked bar is manned by friendly staff thoroughly educated in the art of adult refreshment. Mixologist Jake Burger's impeccable, approachable directory of discerning drinks is the last word on sophisticated intoxication. Ginger Pig pies are on hand to soak up the alcohol.

Shops & services

Cowshed

119 Portland Road, W11 4LN (7078 1944, www.cowshedclarendoncross.com). Holland Park tube. **Open** 9am-8pm Mon-Fri; 9am-7pm Sat; 10am-5pm Sun. **Map** p221 A3 ⓬ **Health & beauty**

The London branch of Cowshed (from Somerset's renowned hotel-spa Babington House) does its country cousin proud. The chic, white ground floor is buzzy, with a tiny café area on one side, and a manicure/pedicure section on the other. For facials, massages and waxing, head downstairs.

Other locations 31 Fouberts Place, Soho, W1 7QG (7534 0870); 115-117 Regents Park Road, Chalk Farm, NW1 8UR (3725 2777); Shoreditch House, Ebor Street, Shoreditch, E1 6AW (7749 4531); 162 Chiswick High Road, Chiswick, W4 1PR (8987 1607).

Honest Jon's

278 Portobello Road, W10 5TE (8969 9822, www.honestjons.com). Ladbroke Grove tube. **Open** 10am-6pm Mon-Sat; 11am-5pm Sun. **Map** p221 A1 ⓭ **Books & music**

Honest Jon's found its way to Notting Hill in 1979, and the owner helped James Lavelle to set up Mo'Wax records. You'll find jazz, hip hop, soul, broken beat, reggae and Brazilian music, as well as the label's own brilliant compilations – the first volumes of the *London is the Place for Me* series, detailing calypso, Afro-jazz and highlife in the post-war years, were a revelation.

Idler Academy

81 Westbourne Park Road, W2 5QH (0845 250 1281, www.idler.co.uk/academy). Royal Oak tube. **Open** 10am-6pm Wed-Sun. **Map** p221 C1 ⓮ **Books & music**

Tom Hodgkinson has made a career out of being idle. He edits *The Idler* magazine, has written books on the subject and now runs this café/bookshop/centre of learning to spread the word further. It's a lovely place, with a tiny patio garden and ample space for lounging inside. The emphasis is not really on food. Stop in for a Monmouth filter coffee, or tea and a slice of cake, and take some intellectual nourishment from bookshelves packed with Plato, Virgil and ukuleles.

Lutyens & Rubinstein

21 Kensington Park Road, W11 2EU (7229 1010, www.lutyensrubinstein.co.uk). Ladbroke Grove tube. **Open** 10am-6pm Mon, Sat; 10am-6.30pm Tue-Fri; 11am-6pm Sun. **Map** p221 B2 ⓯ **Books & music**

Lutyens & Rubinstein sells a beautifully arranged selection of literary fiction and general non-fiction. The core stock was put together by the owners canvassing hundreds of readers on the books they'd most like to find in a bookshop; thus every book stocked is sold because somebody has recommended it. The result is an appealing alternative to the homogeneous chain bookshops, with some unusual titles available. As well as books, the shop stocks a small range of stationery, greetings cards, paperweights, local honey and literary-inspired scents from CB I Hate Perfume.

Portobello Road Market

Portobello Road, W10 (www.portobelloroad.co.uk). Ladbroke Grove or Notting Hill Gate tube. **Open** *General* 9am-6pm Mon-Wed; 9am-1pm Thur; 7am-7pm Fri, Sat. *Antiques* 6am-4pm Fri, Sat. **No credit cards. Map** p221 B3 ⓰ **Market**

Best known for antiques and collectibles, this is actually several markets rolled into one: antiques start at the Notting Hill end; further up are food stalls; under the Westway and along the walkway to Ladbroke Grove are emerging designer and vintage clothes on Fridays (usually marginally less busy) and Saturdays (invariably manic).

Sasti

6 Portobello Green Arcade, 281 Portobello Road, Notting Hill, W10 5TZ (8960 1125, www.sasti.co.uk). Ladbroke Grove tube. **Open** 10am-6pm Mon-Sat; noon-5pm Sun. **Map** p221 A1 ⓱ **Children**

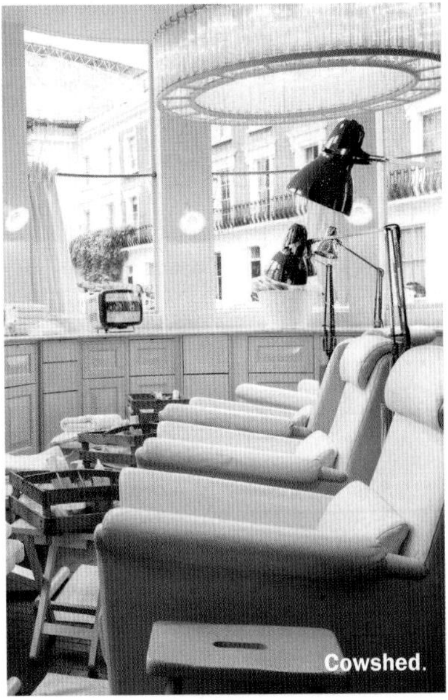
Cowshed.

EXPLORE

This affordable children's boutique sells delightfully fun clothes for little girls and boys. Perennial best-sellers include the bunny dresses, flower-covered skirts, bus pyjamas, nursery rhyme blouses and kitten scarves. Apart from its own-label clothes, Sasti also stocks items from Pixie Dixie.

KENSINGTON & HOLLAND PARK

High Street Kensington or Holland Park tube.

Just off **Kensington High Street**, a smart but rarely intoxicating shopping drag, an array of handsome squares are lined with grand 19th-century houses, many of which still serve as single-family homes for the wealthy. Linking with Notting Hill (*see p220*) to the north, **Kensington Church Street** has many antique shops selling furniture so fine you would probably never dare use it. **St Mary Abbots** (http://smanews.weebly.com), at the junction of Church Street and High Street, is a Victorian neo-Gothic church. It was built – on the site of the 12th-century original – by Sir George Gilbert Scott between 1869 and 1872. Past worshippers have included Isaac Newton and William Wilberforce. As well as beautiful stained-glass windows, it has London's tallest spire (278 feet).

Across the road is a striking art deco building, once the department store Barkers but now organic food giant **Whole Foods Market** (*see p225*). South down Derry Street, past the entrance to the **Roof Gardens** – a restaurant and private members' club with flamingos and a stream, 100 feet above central London – is Kensington Square,

DESIGNS ON KENSINGTON

The new museum premises that are a design classic in themselves.

Throughout his career, Terence Conran has been a pioneer of great design in everyday life, and it was he who decided, more than a quarter of a century ago, that London must have a Design Museum (*see p63*). The museum opened in 1989, in one of the warehouses of Shad Thames that had been left dilapidated when major shipping left the Pool of London. The premises were soon unrecognisable, as a clean-lined white building emerged from the fabric of a 1940s banana warehouse. Currently some 200,000 visitors a year come to see changing exhibitions such as global architect Zaha Hadid's debut solo show.

With the arrival of a new director, Deyan Sudjic, in 2006, ambitious plans began to be hatched: for one thing, there had never been enough room to show off the museum's own design collection. Eyes turned to the Grade II*-listed former Commonwealth Institute on Kensington High Street. Opened in 1962, but closed since 2002, it is a distinctive place, built to look like a tent, with a remarkable hyperbolic paraboloid roof (made of 25 tonnes of copper mined in what was then Rhodesia).

The new museum will be designed by John Pawson, at a cost of £80m (£17m of which is coming from Conran). As well as bringing a classic modernist building back into use, there will be three times as much gallery space. And access to the permanent collection – to open in 2015 – will be free.

which has a mighty concentration of blue plaques. The writer William Thackeray lived at no.16 and the painter Edward Burne-Jones at no.41; at no.18, John Stuart Mill's maid made her bid for 'person from Porlock' status by using Carlyle's sole manuscript of *The French Revolution* to light the fire. The houses, though much altered, date from the development of the square in 1685, and were surrounded by fields until 1840.

Further west is one of London's finest green spaces: **Holland Park**. Along its eastern edge, Holland Walk is one of the most pleasant paths in central London, but the heart of the park is the Jacobean **Holland House**. Left derelict after World War II, it was bought by the London County Council in 1952; the east wing now houses the city's best-sited youth hostel (*see p254*). In summer, open-air theatre and opera are staged on the front terrace. Three lovely formal gardens are laid out near the house. A little further west, the Japanese-style Kyoto Garden has huge koi carp and a bridge at the foot of a waterfall.

To the south of the park are another two historic houses: **18 Stafford Terrace** and, extensively refurbished, **Leighton House** (for both, *see below*), as well as the Commonwealth Institute, soon to be home to the **Design Museum** (*see below*).

Sights & museums

18 Stafford Terrace

18 Stafford Terrace, W8 7BH (tours 7602 3316, www.rbkc.gov.uk). High Street Kensington tube. **Open** (pre-booked tours only) *Mid Sept-mid June* 11.15am, 2.15pm Wed; 11.15am, 1pm, 2.15pm, 3.30pm Sat, Sun. **Tours** £8; £3-£6 reductions. **Map** p221 C6 ⓲

The home of cartoonist Edward Linley Sambourne was built in the 1870s and has almost all of its original fittings and furniture. At the weekend, tours (except at 11.15am) are led by an actor in period costume.

▶ *If you enjoy the costume tours here, try those at Benjamin Franklin House; see p146.*

Design Museum

Kensington High Street, W14 8ND (7403 6933, http://designmuseum.org/). High Street Kensington tube. **Map** p221 C6 ⓳

The Design Museum is due to open in a remodelled Commonwealth Institute building in 2015; for details, *see p224* **Designs on Kensington**.

▶ *Until the new premises are ready, the museum remains open in its Shad Thames site; see p63.*

★ Leighton House

12 Holland Park Road, W14 8LZ (7602 3316, www.rbkc.gov.uk). High Street Kensington tube. **Open** 10am-5.30pm Mon, Wed-Sun. *Tours* 3pm Wed (other times by appointment only). **Admission** £5; £3 reductions. **Map** p221 B6 ⓴

In the 1860s, artist Frederic Leighton commissioned a showpiece house. Behind the sternly Victorian red-brick façade, he made sure it was full of treasures from all over the world, as well as his own works and those of his contemporaries. The house is decorated in high style: magnificent downstairs reception rooms designed for lavish entertaining; a dramatic staircase leading to a light-filled studio that takes up most of the first floor; and, above all, the Arab Hall, which showcases Leighton's huge collection of 16th-century Middle Eastern tiles. The only private space in the whole house is a tiny single bedroom.

Restaurants

Clarke's

124 Kensington Church Street, W8 4BH (7221 9225, www.sallyclarke.com). Notting Hill Gate tube. **Open** 8am-10pm Mon-Sat. **Main courses** £20-£27.50. **Map** p221 D4 ㉑ **Modern European**

At Clarke's, that irritatingly overused 'best ingredients, simply prepared' phrase is actually true; a salad of peas, baby broad beans, spinach and grilled courgette looks like spring on a plate, while roast salmon fillet is a gorgeous deep pink, set off by explosively sweet baked tomatoes and olives. Chef-proprietor Sally Clarke has been espousing the 'seasonal and local' ethic since the mid 1980s. There's also a deli across the road, where goodies include Clarke's bread, at 1 Campden Street, W8 7EP, 7229 2190.

Yashin

1A Argyll Road, W8 7DB (7938 1536, www.yashinsushi.com). High Street Kensington tube. **Open** noon-2.15pm, 6-10pm daily. **Dishes** £3.50-£24.80. **Map** p221 C6 ㉒ **Sushi**

Yashin's exterior looks more like a smart French brasserie than a Japanese restaurant. But the centrepiece sushi counter gives the game away as soon as you step inside. Set on the dark green tiles behind the team of *itamae* (sushi chefs), a neon sign reads 'without soy sauce', and this is how the chefs ask you to eat your artfully crafted sushi. In place of a dunking, each piece is finished with its own flavourings – perhaps a dab of tangy ume plum paste, a spoon of tosa jelly, or a quick blast from a blowtorch. **Other location** 117-119 Old Brompton Road, South Kensington, SW7 3RN (7373 3990).

Shops & services

Whole Foods Market

63-97 Kensington High Street, W8 5SE (7368 4500, www.wholefoodmarket.com). High Street Kensington tube. **Open** 8am-10pm Mon-Sat; 10am-6pm Sun. **Map** p221 D6 ㉓ **Food & drink**

The London flagship of the American health-food supermarket chain occupies the handsome deco building that was once Barkers department store. There are several eateries on the premises. **Other locations** throughout the city.

Further Afield

London is an old city – there are Bronze Age remains on the Vauxhall foreshore – and one that industrialised early, opening the world's first underground railway in 1863. Thus it is both large (600 square miles) and dense in historic attractions. In this chapter, we try to gather the most interesting self-contained areas of the city, and round up the single attractions worthiest of your attention.

Sigmund Freud, Karl Marx and John Keats all settled in north London: find out why among the grand squares of Islington or in villagey Hampstead and Highgate; Camden has its own chapter *(see pp188-195)*. In east London – not at all the same thing as the East End (*see pp196-211)* – we highlight Docklands and the Olympic Park, as well as hipster Dalston and rapidly gentrifying Hackney, on the northern fringe of the East End proper. After that, head 'south of the river' – where, apocryphally, black cabbies refuse to go – for Greenwich (in its own chapter, *see pp212-217*) and once-troubled Brixton.

Highgate Cemetery.

Don't Miss

1 Kenwood House 17th-century country manor house (p229).

2 William Morris Gallery Home of the man behind the fabric (p233).

3 Highgate Cemetery Victorian tombs and Karl Marx's grave (p230).

4 Ottolenghi Flagship brasserie from the cookbook star (p232).

5 Queen Elizabeth Olympic Park Flowers, waterways and art (p237).

HAMPSTEAD

Hampstead tube, or Gospel Oak or Hampstead Heath rail.

It may have been absorbed into London during the city's great Victorian expansion, but hilltop Hampstead still feels like a Home Counties' village. It has long been a favoured roost for literary and artistic types: Keats and Constable lived here in the 19th century, and sculptors Barbara Hepworth and Henry Moore took up residence in the 1930s. However, the area is now popular with City workers, who are among the only people able to afford what is some of London's priciest property.

The undisputed highlight of the district is **Hampstead Heath**, the vast and in places wonderfully overgrown tract of countryside between Hampstead village and Highgate that is said to have inspired CS Lewis's Narnia. The heath covers 791 acres of woodland, playing fields, swimming ponds and meadows of tall grass that attract picnickers and couples in search of privacy.

The south end of the heath is where you'll find dinky Hampstead village, all genteel shops and cafés, restaurants and lovely pubs such as the **Holly Bush** (*see p230*). While you're there, tour the gorgeous sunken gardens and antique collection at **Fenton House** (*see p229*) or gaze at the stars from the **Hampstead Scientific Society Observatory** (Lower Terrace, www.hampsteadscience.ac.uk/astro), open on clear Friday and Saturday evenings and Sunday lunchtimes from mid September to mid April. A stroll along nearby Judges Walk reveals a line of horse chestnuts and limes virtually unchanged since they appeared in a Constable painting in 1820. Constable was buried nearby at **St John-at-Hampstead Church** (7794 5808, www.hampsteadparishchurch.org.uk), as was the comedian Peter Cook. At the top of Hampstead, North End Way divides the main heath from the wooded West Heath, one of London's oldest gay cruising areas (but perfectly family-friendly by day). Just off North End Way is Hampstead's best-kept secret, the secluded and charmingly overgrown **Hill Garden & Pergola** (open 8.30am-dusk daily), which was built by Lord Leverhulme using soil from the excavation of the Northern line's tunnels.

East of Hampstead tube, a maze of postcard-pretty residential streets shelters **Burgh House** (New End Square, 7431 0144, www.burghhouse.org.uk), a Queen Anne house with a small local history museum and gallery. Also in the area are **2 Willow Road** (*see below*), architect Ernö Goldfinger's self-designed 1930s residence, and **40 Well Walk**, Constable's home for the last ten years of his life. Downhill towards Hampstead Heath Overground station is **Keats House** (*see p229*). Further west, and marginally closer to Finchley Road tube, is the **Freud Museum** (*see p229*), while the contemporary art exhibitions of **Camden Arts Centre** (*see 229*) are almost opposite Finchley Road & Frognal Overground station.

Sights & museums

2 Willow Road

2 Willow Road, NW3 1TH (7435 6166, www.nationaltrust.org.uk). Hampstead tube or Hampstead Heath rail. **Open** *Mar-Oct* 11am-5pm Wed-Sun. *Tours* 11am, noon, 1pm, 2pm Wed-Sun.

Admission £6; £3 children; free under-5s; £15 family. *Joint ticket with Fenton House £9.*
A surprising addition to the National Trust's collection of historic houses, this small modernist building was designed by Hungarian-born architect Ernö Goldfinger. The house was made to be flexible, with ingenious movable partitions and folding doors. Home to the architect and his wife until their deaths, it contains a fine, idiosyncratic collection of art by the likes of Max Ernst and Henry Moore. Goldfinger also designed Notting Hill's Trellick Tower.

Camden Arts Centre

Arkwright Road, NW3 6DG (7472 5500, www.camdenartscentre.org). Finchley Road tube or Finchley Road & Frognal rail. **Open** 10am-6pm Tue, Thur-Sun; 10am-9pm Wed. **Admission** free.
Under the directorship of Jenni Lomax, Camden Arts Centre has eclipsed larger venues. The annual artist-curated shows – sculpture, automata, film works – have been among the most memorable in recent history. The Centre also hosts a comprehensive programme of talks, events and workshops and boasts a good bookshop and a great café, which opens on to a surprisingly tranquil garden.

Fenton House

3 Hampstead Grove, NW3 6RT (7435 3471, www.nationaltrust.org.uk). Hampstead tube. **Open** *Mar-Oct* times vary; check website for details. **Admission** *House & gardens* £6.50; £3 reductions; £16 family; free under-5s. *Gardens* £2. *Joint ticket with 2 Willow Road* £9.
Set in a gorgeous garden, with a 300-year-old apple orchard, this manor house is notable for its 17th- and 18th-century harpsichords, virginals and spinets, which are still played at lunchtime and evening concerts (phone for details). Also on display are European and Chinese porcelain, Chippendale furniture and some artful 17th-century needlework.

Freud Museum

20 Maresfield Gardens, NW3 5SX (7435 2002, www.freud.org.uk). Finchley Road tube. **Open** noon-5pm Wed-Sun. **Admission** £6; £3-£4.50 reductions; free under-12s.
Driven from Vienna by the Nazis, Sigmund Freud lived in this quiet house in north London with his wife Martha and daughter Anna until his death in 1939. Now a museum with imaginative temporary exhibitions, the house displays Freud's antiques, art and therapy tools, including his famous couch. Unusually, the building has two blue plaques, one for Sigmund and another for Anna, a pioneer in child psychiatry.

Keats House

Keats Grove, NW3 2RR (7332 3868, www.cityoflondon.gov.uk/keatshousehampstead). Hampstead tube, Hampstead Heath rail or bus 24, 46, 168. **Open** *Mar-Oct* 1-5pm Tue-Sun. *Nov-Feb* 1-5pm Fri-Sun. **Admission** £5; £3 reductions; free under-18s.
Keats House was the Romantic poet's last British home before tuberculosis forced him to Italy and death at the age of only 25. A leaflet guides you through each room, starting from the rear, as well as providing context for Keats's life and that of his less famous friend and patron, Charles Brown. Painstaking renovation has ensured the decorative scheme is entirely accurate, down to pale pink walls in Keats's humble bedroom. The garden, in which he wrote 'Ode to a Nightingale', is particularly pleasant.

★ FREE Kenwood House/Iveagh Bequest

Hampstead Lane, NW3 7JR (8348 1286, www.english-heritage.org.uk). Hampstead tube, or Golders Green tube then bus 210. **Open** 9am-4pm daily. **Admission** free.
Set in lovely grounds at the top of Hampstead Heath, Kenwood House is every inch the country manor house. Built in 1616, the mansion was remodelled in the 18th century for William Murray, who made the pivotal court ruling in 1772 that made it illegal to own slaves in England. The house was purchased by brewing magnate Edward Guinness, who was kind enough to donate his art collection to the nation in 1927. It reopened in 2014 after extensive, splendid renovations, returning the interiors to a state that enhances such highlights as Vermeer's *The Guitar Player*, Gainsborough's *Countess Howe*, and one of Rembrandt's finest self-portraits (dating to c1663).

Restaurants

★ Bull & Last

168 Highgate Road, NW5 1QS (7267 3641, www.thebullandlast.co.uk). Kentish Town tube/rail then bus 214, C2, or Gospel Oak rail then bus C11. **Open** noon-11pm Mon-Thur; 9am-midnight Fri, Sat; 9am-10.30pm Sun. **Main courses** £8.50-£22. **Gastropub**
For a place with such a good reputation for its food, the Bull & Last is refreshingly pubby: heavy wooden furniture, velvet drapes, stuffed animals and old prints decorate both the bar and the upstairs dining room. The latter is a calmer and cooler place to eat than the ground-floor bar, and allows diners to focus on dishes such as king scallop carpaccio with pink grapefruit, crème fraîche, coriander and vinaigrette, or pig's cheek with watermelon pickle, basil and sesame. There are (big) roasts at weekends, a changing selection of beers and ciders from small breweries and a decent wine list.

★ Wells

30 Well Walk, NW3 1BX (7794 3785, www.thewellshampstead.co.uk). Hampstead tube or Hampstead Heath rail. **Open** Food served noon-3pm, 6-10pm Mon-Fri; noon-4pm, 7-10pm Sat; noon-4pm, 7-9.30pm Sun. **Main courses** £11.50-£16.75. **Gastropub**

EXPLORE

The dining rooms above this very soigné Georgian pub are a useful addition to Hampstead's relatively limited restaurant scene. The menu is appealing without being faddish or daring. Perfectly grilled scallops with crisp bacon, samphire and shallot and rocket purées might be followed by crisp-skinned sea bass on tender fennel, courgette, chorizo, green beans and red pepper; there's also a section of the menu devoted to steaks. Add solicitous service and well-chosen wines at friendly prices and the Wells is a winner.

Pubs & bars

The **Horseshoe** (28 Heath Street, NW3 6TE, 020 7431 7206) in Hampstead is an excellent gastropub which doesn't disappoint on the own-brewed ale front.

★ Holly Bush

22 Holly Mount, NW3 6SG (7435 2892, www.hollybushhampstead.co.uk). Hampstead tube or Hampstead Heath rail. **Open** noon-11pm Mon-Sat; noon-10.30pm Sun. *Food served* noon-3pm, 6-10pm Mon-Fri; noon-4pm, 6-10pm Sat; noon-8pm Sun.

As the trend for gutting old pubs claims yet more Hampstead boozers, this place's cachet increases. Located on a quiet hilltop backstreet, it was built as a house in the 1790s and used as the Assembly Rooms in the 1800s, before becoming a pub in 1928. A higgledy-piggledy air remains, with three low-ceilinged bar areas and one bar counter at which are poured decent pints. Sound food and a good choice of wines by the glass are further draws.

EXPLORE

HIGHGATE

Archway or Highgate tube.

Taking its name from the tollgate that once stood on the High Street, Highgate is inexorably linked with London's medieval mayor, Richard 'Dick' Whittington. As the story goes, the disheartened Whittington, having failed to make his fortune, fled the City as far as Highgate Hill, but turned back when he heard the Bow Bells peal out 'Turn again, Whittington, thrice Mayor of London'. Today, the area is best known for the atmospheric grounds of **Highgate Cemetery** (*see right*). Adjoining the cemetery is pretty **Waterlow Park**, created by low-cost housing pioneer Sir Sydney Waterlow in 1889, with ponds, a mini-aviary, tennis courts and a cute garden café in 16th-century **Lauderdale House** (8348 8716, www.lauderdalehouse.co.uk), former home of Charles II's mistress, Nell Gwynn. North of Highgate tube, shady **Highgate Woods** are preserved as a conservation area, with a nature trail, an adventure playground and a café that hosts live jazz during the summer.

Sights & museums

★ Highgate Cemetery

Swains Lane, N6 6PJ (8340 1834, www.highgate-cemetery.org). Archway tube. **Open** *East Cemetery* Mar-Oct 10am-5pm Mon-Fri; 11am-5pm Sat, Sun. Nov-Feb 10am-4pm Mon-Fri; 11am-4pm Sat, Sun. *West Cemetery* by tour only. **Admission** £4; free under 18s. *Tours* £12; £6 reductions.

The final resting place of some very famous Londoners, Highgate Cemetery is a wonderfully overgrown maze of ivy-cloaked Victorian tombs and time-shattered urns. Visitors can wander at their own pace through the East Cemetery, with its memorials to Karl Marx, George Eliot and Douglas Adams, but the most atmospheric part of the cemetery is the foliage-shrouded West Cemetery, laid out in 1839. Only accessible on an organised tour (book ahead, dress respectfully and arrive 30mins early), the shady paths wind past gloomy catacombs, grand Victorian pharaonic tombs, and the graves of notables such as poet Christina Rossetti, scientist Michael Faraday and poisoned Russian dissident Alexander Litvinenko.

► *The cemetery closes during burials, so call ahead before you visit. Note that children under eight are not allowed in the West Cemetery.*

Pubs & bars

Bull

13 North Hill, N6 4AB (8341 0510, www.thebullhighgate.co.uk). Highgate tube. **Open** noon-11.30pm Mon-Thur; noon-midnight Fri, Sat; noon-10.30pm Sun. *Food served* noon-10pm Mon-Sat; noon-9pm Sun. **Main courses** £11-21.50.

First impressions would suggest the Bull is just another suburban gastropub, but note the enamelled beer memorabilia on the walls and garlands of hop flowers: this pub holds beer in extremely high esteem. You might catch a glimpse of the Willy Wonka tubing and brass vats of the brewing equipment, and the beer taps reveal almost nothing recognisable from the average high-street chain pub. Five of the pumps dispense the fine products of the

IN THE KNOW
BEAUTY ON THE INSIDE

Printer Emery Walker was a friend and colleague of William Morris, the founder of the Arts and Crafts Movement, and his house at **7 Hammersmith Terrace** is an immaculately preserved time capsule of a perfectly realised Arts and Crafts home. Tours take place every Saturday from April to October and by prior arrangement. See www.emerywalker.org.uk for further details.

Holly Bush.

London Brewing Company, made on the premises, and keg fonts advertise the likes of Sierra Nevada Torpedo and Veltins Pils.

ISLINGTON

Angel tube or Highbury & Islington tube/rail.

Islington started life as a country village beside one of Henry VIII's expansive hunting reserves. It soon became an important livestock market supplying the Smithfield meat yards, before being enveloped into Greater London. The 19th century brought industrial development along the Regent's Canal and later industrial decay, but locals kept up their spirits at the area's music halls, launchpads for such working-class heroes as Marie Lloyd, George Formby and Norman Wisdom. From the 1960s, there was an influx of arts and media types, who gentrified the Georgian squares and Victorian terraces and opened cafés, restaurants and boutiques around Upper Street and Essex Road. It is now a suburban bower of the *Guardian*-reading middle classes.

Close to Angel station on Upper Street, the **Camden Passage** antique market bustles with browsing activity on Wednesdays and Saturdays. The music halls have long gone, but locals still take advantage of the celluloid offerings at the **Screen on the Green** (*see p255* **Everyman & Screen Cinemas**) and the stage productions at the **Almeida** theatre (*see p289*).

East of Angel, Regency-era **Canonbury Square** was once home to George Orwell (no.27) and Evelyn Waugh (no.17A). One of the handsome townhouses now contains the **Estorick Collection of Modern Italian Art** (*see below*). Just beyond the end of Upper Street is **Highbury Fields**, where 200,000 Londoners fled in 1666 to escape the Great Fire. The surrounding district is best known as the home of Arsenal Football Club, who abandoned the charming Highbury Stadium in 2006 for the gleaming 60,000-seater behemoth that is the **Emirates Stadium** (Ashburton Grove, N7 7AF). Fans can either take a fine self-guided audio tour of the stadium or check out the memorabilia at the **Arsenal Museum** (7619 5000, www.arsenal.com). Dedicated football fans will enjoy walking a couple of blocks east to Avenell Road, where Archibald Leitch's palatial East Stand has been preserved as offices; on parallel Highbury Hill, a single painted house marks the entrance to the vanished West Stand.

Sights & museums

Estorick Collection of Modern Italian Art

39A Canonbury Square, N1 2AN (7704 9522, www.estorickcollection.com). Highbury & Islington tube/rail or bus 271. **Open** 11am-6pm Wed-Sat; noon-5pm Sun. **Admission** £5; £3.50 reductions; free under-16s, students.

Originally owned by American political scientist and writer Eric Estorick, this is a wonderful depository of early 20th-century Italian art. It is one of the world's foremost collections of futurism, Italy's brash and confrontational contribution to international modernism. The four galleries are full of movement, machines and colour, while the temporary exhibits meet the futurist commitment to fascism full on. There is also a shop and café.

Restaurants

Ottolenghi

287 Upper Street, N1 2TZ (7288 1454, www.ottolenghi.co.uk). Angel tube or Highbury & Islington tube/rail. **Open** 8am-10.30pm Mon-Sat; 9am-7pm Sun. **Main courses** £11.50-£16.70. **Café**

Hit cookbooks have made this flagship branch of the burgeoning Ottolenghi empire a point of pilgrimage for foodies the world over. French toast made from brioche and served with crème fraîche and a thin berry and muscat compote makes a heady start to the day. Or there's welsh rarebit, scrambled eggs with smoked salmon or a lively chorizo-spiked take on baked beans served with sourdough, fried egg and black pudding. In the evening (when bookings are taken), the cool white interior works a double shift as a smart and comparatively pricey restaurant serving elegant fusion dishes for sharing. Expect the likes of grilled quail with smoked chilli chocolate sauce, potato, pak choi and sesame – and expect to have trouble snaring a table.

Ottolenghi.

Other locations 63 Ledbury Road, Notting Hill, W11 2AD (7727 1121); 13 Motcomb Street, Belgravia, SW1X 8LB (7823 2707).

▶ *For more Yotam Ottolenghi food in a restaurant setting, try Nopi (21-22 Warwick Street, W1B 5NE, 7494 9584).*

Smokehouse

63-69 Canonbury Road, N1 2DG (7354 1144, www.smokehouseislington.co.uk). Highbury & Islington tube/rail. **Open** 6-10pm Mon-Fri; 11am-4pm, 6-10pm Sat; noon-9pm Sun. **Main courses** £12.50-£25. **Barbecue**

In the Big Smoke, chef Neil Rankin has become a high priest of barbecue. Trendy though the menu seems – it includes French bistro dishes, carefully sourced British produce and even Korean flavours – the mutton chops come from the grill, not the barman's cheeks, and they come fatty and full-flavoured. Mullet is smoked, cut into translucent slivers and served with white pickled clams, radishes and sea purslane. Pit-roasted corn on the cob, slathered with buttery smoked béarnaise sauce, shows that a barbecue expert doesn't just cook flesh.

★ Trullo

300-302 St Paul's Road, Islington, N1 2LH (7226 2733, www.trullorestaurant.com). Highbury & Islington tube/rail. **Open** 12.30-3pm, 6-10.30pm Mon-Sat; 12.30pm-3pm Sun. **Main courses** £14-£30. **Italian**

While evenings are still busy-to-frantic in this two-floored contemporary trattoria, lunchtime finds Trullo calm and the cooking relaxed and assured. A bargain £15 set menu gleans two courses (primi plus either antipasti or dessert) from a daily-changing menu. Grills and roasts from the carte might include Black Hampshire pork chop and cod with cannellini beans and mussels, while pappardelle with beef shin ragù has been a staple since Trullo's early days and remains a silky substantial delight.

Pubs & bars

The **Old Queen's Head** (*see p267*) is a boisterous and lively pub.

★ 69 Colebrooke Row

69 Colebrooke Row, Islington, N1 8AA (07540 528593, www.69colebrookerow.com). Angel tube. **Open** 5pm-midnight Mon-Wed, Sun; 5pm-1am Thur; 5pm-2am Fri, Sat.

It's not easy to get a seat in this flagship of bar supremo Tony Conigliaro without booking. Punters come for the outstanding cocktails; some of them may push the boundaries of what can be put in a glass, but they always maintain the drinkability of

ONE OF A KIND HISTORIC HOUSES

Places where the high, mighty – and mighty eccentric – lived.

Chiswick House

Burlington Lane, W4 2RP (8995 0508, www.chgt.org.uk). Hammersmith tube then bus 190, or Chiswick rail. **Open** *Apr-Oct* 10am-6pm Mon-Wed, Sun. *Oct-Nov* 10am-5pm Mon-Wed, Sun. **Admission** £6.10; £3.70-£5.50 reductions; £15.90 family; free under-5s.

Richard Boyle, third Earl of Burlington, designed this Palladian villa in 1725 as a place to entertain the artistic and philosophical luminaries of his day. The Chiswick House & Gardens Trust has restored the brilliant gardens (free entry) to the original design. The restoration was helped by details from a painting by Dutch landscape artist Pieter Andreas Rysbrack (c1685-1748), which can be seen here. There's an impressive café too (8995 6356, www.chiswickhousecafe.co.uk), built in startingly effective modern style.

Ham House

Ham Street, Richmond, Surrey TW10 7RS (8940 1950, www.nationaltrust.org.uk/hamhouse). Richmond tube/rail then bus 371. **Open** check website for details. **Admission** £10; £5 reductions; £25 family; free under-5s.

Built in 1610 for one of James I's courtiers, Thomas Vavasour, this lavish red-brick mansion is full of period furnishings, rococo mirrors and ornate tapestries. The restored formal grounds also attract attention: there's a lovely trellised Cherry Garden and some lavender parterres. The tearoom turns out historic dishes using ingredients from the Kitchen Gardens.

FREE Hogarth's House

Hogarth Lane, Great West Road, W4 2QN (8994 6757). Turnham Green tube or Chiswick rail. **Open** noon-5pm Tue-Sun. **Admission** free; donations appreciated.

Recently reopened after refurbishment, this was the country retreat of the 18th-century artist and social commentator William Hogarth. On display are some famous engravings, including *Gin Lane*, *Marriage à la Mode* and a copy of *Rake's Progress*, and plenty of biographical information. Despite the setting on a horrid main road, the garden is charming – and amazingly tranquil.

Strawberry Hill.

Strawberry Hill

268 Waldegrave Road, Twickenham, Middx TW1 4ST (8744 1241, www.strawberryhillhouse.org.uk). Richmond tube then bus R68, or Strawberry Hill rail. **Open** *Mar-Nov* 2-6pm Mon-Wed; noon-6pm Sat, Sun. **Admission** £12; £6 reductions; free under-16s.

Antiquarian Horace Walpole, who created the Gothic novel with his book *The Castle of Otranto*, laid the groundwork for the Gothic Revival of Victorian times as early as the 1700s. Pre-booked tickets, timed at 20-minute intervals, allow you to explore the crepuscular nooks and crannies of his 'play-thing house', this 'little Gothic castle'.

★ FREE William Morris Gallery

Lloyd Park, Forest Road, E17 4PP (8496 4390, www.wmgallery.org.uk). Walthamstow Central tube/rail or bus 34, 97, 215, 275. **Open** 10am-5pm Wed-Sun. **Admission** free; donations appreciated.

Artist, socialist and source of flowery wallpaper, William Morris lived here between 1848 and 1856. There are plenty of designs in fabric, stained glass and ceramic on show, produced by Morris and his acolytes. Excellent refurbishments improved the displays (which show off the medieval-style helmet and sword Morris used as props for murals, and the satchel from which he distributed political tracts) and created a popular tea room.

the classics. Take the Terroir, for instance, which lists as its ingredients 'distilled clay, flint and lichen', and tastes wonderfully like a chilled, earthy, minerally vodka. It's made in Conigliaro's upstairs laboratory, which also produces bespoke cocktail ingredients such as Guinness reduction, paprika bitters, rhubarb cordial and pine-infused gin. There's a subtle jazz-age vibe and – on certain nights – a pianist belts out swinging standards.

Shops & services

Islington isn't the shopping area it once was – many of the boutiques have vanished to be replaced by chainstores – but Upper Street still rewards a stroll.

Flashback

50 Essex Road, Islington, N1 8LR (7354 9356, www.flashback.co.uk). Angel tube then bus 38, 56, 73, 341. **Open** 10am-7pm Mon-Sat; 11.30am-6pm Sun. **Books & music**

Stock is scrupulously organised at this second-hand treasure trove. The ground floor is dedicated to CDs, while the basement is vinyl-only: an ever-expanding jazz collection jostles for space alongside soul, hip hop and a carpal tunnel-compressing selection of library sounds. A range of rarities is pinned in plastic sleeves to the walls. The shop also sells new vinyl. **Other location** 114 Crouch Hill, Stroud Green, N8 9DX (8342 9633).

Smug

13 Camden Passage, Islington, N1 8EA (7354 0253, www.ifeelsmug.com). Angel tube. **Open** noon-5pm Tue, Sun; 11am-6pm Wed, Fri, Sat; noon-7pm Thur. **Homewares**

Graphic designer Lizzie Evans has decked out this lovely lifestyle boutique with all her favourite things. You'll be treated to a well-edited selection of home accessories (owl ceramic candlesticks, say), plus vintage homewares (Welsh blankets, 1960s Formica furniture), colourful cushions, Pixie make-up, home-made brooches, old-fashioned notebooks, retro Casio watches and a range of graphic-print men's T-shirts.

DALSTON & HACKNEY

Dalston Kingsland, Dalston Junction, London Fields or Hackney Central rail.

The opening of the East London line in 2010 leaves even bus-averse visitors few excuses to ignore this part of town. Occupying the area around the junction of Balls Pond Road and Kingsland Road, scruffy Dalston may be summed up these days by African-flavoured Ridley Road market: routinely praised by hipsters for its authentic cultural mix, it's still 'real' enough that some stallholders were caught selling 'illicit' meat in 2012. Safer to head to one of the delicious Turkish *ocakbaşı* (grill restaurants) along Stoke Newington Road, although the throngs of hipsters OMGing over sharing plates and the latest 'dirty' food pop-up are the current zeitgeist. In truth, even as the brand managers descend, Dalston remains a cool and lively part of London – with several establishments now well established. All tribes play together happily enough at the appealingly urban **Dalston Jazz Bar** (4 Bradbury Street, 7254 9728), the brilliant **Vortex Jazz Club** (*see p277*) and **Café Oto** (*see p276*). Also near the Overground station is an appealing 'micropark', the delightfully urban **Dalston Eastern Curve Garden** (3 Dalston Lane, E8 3DF, http://dalstongarden.org).

Neighbouring **Stoke Newington** is the richer cousin of Dalston and poorer cousin of Islington. At weekends, pretty **Clissold Park** (www.clissoldpark.com) is overrun with picnickers and mums pushing prams. Most visitors head to Stoke Newington for bijou **Church Street**. This curvy road is lined with second-hand bookshops, cute boutiques and kids' stores, and superior cafés and restaurants – Keralan vegetarian restaurant **Rasa** (no.55, 7249 0344) is probably the best of them. Another local highlight is **Abney Park Cemetery** (www.abney-park.org.uk), a wonderfully wild, overgrown Victorian boneyard and nature reserve.

Alongside Stoke Newington to the east, Hackney has few blockbuster sights, but is one of London's fastest changing areas – a pioneer in the current wave of gentrification. Its administrative centre is Town Hall Square on Mare Street, where you'll find a century-old music hall, the **Hackney Empire** (291 Mare Street, 8985 2424, www.hackney empire.co.uk); an art deco town hall; a multiscreen cinema in the old Victorian library; and the fine little **Hackney Museum** (1 Reading Lane, 8356 3500, www.hackney.gov.uk/cm-museum.htm), in the 21st-century library. Opposite, an ambitious failed music venue has become a successful cinema (**Hackney Picturehouse**; *see p255*). Within walking distance to the east is the historic **Sutton House**.

Sights & museums

Sutton House

2-4 Homerton High Street, E9 6JQ (8986 2264, www.nationaltrust.org.uk). Bethnal Green tube then bus 254, 106, D6, or Hackney Central rail. **Open** times vary; check website for details. **Admission** £3.50; £1 reductions; £6.90 family; free under-5s, National Trust members.

Smug.

Built in 1535 for Henry VIII's first secretary of state, Sir Ralph Sadleir, this red-brick Tudor mansion is east London's oldest home. Now beautifully restored in authentic original decor, with a real Tudor kitchen to boot, it makes no secret of its history of neglect: even some 1980s squatter graffiti has been preserved. The house closes for January each year.

Restaurants

19 Numara Bos Cirrik

34 Stoke Newington Road, N16 7XJ (7249 0400, www.cirrik1.co.uk). Dalston Kingsland rail. **Open** noon-midnight daily **Main courses** £9.50-£13.50. **Turkish**

Benefiting from Dalston's gentrification, 19 Numara Bos Cirrik has firmly established itself as the hipsters' ocakbası of choice, yet standards haven't slipped at this ever-busy joint: starting with bread that's piping-hot, feather-light, smoky and carrying hints of onion and tomato. The pide is every bit as good, while the likes of lamb beyti perfectly balance garlic, chilli and smoky charcoal tones.

Tina, We Salute You

47 King Henry's Walk, N1 4NH (3119 0047, www.tinawesaluteyou.com). Dalston Kingsland rail or bus 38. **Open** 8am-6pm Mon-Fri; 10am-6pm Sat, Sun. **Main courses** £4-£6. **No credit cards. Café**

Tina's puts you instantly at ease: the large communal table in the middle (sofas and a handful of pavement tables also available for early arrivers) – populated with help-yourself jars of Marmite and jam, and locals helping each other with the *Guardian* crossword – feels like your best friend's kitchen table. Owners Danny and Steve make all the cakes at home, but there's also a comforting breakfast menu (poached eggs, pancakes with berries, porridge) that eases itself into lunch (toasted sandwiches, bagels, ploughman's). Tina's also serves good coffee; expand your tastes beyond the usual latte with a Gibraltar (between a mini latte and a large macchiato).

★ Towpath

Regent's Canal towpath, between Whitmore Bridge and Kingsland Road Bridge, N1 5SB (no phone). **Open** *Mar-Nov* 8am-dusk Tue-Fri; 9am-dusk Sat, Sun. **Main courses** £3-£8. **Café**

This simple operation on Regent's Canal towpath was a novelty when it opened in 2010. Its four shallow units continue to lure passing walkers and cyclists with its original setting and enticing food and drink, even with a couple of more elaborate restaurants now on the same block. Wing a table in the sunshine on a summer's day, and you might end up staying for hours. Relaxed entertainment is provided by coots tending their nests and passing bikes whizzing by, as you tuck into delicious grilled cheese sandwiches and decent coffee.

Pubs & bars

★ Cock Tavern

315 Mare Street, E8 1EJ (www.thecocktavern.co.uk). Hackney Central rail. **Open** from noon daily.

The Cock Tavern is the sort of place you walk into and think: This is a bloody good pub. It's dark, uncomplicated and resonant with merry conversation. Put simply, it's a room for grown-ups to stand in and drink beer. It's timelessly classic: aside from the Victorian beards on the bar staff, it could be any era between 1920 and 2013 in here. It's usually rammed here, and it's mainly down to the fabulous beer and cider: the pub cellar is now home to the Howling Hops microbrewery, whose output is mostly drunk in the Cock. A few guests pop up too among the 22 taps, but with a home-brewed selection this good, you might not need them. To fill you up there's gloriously simple food. A bartop cabinet displays Scotch eggs and pork pies, and there's a jar of pickled eggs.

Railway Tavern

2 St Jude Street, N16 8JT (020 0011 1195). Dalston Kingsland rail. **Open** 4-11pm Mon-Fri; noon-midnight Sat; noon-10.30pm Sun.

The Railway Tavern has been given a thoughtful makeover, with a few bits of artful railway ephemera here and there. Food is Thai; musicians frequently play, but visit for the beers. There are six regularly changing real ales on tap, and they're often made in London – from Redemption, Brodie's or the East London Brewing Company, for instance. On the keg taps are Meantime London Lager, König Pilsner, Black Isle Porter and Brewdog's 5am Saint. The bottles pay homage to the microbrewing nous of the Americans. The brews are served in handled, dimpled pint mugs: magic.

Shops & services

For a fashion show and farmers' market in one, head to Hackney's **Broadway Market** on Saturday.

Aquascutum

7-8 Chatham Place, E9 6LT (3478 0928, www.aquascutum.co.uk). Hackney Central or Homerton rail. **Open** 10am-6.30pm Mon-Fri; 9am-6pm Sat; 11am-5pm Sun. **Fashion**

The Aquascutum outlet shop is bang opposite Burberry's factory shop (29-31 Chatham Place, E9 6LP, 8328 4287) – meaning it gets a nice cut of the tourist traffic that comes to this unlikely spot in east London. In many ways, the Aquascutum store is superior to its neighbour. For a start, it's cheaper – a perfect cashmere knit is around £70 (down from £230) and a classic Harrington jacket is £150 (from £300). And, unlike other sale shops crammed with tat and inferior made-for-sale products, this one has the feel of a luxury store.

► *Also in Hackney, the Pringle of Scotland Outlet, 86 Morning Lane, E9 6NA (www.pringlescotland.com) has argyle sweaters, cashmere twinsets and polo shirts at 50% or more off their original price.*

LN-CC

18-24 Shacklewell Lane, E8 2EZ (3174 0726, www.ln-cc.com). Dalston Kingsland rail. **Open** by appointment only. **Fashion, books & music**

LN-CC, otherwise known as the Late Night Chameleon Club, is as mysterious as its name suggests. Accessed by appointment via a basement-level door in an unlikely Shacklewell warehouse building, the store is a Tim Burton-like wonderland rendered in natural wood with a secret dancefloor, tree house, listening library and London's most unique edit of super-rare fashion. Ostensibly a showroom for internet boutique LN-CC.com, the space is a gallery for upscale design, selling super-posh brands like Rik Owens, Givenchy, Lanvin and any number of hard-to-pronounce rarities (try saying shoe brand 'Cherevichkiotvichki' after one too many shandies). With vinyl, art books and eyewear, and stock separated into different themed zones, LN-CC is a shop like no other.

Olympic Park.

IN THE KNOW ALL ABOARD!

Transport boffins and fans of design classics: the **London Transport Museum** (*see p138*) opens its Acton depot to visitors on a few weekends a year. This west London warehouse contains over 370,000 objects that wouldn't fit into the Covent Garden premises, including vehicles – a 1950s Routemaster bus prototype among them – and vintage posters and uniforms. See www.ltmuseum.co.uk for details.

OLYMPIC PARK

The Olympic Park, scene of the 2012 Games, is a square mile of the Lower Lea Valley in east London. Closed between the end of the Paralympics and spring 2014, it is now fully open. After a sporting summer that exceeded most predictions – and won over many critics – the Games are long gone and only the contentious business of 'legacy' remains: arguments over what benefits have been brought to Londoners by the £8.77bn spent on the Games may continue for generations, but the physical legacy of the post-Games Olympic Park – officially renamed the **Queen Elizabeth Olympic Park** (www.queenelizabetholympic park.co.uk) in January 2013 – is becoming clear.

The immaculate parklands to the north had already been launched in summer 2013, their paths and waterways enhanced by the new Timber Lodge with its café. Next came the Zaha Hadid-designed **Aquatics Centre** (£3.50-£4.50 adults, £2-£2.50 reductions), open for public swimming and diving sessions, followed by the **VeloPark**, home to road, track, BMX and mountain biking, and the southern section of the park. The latter comprises all the remaining parkland, including children's play areas, four walking trails, a couple of dozen public artworks, plus the **ArcelorMittal Orbit** (*see right*). All that remains is the Olympic Stadium, which is currently being retooled (including the addition of a roof over the seats). It is due to reopen for the Rugby World Cup in 2015, before West Ham football club take up permanent residence in 2016. Further ahead, the venue wil host the 2017 IAAF World Championships and 2017 IPC World Athletics Championships. In the meantime, it will continue to host music events Hard Rock Calling and the Wireless Festival. For a good vantage point on the park, head to **Moka East** (*see right*) in the View Tube. And if you've a little time on your hands, stroll south along the Lea towards the Thames to **Three Mills Island** (*see right*), or north.

Sights & museums

ArcelorMittal Orbit

Queen Elizabeth Olympic Park (www.queen elizabetholympicpark.co.uk). Stratford tube/ rail/DLR or West Ham tube/rail. **Open** check website for details. **Admission** £15; £7-£12 reductions; £40 family.

Perhaps the most dramatic structure in the Olympic Park, overlooking the Olympic Stadium, is the Orbit. Designed by sculptor Anish Kapoor and engineer Cecil Balmond, it is red, 374 feet tall and not much loved by locals. The peripheral location – compared to both Shard (*see p63*) and Eye (*see p51*) – makes the view interesting rather than breathtaking, but Kapoor's arty mirrors inside are really fun.

Three Mills

Three Mill Lane, E3 3DU (8980 4626, www. housemill.org.uk). Bromley-by-Bow tube. **Tours** *May-Oct* 1-4pm Sun. **Admission** £3; £1.50 reductions; free under-16s. **No credit cards**.

Just south of the Olympic Park, this island on the River Lea takes its name from the three mills that ground flour and gunpowder here. The House Mill, built in 1776, is the oldest and largest tidal mill in Britain and is occasionally opened to the public. Even when it's closed, the island provides pleasant walks that can feel surprisingly rural. Victorian sewer engineer Sir Joseph Bazalgette's extraordinary, Byzantine Abbey Mills Pumping Station can be seen nearby.

Restaurants

Moka East

View Tube, Marshgate Lane, E15 2PJ (www.theviewtube.co.uk). Pudding Mill Lane DLR. **Open** 9am-5pm daily. **Café**.

Set up as a viewing point during the construction of the Olympic Park, this café is housed in stacked-up acid-green shipping containers. It's now run by the family behind Mario's Cafe – sung about by St Etienne, and one of London's proper old-fashioned caffs. Breakfast options include standard bacon, sausage and eggs, and also muesli with yoghurt and berries, and even kippers. The café is right in front of the Olympic Stadium – Anish Kapoor's ArcelorMittal Orbit sculpture is directly opposite.

Shops & services

Westfield Stratford City

Great Eastern Road, E20 (8221 7300, www. westfield.com/stratfordcity). Stratford tube/DLR/ rail. **Open** 10am-9pm Mon-Fri; 9am-9pm Sat; noon-6pm Sun. **Mall**

This £1.45bn retail behemoth snakes through what was the London Olympic site, with 300 retail units – including gigantic branches of high-street brands John Lewis, Marks & Spencer and Waitrose – 70 restaurants, bars and cafés, and a 17-screen digital cinema.

ONE OF A KIND ATTRACTIONS

Sightseeing treats off the beaten track.

★ Dulwich Picture Gallery

Gallery Road, Dulwich, SE21 7AD (8693 5254, www.dulwichpicturegallery.org.uk). North Dulwich or West Dulwich rail. **Open** 10am-5pm Tue-Fri; 11am-5pm Sat, Sun. **Admission** £6; free-£5 reductions. Special exhibitions £11; free-£10 reductions.

This bijou attraction was designed by Sir John Soane in 1811 as the first purpose-built gallery in the UK. It's a beautiful space that shows off Soane's ingenuity with lighting effects. The gallery displays a small but outstanding collection of work by Old Masters, offering a fine introduction to the Baroque era through works by Rembrandt, Rubens, Poussin and Gainsborough.

Dulwich Picture Gallery.

★ FREE Horniman Museum

100 London Road, Forest Hill, SE23 3PQ (8699 1872, www.horniman.ac.uk). Forest Hill rail or bus 122, 176, 185, 363, P4, P13. **Open** 10.30am-5.30pm daily. **Admission** free; donations appreciated. Temporary exhibitions prices vary. *Aquarium* £3; £1.10 reductions; £7 family; free under-3s.

The Horniman is an eccentric-looking art nouveau building with extensive gardens. The Natural History gallery is dominated by an ancient walrus (overstuffed by Victorian taxidermists, who thought they ought to get the wrinkles out of the animal's skin) and ringed by glass cabinets containing pickled animals, stuffed birds and insect models. Other galleries include African Worlds and the Centenary Gallery, which focuses on world cultures. The Music Gallery contains hundreds of instruments: their sounds can be unleashed via touch-screen tables. The showpiece Aquarium is a series of tanks and rockpools covering seven distinct aquatic ecosystems.

London Museum of Water & Steam

Green Dragon Lane, Brentford, Middx TW8 0EN (8568 4757, www.kbsm.org). Gunnersbury tube/rail or Kew Bridge rail. **Open** 11am-4pm daily. **Admission** £11.50; £5-£10 reductions; free under-5s.

This Victorian pumping station is a reminder that steam wasn't just used for powering trains but also for supplying water to the citizens of an expanding London. Home to an extraordinary collection of engines, it now has a great array of new interactives, a dressing-up box and even a miniature steam train. The engines crank into action at weekends and Bank Holidays.

Lord's Tour & MCC Museum

St John's Wood Road, St John's Wood, NW8 8QN (7616 8500, www.lords.org). St John's Wood tube. **Open** *Tours* phone or check website for details. **Admission** £18; £12 reductions; free under-5s; £49 family.

Lord's is more than just a famous cricket ground. As the headquarters of the Marylebone Cricket Club (MCC), it is official guardian of the sport's rules. The museum's highlight is the tiny urn containing the Ashes (the coveted trophy never leaves Lord's, so it's still here despite England's pitiful capitulation in 2013/14). There's also memorabilia celebrating legends of the game.

South London Gallery

65 Peckham Road, Peckham, SE5 8UH (7703 6120, www.southlondongallery.org). Oval tube then bus 436, or Elephant & Castle tube/rail then bus 12, 171. **Open** 11am-6pm Tue, Thur-Sun; 10am-9pm Wed.

In 1891, William Rossiter opened the pioneering South London Fine Art Gallery. A century later, renamed the South London Gallery, it found new renown as first exhibitor of *Everyone I Have Ever Slept With 1963-1995*, Tracey Emin's infamous tent. A £1.8m

EXPLORE

extension in 2010 added a great café, two exhibition spaces and a resident artist's flat, and helps to keep it on the cutting edge as a contemporary art venue.

Thames Barrier
1 Unity Way, Woolwich, SE18 5NJ (8305 4188, www.environment-agency.gov.uk/thamesbarrier). Woolwich Dockyard rail, or North Greenwich tube then bus 472. **Open** 10.30am-5pm Thur-Sun. **Admission** £3.75; £2.25-£3.25 reductions; free under-5s.
This adjustable dam came into its own in the terrible floods of 2014. The shiny silver fins, lined up across Woolwich Reach, are an impressive sight. Built in 1982 at a cost of £535m, the barrier is regularly in action for maintenance purposes; check the website for a current timetable. To learn more, look around the learning centre, where you'll find an account of the 1953 flood that led to the barrier's construction, as well as displays on Thames wildlife. There's a pleasant café with picnic benches.

World Rugby Museum/ Twickenham Stadium
Twickenham Rugby Stadium, Rugby Road, Twickenham, Middx TW1 1DZ (8892 8877, www.rfu.com). Hounslow East tube then bus 281, or Twickenham rail. **Open** *Museum* 10am-5pm Tue-Sun. *Tours* Check website for times. **Admission** £16; £10 reductions; free under-5s.
Twickenham Stadium is the home of English rugby union. Guided tours take in the England dressing room, the players' tunnel and the Royal Box. Memorabilia charts the game's development from the late 19th century, and there's a scrum machine.

Wembley Stadium
Stadium Way, Wembley, Middx HA9 0WS (0844 980 8001, www.wembleystadium.com). Wembley Park tube or Wembley Stadium rail.
Lord Foster's 2007 Wembley redesign is impressive, and the guided tours of the 90,000-seat stadium give a fantastic flavour of the venue's history: here England won their only World Cup in 1966, and the crossbar from which Hurst's disputed goal bounced is in one of the cafés.

Wimbledon Lawn Tennis Museum
Museum Building, All England Lawn Tennis Club, Church Road, SW19 5AE (8946 6131, www.wimbledon.org/museum). Southfields tube. **Open** 10am-5pm daily; ticket holders only during championships. **Admission** (incl tour) £22; £13-£19 reductions; free under-5s.
Highlights at this popular museum on the history of tennis include a 200º cinema screen that allows you to find out what it's like to play on Centre Court and a re-creation of a 1980s men's dressing room, complete with a 'ghost' of John McEnroe. Visitors can also enjoy a behind-the-scenes tour.

★ WWT Wetland Centre
Queen Elizabeth's Walk, Barnes, SW13 9WT (8409 4400, www.wwt.org.uk). Hammersmith tube then bus 283, Barnes rail. **Open** *Apr-Oct* 9.30am-6pm daily. *Nov-Mar* 9.30am-5pm daily. **Admission** £12.35; £6.90-£9.20 reductions; free under-4s.
The 43-acre Wetland Centre is four miles from central London, but feels a world away. Quiet ponds, rushes, rustling reeds and wildflower gardens all teem with bird life – some 150 species. There are over 300 varieties of butterfly, 20 types of dragonfly and four species of bat. You can explore water-recycling initiatives in the RBC Rain Garden or check out the interactive section: pilot a submerged camera around a pond, learn about the life-cycle of a dragonfly or make waves in a digital pool.

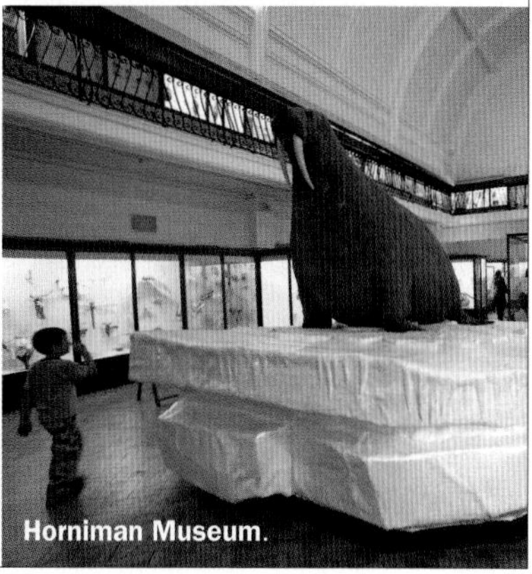
Horniman Museum.

EXPLORE

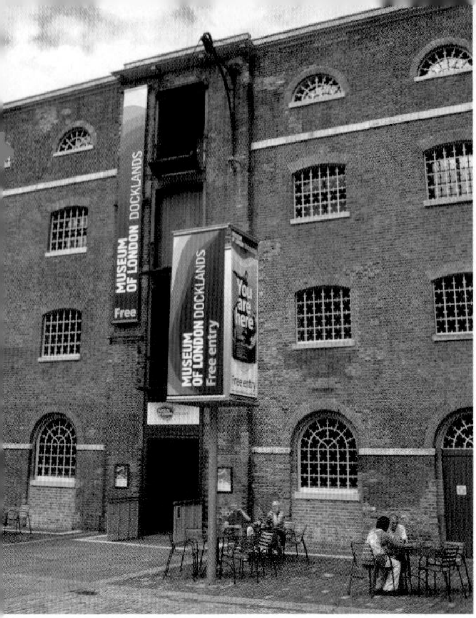

Museum of London Docklands.

DOCKLANDS

London's docks were fundamental to the prosperity of the British Empire. Between 1802 and 1921, ten separate docks were built between Tower Bridge in the west and Woolwich in the east. These employed tens of thousands of people. Yet by the 1960s, the shipping industry was changing irrevocably. The new 'container' system of cargo demanded larger, deep-draught ships, as a result of which the work moved out to Tilbury, from where lorries would ship the containers into the city. By 1980, the London docks had closed.

The London Docklands Development Corporation (LDDC), founded in 1981, spent £790m of public money on redevelopment during the following decade, only for a country-wide property slump in the early 1990s to leave the shiny new high-rise offices and luxury flats unoccupied. Nowadays, though, as a financial hub, Docklands is a booming rival to the City, with an estimated 90,000 workers commuting to the area each day, on improved transport links. For visitors, regular **Thames Clippers** (0870 781 5049, www.thamesclippers.com) boat connections with central London and the **Docklands Light Railway** (DLR) make the area easily accessible.

The **Isle of Dogs** is where you'll find Canary Wharf. The origin of the name 'Isle of Dogs' remains uncertain, but the first recorded use is on a map of 1588; one theory claims Henry VIII kept his hunting dogs here. In the 19th century, a huge system of docks and locks transformed what had been just drained marshland; in fact, the West India Docks cut right across the peninsula, so the Isle of Dogs did eventually become true to its name.

Almost all the interest for visitors is to be found in the vicinity of Cesar Pelli's dramatic **One Canada Square**, which was the country's tallest habitable building between 1991 and 2012, when it was topped by the Shard (*see p51*). The only slightly shorter HSBC and Citigroup towers joined it in the noughties, and clones are springing up thick and fast. Shopping options are limited to the mall beneath the towers (www.mycanarywharf.com), but you'll find a calm but crisp Japanese garden beside Canary Wharf tube station. Across a floating bridge over the dock to the north, there's the brilliant **Museum of London Docklands** (*see p241*).

It's also well worth hopping on the DLR and heading south to **Island Gardens** station at the tip of the Isle of Dogs. From narrow Island Gardens park, there's a famous Greenwich view – and the entrance to the Victorian pedestrian tunnel. Nearby to the north, at **Mudchute Park & Farm** (Pier Street, 7515 5901, www.mudchute.org), a complete farmyard of animals ruminate in front of the skyscrapers.

Further east (get off at East India DLR), the Lea River empties into the Thames at **Bow Creek**, almost directly opposite the white, deflated balloon of the O2 Arena (*see p271*). Here, **Trinity Buoy Wharf** (64 Orchard Place, E14 0JW, www.trinitybuoywharf.com) is pure incongruity. Built in the early 1800s, it was a depot and repair yard for shipping buoys, and it was here, in the 1860s, that James Douglass – later designer of the fourth Eddystone Lighthouse – built London's only lighthouse. Open to the public every weekend from 11am to 4pm (5pm in summer), the lighthouse is the perfect setting for the haunting *Longplayer* sound installation (http://longplayer.org).

A couple more stops east give you access to the **Royal Docks** – get off at Royal Victoria or Royal Albert – as well as the ExCeL conference centre, a docked steamship and a new attraction, the black and pointy **Crystal** (*see below*). You can also cross the slightly hair-raising, high white bridge from ExCeL to find two historic ships: a red lightship and, floating on a raft to preserve it, **SS Robin** (www.ssrobin.org), a steamship so rare it is included (with the *Cutty Sark* and HMS *Belfast*) in the National Historic Fleet. It's due to reopen to the public in 2014. Head south towards the Thames and you'll find the beautiful **Thames Barrier Park**. Opened in 2001, this was London's first new park in half a century. It has a lush sunken garden of waggly hedges and offers perhaps the best views from land of the Thames Barrier (*see p239*). If you don't fancy walking, enter the park from Pontoon Dock DLR.

Unless you're checking in at **London City Airport** (*see p365*), keep on the DLR as far as King George V to get a free ferry (every 15mins daily, 8853 9400) that chugs pedestrians and cars across the river, or stay in your carriage as the DLR passes under the river all the way to its final stop at Woolwich Arsenal.

Restaurants

FREE Crystal

Royal Victoria Dock, 1 Siemens Brothers Way, E16 1GB (7055 6400, http://thecrystal.org). Royal Victoria DLR. **Open** 10am-5pm Tue-Sat; 10am-7pm Sun. *Café* 8.30am-5pm Mon-Fri; 10am-7pm Sat, Sun. **Admission** free.

The Crystal attempts to explain in an engaging fashion how cities work, and how they might meet the challenges of global warming, population growth, ageing and the shortage of key resources, especially water. The two floors of interactives are slick and fun: beat the computer at face recognition, or plan the transport for different cities. There's a good café too.

★ Emirates Air Line

North terminal *27 Western Gateway, E16 4FA. Royal Victoria DLR.*
South terminal *Edmund Halley Way, SE10 0FR. North Greenwich tube.*
Both Open 7am-9pm Mon-Fri; 8am-9pm Sat; 9am-9pm Sun. **Tickets** £4.30 single; £2.20 5-15s, free under-5s.

Arguments for a cable car across the Thames as a solution to any of London's many transport problems are, at best, moot, but its value as a tourist thrill is huge. The comfy pods zoom 295ft up elegant stanchions at a gratifying pace. Suddenly there are brilliant views of the expanses of water that make up the Royal Docks, the ships on the Thames, Docklands and the Thames Barrier. Good fun and good value – but note that the cable car may not run in high winds.

▶ *Tickets are cheaper if you use an Oyster card, and you'll avoid any ticket desk queues.*

★ Museum of London Docklands

No.1 Warehouse, West India Quay, Hertsmere Road, E14 4AL (7001 9844, www.museumindocklands.org.uk). Canary Wharf tube or West India Quay DLR. **Open** 10am-6pm daily. **Admission** free. *Temporary exhibitions* vary; check website for details.

Housed in a 19th-century warehouse (itself a Grade I-listed building), this museum explores the complex history of London's docklands and the river over two millennia. Displays spreading over three storeys take you from the arrival of the Romans all the way to the docks' 1980s closure and the area's subsequent redevelopment. The Docklands at War section is very moving, while a haunting new permanent exhibition sheds light on the dark side of London's rise as a centre for finance and commerce, exploring its involvement in the slave trade. You can also walk through full-scale mock-ups of a quayside and a dingy riverfront alley. Temporary exhibitions are set up on the ground floor, where you'll also find a café and a docks-themed play area. Just like its elder brother, the Museum of London (*see p55*), the MoLD has a great programme of screenings and special events.

Restaurants

Jamie's Italian

Unit 17, 2 Churchill Place, Canary Wharf, E14 5RB (3002 5252, www.jamieoliver.com). Canary Wharf tube/DLR. **Open** 11.30am-11pm Mon-Fri; noon-11pm Sat; noon-10.30pm Sun. **Main courses** £9.95-£24. **Italian**

The vivacity and personality of the cooking makes Jamie Oliver's most successful concept an appealing choice. This likeable chain serves dishes such as grilled free-range chicken with garlic and rosemary with a tomato, caper, chilli and olive sauce; spaghetti alla norma, with aubergines, oregano, chilli and basil in a tomato sauce. All are punchily flavoured, thoughtfully sourced and served with panache. **Other locations** throughout the city.

Yi-Ban

London Regatta Centre, Dockside Road, E16 2QT (7473 6699, www.yi-ban.co.uk). Royal Albert DLR. **Open** noon-11pm Mon-Sat; 11am-10pm Sun. **Main courses** £6-£50. **Chinese**

Visiting Yi-Ban by public transport can be a disconcerting experience, involving a trip on the DLR to Royal Albert station, then a walk along a deserted road and across a large car park to the first floor of the grey concrete box that is the London Regatta Centre. Once inside, you're greeted by a spacious room lined with floor-to-ceiling windows offering striking views across the dock of planes taking off and landing at City Airport. The menu is extensive, with Vietnamese as well as Chinese dishes, a particularly good selection of seafood and a dozen hotpots including sea cucumber and 'duck's web' (the foot). Note that the restaurant gets very busy at weekends, so it's wise to book.

VAUXHALL & BRIXTON

Stockwell tube, or Brixton or Vauxhall tube/rail.

The area now known as Vauxhall was, in the 13th century, home to a house owned by one Falkes de Bréauté, a soldier rewarded for carrying out King John's dirtier military deeds. Over time, Falkes' Hall became Fox Hall and finally Vauxhall. Vauxhall's heyday was in the 18th century when the infamous Pleasure Gardens, built back in 1661, reached the height of their popularity, a mingling of wealthy and not-so-wealthy, with everyone getting into trouble on 'lovers' walks'. When the Gardens closed in 1859, the area became reasonably respectable – all that remains is Spring Garden, behind popular gay haunt the Royal Vauxhall Tavern (aka **RVT**; *see p259*). For a glimpse of old Vauxhall head to **Bonnington Square**. Down on the river is the cream and emerald ziggurat designed by Terry Farrell for the Secret Intelligence Service (formerly MI6).

At the top end of the South Lambeth Road, **Little Portugal** – a cluster of Portuguese cafés, shops and tapas bars – is an enticing oasis. At the other end, **Stockwell** is prime commuter territory, with little to lure visitors except some charming Victorian streets: Albert Square, Durand Gardens and Stockwell Park Crescent; van Gogh was briefly resident at 87 Hackford Road.

South of Stockwell is **Brixton**, a lively hub of clubs and music. The town centre has been enjoying significant redevelopment, with Windrush Square completed at the end of Coldharbour Lane in 2010. The square's name is significant: HMS *Windrush* was the boat that brought West Indian immigrants from Jamaica in 1948. They were hardly welcomed, but managed to make Brixton a thriving community. As late as the 1980s, tensions were still strong, as the Clash song 'Guns of Brixton' famously illustrates. The rage of the persecuted black community, still finding themselves isolated and under suspicion decades after arriving, is better expressed by dub poet Linton Kwesi Johnson – try 'Sonny's Lettah (Anti-Sus Poem)' for starters. The riots of 1981 and 1985 around Railton Road and Coldharbour Lane left the district scarred for years.

Now, most visitors come to Brixton for Brixton Village (*see p243*). The two covered arcades date to the 1920s and '30s and have been – with Market Row – Grade II-listed. The district's main roads are modern and filled with chain stores, but there's also some attractive architecture – check out the **Ritzy Cinema** (Brixton Oval, Coldharbour Lane, 0871 902 5739, www.picturehouses.co.uk), dating to 1911. Brixton's best-known street, **Electric Avenue**, got its name when, in 1880, it became one of the first shopping streets to get electric lights.

Minutes south of Brixton's hectic centre, flanked by Tulse Hill and Dulwich Road, **Brockwell Park** (www.brockwellpark.com) is one of London's most underrated green spaces. Landscaped in the early 19th century for a wealthy glass-maker, the park contains his Georgian country house – now a café – an open-air swimming pool, bowling green, walled rose garden and miniature railway. Each July, there's an enjoyable traditional country fair. If that doesn't seem bucolic enough, visit **Brixton Windmill** (*see below*) just off Brixton Hill a little further west.

IN THE KNOW CHART OF ART

If you want to get a grip on the lively art scene south of the river, check out the **South London Art Map** (www.southlondonartmap.com), which provides listings, a print map (also with a Google link) and the likes of downloadable audio tours. It also organises late openings on the last Friday of every month.

Sights & museums

FREE Brixton Windmill

Windmill Gardens, off Blenheim Gardens, SW2 5BZ (www.brixtonwindmill.org). Brixton tube. **Open** pre-booked tours Apr-Oct; see website for details. **Admission** free.

Built in 1816 and in service until 1934, Brixton Windmill reopened to the public in 2011, and had already won several tourism and heritage awards in 2012. There are about 20 open days a year, during which you can visit without booking (but may have to queue: there isn't much room in the windmill), but the 30-45min pre-booked guided tours give access to the upper floors – and are a fascinating glimpse into a lost London industry.

Restaurants

Brunswick House Café

30 Wandsworth Road, Vauxhall Cross, Vauxhall SW8 2LG (7720 2926, www.brunswickhouse.co). Vauxhall tube/rail. **Open** 9.30am-10.30pm Mon-Fri; 10am-10.30pm Sat; noon-4pm Sun. **Main courses** £11.80-£17. **Brasserie**

Brixton Village.

This Georgian mansion, a tiny beacon of classic calm amid the high-rise apartments and noisy chaos of Vauxhall Cross, has no trouble packing in a young, high-spending clientele. Some are simply stopping by for a cocktail while perusing the desirable bric-a-brac on offer from architectural salvage company Lassco, but most are here to meet, drink, eat and generally enjoy the place's markedly non-corporate hospitality. It's an appealing combination of boho-chic comfort and minimalist menu presentation.

★ Franco Manca

4 Market Row, Electric Lane, Brixton, SW9 8LD (7738 3021, www.francomanca.co.uk). Brixton tube/rail. **Open** noon-5pm Mon; noon-10.30pm Tue-Thur, Sun; noon-11pm Fri, Sat.
Main courses £4.50-£7.50. **Pizza**
With its top-notch, UK-sourced (when possible) ingredients, speedy and friendly service, and rapid turnover, the original Brixton branch of Franco Manca remains, for our money, the best pizza joint in London. Both indoor and outdoor seating overlooks the bustling market arcade. Here you can sate a craving for genuine, Neapolitan-style pizza, with a flavourful slow-rise sourdough crust and a variety of traditional and innovative toppings.
Other locations throughout the city.

Pubs & bars

Crown & Anchor

246 Brixton Road, Brixton, SW9 6AQ (7737 0060, www.crownandanchorbrixton.co.uk). Stockwell tube or Brixton tube/rail. **Open** 4.30-11pm Mon-Thur; 4.30pm-11.30pm Fri; noon-midnight Sat; noon-11pm Sun. *Food served* 5-10pm Mon-Fri; noon-10pm Sat; noon-8pm Sun
The most exciting feature of this pub after a back-to-basics restoration is the lengthy bar with its endless fonts: seven cask ales, 14 keg beers and ciders. Clued-up staff are keen to recommend and offer tasting notes and samples. It's a friendly, unpretentious place, devoted to great beer.

Shops & services

★ Brixton Village

Corner of Coldharbour Lane & Brixton Station Road, SW9 8PR (7274 2990, http://brixtonmarket.net). Brixton tube/rail. **Open** 6am-6pm Mon; 6am-11.30pm Tue-Sun; check website for opening hours of individual shops. **Mall**
Once almost forgotten, Granville Arcade has found a new lease of life. It originally opened in 1937, when it was proclaimed 'London's Largest Emporium', and in the 1960s became a Caribbean market. But by the 1990s, many of the arcade's units were unoccupied and its old art deco avenues were falling into a dilapidated state. In 2009, Lambeth Council called in urban regeneration agency Space Makers, which launched a competition for local entrepreneurs to apply for a unit. It then awarded the best initiatives a place on site, and renamed the space Brixton Village, in line with its eclectic, locally minded new contents – from bijoux bakeries and vintage boutiques to international eateries and fledgling fashion labels. Highlights here include Margot Waggoner's Leftovers (unit 71), with its Marseille lace and vintage sailor dresses, and Binkie and Tabitha's Circus (unit 70), which juxtaposes retro glassware with an assortment of socialist literature.

Arts & Entertainment

Children

London has a lot to offer young visitors. Its museums go out of their way to engage the minds of children with enjoyable events, there are gorgeous parks and playgrounds, brilliant theatres with child-oriented productions and world-famous attractions. Many of these, such as the Natural History Museum and the Science Museum, are free; many of those that aren't, such as the Tower of London, give you a lot of fun for your entry fee.

Plan carefully, but don't try to cram too much into one day. Sometimes, the most fun happens in the gaps between the official itinerary – lots of kids get a big kick just from using public transport.

For children's festivals (and the many more events that aren't specifically for children but will be enjoyed by them), *see pp30-41*.

WHERE TO GO

South Bank & Bankside

This is one of the all-time favourite spots for a family day out in London. Just strolling along the wide riverside promenade will lead you past skateboarders, installations, street artists, book stalls and, often, free performances. The expensive end is around **London Eye** (*see p51*), **London Aquarium** (*see p54*) and the **London Dungeon** (*see p51*). Moving east, visit the **Southbank Centre** (*see p50 and p282*), where free shows and workshops take place in holidays and weekends in the Clore Ballroom. Don't miss Jeppe Hein's *Appearing Rooms* play fountains in summer. Next, the **National Theatre** (*see p285*) usually offers free entertainment outside during the summer.

Keep going along the riverbank, past Gabriel's Wharf, a riverside cluster of restaurants and shops, to reach **Tate Modern** (*see p56*). Tate Modern is a day out in itself, with its dramatic Turbine Hall, free family trails and a Bloomberg Learning Zone on Level 5. At weekends and in school holidays, age-appropriate activity packs are available from Level 3. (There's a boat service from here to **Tate Britain**; *see p77*.)

Once you've emerged, pick up the Bankside Walk, ducking under the southern end of Southwark Bridge. Walk down cobbly Clink Street towards the **Golden Hinde** (*see p60*) and **Southwark Cathedral** (*see p60*), having passed the **Clink Prison Museum** (*see p60*), a cheaper alternative to the London Dungeon. From Tooley Street, march through Hays Galleria to regain the riverside path, which takes you to the excellent warship museum **HMS Belfast** (*see p63*) and on, past the dancing fountains, to **City Hall** and **Tower Bridge** (*see p186*).

The City

It seems pricey, but the **Tower of London** (*see p186*) is a top day out for all ages. If it is free stuff you're after, though, the **Museum of London** (*see p179*) is superb. Its Galleries of Modern London put interactivity and drama at the heart of exciting exhibits, but there are dressing-up boxes throughout, and lots of storytelling sessions and workshops. Nearby, in the **Bank of England Museum** (*see p182*), kids can try to lift a gold bar – by reaching into an otherwise sealed box, so no bank heist is possible.

Kings Cross & Bloomsbury

Children are captivated by the mummies at the **British Museum** (*see p150*). However, the size of the collection can make it overwhelming. The beautifully produced and well-conceived free trails for different ages take a theme and lead families around an edited selection (available in the Paul Hamlyn Library). Alternatively, there are regular events and workshops or free backpacks for kids, filled with puzzles and games. For weekends and school holidays, the Ford Centre for Young Visitors provides a picnic-style eating area.

Central London's best playground, **Coram's Fields** (*see p251*), is close, and the nearby **Foundling Museum** (*see p151*) is well worth a visit to learn how orphans used to be treated.

Futher play opportunities are to be found a 15-minute walk north at King's Cross, where the lovely illuminated fountains of **Granary Square** (*see p157*) can be frolicked through, and there's the green tranquillity of **Camley Street** nature reserve (*see p249*) just across the canal.

Covent Garden & the Strand

At the lively **London Transport Museum** (*see p138*), children can make believe they are driving a bus or riding in a horse-drawn carriage. They love the numbered stamp trail too. The museum also has a programme of school-holiday events. Across the Piazza, the acts in front of **St Paul's Covent Garden** (*see p140*) are worth watching. On the south side of the Strand, **Somerset House** (*see p147*) allows kids to play outside among the fountains in summer and skate on the winter ice rink. There are also regular art workshops.

Trafalgar Square

London's central square (www.london.gov.uk/trafalgarsquare) has been a free playground for children since time immemorial – watch out for the imperious, bright-blue cock (on the Fourth Plinth until Feb 2015). Festivals take place most weekends. Even if all is quiet in the square, the **National Gallery** (*see p68*) has paper trails and audio tours, as well as workshops for teens and three- to five-year-olds. For five- to 11-year-olds, the **National Portrait Gallery** (*see p69*) runs Family Art Workshops at weekends and during the school holidays.

Just nearby, **St Martin-in-the-Fields** (*see p60*) has London's only brass-rubbing centre, as well as a fine café that does plenty of the type of food that goes down well with children.

South Kensington

Top of any Grand Day Out itinerary is this cultural goldmine. The **Science Museum** (*see p90*) offers heaps of excitement, with six play zones for all ages, from the Garden in the basement for under-sixes to the new Atmosphere gallery upstairs, where children can use touchscreens to learn about climate change. Dinosaur fans won't rest until they've visited the **Natural History Museum** (*see p87*), and seen the animatronic beasties in action. An ice rink in winter also draw the crowds. The **Victoria & Albert Museum** (*see p90*) marks interactive

London Transport Museum.

displays on its floorplan. Its free weekend and school holiday drop-in family events (featuring trails, activity backpacks, and interactive workshops) provide great ways of focusing on the collection. (Its sister gallery, Bethnal Green's **V&A Museum of Childhood**, *see p209*, has an excellent programme of events for children.) The same rule applies for all of them, but especially the Science Museum and NHM: arrive as early in the day as you can to avoid the screaming throngs.

Greenwich

Magical Greenwich provides a lovely day out away from the mayhem of the West End. Arrive by boat to appreciate its riverside charms, then take time to check out the restored **Cutty Sark** (*see p212*) and excellent **Discover Greenwich** (*see p212*). Next, head to the very child-friendly **National Maritime Museum** (*see p213*), where there's a boat simulator to pilot and a whole room of interactives. From here it's a pleasant leg-stretch in the Royal Park for views from the top of the hill, crowned by the **Royal Observatory & Planetarium** (*see p214*). When the stars come out, keep an eye out for the luminous green Meridian Line that cuts across the sky towards the city.

Further north, the **Emirates Air Line** cable car is an exciting way to cross the river. It runs from North Greenwich tube to the Royal Victoria Dock DLR (*see p249* **In the Know**).

EATING & DRINKING

Other restaurants particularly suitable for children include **Inn the Park** (*see p81*) and **Gallery Mess** (*see p99*).

Big Red Bus

30 Deptford Church Street, Deptford, SE8 4RZ (3490 8346, www.bigredpizza.co.uk). Deptford Bridge DLR. **Open** 5-10.30pm Tue, Wed; 5-11pm Fri; noon-1am Sat; noon-6.30pm Sun. **Main courses** £6.50-£11.

Kids love this pizzeria – inside an old double-decker bus. You can either sit inside, or on the pretty decked terrace. It's beside the DLR, so travel is easy, and the nearby Creekside Centre (*see p250*) makes a good excursion.

Frizzante@Hackney City Farm

1A Goldsmith's Row, Hackney, E2 8QA (7739 2266, www.frizzanteltd.co.uk). Hoxton rail. **Open** 10am-4.30pm Tue, Sat, Sun; 10am-10pm Wed, Fri; 10am-4pm, 7-11pm Thur. **Main courses** £7.50-£14.

Trot around the pigs, poultry and sheep outside, then settle down to eat their relatives (or stick to vegetarian options). The oilcloth-covered tables always heave with families tucking into healthy nosh, including big farm breakfasts.

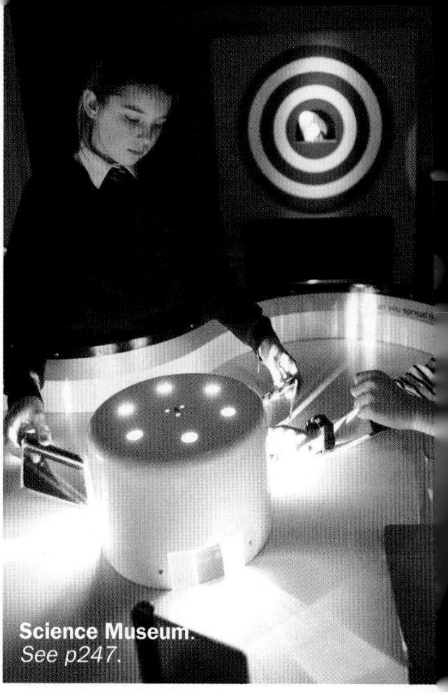

Science Museum. *See p247.*

Gracelands

118 College Road, Kensal Green, NW10 5HD (8964 9161, www.gracelandscafe.com). Kensal Green tube/rail. **Open** 8.30am-4.30pm Mon-Fri; 9am-4.30pm Sat; 9.30am-2.30pm Sun. **Main courses** £7-£13.

While many places claim to be child-friendly, this café really means it, with its toy-filled play area, a healthy tots-own menu (£3.70 for the likes of pasta bolognese or sausage and mash), and chefs cooing at high-chair diners from the open-plan kitchen. For grown-ups, the burger, made from 21-day matured beef, has proper foodie pedigree and the salads are unfailingly excellent.

Mudchute Kitchen

Mudchute Park & Farm, Pier Street, Isle of Dogs, Docklands, E14 3HP (3069 9290, www.mudchute.org). Mudchute DLR. **Open** 9.30am-4pm Fri-Sun. **Main courses** £2.50-£9.

A farm fenced in by skyscrapers is an amusing place for anyone to eat lunch, but Mudchute is ideal for families. You can eat at farmhouse kitchen tables in the courtyard, while your babies roll around on a big futon or in the toy corner, or in the spacious interior. Frizzante (*see left*) took over in 2011, which means the food is excellent.

Rainforest Café

20 Shaftesbury Avenue, Piccadilly, W1D 7EU (7434 3111, www.therainforestcafe.co.uk). Piccadilly Circus tube. **Open** noon-10pm Mon-Fri; 11.30am-8pm Sat; 11.30am-10pm Sun. During school holidays the restaurant

is open at 11.30am every day. **Main courses** £12.95-£18.90. **Map** p399 K7.
This themed restaurant is designed to thrill children with animatronic wildlife, cascading waterfalls and jungle sound-effects. The menu has lots of family-friendly fare, from 'paradise pizza' and 'Bamba's bangers' to amusing dishes for grown-ups. The children's menu costs £12.50 for two courses.

★ Tate Modern Café

Tate Modern, Sumner Street, Bankside, SE1 9TG (7401 5014, www.tate.org.uk). Southwark tube or London Bridge tube/rail. **Open** 10am-5.30pm Mon-Thur; 10am-8.30pm Fri; 9am-6.30pm Sat; 9am-5.30pm Sun. **Main courses** £7.50-£13. **Map** p402 O7.
In addition to views from the windows framing the busy River Thames, there are literacy and art activities on the junior menu, handed out with a pot of crayons. Children can choose haddock fingers with chips, pasta bolognese with parmesan or a ham and cheese bake with focaccia, finished off with ice-cream or a fruit salad; a free children's main is offered when an adult orders a regular main. There is also a 'teen menu' of reduced-price dishes from the adult menu.

That Place on the Corner

1-3 Green Lanes, Stoke Newington, N16 9BS (7704 0079, www.thatplaceonthecorner.co.uk). Canonbury rail then bus 73, 141, 341. **Open** 9.15am-6pm Mon-Fri; 9.30am-3pm Sat. Closes Sat for functions; phone ahead. **Main courses** £4.50-£8.50.
London's only child-friendly café that won't allow unaccompanied grown-ups to enter. Even better, children's needs are provided for by a library, a puppet theatre, two play areas and a dressing-up corner, as well as classes in baking, dance and music. The menu sticks to the trusted formula of pasta, panini and big breakfasts, but also offers some brasserie staples.

IN THE KNOW
EMIRATES AIR LINE

A thrilling ride on the **Emirates Air Line**, London's first urban cable car, is a surefire hit with children. Running from the Greenwich Peninsula to Royal Victoria Dock and ascending to nearly 300 feet above the Thames, with London's landmarks jostling for attention below – this is no mere expensive attraction, but part of London's transport system, with its own special line marked on the tube map. Adult trips using Oyster pay-as-you-go cost £3.20; for 5- to 15-year-olds with Oyster card, it costs £1.60; under-5s travel free.

ENTERTAINMENT

City farms & zoos

There's always something new at **ZSL London Zoo** (*see p195*); the admission charge seems high, but it's a guaranteed winner (*see also p250* **Meet the Animals**). Easier on the budget is the adorable **Battersea Park Children's Zoo** (www.batterseaparkzoo.co.uk), where ring-tailed lemurs, giant rabbits, inquisitive meerkats and kune kune pigs are among the inhabitants.

City farms all over London charge nothing to get in. Try **Freightliners City Farm** (www.freightlinersfarm.org.uk) and **Kentish Town City Farm** (www.aapi.co.uk/cityfarm) or, in the east, **Mudchute City Farm** (www.mudchute.org) and **Hackney City Farm** (www.hackneycityfarm.co.uk), both of which have terrific cafés (for both, *see p248*).

Puppets

★ Little Angel Theatre

14 Dagmar Passage, off Cross Street, Islington, N1 2DN (7226 1787, www.littleangeltheatre.com). Angel tube or Highbury & Islington tube/rail. **Box office** 10am-6pm Mon-Fri; 9am-4pm Sat, Sun. **Tickets** £5-£14. **Map** p400 O1.
London's only permanent puppet theatre is set in a charming old Victorian temperance hall. All aspects of puppetry are covered, with themes, styles and stories drawn from a broad array of traditions. There's a Saturday Puppet Club and a youth puppet theatre. Shows are often for fives and above.

Puppet Theatre Barge

Opposite 35 Blomfield Road, Little Venice, W9 2PF (07836 202745 summer, 7249 6876 winter, www.puppetbarge.com). Warwick Avenue tube. **Box office** 10am-6pm daily. **Tickets** £10; £8.50 reductions.
This intimate waterborne stage is the setting for quality puppet shows that put a modern twist on traditional tales, such as *Mr Rabbit meets Brer Santa* and *The Flight of Babuscha Baboon*. The barge is moored here between October and July; shows themselves are held at 3pm on Saturday and Sunday, and daily during school holidays, plus some matinées. During the summer, the barge also holds performances in Richmond.

Science & nature

FREE Camley Street Natural Park

12 Camley Street, King's Cross, N1C 4PW (7833 2311, www.wildlondon.org.uk). King's Cross tube/rail. **Open** 10am-5pm Mon-Fri, Sun (closes at 4pm in winter). **Admission** free.
A small but thriving green space on the site of a former coal yard, Camley Street is near the heart

of the renovated King's Cross. London Wildlife Trust's flagship reserve, it hosts pond-dipping and nature-watching sessons for children, and its wood-cabin visitor centre is used by the Wildlife Watch Club.

FREE Creekside Centre

14 Creekside, Greenwich, SE8 4SA (8692 9922, www.creeksidecentre.org.uk). Deptford Bridge or Greenwich DLR, or bus 53, 177, 188. **Open** phone for details. **Admission** free.

Deptford Creek is a tributary of the Thames and this centre allows visitors to explore its surprisingly diverse wildlife and rich heritage. Low-tide walks take place on selected weekend days for accompanied eight-year-olds and above and there's also a programme of puppet theatre. Events vary (and some charge a fee), so phone ahead for the programme.

★ WWT Wetland Centre

Queen Elizabeth's Walk, Barnes, SW13 9WT (8409 4400, www.wwt.org.uk/london). Hammersmith tube then bus 33, 72, 209 (alight at Red Lion pub). **Open** *Summer* 9.30am-6pm daily. *Winter* 9.30am-5pm daily. **Admission** £11.65 (incl donation); £8.70 reductions; £6.50 4-16s; free under-4s; £32.50 family (2+2). *Tours* free.

This wetland reserve is one of London's best-kept secrets. If you can get children past the giant snakes and ladders game (with giant dice), there are 104 acres for them to stretch their legs in, along paths that take them past the main lake, reed beds, ponds and wetland meadows, as well as one of the best playgrounds in London. A series of interactive exhibits exploring the environment was added in 2010.

Theatre

Polka Theatre

240 Broadway, Merton, SW19 1SB (8543 4888, www.polkatheatre.com). South Wimbledon tube or Wimbledon tube/rail, then bus 57, 93, 219, 493. **Box office** (by phone and in person) 9.30am-4.30pm Tue-Fri; 10am-4.30pm Sat; noon-4.30pm Sun. **Tickets** £9-£16.

This children's theatre pioneer has been up and running since 1979. Daily shows are staged by touring companies in the main auditorium, while shorter works for babies and toddlers take over at the Adventure Theatre once a week.

MEET THE ANIMALS

Helping children to get even closer to their furry favourites.

A trip to any zoo is a brilliant family day out. **London Zoo** (*see p195*) continues its transformation year on year, with its animals rehoused in imaginative enclosures and interactive elements introduced across the site. Perhaps the most exciting addition for younger visitors has been Gorilla Kingdom, where you can get to within a foot of the gorillas – albeit separated from them by reinforced glass. The lovely beasts also have a big area of landscaped greenery to explore.

To meet animals without reinforced glass, head to the Children's Zoo. Here, kids can groom goats and sheep, meet the llamas, climb with coatis, expore tunnels in the Roots Zone or listen to a story in the tipi. Children also love Animals in Action, an event held every day at noon in the Amphitheatre. It's a chance to come virtually face to face with parrots, owls, rats, meerkats and more, demonstrating their natural behaviour – flying (low, you may have to duck), leaping, climbing, and walking along a rope in the case of a demonstration of just how easily rats found their way on to ships.

Older children (11-16s) with a well-developed interest in animals might enjoy being a junior keeper for a day. The programme, run during school holidays, has groups of up to five youngsters mucking out, grooming, feeding, and helping with life enrichment programmes for animals such as giraffes, meerkats and llamas. The website (www.zsl.org) has more details of all the zoo's animals and events.

Coram's Fields.

Unicorn Theatre

147 Tooley Street, Bankside, SE1 2HZ (7645 0560, www.unicorntheatre.com). London Bridge tube/rail. **Box office** 9.30am-6pm Mon-Fri; 10am-6pm Sat; noon-5pm Sun. **Tickets** £9-£22; £7-£13 reductions. **Map** p403 Q8.

This light, bright building, with a huge white unicorn in the foyer, has two performance spaces. Its small ensemble company performs in all shows and focuses on an outreach programme for local children.

Theme parks

There are several theme parks within easy reach of London. Heading out west, **Legoland** (Winkfield Road, Windsor, Berks SL4 4AY, 0871 222 2001, www.legoland.co.uk) has rides including the wet 'n' wild Viking's River Splash, and the extraordinary Miniland London, made of 13 million Lego bricks. **Thorpe Park** (Staines Road, Chertsey, Surrey KT16 8PN, 0871 663 1673, www.thorpepark.com) has the fastest rollercoaster in Europe, called Stealth, and the terrifying horror-movie ride, Saw; it's best for older kids and teens. **Chessington World of Adventures** (Leatherhead Road, Chessington, Surrey KT9 2NE, 0871 663 4477, www.chessington.com) is a gentler option. This theme park is partly a zoo, and children can pay to be zoo keeper for a day.

Likely to be on any child's visiting wishlist is the new Harry Potter studio tour near Watford, a short journey north of town; *see p301* **Warner Bros Studio Tour London.**

For a day with less of an adrenaline rush, try **Bekonscot Model Village** (Warwick Road, Beaconsfield, Bucks HP9 2PL, 01494 672919, www.bekonscot.com), a haven of vintage miniature villages with a ride-on train. To the north, **Butterfly World** (Miriam Lane, Chiswell Green, Herts AL2 3NY, 01727 869203, www.butterflyworldproject.com) is designed to look like a huge butterfly head from the air with a 330-foot diameter walk-through biome (the butterfly's eye). There's also a walk-through butterfly tunnel and butterfly breeding house.

SPACES TO PLAY

London's parks are lovely. **Hyde Park** (*see p92*) and **St James's Park** (*see p80*) are very central, but it isn't much further to **Regent's Park** (*see p195*), and **Greenwich Park** (*see p210*) is easily reached by river.

FREE Coram's Fields

93 Guilford Street, Bloomsbury, WC1N 1DN (7837 6138, www.coramsfields.org). Russell Square tube. **Open** *Apr-Sept* 9am-7pm daily. *Oct-Mar* 9am-dusk daily. **Admission** free (adults admitted only if accompanied by child under 16). **No credit cards. Map** p397 L4.

This historic site dates to 1747, when Thomas Coram established the Foundling Hospital, but only opened as a park in 1936. It has sandpits, a small petting zoo, ride-on toys and playgrounds for different age groups.

► *For the Foundling Hospital's museum, see p151.*

★ FREE Diana, Princess of Wales Memorial Playground

Near Black Lion Gate, Broad Walk, Kensington Gardens, South Kensington, W8 2UH (7298 2141, www.royalparks.gov.uk). Bayswater or Queensway tube. **Open** *Summer* 10am-6.45pm daily. *Winter* 10am-dusk daily. **Admission** free; adults admitted only if accompanied by under-12s. **Map** p393 E8.

Bring buckets and spades, if you can, to this superb playground: the huge, central pirate ship is moored in a sea of sand. Other attractions include a tepee camp and a treehouse encampment, and excellent provision is made for children with special needs.

Discover Children's Story Centre

383-387 High Street, Stratford, E15 4QZ (8536 5555, www.discover.org.uk). Stratford tube/rail/DLR. **Open** 10am-5pm Tue-Fri; 11am-5pm Sat, Sun. *School holidays* 10am-5pm Mon-Fri; 11am-5pm Sat, Sun. **Admission** £5; £18 family of 4; free under-2s.

The UK's first creative learning centre for children is committed to promoting diversity and providing learning opportunities for socially and economically disadvantaged children. The main floor offers all sorts of imaginative exploration, while downstairs houses temporary interactive exhibitions. The garden is fun.

Film

Londoners still seem to have a feel for the romance of film that suburban multiplexes just can't satisfy. Perhaps that's why there's such a lively and varied range of screenings in the capital. Giant picture palaces hosting red-carpet premières attended by A-list actors? Check out the Odeon Leicester Square. Cheap-as-chips repertory cinema? The Prince Charles is right around the corner. Refurbished art deco gems? Try the gorgeous, historic Phoenix or the Rio in Dalston. A world-class film festival? Happens every autumn. Outdoor screenings in remarkable settings, ciné clubs, film seasons devoted to every genre and national cinema under the sun? Yes, yes and yes. So get some popcorn and sit yourself down.

WHERE TO GO

Leicester Square underwent a major and much-needed facelift in 2011, and has the biggest first-run cinemas and stages most of the big-budget premières – but it also has the biggest prices. By contrast, the independents provide a cheaper and often more enjoyable night out, and they often show films that wouldn't come within a million miles of a red carpet.

Among the rep cinemas, the British Film Institute's flagship venue gets top billing. **BFI Southbank** (*see p256*) screens seasons exploring and celebrating various genres of cinema and TV. It also has a brilliant bar. After the BFI, London's best repertory cinema is found at the **Riverside Studios** (*see p256*), where you'll find special seasons and film events.

Unexpected venues for film-viewing include the big museums and galleries. The **British Museum** (*see p150*), **National Gallery** (*see p68*), **Imperial War Museum** (*see p55*) and **Tate Modern** (*see p56*) all have regular screenings themed to their temporary exhibitions. Several luxury hotels open their screening rooms to the public; those at the **Soho Hotel** (*see p348*), **Charlotte Street Hotel** (*see p343*), **Covent Garden Hotel** (*see p346*) and **One Aldwych** (*see p347*) are favourites. Films in these luxe surroundings usually include drinks, lunch, dinner or tea, for an all-inclusive price.

Outdoor summertime screens have popped up across the capital. The most glamorous is the **Somerset House Summer Screen** (www.somersethouse.org.uk/film) and Park Nights at the **Serpentine Gallery** (*see p94*). Fans of memorabilia can check out the **London Film Museum** (*see p138*), but the latest trend is to mix cinema with other forms of entertainment, and to screen the films in a range of unusual locations (*see p255* **In the Know**).

The lowdown

Consult *Time Out* magazine's weekly listings or visit www.timeout.com/film for full details of what's on and performance times; note that the programmes change on a Friday. Films released in the UK are classified as follows: **U** – suitable for all ages; **PG** – open to all, parental guidance is advised; **12A** – under-12s only admitted with an over-18; **15** – no one under 15 is admitted; **18** – no one under 18 is admitted.

FIRST-RUN CINEMAS

Central London

Barbican

Silk Street, the City, EC2Y 8DS (7638 8891, www.barbican.org.uk). Barbican tube or Moorgate tube/rail. **Tickets** £13.50; £7-£8.50 reductions; £4 Mon. **Screens** 3. **Map** p400 P5.

Two new (small) screens have been added – at the corner of Beech Street and Whitecross Street – bringing the Barbican Centre's total number of screens back to three (the excellent Cinema 1 remains within the Barbican Centre proper). Expect new releases of quality world and independent films, as well as themed series.

Curzon Cinemas

Chelsea *206 King's Road, SW3 5XP (0871 703 3990). Sloane Square tube then bus 11, 19, 22, 319.* **Screens** 1. **Map** p395 E12.
Mayfair *38 Curzon Street, W1J 7TY (0871 703 3989). Green Park or Hyde Park Corner tube.* **Screens** 2. **Map** p398 H8.
Soho *99 Shaftesbury Avenue, W1D 5DY (0871 703 3988). Leicester Square tube.* **Screens** 3. **Map** p399 K6.
All *www.curzoncinemas.com.* **Tickets** £8-£14.50; £6-£11.50 reductions.
Expect a superb range of shorts, rarities, double-bills and seasons alongside new international releases across the small Curzon chain. There's 1970s splendour in Mayfair (it's sometimes used for premières) and comfort in Chelsea, which is perfect for a Sunday screening after a King's Road brunch. But the coolest of the bunch is the Soho outpost, which has a buzzing café, a decent basement bar and sometimes themes its eating and drinking spaces to tie in with event releases.

★ ICA Cinema

Nash House, the Mall, SW1Y 5AH (7930 0493, 7930 3647 tickets, www.ica.org.uk). Charing Cross tube/rail. **Tickets** £7-£10; £8 reductions. **Screens** 2. **Map** p399 K8.
London's small contemporary arts centre (*see p81*) has met its brief not only by screening an eclectic range of cinema, but by distributing some of the most noteworthy films of recent years. After an uninspiring few years, there are signs of a renaissance under new leadership. Serious types can often be seen discussing the evening's programme afterwards in the ICA Café.

FILM FESTIVALS

There's a celebration of movies every season in London.

There's a film festival in the capital on pretty much any given week during the year, but the **London Film Festival** (www.bfi.org.uk/lff, Oct) is far and away the most prestigious. Nearly 200 new British and international features are screened, mainly at the BFI Southbank and Leicester Square's Vue West End. It's preceded by the leftfield **Raindance Festival** (www.raindance.co.uk), with a terrific shorts programme. Relatively new, and in the big league, is a London offshoot of Robert Redford's **Sundance Festival** (www.sundance-london.com), in April.

Highlighting the importance of the city's LGBT communities, the **London Lesbian & Gay Film Festival** (7928 3232, www.bfi.org.uk/llgff, late Mar) is the UK's third largest film festival. Also in spring are **Human Rights Watch International Film Festival** (7713 1995, www.hrw.org/iff, mid-late Mar) and the **East End Film Festival** (www.eastendfilmfestival.com, late Apr), which has a special fondness for films starring London.

Several festivals screen the output of a particular foreign territory. Among them are the Polish Cultural Institute's **Kinoteka** (www.kinoteka.org.uk, Mar); the **London Turkish Film Festival** (www.ltff.co.uk, Nov-Dec); the wonderful **Mosaïques** festival (Ciné Lumière, www.institut-francais.org.uk/mosaiques, June); and the **French Film Festival** (www.frenchfilmfestival.org.uk, Ciné Lumière, Nov), which shows off the best of new French cinema.

London Film Festival.

Short films hog the limelight at the **London Short Film Festival** (www.shortfilms.org.uk, Jan), while September's **London International Animation Festival** (www.liaf.org.uk) screens 300 or more animated shorts from around the globe. The **Portobello Film Festival** (www.portobellofilmfestival.com, early Sept) offers an eclectic programme of free screenings, while a noble addition to the schedule since June 2011 is the **Open City London Documentary Festival** (www.opencitylondon.com, June), which is organised by and takes place mainly at University College London.

ESSENTIAL LONDON FILMS

We pick out six of the capital's star turns.

Passport to Pimlico.

BLOWUP
dir Michelangelo Antonioni, 1966
It's Swinging London, and a fashion photographer (David Hemmings) is at a loose end, having ditched his jobs for the day. He wanders into Maryon Park and when he develops the pictures he takes there, they appear to show a murder. Music from the Yardbirds.

CROUPIER
dir Mike Hodges, 1998
Thriller set in the nocturnal world of London's casinos and after-hours drinking clubs. Jack Manfred is an aspiring writer going nowhere fast. To make some cash he falls back on his old skills as a croupier. Soon, the job plunges him into a dangerous world where the rules are waiting to be broken.

FRENZY
dir Alfred Hitchcock, 1972
Covent Garden was still a fruit and veg market when this was made, and a serial killer is on the loose in the area, raping and strangling women. Fruit merchant Robert Rusk is revealed to viewers as the murderer, but suspicion falls on his friend, Richard Blaney. Will the real culprit be uncovered?

LONDON
dir Patrick Keiller, 1994
Lying at the point where documentary meets fiction, the film follows the travels of an unseen narrator around London with his friend/ex-lover to research English Romanticism. But events soon distract the pair from their planned focus. A fascinating study of 1990s London in the era of the Major government.

PASSPORT TO PIMLICO
dir Henry Cornelius, 1949
An antidote to the grimness of post-war austerity, cosy Ealing comedy *Passport to Pimlico* sees the citizens of that area of London discover that they are really Burgundians and declare independence. So it's out with the ration books and in with free-for-all shopping, boozing and jollity.

PERFORMANCE
dir Nicolas Roeg, 1970
Roeg's complex visual kaleidoscope sees an enforcer for a protection racket (James Fox) involved in murder and forced to hide from retribution in a Notting Hill basement. There, as he waits to escape abroad, he gets involved with a fading pop star (Mick Jagger) brooding over the loss of his powers of incantation.

Odeon Leicester Square
Leicester Square, WC2H 7LQ (0871 224 4007, www.odeon.co.uk). Leicester Square tube. **Tickets** £13-£22.50; £7-£17 reductions. **Screens** 6. **Map** p399 K7.

You'll often find the red carpets and crush barriers up outside this art deco gem – it's the city's leading site for star-studded premières and hosts the opening and closing nights of the London Film Festival. If you're lucky, you might catch one of the silent film screenings, with accompaniment on a 1937 Compton organ. Otherwise, it's a diet of big-volume mainstream hits.

Neighbourhood London

Electric Cinema
191 Portobello Road, Notting Hill, W11 2ED (7908 9696, www.electriccinema.co.uk). Ladbroke Grove or Notting Hill Gate tube. **Tickets** £15.50-£18 adult; £10 children. **Screens** 1. **Map** p404 X4.

The Electric had gone from past-it fleapit to luscious luxury destination with leather seats and sofas, footstools and a bar inside the auditorium when it was hit by a kitchen fire in the Electric Brasserie next door in 2012. It reopened at the end of that year with a restored interior, upgraded sound system and digital projection, and comfy new seats.

Everyman & Screen Cinemas
Everyman *5 Hollybush Vale, Hampstead, NW3 6TX. Hampstead tube.* **Tickets** £11; £9 reductions. **Screens** 2.

Screen on the Green *83 Upper Street, Islington, N1 0NP. Angel tube.* **Tickets** £10-£12; £9 reductions. **Screens** 2. **Map** p400 O2.

Both *0871 906 9060, www.everymancinema.com.*

London's most elegant cinema, the Everyman has a glamorous bar and two-seaters (£30) in its 'screening lounges', complete with foot stools and wine coolers. Everyman now also owns three former Screen cinemas, of which Islington's Screen on the Green is the best – carefully refurbished in 2009, it lost seats to make space for the more comfortable kind, gained an auditorium bar and a stage for live events, but kept its lovely exterior neon sign.

Hackney Picturehouse
270 Mare Street, Hackney, E8 1HE (0871 902 5734, www.picturehouses.co.uk). Hackney Central or London Fields rail. **Tickets** £6-£11.50; £4-£10 reductions. **Screens** 4.

Opened in autumn 2011, the four-screen Hackney Picturehouse is the newest of the Picturehouse chain, and has become the flagship cinema for a borough woefully served for film. As well as showing the more interesting new releases and hosting festivals and seasons geared towards the diverse local community, the Picturehouse has an excellent café and the Attic, a performance space.

★ Phoenix
52 High Road, East Finchley, N2 9PJ (8444 6789, www.phoenixcinema.co.uk). East Finchley tube. **Tickets** £6-£9.50; £6 reductions. **Screens** 1.

Built in 1910 and revamped in the 1930s, the Grade II-listed Phoenix has recently been restored to its copper and gold, art deco glory. It has real old-fashioned glamour, and is London's oldest cinema to have remained in continuous operation. Owned by a charitable trust, it runs a varied programme including theatre and opera transmissions. The best cinema in north London. *Photo p256.*

Rio Cinema
107 Kingsland High Street, Dalston, E8 2PB (7241 9410, www.riocinema.org.uk). Dalston Kingsland rail. **Tickets** £10; £8 reductions. **Screens** 1.

Another great deco survivor, restored to its original sleek lines, the Rio is east London's finest independent. Alongside mainstream releases, the Rio is well known for its Turkish and Kurdish film festivals.

Vue Westfield London
Westfield London, Shepherd's Bush, W12 7GF (0871 224 0240, www.myvue.com). White City or Wood Lane tube, or Shepherd's Bush tube/rail. **Tickets** check website for details. **Screens** 14.

At this Vue multiplex, all the screens are digital, with five 3D-ready and two 18m by 10m whoppers. The main rooms are functional black boxes with good sightlines, but you can also fork out for over-18s 'Scene' screens: you get reclining chairs and access to a private bar and a cloakroom. There's a branch at the Westfield centre in Stratford.

Other locations throughout the city.

REPERTORY CINEMAS

Several first-run cinemas also offer rep-style fare – check www.timeout.com for locations.

★ BFI Southbank
South Bank, SE1 8XT (7928 3232 tickets, www.bfi.org.uk). Embankment tube or Waterloo tube/rail. **Tickets** £12; £8.50 reductions. **Screens** 4. **Map** p399 M8.

IN THE KNOW SECRET CINEMA

Go on the website (www.secretcinema.org) and book yourself a couple of tickets for a rollercoaster ride of a film experience. Venue and a theme for costumes are announced just 24 hours before curtain-up. It's an immersive experience, in a setting transformed to fit in with your film. This may give you a clue, but you won't know for sure until the film starts rolling.

The BFI's success is still built on its core function: thought-provoking seasons giving film-fans the chance to enjoy rare and significant British and foreign films. A terrific place to enjoy rare movies.
▶ *The BFI's Mediatheque gives you free access to its huge film and documentary archive.*

Ciné Lumière

Institut Français, 17 Queensberry Place, South Kensington, SW7 2DT (7871 3515, www.institut-francais.org.uk). South Kensington tube. **Tickets** £8-£10; £6-£8 reductions; £8 Mon. **Screens** 1. **Map** p395 D10.
Ciné Lumière reopened in 2009 with better seating and a refreshed art deco interior. No longer screening French films only (there are still, however, regular French previews and classics), the Lumière is a standard-bearer for world cinema in the capital.

Prince Charles

7 Leicester Place, off Leicester Square, WC2H 7BY (7494 3654, www.princecharlescinema.com). Leicester Square tube. **Tickets** £6.50-£10; £4-£6 reductions. **Screens** 2. **Map** p399 K7.
Central and cheap, the Prince Charles is just up an alley from the pricey Leicester Square monsters, but even films on the new screen are a bargain. Perfect for catching up on still-fresh films you missed first time round, it is renowned for riotous singalong screenings and cult programming such as *The Room*, billed as 'the worst film ever made' and shown to a packed house once a month.

★ Riverside Studios

Crisp Road, Hammersmith, W6 9RL (8237 1111, www.riversidestudios.co.uk). Hammersmith tube. **Tickets** £8.50; £7.50 reductions. **Screens** 1.
The Riverside offers a superb programme of films and has become well known for inventive double-bills.

IMAX

BFI IMAX

1 Charlie Chaplin Walk, South Bank, SE1 8XR (0330 333 7878, www.bfi.org.uk/imax). Waterloo tube/rail. **Tickets** £16.60-£20.70; £11.40-£15 reductions. **Screens** 1. **Map** p399 M8.
London's biggest screen mixes made-for-IMAX fare and scenery-heavy documentaries with mainstream blockbusters, such as Harry Potter films.

OUTDOOR SCREENINGS

The best known open-air screenings are those at **Somerset House**, but you can find plenty more – some in unusual locations. **Free Film Festivals** (www.freefilmfestivals.org) puts on free outdoor screenings in interesting public spaces in south-east London. The Scoop (*see p62*) is the location for summer screenings as part of **More London Free Festival** (www.morelondon.com), while **Pop Up Screens** (www.popupscreens.co.uk) shows popular films in parks in west London.

Rooftop Film Club

Queen of Hoxton, 1-5 Curtain Road, Hoxton, EC2A 3JX (www.rooftopfilmclub.com). **Tickets** £13.
In summer, the rooftop garden at this bar/club/arts collective screens around five films a week. Tickets are only available online; see the website for details.

Somerset House

The Strand, WC2R 1LA (7845 4600, www.somersethouse.org.uk/film). **Tickets** vary. **Map** p399 M7.
This summer season takes place in the lovely neo-classical courtyard of Somerset House; tickets sell out way in advance. Bring a picnic and cushions.

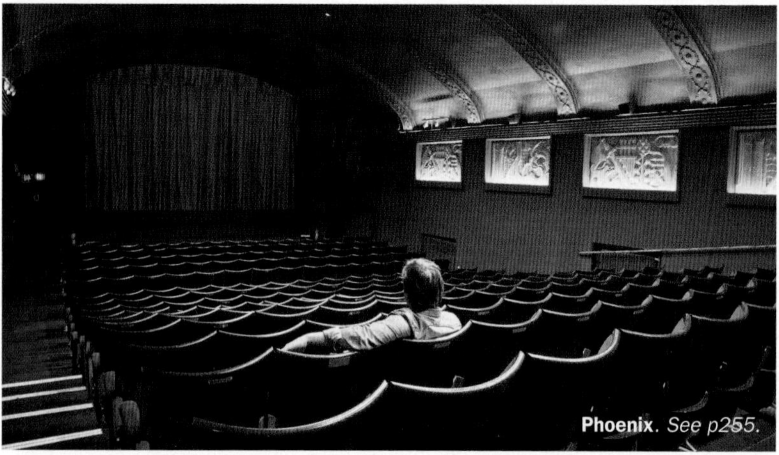

Phoenix. *See p255.*

ARTS & ENTERTAINMENT

Gay & Lesbian

After the minor disaster of World Pride 2012 – funding shortfalls meant there weren't even floats for the traditional parade – London's LGBT community were relieved at the success of Pride 2013; the new organisers of London's showpiece gay festival even managed to arrange good weather in what was otherwise a miserable June. Despite the controversy of London's headline homo event, smaller, more DIY goings-on continue to thrive in the city. Whatever your taste in music, from thunderous indie to thumping disco, you'll find somewhere that specialises in it, in a nightlife scene that runs around the clock and throughout the week. Off the dancefloor, the scene is more varied still, with cabaret nights, literary salons and plays, and a major gay and lesbian film festival.

THE GAY SCENE IN LONDON

Roughly speaking, London's gay scene is split into three distinct zones: **Soho**, **Vauxhall** and **east London**. Each of these three districts has its own character: in a nutshell, Soho is the most mainstream, Vauxhall is the most decadent and east London is the most outré.

Centred on Old Compton Street, the Soho scene continues to attract the crowds. Luvvies take in a singalong at the **Green Carnation**, fit freaks work out at **Sweatbox** and everyone else mills around the plethora of gay-slanted bars and cafés. And just down the road, close to Charing Cross Station, sits the legendary **Heaven**, home to **G-A-Y**. If your dream has always been to see Madonna or Kylie in a club, here's your chance – the list of singers who've done live PAs here reads like a *Who's Who* of squeal-tastic gay pop icons.

Down south, Vauxhall is more hedonistic. You could arrive in London on a Friday evening and dance non-stop here for an entire weekend before flying out of town again, with venues such as the **RVT,** the Eagle (home to the superb **Horse Meat Disco**) and **Popstarz** providing great alternatives to the standard Vauxhall offerings of throngs of shirtless, sweaty chaps.

The most alternative and creative of the capital's queer scenes is in east London. In the likes of the **George & Dragon** and **Dalston Superstore**, you'll be rubbing shoulders with fashion and music's movers and shakers (plus assorted straight folk), to soundtracks built by ferociously underground DJs. With so much coolness going on, it can get a little snooty, but a lot of the bars and clubs round Shoreditch and Dalston are also properly mixed, which makes the area ideal for a night out with straight mates.

Keen to cut to the chase? **Chariots** is the sauna chain of choice, although **Vault 139** and **Pleasuredrome** (Arch 124, Cornwall Road, Waterloo, SE1 8XE, 7633 9194, www.pleasuredrome.com) also have their followers. Most regular bars don't have backrooms, but some club nights in Vauxhall can get raunchy. The monthly **Hard On** (www.hardonclub.co.uk) is the top pick on the calendar for lovers of fetish and leather.

It was a blow for London's lesbian scene when the Candy Bar – the city's first full-time drinking den for lesbians – closed in early 2014, though rumour has it that **Ku** (*see p262*) may open a women's bar as a replacement, and the basement venue **She Soho** (23A Old Compton Street, W1D 5LB, http://she-soho.com) was due

Pride London. See p35.

to open in Soho as we went to press. Monday or Wednesday at **Retro** are good choices, and the women-only **Glass Bar** (www.theglassbar.org.uk), which lost its own premises a few years ago, now runs various events. There's also the glam **Bijou Cocktail Club** on the second Saturday of the month at Rudds bar in the City (148 Queen Victoria Street, EC4V 4BY, www.elysionevents.co.uk).

New stand-alone nights for clubbing, cabaret and entertainment of all kinds pop up all the time, but Bird Club at the **Bethnal Green Working Men's Club** (*see p277*), exclusive Code at **Green Carnation** (*see p261*) and Ruby Tuesdays at **Ku** (*see p262*) are recommended. Over the last decade, **100% Babe** at the Roxy (3-5 Rathbone Place, Fitzrovia, W1P 1DA, 7636 1598, www.theroxy.co.uk) has become an institution. It happens every Sunday night before a bank holiday – expect house music, feel-good floorfillers and a party mood. And queer performance nights Duckie (hosted by Amy Lamé) and Bar Wotever at **RVT** (*see p259*) are popular with both the girls and the boys. For culture vultures, there's literary salon **Polari** (www.polariliterarysalon.co.uk), held every month at the Southbank Centre.

Lastly, special mention should go to the **NYC Downlow**, a travelling homo disco straight out of 1970s New York that you can catch at festivals across the country (http://thedownlowradio.com/the-downlow) including **Lovebox** (*see p35*), the Sunday of which competes with **Summer Rites** (http://summerritesevents.com) in Shoreditch Park for the title of London's gayest festival.

RESTAURANTS & CAFÉS

More or less every café and restaurant in London welcomes gay custom. Certainly nowhere in or around Soho will so much as bat an eyelid at you and your other half having a romantic dinner. For thirtysomething lesbians, there are fun cocktail evenings amid the mom-and-pop Italian vintage decor of **Star at Night** (22 Great Chapel Street, Soho, W1F 8FR, 7494 2488, www.thestaratnight.com, open 6-11.30pm Tue-Sat) – by day, it's a greasy spoon.

Balans

60 Old Compton Street, Soho, W1D 4UG (7439 2183, www.balans.co.uk). Leicester Square or Piccadilly Circus tube. **Open** 8am-2am Mon-Thur; 8am-4am Fri, Sat; 7.30am-2am Sun. **Admission** £2.50 after midnight Mon-Sat. **Map** p397 K6.
The gay café-restaurant of choice for many years, Balans is all about location, location, location (plus hot waiters, decent food and ridiculous opening hours). Situated across from Compton's bar and next door to Clone Zone, it's the beating heart of the Soho scene. The nearby Balans Café (no.34) serves a shorter version of the menu. Both are open almost all night and are good for a post-club bite.
Other locations throughout the city.

NIGHTCLUBS

London's club scene is particularly subject to change: venues close, nights end and new soirées start. Check *Time Out* magazine or www.timeout.com for details on what's on when you're here.

If you want to stay up all night and next day as well, head to **Vauxhall**. At **Fire** (South

Lambeth Road, SW8 1UQ, www.fireclub.co.uk), popular nights include Orange, a Sunday staple. Still in Vauxhall, on the Albert Embankment, try **Union** (no.66, www.clubunion.co.uk) and **Area** (nos.67-68, www.arealondon.net). If you're near Old Street, keep an eye on **East Bloc** (217 City Road, EC1V 1JN, www.eastbloc.co.uk).

Club Kali

Dome, 1 Dartmouth Park Hill, Tufnell Park, N19 5QQ (7272 8153, www.clubkali.com). Tufnell Park tube. **Open** 10pm-3am 3rd Fri of mth. **Admission** £8; £5 reductions.

The world's largest LGBT Asian dance club offers Bollywood, bhangra, Arabic tunes, R&B and dance classics spun by DJs Ritu, Riz & Qurra.

Exilio Latin Dance Club

Venues vary; see website for details (07956 983230, www.exilio.co.uk). **Open** 9.30pm-2.30am every other Sat. **Admission** £6-£12. **No credit cards.**

This is London's principal queer Latino club, held in various locations, with girls and guys getting together for merengue, salsa, cumbia and reggaeton.

Heaven

Underneath the Arches, Villiers Street, Covent Garden, WC2N 6NG (7930 2020, www.heavennightclublondon.com). Embankment tube or Charing Cross tube/rail. **Open** 11pm-5.30am Mon; 11pm-4am Thur, Fri; 10.30pm-5am Sat. **Admission** prices vary. **No credit cards.** **Map** p399 L7.

London's most famous gay club is a bit like *Les Misérables* – it's camp, it's full of history, and tourists love it. Popcorn (Mon) has long been a good bet, but it's really all about G-A-Y (Thur-Sat). For years, divas with an album to flog (Madonna, Kylie, Girls Aloud) have turned up to play here at the weekend.

★ Horse Meat Disco

Eagle London, 349 Kennington Lane, Vauxhall, SE11 5QY (7793 0903, www.eaglelondon.com). Vauxhall tube/rail. **Open** 8pm-3am Sun. **Admission** £6. **No credit cards.**

Not your average gay club. Skinny Soho boys and fashionistas rub shoulders with scally lads and bears in a traditional old boozer. The hip soundtrack is an inspired mix of Studio 54, New York punk and new wave. As one *Time Out* critic put it: 'If you ever wished you could hang out in a club like the one in *Beyond the Valley of the Dolls* or *Scarface*, you'll love Horse Meat Disco.' A must. *Photo p260.*

▶ *When Horse Meat isn't in residence, the Eagle is a hub for those wishing to try a bit of leather without a strict dress code.*

Popstarz

www.popstarz.org. **Open** 10pm-5am Fri. **Admission** £3 before 11pm, then £5-£8.

What G-A-Y is to cheese, Popstarz is to indie. It's studenty, drunken, attitude-free and popular – so popular, in fact, that the club has spawned imitators from New York to Paris. There are also occasional PAs from in-demand acts.

▶ *Having settled at various London locations since it began in 1995, Popstarz is currently itinerant, moving to a new venue each month. Check the website for the latest venue – and a map.*

★ RVT

Royal Vauxhall Tavern, 372 Kennington Lane, Vauxhall, SE11 5HY (7820 1222, www.rvt.org.uk). Vauxhall tube/rail. **Open** 7pm-midnight Mon, Wed, Thur; 6pm-midnight Tue; 7pm-2am Fri; 9pm-2am Sat; 2pm-midnight Sun. **Admission** £5-£7.

This pub turned legendary gay cabaret venue, a much-loved stalwart on the scene for years, operates an anything-goes booking policy. The most famous fixture is Saturday's queer performance night Duckie (www.duckie.co.uk), with Amy Lamé hosting acts at midnight that range from strip cabaret to porn puppets. On Sundays there's S.L.A.G.S/Chill-out, with house spun by DJ Simon Le Vans at 2pm, followed by cabaret from Charlie Hides at 5.30pm and guest DJs from 7.30pm. The aim is always to please the crowd of regulars, reliably vocal with their feedback. Punters verge on the bear, but the main dress code is 'no attitude'. *Photo p261.*

Vogue Fabrics

66 Stoke Newington Road, Dalston, N16 7XB (http://voguefabricsdalston.com/club). Dalston Junction or Dalston Kingsland rail. **Open** 10pm-7am Fri, Sat. **Admission** £3-£5 Fri, Sat. **No credit cards.**

Small, sweaty and seemingly illegal (but in fact perfectly legitimate), Vogue Fabrics is the place to come if you like your nights messy and your men of the bear and otter variety. While the regular parties come and go, the electro-, disco-, Italo-pumpin' Dirtbox remains a favourite.

► *A little boy-heavy? The guys behind Dirtbox run Dick and Fanny (www.dickandfanny.tumblr.com).*

XXL

1 Invicta Plaza, South Bank, SE1 9UF (www.xxl-london.com). Southwark tube. **Open** 10pm-3am Wed; 10pm-6am Sat. **Admission** £15. **No credit cards. Map** p402 O7.

The world's biggest club – naturally! – for bears and their friends, XXL is nirvana for chubbier, hairier and blokier gay men and their twinky admirers. Note the new venue.

PUBS & BARS

Unless otherwise stated, the pubs and bars listed here are open to both gay men and lesbians.

Barcode Vauxhall

Arch 69, Goding Street, Vauxhall, SE11 5AW (7582 4180, www.bar-code.co.uk). Vauxhall tube/rail. **Open** 8pm-4am Thur; 8pm-8am Fri, Sat; 8pm-3am Sun. **Admission** £6, £8 after midnight.

Prior to the arrival of Barcode Vauxhall, Vauxhall was mostly for clubbing, with those oh-so-necessary pre-dance drinks to be enjoyed anywhere-else-but-here. Now those pre-dancing punters are joined by folks just after a drink at this massive, lavish venue, which generally attracts a blokey-ish crowd despite its shiny, sparkly surfaces.

Horse Meat Disco. *See p259.*

★ Dalston Superstore

117 Kingland High Street, Dalston, E8 2PB (7254 2273, http://dalstonsuperstore.com). Dalston Kingsland rail. **Open** 11am-2am Mon-Wed; 11am-2.30am Thur; 11am-4am Fri; 10am-4am Sat; 10am-2.30am Sun.

The opening of this gay arts space-cum-bar a few years back cemented Dalston's status as the final frontier of the East End's gay scene. Come during the day for the café grub (the food's good and breakfast is quite a trendy scene), Wi-Fi and art exhibitions on the walls; at night, you can expect queues for an impressive roster of guest DJs spinning anything from garage to pop. Regular dates, such as Sunday's Tutti Frutti (soul, disco and house), are well worth putting in the diary. The guys behind Dalston Superstore also run Trailer Trash (www.clubtrailertrash.com), a roaming club night that pulls in a fashion-forward pack of partiers. *Photo p262.*

Freedom Bar

66 Wardour Street, Soho, W1F OTA (7734 0071, www.freedombarsoho.com). Leicester Square or Piccadilly Circus tube. **Open** 4pm-3am Mon-Thur; 2pm-3am Fri, Sat; 2-10.30pm Sun. **Admission** £5 after 10pm Fri, Sat. **Map** p396 J6.

A glitzy cocktail lounge and DJ bar, spread over two floors. The glam ground-floor bar attracts a fashion-conscious crowd, who sip cocktails among chandeliers, zebra-print banquettes and Venetian mirrors. A few 'strays' and dolled-up gal pals add colour. The large basement club and performance space hosts weekday cabaret and gets busy with the gay party crowd over the weekend.

G-A-Y Bar

30 Old Compton Street, Soho, W1D 4UR (7494 2756, www.g-a-y.co.uk). Leicester Square or Tottenham Court Road tube. **Open** noon-midnight daily. **Map** p397 K6.

The G-A-Y night at Heaven (*see p259*) gets the celebrity cameos, but this popular bar is still a shrine to queer pop idols, with nightly drinks promos every time they play a video from the current diva du jour. There's also a women's bar in the basement, called (delightfully) Girls Go Down – popular with flirty, studenty lesbians, loathed by most older women.

► *G-A-Y bar's plush late-night sibling, G-A-Y Late, is round the corner at 5 Goslett Yard.*

George & Dragon

2 Hackney Road, Bethnal Green, E2 7NS (7012 1100). Old Street tube/rail or Hoxton rail. **Open** 6pm-midnight Mon-Thur, Sat, Sun; 5pm-midnight Fri. **Map** p401 S3.

ARTS & ENTERTAINMENT

RVT. *See p259.*

The location of this mini-pub ensures a stylish and up-for-it clientele, while the decor (a wall-mounted horse's head, creepy puppets, random garbage) keeps the vibe fun. The music – pop, indie and accessible electronica – is often delivered with a sense of humour. Gay or not, it's one of London's best boozers.
▶ *Wondering where everyone went at closing time? To the Joiners Arms, of course (see right).*

Green Carnation

4-5 Greek Street, Soho, W1D 4DB (8123 4267, www.greencarnationsoho.co.uk). Tottenham Court Road tube. **Open** 4pm-2am Mon-Sat; 4pm-12.30am Sun. **Admission** £5 after 11pm Mon-Sat. **Map** p397 K6.
The Green Carnation had a major refit a few years back, to spectacular effect. Head upstairs for cocktails in posh surroundings, with chandeliers and piano music. There's a bar and a dancefloor downstairs. It's a haven for West End Wendies, always on hand to belt out a minor Sondheim in the wee hours.

Hoist

Arches 47B & 47C, South Lambeth Road, Vauxhall, SW8 1RH (7735 9972, www.thehoist.co.uk). Vauxhall tube/rail. **Open** 9pm-1am Wed; 10pm-3am Fri; 10pm-4am Sat; 2pm-2am Sun. **Admission** £6 Fri, Sun; £2-£10 Sat. **No credit cards**.
One of only two genuine leather bars in town, this club sits under the arches and makes the most of its underground and industrial setting. The Saturday night event SBN (Stark Bollock Naked) gives you the tone of the place; leather, uniforms, rubber, skinhead or boots are the usual dress code. Strictly no trainers.

Joiners Arms

116-118 Hackney Road, Bethnal Green, E2 7QL (www.thejoinershoreditch.com). Old Street tube/rail or Hoxton rail. **Open** 5pm-2am Mon-Wed; 5pm-3am Thur; 5pm-4am Fri, Sat; 2pm-2am Sun. **Map** p401 S3.
Love it or loathe it, come midnight this is where all the gays in Shoreditch end up. A mix of fashion types, queer East End geezers and tourists cabbing it from Soho get down to the sounds of pop, house and electro. The queue for the loos is obscene and the vibe can be obnoxiously trendy, but on the whole the Joiners Arms is friendly, drunken and fun. Word to the wise: Sunday nights are often where it's at.

★ Ku

30 Lisle Street, Chinatown, WC2H 7BA (7437 4303, www.ku-bar.co.uk). Leicester Square or Piccadilly Circus tube. **Open** noon-3am Mon-Sat; noon-midnight Sun. **Map** p399 K7.

With a string of awards to its name, Ku must be doing something right. Formerly known as West Central, it has morphed from a mediocre space into a popular bar and club that offers everything from film nights to comedy. The sheer variety of club nights (which are held in the basement) is impressive. The choice ranges from Sandra D's Ruby Tuesdays for lesbians, to drag queen Vicki Vivacious on Wednesdays and the Ku DJ Quest Winners – Doug Silva and Athanas Sak – on Saturday nights.

Dalston Superstore. *See p260.*

► *Ku also runs a three-floor bar-club in the heart of the local scene, on the corner of Frith and Old Compton streets. Serious competition for G-A-Y, then.*

KW4

77 Hampstead High Street, Hampstead, NW3 1RE (7435 5747, www.kingwilliamhampstead.co.uk). Hampstead tube or Hampstead Heath rail. **Open** 11am-11pm Mon-Thur; 11am-midnight Fri-Sun.

The perfect evening ending (or beginning) to time spent on the heath, this fabulous old local – the King William IV, or King Willy to those with longer memories – attracts a very Hampstead crowd (read: well-off and ready for fun). On summer weekends, the cute little beer garden tends to fill up with a mix of gay and straight punters keen to put down their shopping bags. The pub is more popular with lesbians in summer too, as a stop-off after a dip in the heath's women's bathing pond.

Manbar

79 Charing Cross Road, Chinatown, WC2H 0NE (7434 2567, www.manbarsoho.com). Leicester Square tube. **Open** 5pm-3.30am Mon-Thur; 3pm-3.30am Fri, Sat; 3-11pm Sun. **Map** p399 K6.

What was once late-night booze and cruise bar 79CXR now has sexy black and red decor on three levels. DJs play remixed versions of current commercial chart hits mixed with cutting-edge dance anthems. Regular nights include Beartrap on Mondays, talent show Spotlight on Tuesdays, and Sunday School – games, magic, performances and more – hosted by award-winning drag queen/cabaret star Myra Dubois.

Retro Bar

2 George Court, off the Strand, Covent Garden, WC2N 6HH (7839 8760, www.retrobarlondon.co.uk). Charing Cross tube/rail. **Open** noon-11pm Mon-Fri; 2-11pm Sat; 2-10.30pm Sun. **Map** p399 L7.

Iggy Pop and Kate Bush are on the walls of this bar, where nights are dedicated to indie rock and 1980s hits (Echo Beach on Thursdays). The crowd is mixed in every sense: gay/straight, gay/lesbian and scene queen/true eccentric. Quiz nights (Tue) are popular, too, and the bar on occasions even relinquishes control of the music and lets punters be the DJ – bring your iPod.

Shadow Lounge

5 Brewer Street, Soho, W1F 0RF (7287 7988, www.theshadowlounge.co.uk). Leicester Square or Piccadilly Circus tube. **Open** 10pm-3am Mon-Sat. **Admission** free Mon; £5 Tue-Thur; £10 Fri, Sat. **Map** p399 K6.

For celebrity sightings, suits, cutes and fancy boots, this is your West End venue. Expect a hefty cover charge and a queue at the weekends, but there's often a sublime atmosphere inside.

ARTS & ENTERTAINMENT

Yard

57 Rupert Street, Soho, W1V 7BJ (7437 2652, www.yardbar.co.uk). Leicester Square or Piccadilly Circus tube. **Open** 4-11.30pm Mon-Wed; 3-11.30pm Thur; 2pm-midnight Fri, Sat; 2-10.30pm Sun. **Map** p399 K6.

Possibly the most reliable gay bar in Soho. Come for the courtyard in summer, stay for the Loft Bar in winter. This unpretentious bar offers a great open-air courtyard in a central location, attracting pretty boys, blokes and lesbians in equal measure.

ADULT CLUBS & SAUNAS

Chariots

1 Fairchild Street, Shoreditch, EC2A 3NS (7247 5333, www.gaysauna.co.uk). Liverpool Street tube/rail or Shoreditch High Street rail. **Open** noon-8am Mon-Fri; noon-9am Sat, Sun. **Admission** £19; £17 reductions. **Map** p401 R4.

Chariots is a sauna chain with outlets all over town. The original is this one in Shoreditch, the biggest and busiest, although not necessarily the best. That accolade probably goes to the one on the Albert Embankment at Vauxhall (nos.63-64, 7247 5333). The Waterloo branch (101 Lower Marsh, 7401 8484) has the biggest sauna in the UK.

Other locations throughout the city.

★ Sweatbox

Ramillies House, 1-2 Ramillies Street, Soho, W1F 7LN (3214 6014, www.sweatboxsoho.com). Oxford Circus tube. **Open** 24hrs daily. **Admission** £16 day; £10 under-25s. **Map** p396 J6.

Sweatbox Soho looks more like a nightclub than a typical gym, with the sleek design offset by friendly staff. Though small, the space is well laid out, with a multigym and a free weights room. Qualified masseurs offer treatments. If that doesn't do the trick, there's a sauna downstairs.

Vault 139

139-143 Whitfield Street, Fitzrovia, W1T 5EN (7388 5500, www.vault139.com). Warren Street tube. **Open** 1pm-1am daily. **No credit cards**. **Map** p396 J4.

Hidden away on a quiet backstreet, Vault 139 is London's most central cruise bar – and it's classy, too, with plush sofas, TV screens and a DJ booth.

IN THE KNOW CAB LORE

'**Vauxhall** has a big one-way system,' says taxi driver Angela. 'After a club, make your way to the bridge, on the south side of the railway, to go north of the river. You'll catch cabs that have come south and are turning back.' If you're in **Soho**, says Peter, another cabbie, 'try and get on to Shaftesbury Avenue, Charing Cross Road or Oxford Street. The Soho sidestreets become very congested at night so not many drivers go there.'

Ku.

Nightlife

To say London has brilliant and diverse nightlife is an understatement, whether clubbing, live music, cabaret or comedy. These days, though, big is rarely best. We have one of the world's largest and most influential nightclubs, Fabric, but as a credible superclub, it stands alone in the city. It's the smaller venues that are really buzzing. In particular, good clubbing is easy to come by along the Kingsland Road strip in Dalston, where you'll find the Nest, Dalston Superstore and a range of party bars. There's more new music from the edge at places such as XOYO and the Shacklewell Arms, the latter proving the London cliché of indie bands in sticky dives endures. London has more than 250 comedy gigs a week, ranging from pub open-mics to arena shows; the Comedy Store is a good place to start. Meanwhile, the alt cabaret scene rolls on: Bethnal Green Working Men's Club and RVT are key venues.

Clubs

In this era of boutique clubbing, London has all the bases covered – you don't even always have to go to a club to have the club experience. Try bowling and boogieing at **Bloomsbury Bowling Lanes** (*see p272*), for example, or dress up for one of the city's burgeoning number of 'vintage'-themed parties. And these days, some of the best events happen in secret warehouse locations, usually in east or south London.

IN THE KNOW DO MORE

The free *Time Out* magazine picks out key highlights of London's nightlife. For much, much more, check out the website: www.timeout.com.

CITY SOUNDS AND TOP NIGHTS

Since the arrival of jungle in the mainstream way back in the 1990s, big, beefy, speakerstack-destroying bass has always been hot in London. Dubstep is huge – and heavy – its reverberating beats sending dancefloors wild across the capital as it continues to morph through urban genres such as funky, future house, bassline, dancehall and 2step – all characterised as UK bass. But revivalists continue to mine any number of genres – disco, psychsoul, UKG (UK Garage)... – anything that will get you dancing. In fact, the days of epoch-defining megaraves is gone, shattered into a thousand microscenes and sound systems that are fleet of foot and quick to respond to the passions of their audience. Upstairs rooms in pubs and the basements of abandoned shops – still especially in east London – are the birthing ground for DJs and promoters who might graduate to more permanent venues – or might vanish without trace. It's a bewildering scene, but thrilling too.

VENUES

Shoreditch was the hub of the capital's nightlife scene for a long time. It has, however, become increasingly commercialised in recent years (witness the trails of hen and office parties between Old Street and Spitalfields) and there's more action elsewhere – though live space and club **XOYO** (*see p268*) is a very welcome addition. The range of nights at **Book Club** (*see p267*), from disco to science drink-and-thinks, is one side of Shoreditch nightlife, but **Plastic People** (*see p267*) is another – still a great venue after all these years: it's amazing what quality sound does for a night out.

The city's cool kids now take the bus north up the Kingsland Road from Shoreditch into **Dalston** and further on into Stoke Newington. The former has much-improved transport connections to the rest of the city since the London Overground arrived at Dalston Junction station, but it can be difficult to find the clubs – even more so what's happening in them. Spend a few moments checking *Time Out* magazine, www.timeout.com/clubs or hunting on Facebook and you'll unearth fabulous happenings at the likes of **Dalston Superstore** (*see p260*), hipster-magnet **Alibi** (91 Kingsland High Street, E8 2PB, 7249 2733, www.thealibilondon.co.uk) or **Dance Tunnel** (95 Kingsland High Street, E8 2PB, 72497865, www.dancetunnel.com), now home to the pioneering and enduringly influential dubstep and bass night, FWD>>.

The appeal of clubbing in the **West End** has steeply declined; with the exception of **Madame JoJo's** (*see p277*), there's little here beside bars, pubs and a lively – but not especially advnenturous – gay scene.

To the north, up in **King's Cross**, **Egg** (200 York Way, N7 9AX, 7871 7111, www.egglondon.net) and the **Big Chill House** (257-259 Pentonville Road, N1 9NL, 7427 2540, www.wearebigchill.com/venues) are all that remain of a former clubbing nexus that was lost to redevelopment. But the **Star of Kings** pub-club (126 York Way, N1 0AX, 7278 9708, www.starofkings.co.uk), with its late licence (at the weekend) and killer sound system, signifies that the area still has hedonistic potential. And the **Lexington** (*see p275*) is known for its rough and ready nights with a studenty feel in its upstairs room – Paris is Burning is a decent electro-house night.

Further north, **Camden** is still very popular – especially with tourists. Indie student hangout **Proud** (*see p267*), teeny pub-rave spot the **Lock Tavern** (*see p267*) and bourbon-soaked gig haunt the **Blues Kitchen** (*see p272*) offer credible nights for London party people too. And **Koko** (*see p270*) runs some of the biggest student nights around – Club NME and Annie Mac Presents.

There's more of interest to the south. The gay village in **Vauxhall** is just as welcoming to open-minded, straight-rolling types, with club promoters looking towards south-of-the-river venues such as **Fire** (South Lambeth Road, SW8 1RT, 3242 0040, www.firelondon.net), which has some big line-ups, and **Hidden** (100 Tinworth Street, SE11 5EQ, 7820 6613, www.hiddenclub.co.uk) as occasional homes for their (largely drum 'n' bass and electronica) parties. The calendar is even fuller at **Corsica Studios** (*see p274*), at Elephant and Castle.

CENTRAL

★ Fabric

77A Charterhouse Street, Clerkenwell, EC1M 3HJ (7336 8898, www.fabriclondon.com). Farringdon tube/rail. **Open** 10pm-6am Fri; 11pm-8am Sat; 11pm-6am Sun. **Admission** £8-£24. **Map** p400 O5.

Fabric is the club that most party people come to see in London, with good reason. Located in a former meatpacking warehouse, it has a well-deserved reputation as the capital's biggest and best club. The line-ups are legendary. Fridays belong to the bass: guaranteed highlights include DJ Hype, with his

Fabric.

DANS LE NOIR ?
Restaurant - Bar - Lounge
Already 1.000.000 guests worldwide
DINING IN THE DARK...
A unique human and sensory experience
30-31 Clerkenwell Green
EC1R 0DU London
Metro: Farringdon
+44 (0) 207 253 1100
booking@danslenoir.com
Online booking: www.danslenoir.com
£8 OFF YOUR BILL*
*On your total bill for a minimum of 2 full menu (drinks not included). Offer till 31st December 2014

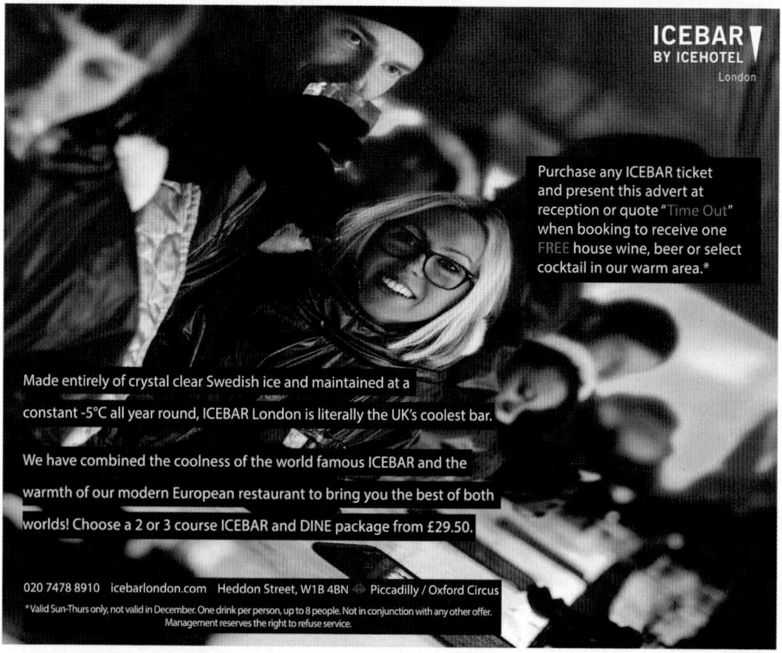
ICEBAR
BY ICEHOTEL
London
Purchase any ICEBAR ticket and present this advert at reception or quote "Time Out" when booking to receive one FREE house wine, beer or select cocktail in our warm area.*
Made entirely of crystal clear Swedish ice and maintained at a constant -5°C all year round, ICEBAR London is literally the UK's coolest bar.
We have combined the coolness of the world famous ICEBAR and the warmth of our modern European restaurant to bring you the best of both worlds! Choose a 2 or 3 course ICEBAR and DINE package from £29.50.
020 7478 8910 icebarlondon.com Heddon Street, W1B 4BN Piccadilly / Oxford Circus
*Valid Sun-Thurs only, not valid in December. One drink per person, up to 8 people. Not in conjunction with any other offer. Management reserves the right to refuse service.

drum 'n' bass and dubstep night Playaz, plus Andy C's Ram Records takeover and Caspa's Dub Police label nights. Saturdays descend into techy, minimal, deep house territory, with the world's most famous DJs regularly making appearances. Be warned: the queues are also legendary. Blag on to the guestlist or buy tickets in advance to avoid a two-hour wait.

NORTH LONDON

Better known as gig venues, **Koko** (*see p270*) and **Barfly** (*see p272*) have good reputations for feisty club nights, and the live music at the **Blues Kitchen** (*see p272*) can really rock.

Lock Tavern

35 Chalk Farm Road, Camden, NW1 8AJ (7482 7163, www.lock-tavern.com). Chalk Farm tube. **Open** noon-midnight Mon-Thur; noon-1am Fri, Sat; noon-11pm Sun. **Admission** free. **Map** p404 X1.

A favourite of artfully distressed rock urchins, it teems with aesthetic niceties inside (cosy black couches and warm wood panels downstairs; open-air terrace on the first floor), but it's the unpredictable after-party vibe that packs in the punters, with big-name DJs regularly providing the tunes.

Old Queen's Head

44 Essex Road, Islington, N1 8LN (7354 9993, www.theoldqueenshead.com). Angel tube. **Open** noon-midnight Mon-Wed, Sun; noon-1am Thur; noon-2am Fri, Sat. **Admission** £4 after 8pm Fri, Sat. **Map** p400 O1.

Pulling in fun-seekers since its relaunch way back in 2006, the Old Queen's Head is another place with long queues at the weekends. There are two floors and outside seating front and back, and during the week you can lounge on battered sofas. Weekends are for dancing, minor league celeb-spotting and chatting up the bar staff, or trying out the private karaoke room.

Proud

Horse Hospital, Stables Market, Camden, NW1 8AH (7482 3867, www.proudcamden.com). Chalk Farm tube. **Open** 11am-1.30am Wed; 11am-2.30am Thur-Sat; 11am-12.30am Sun. **Admission** free-£10. **Map** p404 W2.

The north London guitar-slingers have given way to dubstep, rock 'n' rave and drum 'n' bass, but the action at this former equine hospital is still rock 'n' roll. Drape yourself – cocktail in hand – over the luxurious textiles in the individual stable-style booths (you must book in advance), sink into deckchairs on the outdoor terrace, or spin around in the main band room at its naughtily themed nights.

EAST LONDON

In addition to the venues below, check out gay hangout the **Dalston Superstore** (*see p260*).

Book Club

100 Leonard Street, Shoreditch, EC2A 4RH (7684 8618, www.wearetbc.com). Old Street tube/rail. **Open** 8am-midnight Mon-Wed; 8am-2am Thur, Fri; 10am-2am Sat; noon-midnight Sun. **Admission** free-£5. **Map** p401 Q4.

The Book Club aims to fuse lively creative events, table tennis (there's a ping pong table and regular tournaments) and late-night drinking. Events range from Electro-Swing, the night that started a huge trend in mashing up vintage sounds with electro beats, to arty think-and-drink workshops.

Nest

36 Stoke Newington Road, Dalston, N16 7XJ (7354 9993, www.ilovethenest.com). Dalston Junction rail. **Open** 9pm-3am Thur; 9pm-4am Fri, Sat. **Admission** free-£7.

We love the Nest, one of Dalston's finest. It's kind of like a corridor, but in a good way, with an industrial chic look. Line-ups are usually great, with music on the dancefloor-focused disco, electro and house end of the spectrum.

★ Oslo

1A Amhurst Road, Hackney, E8 1LL (3553 4831, www.oslohackney.com). Hackney Central rail. **Open** check website for details.

See p269 **Come In, It's Cold Outside**.

Plastic People

147-149 Curtain Road, Shoreditch, EC2A 3QE (7739 6471, www.plasticpeople.co.uk). Old Street tube/rail. **Open** 9.30pm-2am Thur; 10pm-4am Fri, Sat. **Admission** free-£15. **Map** p403 R4.

Proud.

ARTS & ENTERTAINMENT

The long-established and ever-popular Plastic People subscribes to the old-school line that all you need for a kicking party is a dark basement and a sound system. The programming remains true to form: deep techno to house, all-girl DJ line-ups and many a star DJ (Thom Yorke, anyone?) squeezing through the doors for a secret gig.

Shacklewell Arms

71 Shacklewell Lane, Dalston, E8 2EB (7249 0810, www.shacklewellarms.com). Dalston Junction rail. **Open** 5pm-midnight Mon-Wed; 5pm-1am Thur; 5pm-3am Fri; noon-3am Sat; noon-midnight Sun. **Admission** free-£8.

The Shacklewell Arms is a magnet for leftfield music. Bands and DJs come from the electronic, lo-fi, chillwave and post-dubstep arenas, contrasting brilliantly with the shabby interior of this former Afro-Caribbean hotspot.

★ XOYO

32-37 Cowper Street, Shoreditch, EC2A 4AP (7354 9993, www.xoyo.co.uk). Old Street tube/rail. **Open/admission** varies; check website for details. **Map** p401 Q4.

There's live music during the week at this 800-capacity venue, but XOYO is first and foremost a nightclub. This former printworks is a bare concrete cell, defiantly taking the 'chic' out of 'shabby chic'. The open space means the atmosphere is always buzzing, as the only place to escape total immersion in the music is the small smoking courtyard outside. The Victorian loft-style space provides effortlessly cool programming and high-profile DJs, while the return of longer residencies – a 12-week stint for Eats Everything, for instance – is old-school in the best way possible.

SOUTH LONDON

Corsica Studios

4-5 Elephant Road, Elephant & Castle, SE17 1LB (7703 4760, www.corsicastudios.com). Elephant & Castle tube/rail. **Open** times vary Mon-Wed, check website for details; 8pm-3am Thur; 10pm-6am Fri, Sat; 7am-3pm Sun. **Admission** free-£15.

An independent warehouse-styled complex, Corsica aims to breed creativity and culture in areas of regeneration. It's certainly rough around the edges with its makeshift bars and toilets but the club nights are second to none: flagship night Trouble Vision boasts the best of bass, while Sunday sees daytime house and techno events. There's also live music: Silver Apples, Acoustic Ladyland and Lydia Lunch have all gigged here.

Electric Brixton

Town Hall Parade, Brixton, SW2 1RJ (7274 2290, www.electricbrixton.com). Brixton tube/rail. **Open** times vary Thur-Sun; check website for details. **Admission** £10-£35.

The Fridge in Brixton was a rave paradise in the early '90s, a stomping ground for the rare groove scene, funky jazz-house and, later, hard dance and psy-trance beats. In 2011, however, it underwent a £1m refit, with new management, and was reborn as Electric Brixton, with a mix of club nights – the likes of Skreamizm with Skream, featuring dubstep with forays into jungle, drum 'n' bass and disco – and live music.

Ministry of Sound

103 Gaunt Street, off Newington Causeway, Elephant & Castle, SE1 6DP (7740 8600, www.ministryofsound.com). Elephant & Castle tube/rail. **Open** 10.30pm-6am Fri; 11pm-7am Sat. **Admission** £10-£20. **Map** p402 O10.

Ministry of Sound was once the epitome of warehouse cool and is still possibly the UK's best-known clubbing venue. Laid out across four bars, five rooms and three dancefloors, there's lots to explore. Trance night the Gallery has made its home at Ministry of Sound on Fridays, while Saturday nights boast big-name DJ takeovers from the likes of Connected, Roger Sanchez and Erick Morillo.

Plan B

418 Brixton Road, Brixton, SW9 7AY (7733 0926, www.plan-brixton.co.uk). Brixton tube/rail. **Open** times vary Fri-Sun, check website for details. **Admission** £5-£12.50.

The decor is industrial chic (exposed brickwork, metal pillars, geometric furnishings) and the music programme rampantly eclectic. This, plus a late licence, happy hour every evening and student discount that ensures the place is very often brimming. Watch out for irregular '90s R&B and hip hop night Supa Dupa Fly.

WEST LONDON

Notting Hill Arts Club

21 Notting Hill Gate, Notting Hill, W11 3JQ (7460 4459, www.nottinghillartsclub.com). Notting Hill Gate tube. **Open** hours vary, but around 7pm-2am Wed-Thur; 6pm-2am Fri; 4pm-2am Sat; 6pm-1am Sun. **Admission** free-£8. **Map** p404 Y4.

Notting Hill Arts Club almost single-handedly keeps this side of town on the radar thanks to its monthly Death2Disco, plus nights such as Juicebox (electro) and NHAC Presents (DJ sets).

Paradise

19 Kilburn Lane, Kensal Green, W10 4AE (8969 0098, www.theparadise.co.uk). Kensal Green tube or Kensal Rise rail. **Open** noon-midnight Mon-Wed; noon-1am Thur; noon-2am Fri, Sat; noon-11.30pm Sun. **Admission** free-£8.

This is a star among the legion of pub-clubs, thanks to its alternative programme of art auctions, burlesque life drawing and late-night club nights, making it more than just a good local hangout.

Music

ROCK, POP & ROOTS

The rest of the country might not like it, but every musician is going to have to come to London: you might find yourself watching a US country star in a tiny basement, an African group under a railway arch or a torch singer in a church – all in one night, if you've any stamina.

Corporations have invested in venues, resulting in positives (improved facilities and sound systems) and negatives (overpriced bars), but there's rough and ready individuality – as well as the newest sounds – in venues like **XOYO** and the **Shacklewell Arms** (for both, *see p268*).

TICKETS & INFORMATION

Your first stop should be www.timeout.com, which lists hundreds of gigs every week. Most venues' websites detail future shows. Check ticket availability before setting out: venues large and small can sell out weeks in advance. The main exceptions are pub venues, which sell tickets only on the day. Many venues offer tickets online via their websites, but beware: most online box offices are operated by ticket agencies, which add booking fees that can raise the ticket price by as much as 30 per cent. Try to pay cash in person if possible; for details of London's ticket agencies, *see p285*.

There's often a huge disparity between door times and stage times; doors may open at 7pm, for instance, but the gigs often don't start until after 9pm. Some venues run club nights after the gigs, which means the show has to be wrapped up by 10.30pm; but at other venues, the main act won't even start until 11pm. If in doubt, call ahead.

COME IN, IT'S COLD OUTSIDE

Does Oslo signal that north-east London's club scene is growing up?

There's a new addition to the growing collection of nightlife venues in north-east London. However, this one isn't a basement dive bar, dilapidated pub or a too-cool-for-school danceteria. Nope, **Oslo** (*see p267*) is a proper, real-life music venue with a decent-sized stage, proper sound system and light rig. The former railway station next to Hackney Central is London's first venue from Nottingham-based promoters DHP Family; it hosts bands most nights of the week, with an impressive selection of club nights at weekends. We're delighted to hear that über-hip city-hopping promoters Dollop were signed up to programme Saturdays, bringing with them some impressive names from the underground – early gigs included World Unknown's Andy Blake and Fatima Al-Qadiri from dear old NYC. Ears ringing? Head downstairs to a restaurant that's open night and day, and a proper bar.

Of course, the era of the dive venue is far from over – after all, they're such fun – but its heartland is in Dalston, roughly splitting the difference between cool Oslo in the north and office-party bothered Shoreditch to the south. The **Shacklewell Arms** (*see p268*), a pub that's never bothered to update its original decor – tropical-themed murals, signs for 'the dancehall' – has become a Dalston staple with its edgy programming. Equally exciting is the **Nest** (*see p267*). The basement club (they mostly are round here) hosts weekend parties crammed with cool electro, disco, house and rock 'n' rave tunes, while its in-house Friday nighter attracts the cream of the electronic DJ crop. The more sophisticated **Dalston Superstore** (*see p260*) spearheaded the area's boogie renaissance in 2009 and still pulls huge crowds on to its intense, pitch-black dance floor. Upstairs, alternative drag cabaret stars whip revellers into shape with sharp one-liners, while a typically east London mix of music plays downstairs – anything from acid house to vogueing stompers.

MAJOR VENUES

In addition to the venues listed below, the **Barbican Centre** (*see p280*), the **Southbank Centre** (*see p282*) and the **Royal Albert Hall** (*see p281*) also stage regular gigs.

Alexandra Palace

Alexandra Palace Way, N22 7AY (8365 2121, www.alexandrapalace.com). Alexandra Palace rail or W3 bus. **Tickets** vary; the promoters rather than the venue sell tickets.

This hilltop landmark venue, adorned with sculptures and frescoes, opened in 1873 as the People's Palace and was devastated by fire twice – once only 16 days after opening, and the second time in 1980. Bar and toilet provision for some of the big shows remains patchy thanks to the layout, but the sound system is beloved of audiophiles – the Pixies chose it for the first London shows when they reformed, and James Murphy for the last UK appearances of LCD Soundsystem.

Eventim Apollo

45 Queen Caroline Street, Hammersmith, W6 9QH (8563 3800 information, 0844 249 4300 tickets, www.eventimapollo.com). Hammersmith tube. **Box office** *In person* 4-8pm performance days. *By phone* 24hrs daily. **Tickets** £10-£43.

This 1930s cinema doubles as a 3,600-capacity all-seater theatre (popular with big comedy acts and children's shows) and a 5,000-capacity standing-room-only gig space, hosting shows by major rock bands and others not quite ready for the O2.

The Forum

9-17 Highgate Road, Kentish Town, NW5 1JY (7428 4099 information, 7428 4099, www.mamacolive.com/theforum). Kentish Town tube/rail. **Box office** *In person* 5.30-9.30pm performance days. *By phone* 24hrs daily. **Tickets** £5-£30. **Map** p400 N2.

Originally constructed as part of a chain of art deco cinemas with a spurious Roman theme (hence the name, the incongruous bas relief battle scenes and imperial eagles flanking the stage), the 2,000-capacity Forum became a music venue back in the early 1980s. Since then, it's been vital to generations of gig-goers, whether they cut their teeth on the Velvet Underground, Ian Dury & the Blockheads, Duran Duran, Killing Joke or the Wu-Tang Clan, all of whom have played memorable shows here.

IndigO2

For listings, see p271 **O2 Arena**.

The little sister of the vast O2 Arena is only little in comparison with the huge expanses of its elder sibling. With a capacity of 2,350 (part-standing room, part-amphitheatre seating, sometimes part-table seating), IndigO2 is impressive in its own right. Its niche roster of MOR acts is dominated by soul, funk, pop-jazz and old pop acts, though it also hosts after-show parties for those headlining at the O2.

★ Koko

1A Camden High Street, Camden, NW1 7JE (0870 432 5527 information, 0844 847 2258 tickets, www.koko.uk.com). Mornington Crescent tube. **Box office** *In person* noon-5pm Mon-Fri (performance days only). *By phone* 24hrs daily. **Tickets** £3-£25. **Map** p404 Z3.

Koko has had a hand in the gestation of numerous styles over the decades. As the Music Machine it hosted a four-night residency with the Clash in 1978; the venue changed its name to Camden Palace in the

KoKo.

'80s, whereupon it became home to the emergent new romantic movement and saw Madonna's UK debut. Later it was one of the first 'official' venues to host acid house events. Since a spruce-up in the early noughties, it has hosted acts as diametrically opposed as Joss Stone and Queens of the Stone Age, not to mention one of Prince's electrifying 'secret' gigs in 2014. Nonetheless, the 1,500-capacity hall majors on weekend club nights – Annie Mac Presents and Club NME – and gigs by indie rockers, from the small and cultish to those on the up.

★ O2 Academy Brixton

211 Stockwell Road, Brixton, SW9 9SL (7771 3000 information, 0844 477 2000 tickets, www.o2academybrixton.co.uk). Brixton tube/rail. **Box office** *In person* 2hrs before doors on performance days. *By phone* 24hrs daily. **Tickets** £10-£40.

Brixton is still the preferred venue for metal, indie and alt rock bands looking to play their triumphant 'Look, ma, we've made it!' headline show. Built in the 1920s, this ex-cinema is the city's most atmospheric big venue. The 5,000-capacity art deco gem straddles the chasm between the pomp and volume of a stadium show and the intimate (read: sweaty) atmosphere of a club. Since becoming a full-time music venue in the '80s, it's hosted names from James Brown to the Stones to Springsteen, Dylan, Prince and Madonna, via the Red Hot Chili Peppers. And with its raked dancefloor, everyone's guaranteed a decent view.

O2 Academy Brixton.

O2 Academy Islington

N1 Centre, 16 Parkfield Street, Islington, N1 0PS (7288 4400 information, 0844 477 2000 tickets, www.o2academyislington.co.uk). Angel tube. **Box office** *In person* noon-4pm Mon-Sat. *By phone* 24hrs daily. **Tickets** £5-£25. **Map** p400 N2.

Located in a shopping mall, this 800-capacity room was never likely to be London's edgiest venue. Still, as a stepping stone between the pubs of Camden and the city's larger venues, it's a good place to catch fast-rising indie acts and re-formed '80s bands, not least because of the great sound system. The adjacent Bar Academy plays host to smaller bands, and also hosts club nights.

★ O2 Arena

Peninsula Square, North Greenwich, SE10 0DX (8463 2000 information, 0844 856 0202 tickets, www.theo2.co.uk). North Greenwich tube. **Box office** *In person* 12.30pm-8pm daily. *By phone* 8am-8pm daily. **Tickets** £10-£100.

The national embarrassment that was the Millennium Dome has been transformed into the city's de facto home of the megagig. The 20,000-seater has outstanding sound, unobstructed sightlines and the potential for artists to perform 'in the round'; shows from even the world's biggest acts (Britney, Led Zep, even – forgive us – One Direction) don't feel very far away. IndigO2 (*see p270*) is on the same site.

O2 Shepherd's Bush Empire

Shepherd's Bush Green, Shepherd's Bush, W12 8TT (8354 3300 information, 0844 477 2000 tickets, www.o2shepherdsbushempire.co.uk). Shepherd's Bush Market tube or Shepherd's Bush tube/rail. **Box office** *In person* 4-6pm performance days. *By phone* 24hrs daily. **Tickets** £10-£40.

Once a BBC television theatre, the Empire's baroque interior exudes a grown-up glamour few venues can match. The environment lends a gravitas to the chirpiest performance, as Lily Allen demonstrated in the flush of her fame. So you can imagine the sensation of seeing the likes of David Bowie or Bob Dylan here. It holds 2,000 standing or 1,300 seated, sightlines are good, the sound is decent (with the exception of the alcove behind the stalls bar and the scarily vertiginous top floor) and the roster of shows is quite varied, with acts at the poppier end of the scale joined by everyone from folkies to grizzled '70s rockers.

★ Roundhouse

Chalk Farm Road, Camden, NW1 8EH (7424 9991 information, 0844 482 8008 tickets, www.roundhouse.org.uk). Chalk Farm tube. **Box office** *In person* 11am-7pm Mon-Fri; 9am-7pm sat, Sun. *By phone* 9am-7pm Mon-Fri; 9am-4pm Sat; 9.30am-4pm Sun. **Tickets** £5-£50. **Map** p404 W1.

The main auditorium's supporting pillars mean there are some poor sightlines at the Roundhouse, but this one-time railway turntable shed (hence the name), which was used for hippie happenings in the 1960s before becoming a famous rock (and punk) venue in the '70s, has been a fine addition to London's music venues since its reopening in 2006. Expect a mix of arty rock gigs (the briefly re-formed Led Zeppelin played here), dance performances, theatre and multimedia events.

Scala

275 Pentonville Road, King's Cross, N1 9NL (7833 2022, www.scala-london.co.uk). King's Cross tube/rail. **Box office** 10am-6pm Mon-Fri. **Tickets** free-£15. **Map** p397 L3.

Although the venue has vacillated between use as a picturehouse and concert hall, the Scala's one consistent trait has been its lack of respect for authority: its stint as a cinema was ended after Stanley Kubrick sued it into bankruptcy for showing *A Clockwork Orange*. Nowadays, it's one of the most rewarding venues to push your way to the front for those cusp-of-greatness shows by big names in waiting – names as varied as the Chemical Brothers and Joss Stone.

Wembley Arena

Arena Square, Engineers Way, Wembley, Middx, HA9 0DH (8782 5500 information, 0844 815 0815 tickets, www.livenation.co.uk/wembley). Wembley Park tube. **Box office** *In person* 10.30am-4.30pm Mon-Fri; noon-4.30pm Sat (performance days only); 1hr before performance start Sun (performance days only). *By phone* 8.30am-8pm Mon-Fri; 8am-6pm Sat; 9am-6pm Sun. **Tickets** £5-£100.

Wembley Arena may have seen its commercial heyday end with the arrival of the O2 Arena (*see p271*), although it is beginning to carve out something of a niche for soul with the Show revue. Still, it's hardly anyone's favourite venue, not least because the food and drink could be better, but most Londoners have warm memories of at least one Arena megagig, and a £30 million refurbishment did much to improve this 12,500-capacity venue.

Club & pub venues

In addition to the venues listed below, a handful of London nightclubs also stage gigs. Try the **Notting Hill Arts Club** (*see p268*), **Madame JoJo's** (*see p277*), **Proud** (*see p267*), **XOYO** (*see p268*) and the **ICA** (*see p81*).

12 Bar Club

22-23 Denmark Place, Soho, WC2H 8NL (7240 2622, www.12barclub.com). Tottenham Court Road tube. **Open** *Café* 11am-7pm Mon-Fri; noon-7pm Sat. *Bar* 7pm-3am Mon-Sat; 7pm-12.30am Sun. *Shows* from 7.30pm; nights vary. **Admission** £5-£13. **Map** p416 X2.

A London treasure, this easy-to-miss hole-in-the-wall venue set among the guitar shops of Denmark Street books a grab-bag of low-key stuff, though its tiny size (it has an audience capacity of 100 and a minuscule stage) dictates a predominance of singer-songwriters.

93 Feet East

150 Brick Lane, Spitalfields, E1 6QL (7770 6006, www.93feeteast.co.uk). Aldgate East tube. **Open** 5-11pm Wed, Thur; 5pm-1am Fri, Sat; 2-10.30pm Sun. *Shows* vary. **Admission** free-£10. **Map** p401 S5.

With three rooms, a balcony and a wraparound courtyard that's great for barbecues, 93 Feet East keeps ticking by maintaining an incredibly broad programme: swing dance classes in the main bar, tech-house DJs, a mix of indie-dance bands and various art-rockers, plus short films, ping pong and cocktails nights, and a variety of arty happenings.

★ 100 Club

100 Oxford Street, Soho, W1D 1LL (7636 0933, www.the100club.co.uk). Oxford Circus tube. **Open** *Shows* vary; check website for details. **Tickets** £8-£17.50. **Map** p416 V1.

The 100 Club is synonymous with punk, having hosted shows by the Sex Pistols, the Clash, Siouxsie and the Banshees and the Buzzcocks. One historic show, in September 1976, featured the Sex Pistols, the Clash and the Damned. These days, though, the famous, 350-capacity basement room is more of a hub for blues rockers, pub rockers and trad jazzers, coming into its own for the odd secret gig by A-list bands such as Primal Scream and Oasis.

Barfly

49 Chalk Farm Road, Camden, NW1 8AN (7424 0800 information, 0844 847 2424 tickets, www.mamacolive.com/thebarfly). Chalk Farm tube. **Open** 3pm-2am Mon, Thur; 3pm-1am Tue, Wed; 3pm-3am Fri, Sat; 3pm-midnight Sun. *Shows* from 7pm daily. **Admission** free-£15. **Map** p404 X1.

This 200-capacity venue is part of London's indie-rock fabric, a key player in the fusion of indie guitars and electro into an unholy, danceable row.

Bloomsbury Bowling Lanes

Basement, Tavistock Hotel, Bedford Way, Bloomsbury, WC1H 9EU (7183 1979, www.bloomsburybowling.com). Russell Square tube. **Open** 4pm-midnight Mon, Tue; 4pm-2am Wed; noon-2am Thur; noon-3am Fri, Sat; noon-midnight Sun. **Admission** varies. **Map** p397 K4.

Offering a late-night drink away from Soho, BBL has been putting on bands and DJs for a while now – and the range of activities make it a playground for grown-ups. As well as the eight lanes for bowling, there's pool by the hour, table football, karaoke booths and, beside the entrance, a small cinema. Music includes regular funk party Funk and Bowl Club, with appearances by the likes of Hackney Colliery Band and DJ Craig Charles.

Blues Kitchen

111 Camden High Street, Camden, NW1 7JN (7387 5277, www.theblueskitchen.com). Camden Town or Mornington Crescent tube. **Open** noon-

ESSENTIAL LONDON ALBUMS

Quintessential city music.

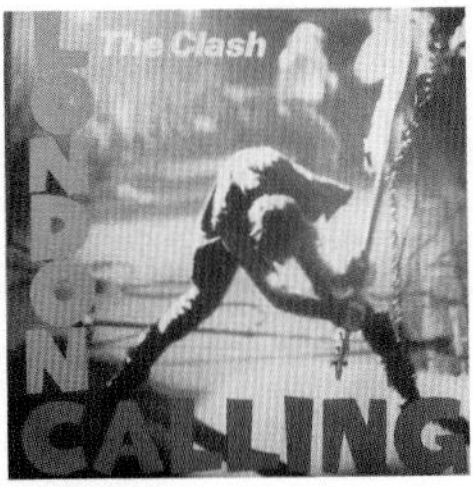

LONDON CALLING
THE CLASH (1979)
Era-defining punk classic, with cover artwork that pays homage to Elvis Presley's first album. The rocking title track now gets all the airplay (from British Airways ads to Olympic Stadium shout-outs), but the West London art school rapscallions put their guitars into a varied set of songs, among them 'The Guns of Brixton'.

NEW BOOTS AND PANTIES!!
IAN DURY (1977)
The title refers to the only clothes a thrifty Dury wouldn't buy from charity shops, and the cover shows him with his son, Baxter. Classic tracks like 'Wake Up and Make Love to Me', 'Billericay Dickie' and 'Clever Trevor' make this some of the finest work by the Essex pub-rock maestro.

PARKLIFE
BLUR (1994)
Launched at the defunct Walthamstow Dog Track, *Parklife* was a hymn to the East End, with the laddish Britpoppers on cheekily good form. 'Girls and Boys', 'End of a Century' and 'To the End' join the iconic 'Parklife' on an album that came to epitomise the emerging 1990s Britpop scene.

TONGUE N' CHEEK
DIZZEE RASCAL (2009)
The east London rapper makes a serious bid for pop superstardom, taking rhymes rough enough for the toughest estates up the charts with him. As well as the lubricious 'Dirtee Disco' and 'Holiday', 'Bonkers' made violent mental derangement seem enough fun to merit an Olympic Opening Ceremony slot.

SOMETHING ELSE
THE KINKS (1967)
Early evidence of Ray Davies' melancholy romanticism lies in the most enduring track on the album that propelled a million moony couples to watch their very own 'Waterloo Sunset'. Listen too for the careful blend of self-deception, veiled homoeroticism and waspish irony on 'David Watts'.

ORIGINAL PIRATE MATERIAL
THE STREETS (2002)
Mike Skinner almost singlehandedly invented geezer rap with his debut album. The keynotes of his later style are already present – wearily lovelorn entreaties and sordid tales of dope-smoking and brandy-toting – often revolving around late late nights at the Dogstar in Brixton.

midnight Mon, Tue; noon-1am Wed, Thur; noon-3am Fri; 10am-3.30am Sat; 10am-1am Sun. **Admission** free; £5 after 9.30pm Fri; £6 after 9pm Sat. **Map** p404 Y3.
The Blues Kitchen combines credible live music (roots blues, rockabilly and so on) with a rather smart interior. The food is spicy New Orleans fare and there's a huge range of American bourbon for sippin'. All in all, it makes for a pleasant Sunday afternoon hangout as well as a late-opening gig venue.

★ Borderline
Orange Yard, off Manette Street, Soho, W1D 4JB (0844 847 2465, www.theborderline.co.uk). Tottenham Court Road tube. **Open** hrs vary. **Admission** £3-£20. **Map** p416 W2.
A small, sweaty dive bar and juke joint right in the heart of Soho, the Borderline has long been a favoured stop-off for touring American bands of the country and blues varieties, though you'll also find a range of indie acts and singer-songwriters going through their repertoire here. Be warned, though, that it can get very cramped.

Bush Hall
310 Uxbridge Road, Shepherd's Bush, W12 7LJ (8222 6955, www.bushhallmusic.co.uk). Shepherd's Bush Market tube. **Open** hrs vary. *Shows* from 7.30pm. **Tickets** £5-£8.
This handsome room has been a dance hall, soup kitchen and snooker club. Now, with original fittings intact, it plays host to big bands performing stripped-down shows, top folk outfits and rising indie rockers.

★ Cecil Sharp House
2 Regent's Park Road, Camden, NW1 7AY (7485 2206, www.cecilsharphouse.org). Camden Town tube. **Open/tickets** vary. **Map** p404 X3.
Headquarters of the British Folk Dance and Song Society, Cecil Sharp House is a great place to visit, even when there isn't any music playing – there's a folk arts education centre and archive open during the day. But the Kennedy Hall performance space boasts a comfortably sprung floor and a well-informed and enthusiastic team of bookers ensuring all angles of trad music are well represented without being preserved in aspic. Events range from regular Scottish ceilidhs to more contemporary alt folk.

Corsica Studios
Elephant Road, Elephant & Castle, SE17 1LB (7703 4760, www.corsicastudios.com). Elephant & Castle tube/rail. **Open** hrs vary. **Tickets** £3-£15. **Map** p402 O10.
Corsica Studios is an independent, not-for-profit arts complex whose ethos is to breed creativity and culture. The flexible performance space is used as one of London's most adventurous live music venues and clubs, supplementing bands with poets, painters and lunatic projectionists. Main nights include Trouble Vision, a mashing of different genres of dance music.

Bloomsbury Bowling Lanes.

Garage
20-22 Highbury Corner, Highbury, N5 1RD (7619 6721 information, 0844 847 1678 tickets, www.mamacolive.com/thegarage). Highbury & Islington tube/rail. **Box office** *By phone* 24hrs daily. **Tickets** £3-£20.
This 650-capacity alt-rock venue reopened in 2009 after three years of impressive refurbishment. It now books an exciting and surprisingly wide-ranging calendar of indie and art rock gigs, from ancient punk survivors such as the Pop Group and Sham 69 to the poppier end of the indie singer-songwriter scale (Fran Healy in the smaller Upstairs, for example).

Green Note
106 Parkway, Camden, NW1 7AN (7485 9899, www.greennote.co.uk). Camden Town tube. **Open** 7-11pm Mon-Thur, Sun; 7pm-midnight Fri, Sat. *Shows* 8.30pm daily. **Tickets** £4-£15. **Map** p404 X3.
A stone's throw from Regent's Park, this cosy little venue and vegetarian café-bar was a welcome addition to the city's roots circuit back in 2005. Singer-songwriters, folkies and blues musicians make up the majority of the gig roster, with a handful of big names in among the listings.

Hoxton Square Bar & Kitchen
2-4 Hoxton Square, Shoreditch, N1 6NU (7613 0709, www.mamacolive.com/hoxton). Old Street tube/rail or Shoreditch High Street rail. **Open** noon-midnight Mon, Sun; noon-1am Tue-Thur; noon-2am Fri, Sat. **Tickets** free-£5 after 10pm Fri, Sat. **Map** p401 R3.
This 450-capacity venue is more than just a place to be seen: the line-ups are always cutting edge and fun, with the HSB&K often hosting a band's first London outing. Get there early or be prepared to queue.

Jazz Café

5 Parkway, Camden, NW1 7PG (7688 8899 information, 0844 847 2514 tickets, www.mamaco live.com/thejazzcafe). Camden Town tube. **Box office** *In person* 10.30am-5.30pm Mon-Sat. *By phone* 24hrs daily. **Tickets** £5-£30. **Map** p404 Y2.

Given its sterling reputation, you wouldn't think that the jazz café was such a newbie on the London music map, converted from a branch of Barclays in 1990. In those days, the support pillars famously boasted the command of 'STFU' – this was a venue that took music seriously. These days, though, the interpretation of jazz is pretty loose, stretching to intimate shows by US hip hop legends (such as De La Soul) and racing certainties (such as Aloe Blacc's incredible UK debut), as well as funk, soul and R&B legends such as Marlena Shaw and Mary J Blige.

★ Lexington

96-98 Pentonville Road, Islington, N1 9JB (7837 5371, www.thelexington.co.uk). Angel tube. **Open** noon-2am Mon-Wed, Sun; noon-3am Thur; noon-4am Fri, Sat. **Tickets** free-£15. **Map** p400 N2.

Effectively the common room for the music industry's perennial sixth form, this 200-capacity venue has a superb sound system in place for the leftfield indie bands that dominate the programme. It's where the hottest US exports often make their London debut: indie greats such as the Drums and Sleigh Bells have cut their teeth here in front of London's most receptive crowds. Downstairs, there's a lounge bar with a vast array of US beers and bourbons, above-par bar food and a Rough Trade music quiz (every Monday).

★ Nest

36 Stoke Newington Road, Dalston, N16 7XJ (7354 9993, www.ilovethenest.com). Dalston Kingsland rail. **Open** hrs vary Mon-Wed, check website for details; 9pm-3am Thur; 9pm-4am Fri, Sat. **Tickets** free-£10.

Formerly the Dalston hipster institution Bardens Boudoir, the Nest retains much of its predecessor's eclectic, forward-looking booking policy, with the benefit of a big money 'distressed industrial' refurbishment and, crucially, much improved toilets.

★ Shacklewell Arms

71 Shacklewell Lane, Dalston, E8 2EB (7249 0810, www.shacklewellarms.com). Dalston Kingsland or Dalston Junction rail. **Open** 5pm-midnight Mon-Wed; 5pm-1am Thur; 5pm-3am Fri; noon-3am Sat; noon-midnight Sun. **Admission** free-£8.

A Dalston location and a roster of sharp acts make the Shacklewell Arms the venue du jour in fashionable hearts. This quirkily decorated gaff has hosted the Horrors, Toy and Haim, among many others.

Underworld

174 Camden High Street, Camden, NW1 0NE (7482 1932, www.theunderworldcamden.co.uk). Camden Town tube. **Box office** *In person* 11am-11pm daily. *By phone* 24hrs daily. **Shows** hrs vary. **Admission** £5-£20. **Map** p404 Y2.

A dingy maze of pillars and bars below Camden, this subterranean oddity is an essential for metal and hardcore fans who want their ears bludgeoned by bands with names such as the Atomic Bitchwax, Skeletonwitch and Decrepit Birth. Tickets are purchased from the World's End pub upstairs.

★ Union Chapel

Compton Terrace, Islington, N1 2XD (7226 1686, www.unionchapel.org.uk). Highbury & Islington tube/rail. **Open** hrs vary. **Tickets** £6-£35.

In 2012, readers of *Time Out* magazine voted Union Chapel their top music venue. The Grade I-listed Victorian Gothic church still holds services and runs a homeless centre, while doubling as an atmospheric gig venue. It made its name hosting acoustic events and occasional jazz shows, becoming a magnet for thinking bands and their fans. These days, you'll also find classy intimate shows from bigger artists such as Paloma Faith. Watch out for the Daylight Music free Saturday afternoon concerts.

★ Windmill

22 Blenheim Gardens, Brixton, SW2 5BZ (8671 0700, http://windmillbrixton.co.uk). Brixton tube/ rail. **Open** *Shows* 8-11pm Mon-Thur; 8pm-1am Fri, Sat; 2-11pm Sun. **Admission** free-£10.

There's a free barbecue every Sunday afternoon in summer; a somewhat scary dog lives on the roof, frightening unsuspecting smokers; and an actual windmill stands in the adjacent park. The Windmill is certainly not your average music venue, but it's been revelling in its rough-around-the-edges eccentricity for years, its unprepossessing exterior a cloak for its dedication to new leftfield music. The Vaccines played here in 2013, though generally the programming is biased towards alt country, alt folk and alt punk. It's worth a visit just to pick up an 'I Believe in Roof Dog' T-shirt.

JAZZ

The international big hitters keep on visiting London, but these are exciting times, too, for the city's homespun jazz scene. Inspired by freewheeling attractions at the **Vortex** (*see p277*) and the sporadic, unhinged **Boat-Ting Club** nights (www.boat-ting.co.uk), acts such as Portico Quartet, Led Bib and Kit Downes Trio have won Mercury Prize nominations with recent albums, and the F-IRE and Loop Collectives are busy nurturing future stars.

In addition to the venues below, the **100 Club** (*see p272*) hosts trad groups, while the **Spice of Life** at Cambridge Circus (6 Moor Street, W1D 5NA, 7437 7013, www.spiceoflife soho.com) has solid mainstream jazz. The **Jazz Café** (*see left*) lives up to its name from time to time; there's a lot of very good jazz at the excellent **Kings Place** (*see p281*); and both the **Barbican** (*see p280*) and the **Southbank Centre** (*see p282*) host dozens of big names. For the increasingly excellent **London Jazz Festival**, *see p40*.

606 Club

90 Lots Road, Chelsea, SW10 0QD (7352 5953, www.606club.co.uk). Imperial Wharf rail or bus 11, 211. **Shows** 8.30pm Mon, Thur, Sun; 7.30pm, 10.15pm Tue, Wed; 9.30pm Fri, Sat. **Admission** (non-members) £8-£12.

Since 1976, Steve Rubie has run this spot, which relocated to this 150-capacity club in 1987. Alongside its Brit-dominated bills, expect informal jams featuring musos who've come from gigs elsewhere. There's no entrance fee as such; bands are funded from a music charge added to bills at the end of the night.

Bull's Head

373 Lonsdale Road, Barnes, SW13 9PY (3437 0134, www.thebullshead.com). Barnes Bridge rail. **Open** noon-11pm Mon-Sat; noon-10pm Sun. *Jazz Club* 8-11pm Mon-Sat; 1-3.30pm, 8.30-11pm Sun. **Admission** £5-£12.

This venerable, ancient Thames-side pub won a reputation for hosting modern jazz in the 1960s but today specialises in mainstream British jazz and swing, with guests such as the Humphrey Lyttelton band. A facelift has added posh pub food and quirkily appealing decor.

★ Café Oto

18-22 Ashwin Street, Dalston, E8 3DL (7923 1231, www.cafeoto.co.uk). Dalston Junction or Dalston Kingsland rail. Café **Open** 8.30am-5.30pm Mon-Fri; 9.30am-5.30pm Sat; 10.30am-5.30pm Sun. *Shows* 8pm. **Admission** £4-£12.

Opened in 2008, this 150-capacity café and music venue can't easily be categorised, though its website offers the tidy definition that it specialises in 'creative new music that exists outside of the mainstream'. That means Japanese noise rockers ('Oto' is Japanese for 'sound'), electronica pioneers, improvising noiseniks and artists from the stranger ends of the rock, folk and classical spectrums.

★ Charlie Wright's International Bar

45 Pitfield Street, Hoxton, N1 6DA (7490 8345, www.charliewrights.com). Old Street tube/rail. **Open** noon-1am Mon-Wed; noon-4am Thur, Fri; 6pm-4am Sat; 6pm-1am Sun. *Shows* from 8pm daily. **Admission** free-£10. **Map** p401 Q3.

When Zhenya Strigalev and Patsy Craig began programming here in 2006, London's jazz fans were given a reason to visit what had been merely a rather good after-hours boozer. Now this agreeably scruffy venue stages a fine jazz programme every night of the week bar Saturday. Gigs don't usually start until 10pm, and run late on Thursdays and Fridays.

Ronnie Scott's.

Forge & Foundry

3-7 Delancey Street, Camden, NW1 7NL (7383 7808, www.forgevenue.org). Camden Town or Mornington Crescent tube. **Open** hrs vary. **Admission** free-£12. **Map** p404 Y3.

Run by a non-profit community organisation, this innovative music/restaurant space incorporates a stunning atrium, and hosts concerts of various sizes and formalities. The programme is skewed heavily to jazz, but also features a carefully curated selection of roots and classical shows. There's an on-site restaurant, the Foundry; you can dine while you listen on a Friday, and there's an interesting Sunday brunch programme.

Pizza Express Jazz Club

10 Dean Street, Soho, W1D 3RW (0845 602 7017, www.pizzaexpresslive.com). Tottenham Court Road tube. **Shows** hrs vary, check website for details. **Admission** £15-£25. **Map** p416 W2.

The upstairs restaurant (7437 9595) is jazz-free, but the 120-capacity basement is one of the best mainstream jazz venues in town. Singers such as Kurt Elling and Lea DeLaria join instrumentalists from home and abroad on the nightly bills.

★ Ronnie Scott's

47 Frith Street, Soho, W1D 4HT (7439 0747, www.ronniescotts.co.uk). Leicester Square or Tottenham Court Road tube. **Shows** 7.15pm-1am Mon-Sat; noon-4pm, 8pm-midnight Sun. **Admission** £20-£50. **Map** p416 W2.

Opened (on a different site) by the British saxophonist Ronnie Scott in 1959, this jazz institution – the setting for Jimi Hendrix's last ever UK performance among many other distinctions – was completely refurbished in 2006. The capacity was expanded to 250, the food got better and the bookings became drearier. Happily,

ARTS & ENTERTAINMENT

though, Ronnie's has got back on track, with jazz heavyweights dominating once more – from trad talents such as Chick Corea to hotly tipped purists such as Kurt Elling to futuristic mavericks such as Robert Glasper. Perch by the rear bar or get table service at the crammed side-seating or more spacious (but noisier) central tables in front of the stage.

★ Vortex Jazz Club

Dalston Culture House, 11 Gillet Street, Dalston, N16 8JN (7254 4097, www.vortexjazz.co.uk). Dalston Kingsland rail. **Shows** 8pm daily. **Admission** £5-£18.

One of the few venues in the city you could visit on spec and be guaranteed to hear something interesting. Along with the nearby Café Oto (*see p276*), the Vortex is one of London's most lovingly curated venues. Jazz is the order of the day, but the Vortex serves it up in kaleidoscopic variety. For the less daring, there's a regular calendar of big band, piano trio, vocal, free improv, world music and folk-oriented sounds each month, as well as some poetry gigs. The Vortex hosts its own strand of the London Jazz Festival and various other forward-thinking events.

Cabaret

To see the best cabaret, head to **Soho Theatre's** downstairs space, host to excellent international performers ranging from European chanteuses to American alternative drag acts; the always interesting **Bethnal Green Working Men's Club** (for both, *see below*); and the even more alternative **RVT** (*see p259*). A recent trend has been for cabaret in posh venues. The **Savoy** (*see p248*) has hosted evenings in the Beaufort Bar mixing burlesque, variety and song; **Brasserie Zédel** (*see p114*) puts on shows at its Crazy Coqs venue; comedy chanteuse Miss Polly Rae is currently in residence on Wednesday and Saturday nights; and the **Hippodrome** (www.hippodromecasino.com), now primarily a casino, also hosts music and cabaret. Again, many of the best cabaret nights are one-off parties in a range of formal and informal venues – wherever you party, bring an open mind.

★ Bethnal Green Working Men's Club

42-44 Pollard Row, Bethnal Green, E2 6NB (7739 7170, www.workersplaytime.net). Bethnal Green tube. **Open** hrs vary; check website for details. **Admission** free-£8.

Sticky red carpet and broken lampshades perfectly suit the programme of quirky lounge, retro rock 'n' roll and fancy-dress burlesque parties here. You might get to watch a spandex-lovin' dance duo or get hip with burlesque starlets on a 1960s dancefloor. The mood is friendly, the playlist upbeat and the air full of artful, playful mischief.

CellarDoor

Zero Aldwych, Covent Garden, WC2E 7D (7240 8848, www.cellardoor.biz). Covent Garden tube. **Open** hrs vary; check website for details. **Admission** varies. **Map** p399 L7.

Some staggeringly clever design means that although there's room for just 60 in this subterranean converted Victorian loo, CellarDoor never feels claustrophobic. Musical-theatre cabaret crooners and drag queens are the order of the day, giving this sleek establishment a vintage feel. Nearly all shows are free and often great fun – EastEnd Cabaret regularly appear and Champagne Charlie's Trash Tuesday open-mic night is an institution.

Madame JoJo's

8-10 Brewer Street, Soho, W1F 0SD (7734 3040, www.madamejojos.com). Leicester Square or Piccadilly Circus tube. **Open** 7.30pm-3am Tue-Sun. **Admission** £3-£15. **Map** p416 W3.

The red and slightly shabby basement space at JoJo's is a beacon for those seeking to escape the West End's post-work chain pubs. The most treasured nights tend towards variety – Kitsch Cabaret is every Saturday night – but its long-running Tuesday nighter, White Heat, still books up-and-coming bands and DJs for a largely indie and student crowd.

Pheasantry

152-154 King's Road, Chelsea, SW3 4UT (0845 602 7017, www.pizzaexpresslive.com). Sloane Square tube. **Shows** 8.30pm, days vary, check website for details. **Admission** varies. **Map** p395 F11.

The successor to the institution that was Pizza on the Park, this jazz and cabaret venue is also part of the Pizza Express stable. The bright, spacious basement space has something of a cruise-ship feel (where does that staircase actually go?) and sightlines aren't always great, but it's the city's premier platform for New York-style jazz singing and musical-theatre-influenced cabaret work, often attracting big names from the West End and across the pond.

St James Studio

12 Palace Street, Victoria, SW1E 5JA (0844 264 2140, www.stjamestheatre.co.uk). Victoria tube/rail. **Open** hrs vary, check website for details. **Admission** £15-£25. **Map** p398 J9.

When it opened in 2012, an integral part of St James Theatre was its downstairs Studio space, a cosy room that plays host to a range of work towards the classic end of the cabaret spectrum, as well as comedy, music and fringe work. Recent highlights have included runs from the sensational interpreter of song Barb Jungrand Peter Straker's barnstorming tribute to the songs of Jacques Brel.

Soho Theatre

For listings, *see p289*.

Soho Theatre's downstairs comedy and cabaret room is a little on the cramped and clattery side, but that doesn't detract from the high calibre of cabaret performers on its stage. There's confident international scope and generous formal breadth to the programming, which ranges from home-grown sensations such as Bourgeois & Maurice and Bryony Kimmings to smoky chanteuses like Lady Rizo and Caroline Nin to hysterical alt-drag acts such as Dina Martina.

Comedy

Explore dingy pubs and clubs where skills are honed, and check out arenas and theatres for the finished act. For weekly line-ups, check *Time Out* magazine and www.timeout.com.

Amused Moose Soho

Moonlighting, 17 Greek Street, Soho, W1D 4DR (7287 3727, www.amusedmoose.com). Leicester Square or Tottenham Court Road tube. **Shows** *Sept-May* 7.45pm Sat. **Admission** £10-£14. **No credit cards. Map** p416 W2.

Hils Jago's rosters are always strong, with names such as Bill Bailey and Eddie Izzard continuing to justify the club's multi-award-winning status. Jago has a lot of special guests who can't be named – in other words, really top names trying out new material – and runs the Amused Moose ComedyAwards; finalists have included Jimmy Carr and Simon Amstell.

Boat Show

Tattershall Castle, Kings Reach, Victoria Embankment, SW1A 2HR (07932 658895, www.boatshowcomedy.co.uk). Embankment tube. **Shows** 8pm Fri, Sat. **Admission** £11-£15. **No credit cards. Map** p399 L8.

The line-ups aboard this floating comedy club situated opposite the London Eye are consistently strong. Ticket prices are reasonable, and for those wishing to party into the small hours, a nightclub follows the comedy every Friday and Saturday at no extra charge.

Canal Café Theatre

Delamere Terrace, Little Venice, W2 6ND (7289 6054, www.canalcafetheatre.com). Royal Oak or Warwick Avenue tube. **Shows** 9.30pm Thur-Sat; 9pm Sun; additional live acts listed in website. **Admission** £8.50-£12.50. **Map** p392 C4.

This charming little theatre, perched on the edge of a canal in Little Venice, offers a number of shows a week. Past performers include Stewart Lee and Pete Firman, and it's a good place to catch young comics and sketch acts, as well as NewsRevue, who have a residency performing their topical sketches and songs every Thursday to Sunday.

Comedy Café

68 Rivington Street, Shoreditch, EC2A 3AY (7739 5706, www.comedycafe.co.uk). Liverpool

Soho Theatre.

Street or Old Street tube/rail. **Shows** 8pm Tue-Sat. **Admission** £7-£12; free Wed. **Map** p401 R4.
The Comedy Café is another purpose-built club set up by a comedian. Noel Faulkner, who worked on trawlers and was wanted by the FBI in his time, now mainly keeps to the back room but, with the emphasis on inviting bills and satisfied punters, his influence can still be felt. The atmosphere is fun and food is an integral part of the experience.

★ Comedy Store
1A Oxendon Street, Soho, SW1Y 4EE (0844 871 7699, www.thecomedystore.co.uk). Leicester Square or Piccadilly Circus tube. **Shows** times vary, check website for details. **Admission** £9-£23.50. **Map** p416 W4.
Alternative line-ups at this, the daddy of British comedy clubs, helped to launch jokers such as Alexei Sayle, Dawn French and Paul Merton. The legendary King Gong show, in which would-be stand-ups are given only as much time on stage as the audience will allow, is on the last Monday of the month.

Downstairs at the King's Head
2 Crouch End Hill, Crouch End, N8 8AA (8340 1028, www.downstairsatthekingshead.com). Finsbury Park tube/rail then bus W7. **Shows** 8pm Tue, Thur, Sat, Sun. **Admission** £3-£11.
Founded in what seems like the comedic pre-history of 1981, this venue is still run with huge enthusiasm by its immensely knowledgeable promoter Pete Grahame. It's an easygoing, comfortable place where comedians can experiment and play around with new material and routines in complete freedom. It's popular with comics doing warm-up shows for TV and tours.

Etcetera Theatre
The Oxford Arms, 256 Camden High Street, Camden, NW1 7BU (7482 4857, www.etcetera theatre.com). Camden Town tube. **Shows** vary; check website for details. **Admission** £3-£10. **No credit cards**. **Map** p404 Y2.
This intimate black box theatre above the Oxford Arms pub is a great place to catch Edinburgh previews, comedy in August's Camden Fringe, and occasionally big names warming up for tours, which in the past have included Russell Brand and We Are Klang.

Feature Spot
The 100 Club, 100 Oxford Street, Soho, W1D 1LL (07956 834135, www.featurespot.co.uk). Oxford Circus or Tottenham Court Road tube. **Shows** vary; check website for details. **Admission** £10-£15. **Map** p416 V1.
Feature Spot's monthly comedy nights often feature in critics' choices lists. Previous acts include Russell Howard, Stephen Merchant, Adam Buxton and Tim Minchin. But whoever's on the bill, you're guaranteed an excellent show.

Funny Side of Covent Garden
Upstairs at The George, 213 the Strand, Aldwych, WC2R 1AP (0844 478 0404, www.thefunny side.info). Covent Garden or Temple tube. **Shows** 8pm Sat. **Admission** £12.50. **Map** p399 M6.
This is an enjoyable club upstairs in a mock Tudor pub, but calling it 'Covent Garden' is a bit of a stretch, geographically speaking – it's on the fringes of the City near the Royal Courts of Justice. Well-known comedians such as Felix Dexter, Josie Long and Phil Kay have all performed here. Funny Side also host occasional gigs on Wednesday and Sunday at Café Koha (11 St Martin's Court, Covent Garden, WC2N 4AJ).

Hen & Chickens
109 St Paul's Road, Highbury Corner, Islington, N1 2NA (7704 2001, www.thehenandchickens theatrebar.co.uk). Highbury & Islington tube/rail. **Shows** times vary. **Admission** £4-£12.50. **No credit cards**.
This dinky, black-box theatre above a cosy Victorian corner pub is well known as the place to see great solo shows, especially from those warming up for a tour. Acts have included Jenny Eclair, Frankie Boyle, Rhona Cameron and Jimmy Carr.

Leicester Square Theatre
Leicester Square Theatre, 6 Leicester Place, Leicester Square, Soho, WC2H 7BX (0844 873 3433, www.leicestersquaretheatre.com). Leicester Square tube. **Shows** vary; check website for details. **Admission** £5-£47. **Map** p416 X4.
With a mixture of mixed-bill shows and solo offerings, the theatre programmes comedy names in the main house, and rising stars in the basement. A favourite of many big-name American comics, the list of names who play here is getting better and better – Stewart Lee in 2014, for example.

Soho Theatre
For listings, *see p289*.
The Soho Theatre is one of the best places to see comics break out of their normal club sets to perform more substantial solo shows. There's always a good mix of home-grown and international talent.

Up the Creek
302 Creek Road, Greenwich, SE10 9SW (8858 4581, www.up-the-creek.com). Greenwich DLR/rail. **Shows** 8.15pm Thur; 8.45pm Fri; 8.30pm Sat; 7.30pm Sun. **Admission** £5 Thur; £10 Fri, £14 Sat; £6 Sun. **Map** p405 W2.
Set up by the late and legendary Malcolm Hardee ('To say that he has no shame is to drastically exaggerate the amount of shame he has,' quipped one critic), this purpose-built club has been around since the 1990s, and it remains to this day one of the best places to enjoy comedy. It's renowned for its lively, not to say bearpit atmosphere, but there's a more chilled-out feel to the 'Sunday Special Club' (www.sundayspecial.co.uk).

Performing Arts

London's classical musicians seem unusually open-minded, with classical nights in pubs and jazz strands at august classical auditoriums. But as well as this mix-and-match aesthetic, passionate purists remain – the Barbican and Royal Festival Hall still deliver a big orchestral punch with the traditional repertoire. Music, of a different stripe, dominates the West End theatre scene too: the biggest attractions remain the indomitable musicals. That's not to say there's no 'proper' drama in the capital, with a couple of current successes having begun life in the National Theatre, the city's flagship publicly funded theatre. And London remains a hub for dance in a way few other cities can match, with even the 80-year-old Royal Ballet producing groundbreaking new work.

Check the free *Time Out* magazine for the performing arts highlights of the week, or check out www.timeout.com for cultural listings.

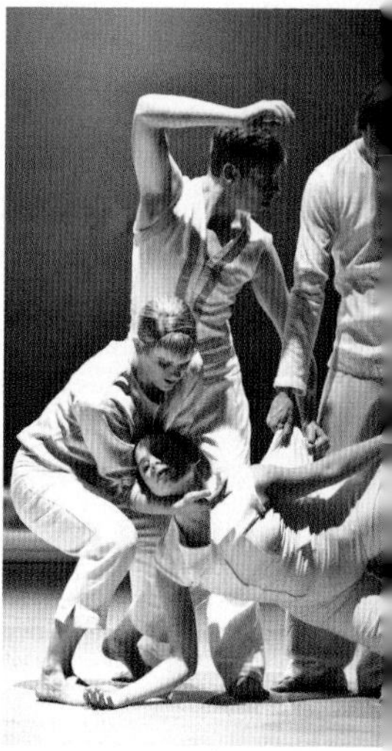

Classical Music & Opera

London's classical scene has never looked or sounded more current, with the **Southbank Centre** (*see p282*), the **Barbican Centre** (*see right*) and **Kings Place** (*see p281*) all working with strong programmes. Even the once-stuffy **Royal Opera House** now leavens its programme with occasional commissions such as Mark-Anthony Turnage's opera *Anna Nicole*, the tragic tale of a Playboy model and her ancient sugar-daddy, and youthful music director Edward Gardner has given the **English National Opera** a spirit of adventure – it will be interesting to see what happens there when he departs in 2015.

Tickets & information

Tickets for most classical and opera events are available direct from the venues, online or by phone. It's advisable always to book ahead. Several venues, such as the Barbican and the Southbank Centre, operate standby schemes, offering unsold tickets at cut-rate prices just before the show. They also have reduced-price tickets for under-26s.

CLASSICAL VENUES

In addition to the major venues below, you can hear what tomorrow's classical music might sound like at the city's music schools, which stage regular concerts by pupils and visiting professionals. Check the websites of the **Royal Academy of Music** (7873 7373, www.ram.ac.uk), the **Royal College of Music** (7591 4314, www.rcm.ac.uk), the **Guildhall School of Music & Drama** (7628 2571, www.gsmd.ac.uk) and **Trinity College of Music** (8305 4444, www.tcm.ac.uk). There's also a trend for top-class classical and contemporary classical music in relaxed – for which read 'alcohol-friendly' – settings (*see p284* **Beer, Bars and Bach**).

★ Barbican Centre

Silk Street, the City, EC2Y 8DS (7638 4141 information, 7638 8891 tickets, www.barbican.org.uk). Barbican tube or Moorgate tube/rail.

Box office 10am-9pm Mon-Sat; noon-9pm Sun. **Tickets** £8-£65. **Map** p400 P5.
Europe's largest multi-arts centre is easier to navigate than ever after a renovation – although 'easier' still isn't quite the same as 'with ease', so allow a little extra time to get to your seat. The programming remains as rich as ever, and the London Symphony Orchestra, guided by principal conductor Valery Gergiev, remains in residence. The BBC Symphony Orchestra also performs an annual series of concerts, and there's a laudable amount of contemporary classical music. Beyond classical, programming falls into a wide range of genres: from Sufi music to New York rock legends.
► *A brand-new concert hall opened in 2014 barely 100 yards from the main external entrance to the Barbican. Milton Court (1 Milton Street, EC2Y 9BH, 7638 8891, www.gsmd.ac.uk) is run by the Guildhall School of Music & Drama and combines a 608-seat concert hall and two smaller theatres.*

Cadogan Hall

5 Sloane Terrace, off Sloane Street, Chelsea, SW1X 9DQ (7730 4500, www.cadoganhall.com). Sloane Square tube. **Box office** *Non-performance days* 10am-6pm Mon-Sat. *Performance days* 10am-8pm Mon-Sat. **Tickets** £15-£50. **Map** p398 G10.
Jazz groups and rock bands have been attracted by the acoustics in this renovated former Christian Science church, but the programming at the austere yet comfortable 900-seat hall is dominated by classical. The Royal Philharmonic are resident; other orchestras also perform, and there's regular chamber music.

★ Kings Place

90 York Way, King's Cross, N1 9AG (0844 264 0321, www.kingsplace.co.uk). King's Cross tube/rail. **Box office** 10am-5pm Mon; noon-7pm Tue-Sun (performance days only). **Tickets** £9.50-£51.50. **Map** p397 L2.
Once a lone pioneer in the revival of King's Cross, Kings Place suddenly finds itself part of the King's Cross Central cultural hub. Beneath seven office floors and a ground-floor restaurant-bar (with prized seats on the canal basin outside, the 400-seat main hall is a beauty, dominated by wood carved from a single, 500-year-old oak tree and ringed by invisible rubber pads that kill unwanted noise that might interfere with the immaculate acoustic. There's also a versatile second hall and a number of smaller rooms for workshops and lectures. The programming is tremendous and includes curated weeks featuring artists as wide-ranging as Schönberg and jazz band AIR. Other strands include chamber music and experimental classical, and there are spoken-word events too.

LSO St Luke's

161 Old Street, the City, EC1V 9NG (7588 1116 information, 7638 8891 tickets, www.lso.co.uk/lsostlukes). Old Street tube/rail. **Box office** 10am-9pm Mon-Sat; noon-9pm Sun. **Tickets** free-£37. **Map** p400 P4.
This Grade I-listed church, built by Nicholas Hawksmoor in the 18th century, was beautifully converted into a performance and rehearsal space by the LSO several years ago. The orchestra occasionally welcomes the public for open rehearsals (book ahead); the more formal side of the programme takes in global sounds alongside classical music, including lunchtime concerts every Thursday that are broadcast on BBC Radio 3.
► *Intrigued by St Luke's obelisk spire? Hawksmoor also designed the brutal spike of Christ Church Spitalfields (see p198) and the mini-ziggurat atop St George's Bloomsbury (see p154).*

Royal Albert Hall

Kensington Gore, South Kensington, SW7 2AP (0845 401 5034, www.royalalberthall.com). South Kensington tube or bus 9, 10, 52, 452. **Box office** 9am-9pm daily. **Tickets** £13-£275. **Map** p395 D9.
In constant use since opening in 1871, with boxing matches, motorshows and Allen Ginsberg's 1965 International Poetry Incarnation among the headline events, the Royal Albert Hall continues to host a very broad programme. The classical side is dominated by the superb BBC Proms (*see p37*), which runs every night for two months in summer and sees a huge array of orchestras and other ensembles battling the difficult acoustics. It's well worth catching a concert that features the thunderous Grand Organ.

St James's Piccadilly

197 Piccadilly, Piccadilly, W1J 9LL (7381 0441, www.sjp.org.uk). Piccadilly Circus tube. **Box office** 10am-5pm Mon-Sat. **Tickets** free-£27. **Map** p398 J7.
This community-spirited Wren church holds free lunchtime recitals (Mon, Wed, Fri at 1.10pm) and offers regular evening concerts in a variety of fields.

IN THE KNOW
A NEW LOOK NATIONAL

Since the 1970s, the National Theatre – Britain's most prominent publicly funded theatre – has occupied a purpose-built, once-controversial, Brutalist building. An ambitious refurbishment project is now under way, to be completed by the end of 2014. Costing £80m, the work should result in what the National's outgoing artistic director Nicholas Hytner describes as 'a dramatic opening up and renewal of Denys Lasdun's 1970s building'. There will be a new main entrance, dedicated learning spaces and a backstage viewing gallery; until then, a bright-red temporary theatre, the Shed, is filling in outside.

St John's, Smith Square

Smith Square, Westminster, SW1P 3HA (7222 1061, www.sjss.org.uk). Westminster tube. **Box office** *Non-performance days* 10am-5pm Mon-Fri. *Performance days* 10am-6pm Mon-Fri. **Tickets** free-£28. **Map** p399 K10.

This curiously shaped 18th-century church – it is said the four-turret design was the result of Queen Anne's demand that architect Thomas Archer make it look like a footstool that she had kicked over – hosts concerts more or less nightly, and Thursday lunchtime recitals too, with everything from symphony orchestras to solo recitals making the most of good acoustics. Down in the crypt are two bars for interval drinks and the Smith Square Bar & Restaurant. The church marks its 300th anniversary in 2014.

St Martin-in-the-Fields

Trafalgar Square, Westminster, WC2N 4JJ (7766 1100, www.stmartin-in-the-fields.org). Charing Cross tube/rail. **Box office** *In person* 8am-5pm Mon, Tue; 8am-9.45pm Wed; 8am-8.30pm Thur-Sat. *By phone* 10am-5pm Mon-Sat. **Tickets** free-£30. **Map** p399 L7.

This church is one of the capital's most amiable and populist venues, hosting performances of the likes of Bach, Mozart and Vivaldi by candlelight, jazz in the crypt's improved café and lunchtime recitals (1pm Mon, Tue, Fri) from young musicians. There's a fine atmosphere in the beautifully restored interior.

► *For more on the church, see p69.*

★ Southbank Centre

Belvedere Road, South Bank, SE1 8XX (7960 4200 information, 0844 875 0073 tickets, www.southbankcentre.co.uk). Embankment tube or Waterloo tube/rail. **Box office** *In person* 10am-8pm daily. *By phone* 9am-8pm daily. **Tickets** £7-£75. **Map** p399 M8.

The centrepiece of the cluster of cultural venues collectively known as the Southbank Centre is the 3,000-seater Royal Festival Hall, which was renovated acoustically and externally to the tune of £90m back in 2007; now the neighbouring 900-seat Queen Elizabeth Hall and attached 365-seat Purcell Room are due a little TLC – plans for refurbishment are in the pipeline. All three programme a wide variety of events – spoken word, jazz, rock and pop gigs – but classical is very well represented. The RFH has four resident orchestras (the London Philharmonic and Philharmonia Orchestras, the London Sinfonietta and the Orchestra of the Age of Enlightenment), and hosts music from medieval motets to Messiaen via Beethoven and Elgar. Beneath this main hall, facing the main bar, the foyer stage puts on hundreds of free concerts each year.

► *For the Hayward Gallery, third leg of the Southbank Centre's tripod, see p51; for more on the thus-far thwarted redevelopment of the Southbank Centre, see p283* **Skaters V the Festival Wing**.

★ Wigmore Hall

36 Wigmore Street, Marylebone, W1U 2BP (7935 2141, www.wigmore-hall.org.uk). Bond Street tube. **Box office** *Non-performance days* 10am-7pm Mon-Sat; 10am-2pm Sun. *Performance days* 10am-7pm daily. **Tickets** £10-£35. **Map** p396 G6.

Built in 1901 as the display hall for Bechstein pianos, this world-renowned, 550-seat concert venue has perfect acoustics for the 400 concerts that take place each year. Music from the classical and romantic periods are mainstays, usually performed by major classical stars to an intense audience, but under artistic director John Gilhooly there has been a broadening in the remit: more baroque and increased jazz (Joshua Redman is curating the Jazz Series), including late-night gigs. Monday lunchtime recitals are broadcast live on BBC Radio 3.

OPERA VENUES

In addition to the two big venues below, look out for performances at the **Linbury Studio**, downstairs at the Royal Opera House, **Cadogan Hall** (*see p281*), summer's **Opera Holland Park** (*see p34* **Festivals**), sporadic appearances by **English Touring Opera** (www.englishtouringopera.org.uk) and much promising work, often directed by big names, at the city's music schools. A small but lively fringe opera scene has sprung up with **OperaUpClose** branching out from its King's Head Theatre base in Islington (www.kingsheadtheatre.com) to play up west at the Soho and Charing Cross Theatres; and the **Charles Court Opera** company doing fine operetta in various small theatres (www.charlescourtopera.com).

English National Opera, Coliseum

St Martin's Lane, Covent Garden, WC2N 4ES (7845 9300 tickets, www.eno.org). Leicester Square tube or Charing Cross tube/rail. **Box office** *In person* 10am-6pm Mon-Sat. *By phone* 24hrs daily. **Tickets** £20-£115. **Map** p399 L7.

Built as a music hall in 1904, the home of the English National Opera (ENO) is in fine condition following a renovation back in 2004. Under the youthful stewardship of music director Edward Gardner, it has offered some fascinating collaborations over the last few years (such as with physical theatre troupe Complicité and Blur's Damon Albarn on *Doctor Dee*) and rare contemporary works (a flamboyant version of Ligeti's *Le Grand Macabre*), but his 'Undress for the Opera', encouraging new, younger audience members to attend some classic operas in their everyday clothes, may be the boldest initiative yet. All works are in English, and prices are cheaper than at the Royal Opera. The £20 Secret Seat offer allows you to book

SKATERS V THE FESTIVAL WING

A clash of cultures at the South Bank's anchor venue.

While it would be cruel to describe our esteemed mayor, Boris Johnson, as a fat lady, it was all over when he sang – or, more accurately, spoke at a planning meeting in January 2014. 'I wholeheartedly support the principle of enhancing the world-class cultural facilities at the Southbank Centre,' he said, 'and am encouraged by many of the aspects of their plans. However, redevelopment should not be at the detriment of the skate park, which should be retained in its current position.' With that, a £120m redevelopment plan, with £20m of Arts Council funding already in place, was off the table.

To explain why requires some context. The cluster of venues now called the **Southbank Centre** (*see p282*) grew up in the area that had hosted the 1951 Festival of Britain, a post-war nationwide celebration of industry, art and commerce. The Royal Festival Hall was the only building to remain afterwards, and was joined a few years later by the interconnected Queen Elizabeth Hall and Purcell Room (opened 1967) and the Hayward (1968; *see p51*), a popular but incoherent cluster of arts venues. In 2007, impressive, hugely expensive renovations to the RFH were completed, and after the grand reopening new artistic director Jude Kelly set about creating a buzz around the place. Temporary installations, food fairs and alfresco dining drew throngs of visitors, but those satellite buildings were falling in dire need of renovation themselves.

In March 2013, ambitious plans were released. The three newer buildings would be encased in a huge glass box – also providing an orchestral performance space/rehearsal room that could be watched from outside – funded in part by the proceeds from new restaurants and shops in the Undercroft.

Unfortunately, since the 1970s – when the walkways to Waterloo station were notorious as a cardboard city for the homeless – the Undercroft had been used by skateboarders, who love riding the abstract concrete shapes of its Brutalist architecture. It was soon regarded as the spiritual home of skaters and BMXers. The Southbank Centre offered them a larger, purpose-built skatepark just down the river, and insisted the commercial properties were essential for the scheme, but protests grew. Perhaps significantly, Nick Hytner – the outgoing director of the neighbouring **National Theatre** (*see p285*) – also raised concerns. Then the mayor, who is able to have the ultimate say in all London planning applications, spoke and the Southbank Centre's Board withdrew the planning proposal. So, for now, we are left with the status quo – and the roar of skateboard wheels on the concrete of the South Bank.

an unallocated seat online – the secret lies in its location in the auditiorium. Wherever it turns out to be, your seat will always be worth at least £25.

★ Royal Opera, Royal Opera House

Covent Garden, WC2E 9DD (7304 4000, www.roh.org.uk). Covent Garden tube. **Box office** 10am-8pm Mon-Sat. **Tickets** £6-£215. **Map** p399 L7.

Thanks to a refurbishment at the start of the century, the Royal Opera House has once again taken its place among the ranks of the world's great opera houses. Critics sometimes suggest that the programming can be a little spotty, especially so given the famously elevated ticket prices. The spine of the programme is, of course, fine productions of the classics, often taking place under the baton of Antonio Pappano. Productions take in favourite composers (Donizetti, Mozart, Verdi) and some modern (Benjamin Britten, Harrison Birtwistle).

▶ *It's not just music at the Opera House. The Royal Ballet is also based here; see p293.*

Theatre

The West End has managed to ride out the recession on a tide of song – in other words, those big-production musicals, the most ancient of which had been hoofing it on the London stage since the late 1980s. Although many of those old-timers have now gone, the format is still hugely popular, thanks to the arrival of a bunch of lively, thoroughly modern new musicals – including smash Broadway hit *The Book of Mormon*. Drama is making a very real comeback too, led by the colossal success of National Theatre transfers *War Horse* and *The Curious Incident of the Dog in the Night-Time*, and a spate of excellent Shakespeare productions. There's no shortage of famous faces either, with David Tennant, Ben Whishaw and Jude Law among the film and TV celebs treading the boards.

The **Donmar Warehouse** (*see p289*) traditionally lures high-profile film stars to

BEER, BARS AND BACH

Classical music, but without the frosty penguin suits.

The vibrancy of London's classical music scene can hardly be doubted, but when you find yourself among reverent octogenarians at some London venues, you might feel you have to be on your best behaviour. Not so at a recent Purcell concert, in the unlikely setting of an east London boozer, where a far younger audience were cajoled into drunkenly singing some of the British maestro's pub ditties – with lyrics not fit for publication in a family guidebook.

This was one of the Orchestra of the Age of Enlightenment's ongoing **Night Shift** series (www.oae.co.uk/thenightshift), where a small group of string players from the orchestra gather in the back rooms of various pubs (notably the Old Queen's Head; *see p267*) to perform such stellar composers as Mozart, Haydn and Handel. There's no attempt to shy away from difficult pieces: the professional and seriously talented performers trust to the combination of their skill and enthusiasm with the relaxed settings to win new audiences to the baroque music they love.

Night Shift isn't alone. For 'classical music in a rock 'n' roll setting', head to the 100 Club (*see p272*) where **Limelight** (www.londonlimelight.co.uk) hosts regular gigs – a mix of classical genres and eras,

Night Shift.

performed by a mix of young up-and-comers and stars such as Danielle De Niese.

Arguably, the pioneer of this thriving informal classical scene is one Gabriel Prokofiev, grandson of the famous Russian composer. He founded **Nonclassical** (www.nonclassical.co.uk), which has now been mixing new classical music and DJs for nearly a decade. Its main home is currently in Hackney at the Shacklewell Arms (*see p275*) but check the Nonclassical website for events across London. Also keep an eye out for occasional concerts from Yellow Lounge (http://yellowlounge.co.uk), a group dedicated to bringing classical music up to date with performances in urban spaces.

perform at its tiny Earlham Street home, while appearances by Kevin Spacey and his stellar chums at the **Old Vic** (*see p286*) have put bums on seats there.

On a smaller scale, Off-West End houses such as the **Young Vic** (*see p292*) and the **BAC** (*see p289*) continue to produce some of London's most exciting, best-value theatre, while the **Barbican Centre** (*see right*) programmes visually exciting and physically expressive work from around the world.

THEATRE DISTRICTS

In strictly geographical terms, the **West End** refers to London's traditional theatre district, a busy area bounded by Shaftesbury Avenue, Drury Lane, the Strand and the Haymarket. Most major musicals and big-money dramas run here, alongside transfers of successful smaller-scale shows. However, the 'West End' appellation is now also applied to other major theatres elsewhere in town, including subsidised venues such as the Barbican Centre (in the City), the National Theatre (on the South Bank) and the Old Vic (near Waterloo).

Off-West End denotes theatres with smaller budgets and smaller capacities. These venues, many of them sponsored or subsidised, push the creative envelope with new writing, often brought to life by the best young acting and directing talent. The Bush is good for up-and-coming writers, while the Almeida and Donmar Warehouse offer elegantly produced shows with the occasional big star.

THE FRINGE

The best places to catch next-generation talent include Battersea's **Theatre 503**, above the Latchmere pub (503 Battersea Park Road, SW11 3BW, 7978 7040, www.theatre503.com), which recently won a Peter Brook Empty Space award for its work with new writers. The theatre above the **Finborough** (118 Finborough Road, SW10 9ED, 0844 847 1652, www.finborough theatre.co.uk), a pub in Earl's Court, attracts national critics with its small but perfectly formed revivals of forgotten classics.

Other venues that are worth investigating include the **Yard** (Queen's Yard, Hackney Wick, E9 5EN, www.theyardtheatre.co.uk), a new 130-seat venue near the Olympic Park, made from recycled materials and playing to a house of local hipsters; the **Southwark Playhouse** (77-85 Newington Causeway, Southwark, SE1 6BD, 7407 0234, www.southwarkplayhouse.co.uk); and the **Menier Chocolate Factory** (53 Southwark Street, Southwark, SE1 1RU, 7378 1713, www.menierchocolatefactory.com), which, like the **Union Theatre** (204 Union Street, Southwark, SE1 0LX, 7261 9876, www.union theatre.biz) has a knack for musicals up-close.

BUYING TICKETS

If there's a specific show you want to see, aim to book ahead. And, if possible, always try to do so at the theatre's box office, at which booking fees are generally smaller than they are with agents such as Ticketmaster (0844 844 0444, www.ticketmaster.co.uk). Shop around: different agencies offer different prices and discounts.

If you're more flexible about your choice of show, consider buying from the **Tkts** booth or taking your chances with standby seats (*see p285* **In the Know**).

THE WEST END

Major theatres

Barbican Centre

For listings, *see p280.*

The annual BITE (Barbican International Theatre Events) season continues to cherry-pick exciting and eclectic theatre companies from around the globe. Watch out, too, for imaginatively leftfield family-friendly theatre and installations during school holidays.

★ National Theatre

South Bank, SE1 9PX (information 7452 3400, tickets 7452 3000, www.nationaltheatre.org.uk). Embankment or Southwark tube, or Waterloo tube/rail. **Box office** 9.30am-8pm Mon-Sat. **Tickets** *Olivier & Lyttelton* £12-£48. **Map** p399 M8.

IN THE KNOW CHEAP SEATS

The **TKTS** booths (Clocktower Building, Leicester Square, Soho, WC2H 7NA, www.tkts.co.uk) sells tickets for big shows at much-reduced rates, either on the day or up to a week in advance. It opens at 9am (11am on Sundays); you can check which shows are available on the website. Before buying, be sure you're at the correct booth, in a stand-alone building on the south side of Leicester Square – the square is ringed with other ticket brokers, where the seats are worse and the prices are higher. Many West End theatres also offer their own reduced-price tickets for shows that haven't sold out on the night; these are known as **'standby' seats**. Some standby deals are limited to those with student ID. The time these tickets go on sale varies from theatre to theatre: check before setting out. Watch out too for cut-price **Travelex tickets** at the National (*see above*) and **'groundling' tickets** (standing) at the Globe (*see p286*).

This concrete monster is the flagship venue of British theatre (it celebrated its 50th birthday in 2013), and no theatrical tour of London is complete without a visit. At the time of writing, one of the theatre's three auditoriums was out of action (the Cottesloe is being refurbished and will reopen as the Dorfman Theatre). In the interim, the big, red, temporary Shed is hosting performances of adventurous work from young writers. At least when new artistic director Rufus Norris takes over from his much-lauded predecessor Nicholas Hytner in April 2015, he'll have some new toys to play with.

The National's various auditoriums have always allowed for different kinds of performance: in-the-round, promenade, even classic proscenium arch. Hytner's artistic directorship, with landmark successes such as Alan Bennett's *The History Boys* and *War Horse,* has shown that the state-subsidised home of British theatre can turn out quality drama at a profit. Productions range from top-notch Shakespeare to reworked foreign classics, and British revivals. An array of recent West End hits (*One Man, Two Guvnors*; *The Curious Incident*) started out at the National. The Travelex season ensures a widening audience by offering tickets for £12, £24 and £34, as does the free outdoor performing arts stage, Watch This Space, each summer – although it's in temporary abeyance while the all-weather Shed is in its spot.

Old Vic

The Cut, Waterloo, SE1 8NB (0844 871 7628, www.oldvictheatre.com). Southwark tube or Waterloo tube/rail. **Box office** *In person* 9am-7.30pm Mon-Fri; 9am-7pm Sat. *By phone* 9am-7.30pm Mon-Fri; 9am-4pm Sat; 9.30am-4pm Sun. **Tickets** £11-£52. **Map** p402 N9.

Oscar-winner Kevin Spacey has been the artistic director here since 2003, and the theatre continues to have commercial success; plays are sometimes a critical hit as well, especially when Spacey himself or one of his stellar Hollywood chums takes to the stage. The Old Vic is a beautiful venue, where programming runs from grown-up Christmas pantomimes to serious drama.

★ Open Air Theatre

Regent's Park, Inner Circle, Marylebone, NW1 4NR (0844 826 4242, www.openairtheatre.com). Baker Street tube. **Tickets** £15-£55. **Map** p396 G3.

The verdant setting of this alfresco theatre lends itself perfectly to summery Shakespeare romps – *A Midsummer Night's Dream* is a regular here. But it's not just the Bard – you'll also find classic American shows, such as hit musical *Porgy and Bess* and Arthur Miller's 1947 drama *All My Sons*.

► *If you don't want to bring a picnic, good-value, tasty food can be bought at the Garden Café; or plump for traditional tea or Pimm's on the lawn.*

★ Royal Court Theatre

Sloane Square, Chelsea, SW1W 8AS (7565 5000, www.royalcourttheatre.com). Sloane Square tube. **Box office** 10am-6pm Mon-Sat. **Tickets** £10-£32. **Map** p398 G11.

From John Osborne's *Look Back in Anger*, staged in the theatre's opening year of 1956, to the numerous discoveries of the past decade, among them Sarah Kane, Joe Penhall and Conor McPherson, the emphasis at the Royal Court has always been on new voices in British theatre. Recently, plenty of politics has been injected into the programme, successfully lowering the age of the audiences in the process – Jez Butterworth's *Jerusalem* with Mark Rylance was a huge hit. Expect to find rude, lyrical new work by first-time playwrights, as well as better established American and European writers with a message. Look out for quality shorts and more of the usual vividly produced British and international work by young writers. Vicky Featherstone took over as artistic director (the first woman in the role) in 2013.

Royal Shakespeare Company

Information 01789 403444, tickets 0844 800 1110, www.rsc.org.uk. **Box office** By phone 10am-6pm Mon-Sat. **Tickets** £5-£67.50.

Britain's flagship company hasn't had a London base since it quit the Barbican in 2002, although it is turning its mind towards finding one now the £100m redevelopment of its home theatres in Stratford-upon-Avon has reached completion. In the meantime, it continues its itinerant existence, sometimes popping up in smaller venues to stage new plays. Recent successes have included David Tennant in *Richard II,* staged at the Barbican in winter 2013/14.

★ Shakespeare's Globe

21 New Globe Walk, Bankside, SE1 9DT (7401 9919, www.shakespearesglobe.com). Southwark tube or London Bridge tube/rail. **Box office** *In person* 10am-5pm Mon-Sat; 10am-4pm Sun. *By phone* 10am-6pm Mon-Sat; 10am-5pm Sun. **Tickets** £5-£100. **Map** p402 O7.

Sam Wanamaker's dream to recreate the theatre where Shakespeare first staged many of his plays has become a successful reality, perhaps reaching its peak with the 2012 Globe to Globe Festival: 85,000 tickets were sold for an ambitious six-week marathon of Shakespeare plays by international casts. Comedy is usually what the Globe does best, but the venue's been on great form for a while under Dominic Dromgoole, with the Shakespeare classics paralleled by new plays on similar themes. The open-air, standing-room Pit tickets are excellent value, if a little marred by low-flying aircraft. A new 340-seater indoor Jacobean theatre, called the Sam Wanamaker Playhouse, opened its doors in January 2014 (*see p287* **Theatre by Candlelight**). For tours, *see p56*.

THEATRE BY CANDLELIGHT

The new old-style playhouse at Shakespeare's Globe.

'I'm told it would take a flamethrower to even char the walls,' says Dominic Dromgoole, the artistic director of **Shakespeare's Globe** (*see p286*), proudly. We're standing in the Sam Wanamaker Playhouse, London's newest, sexiest theatre and the intimate indoor sibling to the boisterous open-air Globe Theatre. It is also made entirely out of wood and lit entirely by candles, but apparently its exquisitely decorated oak frame can withstand the fieriest of conflagrations. That's good: it was a fire that did for the original, Elizabethan Globe.

What the first Globe didn't have was a bijou indoor venue. But Shakespeare and his King's Men theatre troupe did have one just down the road, on which the Wanamaker is modelled.

'They wanted to get into an indoor theatre much earlier than they in fact did,' says Dromgoole, the sweary showman whose colourful tenure has been such a success for the Globe. 'They bought the Blackfriars [a former priory] in 1592, but they were told to f**k off when they tried to do plays because there were lots of puritans around who complained about the noise. So they only finally moved there in 1609.'

By that time Elizabeth's golden age was over and the unpopular James I had the throne. Shakespeare's plays got darker and weirder, and the new generation of Jacobean playwrights started writing claustrophobic, blood-soaked revenge tragedies for candlelit indoor spaces. Foremost is John Webster's bleak 1612 masterpiece *The Duchess of Malfi*, which made the perfect opener for the new theatre, a long-delayed cornerstone of Wanamaker's original plans.

The new theatre is a rich, dark space, embellished with gold, with a beautiful ornate ceiling, built to feel even smaller than its 340-seat capacity. 'Hopefully it'll be an erotic space,' says Dromgoole, 'in the right way. The concentration of bodies in a small, dark room should carry some charge – and it should hopefully be fun as well.'

The rest of the inaugural season was delightfully unfamiliar, taking in 1607 meta-comedy *The Knight of the Burning Pestle* and 1645 opera *L'Ormindo*, a hook-up with the Royal Opera House. Notably, there was no Shakespeare, and the prices mark this as a more exclusive venue than the £5-a-pop Globe – tickets for *L'Ormindo* topped out at a hearty £100 (still not bad for opera).

'In some ways you're observing what went wrong,' concedes Dromgoole of the all-17th-century repertoire, 'the movement away from a citizen's theatre. But it's hard to deny the power of the plays, and if we can bring them back into people's imaginations then that's a benefit that can filter out to everybody. There's no denying it's exclusive. But our prices are still lower than the commercial sector. In fact, it's a f**king bargain!'

Long-runners & musicals

★ Billy Elliot the Musical
Victoria Palace Theatre, Victoria Street, Victoria, SW1E 5EA (0844 248 5000, www.billyelliotthe musical.com). Victoria tube/rail. **Box office** 10am-8.30pm Mon-Sat. **Tickets** £20.50-£96. **Map** p398 H10.
The combination of Elton John's music and a heart-melting yarn about a northern working-class lad with a talent for ballet has scooped more awards internationally than any other British musical and launched the careers of dozens of young Billies.

The Book of Mormon
Prince of Wales Theatre, Coventry Street, Soho, W1D 6AS (0844 482 5115, www.bookofmormon london.com). Piccadilly Circus tube. **Box office** 10am-8pm Mon-Sat. **Tickets** £37.50-£152. **Map** p399 K7.
South Park creators Trey Parker and Matt Stone's smash musical about the absurdities of Mormonism is not as shocking as you might expect. There's lots of swearing and close-to-the-bone jokes, but beneath it all, this is a big-hearted affair that pays note-perfect homage to the spirit and sounds of Broadway's golden age. And it's very, very funny.

The Curious Incident of the Dog in the Night-Time
Gielgud Theatre, 35 Shaftesbury Avenue, Soho W1D 6AR (7492 1548, 0844 482 5130, www. delfontmackintosh.co.uk). Piccadilly Circus tube. **Box office** 8am-8pm Mon-Fri; 9am-7pm Sat. **Tickets** £32-£108. **Map** p397 L6.
Another hit West End transfer from the National Theatre, this adaptation of Mark Haddon's best-selling novel about a boy with Asperger syndrome is illuminating, touching and consistently surprising. With a wonderful graph-paper set, imaginative choreography and a strong young cast, it's deservedly garnered seven Oliviers and heaps of critical praise.

Jersey Boys
Piccadilly Theatre, 16 Denman Street, Soho W1D 7DY (0844 412 6666,www.jerseyboyslondon.com). Piccadilly Circus tube. **Box office** *In person* 10am-8pm Mon-Sat. *By phone* 24hrs daily. **Tickets** £22.50-£114. **Map** p398 J7.
This Broadway import had the critics singing the praises of Ryan Molloy, who hits the high notes in Frankie Valli & the Four Seasons' doo-wop standards. The well-trodden storyline of early struggle, success and break-up is elevated by pacy direction.

Les Misérables
Queen's Theatre, 51 Shaftesbury Avenue, Soho, W1D 6BA (0844 482 5160, www.lesmis.com). Leicester Square or Piccadilly Circus tube. **Box office** *In person* 10am-7.45pm Mon-Sat. *By phone* 24hrs daily. **Tickets** £14.50-£97. **Map** p399 K7.

Young Vic. *See p292.*

The RSC's version of Boublil and Schönberg's musical first came to the London stage in 1985 – and no fewer than three celebratory versions ran simultaneously on one October night in 2010. The version currently at the Queen's should manage a few more anniversaries, which has good and bad consequences. When actors have been singing these songs since their first audition, it's easy to take it that half-inch too far. Still, the voices remain lush, the revolutionary sets are film-fabulous, and the lyrics and score (based on Victor Hugo's novel) will be considerably less trivial than whatever's on next door.

★ Matilda the Musical
Cambridge Theatre, 32-34 Earlham Street, Covent Garden, WC2H 9HU (0844 800 1110, www.matildathemusical.com). Covent Garden tube or Charing Cross tube/rail. **Box office** *In person* 10am-8pm Mon-Sat. *By phone* 10am-6pm Mon-Sat. **Tickets** £5-£97.50. **Map** p397 L6.
Adapted from Roald Dahl's riotous children's novel, with songs by superstar Aussie comedian Tim Minchin, this RSC transfer received rapturous reviews on its first outing in Stratford-upon-Avon and has been going strong ever since, winning multiple Olivier awards.

The Mousetrap
St Martin's Theatre, West Street, Cambridge Circus, Covent Garden, WC2H 9NZ (0844 499 1515, www.the-mousetrap.co.uk). Leicester Square tube. **Box office** 10am-8pm Mon-Sat. **Tickets** £17.50-£65. **Map** p397 K6.
Running in the West End since 1952, Agatha Christie's drawing-room whodunnit is a murder mystery Methuselah, and will probably still be booking when the last trump sounds.

ARTS & ENTERTAINMENT

★ War Horse

New London Theatre, Drury Lane, Covent Garden, WC2B 5PW (0844 412 2708, www.nationaltheatre.org.uk/warhorse). Covent Garden tube. **Box office** *In person* 10am-7.30pm Mon-Sat. *By phone* 24hrs daily. **Tickets** £15-£90. **Map** p397 L6.

Transferred from the National Theatre, *War Horse* is an incredibly moving piece of theatre (and a massive critical and popular hit). The play is based on Michael Morpurgo's children's novel about a horse separated from his young master and spirited off to World War I. Bereft Albert duly signs up, to seek Joey in the mud and carnage of the Flanders front. The real stars are the extraordinary puppet horses. Each visibly manipulated by three actors, who make them gallop, pant and emote as clearly as any human actor, these plywood and leather frames become astonishingly expressive beasts.

OFF-WEST END THEATRES

Almeida

Almeida Street, Islington, N1 1TA (7359 4404, www.almeida.co.uk). Angel tube. **Box office** *In person & by phone* 10am-6pm Mon-Fri. **Tickets** £10-£69.50. **Map** p400 O1.

Well groomed and with a rather funky bar, the Almeida turns out thoughtfully crafted theatre for grown-ups. Recent hits have included *Chimerica*, Lucy Kirkwood's exhilarating political thriller about China and America (which transferred to the West End). In summer, the month-long Almeida Festival brings over 50 new works to the building, including the bar and dressing rooms. Rupert Goold took over as artistic director in 2013 and immediately made his mark with *American Psycho*, a musical adaptation of the Bret Easton Ellis novel starring *Doctor Who*'s Matt Smith.

★ Battersea Arts Centre (BAC)

Lavender Hill, Battersea, SW11 5TN (7223 2223, www.bac.org.uk). Clapham Common tube, Clapham Junction rail or bus 77, 77A, 345. **Box office** *In person & by phone* 10am-6pm Mon-Fri; 3-6pm Sat. **Tickets** £5-£25; pay what you can.

Housed in the old Battersea Town Hall, the forward-thinking BAC hosts young theatre troupes; expect quirky, fun and physical theatre from the likes of cult companies Kneehigh, 1927 and highly acclaimed international innovators Forced Entertainment.

★ Bush

7 Uxbridge Road, Shepherd's Bush, W12 8LJ (8743 5050, www.bushtheatre.co.uk). Shepherd's Bush Market tube. **Box office** *In person & by phone* noon-7.30pm Mon-Sat (performance days); noon-8pm Mon-Fri (non-performance days). **Tickets** £10-£19.50.

Occupying the former Shepherd's Bush public library, the Bush punches well above its weight, with well-designed productions and an impressive record of West End transfers. It's famous for its new writers, among them Stephen Poliakoff and David Edgar.

★ Donmar Warehouse

41 Earlham Street, Covent Garden, WC2H 9LX (0844 871 7624, www.donmarwarehouse.com). Covent Garden or Leicester Square tube. **Box office** *In person* 10am-6pm Mon-Sat. *By phone* 9am-10pm Mon-Sat; 10am-8pm Sun. **Tickets** £7.50-£35. **Map** p397 L6.

The Donmar is less a warehouse than a boutique chamber. Award-winning artistic director Michael Grandage kept the venue on the fresh, intelligent path established by Sam Mendes, and his successor, Josie Rourke, is continuing the good work. The Donmar's combination of artistic integrity and intimate size, with audience right alongside the stage, has proved hard to resist, with many high-profile film actors appearing: among them Nicole Kidman, Gwyneth Paltrow, Ewan McGregor and Tom Hiddleston.

Gate Theatre

Prince Albert, 11 Pembridge Road, Notting Hill, W11 3HQ (7229 0706, www.gatetheatre.co.uk). Notting Hill Gate tube. **Box office** *By phone* 10am-6pm Mon-Fri. *In person* 6.30-8pm Mon-Fri; 2-4pm, 6.30-8pm Sat. **Tickets** £20; £15 reductions. **Map** p404 Z6.

A doll's house of a theatre, with rickety wooden chairs as seats, the Gate is the only producing theatre in London dedicated to international work.

★ Lyric Hammersmith

Lyric Square, King Street, Hammersmith, W6 0QL (8741 6850, www.lyric.co.uk). Hammersmith tube. **Box office** *By phone* 10am-5.30pm Mon-Sat. *In person* 9.30am-7.30pm on performance days. **Tickets** £12.50-£35.

Artistic director Sean Holmes launched his tenure in 2009 with a pledge to bring writers back into the building, making space for neglected modern classics and new plays alongside the cutting-edge physical and devised work for which the Lyric is known. The building is currently undergoing a major facelift (due for completion in spring 2014), which will add a two-storey extension including drama, dance and recording studios, a cinema and a new café and bar.

Soho Theatre

21 Dean Street, Soho, W1D 3NE (7478 0100, www.sohotheatre.com). Tottenham Court Road tube. **Box office** *In person* 9am-9.30pm Mon-Sat. *By phone* 10am-10pm Mon-Sat. **Tickets** £5-£37.50. **Map** p395 K6.

Its cool blue neon lights and front-of-house café help it to blend into the Soho landscape, but this theatre has made a name for itself since opening in 2000. It attracts a young, hip crowd and plays very effectively to the theatre/comedy/cabaret crossover scene.

▶ *For comedy at the Soho, see p277. For cabaret, see p279.*

THE BEST OF THE WEST END

A selection of shows from London's theatreland.

READ THE BOOK? SEEN THE FILM? NOW HERE'S THE MUSICAL

It may not be strictly West End, but the musical adaptation of Bret Easton Ellis's novel *American Psycho* is making waves at Islington's Almeida Theatre (*see p289*). Matt Smith stars as murderous yuppie Patrick Bateman, taking out his frustrations with 1980s competitive materialism with an axe. It couldn't be more different to *The Full Monty* (Noël Coward Theatre, St Martin's Lane, WC2N 4AU, 0844 482 5141, www.delfontmackintosh.co.uk). The 1997 film, about unemployed men in post-industrial Sheffield taking to the stage as strippers, was a cracker and now the show is on stage. It's complemented by songs from the soundtrack, and we think it's going to be hot stuff (or just bloody funny). Staying in the north, and also a film spin-off, *Billy Elliot* (*see p288*) is the story of a young boy's ambitions to leave gritty mining-town masculinity behind and embrace ballet. Told against a backdrop of the 1984 miners' strike, it continues to charm as a glorious comedy – and near-tragedy – of dissonant values and shifting perceptions.

Talking of gritty masculinity, Tim Rice's adaptation of the semi-autobiographical novel by James Jones, *From Here to Eternity* (Shaftesbury Theatre, 210 Shaftesbury Avenue, WC2H 8DP, 020 7379 5399, www.shaftesburytheatre.com), following the lives, loves and violent deaths of a group of GIs posted to Hawaii in 1941, hardly seems the stuff that musicals are made of. The rugged production strikes an appropriate tone, but the shadow of the film – with its famous love-in-the-waves scene with Deborah Kerr and Burt Lancaster – looms large. Last, and maybe least, the stage version of the peerless 1987 '60s-era awakening-sexuality film *Dirty Dancing* (Piccadilly Theatre, 4 Denman Street, W1D 7DY, 0844 871 7618, www.ambassadortickets.com) continues to fill seats with women of a certain age. By the time dancer Johnny bounds through the stalls to rescue Baby from her corner, there's just enough adrenaline in the auditorium to make a triumph of that famous lift. But we won't promise you 'the time of your life'...

The Book of Mormon.

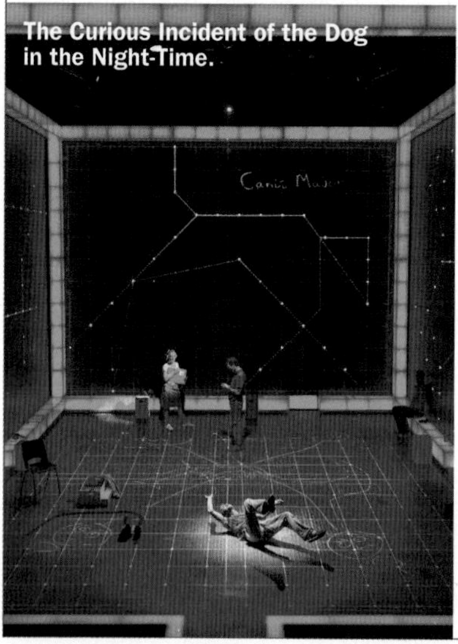

The Curious Incident of the Dog in the Night-Time.

MAKE 'EM LAUGH

The Broadway smash musical *The Book of Mormon* (*see p288*) hit our shores in 2013, with its crazy tale of mismatched but equally clueless Mormon missionaries posted to Uganda. Part buddy story, part tale of how trying to fix things in other countries doesn't always work, this whip-sharp but warm-hearted show has been a big hit here too.

Meanwhile, reality TV gets the comedy treatment in *I Can't Sing! – The X Factor Musical* at the London Palladium (8 Argyll Street, W1F 7TF, 7492 9930, www.londonpalladium.org). Hotly anticipated, this musical comedy written by comedian Harry Hill takes on the monster TV talent show of the same name.

WEST END TRANSFERS

The public National Theatre (*see p285*) has given birth to plays that have transferred to the West End following successful National runs. The most successful – and a huge money-spinner for the National – is *War Horse* (*see p289*), the story of a Devon lad who experiences the horrors of World War I to be reunited with his horse pal Joey. Michael Morpurgo's original story was for children and may seem formulaic at times, but wonderful life-size horse marionettes, skeletally modernist in form but utterly, magically alive thanks to their talented army of puppeteers, make the show. Another successful transfer, *The Curious Incident of the Dog in the Night-Time*, meanwhile, acquired another level of curiosity when part of the roof collapsed in torrential rain during a performance at the Apollo Theatre in late 2013, ending its run there. The show, the story of a 15-year-old boy with Asperger syndrome who embarks upon a journey to solve the mystery of who killed his neighbour's dog, will resume at the Gielgud Theatre from June 2014 (35 Shaftesbury Avenue, W1D 6AR, 0844 482 5130, www.delfontmackintosh.co.uk).

War Horse.

JUKEBOX MUSICALS

You know, the ones where they take back catalogues and wind a story around the songs. They're a strange hybrid but some of these shows have run and run. There's joyful *Mamma Mia!* (Novello Theatre, Aldwych, WC2B 4LD, 0844 544 3830, www.delfontmackintosh.co.uk), with love and Abba songs on a Greek island; *Jersey Boys* (*see p288*), which eschews the made-up plot in favour of a straightforward telling of the story of the Four Seasons, accompanied by their wonderful songs; *Thriller Live* (Lyric Theatre, 29 Shaftesbury Avenue, W1D 7ES, 0844 544 3830, www.nimaxtheatres.com), pure Michael Jackson with dazzling dancing, held together by the loosest of narratives; and *We Will Rock You* (Dominion Theatre, 268-269 Tottenham Court Road, W1T 7AQ, 0844 847 1775, www.dominiontheatre.com), Queen's back catalogue threaded into Ben Elton's depiction of a dystopian future where live music is banned.

OLD FAITHFULS

Whodunnit *The Mousetrap* (*see p288*) has been churning out performances since 1952, and shows no signs of stopping despite its decrepitude. There's more life to be found in long-running musicals. The brilliantly skilful *Lion King* (Lyceum Theatre, 21 Wellington Street, WC2E 7RQ, 0844 871 3000, www.lyceumtheatrelondon.com) scores with its astonishing theatricality. Techniques from all over the world – African masks, Japanese kabuki costumes, Malaysian shadow puppetry – are smashed together with Elton John's songs in an explosion of spectacle in this take on the original Disney film. Derided by many as 'opera lite', *Les Miserables* (*see p288*) nevertheless has a huge fan base, who love the bombast and power vocals of the 19th-century French barricades melodrama.

Theatre Royal Stratford East

Gerry Raffles Square, Stratford, E15 1BN (8534 0310, www.stratfordeast.com). Stratford tube/rail/DLR. **Box office** *In person & by phone* 10am-6pm Mon-Sat. **Tickets** £5-£24.

The Theatre Royal Stratford East is a community theatre, with many shows written, directed and performed by black or Asian artists. Musicals are big here – *The Harder They Come* went on to West End success – but there is also a Christmas pantomime and harder-hitting fare.

Tricycle

269 Kilburn High Road, Kilburn, NW6 7JR (information 7372 6611, tickets 7328 1000, www.tricycle.co.uk). Kilburn tube. **Box office** *In person & by phone* 10am-9pm Mon-Sat; 2-9pm Sun. **Tickets** £8-£29.

Passionate and political, the Tricycle consistently finds original ways into difficult subjects. It has pioneered its own genre of 'tribunal' docu-dramas.

★ Wilton's Music Hall

Graces Alley, off Ensign Street, Whitechapel, E1 8JB (7702 2789, www.wiltons.org.uk). Aldgate East or Tower Hill tube. **Box office** 10am-6pm Mon-Fri. **Tickets** £13-£25. **Map** p403 S7.

London's last surviving example of the giant music halls that flourished in the mid 19th century, Wilton's once entertained the masses with acts ranging from Chinese performing monkeys to acrobats, contortionists to opera singers. It was here that the can-can first scandalised London. Roughly 150 years later, Wilton's is still a theatre, offering an atmospheric stage for everything from situation-specific Bach to immersive theatre to magic.

★ Young Vic

66 The Cut, Waterloo, SE1 8LZ (7922 2922, www.youngvic.org). Waterloo tube/rail. **Box office** 10am-6pm Mon-Sat. **Tickets** £10-£35. **Map** p402 N8.

As the name suggests, this Vic (actually now in its forties) has more youthful bravura than its older sister up the road, and draws a younger crowd, who pack out the open-air balcony at its restaurant and bar on the weekends. They come to see European classics with a modern edge, new writing with an international flavour and collaborations with leading companies. Recent winners have included hard-hitting race musical *The Scottsboro Boys*, and the theatre has been attracting some starry acting talent, with both Chiwetel Ejiofor and Gillian Anderson having appeared. *Photo p288.*

Dance

London is the home of two long-established classical dance companies. The **Royal Ballet**, founded in 1931 and resident at the Royal Opera House (*see p284*), is a company of global stature, which recently lured star Russian ballerina Natalia Osipova to join its ranks. The Royal's (friendly) rival is **English National Ballet**, a touring company founded in 1950 that performs most often at the Coliseum (*see below*) and, for the regular *Swan Lake* 'in the round', at the **Royal Albert Hall** (*see p281*). Its busy artistic director, Tamara Rojo, is also a principal dancer with the company. On the contemporary side, London is the base for internationally acclaimed choreographers including Akram Khan, Hofesh Shechter and Wayne McGregor.

MAJOR VENUES

Barbican Centre

For listings, see p280.

Conceived in the 1960s and completed in 1982, the Barbican attracts and nurtures experimental dance, especially in the perfectly intimate Pit Theatre.

Coliseum

For listings, see p282.

Once a music hall, the Coliseum is in fine condition following a renovation in 2004. The English National Ballet performs here, along with the likes of the Peter Schaufuss Ballet and visiting Russian ballet companies.

★ The Place

17 Duke's Road, Bloomsbury, WC1H 9PY (7121 1100, www.theplace.org.uk). Euston tube/rail. **Box office** *In person & by phone* 10.30am-6pm Mon-Sat; 10.30am-8pm on performance days. **Tickets** £11-£14. **Map** p399 K3.

The Place.

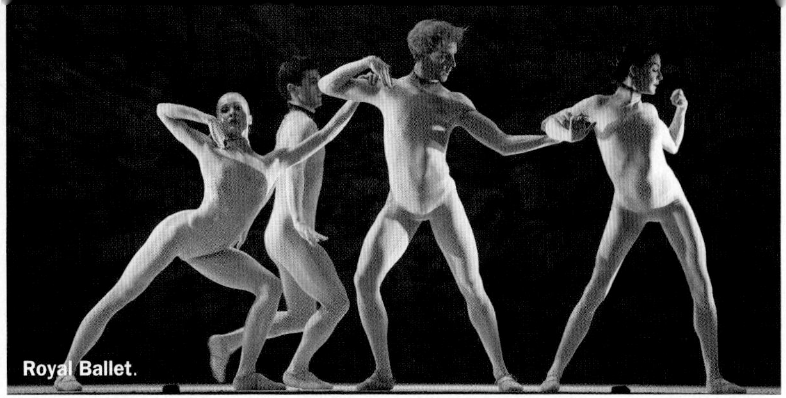
Royal Ballet.

For genuinely emerging dance, look to the Place. The theatre is behind the biennial Place Prize for choreography, which rewards the best in British contemporary dance as well as regular seasons of new work such as Resolution! (short works; Jan/Feb) and Spring Loaded (Apr/May).

★ Royal Opera House

For listings, see p284.

For the full ballet experience, nothing beats the Royal Opera House, home of the Royal Ballet. The current incarnation of the building is an appropriately grand space in which to see dreamy ballerinas including Marianela Nuñez and Lauren Cuthbertson. There's edgier fare in the Linbury Studio Theatre. Royal Ballet in Rehearsal sessions offer a rare – and thrillingly close-up – glimpse behind the scenes. The 90-minute sessions are held in the Clore Studio Upstairs, with a capacity of 170. This is ballet at its most stripped down: no sets, no exquisite costumes and no grand stage. Instead, there's just the piano, the squeak of shoes on the scuffed grey floor, and the intense concentration of the dancers.

★ Sadler's Wells

Rosebery Avenue, Finsbury, EC1R 4TN (0844 412 4300, www.sadlerswells.com). Angel tube. **Box office** *In person & by phone* 10am-8pm Mon-Sat. **Tickets** £8-£60. **Map** p402 N3.

Purpose-built in 1998 on the site of a 17th-century theatre of the same name, this dazzling complex is home to impressive local and international performances of contemporary dance in all its guises. The Lilian Baylis Studio offers smaller-scale new works and works-in-progress, and the Peacock Theatre (on Portugal Street in Holborn) operates as a satellite venue.

Southbank Centre

For listings, see p282.

From international contemporary dance to hip hop to physical theatre to South Asian dance, there's an eclectic programme at the cluster of venues collectively known as the Southbank Centre: the mammoth RFH, the medium-sized Queen Elizabeth Hall, the intimate Purcell Room and the riverside terrace.

OTHER VENUES

Greenwich Dance

Borough Hall, Royal Hill, Greenwich, SE10 8RE (8293 9741, www.greenwichdance.org.uk). Greenwich DLR/rail. **Box office** 9am-9pm Mon-Fri; 9am-3pm Sat. **Tickets** free-£20. **Map** p405 W3.

This art deco venue in Greenwich hosts classes and workshops and a regular tea dance, as well as unique cabaret nights, which deliver entertaining dance performances in short bursts.

Laban Centre

Creekside, Deptford, SE8 3DZ (8305 9300, 8463 9100 tickets, www.trinitylaban.ac.uk). Deptford DLR or Greenwich DLR/rail. **Open** *In person & by phone* 10am-5pm Mon-Fri. **Tickets** £4-£15 for the centre's own events.

Originally founded (in Manchester) by the innovative and influential movement theoretician Rudolf Laban (1879-1958), in 2005 the Laban Centre joined forces with Trinity College of Music to create the first ever UK conservatoire for music and dance. The centre was designed by Herzog & de Meuron of Tate Modern fame and features a curving, multi-coloured glass frontage. The stunning premises include a 300-seat auditorium and are home to Transitions Dance Company.

► *Also in Deptford, the Albany (Douglas Way, SE8 4AG, 8692 4446, www.thealbany.org.uk) specialises in hip hop theatre.*

Rich Mix

35-47 Bethnal Green Road, Shoreditch, E1 6LA (7613 7498 box office, www.richmix.org.uk). Shoreditch High Street rail. **Box office** *In person & by phone* 9am-11pm Mon-Fr; 10am-11pm Sat, Sun. **Tickets** free-£18. **Map** 401 4S.

A cinema and arts centre that offers regular dance events (often in the street dance and hip hop genres) alongside music, comedy, spoken word and theatre. Quality can be variable, but enthusiasm levels are high.

Escapes & Excursions

Escapes & Excursions

You'll never run out of things to do in London. But everyone who lives here feels an irresistible urge to leave occasionally, so why would visitors be any different? And with good train services out of London, it's easy to reach some interesting destinations in under two hours. We also list a few stellar day trips on the outskirts of the city, such as Hampton Court and Kew Gardens, which can be reached in less than an hour.

GETTING AROUND

All of the destinations included in this chapter are within easy reach of London. For the main attractions, we've included details of opening times and admission prices, but be aware that these can change without notice: always phone to check.

By train

Britain's rail network is generally reliable. However, ticket prices on some services are high, and with different rail companies sharing some routes, it's easy to inadvertently pay too much or buy a ticket that limits your options. Factor in varying definitions of peak and off-peak travel and you'll usually be better off discussing your needs at a ticket office window, than buying blind at a machine. If more than two of you are travelling, ask about family and group tickets, which offer excellent value.

The website www.nationalrail.co.uk has a good journey planner and gives live advice on engineering works and other delays, which are a regular occurence, particularly at weekends. You can buy tickets on the website, too, but there's generally no advantage, unless your journey takes you outside the south-eastern network (in which case, the further ahead you purchase, the lower the price). National Rail's phone number is 0845 748 4950.

If you need extra help, there are rail travel centres in London's mainline stations, as well as at Heathrow and Gatwick airports. Staff can give you guidance on timetables and booking.

By coach

Coaches operated by National Express (0871 781 8181, www.nationalexpress.com) run throughout the country. Services depart from Victoria Coach Station (164 Buckingham Palace Road, SW1W 9TP, 0871 781 8178, www.tfl.gov.uk), which is ten minutes' walk from Victoria rail and tube stations. Green Line Travel (0871 200 2233, www.greenline.co.uk) also operates coaches.

One-offs

ARUNDEL CASTLE

With its hilltop castle and cathedral and the River Arun running beneath, Arundel looks more like a stage set for a medieval period drama than a real town. What's more, it's only 90 minutes from London by rail (trains leave from Victoria station).

Arundel Castle originated at the end of the 11th century and has been the family home of the Dukes of Norfolk and their ancestors for

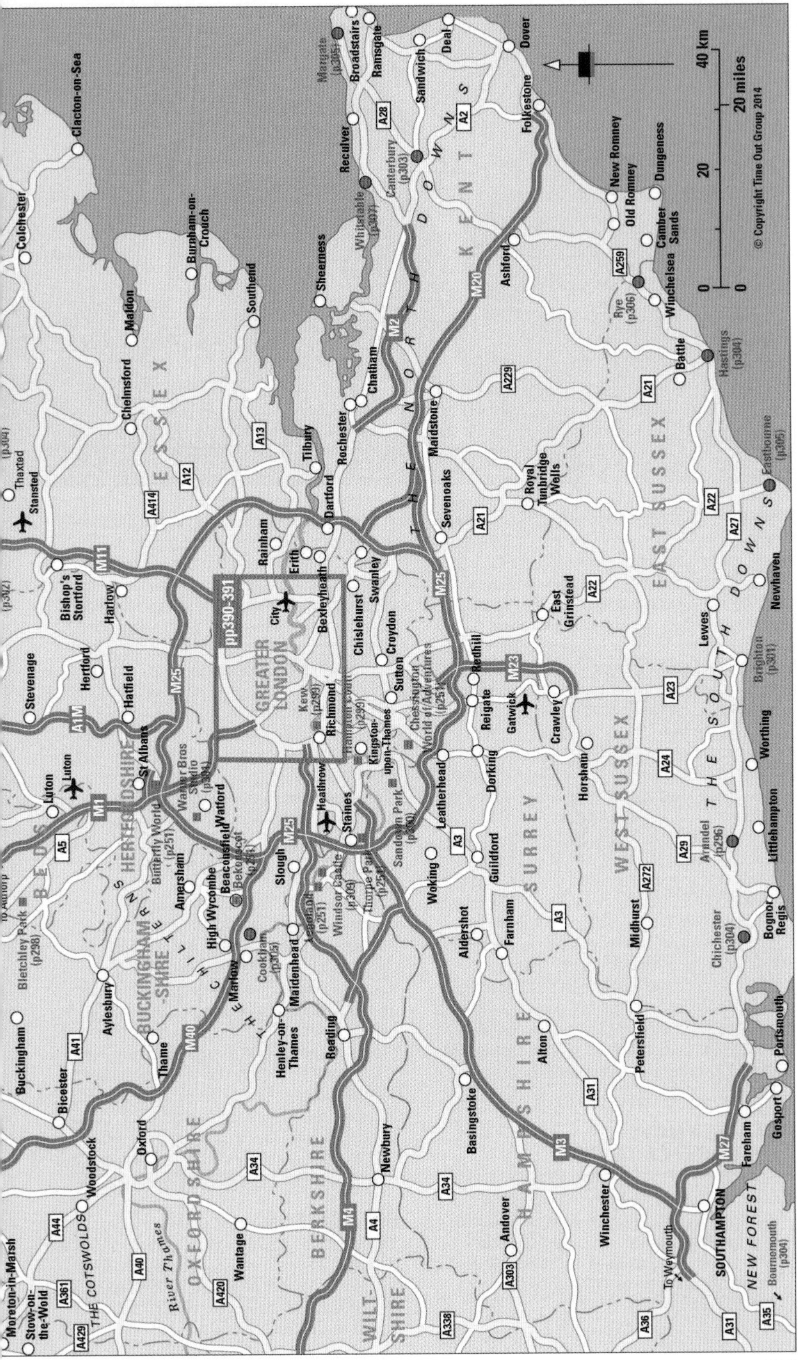
Clacton-on-Sea
Colchester
Burnham-on-Crouch
Maldon
Southend
Chelmsford
Sheerness
Whitstable (p307)
Canterbury (p303)
Reculver
Margate (p308)
Broadstairs
Ramsgate
Sandwich
Deal
Dover
Folkestone
New Romney
Old Romney
Dungeness
Camber Sands
Winchelsea
Rye (p306)
Hastings (p304)
Battle
Ashford
Maidstone
Chatham
Rochester
Tilbury
Dartford
Thaxted
Stansted
Bishop's Stortford
Harlow
Stevenage
Hertford
Hatfield
St Albans
Luton
Watford
Warner Bros Studio (p304)
Butterfly World (p251)
Amersham
Beaconsfield
Bekonscot (p251)
High Wycombe
Marlow
Cookham (p305)
Maidenhead
Slough
Windsor Castle (p309)
Legoland (p251)
Thorpe Park (p251)
Staines
Heathrow
Henley-on-Thames
Reading
Aylesbury
Thame
Buckingham
Bicester
Bletchley Park (p298)
Oxford
Woodstock
Wantage
Newbury
Basingstoke
Andover
Winchester
Southampton
Fareham
Gosport
Portsmouth
Petersfield
Alton
Farnham
Aldershot
Woking
Guildford
Leatherhead
Dorking
Reigate
Redhill
Gatwick
Crawley
Horsham
East Grinstead
Sevenoaks
Royal Tunbridge Wells
Lewes
Brighton (p301)
Newhaven
Eastbourne (p305)
Worthing
Littlehampton
Arundel (p296)
Bognor Regis
Chichester (p304)
Midhurst
Rainham
Erith
Bexleyheath
Swanley
Chislehurst
Croydon
Sutton
Kingston-upon-Thames
Hampton Court (p299)
Richmond
Kew (p299)
City
Chessington World of Adventures (p251)
Sandown Park (p300)
GREATER LONDON
pp390-391
Moreton-in-Marsh
Stow-on-the-Wold
THE COTSWOLDS
River Thames
To Weymouth
Bournemouth (p304)
NEW FOREST
ESSEX
KENT
THE NORTH DOWNS
THE SOUTH DOWNS
EAST SUSSEX
WEST SUSSEX
SURREY
HAMPSHIRE
BERKSHIRE
WILTSHIRE
OXFORDSHIRE
BUCKINGHAMSHIRE
HERTFORDSHIRE
BEDS
CHILTERN HILLS
M1
M11
M25
M2
M20
M23
M3
M4
M40
M27
A1M
A2
A28
A259
A229
A21
A22
A27
A23
A24
A29
A272
A3
A31
A34
A4
A303
A338
A36
A35
A12
A13
A414
A5
A41
A44
A40
A361
A420
A429
0
20
40 km
20 miles
© Copyright Time Out Group 2014

Bletchley Park.

more than 850 years. Aside from the occasional reversion to the throne, it's one of the longest inhabited aristocratic houses in England. In 1643, during the Civil War, the castle was besieged by General Waller (for Parliament) and the defences were partly demolished. Happily, many of the original features – such as the crenellated Norman keep, gatehouse and barbican, and the lower part of Bevis Tower – survived. The castle was almost completely rebuilt in the late 19th century.

The castle is worth exploring for its collection of paintings by Van Dyck, Gainsborough and Reynolds, among others, as well as its tapestries and furniture, and the gorgeous FitzAlan Chapel. Other treasures include a 14th-century two-handed sword, a jousting saddle (thought to be the only one in existence) and a silver icon of the Virgin and Child by Fabergé. A new formal garden was opened in 2008 as a tribute to Thomas Howard, 14th Earl of Arundel (1585-1646), known as 'the Collector'. An organic kitchen garden has been recreated, but the over-the-top decorations are based on what the Collector is thought to have enjoyed at his house in London. There's also a restaurant, café and gift shop. At weekends, outdoor events include medieval-style encampments with jousting and archery displays.

The castle is Arundel's main attraction, but the town has plenty of other delights, ranging from a disproportionate number of good eateries, wine bars, and independent shops, to the natural delights of the WWT Arundel Wetland Centre.

Arundel Castle

High Street, Arundel, West Sussex, BN18 9AB (01903 882173, www.arundelcastle.org). **Open** *Apr-Oct* 10am-5pm Tue-Sun; also Mon in Aug (last admission 4pm). **Admission** £9-£18; £9-£15.50 reductions; £41-£45 family.

BLETCHLEY PARK

The code-breaking centre – which famously broke the Nazi's Enigma cypher machine – remained shrouded in mystery until declassification after the Cold War. Bletchley's displays cover the story of its code-breakers and machines, and a new multimedia guide helps visitors to get the most from their visit; there's a special one for children too. There's also a computer museum (for which there's a separate charge), and the centre is surrounded by parkland. It's all easily accessible from London by rail (the journey north from Euston to Bletchley takes less than an hour, and the complex is close to Bletchley station).

Bletchley Park

The Mansion, Bletchley Park, Sherwood Drive, Bletchley, Milton Keynes, MK3 6EB (01908 640404, www.bletchleypark.org.uk). **Open** *Mar-Oct* 9.30am-5pm daily. *Nov-Feb* 9.30am-4pm aily. **Admission** £15; £9-£13 reductions.

IN THE KNOW CHILDREN'S TRIPS

Surefire winning trips for children around the London area include **Butterfly World**, **Thorpe Park** (home of Europe's fastest rollercoaster), **Legoland** and **Chessington World of Adventures** (with zoo). For all, *see p251.*

HAMPTON COURT PALACE

This spectacular palace, once owned by Henry VIII, is just a half-hour journey from central London. It was built in 1514 by Cardinal Wolsey, the high-flying Lord Chancellor, but Henry liked it so much he seized it for himself in 1528. For the next 200 years it was a focal point of English history: Elizabeth I was imprisoned in a tower by her jealous and fearful elder sister Mary I; Shakespeare gave his first performance to James I in 1604; and, after the Civil War, Oliver Cromwell was so besotted by the building he ditched his puritanical principles and moved in to enjoy its luxuries.

Centuries later, the rosy walls of the palace still dazzle. Its vast size can be daunting, so it's a good idea to take advantage of the guided tours. If you do decide to go it alone, start with Henry VIII's State Apartments, which include the Great Hall, noted for its beautiful stained-glass windows and elaborate religious tapestries; in the Haunted Gallery, the ghost of Catherine Howard – Henry's fifth wife, executed for adultery in 1542 – can reputedly be heard shrieking. The King's Apartments, added in 1689 by Wren, are notable for a splendid mural of Alexander the Great, painted by Antonio Verrio. The Queen's Apartments and Georgian Rooms feature similarly elaborate paintings, chandeliers and tapestries. The Tudor Kitchens are great fun, with their giant cauldrons, fake pies and blood-spattered walls.

More extraordinary sights await outside, where the exquisitely landscaped gardens contain topiary, Thames views, a reconstruction of a 16th-century heraldic garden and the famous Hampton Court maze.

★ Hampton Court Palace

East Molesey, Surrey KT8 9AU (0844 482 7777, www.hrp.org.uk). Hampton Court rail, or riverboat from Westminster or Richmond to Hampton Court Pier (Apr-Oct). **Open** *Palace* Apr-Oct 10am-6pm daily; Nov-Mar 10am-4.30pm daily. *Park* dawn-dusk daily. **Admission** *Palace, courtyard, cloister & maze* £18.15; £9.08-£15.40 reductions; £46.75 family; free under-5s. *Maze only* £4.40; £2.75 reductions. *Gardens only* Apr-Oct £5.72; £4.84 reductions; free under-15s. Nov-Mar free to all.

ROYAL BOTANIC GARDENS (KEW GARDENS)

Kew's lush, landscaped beauty represents the pinnacle of our national gardening obsession. From the early 1700s until 1840, when the gardens were given to the nation, these were the grounds for two fine royal residences – the White House and Richmond Lodge. Early resident Queen Caroline, who was wife of George II, was very fond of exotic plants brought back by botanists voyaging to far-flung parts of the world. In 1759, the renowned 'Capability' Brown was employed by George III to improve on the work of his predecessors here, William Kent

Hampton Court Palace.

Royal Botanic Gardens (Kew Gardens).

and Charles Bridgeman. Thus began the shape of the extraordinary garden that today attracts hundreds of thousands of visitors each year.

Covering half a square mile, Kew feels surprisingly big – pick up a map at the ticket office and follow the handy signs. Head straight for the 19th-century greenhouses, filled to the roof with plants – some of which have been here as long as the enormous glass structures themselves. The sultry Palm House holds tropical plants: palms, bamboo, tamarind, fig and mango trees, and fragrant hibiscus and frangipani. The Temperate House (closed for 2014) features *Pendiculata sanderina*, the Holy Grail for orchid hunters, with three-foot petals.

Also worth seeking out are the Princess of Wales Conservatory, divided into ten climate zones; the Marine Display, downstairs from the Palm House (it isn't always open, but when it is you can see the delightful seahorses); the lovely, quiet indoor pond of the Waterlily House (closed in winter); and the exquisite Victorian botanical drawings found in the fabulous Marianne North Gallery. The Xstrata Treetop Walkway has been a hugely popular addition to the gardens, giving a completely different woodland walk 60 feet up in the leaf canopy.

Though Kew's main appeal is the Gardens, the area rewards further exploration. Much of Kew has a rarified air, with leafy streets that lead you into a quaint world of teashops, tiny bookstores and gift shops, a sweet village green, ancient pubs and pleasant riverside paths.

► *Britain's smallest royal palace is also within the gardens: Kew Palace (www.hrp.org.uk/KewPalace; closed Oct-Mar; entry included in Gardens admission price) dates back to the 18th century.*

★ Royal Botanic Gardens (Kew Gardens)

Kew, Richmond, Surrey TW9 3AB (8332 5655, www.kew.org). Kew Gardens tube/rail, Kew Bridge rail or riverboat to Kew Pier. **Open** times vary; check website for details. **Admission** £16; £14 reductions; free under-17s.

SANDOWN PARK

Sandown is attractively sited in a natural amphitheatre and is the winner of several 'Racecourse of the Year' awards. Racing takes place all year round, with April's Gold Cup the highlight of the jumping season and the Coral-Eclipse Stakes in July the main feature of the flat programme – both pushing horses to the limit on Sandown's infamous hill finish. There's also a run of summer evening meetings, most also featuring live music. Families are welcome; a free creche is available for under-fives on Saturdays, and there's a dedicated picnic area during the summer.

Sandown Park

Sandown Park Racecourse, Esher Station Road, Esher, Surrey KT10 9AJ (01372 464348, www.sandown.co.uk). **Open** times vary according to racing schedule. **Admission** varies; check website for details.

WARNER BROS STUDIO TOUR

Warner Bros Studios in Leavesden, near Watford on the outskirts of London, is where all eight Harry Potter blockbusters were created. For followers of the bespectacled child-wizard, the Harry Potter Studio Tour offers a rare opportunity to learn just how JK Rowling's magical world was brought to life in the highest-grossing film series of all time. The Leavesden Studios, a former aircraft hangar 20 miles north-west of London, are spread over 150,000 square feet. The two- to three-hour walking tour takes in such iconic sets as Hagrid's hut and the Gryffindor common room, plus it offers the chance to check out the special effects, animatronics, props and costumes used in the films. One of the highlights for many fans will be the set of the Great Hall. First seen in *Harry Potter and the Philosopher's Stone* and designed by BAFTA-winning production designer Stuart Craig, the hall is 120 feet long and 40 feet wide with a solid stone floor and the original tables and benches where Daniel Radcliffe, Emma Watson et al once sat. Dumbledore's office will alsobe of interest to the fans – it was built for *Harry Potter and the Chamber of Secrets* and is home to the Sorting Hat, the Sword of Gryffindor and Albus Dumbledore's desk.

The Leavesden Studios are just off the A405, less than 3 miles from Watford town centre. Fast trains go direct from London Euston in less than 20 minutes; a shuttle bus to the studios runs from Watford Junction station.

Warner Bros Studio Tour
Leavesden Studios, near Watford (08450 840 900, www.wbstudiotour.co.uk). **Open** *Tours* 10am-4pm Mon-Fri; 9am-6.30pm Sat, Sun. **Admission** (tickets must be booked in advance) £30 adults, £22.50 children, £89 family.

Towns & Cities

BRIGHTON

With its bracing sea air and whiff of scandal, Brighton has been a favoured day trip for Londoners ever since the 19th century, when the pleasure-loving Prince Regent decamped to the southern coast to escape his father's watchful eye. Its Regency heyday left a rich legacy of stately seafront terraces and squares to rival those of Bath, in contrast to the elaborate domes and minarets of the **Royal Pavilion** (0300 029 0900, www.royal pavilion.org.uk) – the Prince's ornate and outlandish country farmhouse-turned-mock-Mughal palace.

Warner Bros Studio Tour.

Brighton.

This is a city that shuns the mainstream and embraces counterculture, with an ebullient gay scene and a packed arts calendar, culminating in the three-week arts extravaganza of the **Brighton Festival** (01273 709709, www.brightonfestival.org). It's also home to a laid-back but fiercely independent shopping scene, encompassing flea markets, art galleries, jewellery shops, delis and boutiques – perfect for a leisurely day of browsing and café-hopping. Further diversions are offered by Brighton Pier and all the traditional seaside resort trappings, not to mention seven miles of coastline – see them all from the Brighton Wheel (01273 722822 www.brightonwheel.com).

Brighton has a ridiculous number of dining possibilities for a town of its size. Easy-going all-day eateries include **Bill's** (the Depot, North Road, 01273 692894, www.bills-website.co.uk), an organic deli and restaurant; **Terre à Terre** (71 East Street, 01273 729051, www.terreaterre.co.uk), an inventive vegetarian restaurant; and any number of coffee shops, cafés and pubs. Also worth a look are the **Basketmakers Arms** (12 Gloucester Road, 01273 689006, www.thebasketmakersarms.co.uk), with its comprehensive selection of cask ales and whiskies; real ale specialist the **Hand in Hand** (33 Upper St James Street, 01273 699595), and the wonderful little **Lion & Lobster** (24 Sillwood Street, 01273 327299, www.thelionandlobster.co.uk).

CAMBRIDGE

Beautiful, intimidating Cambridge has the feel of an enclosed city, but pluck up the courage to pass through those imposing gates with their stern porters: within and behind the colleges are pretty green meadows and the idle River Cam, a place where time seems to have stopped back in the 18th century.

Each of the 31 Cambridge colleges is an independent entity, so entry times (and, for the more famous ones, prices) vary considerably: www.cam.ac.uk/colleges has the details. But Cambridge isn't only about the colleges. The **Fitzwilliam Museum** (01223 332900, www.fitzmuseum.cam.ac.uk) has a superb collection of paintings and sculpture (by Titian, Modigliani and Picasso), as well as ancient artefacts from Egypt, Greece and Rome, and it's just one of many museums in Cambridge. A short walk south, the 40 relaxing acres of the **Botanic Gardens** (01223 336265, www.botanic.cam.ac.uk) have 8,000 plants. One of the real treats during a visit to Cambridge is **Kettle's Yard** (01223 748100, www.kettlesyard.co.uk), once Tate curator Jim Ede's home and now a magnificently atmospheric collection of early 20th-century artists – Miró, Brancusi, Hepworth – arranged just as he left it.

Behind the main colleges, the beautiful meadows bordering the willow-shaded Cam are known as the Backs. Carpeted with crocuses in spring, the Backs are idyllic for summer strolling and punting. Punts can be hired; **Scudamore's Boatyard** (01223 359750, www.scudamores.com) is the largest operator.

The **Cambridge Chop House** (1 King's Parade, 01223 359506, www.cambscuisine.com) is a great come-one-come-all bistro opposite King's College, where you can tuck into British comfort food and draught ales. Nearby, the busy subterranean **Rainbow Café** (9A King's Parade, 01223 321551, www.rainbowcafe.co.uk) serves cheap, hearty vegetarian food. The legendary **Fitzbillies** (51-52 Trumpington Street, 01223 352500, www.fitzbillies.com), loved by generations of students, is still the place for tucking into a Chelsea bun or teatime treat.

Cambridge has many creaky old inns in which to settle down and enjoy one of the city's decent local ales. The **Eagle** on Benet Street (01223 505020) is the most famous, but there are many others, including the **Pickerel Inn** (30 Magdalene Street, 01223 355068) and, down a back alley a little off the beaten track, the sweet little **Free Press** (Prospect Row, 01223 368337, www.freepresspub.com).

Tourist Information Centre *Peas Hill, Cambridge, CB2 3AD (0871 226 8006, www.visitcambridge.org).* **Open** *Apr-Sept* 10am-5pm Mon-Sat; 11am-3pm Sun. *Oct-Mar* 10am-5pm Mon-Sat.

CANTERBURY

The home of the Church of England since St Augustine became the first archbishop of Canterbury in 597, this ancient city is rich in atmosphere, with many soaring spires and enchanting medieval streets. The town's busy tourist trade and large university provide a counterweight to all this history. Everything you want to see, do or buy in Canterbury is within walking distance. And that includes the seaside – at least, it does if you fancy a long (seven-mile) walk or cycle along the Crab & Winkle Way, a disused railway line to pretty Whitstable (*see p207*).

The main sight is glorious **Canterbury Cathedral** (01227 762862, www.canterbury-cathedral.org); inside, you'll find superb stained glass, stone vaulting and a vast Norman crypt. A plaque near the altar marks what is believed to be the spot where Archbishop Thomas Becket was murdered; the Trinity Chapel contains the site of the original shrine, plus the tombs of Henry IV and the Black Prince.

A pilgrimage to Becket's tomb was the focus of one of the earliest and finest long poems in English literature: Geoffrey Chaucer's *Canterbury Tales*, written in the 14th century. At the **Canterbury Tales exhibition** (St Margaret's Street, 01227 479227, www.canterburytales.org.uk), two minutes from the cathedral, visitors are given a device that they point at tableaux inspired by Chaucer's tales of

Canterbury Cathedral.

ART GALLERIES OUTSIDE LONDON

Contemporary buildings, unusual collections and local artists.

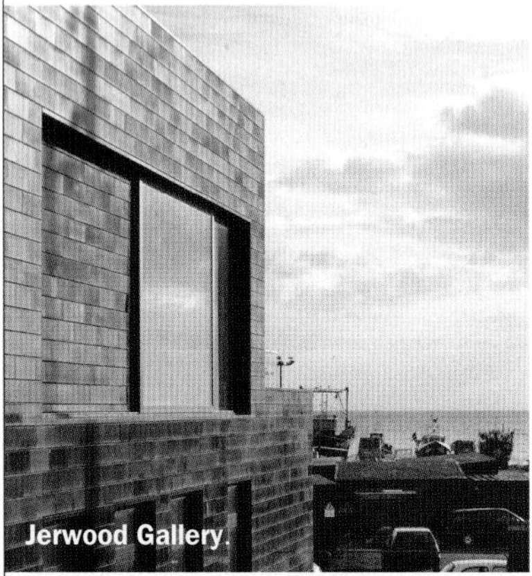

Jerwood Gallery.

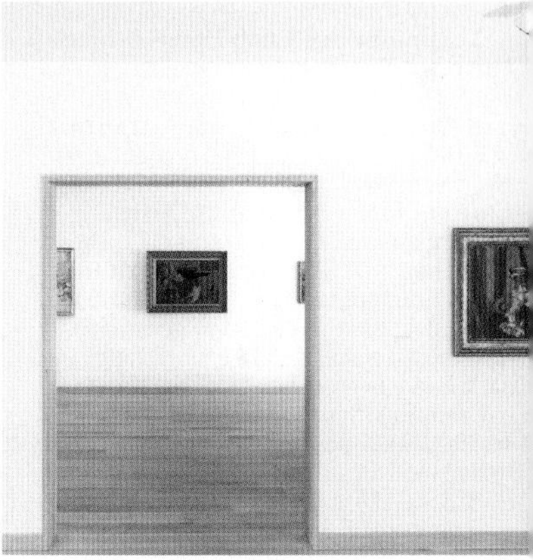

Fry Art Gallery, Saffron Walden
If the Towner (*see p205*) could be said to be the home of Eric Ravilious, the Fry is that of Ravilious's good friend Edward Bawden, who is represented here by almost 600 works of art. All of the work displayed here is by artists who were part of a creative community that flourished in and around the nearby village of Great Bardfield before and after World War II. It's a terrific collection, stuffed with prints, paintings, illustrations, wallpapers and decorative designs.
Castle Street, Saffron Walden, Essex CB10 1BD (01799 513779, www.fryartgallery.org). **Open** *Easter Sunday-end Oct* 2-5pm Tue, Thur, Fri; 11am- 5pm Sat; 2.15-5pm Sun. **Admission** free.

Jerwood Gallery, Hastings
Set on the shingle beach close to the fishing boats, the Jerwood Gallery's 2,000 black exterior tiles blend in with the tarred boards of the nearby fishermen's net huts. The aim of the gallery (opened in 2012) is to provide public access to the Jerwood Collection, a significant collection of modern British art. As well as figurative and abstract works from the period between World War I and the 1960s, it holds contemporary pieces by artists such as Maggi Hambling and Prunella Clough. Check the website for regular changing exhibitions. The café has an outside terrace with lovely views across the beach.
Rock-a-Nore Road, Hastings, East Sussex, TN34 3DW (01424 728377, www.jerwood gallery.org). **Open** 11am-5pm Tue-Fri; 11am-6pm Sat, Sun. **Admission** £8; £5.50 reductions.

Pallant House Gallery, Chichester
This lovely gallery has an outstanding collection of 20th-century British art, featuring works by Henry Moore, Peter Blake, Bridget Riley, Lucian Freud, Walter Sickert, Graham Sutherland and many more. Exciting contemporary art shows and installations and a gallery dedicated to printmakers add to the appeal. The extensive bookshop specialises in modern British art and has a large selection of rare out-of-print books. There's also a restaurant, Baskervilles.
9 North Pallant, Chichester, West Sussex, PO19 1TJ (01243 774557, www.pallant. org.uk). **Open** 10am-5pm Tue, Wed, Fri, Sat; 10am-8pm Thur; 11am-5pm Sun. **Admission** £9; free-£5.50 reductions. Half-price Tue.

Russell-Cotes Art Gallery & Museum, Bournemouth
The Russell-Cotes is housed in one of Bournemouth's few remaining Victorian villas – an eccentric-looking turret-topped affair, filled to the rafters with treasures. A rare survivor as the residence of a Victorian private collector, planned and perpetuated as a permanent art museum, it's as utterly

absorbing as its exterior would suggest, and packed with thousands of curios, artefacts and artworks from around the globe – including more than 1,000 oil paintings and an awful lot of female nudes. It's perched on the clifftops, and the café and gardens have great views.
Russell-Cotes Road, East Cliff, Bournemouth, Dorset BH1 3AA (01202 451858, russell-cotes.bournemouth.gov.uk). **Open** 10am-5pm Tue-Sun. **Admission** *Apr-Sept* £5; free-£4 reductions; £15 family. *Oct-Mar* free.

Stanley Spencer Gallery, Cookham
Sir Stanley Spencer lived in Cookham for much of his life, and made it the subject of many of his paintings and drawings, some 100 of which are gathered here. While the big guns – the likes of *The Resurrection, Cookham* and *Shipbuilding on the Clyde* – are housed in galleries such as the Tate and Imperial War Museum, there's a very impressive collection of work on display. It's also a rare delight to be able to explore the relationship between an artist and his surroundings. The gallery's website details an hour-long ramble you can take around the village that passes many of the subjects and locations of Spencer's paintings.
High Street, Cookham, Berkshire SL6 9SJ (01628 471885, www.stanleyspencer.org.uk). **Open** Apr-Oct 10.30am-5.30pm daily. Nov-Mar 11am-4.30pm Thur-Sun. **Admission** £5; free-£4 reductions.

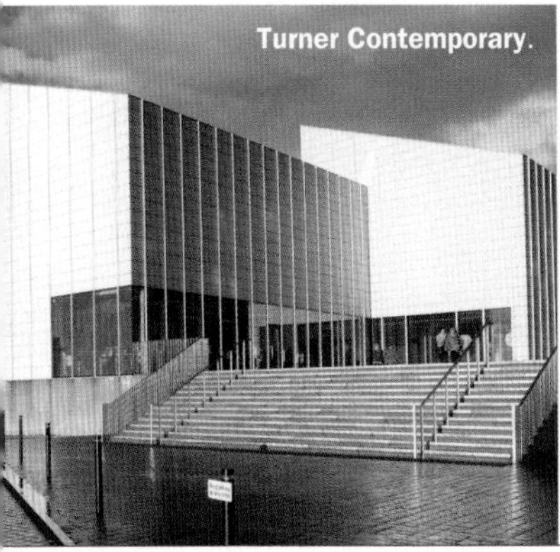
Turner Contemporary.

Towner Gallery.

Towner Gallery, Eastbourne
The town's new £8.5 million Rick Mather-designed gallery became home to more than 4,000 works of art in 2009, with pieces by Vanessa Bell, Tacita Dean, Olafur Eliasson, Anya Gallaccio, Picasso, Wolfgang Tillmans and Eric Ravilious. Ravilious is the name anyone usually associated with the Towner, and with good reason; the artist's work is a key element of the collection, and includes everything from woodcuts to the posters he designed for London Transport and the ceramics he created for Wedgwood.
Devonshire Park, College Road, Eastbourne, East Sussex N21 4JJ (01323 434660, www.townereastbourne.org.uk). **Open** 10am-5pm Tue-Sun. **Admission** free.

Turner Contemporary, Margate
The dramatic silver structure of the Turner Contemporary has a lot of weight on its shoulders: the fortunes of Margate are inextricably tied to its success. The £17 million project opened in April 2011 with an exhibition that used one of JMW Turner's paintings as the centrepiece for new commissions by Daniel Buren, Russell Crotty, Ellen Harvey and Conrad Shawcross, as well as works by Teresita Fernandez and Douglas Gordon, and the programme has remained consistently interesting. Further pluses are the café and the sweeping views.
The Rendezvous, Margate, Kent CT9 1HG (01843 233000, www.turnercontemporary.org). **Open** 10am-6pm Tue-Sun. **Admission** free.

a knight, a miller, a wife of Bath, and others, enabling them to hear the rollicking stories that Chaucer brought to vivid life.

Other places of interest are the **Beaney House of Art & Knowledge** (High Street, 01227 378100, www.thebeaney.co.uk), a monument to high Victorian values and a notable art museum, and **Eastbridge Hospital** (25 High Street, 01227 471688, www.eastbridge hospital.org.uk) – founded to provide shelter for pilgrims – where visitors can admire the undercroft with its Gothic arches, the Chantry Chapel, the Pilgrims' Chapel and the refectory with an enchanting early 13th-century mural showing Christ in Majesty. There's also the **Roman Museum** (Butchery Lane, 01227 785575, www.canterbury.co.uk/museums) and the ruins of **St Augustine's Abbey** (Longport, 01227 767345, www.english-heritage.org.uk).

Canterbury has plenty of eating and drinking options: the **Goods Shed** (Station Road West, 01227 459153, www.thegoodsshed.co.uk) occupies a lofty Victorian building, which was formerly a railway freight store. Only ingredients on sale in the farmers' market below are used in the restaurant.

Pub-wise, most of the better ones are owned by local brewery Shepherd Neame. The best for real ales is the **Unicorn** (61 St Dunstan's Street, 01227 463187, www.unicorninn.com), which also has a great pub garden for summer drinking. Built in 1370, the **Parrot** (1-9 Church Lane, St Radigands, 01227 454170, www.theparrotcanterbury.com) is the oldest pub in Canterbury and serves a good choice of ales and cider in a charming setting. The refurbished **White Hart** (Worthgate Place, 01227 765091, www.whitehartcanterbury.co.uk) is also a good bet.

Tourist Information Centre *18 High Street, Canterbury, CT1 2RA (01227 378100, www.canterbury.co.uk).* **Open** 9am-5pm Mon-Wed, Fri, Sat; 9am-7pm Thur; 10am-5pm Sun.

RYE

Almost too quaint to be true, Rye is a photogenic jumble of Norman, Tudor and Georgian architecture perched on one of the area's few hills. The well-preserved, attractive centre is a joy to walk around, with lots of shops, pubs and cafés, plus a fetching harbour area. Although much of the place is given over to genteel tourism, it remains a working town, with enough real stores and down-to-earth pubs – and a commercial fishing fleet – to prevent there being a theme park atmosphere. It's easy to get to by rail (the walk from the station to the heart of town takes about a minute).

The place has history galore – it became a Cinque port in the 13th century but declined in importance as access to the sea changed over the years; by the 18th century smuggling played a big role in the town's economy. Soak up the atmosphere and architecture by investigating cobbled streets such as West

Mermaid Inn, Rye.

Street, Mermaid Street and also Church Square. From here there are wonderful views, especially if you make the climb to the top of 900-year-old St Mary's church.

Henry James lived in Rye for years, at **Lamb House** on West Street; later residents include novelists EF Benson and Rumer Godden. It's owned by the National Trust and has limited opening times, but these do include Saturday afternoons, late March-late October (see www.nationaltrust.org.uk for details).

Finding somewhere to eat is easy – the streets are lined with decent options, from cheap and cheerful eateries such as **Anatolian Kebab** (16A Landgate, 01797 226868), **Kettle o' Fish** (25 Wish Street, 01797 223684) and **Simply Italian** (the Strand, 01797 226024) to destination restaurants such as the **Fish Café** (17 Tower Street, 01797 222226, www.thefishcafe.com), the **George** (98 High Street, 01797 222114, www.thegeorgeinrye.com) or the **Landgate Bistro** (5-6 Landgate, 01797 222829, www.landgatebistro.co.uk) – and you're never far away from a teashop. There's a good array of pubs too: have a drink in the **Mermaid Inn** (Mermaid Street, 01797 223065, www.mermaidinn.com) for its olde worlde charm and collection of signed photographs, or soak up the view in the beer garden at the **Ypres Castle Inn** (Gun Gardens, 01797 223248, www.yprescastleinn.co.uk) with a pint of Timothy Taylor.

East from Rye lies other-worldly **Romney Marsh**, flat as a pancake and laced with cycle paths. Bikes can be hired from **Rye Hire** (1 Cyprus Place, Rye, 01797 223033, www.ryehire.co.uk) and are an ideal way to explore the lonely medieval churches that dot the level marsh, or to access the vast sandy beach of Camber Sands.

Tourist Information Centre *4-5 Lion Street, Rye, TN31 7LB (01797 229049, www.visitrye.co.uk).* **Open** *Apr-Sept* 10am-5pm daily. *Oct-Mar* 10am-4pm daily.

WHITSTABLE

The image of Whitstable as a weekend bolt hole for London's middle classes is not undeserved, but this lovely old coastal town has enough character to withstand total gentrification – and it's still very much a working fishing town. To learn about the town's history, pop into **Whitstable Museum** (Oxford Street, 01227 276998, www.canterbury.co.uk). Exhibits include a display devoted to the town's most famous fan, Peter Cushing, who bought a seafront house here in 1959. It includes film stills, props and examples of the actor-turned-painter's art.

Whitstable has smartened itself up for visitors – for example, many of the old fishermen's huts on the seafront have been

Whitstable.

fashioned into holiday retreats – but it doesn't pander. Much of the town looks as it always has, from the Island Wall with its mid 19th-century cottages to the little alleys once used by fishermen to cut through the town to the sea (Squeeze Gut Alley is so narrow that many have to walk through it sideways). The main streets, running north from Oxford Street to High Street to Harbour Street, all lead towards the seafront and harbour. Here you'll find a selection of small shops, galleries and cafés. Look out for **Oxford Street Books** (01227 281727, www.oxfordstreetbooks.com), where every nook and cranny is stuffed with second-hand books, and the **Cheese Box** (60 Harbour Street, 01227 273711, www.thecheesebox.co.uk), a fantastic deli.

North from Harbour Street to Tower Hill, Whitstable Castle sits on the border of Whitstable and the suburb of Tankerton. The recently restored castle and grounds is a good place to take in some sea air. If you climb to the top of the hill you'll come out opposite **Tower Hill Tea Gardens**, an idyllic and often quiet spot with sea views.

Running parallel to the shingle beach is Island Row, lined with pretty cottages; walk east to reach the harbour. Low tide reveals a natural spit of shingle on a clay bank, known as the Street. You can walk it for about half a mile, on the last of the town's land to the north, the rest having been eroded and swallowed by the sea. Keep an eye on the rising tide, though.

Whitstable has been praised for its oysters since Juvenal shucked a few here a couple of thousand years ago. These days, try them at the **Whitstable Oyster Festival** (www.whitstableoysterfestival.co.uk, July-Aug), or at the **Crab & Winkle** (South Quay, 01227 779377, www.crabandwinklerestaurant.co.uk), the **Pearson's Arms** (Sea Wall, 01227 773133, www.pearsonsarmsbyrichardphillips.co.uk), **English's of Whitstable** (48 Harbour Street, 01227 273373, www.thetapas.co.uk) or **Wheelers Oyster Bar** (8 High Street, 01227 273311, www.wheelersoysterbar.com) – or you could push the boat out at the

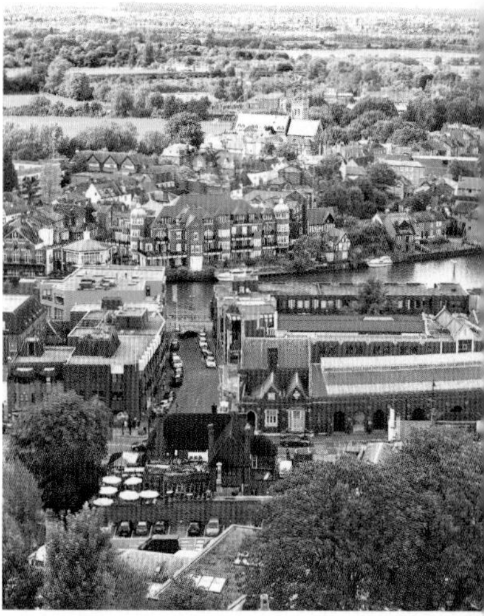

WALKS

Enjoy the outdoors on foot.

South-east England is blessed with many long-distance paths, short sections of which can often be walked in a day out from London: among the best are the Greensand Way (Surrey and Kent), the North Downs Way (Surrey and Kent) and the South Downs Way (Hampshire, Sussex). There's also the Thames Path, which runs from source to sea, taking in the Cotswolds, Oxford, Henley, Windsor and central London, to the Thames Barrier. More information can be found at www.nationaltrail.co.uk.

For many more walks from London, all using public transport, buy a copy of *Time Out Country Walks*, volumes I and II, or see www.timeout.com (country walks outside London) or www.walkingclub.org.uk.

Windsor.

Whitstable Oyster Fishery Company (Royal Native Oyster Stores, Horsebridge, 01227 276856, www.whitstableoystercompany.com), a handsome building in a prime position on the beach. There are plenty of takeaway options too – try the fish market on South Quay (01227 771245; there are barbecues here in summer). For fish and chips, **VC Jones** is a favourite (25 Harbour Street, 01227 272703, www.vcjones.co.uk).

WINDSOR

The direct line from Waterloo station to Windsor & Eton Riverside (taking just under an hour) offers pleasing views of Windsor Castle as you roll into town. The castle (Her Majesty is in residence if the royal standard is flying) is immediately before you, as is the start of the 4,800-acre Great Park's Long Walk – a three-mile stretch of surfaced path that leads from the castle to the Copper Horse statue atop Snow Hill depicting George III. Windsor town centre offers high-class shopping at a less frenetic pace than London, while Eton College and the River Thames are further attractions.

The sights at **Windsor Castle** (01753 831118, www.royalcollection.org.uk) – the Queen's weekend pad and the world's biggest occupied castle – run from works by Rembrandt, Rubens, Gainsborough and Van Dyck, to Edward Lutyens's elaborate Queen Mary's Dolls' House, complete with flushing loos. Or you may prefer to leave the changing guards, castle tours and souvenir shops behind, and set off on a walk through the Great Park.

Depending on the timing of your walk, you might stop at the lovely **Two Brewers** (34 Park Street, SL4 1LB, 01753 855426, www.twobrewerswindsor.co.uk) first. Get back on track and the greatest joy of the Long Walk promenade soon becomes clear. You don't need a map. Simply relax and let your mind wander as you march ahead admiring gnarly old oak trees and – a little further along – the resident red deer.

Should you fancy straying from the path, there are ample, well-signposted diversions. One of the most fascinating is **Frogmore House and the Royal Mausoleum** (final resting place of Prince Albert and Queen Victoria, www.royalcollection.org.uk), set in the private Home Park. You'll have to plan ahead to visit it as the former royal residence is only open to the public for two weekends a year – typically August bank holiday weekend and another in either May or June. The landscaped gardens are vast and impressive, with tulip trees and giant redwoods among the many historic plantings.

Stay away from such detours and your walking efforts will be rewarded as you ascend Snow Hill for stunning views of the castle and beyond (the arch of Wembley Stadium can be seen on a clear day).

For lunch, however, you'll need to take a left as you face the Copper Horse and walk towards Bishops Gate and the cosy **Fox & Hounds** (Bishops Gate, Englefield Green, Surrey, 01784 433098, www.thefoxandhoundsrestaurant.co.uk). Warming in winter and spot on for summer alfresco drinking, this atmospheric pub is a popular local choice.

In Focus

History

The making of modern London.

Over the 2,000 years since London began life as a small trading station by a broad, marshy river, the city has faced plague and invasion, fire and war, religious turbulence and financial turmoil. There have been natural disasters and acts of terrorism, all borne by Londoners with a characteristic upbeat pessimism until the moment arrives when the frenzy of commerce can begin again. More than anything, this city's past is a tale of resilience.

In the City, Wren churches – built from the ruins of the Great Fire – have walls still blackened by the German incendiary bombs dropped during the Blitz, and shrapnel scars around Cleopatra's Needle beside the Thames remain from a World War I biplane raid. A fragment of glass, deeply embedded in a wall at the Old Bailey, tells of an IRA terrorist attack back in 1973, while 52 austere steel columns in Hyde Park commemorate those killed by suicide bombers in the summer of 2005.

Evidence of strife is everywhere in this city, and the true Londoner will cheerfully insist there's more and worse to come. Just don't bet against them handling their portion of strife with aplomb.

LATIN LESSONS

The city's origins are hardly grand. Celtic tribes lived in scattered communities along the banks of the Thames before the Romans arrived in Britain – creating what archaeologists describe as a 'ritual landscape': a dispersed region of monuments (*see p317* **London under London**) – but there's no evidence of a settlement that we might recognise as the seed of the future metropolis before the invasion of the Emperor Claudius in AD 43. During his conquest, the Romans forded the Thames at its shallowest point (probably near today's London Bridge) and, later, built a timber bridge there. A settlement developed on the north side of this crossing.

Over the next two centuries, the Romans built roads, towns and forts in the area. Progress was halted in AD 61 when Boudicca, the widow of an East Anglian chieftain, rebelled against the imperial forces who had seized her land, flogged her and raped her daughters. She led the Iceni in a revolt, destroying the Roman colony at Colchester before marching on London. The Romans were massacred and their settlement razed.

After order was restored, London was rebuilt; around AD 200, a two-mile-long, 18-foot-high wall was put up around it. Chunks of the wall survive today; the early names of the original gates – Ludgate, Bishopsgate, Newgate, and Aldgate – are preserved on the map of the modern city, with the street known as London Wall tracing part of its original course. But through to the fourth century, racked by invasions and internal strife, the Roman Empire was clearly in decline. In 410, the last troops were withdrawn, and London became a ghost town.

INTO THE DARK

During the fifth and sixth centuries, history gives way to legend. The Saxons crossed the North Sea; apparently avoiding the ruins of London, they built farmsteads and trading posts outside the city walls. Pope Gregory sent Augustine to convert the English to Christianity in 596; Mellitus, one of his missionaries, was appointed the first Bishop of London, founding a cathedral dedicated to St Paul inside the old city walls in 604.

From this period, the history of London is one of expansion. Writing in 731, monk and writer the Venerable Bede described 'Lundenwic' as 'the mart of many nations resorting to it by land and sea'. Yet the city faced a new danger during the ninth century: the Vikings. The city was ransacked in 841 and again in 851, when Danish raiders returned with 350 ships. It was not until 886 that King Alfred of Wessex, Alfred the Great, regained the city, re-establishing London as a major trading centre.

Throughout the tenth century the city prospered. Churches were built, parishes established and markets set up. However, the 11th century brought more harassment from the Vikings, and the English were forced to accept a Danish king, Cnut (Canute, 1016-35), during whose reign London replaced Winchester as the capital of England.

After a brief spell under Danish rule, the country reverted to English control in 1042 under Edward the Confessor, who devoted himself to building England's grandest church two miles west of the City on an island in the river marshes at Thorney: 'the West Minster' (Westminster Abbey). Just a week after the consecration, he died. London now had two hubs: Westminster, centre of the royal court, government and law; and the City of London, centre of commerce.

On Edward's death, foreigners took over. Duke William of Normandy was crowned king on Christmas Day 1066, having defeated Edward's brother-in-law Harold at the Battle of Hastings. The pragmatic Norman resolved to win over the City merchants by negotiation rather than force, and in 1067 granted the burgesses and the Bishop of London a charter – still available to researchers in the London Metropolitan Archives – that acknowledged their rights and independence in return for taxes. He also ordered strongholds to be built at the city wall 'against the fickleness of the vast and fierce population', including the White Tower (the tallest building in the Tower of London) and the now-lost Baynard's Castle that stood at Blackfriars.

PARLIAMENT AND RIGHTS

In 1295, the Model Parliament, held at Westminster Hall by Edward I and attended by barons, clergy and representatives of

Boudicca leading an uprising against the Romans.

knights and burgesses, agreed the principles of English government. The first step towards establishing personal rights and political liberty, not to mention curbing the power of the king, had already been taken in 1215 with the signing of the Magna Carta by King John. Then, in the 14th century, subsequent assemblies gave rise to the House of Lords and the House of Commons. During the 12th and 13th centuries, the king and his court travelled the kingdom, but the Palace of Westminster was now the permanent seat of law and government; noblemen and bishops began to build palatial houses along the Strand from the City to Westminster, with gardens stretching down to the river.

Relations between the monarch and the City were never easy. Londoners guarded their privileges, and resisted attempts by kings to squeeze money out of them to finance wars and construction projects. Subsequent kings were forced to turn to Jewish and Lombard moneylenders, but the City merchants were intolerant of foreigners too.

The self-regulation privileges granted to the City merchants under Norman kings were extended by the monarchs who followed – in return for finance. In 1191, the City of London was recognised by Richard I as a self-governing community; six years later, it won control of the Thames. In 1215 King John confirmed the city's right 'to elect every year a mayor', a position of authority with power over the sheriff and the Bishop of London. A month later, the mayor joined the rebel barons in signing the Magna Carta.

Over the next two centuries, the power and influence of the trade and craft guilds (later known as the City Livery Companies) increased as dealings with Europe grew. The City's markets drew produce from miles around: livestock at Smithfield, fish at Billingsgate, poultry at Leadenhall. The street markets ('cheaps') around Westcheap (now Cheapside) and Eastcheap were crammed with a variety of goods. The population within the city walls grew from about 18,000 in 1100 to well over 50,000 in the 1340s.

WAKE UP AND SMELL THE ISSUE

Lack of hygiene became a serious problem. Water was provided in cisterns, but the supply, more or less direct from the Thames, was limited and polluted. The street of Houndsditch was so named because Londoners threw their dead animals into the furrow there; in the streets around Smithfield (the Shambles), butchers dumped entrails into the gutters. These conditions helped to foster the greatest catastrophe of the Middle Ages: the Black Death of 1348 and 1349, which killed about 30 per cent of England's population. The plague came to London from Europe, carried by rats on ships, and was to recur in London several times during the next three centuries.

Disease left the harvest short-handed, causing unrest among the peasants whose labour was in such demand. Then a poll tax of a shilling a head was imposed. It was all too much: the Peasants' Revolt began in 1381. Thousands marched on London, led by Jack Straw from Essex and Wat Tyler from Kent; the Archbishop of Canterbury was murdered and hundreds of prisoners were set free. After meeting the Essexmen near Mile End, the 14-year-old Richard II rode out to the rioters at Smithfield and spoke with Tyler. During their discussion, Tyler was fatally stabbed by the Lord Mayor; the revolt collapsed and the ringleaders were hanged. But no more poll taxes were imposed.

ROSES, WIVES AND THE ROYAL DOCKS

Its growth spurred by the discovery of America and the opening of ocean routes to Africa and the Orient, London became one of Europe's largest cities under the Tudors (1485-1603). The first Tudor monarch, Henry VII, had ended the Wars of the Roses by might, defeating Richard III at the Battle of Bosworth and, by policy, marrying Elizabeth of York, a daughter of his rivals. By the time his son took the throne, the Tudor dynasty was firmly established. But progress under Henry VIII was not without its hiccups. His first marriage to Catherine of Aragon failed to produce an heir, so in 1527 he determined the union should be annulled. When the Pope refused to co-operate, Henry defied the Catholic Church, demanding to be recognised as Supreme Head of the Church in England and ordering the execution of anyone who opposed the plan (including Sir Thomas More, his otherwise loyal chancellor). The subsequent dissolution of the monasteries transformed the face of the medieval city.

When not transforming the politico-religious landscape, Henry found time to develop a professional navy, founding the Royal Dockyards at Woolwich in 1512. He also established palaces at Hampton Court and Whitehall, and built a residence at St James's Palace. Much of the land he annexed for hunting later became today's Royal Parks, among them Greenwich Park, Hyde Park and Regent's Park.

RENAISSANCE MEANS REBIRTH

Elizabeth I's reign (1558-1603) saw the founding of the Royal Exchange in 1566, which enabled London to emerge as Europe's commercial hub. Merchant venturers and the first joint-stock companies established new trading enterprises, as pioneering seafarers Francis Drake, Walter Raleigh and Richard Hawkins sailed to the New World. As trade grew, so did London: it was home to some 200,000 people in 1600, many living in dirty, overcrowded conditions. The most complete picture of Tudor London is given in John Stow's *Survey of London* (1598), a fascinating first-hand account by a diligent Londoner whose monument stands in the church of St Andrew Undershaft.

These were the glory days of English drama. The Rose (1587) and the Globe (1599, now recreated; *see p37*) theatres were erected at Bankside, providing homes for the works of popular playwrights William Shakespeare and Christopher Marlowe. Deemed officially 'a naughty place' by royal proclamation, 16th-century Bankside was a vibrant mix of entertainment and 'sport' (bear-baiting, cock-fighting), drinking and whoring – and all within easy reach of the City, which had outlawed theatres in 1575.

In 1605, two years after the Tudor dynasty ended with Elizabeth's death, her Stuart successor, James I, escaped assassination on 5 November, when Guy Fawkes was found underneath the Palace of Westminster. Commemorated with fireworks each year as Bonfire Night, the Gunpowder Plot had been hatched in protest at the failure to improve conditions for the persecuted Catholics, but only resulted in an intensification of anti-papist sentiment. James I is more positively remembered for hiring Inigo Jones to design court masques (musical dramas) and London's first influential examples of the classical Renaissance architectural style: the Queen's House (1616; *see p216*), the Banqueting House (1619; *see p75*) and St Paul's Covent Garden (1631; *see p140*).

LONDON UNDER LONDON

Redevelopment and railworks have uncovered ancient artefacts.

Just as many university archaeology departments are being scaled back or amalgamated due to government cuts, the archaeological picture of London is becoming far, far richer.

The key driver of this is Crossrail (*see p21*). Driven east–west under London, this extraordinary civil engineering effort has uncovered so much historic material that an exhibition was mounted at their offices in 2014: Roman skulls, a medieval plague pit and even Bronze Age remains have been recovered before the vast boring machines got to work. The whole story is at www.crossrail.co.uk/sustainability/archaeology/.

Temple of Mithras.

The City's voracious appetite for new buildings has also played its part. The development of a new HQ for Bloomberg has uncovered what some have called 'the Pompeii of the North'. A sewage-bearing lost river called the Walbrook would have to play the role of the Grand Canal in that analogy, but the recovery of some 10,000 small finds is impressive. It was here that the Roman Temple of Mithras was discovered, in a blaze of publicity, back in 1954. Builders had stumbled across the head of a young Roman god; archaeologists then uncovered a temple, dating from the AD 240s, to the bull cult of Mithras. What was left of it was plonked, in public view, on top of a car park. Now an original column has been found *in situ*, which will help a more careful reconstruction of the temple for the public.

Not far to the north-east, a piece of first-century AD sculpture – so well preserved it was originally considered a Victorian imitation – was found by Museum of London archaeologists in late 2013 on the site of a new hotel. The 'Eagle of the Minories' (pictured) is so detailed you can see the snake in its claw.

And our knowledge is reaching back far further than the Romans. In 2010, a series of 6,000-year-old stakes were discovered on the foreshore at Vauxhall. Initially thought to be a pier or the end of a bridge, it is now suggested they are a deposition platform – a sacred site from which objects of great value could be sacrificed to the river. Certainly an extraordinary number of objects – some as fine as the British Museum's Battersea Shield – have been recovered from the Thames. Along with ancient manmade mounds from Greenwich to Westminster, the whole of London is beginning to be recognised as a prehistoric ritual landscape, an area of artificial monuments and natural landmarks choreographed across a vast area.

Fleeing the Great Fire of London, 1666.

ROYALISTS AND ROUNDHEADS

Charles I succeeded his father in 1625, but gradually fell out of favour with the City of London and an increasingly independent-minded Parliament over taxation. The country slid into civil war (1642-49), the supporters of Parliament (the Roundheads, led by Puritan Oliver Cromwell) opposing the supporters of the King (the Royalists).

Both sides knew that control of the country's major city and port was vital for victory, and London's sympathies were with the Parliamentarians. In 1642, 24,000 citizens assembled at Turnham Green to face Charles's army, but the King withdrew. The move proved fatal: Charles never threatened the capital again, and was eventually found guilty of treason. Taken to the Banqueting House in Whitehall on 30 January 1649, he declared himself a 'martyr of the people' and was beheaded. A commemorative wreath is still laid at the site of the execution on the last Sunday in January each year.

For the next decade, the country was ruled as a Commonwealth by Cromwell. But his son Richard's subsequent rule was brief: due to the Puritans closing theatres and banning Christmas (a Catholic superstition), the Restoration of the exiled Charles II in 1660 was greeted with great rejoicing. The Stuart king had Cromwell exhumed from Westminster Abbey, and his body was hung in chains at Tyburn (near modern-day Marble Arch). His severed head was displayed on a pole outside the abbey until 1685.

PLAGUE, FIRE AND REVOLUTION

The year 1665 saw the most serious outbreak of bubonic plague since the Black Death, killing nearly 100,000. Then, on 2 September 1666, a second disaster struck. The fire that spread from a carelessly tended oven in Thomas Farriner's baking shop on Pudding Lane raged for three days and consumed four-fifths of the City.

The Great Fire at least allowed planners the chance to rebuild London as a modern city. Many blueprints were considered, but Londoners were so impatient to get on with business that the City was reconstructed largely on its medieval street plan (albeit in brick and stone rather than wood). The prolific Sir Christopher Wren oversaw work on 51 of the 54 rebuilt churches. Among them was his masterpiece: the new St Paul's, completed in 1710 and effectively the world's first Protestant cathedral.

In the wake of the Great Fire, many well-to-do City dwellers moved to new residential developments west of the old quarters, an area subsequently known as the West End. In the City, the Royal Exchange was rebuilt, but merchants increasingly used the new coffeehouses to exchange news. With the expansion of the joint-stock companies and the chance to invest capital, the City emerged as a centre not of manufacturing but of finance. Even at this early stage, economic instability was common: the 1720 financial disaster known as the South Sea Bubble ruined even Sir Isaac Newton.

Anti-Catholic feeling still ran high. The accession in 1685 of Catholic James II aroused such fears of a return to papistry that a Dutch Protestant, William of Orange, was invited to take the throne with his wife, Mary Stuart (James's daughter). James fled to France in 1688 in what became known (by its beneficiaries) as the 'Glorious Revolution'. It was during William's reign that the Bank of England was founded, initially to finance the King's religious wars with France.

CREATION OF THE PRIME MINISTER

In 1714, the throne passed to George, the Hanover-born great-grandson of James I. The German-speaking king (he never learned English) became the first of four Georges in the Hanoverian line.

During George I's reign (1714-27), and for several years after, Sir Robert Walpole's Whig party monopolised Parliament. Their opponents, the Tories, supported the Stuarts and had opposed the exclusion of the Catholic James II. On the king's behalf, Walpole chaired a group of ministers (the forerunner of today's Cabinet), becoming, in effect, Britain's first prime minister. Walpole was presented with 10 Downing Street (built by Sir George Downing) as a residence; it remains the official prime ministerial home.

During the 18th century, London grew with astonishing speed. New squares and terraced streets spread across Soho, Bloomsbury, Mayfair and Marylebone, as wealthy landowners and speculative developers cashed in on the new demand for leasehold properties. South London also became more accessible with the opening of the first new bridges for centuries: Westminster Bridge (opened 1750) and Blackfriars Bridge (completed 1769) joined London Bridge, previously the only Thames crossing.

GIN-SOAKED POOR, NASTY RICH

In London's older districts, people were living in terrible squalor. Some of the most notorious slums were located around Fleet Street and St Giles's (north of Covent Garden), only a short distance from fashionable residences. To make matters worse, gin ('mother's ruin') was readily available at low prices; many poor Londoners drank excessive amounts in an attempt to escape the horrors of daily life. The well-off seemed complacent, amusing themselves at the popular Ranelagh and Vauxhall Pleasure Gardens or with trips to mock the patients at the Bedlam lunatic asylum. Public executions at Tyburn were popular events in the social calendar; it's said that 200,000 people gathered to see the execution (after he had escaped from prison four times) of the folk-hero thief Jack Sheppard in 1724.

The outrageous imbalance in the distribution of wealth encouraged crime, and there were daring daytime robberies in the West End. Reformers were few, though there were exceptions. Henry Fielding, author of the picaresque novel *Tom Jones*, was also an enlightened magistrate at Bow Street Court. In 1751, he and his blind half-brother John set up a volunteer force of 'thief-takers' to back up the often ineffective efforts of the parish constables and watchmen who were, until then, the city's only law-keepers. This crime-busting group of proto-cops, known as the Bow Street Runners, were the earliest incarnation of today's Metropolitan Police (established in 1829).

Meanwhile, five major new hospitals were founded by private philanthropists. St Thomas's and St Bartholomew's were long-established monastic institutions for the care of the sick, but Westminster (1720), Guy's (1725), St George's (1734), London (1740) and the Middlesex (1745) went on to become world-famous teaching hospitals. Thomas Coram's Foundling Hospital (*see p151*) was another remarkable achievement.

INDUSTRY AND CAPITAL GROWTH

It wasn't just the indigenous population of London that was on the rise. Country folk, whose common land had been replaced by sheep enclosures, were faced with a choice between starvation wages or unemployment, and so drifted into the towns. Just outside the old city walls, the East End drew many poor immigrant labourers to build the docks towards the end of the 18th century. London's total population had grown to one million by 1801, the largest of any city in Europe. By 1837, when Queen Victoria came to the throne, five more bridges and the capital's first passenger railway (from Greenwich to London Bridge) gave hints of huge expansion.

As well as being the administrative and financial capital of the British Empire, London was its chief port and the world's largest manufacturing centre. On the one hand, it had splendid buildings, fine shops, theatres and museums; on the other, it was a city of poverty, pollution and disease. Residential areas were polarised into districts of fine terraces maintained by squads of servants and overcrowded, insanitary slums.

The growth of the metropolis in the century before Victoria came to the throne had been spectacular, but during her reign (1837-1901), thousands more acres were covered with roads, houses and railway lines. If you visit a street within five miles of central London, its houses will be mostly Victorian. By the end of the 19th century, the city's population had swelled to more than six million, an incredible growth of five million in just 100 years.

Despite social problems of the Victorian era, memorably depicted in the writings of Charles Dickens, by the turn of the century steps were being taken to improve conditions for the majority of Londoners. The Metropolitan Board of Works installed an efficient sewerage system, street lighting and better roads. The worst slums were replaced by low-cost housing schemes funded by philanthropists such as the American George Peabody, whose Peabody Donation Fund continues to provide subsidised housing to the working classes. The London County Council (created in 1888) also helped to house the poor.

The Victorian expansion would not have been possible without an efficient public transport network with which to speed workers into and out of the city from the new suburbs. The horse-drawn bus appeared on London's streets in 1829, but it was the opening of the first passenger railway seven years later that heralded the commuters of the future. The first underground line, which ran between Paddington and Farringdon Road, opened in 1863 and proved an instant success, attracting 30,000 travellers on the first day. The world's first electric track in a deep tunnel – the 'tube' – opened in 1890 between the City and Stockwell, later becoming part of the Northern line.

THE CRYSTAL PALACE

If any single event symbolised this period of industry, science, discovery and invention, it was the Great Exhibition of 1851. Prince Albert, the Queen's Consort, helped to organise the triumphant showcase, for which the Crystal Palace, a vast building of iron and glass, was erected in Hyde Park. It looked like a giant greenhouse; hardly surprising as it was designed not by a professional architect but by the Duke of Devonshire's gardener, Joseph Paxton. Condemned by art critic John Ruskin as the model of dehumanisation in design, the Palace came to be presented as the prototype of modern architecture. During the five months it was open, the Exhibition drew six million visitors. The profits were used by the Prince Consort to establish a permanent centre for the study of the applied arts and sciences; the enterprise survives today in the South Kensington museums of natural history, science, and decorative and applied arts (*see p87-90*), and in three colleges (of art, music and science). After the Exhibition closed, the Crystal Palace was moved to Sydenham and used as an exhibition centre until it burned down in 1936.

ZEPPELINS ATTACK FROM THE SKIES

London entered the 20th century as the capital of the largest empire in history. Its wealth and power were there for all to see in grandstanding monuments such as Tower Bridge (*see p186*) and the Midland Grand Hotel at St Pancras Station (*see p344*), both of which married the retro stylings of High Gothic with modern iron and steel technology. During the brief reign of Edward VII (1901-10), London regained some of the gaiety and glamour it had lacked in the later years of Victoria's reign. Parisian chic came to London with the opening of the Ritz; Regent Street's Café Royal hit the heights as a meeting place for artists and writers; gentlemen's clubs proliferated; and 'luxury catering for the little man' was provided at the new Lyons Corner Houses (the Coventry Street branch held 4,500 people).

IN THE BLUE CORNER

Celebrate the salvation of the English Heritage blue plaque scheme.

Ever wondered where the diving helmet was invented? Look up on Denmark Street and a blue plaque will tell you: German inventor Augustus Siebe did so, at no.5. Hundreds such geolocated snippets of history are dotted around London, providing delight to curious passersby.

The first blue plaque celebrating a notable Londoner was erected in 1867, when the Royal Society for Arts put up a memorial at the (now demolished) birthplace of Lord Byron. To be eligible for consideration for a blue plaque, a person must have been dead for 20 years or born more than a century ago (so, for instance, nothing yet celebrating Paul McCartney), and a building associated with them must survive (which is why there's no blue plaque honouring Shakespeare).

ENGLISH HERITAGE
JOHN
LENNON
1940-1980
Musician
and Songwriter
lived here in
1968

The low-key scheme found increased popularity under the auspices of the London County Council (LCC, 1901-65) and the Greater London Council (GLC, 1965-85); when the GLC was shut, the scheme passed to English Heritage (www.english-heritage.org.uk), who administered it quite happily until the start of 2013, when it announced that – in the face of 34% cuts to government funding – the scheme would have to be stopped, a few years short of its 150th birthday.

But the scheme is much loved: private benefactors duly stepped in to stump up the £4,000 each plaque costs, including research, the plaque itself and installation. So for the foreseeable future, blue plaques seem secure.

In any case, the popularity of the scheme has seen it spawn many imitators. Some are operated by councils: Westminster City Council has a green plaque scheme, while Camden prefers brown and Southwark favours a rich, dark blue. And they aren't all round: the City of London goes for square plaques (often placed at eccentric heights – down by your ankles or way up above your head). Other schemes are run by groups such as Equity and the British Film Institute, and some companies have got in on the act: HMV unveiled one after they left their old Oxford Street store (at no.363, to which they returned in 2013), while Bentley erected one for the first car they produced (near Baker Street). There's even a black plaque: on Porchester Square, for Szmul Zygielbojm, a Polish trade unionist who killed himself 'nearby' in 1943 in despair at the world's indifference to Jewish suffering.

Many plaques look official but aren't: the perfect tones and font for the blue plaque to 'film-maker Monty Python' above the comic troupe's old HQ in Neal's Yard. There are even plaques to fictional characters, such as Great Russell Street's tribute to Charles Kitterbell from Charles Dickens' *Sketches by Boz.* Dickens, incidentally, is London's most plaqued former resident: there are 11 devoted to him, the most recent of them unveiled at 22 Cleveland Street, Fitzrovia, in summer 2013. And increasing numbers of plaques have been privately erected, either by local enthusiasts or by businesses hoping to enhance the prestige of their property – publicising the fact that a famous architect built your terraced house could easily bump the value up by a few grand; if you can rustle up a poet or a rockstar, you're probably quids in.

Aftermath of a German bombing raid in the first days of the Blitz.

Road transport, too, was revolutionised in this period. By 1911, horse-drawn buses were abandoned, replaced by motor cars, which put-putted around the city's streets, and the motor bus, introduced in 1904. Disruption came in the form of devastating air raids during World War I (1914-18). Around 650 people lost their lives in Zeppelin raids, but the greater impact was psychological – the mighty city and its populace had experienced helplessness.

CHANGE, CRISIS AND SHEER ENTERTAINMENT

Political change happened quickly after the war. At Buckingham Palace, the suffragettes had fiercely pressed the case for women's rights before hostilities began, and David Lloyd George's government averted revolution in 1918-19 by promising 'homes for heroes' (the returning soldiers). It didn't deliver, and in 1924 the Labour Party, led by Ramsay MacDonald, formed its first government.

A live-for-today attitude prevailed in the Roaring '20s among the young upper classes, who flitted from parties in Mayfair to dances at the Ritz. But this meant little to the mass of Londoners, who were suffering in the post-war slump. Civil disturbances, brought on by the high cost of living and rising unemployment, resulted in the nationwide General Strike of 1926, when the working classes downed tools en masse in support of striking miners. Prime Minister Baldwin encouraged volunteers to take over the public services, and the streets teemed with army-escorted food convoys, aristocrats running soup kitchens and students driving buses. After nine days of chaos, the strike was finally called off.

The economic situation only worsened in the early 1930s following the New York Stock Exchange crash of 1929. By 1931, more than three million Britons were jobless. During these years, the London County Council (LCC) began to have a greater impact on the city, clearing slums and building new houses, creating parks and taking control of public services. All the while, London's population increased, peaking at nearly 8.7 million in 1939 – the city has only recently begun to close in again on that kind of population, with the most recent census (2011) counting 8.17m residents. To accommodate the influx, the suburbs expanded, particularly to the north-west with the extension of the Metropolitan line to an area that became known as 'Metroland'. Identical gabled houses sprang up in their thousands.

At least Londoners were able to entertain themselves with film and radio. Not long after London's first radio broadcast was beamed from the roof of Marconi House in the Strand in 1922, families were gathering around huge Bakelite wireless sets to hear the BBC (the British Broadcasting Company; from 1927 the British Broadcasting

Corporation). TV broadcasts started on 26 August 1936, when the first telecast went out from Alexandra Palace, but few Londoners could afford televisions until the 1950s.

BLITZKRIEG

Abroad, events had taken on a frightening impetus. Neville Chamberlain's policy of appeasement towards Hitler's Germany collapsed when the Germans invaded Poland. Britain duly declared war on 3 September 1939. The government implemented precautionary measures against air raids, including the evacuation of 600,000 children and pregnant mothers, but the expected bombing raids didn't happen during the autumn and winter of 1939-40 (the so-called 'Phoney War'). Then, in September 1940, hundreds of German bombers dumped explosives on east London and the docks, destroying entire streets and killing or injuring more than 2,000 in what was merely an opening salvo. The Blitz had begun. Raids on London continued for 57 consecutive nights, then intermittently for a further six months. Londoners reacted with stoicism, famously asserting 'business as usual'. After a final raid on 10 May 1941, the Nazis had left a third of the City and the East End in ruins.

From 1942 onwards, the tide began to turn, but Londoners had a new terror to face: the V1 or 'doodlebug'. Dozens of these deadly, explosive-packed, pilotless planes descended on the city in 1944, causing widespread destruction. Later in the year, the more powerful V2 rocket was launched. The last fell on 27 March 1945 in Orpington, Kent, around six weeks before Victory in Europe was declared on 8 May 1945.

'NEVER HAD IT SO GOOD'

World War II left Britain almost as shattered as Germany. Soon after VE Day, a general election was held and Winston Churchill was defeated by the Labour Party under Clement Attlee. The new government established the National Health Service in 1948, and began a massive nationalisation programme that included public transport, electricity, gas, postal and telephone services. For most people, however, life remained regimented and austere. In war-ravaged London, local authorities struggled with a critical shortage of housing. Prefabricated bungalows provided a temporary solution for some (60 years later, six prefabs on the Excalibur estate in Catford, south-east London, were given protection as buildings of historic interest), but the huge new high-rise housing estates that the planners devised proved unpopular with their residents.

There were bright spots. London hosted the Olympic Games in 1948; three years later came the Festival of Britain, resulting in the first full redevelopment of the riverside site into the South Bank (now Southbank) Centre. As the 1950s progressed, life and prosperity returned, leading Prime Minister Harold Macmillan in 1957 to proclaim that 'most of our people have never had it so good'. However, Londoners were leaving. The population dropped by half a million in the late 1950s, causing a labour shortage that prompted huge recruitment drives in Britain's former colonies. London Transport and the National Health Service were both particularly active in encouraging West Indians to emigrate to Britain. Unfortunately, as the Notting Hill race riots of 1958 illustrated, the welcome these new immigrants received was rarely friendly. Still, there were several areas of tolerance: Soho, for instance, which became famous for its mix of cultures and the café and club life they brought with them.

THE SWINGING '60S

By the mid 1960s, London had started to swing. The innovative fashions of Mary Quant and others broke the stranglehold Paris had on couture: boutiques blossomed along the King's Road, while Biba set the pace in Kensington. Carnaby Street became a byword for hipness as the city basked in its new-found reputation as music and fashion capital of the world – made official, it seemed, when *Time* magazine devoted its front cover to 'swinging London' in 1966. The year of student unrest in Europe, 1968, saw the first issue of *Time Out* hit the streets in August; it was a fold-up sheet, sold for 5d. The decade ended with the Rolling Stones playing a free gig in Hyde Park that drew around 500,000 people.

Then the bubble burst. Many Londoners remember the 1970s as a decade of economic strife, the decade in which the IRA began its bombing campaign on mainland

Britain. After the Conservatives won the general election in 1979, Margaret Thatcher instituted an economic policy that cut public services and widened the gap between rich and poor. Riots in Brixton (1981) and Tottenham (1985) were linked to unemployment and heavy-handed policing, keenly felt in London's black communities. The Greater London Council (GLC), led by Ken Livingstone, mounted vigorous opposition to the government with a series of populist measures, but it was abolished in 1986.

Time Out
'We control the streets of London and that's all there is to it.'

THINGS CAN ONLY GET BETTER?

In May 1997, the British electorate ousted the Tories and gave Tony Blair's Labour Party the first of three election victories. Blair left London with two significant legacies. First, the government commissioned the Millennium Dome, whose turn-of-the-century celebrations it hoped would be a 21st-century rival to the Great Exhibition of 1851. Instead, the Dome ate £1 billion and became a national joke. However, as Labour's fortunes declined, the Dome's saw an upturn. As the O2 Arena (*see p271*), it has hosted concerts by the likes of Prince and Lady Gaga; as the North Greenwich Arena, it was a key venue in the London 2012 Olympic and Paralympic Games. Second, following a referendum, Labour instituted the Greater London Assembly (GLA) and London mayoralty. Thus 2000 saw Ken Livingstone return to power as London's first directly elected mayor. He was re-elected in 2004, a thumbs-up for policies that included a traffic congestion charge. Summer 2005 brought elation, as London won the bid to host the 2012 Games, and devastation the very next day, as bombs on tube trains and a bus killed 52 people and injured 700.

Aided by support from the suburbs, which felt neglected by Livingstone, thatch-haired Tory Boris Johnson became mayor in 2008 with a healthy majority, and again in May 2012 by a slim margin. Publicity-friendly early policies, such as the introduction of a bike rental scheme and the development of an updated Routemaster bus (both launched as self-financing through a combination of revenue and private sponsorship) and the locally popular scrapping of the western extension of the Congestion Charge, began to unravel in the face of a relentlessly cost-cutting national Conservative-Liberal Democrat coalition government – public transport costs in London continue their relentless rise under Johnson. The disturbing riots and looting of August 2011, whose flashpoint was again in Tottenham, brought issues of youth unemployment, alienation and policing to the fore; how to build enough affordable housing for Londoners is another major problem that Johnson seems unlikely to solve. The 2012 Olympics and Paralympics were an unbridled success, yet the promised 'legacy' of improvements at a local level in some of London's poorest areas remains frustratingly elusive.

All of which should make the next mayoral election in 2016 very interesting, especially since Johnson has ruled himself out of contention for a further term. With London's population continuing to grow, rocketing house prices and benefit cuts forcing major demographic shifts, the vast new Crossrail train link burrowing its way right under the city, and whole new districts growing out of the remains of the old – King's Cross and the Olympic Park may well be matched in ambition by the reworking of Battersea Power Station and the rebirth of Vauxhall – the city's future looks as turbulent as its past.

KEY EVENTS

43 The Romans invade; the settlement of Londinium is founded on the remains of an ancient ritual landscape.
61 Boudicca burns Londinium; the city is rebuilt and made provincial capital.
200 A city wall is built.
410 Roman troops evacuate Britain.
c600 Saxon London is built to the west.
841 The Norse raid for the first time.
c871 The Danes occupy London.
886 Alfred the Great takes London.
1042 Edward the Confessor builds a palace and 'West Minster' upstream.
1066 William I is crowned in Westminster Abbey.
1078 The Tower of London is begun.
1123 St Bart's Hospital is founded.
1197 Henry Fitzalwin is the first mayor.
1215 The mayor signs the Magna Carta.
1240 First Parliament at Westminster.
1290 Jews are expelled from London.
1348 The Black Death arrives.
1381 The Peasants' Revolt.
1397 Richard Whittington is Lord Mayor.
1476 William Caxton sets up the first printing press at Westminster.
1534 Henry VIII cuts England off from the Catholic Church.
1555 Martyrs burned at Smithfield.
1565 Sir Thomas Gresham proposes the Royal Exchange.
1572 First known map of London.
1599 The Globe Theatre opens.
1605 Guy Fawkes's plot to blow up James I fails.
1642 The start of the Civil War.
1649 Charles I is executed; Cromwell establishes Commonwealth.
1665 Outbreak of the Great Plague.
1666 The Great Fire.
1675 Building starts on the new St Paul's Cathedral.
1694 The Bank of England is set up.
1766 The city wall is demolished.
1773 The Stock Exchange is founded.
1824 The National Gallery is founded.
1836 The first passenger railway opens; Charles Dickens publishes *The Pickwick Papers*, his first novel.
1851 The Great Exhibition takes place.
1858 The Great Stink: pollution in the Thames reaches hideous levels.
1863 The Metropolitan line opens as the world's first underground railway.
1866 London's last major cholera outbreak; the Sanitation Act is passed.
1868 The last public execution is held at Newgate prison (now the Old Bailey).
1884 Greenwich Mean Time is established as a global standard.
1888 Jack the Ripper prowls the East End; London County Council is created.
1890 The Housing Act enables the LCC to clear the slums; the first electric underground railway opens.
1897 Motorised buses are introduced.
1908 London hosts the Olympic Games for the first time.
1915 Zeppelins begin three years of bombing raids on London.
1940 The Blitz begins.
1948 London again hosts the Olympic Games; forerunner of the Paralympics, the Stoke Mandeville Games are organised by neurologist Sir Ludwig Guttman.
1951 The Festival of Britain is held.
1952 The last 'pea-souper' smog.
1953 Queen Elizabeth II is crowned.
1981 Riots in Brixton.
1982 The last London docks close.
1986 The Greater London Council is abolished.
1992 One Canada Square tower opens on Canary Wharf.
2000 Ken Livingstone becomes London's first directly elected mayor; Tate Modern and the London Eye open.
2005 The city wins its bid to host the 2012 Games; suicide bombers kill 52 on public transport.
2008 Boris Johnson becomes mayor.
2010 Hung parliament leads to new Conservative–Lib Dem coalition.
2011 Riots and looting around the city.
2012 London 2012 Olympic Games and Paralympic Games take place.
2013 Opening of the 87-storey Shard, the EU's tallest building.

Architecture

A wonderful jumble of world-class buildings.

Long before Britain began emerging from recession, London had already started to build. Rafael Viñoly's 'Walkie Talkie', 38 curvaceous storeys at 20 Fenchurch Street, should open as this guide hits the shelves, with Richard Rogers's even taller 'Cheesegrater' to join it later in 2014. These are only the latest of a 'cluster' of City skyscrapers – the Gherkin, Tower 42 and Heron Tower – that are looked down on by Renzo Piano's 1,016-foot-tall Shard, the vast spike that opened on the opposite bank of the Thames in 2012.

For all the annual lists of London's worst new buildings, the best modern architecture is swiftly appreciated; other buildings become classics over time: the BT Tower, National Theatre and Barbican are all once-hated structures that are now dearly loved. None of which is new: in the 17th century, the authorities objected to Wren's magnificent St Paul's Cathedral because it looked too Roman Catholic for their Anglican sensibilities.

In fact, London's defining characteristic is its aesthetically unhappy mix of buildings, a mess of historic bits and modern bobs that gives the city a unique capacity to surprise and delight.

ENTRY TO THE TRAITORS' GATE

Tower of London.

ANCIENT STREETS, NEW CITY

Modern London sprang into being after the Great Fire of 1666, which destroyed four-fifths of the City of London, burning 13,200 houses and 89 churches. The devastation was explicitly commemorated by Sir Christopher Wren's 202-foot **Monument** (*see p185*), but many of the finest buildings in the City stand testament to his talent as the architect of the great remodelling, and to the work of his successors.

London had been a densely populated place built largely of wood, and fire control was primitive. It was only after the three-day inferno that the authorities insisted on a few basic regulations. Brick and stone became the construction materials of choice, and key streets were widened to act as firebreaks. Yet, despite grand, Classical proposals from several architects (Wren among them), London reshaped itself around its old street pattern, and some structures that survived the Fire still stand as reminders of earlier building styles. Chief of these are the City's fragments of Roman wall (Tower Hill tube station and the grounds of the Museum of London, *see p179*, have good examples) and the central Norman keep at the **Tower of London** (*see p186*), begun soon after William's 1066 conquest and extended over the next 300 years; the Navy saved the Tower from the flames by blowing up surrounding houses before the inferno could reach it.

Another long-standing building, **Westminster Abbey** (*see p76*) was begun in 1245 when the site lay far outside London's walls; it was completed in 1745 by Nicholas Hawksmoor's distinctive west towers. The abbey is the most French of England's Gothic churches, but the chapel – begun by Henry VII – is pure Tudor. Centuries later, the American writer Washington Irving gushed: 'Stone seems, by the winning labour of the chisel, to have been robbed of its weight and density, suspended aloft, as if by magic.'

A LATE FLOWERING

The European Renaissance came late to Britain, making its London debut with Inigo Jones's 1622 **Banqueting House** (*see p75*). The sumptuously decorated ceiling, added in 1635 by Rubens, celebrated the Stuart monarchy's Divine Right to rule, although 14 years later King Charles I provided a greater spectacle as he was led from the room and beheaded on a stage outside. Tourists also have Jones to thank for **St Paul's Covent Garden** (*see p140,* and the precise little **Queen's House** (*see p216*) in Greenwich, but they're not his only legacies. He mastered the art of piazzas (notably at Covent Garden), porticos and pilasters, changing British architecture forever. His work influenced the careers of succeeding generations of architects and introduced a habit of venerating the past that it would take 300 years to kick.

Nothing cheers a builder like a natural disaster, and one can only guess at the relish with which Wren and co began rebuilding after the Fire. They brandished Classicism like a new broom: the pointed arches of English Gothic were rounded off, Corinthian columns made an appearance and church spires became as complex, frothy and multi-layered as a wedding cake.

Wren blazed the trail with his daring plans for **St Paul's Cathedral** (*see p176*), spending an enormous (for the time) £500 on just the oak model of his proposal. But the scheme, incorporating a Catholic dome rather than a Protestant steeple, was too Roman for the establishment and the design was rejected. Wren quickly produced a redesign and gained planning permission by incorporating a spire, only to set about a series of mischievous U-turns to give us the building, domed and heavily suggestive of an ancient temple, that survives to this day.

Wren's baton was picked up by Nicholas Hawksmoor and James Gibbs, who benefited from a 1711 decree that 50 extra churches should be built using the money raised by a tax on coal. Gibbs became busy around Trafalgar Square with the steepled Roman temple of **St Martin-in-the-Fields** (*see p69*), as well as the Baroque **St Mary-le-Strand** and the tower of **St Clement Danes** (for both, *see p146*). His work was well received, but the more experimental Hawksmoor had a rougher ride. For one thing, not everyone admired his stylistic innovations; for another, even fewer approved of his financial planning, or lack of it: **St George's Bloomsbury** (*see p154*) cost three times its £10,000 budget and took 15 years to build. Nonetheless, Hawksmoor designed, in whole or in part, eight new places of worship. Like Wren, Hawksmoor loved the Classical temple, a style at odds with the Act's insistence on spires. **St George-in-the-East**, **St Anne Limehouse** and **St Mary Woolnoth** (*see p182*) are all unorthodox resolutions of this contradiction, but the 'spire' of St George's Bloomsbury is the barmiest. Apeing the Mausoleum of Halicarnassus, Hawksmoor created a peculiar stepped pyramid design, plopped a giant statue of George I in a toga on top and then added unicorns and lions. Hawksmoor's ruinous overspends were one reason why just a dozen of the proposed 50 churches were built.

After action, reaction: one of a large family of Scottish architects, Robert Adam found himself at the forefront of a movement that came to see Italian Baroque as a corruption of the real thing, with architectural exuberance dropped in favour of a simpler interpretation of ancient forms. The best surviving work of Robert and his brothers

St Paul's Cathedral.

Kenwood House.

James, John and William can be found in London's great suburban houses, including **Kenwood House** (*see p229*), but the project for which they're most famous no longer stands: the cripplingly expensive Adelphi housing estate. Almost all of the complex was pulled down in the 1930s and replaced by an office block, apart from the **Royal Society of Arts** building, just off the Strand on John Adam Street.

SOANE AND NASH

Just as the first residents were moving into the Adelphi in the early 1770s, a young unknown called John Soane was embarking on a domestic commission in Ireland. It was never completed, but Soane eventually returned to London and went on to build the **Bank of England** (*see p181*) and **Dulwich Picture Gallery** (*see p238*). The Bank was demolished between the wars, leaving only the perimeter walls of Soane's masterpiece, but his gracious Stock Office has been reconstructed in the Bank's museum (*see p182*). A further glimpse of what the bankers might have enjoyed can be gleaned from his own house, the quirkily marvellous and recently extended **Sir John Soane's Museum** (*see p165*), an exquisite architectural experiment.

A near-contemporary of Soane's, John Nash was a less talented architect, but his contributions – among them the inner courtyard of **Buckingham Palace** (*see p80*), the **Theatre Royal Haymarket** and **Regent Street** (*see p113*) – have comparable influence in the look of contemporary London to those of Wren. Regent Street began as a proposal to link the West End to the planned park further north, as well as a device to separate the toffs of Mayfair from the riff-raff of Soho; in Nash's own words, a 'complete separation between the Streets occupied by the Nobility and Gentry, and the narrow Streets and meaner houses occupied by mechanics and the trading part of the community'.

By the 1830s, the Classical form of building had been established in England for some 200 years, but this didn't prevent a handful of upstarts from pressing for change. In 1834, the **Houses of Parliament** (*see p75*) burned down, leading to the construction of Sir Charles Barry's Gothic masterpiece. Barry sought out Augustus Welby Northmore Pugin. Working alongside Barry, if not always in agreement with him (of Barry's symmetrical layout, Pugin famously remarked, 'All Grecian, sir. Tudor details on a Classic body'), Pugin created a Victorian fantasy that would later be condemned as the Disneyfication of history.

Houses of Parliament.

Royal Courts of Justice.

GETTING GOTHIC

This was the beginning of the Gothic Revival, a move to replace what was considered to be foreign and pagan with something that was native and Christian. Architects would often decide that buildings weren't Gothic enough; as with the 15th-century Great Hall at the **Guildhall** (*see p182*), which gained its corner turrets and central spire only in 1862. The argument between Classicists and Goths erupted in 1857, when the government hired Sir George Gilbert Scott, a leading light of the Gothic movement, to design a new home for the Foreign Office. Scott's design incensed anti-Goth Lord Palmerston, then prime minister, whose diktats prevailed. But Scott exacted his revenge by building an office in which everyone hated working, and by going on to construct wonderful Gothic edifices all over town, among them the **Albert Memorial** (*see p87*) and what is now the **Renaissance St Pancras** hotel (*see p344*), which still forms the front of St Pancras train station (*see p156*).

St Pancras was completed in 1873, after the Midland Railway commissioned Scott to build a London terminus that would dwarf that of its rivals next door at King's Cross. Using the project as an opportunity to show his mastery of the Gothic form, Scott built an asymmetrical castle that obliterated views of the train shed behind, itself an engineering marvel completed earlier by William Barlow.

Other charming, imposing neo-Gothic buildings around the city include the **Royal Courts of Justice** (*see p173*), the **Natural History Museum** (*see p87*) and **Tower Bridge** (*see p186*). Under the influence of the Arts and Crafts movement, medievalism morphed into such mock Tudor buildings as the wonderful half-timbered **Liberty** department store (*see p115*).

BEING MODERN

World War I and the coming of modernism led to a spirit of renewal and a starker aesthetic. **Freemasons' Hall** (*see p140*) and the BBC's **Broadcasting House** (*see p103*) are good examples of the pared-down style of the 1920s and '30s, but perhaps the finest example of between-the-wars modernism can be found at **London Zoo** (*see p195*). Built by Russian émigré Bertold Lubetkin and the Tecton group, the spiral ramps of the former Penguin Pool were a

Lloyd's of London.

Heron Tower.

showcase for the possibilities of concrete. The material was also put to good use on the London Underground, enabling the quick, cheap building of cavernous spaces with sleek lines and curves: the collaboration between London Underground supremo Frank Pick and architect Charles Holden created design masterpieces such as **Southgate** and **Arnos Grove stations** at the north end of the Piccadilly line, and **Chiswick Park station** to the west of the District line, as well as the transport headquarters at **55 Broadway** – which featured sculptures by modern masters Jacob Epstein, Eric Gill and Henry Moore. Further innovations were employed on the gorgeous **Daily Express** building (121-128 Fleet Street), built in 1931 using the pioneering 'curtain wall' construction, its radical black vitrolite and glass façade hung on an internal frame.

The bombs of World War II left large areas of London ruined, providing another opportunity for builders to cash in. Lamentably, the city was little improved by the rebuild; in many cases, it was left worse off. The destruction left the capital with a dire housing shortage, so architects were given a chance to demonstrate the grim efficiency with which they could house large numbers of families in tower blocks. There were post-war successes, however, including the **Royal Festival Hall** (*see p50*) on the South Bank. The sole survivor of the 1951 Festival of Britain, the RFH was built to celebrate the end of the war and the centenary of the Great Exhibition, held in 1851 and responsible for the foundation in South Kensington of the Natural History Museum, the Science Museum and the V&A. Next to the RFH, the **Hayward Gallery** (*see p51*) is an exemplar of the 1960s vogue for Brutalist architecture, a style more thoroughly explored at the **Barbican** (*see p178*).

HERE COME THE STARCHITECTS

The 1970s and '80s offered up a pair of alternatives to concrete: postmodernism and high-tech. The former is represented by César Pelli's blandly monumental **One Canada Square** (*see p240*) in Docklands, an oversized obelisk that's perhaps the archetypal expression of late '80s architecture – and whose impact is hard to imagine now it stands in a copse of inferior office blocks. Richard Rogers's high-tech **Lloyd's of London** building (*see p183*) is much more widely admired. A clever combination of commercial and industrial aesthetics that adds up to one of the most significant British buildings since the war, it was mocked on completion in 1986; opposite, Rogers' 48-storey **122 Leadenhall Street** ('the Cheesegrater') is now under way again, while nearby Bishopsgate has both the City's current tallest building, the 755-foot, 46-storey **Heron Tower**, and the footings of the building that will soon exceed it: the **Pinnacle** ('the Helter Skelter'), planned to reach 945 feet.

Apart from Rogers, the city's most visible contemporary architect has been Norman Foster, whose **City Hall** and **30 St Mary Axe** (aka 'the Gherkin'; *see p184*) caught up with Big Ben and black taxis as movie shorthand for 'Welcome to London!' – only to be overtaken in 2012 by the giant glass spike of Renzo Piano's **Shard** (*see p63*), on the opposite bank of the Thames. Foster's prolific practice set new standards in sports design with the soaring arch of the new **Wembley Stadium** (*see p239*); the exercise in complexity that is the £100 million Great Court at the **British Museum** (*see p150*) did the same for London's cultural gem. The Great Court is the largest covered square in Europe, but each of the 3,300 triangular glass panels that make up its roof is unique.

LOOKING AT LONDON

Get the inside view on the city's architecture.

Both the **Architectural Association** (36 Bedford Square, WC1B 3ES, 7887 4000, www.aaschool.ac.uk; closed Sun) and **Royal Institute of British Architects** (66 Portland Place, W1B 1AD, 7580 5533, www.architecture.com; closed Sun) have terrific exhibitions on different aspects of architecture, but for a focused look at London's architectural future, get off the tube at Goodge Street and visit **New London Architecture** (26 Store Street, WC1E 7BT, 7636 4044, www.newlondon architecture.org; closed Sun). NLA's centrepiece is a 39-foot-long scale model of the city, with all major developments with planning permission marked in white. Around the model, boards have copious information on key new buildings, providing real insight into the city's recent and future architecture and plans. In addition, Open-City's **Open House London** festival (*see p39*) is the key date in the architecture calendar each year. It does a terrific job of getting locals engaged with their city by giving public access to amazing buildings of all ages that are normally inaccessible.

New London Architecture.

King's Cross station.

Much new architecture is to be found cunningly inserted into old buildings. Herzog & de Meuron's fabulous transformation of a Bankside power station into **Tate Modern** (*see p56*) is the most famous example – the firm aims to repeat its success with an ambitious new extension, the bottom of which opened in 2012 as The Tanks. We must wait until, perhaps, 2016 to see the pyramid folded out of origami that will loom above. Equally groundbreaking was Future Systems' NatWest Media Centre at **Lord's Cricket Ground** (St John's Wood Road, NW8 8QN). Built from aluminium in a boatyard and perched high above the pitch, it's one of London's most daring constructions to date, especially given the traditional setting.

LOCAL COLOUR AND OPEN ARTS

Architecture hasn't all been about headline projects and eye-troubling commercial developments. Will Alsop's multicoloured **Peckham Library** (122 Peckham Hill Street) helped to redefine community architecture in 2000, and architects have continued to play a major role in redefining public libraries. David Adjaye subsequently designed the **Idea Stores** (www.ideastore.co.uk) in Poplar (1 Vesey Path, East India Dock Road) and Whitechapel (321 Whitechapel Road), with a crisp, softened industrial aesthetic that is a world away from the familiar Victorian versions, while at the end of 2011 Piers Gough's upside-down pyramid, **Canada Water Library** (21 Surrey Quays Road), provided a focus for a rather incoherent district in south-east London. The subtle Robbrecht en Daem expansion of **Whitechapel Gallery** (*see p204*) into the stylistically very different former library next door reversed this process, giving a new democratic openness to a pair of landmark Victorian buildings.

THE END – OR BEGINNING? – OF THE MEGABUILDS

In the north of London, the transformation of King's Cross is approaching its conclusion. Here you'll find the reopened St Pancras International station, a refurbished **King's Cross station** with a spectacular new roof, the new-build office/concert venue **Kings Place** (*see p281*) and **Central St Martins** art college, in a redeveloped Victorian granary on a fine new square with geometric, choreographed fountains and terracing down to the canal. This 67-acre brownfield redevelopment, King's Cross Central (*see p157* **Hip to Be a Square**), will eventually also comprise 1,900 new homes, serviced by 20 new streets and another four squares, in a part of London that has its very own new postcode: N1C.

Even more impressive – and also with its own postcode, E20, cannily borrowed from the fictional London borough in long-running

BBC TV soap opera *EastEnders* – is the **Olympic Park** (*see p237*). Having admirably fulfilled its function as the major venue for the 2012 Olympics and Paralympics, it is now being made fit for public ('legacy' in the jargon) use – and the taxpayer may expect rather a lot from a project for which the original budget of £2.4bn had to be increased to an eye-watering £9.3bn, apparently due to a failure to include VAT and security costs. In the short term, the Park's temporary venues are being stripped out, leaving the Olympic Stadium, the beautiful wood-clad Velodrome (to be centrepiece of a VeloPark that will add a cycle trail to the Olympic BMX track), Zaha Hadid's stunning Aquatics Centre (finally without its disfiguring temporary seating stands), the Copper Box, the ugly media centre, the water-based hockey pitches (migrating north to Eton Manor), the Athletes' Village (renamed 'East Village') and, presiding over it all, the cordially loathed red spirals of the Anish Kapoor-designed **ArcelorMittal Orbit** – which, we suspect, will gradually turn out to be rather

ArcelorMittal Orbit.

Westfield Stratford City.

popular when the southern section reopens to the public in 2014 as the 500-acre Queen Elizabeth Olympic Park.

While the value of the Olympic 'legacy' will be fought over for a long time, changes have been seen around other 2012 Games venues: new 'town centres' at Stratford, on the eastern flank of the Olympic Park, where the **Westfield Stratford City** mall (*see p237*) has been doing serious business, and in Woolwich; the £30m Siemens sustainability centre on the Royal Docks, linked across the Thames by Mayor Boris Johnson's latest vanity project – the **Emirates Air Line** cable car (*see p249*) – to the **O2 Arena** (*see p271*), with its own cluster of new buildings, including a university campus. Planners have pointed to this bit of London, start of the 'Thames Gateway', as the city's future for many years now – that possibility is now underpinned by the beginning of the colossally ambitious **Crossrail** project. Not due for completion until 2018, this railway is already worming its way under key areas of the city, including Oxford Street, to connect suburbs to the east and west with the centre of London. It is an extraordinary feat of civil engineering.

Are we on the way to a better future city? The arguments on both sides are fierce. But one thing is clear: heading up, out and under, we are well on our way to a bigger future London.

Essential Information

Hotels

It's a sign of London's continual financial pulling power that, even in these lean times, luxury hotels continue to flourish. The London Edition is perhaps the most striking addition in terms of expensive good looks, though the Ace Hotel wins out when it comes to hipster credentials. Things are also lively among the Victorian and Edwardian grandes dames, with the recently refitted Savoy, and St Pancras Renaissance now joined by the Great Northern Hotel. Elsewhere, there's action in the field of modish, moderately priced hotels that have finally decided to follow the pioneering Hoxton, such as Z Soho, citizenM and Qbic. On the whole, though, room prices remain high. Significantly, Dean Street Townhouse, its slightly younger sibling Shoreditch Rooms and One Leicester Street offer 'tiny' or 'post-supper' rooms at lower-than-you-might-fear rates. The popularity of hip new B&Bs and no-frills hotel concepts speaks to the same need.

OUR LISTINGS

Hotels in this chapter are classified according to the average price of a double room. You can expect to pay more than £300 a night for hotels in the **Deluxe** category, £200-£300 for **Expensive** hotels, £100-£200 for **Moderate** properties and under £100 a night for hotels listed as **Budget**.

The classfications we use are just a guide. A hotel's rates can vary widely, both top to bottom and over the course of the year. As a rule, it's best to book as far ahead as possible, and always try hotels' own websites first: many offer special online deals throughout the year. If you do arrive in town without a bed booked, staff at **Visit London** (1 Lower Regent Street, 0870 156 6366, www.visitlondon.com) will be happy to help you out. Be aware that a few hotels don't include VAT in the rates they quote. And watch out for added extras. If you're bringing a car (not recommended), always check with the hotel before you arrive: few central hotels offer parking, and those that do charge steeply for it.

THE SOUTH BANK & BANKSIDE

Moderate

Bermondsey Square Hotel
Bermondsey Square, Tower Bridge Road, SE1 3UN (0870 111 2525, www.bespokehotels.com). Borough tube or London Bridge tube/rail.
Rooms 80. **Map** p403 Q10.
This is a deliberately kitsch new-build hotel on a newly developed square. Loft suites are named after the heroines of psychedelic rock classics (Lucy, Lily and so on); some have private terraces or a hammock, or Japanese baths. Rooms have classic discs on the walls, and you can kick your heels from the suspended Bubble Chair at reception. But, although occupants of the Lucy suite get a multi-person jacuzzi (with a great terrace view), the real draw isn't the gimmicks – it's well-designed rooms, with free Wi-Fi, for competitive prices. The restaurant-bar, Gregg's Bar & Grill, which serves British food, can be a bit hit-or-miss, but the bar's lounge area is a good spot to relax in and the hotel's staff are happy and helpful.

★ citizenM London Bankside

20 Lavington Street, SE1 0NZ (3519 1680, www.citizenm.com). Southwark tube or Blackfriars tube/rail. **Rooms** 192. **Map** p402 O8.
This casual new-build is a superbly well-designed addition to London's affordably chic hotels. *See p357* **Going Dutch**.

Park Plaza County Hall

1 Addington Street, SE1 7RY (7021 1800, www.parkplaza.com). Waterloo tube/rail.
Rooms 398. **Map** p399 M9.
Park Plaza County Hall is an enthusiastically – if somewhat haphazardly – run new-build. Each room has its own kitchenette with microwave and sink, plus free Wi-Fi, and room sizes aren't bad across the price range (and the floor-to-ceiling windows help to make them feel bigger). There's a handsomely vertiginous atrium, enabling you to peer down into the central restaurant from the frustratingly infrequent glass lifts, the ground-floor bar is buzzy with business types after working hours and the Italian restaurant serves pizzas from a clay oven. Nearby, at the southern end of Westminster Bridge, is the gargantuan Park Plaza Westminster Bridge (200 Westminster Bridge Road, SE1 7UT). Opened in 2010, it's London's largest new-build hotel for four decades.

Premier Inn London County Hall

County Hall, Belvedere Road, SE1 7PB (0871 527 8648, www.premierinn.com). Waterloo tube/rail.
Rooms 314. **Map** p399 M8.
Its position right by the London Eye, the Thames, Westminster Bridge and Waterloo Station is a gift for out-of-towners on a bargain weekend break. Extra points are garnered for its friendly and efficient staff, making this newly refurbished branch of the Premier Travel chain the acceptable face of budget convenience. Check-in is quick and pleasant; rooms are spacious, clean and warm with comfortable beds and decent bathrooms with very good showers. Breakfast, a buffet-style affair in a comfortable dining room, is extra but provides ballast for a day of sightseeing/shopping, or indeed meetings. Wi-Fi costs £3 a day, but guests get a 30-minute free session.

IN THE KNOW BUYER BEWARE

Many high-end hotels charge extra for services that some travellers assume will be free, most commonly internet access and breakfast. Always check in advance if you're blowing the budget for a treat.

THE CITY

Deluxe

Andaz Liverpool Street

40 Liverpool Street, EC2M 7QN (7961 1234, www.london.liverpoolstreet.andaz.com). Liverpool Street tube/rail. **Rooms** 267. **Map** p403 R6.
A faded railway hotel until its £70m Conran overhaul in 2000, the red-brick Great Eastern became in 2007 the first of Hyatt's new Andaz portfolio. The new approach means out with gimmicky menus,

Andaz Liverpool Street.

closet-sized minibars and even the lobby reception desk, and in with down-to-earth, well-informed service and eco-friendliness. The bedrooms still wear style-magazine uniform – Eames chairs, Frette linens – but free services (local calls, wireless internet, healthy minibar) are an appreciated touch. There's serious British dining in the 1901 restaurant in the magnificent former ballroom with stained-glass dome, plus a Japanese restaurant, a pub and a champagne bar on site.

Expensive

DoubleTree by Hilton

7 Pepys Street, EC3N 4AF (7709 1000, http://doubletree3.hilton.com). Tower Hill tube. **Rooms** 583. **Map** p403 R7.

As you turn from the Tower of London and Tower Bridge among anonymous modern buildings to reach the DoubleTree, you might feel your heart sink. Keep your spirits up: the hotel looks a bit dull, but it has unexpectedly brilliant views. Even if you aren't lucky enough to stay in the spacious Thames suite, the 12th-floor SkyLounge bar, with its outside terrace, looks over the rooftops to provide a fine Thames vista. We were sad that Mint sold its mini-chain of hotels, but – under Hilton – service here remains smooth and smiley, and the room technology (including free Wi-Fi) and fittings top-class.

Montcalm London City

52 Chiswell Street, EC1Y 4SD (7374 2988, www.themontcalmlondoncity.co.uk). Barbican tube or Moorgate tube/rail. **Rooms** 235. **Map** p400 P5.

Montcalm London City stands on the former site of the 18th-century Whitbread brewery. The service is welcoming, the decor very much old meets new: brickwork and an original art deco staircase sit with Swarovski crystal chandeliers and spotlight flooring. All rooms have lime green and brown furnishings and are fitted with slick digital doorbell, housekeeping and privacy sensors, but the furniture arrangement is a little cramped and, despite the media-hubs and flatscreen TVs, there's a sense the place was designed by committee – too many good ideas, not enough coherence. The hotel's modern restaurant and cocktail bar is a cracker, though.

★ South Place Hotel

3 South Place, EC2M 2AF (3503 0000, www.southplacehotel.com). Moorgate or Liverpool Street tube/rail. **Rooms** 80. **Map** p401 Q5.

D&D runs some of the swankiest restaurants in London, so much was expected of its first hotel. South Place delivers. It manages the difficult balance of sufficient formality to keep expense-accounters satisfied their needs are being attended to, with enough levity for you to want to spend the evening indoors. The muted top-floor Angler restaurant is a superbly oiled operation, there's a pretty interior courtyard garden bar, and the ground-floor 3 South Place bar-diner segues neatly from smooth breakfast operation to boisterous bar. The attention to detail impresses: from conversation-piece art (wire high-heels in one cabinet, a light feature of suspended aeroplanes, steampunk drawings) to touch controls in the rooms, or the Bond-themed pool room and library complete with vinyl and turntable.

Threadneedles

5 Threadneedle Street, EC2R 8AY (7657 8080, www.hotelthreadneedles.co.uk). Bank tube/DLR. **Rooms** 74. **Map** p403 Q6.

Threadneedles boldly slots some contemporary style into a fusty old dame of a building in the heart of the City; it was formerly the grand Victorian HQ of the Midland Bank, bang next to the Bank of England and the Royal Exchange. The etched glass-domed rotunda of the lobby soars on columns over an artful array of designer furniture and shelving that looks like the dreamchild of some powerful graphics software – it's a calm space, but a stunning one. The bedrooms are individual, coherent and soothing examples of City-boy chic, in muted beige and textured tones, with limestone bathrooms and odd views of local landmarks: St Paul's, Tower 42 and the Lloyd's building. Drinks are served under the stained-glass central dome, and the pillared restaurant is an impressive space too. It's all well run and well thought out. *Photo p342.*

Moderate

Apex London Wall

7-9 Copthall Avenue, EC2R 7NJ (7562 3030, www.apexhotels.co.uk). Bank tube or Moorgate tube/rail. **Rooms** 89. **Map** p403 Q6.

The mini-chain's second London hotel shares the virtues of the first (Apex City of London, 1 Seething Lane, 7702 2020). The service is obliging, the rooms are crisply designed with all mod cons, and there are comforting details – rubber duck in the impressive bathrooms, free jelly beans, free local calls and internet, kettle and iron provided. The City of London branch has the better location for tourists, a short walk from the Tower of London, but this one is handier for business. From the suites, a terrace peers over commercial buildings, but the view from the restaurant – of the flamboyantly sculpted frieze on a business institute – is rather pleasing. Prices are decent for the City location, but book well ahead to get the best deals.

HOLBORN & CLERKENWELL

Expensive

Malmaison

Charterhouse Square, EC1M 6AH (7012 3700, www.malmaison.com). Barbican tube. **Rooms** 97. **Map** p400 O5.

Threadneedles. See p341.

Malmaison is deliciously located, looking out on a lovely cobbled square on the edge of the Square Mile, near the bars, clubs and better restaurants of the East End. This being design-conscious Clerkenwell, it's no surprise that the decor throughout makes a cool statement (note the Veuve Clicquot ice buckets built into the love seats at reception). The rooms overlooking the square are the pick of the bunch, with the best of the views and morning sunshine that pours through large sash windows on to big, white firm beds. Gripes? The muted, business-friendly decor in the rooms is a bit of a let-down after the dark and sultry foyer. There's smiley service downstairs in the lovely basement brasserie, and internet usage is free.

★ Rookery

12 Peter's Lane, Cowcross Street, EC1M 6DS (7336 0931, www.rookeryhotel.com). Farringdon tube/rail. **Rooms** 33. **Map** p400 O5.

Sister hotel to Hazlitt's (*see p349*), the Rookery has long been something of a celebrity hideaway deep in the heart of Clerkenwell. Its front door is satisfyingly hard to find, especially when the streets around are teeming with Fabric (*see p365*) devotees; the front rooms can be noisy on these nights, but the place is otherwise as creakily calm as a country manor house. Once inside, guests enjoy an atmospheric warren of rooms, each individually decorated in the style of a Georgian townhouse: huge clawfoot baths, elegant four-posters, antique desks, old paintings amd brass shower fittings. Modernity isn't forgotten though: there's free Wi-Fi. There's an honesty bar in the bright and airy drawing room at the back, which opens on to a sweet little patio. The ground-floor suite has its own hallway, a cosy boudoir and a subterranean bathroom. Topping it all is the huge split-level Rook's Nest suite, which has views of St Paul's Cathedral.

★ Zetter

86-88 Clerkenwell Road, EC1M 5RJ (7324 4444, www.thezetter.com). Farringdon tube/rail. **Rooms** 59. **Map** p400 O4.

Zetter is a fun, laid-back, modern hotel with some interesting design notes. There's a refreshing lack of attitude and a forward-looking approach, with friendly staff and firm eco-credentials (such as free Brompton bikes for guests' use). The rooms, stacked up on five galleried storeys around an impressive atrium, look into an intimate and recently refreshed bar area. They are smoothly functional, but cosied up with choice home comforts such as hot-water bottles and old Penguin paperbacks, as well as having walk-in showers with REN smellies. The superlative Bistrot Bruno Loubet downstairs, and the fabulous Zetter Townhouse (*see p171*) in a historic building just across the square – with its excellent cocktail bar – have only served to widen the place's already considerable appeal.

Moderate

★ Fox & Anchor

115 Charterhouse Street, EC1M 6AA (7250 1300, www.foxandanchor.com). Barbican tube or Farringdon tube/rail. **Rooms** 6. **Map** p400 O5.

Check in at the handsome attached boozer (*see p171*) and you'll be pointed to the separate front entrance, with its lovely floor mosaic, and a handful of well-appointed, atmospheric and surprisingly luxurious rooms. All are different, but the high-spec facilities (big flatscreen TV, clawfoot bath and drench shower) and quirky attention to detail (bottles of ale in the minibar, the 'Nursing hangover' privacy signs) are common throughout. Expect some clanking noise in the early mornings, but proximity to the historic Smithfield meat market also means you get a feisty fry-up in the morning in the pub.

BLOOMSBURY, KING'S CROSS & FITZROVIA

Deluxe

Charlotte Street Hotel
15-17 Charlotte Street, W1T 1RJ (7806 2000, www.firmdale.com). Goodge Street or Tottenham Court Road tube. **Rooms** 52. **Map** p397 K5.
Now a fine exponent of Kit Kemp's much imitated fusion of flowery English and avant-garde, this gorgeous hotel was once a dental hospital. Public rooms have Bloomsbury Set paintings by the likes of Duncan Grant and Vanessa Bell, while bedrooms mix English understatement with bold flourishes. The huge, comfortable beds and trademark polished granite and oak bathrooms are suitably indulgent, and some rooms have unbelievably high ceilings. The Oscar restaurant and bar are classy and busy with a smart crowd of media and ad people. At 5pm on Sundays the mini-cinema holds screenings. *Photo p344.*

Sanderson
50 Berners Street, W1T 3NG (7300 1400, www.morganshotelgroup.com). Oxford Circus tube. **Rooms** 150. **Map** p396 J5.
No designer flash in the pan, the Sanderson remains a statement hotel, a Schrager/Starck creation that takes clinical chic in the bedrooms to new heights. Colour is generally conspicuous by its absence. The design throughout is all flowing white net drapes, gleaming glass cabinets and retractable screens. The residents-only Purple Bar sports a button-backed purple leather ceiling and fabulous cocktails; in particular, try the Vesper. The 'billiard room' has a purple-topped pool table, surrounded by strange tribal adaptations of classic dining room furniture.

Expensive

Myhotel Bloomsbury (11-13 Bayley Street, WC1B 3HD, 7667 6000, www.myhotels.com) is a grown-up, urban brother to myhotel Chelsea (*see p256*), giving the trademark Asian touches a masculine, minimalist twist.

★ Great Northern Hotel
King's Cross St Pancras Station, Pancras Road, N1C 4TB (3388 0800, www.gnhlondon.com). King's Cross tube/rail. **Rooms** 91. **Map** p397 L3.
Designed by Lewis Cubitt, the city's first railway hotel (take that, St Pancras Renaissance) opened in 1854, part of the Victorian railway explosion. It has had plenty of rough times since then, not least the 12 years it was dark, but almost £40m of renovation have recreated the place as a classic. The furniture is by artisans and, in many cases, bespoke: witness the Couchette rooms, each with a double bed snugly fitted into the window to playfully echo sleeper carriages; the neatly upholstered bedside cabinets; or the ceiling lights raised and lowered by fabulously steampunk pulleys. You're not expected to suffer the privations of a Victorian traveller, though: free Wi-Fi, film and music libraries on the 40in TV, Egyptian cotton sheets and walk-in showers are all standard. There's no room service but each floor has a simply charming pantry, full of jars of vintage sweets, a stand of fresh cakes, tea and coffee, newspapers and books – even a USB printer. There's also Plum + Spilt Milk, a grand restaurant with a quiet bar, on the first floor, while the busy ground-floor Great Northern Bar has direct access to the station. *Photo p345.*

IN THE KNOW ONES TO WATCH

London has plenty of new hotels in the pipeline – these, all due to open in 2014, are the most exciting.

The Beaumont
8 Balderton Street, Mayfair, W1K 6TF (www.thebeaumont.com).
The first hotel (with 73 rooms) from leading restaurateurs Jeremy King and Chris Corbin, housed in a Grade II-listed art deco ex parking garage. Due to open in autumn.

Ham Yard Hotel
www.firmdalehotels.com.
The latest from Kit Kemp (**Charlotte Street**, *see left;* **Haymarket Hotel**, *see p354;* **Soho Hotel**, *see p348*) – a new flagship venture just off Piccadilly Circus, including a 90-room hotel with restaurant, bar, cinema and bowling alley, plus apartments and shops. Due in May.

Mondrian London
20 Upper Ground, Southwark, SE1 9PF (3747 1000, www.morganshotelgroup.com).
The iconic Sea Containers House on the South Bank is the setting for this 359-room luxury hotel from the group behind the **Sanderson** (*see left*) and **St Martins Lane** (*see p347*). Due late spring.

Shangri-La Hotel at the Shard
www.shangri-la.com/london/shangrila.
The much delayed Shangri-La offers 202 rooms on the 34th-52nd floors of the pointy skyscraper. Due early May.

Zetter Seymour Street
28-30 Seymour Street, Marylebone, W1H 7JB (www.thezetter.com).
We love the **Zetter** in Clerkenwell (*see p342*), so a new hotel is very exciting. Scheduled for late summer.

London Edition

10 Berners Street, W1T 3NP (http://edition-hotels.marriott.com/london). Oxford Circus or Tottenham Court Road tube. **Rooms** 173. **Map** p396 J6.

The London Edition makes a big impact as you walk into its grand hall of a lobby, complete with double-height rococo ceilings, floor-to-ceiling windows and marble pillars. And there's more to the space: it's the setting for the lobby bar, with an eclectic mix of comfortable, snazzy seating: sofas with faux-fur throws and wing-backed chairs, plus a blackened steel bar, a real fire and a colossal silver egg-shaped object hanging where you might expect a chandelier. Off on one side is the equally opulent Berners Tavern (*see p159*), where Jason Atherton is executive chef. With banquette seating and many paintings, it has the vibe of a grand café and a brasserie-style menu to match. Hidden away at the back of the public area is the clubby, wood-panelled Punch Room bar where the speciality is – you've guessed it – punch. Bedrooms are a contrast: akin to lodges or dachas, with matte oak floors, wood-panelled walls and more faux-fur throws tossed on luxurious beds. Larger rooms come with sofas, some have large furnished terraces and all have rainforest showers, Le Labo toiletries (with the hotel's woody signature scent), iPod docks and free Wi-Fi. *Photo p346.*

St Pancras Renaissance

Euston Road, NW1 2AR (7841 3540, www.marriott.com). King's Cross tube/rail. **Rooms** 245. **Map** p397 L3.

A landmark hotel in every sense of the word, the St Pancras Renaissance is the born-again Midland Grand, the pioneering railway hotel designed into the station's imposing Gothic Revival frontage. It opened in 1873 but fell into disuse in the 20th century (except for appearances as a Harry Potter backdrop and in the Spice Girls' 'Wannabe' video, among other screen roles). The Renaissance group (fittingly) has done a beautiful and painstaking job of restoring it to its breathtaking, Grade I-listed best while adding modern comforts. The 120 rooms and suites in the historic hotel (there's a new wing too) have high ceilings, original features and awesome views over the station concourse or forecourt. Facilities are high-spec – Bose stereo, Nespresso machines, REN toiletries, marble baths – and the furniture is modern classic in style. Design is sensitive to the context, re-using motifs from the original decor in the carpets, for example. The subterranean spa includes saunas, a steam room and a Victorian tiled relaxation pool. Public areas, including both restaurants (for the Booking Office, *see p158*) and the gorgeous grand staircase, are similarly splendid. London loves it.

Moderate

Academy

21 Gower Street, WC1E 6HG (7631 4115, www.theacademyhotel.co.uk). Goodge Street tube. **Rooms** 49. **Map** p397 K5.

The Academy goes for the country intellectual look to suit Bloomsbury's studious yet decadent history. It's made up of five Georgian townhouses, and provides in all its rooms a tranquil generosity of space that's echoed in the Georgian squares sitting serenely between the arterial traffic rush of Gower Street and Tottenham Court Road. There's a restrained country-house style in the summery florals and checks and a breath of sophistication in the handsome, more plainly furnished suites. The library and conservatory open on to fragrant walled gardens where drinks and breakfast are served in summer.

Charlotte Street Hotel. *See p343.*

Great Northern Hotel. *See p343.*

Harlingford Hotel

61-63 Cartwright Gardens, WC1H 9EL (7387 1551, www.harlingfordhotel.com). Russell Square tube or Euston tube/rail. **Rooms** 40. **Map** p397 L4.

An affordable hotel with tons of charm in the heart of Bloomsbury, the perkily styled Harlingford has light airy rooms with evident boutique aspirations, and free Wi-Fi. The decor is lifted from understated sleek to quirky with the help of vibrant colour splashes from coloured glass bathroom fittings and mosaic tiles – overall, the hotel has something of a Scandinavian feel. The crescent it's set in has a lovely and leafy private garden where you can lob a tennis ball about or just dream under the trees on a summer's night.

Morgan

24 Bloomsbury Street, WC1B 3QJ (7636 3735, www.morganhotel.co.uk). Tottenham Court Road tube. **Rooms** 21. **Map** p397 K5.

This brilliantly located, comfortable and reasonably priced hotel in Bloomsbury is done out in neutral shades. The rooms are well equipped and all are geared up for the electronic age with wireless, voicemail, flatscreen tellies with Freeview, and air-conditioning. A good, slap-up English breakfast is served in a good-looking room with wood panelling, London prints and blue and white china plates. The spacious flats are excellent value.

Rough Luxe

1 Birkenhead Street, WC1H 8BA (7837 5338, www.roughluxe.co.uk). King's Cross tube/rail. **Rooms** 9. **Map** p397 L3.

In a bit of King's Cross that's choked with ratty B&Bs and cheap chains, this Grade II-listed property takes shabby chic to extremes with artfully distressed walls, torn wallpaper, signature works of art, and old-fashioned TVs that barely work. It even retains the sign for the hotel that preceded Rough Luxe: 'Number One Hotel'. All rooms have free wireless internet, but otherwise have totally different characters: there's the one with the free-standing copper tub, the one with the rose motif and so on. The set-up is flexible, too: rooms with shared bathrooms can be combined for group bookings, and the owners are more than happy to chat with guests over a bottle of wine in the back courtyard where a great breakfast is served. A place to stay if you're looking for somewhere different from the norm.

Budget

Clink78

78 King's Cross Road, WC1X 9QG (7183 9400, www.clinkhostels.com). King's Cross tube/rail. **Beds** 717. **Map** p397 M3.

Located in a listed ex-courthouse, the Clink set the bar high for party-style hosteldom when it opened a few years back. There was the setting: the hostel retains the superb original wood-panelled lobby and courtroom where the Clash once stood before the beak. Then there's the urban-chic ethos that permeates the whole enterprise, from the strealined red reception counter to the Japanese-style 'pod' beds. A thorough redesign of the public areas and licensed café/bar downstairs, with computer screens for internet access (£2/hr), has given things a new rock 'n' roll fillip, with street-art decor and more comfortable furniture to enhance the place's good-time vibe. Clink261 – a rebrand of the nearby Ashlee House, which had its public areas pepped up in 2010 – might be a better choice for older and calmer hostellers.

Other location Clink261, 261-265 Gray's Inn Road, Bloomsbury, WC1X 8QT (7183 9400).

London Edition. *See p344.*

Jenkins Hotel

45 Cartwright Gardens, WC1H 9EL (7387 2067, www.jenkinshotel.demon.co.uk). Russell Square tube or Euston tube/rail. **Rooms** 19. **Map** p397 K3.

This well-to-do Georgian beauty has been a hotel since the 1920s, and was refurbished in 2013. It still has an atmospheric, antique air, although the rooms have mod cons enough – TVs, mini-fridges, tea and coffee, and free Wi-Fi. Its looks have earned it a role in *Agatha Christie's Poirot*, but it's not chintzy, just floral. The breakfast room is handsome, with snowy cotton tablecloths and Windsor chairs.

YHA London Central

104 Bolsover Street, W1W 5NU (0845 371 9154, www.yha.org.uk). Great Portland Street tube. **Beds** 302. **Map** p396 J5.

The Youth Hostel Association's newest hostel is one of its best – as well as being one of the best hostels in London. The friendly and well-informed receptionists are stationed at a counter to the left of the entrance, in a substantial café-bar area. The basement contains a well-equipped kitchen and washing areas; above it, five floors of clean, neatly designed rooms, many en suite. Residents have 24hr access and the location is quiet but an easy walk from most of central London.

Other locations throughout the city.

COVENT GARDEN & THE STRAND

Deluxe

★ Corinthia

Whitehall Place, SW1A 2BD (7930 8181, www.corinthia.com). Embankment tube or Charing Cross tube/rail. **Rooms** 294. **Map** p399 L8.

Firmly in the grand hotel tradition, the Corinthia became a hotel after years as government offices. The colossal, modish chandelier (with 1,000 clear crystal globes, plus one in red) in the expansive lobby complete with central dome; the dark wood and silk-covered walls in the high-spec rooms; the luxurious bathrooms with pool-like oval baths: everything is as you would expect for a hotel in this price range, and it's done well and with a light, modern touch that avoids self-importance or stuffiness. The Espa spa and subterranean pools (with jacuzzi, steam room, sauna and hot seats) form a complex over two floors. Espa products are in bathrooms too. Afternoon tea is a stylish affair, served in the lobby. The Bassoon bar is an intimate, after-dark space, while the Northall restaurant serves British food in a dramatic circular space with floor-to-ceiling windows.

★ Covent Garden Hotel

10 Monmouth Street, WC2H 9HB (7806 1000, www.firmdalehotels.com). Covent Garden, Leicester Square or Tottenham Court Road tube. **Rooms** 58. **Map** p397 L6.

The excellent location in the heart of London's theatre district and tucked-away screening room of this Firmdale hotel ensure that it continues to attract starry customers, with anyone needing a bit of privacy able to retreat upstairs to the lovely panelled private library and drawing room. In the guestrooms, Kit Kemp's distinctive style mixes pinstriped wallpaper, pristine white quilts and floral upholstery with bold, contemporary elements; each room is unique, but each has the Kemp trademark upholstered mannequin and granite and oak bathroom. On the ground floor, the 1920s Paris-style Brasserie Max and its retro zinc bar retain their buzz – outdoor tables give a perfect viewpoint on Covent Garden boutique life in summer.

ME by Meliá London

336-337 the Strand, WC2R 1HA (0845 601 8980, www.melondonuk.com). Covent Garden or Temple tube or Charing Cross tube/rail. **Rooms** 157. **Map** p399 M7.

London's first ME by Meliá – its predecessors are in Madrid, Barcelona, Cancún, Cabo San Lucas and Vienna – is a beauty. Designed by Foster + Partners, the finishes are expensive and carefully modelled on what was there before – respecting the lines of Marconi House, the first BBC radio broadcaster. But it now contains a genuinely breathtaking internal atrium, a pyramid nine floors tall, coolly minimal in style – and starting not at ground floor, but from the first. Here guests can sit and calmly sip champagne as they're checked in by personal 'Aura managers'. In the rooms, the tech and textile details are all taken care of, naturally, but idiosyncratic design touches include triangular windows you can't resist stepping into to peer up and down the Aldwych. The social spaces have different moods neatly covered: from a bling American steakhouse and a basement events space into which cars can be driven, via a more relaxed Italian restaurant, up to Radio, the rather elegant tenth-floor roof terrace bar, where Thames-side seats and exceptional views are hugely in demand.

One Aldwych

1 Aldwych, WC2B 4BZ (7300 1000, www.one aldwych.com). Covent Garden or Temple tube or Charing Cross tube/rail. **Rooms** 105. **Map** p399 M7.

You only have to push through the front door and enter the breathtaking Lobby Bar to know that you're in for a treat. Despite the building's weighty history – the 1907 building was once the offices of the *Morning Post* – One Aldwych is a thoroughly modern establishment, with Frette linen, bathroom mini-TVs and an environmentally friendly loo-flushing system. Flowers and fruit are replenished daily, and a card with the next day's weather forecast appears at turndown. One of two on-site restaurants, Axis, serves modish British food with an emphasis on foraged ingredients. The location is perfect for the West End theatres and has become popular with attendees of London Fashion Week, particularly since many of the events are now held in nearby Somerset House. The three round corner suites are very romantic, and a cosy screening room, excellent spa and a downstairs swimming pool where soothing music is played may dissuade you from ever stepping outside.

St Martins Lane Hotel

45 St Martin's Lane, WC2N 4HX (7300 5500, www.morganshotelgroup.com). Leicester Square tube or Charing Cross tube/rail. **Rooms** 204. **Map** p399 L7.

When it opened over a decade ago, the St Martins was the toast of the town. The flamboyant, theatrical

ME by Meliá London.

lobby was constantly buzzing, and guests giggled like schoolgirls at Philippe Starck's playful decor. The Starck objects – such as the giant chess pieces and gold tooth stools in the lobby – remain, but the space, part of the Morgans Hotel Group, lacks the impact of its heyday. There's still much to be impressed by: the all-white bedrooms have comfortable minimalism down to a T, with floor-to-ceiling windows, gadgetry secreted in sculptural cabinets and sleek limestone bathrooms with toiletries from the spa at sister property Sanderson (*see p343*).

Savoy

The Strand, WC2R 0EU (7836 4343, www.fairmont.com/savoy-london). Covent Garden or Embankment tube, or Charing Cross tube/rail. **Rooms** 268. **Map** p399 L7.

The superluxe, Grade II-listed Savoy reopened after more than £100m of renovations in autumn 2010 – the numerous delays testimony to the difficulty of bringing a listed building, loved by generations of visitors for its discreet mix of Edwardian neoclassical and art deco, up to scratch as a modern luxury hotel. Built in 1889 to put up theatregoers from Richard D'Oyly Carte's Gilbert & Sullivan shows, the Savoy is the hotel from which Monet painted the Thames, where Vivien Leigh met Laurence Olivier, where Londoners learned to love the martini. The famous cul-de-sac at the front entrance now has a garden of new topiary and centrepiece Lalique crystal fountain, but the welcome begins before you arrive with a phone call to ascertain your particular requirements. There's a new tearoom with glass-roofed conservatory; the leather counter of the new Beaufort champagne bar is set on a stage that once hosted big bands for dinner dances; and the Savoy Grill is again under the control of Gordon Ramsay's company. Highlight of the fitness and beauty centre is a pool in its own atrium, with a jet-stream for those who choose to swim against the current. Traditionalists can relax, though: the American Bar remains unchanged.

IN THE KNOW NO FRILLS

Chain hotels aren't covered in this chapter, unless they're new, especially well located (**Premier Inn London County Hall**; *see p339*) or otherwise unusually praiseworthy. This is simply because the internal logic of chain hotels is that one should be as similar as possible to another, with reliability one major virtue – and price the other. You can find double rooms for around £100 at **Holiday Inn** and **Holiday Inn Express** (www.ihg.com/holidayinn), **Ibis** (www.ibishotel.ibis.com) and **Travelodge** (www.travelodge.co.uk).

A relatively new development has been the 'no-frills' approach – very low rates, with nothing inessential included. Airline-offshoot **EasyHotel** (www.easyhotel.com) was the first, but it now faces a challenge from **Tune** (www.tunehotels.com), which now has four London hotels; the first is located not far inland from the South Bank, across the river from the Houses of Parliament. Rooms are usually around £75 a night.

If you've got an awkward departure time from Gatwick or Heathrow, consider the neat 'pod' rooms at a **Yotel** (www.yotel.com); a four-hour stay will cost around £60. And opening in May 2014 at Gatwick is London's first **Bloc** hotel (www.blochotels.com) – a high-tech, no-frills enterprise.

SOHO & LEICESTER SQUARE

Deluxe

Soho Hotel

4 Richmond Mews, W1D 3DH (7559 3000, www.firmdale.com). Piccadilly Circus or Tottenham Court Road tube. **Rooms** 91. **Map** p397 K6.

You'd hardly know you were in the heart of Soho once you're inside Firmdale's edgiest hotel: the place is wonderfully quiet, with what was once a car park now feeling like a converted loft building. The big bedrooms exhibit a contemporary edge, with modern furniture, industrial-style windows and nicely planned mod cons (digital radios as well as flatscreen TVs), although they're also classically Kit Kemp with bold stripes, traditional florals, plump sofas, oversized bedheads and upholstered tailor's dummies. The quiet drawing room and other public spaces feature groovy colours while Refuel, the loungey bar and restaurant, has an open kitchen and, yes, a car-themed mural.

W London Leicester Square

10 Wardour Street, W1D 6QF (7758 1000, www.wlondon.co.uk). Leicester Square tube. **Rooms** 192. **Map** p399 K7.

The old Swiss Centre building on the edge of Leicester Square has been demolished and in its place is the UK's first W Hotel. The W brand has made its name with a series of hip hotels around the world that offer glamorous bars, classy food and functional but spacious rooms. The London W is no exception: Spice Market gets its first UK site within the hotel; Wyld is a large nightclub/bar space aiming to become the Met Bar for a new decade, and the W lounge aims to bring New York's cocktail lounge ethos to London. The rooms – 192 of them, across ten storeys – are well equipped and decent-sized, and FIT (the hotel's state-of-the-art fitness facility), next to the pale and serene Away spa on the sixth floor, offers fine views over Soho. Also of note is the W's

Z Soho. *See p350.*

gobsmacking exterior: the entire hotel is veiled in translucent glass, which is lit in different colours through the day.

Expensive

★ Dean Street Townhouse & Dining Room

69-71 Dean Street, W1D 3SE (7434 1775, www.deanstreettownhouse.com). Leicester Square or Piccadilly Circus tube. **Rooms** 39. **Map** p397 K6.

This Grade II-listed, 1730s townhouse has been converted into another winning enterprise from the people behind Soho House members' club, Shoreditch Rooms (*see p362*) and High Road House (*see p363*). To one side of a buzzy ground-floor restaurant are four floors of bedrooms that run from full-size rooms with early Georgian panelling and reclaimed oak floors to half-panelled 'Tiny' rooms that are barely bigger than their double beds – but can be had from the website for as little as £100. The atmosphere is gentleman's club cosy (there are cookies in a cute silver Treats container in each room), but modern types also get rainforest showers, 24hr room service, Roberts DAB radios, free wireless internet and big flatscreen TVs. Even the calm little library room behind reception manages to be both low-key and luxurious.

★ Hazlitt's

6 Frith Street, W1D 3JA (7434 1771, www.hazlittshotel.com). Tottenham Court Road tube. **Rooms** 30. **Map** p397 K6.

Four Georgian townhouses comprise this absolutely charming place, named after William Hazlitt, the spirited 18th-century essayist who died here in abject poverty. With flamboyance and staggering attention to detail the rooms evoke the Georgian era, all heavy fabrics, fireplaces, free-standing tubs and exquisitely carved half-testers, yet modern luxuries – air-conditioning, free Wi-Fi, TVs in antique cupboards and double-glazed windows – have been subtly attended to as well. It gets creakier and more crooked the higher you go, culminating in enchanting garret single rooms with rooftop views. Of seven new bedrooms, the main suite is a real knock-out: split-level, with a huge eagle spouting water into the raised bedroom bath and a rooftop terrace with sliding roof, it's a joyous extravaganza. Entertainingly, from the back alley outside, the extension has been made to look like 1700s shopfronts.

Moderate

★ One Leicester Street

1 Leicester Street, off Leicester Square, WC2H 7BL (3301 8020, http://oneleicesterstreet.com). Leicester Square or Piccadilly Circus tube. **Rooms** 15. **Map** p399 K7.

The first thing you'll probably notice about this hotel is the awning and streetside terrace of its fine restaurant – the hotel's discreet entrance is on Lisle Street. Through it you'll find a cramped reception area, with stairs up to a sweet little first-floor bar that serves excellent cocktails (well worth remembering if you're ever in Leicester Square). The hotel was taken over from St John restaurant (*see p170*) in 2013 by Singaporean hotelier Peng Loh, who is also behind the Town Hall (*see p361*). Some touches are familiar from there – the nacreous tiles in the classy bathrooms, for instance –

but otherwise the stripped-back aesthetic is very St John: simple comfort, but with all essentials in place. The top-floor suite is a beautifully lit eyrie.

Budget

Z Soho
17 Moor Street, W1D 5AP (3551 3700, www.thezhotels.com). Leicester Square or Tottenham Court Road tube. **Rooms** 85. **Map** p397 K6.
For the money, the Z is a cast-iron bargain. First, the location is superb: it really means Soho, not a short bus-ride away – the breakfast room/bar exits on to Old Compton Street. Then there's the hotel itself, which is surprisingly chic – especially the unexpected interior courtyard, with open 'corridors' stacked above it, and room to sit and drink or smoke at the bottom – and very cheerfully run, down to free wine and nibbles of an evening. The rooms are quite handsome, and have everything you need, from a little desk to free Wi-Fi, but not much more. Including space: expect beds (perhaps a little short for anyone over 6ft tall) to take up most of the room, a feeble shower, and no wardrobes or phones in the rooms. A great little hotel – in both senses. *Photo p349.*
Other location Z Victoria, 5 Lower Belgrave Street, Victoria, SW1W 0NR.

OXFORD STREET & MARYLEBONE

Expensive

Cumberland
Great Cumberland Place, off Oxford Street, W1H 7DL (0871 376 9014, www.guoman.com). Marble Arch tube. **Rooms** 1,019. **Map** p393 F6.
Perfectly located by Marble Arch tube, the Cumberland is a bit of a monster: in addition to the 900 rooms in the main block, there are another 119 in an annexe down the road. The echoing, rather chaotic lobby has some dramatic modern art and sculptures, as well as an impressive but somewhat severe waterfall. The rooms are minimalist, with acid-etched headboards, neatly modern bathrooms and plasma TVs – nicely designed, but rather small. There's dining in the Brasserie, plus Carbon, a boisterous, trash-industrial style, late-night DJ bar, and the quieter Momentus champagne bar. Weekend breakfasts can feel like feeding the 5,000.

Dorset Square
39-40 Dorset Square, NW1 6QN (7723 7874, www.dorsetsquarehotel.co.uk). Marylebone tube/rail. **Rooms** 38. **Map** p393 F4.
Grown-up greys are a backdrop for splashes of orange-red and midnight blue, with bold patterns completing a sophisticated modish meets traditional look – the hallmark of owners Firmdale. The Regency townhouse has comfortable, spacious bedrooms,

Dorset Square.

many looking on to the leafy private square; bathrooms are in granite and glass, with Miller Harris products. Downstairs is a comfortable lounge with a fireplace and the Potting Shed restaurant and bar. This property was actually Firmdale's first hotel. It was sold in 2002, but the company bought it again and refurbished it, reopening it in summer 2012.

Montagu Place
2 Montagu Place, W1H 2ER (7467 2777, www.montagu-place.co.uk). Baker Street tube. **Rooms** 16. **Map** p396 G5.
A small, fashionable townhouse hotel, Montagu Place fills a couple of Grade II-listed Georgian residences with sharply appointed rooms graded according to size. The big ones are entitled Swanky, and have king-size beds and big bathrooms – some have narrow front terraces. More modest in size, the Comfy category has queen-size beds and, being at the back of the building, no street views. All rooms have a cool and trendy look, with cafetières and ground coffee instead of Nescafé sachets, as well as flatscreen TVs and free Wi-Fi. The decision to combine bar and reception desk (situated at the back of the house) means you can get a drink at any time and retire to the graciously modern lounge. Service is at once sharp and very obliging.

Moderate

Sumner
54 Upper Berkeley Street, W1H 7QR (7723 2244, www.thesumner.com). Marble Arch tube. **Rooms** 19. **Map** p393 F6.
The Sumner's cool, deluxe looks have earned it many fans, not least in the hospitality industry, where it has won a number of awards. You won't be at all surprised when you get here: from the soft dove

and slatey greys of the lounge and halls you move up to glossily spacious accommodation with brilliant walk-in showers. The breakfast room feels soft and sunny, with a lovely, delicate buttercup motif and vibrant Arne Jacobsen chairs to cheer you on your way to the museums, but the stylishly moody front sitting room is also a cosy gem.

22 York Street

22 York Street, W1U 6PX (7224 2990, www.22yorkstreet.co.uk). Baker Street tube.
Rooms 10. **Map** p396 G5.
Bohemian French chic – white furniture, palest pink lime-washed walls, mellow wooden floors, subtly faded textiles and arresting *objets d'époque* – makes this delightfully unpretentious bed and breakfast in the heart of Marylebone a sight to behold. It doesn't announce itself from the outside, so you feel as if you've been invited to stay in someone's arty home, especially when you're drinking good coffee at the gorgeous curved table that dominates the breakfast room-cum-kitchen. Guests are also given free rein with the hot beverages in a lounge full of knick-knacks upstairs, while a cluttered smaller room downstairs has an internet station (the Wi-Fi is free). All rooms are a decent size and have en suite baths, a rarity at this price and in this part of London.

PADDINGTON, BAYSWATER & NOTTING HILL

Expensive

Portobello Hotel

22 Stanley Gardens, W11 2NG (7727 2777, www.portobellohotel.com). Holland Park or Notting Hill Gate tube. **Rooms** 21. **Map** p404 Y5.
The Portobello is a hotel with approaching half a century of celebrity status, having hosted the likes of Johnny Depp, Kate Moss and Alice Cooper, who used his tub to house a boa constrictor. It remains a pleasingly unpretentious place, with a more civilised demeanour than its legend might suggest. There is now a lift to help rockers who are feeling their age up the five floors, but there's still a 24hr guest-only bar downstairs for those who don't yet feel past it. The rooms are themed – the superb basement Japanese Water Garden, for example, has an elaborate spa bath, its own private grotto and a small private garden – but all are stylishly equipped with a large fan, tall house plants, free Wi-Fi and round-the-clock room service.

Moderate

Hotel Indigo London Paddington

16 London Street, W2 1HL (7706 4444, www.ichotelsgroup.com). Paddington tube/rail.
Rooms 64. **Map** p393 D6.
This boutique property from the people behind Crowne Plaza and Holiday Inn has a relaxed all-day bar-restaurant, sharp-witted and friendly staff, and rooms with all mod cons (excellent walk-in showers rather than baths) – the smaller and cheaper attic rooms have most character. All have free Wi-Fi. The decor is a bit try-hard: a clinical white foyer gives on to acid-bright striped carpets and wardrobe interiors that are an assault by psychedelic swirl. Photographs of Paddington past and ingenious ceiling strips of sky show how less could have been more. A second Hotel Indigo (142 Minories, EC3N 1LS, 7265 1014) opened in 2010, and a third in 2012 in Earl's Court (33-34 Barkston Gardens, SW5 0EW).

La Suite West
See p352.

★ La Suite West

41-51 Inverness Terrace, W2 3JN (7313 8484, www.lasuitewest.com). Bayswater or Queensway tube. **Rooms** 80. **Map** p392 C6.

A typical row of west London townhouses on the outside, La Suite has been transformed on the inside by designer Anouska Hempel, with sleek lines and a black and white palette – the antithesis of her maximalist Blakes (*see p356*). A discreet side entrance leads into a long minimalist reception area with open fire and a zen-like feel. An Asian influence persists in the rooms, with slatted sliding screens for windows, wardrobe and bathrooms helping to make good use of space (which is limited in the cheaper rooms). Thoughtfully designed white marble bathrooms, with rainforest shower and bath, give a feeling of luxury despite not being huge. The large terrace running along the front of the building, with trees planted for an arbour-like effect, is a big summer asset for drinks, lunch or dinner, and the Raw vegetarian restaurant is an unusual take on hotel dining. All in all, clever design, a friendly vibe and – importantly – keen pricing make for a great hotel for this price range. Highly recommended. *Photo p351.*

New Linden

59 Leinster Square, W2 4PS (7221 4321, www.newlinden.co.uk). Bayswater tube. **Rooms** 50. **Map** p392 B6.

Modern, modish and moderately priced – that's the Mayflower Group for you. This is its Bayswater baby. It looks very cool, however, and it is a fantastically comfortable place to stay. The lobby and lounge are slick and glamorous – there's a beautiful teak arch in the lounge and the rooms are low-key with some vibrant, twirly eastern influences. Some of the larger family rooms retain their elaborate period pillars and cornicing. The bathrooms are a symphony in marble; the walk-in showers have deluge heads. There's a pleasant little patio, upstairs at the back, for morning coffee and evening drinks.

Vancouver Studios

30 Prince's Square, W2 4NJ (7243 1270, www.vancouverstudios.co.uk). Bayswater or Queensway tube. **Rooms** 51. **Map** p392 B6.

Step into the hall or comfortably furnished sitting room of this imposing townhouse and it feels like the gracious home of a slightly dotty uncle, with decor in the public spaces comprising colonial swords and historic prints. The studio or apartment accommodation is more modern in tone. Each room has its own style – from cool contemporary lines to a softer, more homely feel – and all are well equipped with kitchen appliances so that guests can do a bit of self-catering, should they wish. There's free Wi-Fi too. Zeus the cat lords it over the building and can show you into the pretty garden with its fountain and heady scent of jasmine – a shady stunner.

Budget

Garden Court Hotel

30-31 Kensington Gardens Square, W2 4BG (7229 2553, www.gardencourthotel.co.uk). Bayswater or Queensway tube. **Rooms** 39. **Map** p392 B6.

Once people have discovered the Garden Court Hotel, they tend to keep coming back, says Edward Connolly, owner-manager of this long-established hotel, with quiet pride. There aren't many places this close to Hyde Park and Portobello Market that give such excellent value for money and impeccable service. The rooms in this grand Victorian terrace have a bright, modern look and plenty of space, and the lounge, with its wood floor, leather-covered furniture, sprightly floral wallpaper and elegant mantelpiece, is a lovely place to linger.

Pavilion

34-36 Sussex Gardens, W2 1UL (7262 0905, www.pavilionhoteluk.com). Edgware Road tube or Marylebone or Paddington tube/rail. **Rooms** 29. **Map** p393 E5.

A hotel that describes itself as 'fashion rock 'n' roll' is never going to be staid, but Danny and Noshi Karne's Pavilion is quite mind-bogglingly excessive. The rooms have attention-grabbing names, such as 'Enter the Dragon' (you've guessed, Chinese themed), 'Honky Tonk Afro' (a tribute to the 1970s) 'Flower Power' (blooming flowery) and 'Cosmic Girl' (way out there, man). They are frequently used for fashion shoots, and the website has an impressive list of celebrities who have rocked up here over the years. Bizarre and voluptuous choice of decor notwithstanding, this crazy hotel actually represents excellent value and has the usual amenities, including free Wi-Fi. You might be disappointed if you want cool contemporary elegance and poncey toiletries – the Pavilion's much more fun than that.

★ Stylotel

160-162 Sussex Gardens, W2 1UD (7723 1026, www.stylotel.com). Edgware Road tube or Marylebone or Paddington tube/rail. **Rooms** 39. **Map** p393 E6.

Partly due to the young manager's enthusiasm, it's hard not to like this place. It's a retro-futurist dream: metal floors and panelling, lots of royal blue (the hall walls, the padded headboards) and pod bathrooms. But the real deal at Stylotel is its bargain studio and apartment (respectively, £120-£150 and £150-£200, with breakfast included), around the corner above a pub. Designed – like the rest of the hotel – by the owner's son, they suggest he's calmed down with age. Here's real minimalist chic: sleek brushed steel or white glass wall panels, simply styled contemporary furniture upholstered in black or white.

PICCADILLY CIRCUS & MAYFAIR

Deluxe

Brown's

Albemarle Street, W1S 4BP (7493 6020, www.roccofortecollection.com). Green Park tube. **Rooms** 117. **Map** p398 J7.

Brown's was opened in 1837 by James Brown, butler to Romantic poet, hedonist and freedom-fighter Lord Byron. The first British telephone call was made from here in 1876, five years after Napoleon III and Empress Eugenie took refuge in one of the considerable suites after fleeing the Third Republic. Ethiopian Emperor Haile Selassie and Rudyard Kipling were also guests. The bedrooms are all large and extremely comfortable, furnished with original art, collections of books and, in the suites, fireplaces; the elegant, classic British hotel restaurant, Hix Mayfair, gives a nod to modernity with a series of contemporary British artworks, including pieces by the likes of Tracey Emin, but the public spaces of the hotel thrum with history. Non-residents can visit: try the afternoon tea in the English Tea Room or sip a cocktail in the classily masculine Donovan Bar.

★ Claridge's

55 Brook Street, W1K 4HR (7629 8860, www.claridges.co.uk). Bond Street tube. **Rooms** 203. **Map** p396 H6.

Claridge's is sheer class and pure atmosphere, with its signature art deco redesign still simply dazzling. Photographs of Churchill and sundry royals grace the grand foyer, as does an absurdly over-the-top Dale Chihuly chandelier. Without departing too far from the traditional, Claridge's restaurant is actively fashionable (Simon Rogan has recently taken over from Gordon Ramsay), and A-listers can gather for champers in the bar. The rooms divide evenly between deco and Victorian style, with period touches such as deco toilet flushes in swanky marble bathrooms. Bedside panels control the mod-con facilities at the touch of a button. If money's no object, opt for a David Linley suite, in duck-egg blue and white, or lilac and silver.

★ Connaught

Carlos Place, W1K 2OAL (7499 7070, www.the-connaught.co.uk). Bond Street tube. **Rooms** 121. **Map** p398 H7.

This isn't the only hotel in London to provide butlers, but there can't be many that offer 'a secured gun cabinet room' for the hunting season. This is traditional British hospitality for those who love 23-carat gold leaf trimmings and stern portraits in the halls, but all mod cons in their room, down to flatscreens in the en suite. Too lazy to polish your own shoes? The butlers are trained in shoe care by the expert cobblers at John Lobb. Both of the bars – gentleman's club cosy Coburg (*see p118*) and cruiseship deco Connaught – and the Hélène Darroze restaurant are very impressive. In the new wing, which doubled the number of guestrooms, there's a swanky spa and 60sq m swimming pool.

Dorchester

53 Park Lane, W1K 1QA (7629 8888, www.thedorchester.com). Hyde Park Corner tube. **Rooms** 250. **Map** p398 G7.

A Park Lane fixture since 1931, the Dorchester's interior may be thoroughly, opulently classical, but the hotel is cutting edge in attitude, providing an unrivalled level of personal service. With the grandest lobby in town, amazing views of Hyde Park, state-of-the-art mod cons and a magnificent spa, it's small wonder the hotel continues to welcome movie stars (the lineage stretches from Elizabeth Taylor to Tom Cruise) and political leaders (Eisenhower planned the D-Day landings here). You're not likely to be eating out, either: the Dorchester employs 90 full-time chefs at the Grill Room, Alain Ducasse and the wonderfully atmospheric China Tang. There's even an angelic tea-room in the new spa: the Spatisserie. A few years ago, the Dorchester opened an entirely new hotel, 45 Park Lane (*see below*), in the former Playboy club premises, almost opposite the entrance to its predecessor.

★ 45 Park Lane

45 Park Lane, W1K 1PN (7493 4545, www.45parklane.com). Hyde Park Corner tube. **Rooms** 46. **Map** p398 G8.

Offspring of the Dorchester, which it faces across a twinkly-treed forecourt, 45 Park Lane opened in late 2011 to immediate acclaim in the style and travel press. It had succeeded resoundingly in the task it had set itself: to translate the famously high standards of the Dorchester into a buzzier, boutiquier, even blingier form. Where the Dorchester offers liveried concierges, 45 Park Lane allocates guests a personal host sharply suited in grey; where the Dorchester can arrange a limo, so can 45 – or lend you a folding bike. Wolfgang Puck brings informal glamour and high-end steaks to the Cut restaurant, and Bar 45 has the largest collection of American wines in the UK. Rooms are standard rectangles given character by well-chosen art, quality furnishings, great views (ask for an upper floor) and considered touches such as a yoga mat, designer glassware and in-safe electrical outlet. Technology is state of the art; enormous flatscreens swing out from the walls; a TV is embedded in the bathroom mirror (to watch from the giant marble bath); and touchscreens control room functions electronically.

Haymarket Hotel

1 Suffolk Place, SW1Y 4HX (7470 4000, www.firmdale.com). Piccadilly Circus tube. **Rooms** 50. **Map** p399 K7.

A terrific addition to Kit Kemp's Firmdale portfolio, this block-size building was designed by John Nash, the architect of Regency London. The public spaces are a delight, with Kemp's trademark combination of contemporary arty surprises and plump, floral sofas. Wow-factors include the bling basement swimming pool and bar (shiny sofas, twinkly roof) and the central location. Rooms are generously sized (as are bathrooms), individually decorated and discreetly stuffed with facilities, and there's plenty of attention from the switched-on staff. The street-side bar and restaurant are top-notch, the breakfast is exquisite.

Metropolitan

19 Old Park Lane, W1K 1LB (7447 1000, www.metropolitan.como.bz). Hyde Park Corner tube. **Rooms** 144. **Map** p398 H8.

The flashier little sister of the Halkin (*see p358*), the Metropolitan may have had its fashion heyday in the 1990s, but it still retains a buzzy, relaxed sense of cool. The Met bar and Nobu restaurant continue to attract celebrities and models, bands such as Kings of Leon still rock up, and many mere mortals drop by to rubberneck. The hotel itself is bright and uncluttered. The rooms are a little clinical and appear ever-so-slightly dated, but pear-wood furnishings, super-soft mattresses and suede throws keep things very comfortable, and the toiletries in the bathrooms are a cut above the usual chuck-away

San Domenico House. *See p356.*

ESSENTIAL INFORMATION

fodder. The hotel's greatest asset, however, is the prime location, overlooking a corner of Hyde Park.

Ritz

150 Piccadilly, W1J 9BR (7493 8181, www.theritzlondon.com). Green Park tube. **Rooms** 134. **Map** p398 J8.

If you like the idea of a world where jeans and trainers are banned and jackets must be worn by gentlemen when dining (the requirement is waived for breakfast), the Ritz is the place for you. Founded by hotelier extraordinaire César Ritz, the hotel is deluxe *in excelsis*. The show-stopper is the ridiculously ornate, vaulted Long Gallery, an orgy of chandeliers, rococo mirrors and marble columns, but all the high-ceilinged, Louis XVI-style bedrooms have been painstakingly renovated to their former glory in restrained pastel colours. But amid the old-world luxury, there are plenty of mod cons including free wireless in most rooms, large TVs and gym. An elegant afternoon tea in the Palm Court (book ahead) is the way in for interlopers.

Expensive

No.5 Maddox Street

5 Maddox Street, W1S 2QD (7647 0200, www.living-rooms.co.uk). Oxford Circus tube. **Rooms** 12. **Map** p396 J6.

This bolthole just off Regent Street is perfect for visiting film directors looking to be accommodated in a chic apartment at a reasonable long-term rate. Here they can shut the discreet brown front door, climb the stairs and flop into a home from home with all contemporary cons, including new flatscreen TVs. The East-meets-West decor is classic 1990s minimalist, but very bright and clean after a gentle refurbishment. Each apartment has a fully equipped kitchen, but room service will shop for you as well as providing usual hotel amenities. There's no bar, but breakfasts and snacks are served, and there's a Thai restaurant (Patara) on the ground floor.

WESTMINSTER & ST JAMES'S

Deluxe

Royal Horseguards

2 Whitehall Court, SW1A 2EJ (0871 376 9033, www.guoman.com). Embankment tube or Charing Cross tube/rail. **Rooms** 280. **Map** p399 L8.

The Royal Horseguards occupies a French château that is discreetly located off Whitehall. The building was designed by Alfred 'Natural History Museum' Waterhouse for the National Liberal Club in 1887, and the club's founder, William Gladstone, the great reformer that he was, probably would have approved of the recent refurbishment of the interior by the Guoman group. It's immaculately clean, 'classic but modern' in style, with welcoming staff. The red-furnished Equus bar has a gentlemen's club-like feel. The bedrooms have useful dressing tables, iPod docks and wonderfully comfortable Hypnos beds, and bathrooms come with a flatscreen TV and Guoman toiletries. The buffet-style breakfasts are ordinary, but from the upper floors the river views of County Hall and the London Eye – whisper it – rival those of the Savoy (*see p348*).

Expensive

Eccleston Square Hotel

37 Eccleston Square, SW1V 1PB (3489 1000, www.ecclestonsquarehotel.com). Pimlico tube or Victoria tube/rail. **Rooms** 39. **Map** 398 H11.

This Grade II-listed Georgian house has been transformed into a smart, urbane and rather masculine boutique hotel, in a palette of grey, black and white, with high-quality fittings such as Italian marble chevron flooring throughout the ground floor and black Murano glass chandeliers. Upstairs, the monochrome continues, with leather headboards, and silk wallpaper and curtains, all in shades of grey. It's in the rooms that the hotel's USP becomes apparent: it's all about the tech. Whether it's the underfloor heating in the bathroom, the lighting or the curtains, it's all operated by finger-tip control pads. The most snazzy is the one that turns the 'smart glass' of the white marble bathroom walls opaque for privacy. (Bath-lovers note that these are eschewed here in favour of rainfall showers.) In addition, every room comes equipped with an iPad (and the Wi-Fi's free). It's all super convenient and comfortable.

Trafalgar

2 Spring Gardens, Trafalgar Square, SW1A 2TS (7870 2900, www.thetrafalgar.com). Charing Cross tube/rail. **Rooms** 129. **Map** p399 K7.

The Trafalgar is part of the Hilton chain of hotels, but you'd hardly notice. The mood is young and dynamic at the chain's first 'concept' hotel, for all that it's housed in the imposing edifice that was once the headquarters of Cunard (this was where the Titanic was conceived). To the right of the open reception is the Rockwell Bar, which is boisterous at night, although thick walls should prevent sound leaking up to the rooms; breakfast downstairs is accompanied by gentler music, sometimes played live. It's the none-more-central location, however, that's the hotel's biggest draw – the handful of corner suites look directly into the square (prices reflect location). Those without their own view can always avail themselves of the little rooftop bar, which is open to the public during the summer months.

Moderate

B+B Belgravia

64-66 Ebury Street, SW1W 9QD (7259 8570, www.bb-belgravia.com). Victoria tube/rail. **Rooms** 17. **Map** p398 H10.

How do you make a lounge full of white and black contemporary furnishings seem cosy and welcoming? Hard to achieve, but the owners have succeeded at B+B Belgravia, which takes the B&B experience to a new level. It's fresh and sophisticated without being hard-edged: there's nothing here that will make the fastidiously design-conscious wince (leather sofa, arty felt cushions, modern fireplace), but nor is it overly precious. A gleaming espresso machine provides 24/7 caffeine, and there's a large but somewhat dark garden to sit out in at the rear.

Windermere Hotel

142-144 Warwick Way, SW1V 4JE (7834 5163, www.windermere-hotel.co.uk). Victoria tube/rail. **Rooms** 19. **Map** p398 H11.

Heading the procession of small hotels that are strung out along Warwick Way, the Windermere is a comfortable, traditionally decked-out London hotel with, thankfully, no aspirations to boutique status. The decor may be showing its age a bit in the hall, but you'll receive a warm welcome and excellent service – there are over a dozen staff for just 19 rooms. There's a cosy basement restaurant-bar, where the breakfasts are top-notch.

Budget

Morgan House

120 Ebury Street, SW1W 9QQ (7730 2384, www.morganhouse.co.uk). Pimlico tube or Victoria tube/rail. **Rooms** 11. **Map** p398 G10.

The Morgan has the understated charm of the old family home of a posh but unpretentious English friend: a pleasing mix of nice old wooden or traditional iron beds, with pretty floral curtains and coverlets in subtle hues, the odd chandelier or big gilt mirror over original mantelpieces, and padded wicker chairs and sinks in every bedroom, along with free Wi-Fi. Though there's no guest lounge, guests can sit in the little patio garden in better weather and, for Belgravia, the prices are a steal.

CHELSEA

Expensive

Myhotel Chelsea

35 Ixworth Place, SW3 3QX (7225 7500, www.myhotels.com). South Kensington tube. **Rooms** 46. **Map** p395 E11.

The Chelsea myhotel feels a world away from its sleekly modern Bloomsbury sister (*see p343*). The Sloane Square branch has an aesthetic that is softer and decidedly more English – with a floral sofa and plate of scones in the lobby, and white wicker headboards, velvet cushions and Bee Kind toiletries in the guestrooms. These feminine touches contrast nicely with the mini-chain's feng shui touches, Eastern-inspired treatment room and sleek aquarium. Breakfast and cold dishes are served in a bar-restaurant with a modernised farmhouse feel, while Pellicano serves Italian food. The central library, which is done out in conservatory style, is simply wonderful. Just pick up a book, sink into one of the ample comfy chairs and listen to the tinkling water feature.

San Domenico House

29-31 Draycott Place, SW3 2SH (7581 5757, www.sandomenicohouse.com). Sloane Square tube. **Rooms** 17. **Map** p395 F11.

Along a quiet terrace of late 19th-century red-stone buildings just off Sloane Square, San Domenico owes much of its tasteful, historic look to previous owner Sue Rogers, the interior designer who transformed this former private residence into a boutique hotel masterpiece. All the categories of guestroom, including the split-level gallery suites and a new junior suite, feature original furnishings or antiques. Royal portraits, Victorian mirrors and Empire-era travelling cases are complemented by fabrics of similar style and taste, offset by contemporary touches to bathrooms. The spacious bedrooms enjoy wide-angle views of London, some from little balconies, and have free Wi-Fi. Breakfasts are taken up to guests or laid out in the room downstairs, while main meals may be taken in the sumptuous coffee room by the lobby.

KNIGHTSBRIDGE & SOUTH KENSINGTON

The landmark **Lanesborough** hotel (7259 5599, www.lanesborough.com) at Hyde Park Corner was closed for renovations at the time of writing, scheduled to reopen in October 2014.

Deluxe

Blakes

33 Roland Gardens, SW7 3PF (7370 6701, www.blakeshotels.com). South Kensington tube. **Rooms** 47. **Map** p395 D11.

As original as when Anouska Hempel opened it in 1983 – the scent of oranges and the twittering of a pair of lovebirds fill the dark, oriental lobby – Blakes and its maximalist decor have stood the test of time, a living casebook for interior design students. Each room is in a different style, with influences from Italy, India, Turkey and China. Exotic antiques picked up on the designer's travels – intricately carved beds, Chinese birdcages, ancient trunks – are set off by sweeping drapery and piles of plump cushions. Downstairs, the Eastern-influenced restaurant caters for a celebrity clientele enticed by the hotel's discreet, residential location.

Gore

190 Queen's Gate, SW7 5EX (7584 6601, www.gorehotel.com). South Kensington tube. **Rooms** 50. **Map** p395 D9.

GOING DUTCH

There's no need to split the bill at London's cheap-chic imports.

Hoxton.

Back in the mists of time – you know... 2009 or so – a hip new hotel opened in arty but then down-at-heel Shoreditch. Its owner reckoned he could give guests all mod cons in small but stylish rooms – at competitive prices. We loved the **Hoxton** (*see p361*), weren't at all surprised it was a success – and awaited a splurge of copy-cat hotels.

A mere three years later, we got our challenger: **citizenM London Bankside** (*see p339*) arrived from the Netherlands. It was affordable, stylish, had a real buzz, and cleverly set itself in the thick of the arty action: right behind Tate Modern (*see p56*).

The ground floor is a slick yet cosy café-bar and reception area: self-check-in, but with staff on hand to help and, when higher-grade rooms are free, offer upgrades. Guests are invited to use it as their 'living room' and – thanks to the neat design – do so. The rooms themselves are tiny but well thought out: there are blackout blinds, free Wi-Fi, drench showers with removable sidehead, storage under the bed and free movies. The rooms are also fun: those blinds are automatic, controlled – like the movies, air-con and funky coloured lighting – from a touch-sensitive tablet.

And what is about the Dutch? In 2013, they're at it again, with the arrival of the sassy, well-located and very affordable **Qbic Hotel London City** (*see p362*).

But the home team hasn't quite given up. It turns out the Hoxton is preparing a local fight-back, with the opening of the Hoxton Holborn at some point in 2014.

citizenM London Bankside.

Number Sixteen.

This fin-de-siècle period piece was founded by descendants of Captain Cook in two grand Victorian townhouses. The lobby and staircase are close hung with old paintings, and the bedrooms all have fantastic 19th-century carved oak beds, sumptuous drapes and shelves of old books. The suites are spectacular: the Tudor Room has a huge stone-faced fireplace and a minstrels' gallery, while tragedy queens should plump for the Venus room and Judy Garland's old bed (and replica ruby slippers). Bistrot 190 provides a casually elegant setting for great breakfasts, while the warm, wood-panelled 190 bar is a charming and elegant setting for cocktails.

Halkin

Halkin Street, SW1X 7DJ (7333 1000, www.comohotels.com/thehalkin). Hyde Park Corner tube. **Rooms** 41. **Map** p398 G9.
Set up by Singaporean fashion mogul Christina Ong (who also owns the Metropolitan; *see p354*), the Halkin marries Eastern charm, style and food with a central and quiet location in Knightsbridge. The rooms, all located off black curved, almost trompe l'oeil wooden corridors, are comfortable and full of Asian artefacts and clever gadgetry (a touch-screen bedside panel controls everything from the air-con to the 'do not disturb' sign on the door). Bathrooms are well equipped and heavy on the marble, and come stocked with a range of products from Ong's Shambhala spa. The Michelin-starred Basque restaurant Ametsa with Arzak Instruction is on the ground floor, and there's tapas and afternoon tea, as well as cocktails, served in the bar.

Milestone Hotel & Apartments

1-2 Kensington Court, W8 5DL (7917 1000, www.milestonehotel.com). High Street Kensington tube. **Rooms** 56. **Map** p392 C8.
Wealthy American visitors make annual pilgrimages here, their arrival greeted by the comforting, gravel tones of their regular concierge, as English as roast beef, and the glass of sherry in the room. Yet amid the old-school luxury (butlers on 24-hour call) thrives inventive modernity (the resistance pool in the spa). Rooms overlooking Kensington Gardens feature the inspired decor of South African owner Beatrice Tillman: the Safari suite contains tent-like draperies and leopard-print upholstery; the Tudor Suite has an elaborate inglenook fireplace, minstrels' gallery and a pouffe concealing a pop-up TV. Afternoon tea is served in the Park Lounge, a glorious melding of library and boudoir.

Expensive

★ Number Sixteen

16 Sumner Place, SW7 3EG (7589 5232, www.firmdalehotels.com). South Kensington tube. **Rooms** 41. **Map** p395 D10.
This may be Kit Kemp's most affordable hotel but there's no slacking in the typical Firmdale hotel style stakes – witness the fresh flowers and origami-ed birdbook decorations in the comfortable drawing room. Bedrooms are generously sized, bright and very light, and carry the Kemp trademark mix of bold and traditional. The whole place has an appealing freshness about it, enhanced by a delicious, large back garden complete with a central water feature. By the time you finish

breakfast in the sweet conservatory, you'll have forgotten you're in the middle of the city.

Moderate

Ampersand

10 Harrington Road, SW7 3ER (7589 5895, www.ampersandhotel.com). South Kensington tube. **Rooms** 111. **Map** p395 D10.

In a Victorian stucco property, Ampersand has a strong design ethos, with dove greys and duck egg blues enlivened by splashes of purples, yellows and reds, bringing together a striking and distinctive look. A whimsical twist on the classic comes from the likes of tall purple padded headboards reaching nearly to the ceiling and dove drawings on the dove-grey walls in the ornithologically inspired deluxe rooms. In the corridors, botanical drawings and representations of scientific instruments reference the museums nearby, while the colourful lounge area – where afternoon tea is served – has deep sofas and studded armchairs in scarlet velvets and kingfisher blues and a multi-coloured teapot collection in a wall cabinet. Breakfast and dining is found downstairs in the white-tiled Mediterranean-oriented Apero restaurant.

Vicarage Hotel

10 Vicarage Gate, W8 4AG (7229 4030, www.londonvicaragehotel.com). High Street Kensington or Notting Hill Gate tube.
Rooms 17. **Map** p392 B8.

Scores of devotees return regularly to this tall Victorian townhouse, which has a great location, tucked in a quiet leafy square just off High Street Ken, hard by Kensington Gardens. It's a comfortable, resolutely old-fashioned establishment – and that's what the punters come for. The refurbished entrance hall is wonderfully grand, with red and gold striped wallpaper, a huge gilt mirror and chandelier. A sweeping staircase ascends from there to an assortment of good-sized rooms, furnished in pale florals and nice old pieces of furniture.

NORTH LONDON

Expensive

York & Albany

127-129 Parkway, Camden, NW1 7PS (7387 5700, www.gordonramsay.com). Camden Town tube. **Rooms** 9. **Map** p404 X3.

Overcommitment to TV and transatlantic enterprises might have knocked a little gloss off Gordon Ramsay's restaurants, but his only hotel is still going strong. Housed in a grand John Nash building that was designed as a coaching house but spent the recent past as a pub, it consists of a restaurant (split over two levels), bar and delicatessen downstairs; above them a selection of nine rooms, handsomely designed by Russell Sage in mellow shades. The decor is an effective mix of ancient and modern, sturdy and quietly charismatic furniture married to modern technology; if you're lucky, you'll have views of Regent's Park from your bedroom window.

Moderate

Colonnade

2 Warrington Crescent, Little Venice, W9 1ER (7286 1052, www.colonnadehotel.co.uk). Warwick Avenue tube. **Rooms** 44. **Map** p392 C4.

Housed in an imposingly sited white mansion, the Colonnade has been lushly done up in interior-designer traditional – lots of swagged curtains, deep opulent colours, luxurious fabrics and careful arrangements of smoothly upholstered furniture. Some of the larger high-ceilinged rooms have had mezzanine floors added. A new restaurant opened in early 2014.

Rose & Crown

199 Stoke Newington Church Street, Stoke Newington, N16 9ES (7923 3337, www.roseandcrownn16.co.uk). Bus 73. **Rooms** 6.

The Rose has always been popular as a pub, but now a separate entrance leads to a contemporary B&B. Landscape gardener Will, who with Diane runs the place, transformed three floors to create individually and tastefully styled guestrooms (drench showers, quality smellies and furnishings), a breakfast room and a sun-catching roof terrace with a large table, a couple of loungers, a patio heater and a view across to central London from the illuminated glow of 13th-century St Mary's Church alongside. Pricier rooms feature a stand-alone bathtub, and the suite by the breakfast room is vast. Truman Brewery touches from yesteryear remain: the pub sign lettering, a finely carved pre-war stair rail and the Mystery Arrow games machine.

Budget

Hampstead Village Guesthouse

2 Kemplay Road, Hampstead, NW3 1SY (7435 8679, www.hampsteadguesthouse.com). Hampstead tube or Hampstead Heath rail. **Rooms** 9.

Owner Annemarie van der Meer loves to point out all the quirky space-saving surprises as she shows you round her wonderful and idiosyncratic bed and breakfast: here's the folding sink, there's the bed that pops out of an antique wardrobe… The special atmosphere at this double-fronted Victorian house, set on a quiet Hampstead street, means that guests return year after year. Each room is uniquely decorated with eclectic furnishings – such as the French steel bathtub in one room – and there's a self-contained studio with its own kitchen. All guests may make use of a range of home comforts, from hot-water bottles to mobile phones, as well as a laptop to borrow and free Wi-Fi. Breakfast (which costs extra) may be taken in the garden that surrounds this lovely property on all four sides.

IT'S ACE IN LONDON

US hotel hipsters hit the city.

The **Ace Hotel** (*see p361*) of New York, Palm Springs, Portland, Seattle and Panama, has landed in London. The group may have a few hotels now, but its approach is nothing like that of a typical chain. In its very singular philosophy, each hotel (and London is no exception) is deeply rooted in its local environment. It starts with a choice of site: in this case in a creative hub that's also near the City. It's matched by a love of craftsmanship, and the use of small, often local, manufacturers to produce beautiful, individual and useful objects for the hotel. In addition, the Ace aims to become a local centre for events, with DJs, live music, screenings and parties most nights.

Most Aces convert buildings that were built for a different use, but in the Shoreditch case, the group took over an old Crowne Plaza hotel; a byproduct is spacious rooms and wide corridors. The look of the rooms is comfortable, a bit bohemian, like a modern urban apartment, with wall-to-wall daybeds/sofas, sturdy oak or metal storage units, round oak tables and beds (and sofas too) covered in luxury denim. Furniture and accessories reflect the Ace appreciation of artisanship. You might find an Ally Capellino leather change box (her shop is just down the road), a CF Martin & Co guitar, or maybe a Rega RP1 turntable and some vintage vinyl. And everyone gets a cosy denim-covered quilt by APC and an individual artwork.

Furniture in public spaces is covered in lovely tweeds from Bute Fabrics (a firm set up to provide employment for ex-servicemen after World War II), matched with walls in distressed concrete and full-height Crittall glass and steel screens. The lobby vibe is egalitarian and informal, with a long communal table with computers and DJs every night. There's a cute juice bar, Lovage, with a window to the street for picking up a juice on your way to work, a nook of a coffee shop from Square Mile Coffee Roasters, a bar tucked into another nook with a skylight and pale bricks in articulated patterns, and flower shop That Flower Shop. And, of course, the wood-clad midcentury-look brasserie Hoi Polloi (*see p206*), serving modish British food until late, with a relaxed bar area that's open all day for no-reservations eating and drinking.

EAST LONDON

Expensive

★ Ace Hotel London Shoreditch

100 Shoreditch High Street, Shoreditch, E1 6JQ (7613 9800, www.acehotel.com/london). Liverpool Street tube/rail or Shoreditch High Street rail. **Rooms** 258. **Map** p401 R4.
See p360 **It's Ace in London.**

Boundary

2-4 Boundary Street, Shoreditch, E2 7DD (7729 1051, www.theboundary.co.uk). Liverpool Street tube/rail or Shoreditch High Street rail. **Rooms** 17. **Map** p401 R4

Design mogul Sir Terence Conran's Boundary Project warehouse conversion was a labour of love. Its restaurants – which include Albion (*see p206*), a downstairs fine-dining establishment and a rooftop bar – are high quality but relaxed, and all 17 bedrooms are beautifully designed. Each has a wet room and handmade bed, but all are otherwise individually furnished with classic furniture and original art. The five split-level suites range in style from the bright and sea-salt fresh Beach to a new take on Victoriana by Polly Dickens, while the remaining rooms (the slightly larger corner rooms have windows along both external walls) are themed by design style: Mies van der Rohe, Eames, Shaker. There's also a charming Heath Robinson room, decorated with the cartoonist's sketches of hilariously complex machines.

Town Hall Hotel

Patriot Square, Bethnal Green, E2 9NF (7871 0460, www.townhallhotel.com). Bethnal Green tube. **Rooms** 98.

A few years back, a grand, Grade II-listed, early 20th-century town hall was transformed into a classy modern aparthotel – despite its unpromising location between a council estate and a scruffy row of shops. The decor is minimal, retaining many features (walnut panelling and marble for the interior, Portland stone outside, stained glass, and fire hoses on old brass reels scattered about) that would be familiar to the local-government bureaucrats who used to toil here, but jazzed up with contemporary art and a patterned aluminium 'veil' that covers the new floor at the top of the building. The pale-toned, spacious apartments are well equipped for self-catering, but hotel luxuries such as free wireless internet and TV/DVD players are also in place. The De Montfort suite is the size of most houses, stretching over three floors, with a living room as big as a council chamber. Viajante restaurant is one of the hottest in town, and is joined by the less formal, also much praised, Corner Room (*see p210*). Under a conservatory roof, there's a narrow basement swimming pool with sparkly tiles.

Moderate

Aloft

One Eastern Gateway, Royal Victoria Dock, E16 1FR (3203 0700, www.aloftlondonexcel.com). Custom House or Prince Regent DLR. **Rooms** 252.

In the (Dock)land where chain mediocrity or bland corporate efficiency prevails, Aloft – a cheaper option from the swanky W chain (*see p348*) – is refreshing. Outside, the design is rather cool, a swoop of shiny surfaces with charming coloured lighting; inside, service is winningly offhand. Shove your credit card into the self-check-in and your key card is dispensed, giving you access to the upper floors by lift, where further funky lighting guides you to your room (nicely finished, masculine decor; remote keyboard to operate the telly; free Wi-Fi; decently appointed wet room). Your card also gets you into the pool and gym, while careless packers have a coin-op mobile phone charger in the lobby. Aloft is right at the exit from the ExCeL conference centre, so Friday night in the bar-diner is lively with post-conference hair being let down.

40 Winks

109 Mile End Road, Stepney, E1 4UJ (7790 0259, 07973 653944, www.40winks.org). Stepney Green tube. **Rooms** 2. **No credit cards.**

Opposite a housing estate and cheap Somali diners, the family home of an interior designer has become the B&B of choice for movie stars and fashion movers. The 'micro-boutique hotel' looks extraordinary (kitchen frescoes, a music room with Beatles drumkit, a lion's head tap in the bath), but each stay is made individual by owner David Carter's commitment to his guests, making them feel they're staying with a fabulous friend rather than just renting a room. Too late to book? Intriguing soirées such as Bedtime Stories (for which everyone must wear pyjamas) open the house to a wider audience. It's flamboyant, fashionable and very cool.

★ Hoxton Hotel

81 Great Eastern Street, Shoreditch, EC2A 3HU (7550 1000, www.hoxtonhotels.com). Old Street tube/rail. **Rooms** 208. **Map** p401 Q4.

Famous for its low rates (including some publicity-garnering £1-a-night rooms), the Hoxton deserves credit for many other things. First, there's the hip Shoreditch location – hip enough for Soho House to have taken over the downstairs bar-brasserie a few years ago. Then there are the great design values (the foyer is a sort of postmodern country lodge, complete with stag's head). Finally, the rooms are well thought out, if mostly rather small, with lots of nice touches – free fresh milk in the fridges, a cold snack for breakfast, free Wi-Fi. Nowadays, there are even three individually designed suites. The downside? Popularity. If you don't book well in advance and plan to visit during the week rather than at the weekend, you could pay as much as at one of the big chains. A major refurbishment was in the pipeline at the time of writing.

★ Shoreditch Rooms

Ebor Street, Shoreditch, E1 6AW (7739 5040, www.shoreditchhouse.com). Shoreditch High Street rail. **Rooms** 26. **Map** p401 S4.

The most recent hotel opening from Soho House members' club (*see also p349* Dean Street Townhouse; *p363* High Road House) might even be the best, perfectly catching the local atmosphere with its unfussy, slightly retro design. The rooms feel a bit like urban beach huts, with pastel-coloured tongue-and-groove, shutters and swing doors to the en suite showers. They feel fresh, bright and comfortable, even though they're furnished with little more than a bed, an old-fashioned phone and DAB radio, and a big, solid dresser (minibar, hairdryer and treats within, flatscreen TV on top). Guests get access to the fine eating, drinking and fitness facilities (yes, a gym, but more importantly an excellent rooftop pool) in the members' club next door. Everything's put together with a light touch, from the 'Borrow Me' bookshelf by the lifts (jelly beans, umbrellas, boardgames) to the room grades: Tiny (from just £105), Small or Small+ (with little rooftop balconies from which to survey the grey horizon).

Budget

Qbic Hotel London City

42 Adler Street, Whitechapel, E1 1EE (no phone, www.qbichotels.com). Aldgate East or Whitechapel tube. **Rooms** 171. **Map** p403 S6.

The second prong of the Dutch invasion of stylish budget hotels (*see p357* **Going Dutch**) is cheaper and more focused on community (working with local cycling charity Bikeworks and Food Cycle, who provide free soup every afternoon) and sustainability: in fact, the hotel was created at the end of 2013 by the incredibly rapid fit-out of a former office building using modular 'Cubi' bedrooms. Rooms are sold at four levels – starting at £59 a night for no view, and increasing in price if you want to see the Whitechapel Road, the inner courtyard or Altab Ali Park. Prices are pegged by keeping down the numbers of staff, which means self check-in and no cash accepted – even vending machines are credit card only. Still, the essentials are covered: TVs in each room, free wireless internet throughout, free snack breakfast or £7.50 for a continental in the natty social space downstairs. The location is gritty but great: minutes from Brick Lane (*see p202*) and the Whitechapel Gallery (*see p204*).

SOUTH-EAST LONDON

Moderate

Church Street Hotel

29-33 Camberwell Church Street, Camberwell, SE5 8TR (7703 5984, www.churchstreethotel.com). Denmark Hill rail or bus 36, 436. **Rooms** 27.

Craftsman José Raido is behind this attractive and original family-run hotel near Camberwell Green. Funky bathroom tiles in the bright, high-ceilinged bedrooms come from Guadalajara, and are thus a perfect match for Mexicana such as imported film posters, while the bed frames were forged by José himself. The colours are as vivid as a Mexican sunset. Bathroom products are organic, as are the pastries and cereals served for breakfast in an icon-filled dining room that also operates as a 24-hour honesty bar. You pay only £90 for a single with shared bathroom, which is a real bargain, and the hotel tapas restaurant, Angels & Gypsies, is a big hit locally.

SOUTH-WEST LONDON

Expensive

★ Bingham

61-63 Petersham Road, Richmond, Surrey TW10 6UT (8940 0902, www.thebingham.co.uk). Richmond tube/rail. **Rooms** 15.

Quality boutique hotel, destination restaurant (under Shay Cooper's award-winning supervision) and sun-filled cocktail bar in one, the Bingham makes excellent use of its superb riverside location by Richmond Bridge. Six of its individually styled and high-ceilinged rooms overlook the Thames; all of them are named after a poet, in honour of the Bingham's artistic past (lesbian aunt-and-niece couple Katherine Harris Bradley and Edith Emma Cooper lived here in the 1890s, regularly hosting members of the Aesthetic Movement while they were in residence). Each room accommodates an ample bathtub and shower, art deco touches to the furnishings and irresistibly fluffy duck-and-goose-feather duvets. Run by the Trinder family for the last 25 years, the Bingham manages to feel both grand and boutique. A treat.

WEST LONDON

Moderate

★ Garret

Troubadour, 263-267 Old Brompton Road, Earl's Court, SW5 9JA (7370 1434, www.troubadour.co.uk). West Brompton tube/rail. **Rooms** 2. **Map** p394 B11.

This idiosyncratic attic apartment is an absolute treat. High above the Troubadour, a 1960s counter-culture café that still hosts poetry and music events, it's unjustly named: yes, the rooms are in the attic and have charming pitched roofs, but there are acres of space for two – and even enough for a small family, if the kids sleep on the pull-out sofa in the lounge-kitchen. The huge, high main bed lies under a skylight and there's a writing desk, but any thought of poetic torment is banished by the well-executed Arts and Crafts decor and fully equipped kitchen area, right down to the cafetière and wines. A new room, the Eleanor, has recently been added.

High Road House

162 Chiswick High Road, Chiswick, W4 1PR (8742 1717, www.highroadhouse.co.uk). Turnham Green tube. **Rooms** 14.

This west London outpost of Nick Jones's ever-fashionable Soho House stable (*see also p349* Dean Street Townhouse; *p362* Shoreditch Rooms) features guestrooms designed by Ilse Crawford, and a members' bar and restaurant above the buzzing ground-floor brasserie. Serving a modern British menu, this has a retro Parisian-bistro-meets-Bloomsbury feel and, as you might expect, the food and service are excellent. Guestrooms are soothing, unadorned, white Shaker Modern with little fizzes of colour (and little hidden treats), the bathrooms well stocked with Cowshed products.

★ Mayflower Hotel

26-28 Trebovir Road, Earl's Court, SW5 9NJ (7370 0991, www.mayflower-group.co.uk). Earl's Court tube. **Rooms** 46. **Map** p394 B11

After fighting on the front lines of the Earl's Court budget-hotel style revolution, the Mayflower's taken the struggle to other parts of London (New Linden; *see p352*). But this is where the lushly contemporary house style evolved, proving that affordability can be opulently chic. The recent complete refurbishment of the hotel, involving public areas and all the guestrooms, shows that it's not resting on its laurels. Hand-carved Asian artefacts complement the richly coloured fabrics. The facilities too are well up to scratch, featuring marble bathrooms, Egyptian cotton sheets, free Wi-Fi and CD players in the rooms.

Rockwell

181-183 Cromwell Road, Earl's Court, SW5 0SF (7244 2000, www.therockwell.com). Earl's Court tube. **Rooms** 40. **Map** p394 B10.

The Rockwell aims for relaxed contemporary elegance – and succeeds magnificently. The listed premises mean that there are no identikit rooms here: they're all different sizes and individually designed, but share gleaming woods and muted glowing colours alongside more sober creams and neutrals. Among the rooms, pleasing eccentricities include a pair of central single rooms with skylights, and basement garden rooms that have tiny patios, complete with garden furniture, looking up at the ground-level bridge that leads on to the garden terrace proper from the handsome bar-restaurant. Each room has a power

Shoreditch Rooms.

shower, Starck fittings and bespoke cabinets in the bathrooms, and triple-glazing ensures you never notice the noisy road just outside.

Twenty Nevern Square
20 Nevern Square, Earl's Court, SW5 9PD (7565 9555, http://www.20nevernsquare.com). Earl's Court tube. **Rooms** 25. **Map** p394 A11.
Only the less-than-posh location of this immaculate boutique hotel keeps the rates reasonable. Tucked away in a private garden square, it feels far from its locale. The modern-colonial style was created by its well-travelled owner, who personally sourced many of the exotic and antique furnishings (as well as those in sister hotel the Mayflower; *see p363*). In the sleek marble bathrooms, toiletries are tidied away in decorative caskets, but the beds are the real stars: from elaborately carved four-posters to Egyptian sleigh styles, all with luxurious mattresses. The vaguely Far Eastern feel extends into the lounge and the airy conservatory, with its dark wicker furniture.

APARTMENT RENTAL

Holiday Serviced Apartments (0845 470 4477, www.holidayapartments.co.uk) and **Palace Court Holiday Apartments** (7727 3467, www.palacecourt.co.uk) specialise in holiday lets. **London Holiday Accommodation** (7265 0882, www.londonholiday.co.uk) offers half a dozen decent-priced self-catering options in the West End and on the South Bank. For serviced apartments, try the South Bank or Earl's Court 'campuses' run by **Think Apartments** (3465 9100, www.think-apartments.com). **Accommodation Outlet** (www.outlet4 holidays.com) is a recommended lesbian and gay agency that has some excellent properties across London in general and in Soho in particular.

CAMPING & CARAVANNING

If putting yourself at the mercy of English weather in a far-flung suburban field doesn't put you off, the difficult transport links into central London might do the job instead. Still, you can't really beat the prices.

Crystal Palace Caravan Club *Crystal Palace Parade, Crystal Palace, SE19 1UF (8778 7155). Crystal Palace rail or bus 3.* **Open** *Mar-Sept* 9am-6pm daily. *Oct-Jan* 9.30am-5.30pm daily.

STAYING WITH THE LOCALS

Several agencies can arrange for individuals and families to stay in Londoners' homes. They include **At Home in London** (8748 2701, www.athomeinlondon.co.uk), **Host & Guest Service** (7385 9922, www.host-guest.co.uk), **London Bed & Breakfast Agency** (7586 2768, www.londonbb.com) and **London Homestead Services** (7286 5115, www.lhslondon.co.uk). There is usually a minimum length of stay.

UNIVERSITY RESIDENCES

During vacations, much of London's dedicated student accommodation is available to visitors. Central locations can make these a bargain.
International Students House *229 Great Portland Street, Marylebone, W1W 5PN (7631 8300, www.ish.org.uk). Great Portland Street tube.* **No credit cards**. **Map** p396 H4.
King's College Conference & Vacation Bureau *Strand Bridge House, 138-142 the Strand, Covent Garden, WC2R 1HH (7848 1700, www.kingsvenues.com). Temple tube.* **No credit cards**. **Map** p399 L7.
LSE *Bankside House, 24 Sumner Street, Bankside, SE1 9JA (7107 5750, www.lsevacations.co.uk). London Bridge tube.* **Map** p402 O8.
The LSE has vacation rentals across town, but Bankside House is the best located.

YOUTH HOSTELS

For Youth Hostel Assocation venues, you can get extra reductions on the rates detailed below if you're a member of the IYHF (International Youth Hostel Federation): you'll pay £3 less a night. Joining costs only £15.95 (£9.95 for under-25s), and can be done on arrival or through www.yha.org.uk prior to departure. All under-18s receive a 25 per cent discount, in any case. YHA hostel beds are arranged either in dormitories or in twin rooms. Our favourite hostels are reviewed (**YHA London Central**, *see p346*; **Clink78**, *see p345*), but those listed below are all handily located across town.

Earl's Court *38 Bolton Gardens, Earl's Court, SW5 0AQ (7373 7083, www.yha.org.uk). Earl's Court tube.* **Open** 24hrs daily. **Map** p394 B11.
Holland Park *Holland Walk, Holland Park, W8 7QU (7937 0748, www.yha.org.uk). Holland Park tube.* **Open** 24hrs daily. **Map** p392 A8.
Meininger *Baden-Powell House, 65-67 Queen's Gate, South Kensington, SW7 5JS (7590 6910, www.meininger-hostels.com). Gloucester Road or South Kensington tube.* **Map** p395 D10.
Oxford Street *14 Noel Street, Soho, W1F 8GJ (7734 1618, www.yha.org.uk). Oxford Circus tube.* **Open** 24hrs daily. **Map** p396 J6.
St Pancras *79-81 Euston Road, King's Cross, NW1 2QE (7388 9998, www.yha.org.uk). King's Cross tube/rail.* **Open** 24hrs daily. **Map** p397 L3.
St Paul's *36 Carter Lane, the City, EC4V 5AB (7236 4965, www.yha.org.uk). St Paul's tube or Blackfriars rail.* **Open** 24hrs daily. **Map** p402 O6.

Getting Around

ARRIVING & LEAVING

By air

Gatwick Airport *0844 892 0322, www.gatwickairport.com. About 30 miles south of London, off the M23.*
Of the three rail services that link Gatwick to London, the quickest is the **Gatwick Express** (0845 850 1530, www.gatwickexpress.com) to Victoria; it takes 30mins and runs 4.30am-12.30am daily. Tickets cost £19.90 single or £34.90 for an open return. Under-16s pay £9.95 for a single and £17.45 for returns; under-5s go free.

Southern (0845 127 2920, www.southernrailway.com) also runs a rail service between Gatwick and Victoria, with trains every 5-10mins (hourly 2-4am and every 15-30mins midnight-2am, 4-6am). It takes about 35mins, and costs £14.40 for a single, £14.50 for a day return (after 9.30am) and £29 for an open period return. Under-16s get half-price tickets; under-5s go free.

If you're staying in King's Cross or Bloomsbury, consider trains run by **First Capital Connect** (0845 748 4950, www.firstcapitalconnect.co.uk) to St Pancras. Tickets are £10 single, £10.40 day return (after 9.30am); £19 for an open return.

A **taxi** to the centre costs about £100 and takes a bit over an hour.

Heathrow Airport *0844 335 1801, www.heathrowairport.com. About 15 miles west of London, off the M4.*
The **Heathrow Express** train (0845 600 1515, www.heathrowexpress.co.uk) runs to Paddington every 15mins (5.12am-11.48pm daily), and takes 15-20mins. Tickets cost £20 single and £34 return (more if you buy on board); under-16s travel at half-price. Many airlines have check-in desks at Paddington Station.

The journey by tube is longer but cheaper. The 50-60min **Piccadilly line** ride into central London costs £5.50 one way (£2.70 under-16s). Trains run every few minutes from about 6am to 12.30am daily (7am-11.30pm Sun).

The **Heathrow Connect** (0845 678 6975, www.heathrowconnect.com) rail service offers direct access to Hayes, Southall, Hanwell, West Ealing, Ealing Broadway and Paddington stations in west and north-west London. The trains run every half-hour, terminating at Heathrow Central (Terminals 1, 2 and 3). From there to Terminal 4 get the free shuttle; between Central and Terminal 5, there's free use of the Heathrow Express. A single from Paddington is £9.50; an open return is £19.

National Express (0871 781 8178, www.nationalexpress.com) runs daily coach services to London Victoria (90mins, 4.20am-22.05pm daily), leaving Heathrow Central bus terminal every 20-30mins. It's £6 for a single (£3 under-16s) or £11 (£5.50 under-16s) for a return.

A taxi into town will cost £45-£85 and take 30-60mins.

London City Airport *7646 0088, www.londoncityairport.com. About 9 miles east of London.*
The Docklands Light Railway (DLR) includes a stop for London City Airport. The journey to Bank station in the City takes around 20mins, and trains run 5.36am-12.16am Mon-Sat, 7.06am-11.16pm Sun. A taxi costs around £35 to central London.

Luton Airport *01582 405100, www.london-luton.com. About 30 miles north of London, J10 off the M1.*
It's a short shuttle bus ride from the airport to Luton Airport Parkway station. From here, the **First Capital Connect** rail service (*see left*) calls at many stations; journey time is 35-45mins. Trains leave every 15mins or so and cost £13.50 single one-way and £23.50 return. Trains between Luton and St Pancras run at least hourly all night.

By coach, the Luton to Victoria journey takes 60-90mins. **Green Line** (0844 801 7261, www.greenline.co.uk) runs a 24hr service. A single is £10 and returns cost £15; under-15s £7 single, £10 return. A taxi to London costs £100-£120.

Stansted Airport *0844 335 1803, www.stanstedairport.com. About 35 miles north-east of London, J8 off the M11.*
The **Stansted Express** train (0845 748 4950, www.stanstedexpress.com) runs to and from Liverpool Street Station; the journey time is 40-45mins. Trains leave every 15mins, and tickets cost £23.40 single, £32.80 return; under-16s travel half-price, under-5s free.

Several companies run coaches to central London. The **National Express** service (0871 781 8178, www.nationalexpress.com) from Stansted to Victoria takes at least 80mins. Coaches run roughly every 30mins (24hrs daily), more at peak times. A single is £10 (£5 for under-16s), return is £18 (£9 for under-16s).

A **taxi** into the centre of London costs around £120.

By coach

Coaches run by **National Express** (0871 781 8178, www.nationalexpress.com), the biggest coach company in the UK, arrive at **Victoria Coach Station** (164 Buckingham Palace Road, SW1W 9TP, 0843 222 1234, www.tfl.gov.uk), a good 10min walk from Victoria tube station. This is where companies such as **Eurolines** (0871 781 8178, www.eurolines.com) dock their European services.

By rail

Trains from mainland Europe run by Eurostar (0843 218 6186, www.eurostar.com) arrive at **St Pancras International** (Pancras Road, Euston Road, N1C 4QP, 7843 7688, www.stpancras.com).

PUBLIC TRANSPORT

Getting around London on public transport is straightforward but it's certainly not cheap.

For lost property, *see p371*.

Information

Details on timetables and other travel information are provided by **Transport for London** (0343 222 1234, www.tfl.gov.uk). Complaints or comments on most forms of public transport can also be taken up with **London TravelWatch** (3176 2999, www.londontravelwatch.org.uk).

Travel Information Centres
TfL's Travel Information Centres provide help with the tube, buses

and DLR. You can find them in **King's Cross tube station**, (7.15am-8pm Mon-Sat; 8.15am-7pm Sun), and in the stations below. Call 0343 222 1234 for more information.

Euston Station 7.15am-7pm Mon-Thur, Sat; 7.15am-8pm Fri; 8.15am-7pm Sun.
Heathrow Terminals 1, 2 & 3 tube station 7.30am-7.30pm daily.
Liverpool Street tube station 7.15am-7pm Mon-Thur, Sat; 7.15am-8pm Fri; 8.15am-7pm Sun.
Piccadilly Circus tube station 7.45am-7pm Mon-Fri; 9.15am-7pm Sat; 9.15am-6pm Sun.
Victoria Station 7.15am-8pm Mon-Sat; 8.15am-7pm Sun.

Fares & tickets

Tube and DLR fares are based on a system of six zones, stretching 12 miles out from the centre of London. A flat cash fare of £4.70 per journey applies across zones 1-3 on the tube, and £5.70 for zones 1-6; customers save up to £2.50 per journey with a pre-pay Oyster card (*see below*). Anyone caught without a ticket or Oyster card is subject to a £80 on-the-spot fine (reduced to £40 if you pay within three weeks).

Oyster cards A pre-paid smart-card, Oyster is the cheapest way of getting around on public transport. You can charge up standard Oyster cards at tube stations, Travel Information Centres (*see p365*), some rail stations and newsagents. There is a £5 refundable deposit payable on each card; to collect your deposit, call 0343 222 1234.

Visitor Oyster cards are available from Gatwick Express outlets, National Express coaches, Superbreak, visit britainshop.com, Oxford Tube coach service and on Eurostar services. The only difference between Visitor Oysters and 'normal' Oysters is that they come pre-loaded with money.

A tube journey in zone 1 using Oyster pay-as-you-go costs £2.20 (80p for under-16s), compared to the cash fare of £4.70. A single tube ride within zones 2, 3, 4, 5 or 6 costs £2.70 (80p for under-16s); single journeys from zones 1 through to 6 using Oyster are £5 (6.30-9.30am, 4-7pm Mon-Fri) or £3 (all other times), or 80p for children. Up to four children under 11 can travel for free when travelling with an adult.

Day Travelcards If you're only using the tube, DLR, buses and trams, using Oyster to pay as you go will always be capped at the same price (or lower – *see below*) as an equivalent Day Travelcard. However, if you're also using National Rail services, Oyster may not be accepted: opt, instead, for a Day Travelcard, a standard ticket with a coded stripe that allows travel across all networks.

Anytime Day Travelcards can be used all day. They cost from £9 for zones 1-2 (£4.50 child), up to £17 for zones 1-6 (£8.50 child). Tickets are valid for journeys begun by 4.30am the next day. The cheaper **Off-Peak Day Travelcard** allows travel after 9.30am Mon-Fri and all day at weekends and public holidays. It costs £8.90 for zones 1-6 (there are no longer different off-peak day Travelcards for zones 1-2 and 1-4). However, Oyster now has day capping of £7 if you're travelling between zones 1-2 off peak, £7.70 between zones 1-4 off peak, and £8.50 between zones 1-6 off peak – in other words, prices that work out cheaper than a day Travelcard, making Oyster pay as you go the cheaper option.

Children Under-5s travel free on buses and trams without the need to provide any proof of identity. Five- to 10-year-olds can also travel free, but need to obtain a 5-10 Zip Oyster photocard. For details, visit www.tfl.gov.uk/tickets or call 0343 222 1234.

An 11-15 Zip Oyster photocard is needed by 11- to 15-year-olds to pay as they go on the tube/DLR and to buy 7-Day, monthly or longer period Travelcards, and by 11- to 15-year-olds to use the tram to/from Wimbledon for free.

Photocards Photocards are not required for 7-Day Travelcards or Bus Passes, adult-rate Travelcards or Bus Passes charged on an Oyster card. For details of how to obtain 5-10, 11-15 or 16+ Oyster photocards, see www.tfl.gov.uk/tickets or call 0343 222 1234.

London Underground

Delays are fairly common, with some lines closing at weekends for engineering works. Trains are hot and crowded in rush hour (7.30-9.30am and 4.30-6.30pm Mon-Fri) – avoid the rush by travelling after 9.30am and you'll also pay less for your fare. The 12 colour-coded lines that together comprise the underground rail system – also known as 'the tube' – remain the quickest way to get around much of London (for a map of the Underground, *see pp414-415*), carrying some 3.5 million passengers every weekday. Comments or complaints are dealt with by **TfL Customer Services** on 0343 222 1234 (8am-8pm daily).

Using the system You can get Oyster cards from www.tfl.gov.uk/tickets, by calling 0343 222 1234, at tube stations, Travel Information Centres, some rail stations and newsagents. Single or day tickets can be bought from ticket offices or machines. You can buy most tickets and top up Oyster cards at self-service machines. Some ticket offices close early (around 7.30pm); carry a charged-up Oyster card to avoid being stranded.

To enter and exit the tube using an Oyster card, simply touch it to the yellow reader, which will open the gates. Make sure you also touch the card to the reader when you exit the tube, or you'll be charged a higher fare when you next use your card to enter a station. On certain lines, you'll see a pink 'validator' – touch this reader in addition to the yellow entry/exit readers and on some routes it will reduce your fare.

To enter using a paper ticket, place it in the slot with the black magnetic strip facing down, then pull it out of the top to open the gates. Exiting is done in much the same way; however, if you have a single journey ticket, it will be retained by the gate as you leave.

Timetables Tube trains run daily from around 5.30am (except Sunday, when they start an hour or so later, and Christmas Day, when there's no service). You shouldn't have to wait more than 10mins for a train; during peak times, services should run every 2-3mins. Times of last trains vary; they're usually around 12.30am daily (11.30pm on Sun). The tubes run all night only on New Year's Eve; otherwise, you're currently limited to night buses (*see p367*). However, there are plans to introduce a limited 24hr weekend service (dubbed the 'Night Tube') from 2015.

Fares The single fare for adults across the network is £4.70 for journeys within zones 1-3; £5.70 for zones 1-6; £7 for zones 1-7; £8.10 for zones 1-9. Using Oyster pay-as-you-go, journeys within zone 1 cost £2.20; zones 1-2 costs £2.20 or £2.80, depending on the time of day; zones 1-6 costs £3 or £5. The single fare for children aged 5-15 is 75p or 80p for any journey in zones 1-6 depending on the time of day. Under-5s travel free.

National Rail & London Overground services

Independently run commuter services co-ordinated by **National Rail** (0845 748 4950, www.nationalrail.co.uk) leave from the city's main rail stations. Visitors heading to south London, or to more remote destinations such as Hampton Court Palace, will need to use these overground services. Travelcards are valid on these services within the right zones, but not all routes accept Oyster pay-as-you-go; check before you travel.

Operated by Transport for London, meaning it does accept Oyster, the **London Overground** is a fabulously useful new service. Originally the rail line ran through north London from Stratford in the east to Richmond in the south-west, with spurs connecting Willesden Junction in the north-west to Clapham Junction in the south-west, and Gospel Oak in the north to Barking in the east, as well as heading north-west from Euston. Then, in 2010, the reopened East London line was incorporated into the Overground network, connecting trains south of the river to trains to the north: effectively, Crystal Palace, West Croydon and New Cross are now connected (via useful, new intermediate stations such as Shoreditch High Street) to Highbury & Islington and the northerly extent of the Overground. Trains run about every 20mins (every half an hour on Sunday), more frequently on popular lines.

Docklands Light Railway (DLR)

DLR trains (7363 9700, www.tfl.gov.uk/dlr) run from Bank station (where they connect with the tube system's Central and Waterloo & City lines) or Tower Gateway, close to Tower Hill tube (Circle and District lines). At Westferry station, the line splits east and south via Island Gardens to Greenwich and Lewisham; a change at Poplar can take you north to Stratford. The easterly branch forks after Canning Town to either Beckton or Woolwich Arsenal. Trains run 5.20am-12.20am daily.

Fares Fares on the DLR are the same as for the tube.

Buses

You must have a ticket or valid pass before boarding any bus in zone 1. You can buy a ticket (or a 1-Day Bus Pass) from machines at bus stops, although they're often not working; better to travel with an Oyster card or some other pass (*see p366*). Inspectors patrol buses at random; if you don't have a ticket or pass, you may be fined £80.

All buses are now low-floor vehicles that are accessible to wheelchair-users and passengers with buggies. The only exceptions are Heritage routes 9 and 15, which are served by the world-famous open-platform Routemaster buses.

Fares Using Oyster pay-as-you-go costs £1.45 a trip; your total daily payment, regardless of how many journeys you take, will be capped at £4.40. Paying with cash at the time of travel costs £2.40 for a single trip – and, from summer 2014, you won't be able to pay directly on board. Under-16s travel for free (using an Under-11 or 11-15 Oyster photocard as appropriate; *see p366*).

Night buses Many bus routes operate 24hrs a day, seven days a week. There are also some special night buses with an 'N' prefix, which run from about 11pm to 6am. Most night services run every 15-30mins, but busier routes run a service around every 10mins. Fares are the same as for daytime buses; Bus Passes and Travelcards can be used at no extra fare until 4.30am of the morning after they expire, with Oyster day-capping in effect until then too.

Green Line buses Green Line buses (0844 801 7261, www.greenline.co.uk) serve the suburbs within 40 miles of London. Its office is opposite **Victoria Coach Station** (*see p365*); services run 24hrs.

Tramlink

In south London, trams run between Beckenham, Croydon, Addington and Wimbledon. Travelcards that cover zones 3, 4, 5 or 6 are valid, as are Bus Passes. Cash fares are £2.40 (£1.45 with Oyster pay-as-you-go).

Water transport

Most river services operate every 20-60mins between 10.30am and 5pm, and may run more often and later in summer. For commuters, **Thames Clippers** (www.thamesclippers.com) runs a service between Embankment Pier and Royal Arsenal Woolwich Pier; stops include Blackfriars, Bankside, London Bridge, Canary Wharf and Greenwich. A standard day roamer ticket (valid 9am-9pm) costs £15, while a single from Embankment to Greenwich is £6.50, or £5.85 for Oyster cardholders.

Westminster Passenger Service Association (7930 2062, www.wpsa.co.uk) runs a daily service from Westminster Pier to Kew, Richmond and Hampton Court from April to October. At around £12 for a single, it's not cheap, but it is a lovely way to see the city, and there are discounts of 33%-50% for Travelcard holders.

Thames River Services (7930 4097, www.westminsterpier.co.uk) operates from the same pier, with trips to Greenwich, Tower Pier and the Thames Barrier. A trip to Greenwich costs £12. Travelcard holders get a third off.

TAXIS

Black cabs

The licensed London taxi, aka 'black cab' (although they now come in many colours), is a much-loved feature of London life. Drivers must pass a test called 'the Knowledge' to prove they know every street in central London, and the shortest route to it.

If a taxi's orange 'For Hire' sign is lit, it can be hailed. If a taxi stops, the cabbie must take you to your destination if it's within seven miles. Fares rise after 8pm on weekdays and at weekends.

You can book black cabs from the 24hr **Taxi One-Number** (0871 871 8710, a £2 booking fee applies, plus 12.5% if you pay by credit card), **Radio Taxis** (7272 0272) and **Dial-a-Cab** (7253 5000; credit cards only, with a booking fee of £2 plus a 12.5% handling charge). Complaints about black cabs should be made to the **Public Carriage Office** (0845 602 7000, www.tfl.gov.uk/pco). Note the cab's badge number, which should be displayed in the rear of the cab and on its back bumper.

Minicabs

Minicabs (saloon cars) are generally cheaper than black cabs, but can be less reliable. Only use licensed firms (look for a disc in the front and rear windows), and avoid those that illegally tout for business in the street: drivers may be unlicensed, uninsured and dangerous.

Trustworthy and fully licensed firms include **Addison Lee** (0844 800 6677), which will text you when the car arrives, and **Ladycars** (8558 9511), which employs only women drivers. Otherwise, text HOME to 60835 ('60tfl'). Transport for London will then text you the numbers of the two nearest licensed minicab operators and the number for Taxi One-Number, which provides licensed black taxis in London. The service costs 35p plus standard call rate. Always ask the price when you book and confirm it with the driver.

DRIVING

London's roads are often clogged with traffic and roadworks, and parking (*see right*) is a nightmare. Walking or using public transport are better options. If you hire a car, you can use any valid licence from outside the EU for up to a year after arrival. Speed limits in the city are generally 20 or 30mph.

Car hire

All firms below have branches at the airport; several also have offices in the city centre.

Alamo *0871 384 1086, www.alamo.co.uk.*
Avis *0844 581 0147, www.avis.co.uk.*
Budget *0844 544 3455, www.budget.co.uk.*
Enterprise *0800 800 227, www.enterprise.com.*
Europcar *0871 384 9900, www.europcar.co.uk.*
Hertz *0843 309 3099, www.hertz.co.uk.*
National *0870 400 4581, www.nationalcar.co.uk.*
Thrifty *01494 751500, www.thrifty.co.uk.*

Congestion charge

Drivers coming into central London between 7am and 6pm Monday to Friday have to pay £10, a fee known as the congestion charge. The congestion charge zone is bordered by Marylebone, Euston and King's Cross (N), Old Street roundabout (NE), Aldgate (E), Tower Bridge Road (SE), Elephant & Castle (S), Vauxhall, Victoria (SW), Park Lane and Edgware Road (W). You'll know when you're about to drive into the charging zone from the red 'C' signs on the road. Enter the postcode of your destination at www.tfl.gov.uk/roadusers/congestioncharging to discover if it's in the charging zone.

Passes can be bought from some newsagents, garages and NCP car parks; you can also pay online at www.tfl.gov.uk/roadusers/congestioncharging, by phone on 0343 222 3333 or by SMS. You can pay any time during the day; payments are also accepted until midnight on the next charging day, although the fee is £12 if you pay then. Expect a fine of £65 if you fail to pay, rising to £130 if you delay payment.

Breakdown services

AA (Automobile Association) *0870 550 0600 information, 0845 788 7766 breakdown, www.theaa.com.*
ETA (Environmental Transport Association) *0845 389 1010, www.eta.co.uk.*
RAC (Royal Automobile Club) *0870 572 2722 information, 0800 828282 breakdown, www.rac.co.uk.*

Parking

Central London is scattered with parking meters, but finding an unoccupied one is usually difficult. Meters cost upwards of £1 for 15mins, and in some areas they are limited to 2hrs. Parking on a single or double yellow line, a red line or in residents' parking areas during the day is illegal, and you may be fined, clamped or towed.

However, in the evening (from 6pm or 7pm in much of central London) and at various times at weekends, parking on single yellow lines is legal and free. If you find a clear spot on a single yellow line during the evening, look for a sign giving the local regulations. Meters also become free at certain times during evenings and weekends. Parking on double yellow lines and red routes is illegal at all times.

NCP 24hr car parks (0845 050 7080, www.ncp.co.uk) are numerous but pricey.

Clamping & vehicle removal

The immobilising of illegally parked vehicles with a clamp is common in London. You'll have to stump up a release fee (£100) and show a valid licence. The payment centre will declamp your car within four hours. If you don't remove your car at once, it may get clamped again, so wait by your vehicle.

If your car has disappeared, it's either been stolen or, if it was parked illegally, towed to a car pound by the local authorities. A release fee of £200 is levied for removal, plus upwards of £21 per day from the first midnight after removal. You'll also probably get a parking ticket of £60-£100 (reduced by 50% if paid within 14 days). Call the **Trace Information Service** hotline (0845 206 8602).

CYCLING

The **Transport for London** (0843 222 1234, www.tfl.gov.uk) cycle hire scheme (nicknamed 'Boris Bikes' after the mayor who introduced them) has been popular enough to see extensions to east and west from the initial central zone of operations, even if suggestions it would be self-funding through sponsorship deals and hiring fees currently seem wide of the mark. The scheme allows when-you-want-it access to a string of bicycle stations across central London. To hire a bike, go to a docking station, touch the 'Hire a cycle' icon and insert a credit or debit card. The machine will print out a five-digit access code, which you then tap into the docking point of a bike, releasing the cycle, and away you go. £2 buys 24-hour access to the bike and the first 30 minutes are free. Serious cyclists should contact the **London Cycle Network** (www.londoncyclenetwork.org.uk) and **London Cycling Campaign** (7234 9310, www.lcc.org.uk).

Despite a rash of cycling fatalities in 2013, riders shouldn't be scared of London's streets – 180 million journeys are made each year by bike. Ride calmly, assertively and obeying the rules of the road; avoid getting caught on the inside of a left-turning bus or lorry; and if you find a road intimidating, get off and walk until you find a quieter route. For TfL's advice, see 'Cycle safety tips' at www.tfl.gov.uk/roadusers/cycling/11598.aspx.

WALKING

The best way to see London is on foot, but the city's street layout is complicated. We've included street maps of central London in the back of this book, as well as area maps in the appropriate chapters for the city's most important districts; the standard Geographers' *London A-Z* and Collins' *London Street Atlas* are useful supplements. There's route advice at www.tfl.gov.uk/getting around, and look out for the yellow-topped 'Legible London' information posts as you stroll around (www.tfl.gov.uk/microsites/legible-london/).

Resources A-Z

TRAVEL ADVICE

For up-to-date information on travel to a specific country – including the latest on safety and security, health issues, local laws and customs – contact your home country government's department of foreign affairs. Most have websites with useful advice for would-be travellers. For information on travelling to the United Kingdom from within the European Union, including details of visa regulations and healthcare provision, see http://europa.eu/travel.

AUSTRALIA
www.smartraveller.gov.au

CANADA
www.voyage.gc.ca

NEW ZEALAND
www.safetravel.govt.nz

REPUBLIC OF IRELAND
www.dfa.ie

UK
www.fco.gov.uk/travel

USA
www.state.gov/travel

ADDRESSES

London postcodes are less helpful than they could be for locating addresses. The first element starts with a compass point – N, E, SE, SW, W and NW, plus the smaller EC (East Central) and WC (West Central). However, the number that follows relates not to geography (unless it's a 1, which indicates central) but to alphabetical order. So N2 is way out in the boondocks (East Finchley), while W2 covers the very central Bayswater.

AGE RESTRICTIONS

Buying/drinking alcohol 18.
Driving 17.
Sex 16.
Smoking 18.

CUSTOMS

Citizens entering the UK from outside the EU must adhere to duty-free import limits:

- 200 cigarettes or 100 cigarillos or 50 cigars or 250g of tobacco
- 4 litres still table wine plus either 1 litre spirits or strong liqueurs (above 22% abv) or 2 litres fortified wine (under 22% abv), sparkling wine or other liqueurs
- other goods to the value of no more than £390

The import of meat, poultry, fruit, plants, flowers and protected animals is restricted or forbidden; there are no restrictions on the import or export of currency if travelling from another EU country. If you are travelling from outside the EU, amounts over €10,000 must be declared.

People over the age of 17 arriving from an EU country are able to import unlimited goods for their own personal use, if bought tax-paid (so not duty-free). For more details, see www.hmrc.gov.uk.

DISABLED

As a city that evolved long before the needs of disabled people were considered, London is difficult for wheelchair users, though access and facilities are slowly improving. The capital's bus fleet is now low-floor for easier wheelchair access; there are no steps for any of the city's trams; and all DLR stations have either lifts or ramp access. However, steps and escalators to the tube and overland trains mean they are often of only limited use to wheelchair users. A blue symbol on the tube map (*see pp414-415*) indicates stations with step-free access. The *Step-free Tube Guide* map is free; call 0843 222 1234 for more details. For London Overground, call 0845 601 4867.

Most major attractions and hotels offer good accessibility, though provisions for the hearing- and sight-disabled are patchier. Enquire about facilities in advance. *Access in London* is an invaluable reference book for disabled travellers. It's available for a £10 donation (sterling cheque, cash US dollars or via PayPal to gordon.couch@virgin.net) from **Access Project** (39 Bradley Gardens, W13 8HE, www.accessinlondon.org).

Artsline *www.artsline.org.uk.*
Information on disabled access to arts and culture.

Can Be Done *Congress House, 14 Lyon Road, Harrow, Middx HA1 2EN (8907 2400, www.canbedone.co.uk). Harrow on the Hill tube/rail.* **Open** 9.30am-5pm Mon-Fri.
Disabled-adapted holidays and tours in London, around the UK and worldwide.

Royal Association for Disability & Rehabilitation *250 City Road, EC1V 8AF (7250 3222, 7250 4119 textphone, www.radar.org.uk). Old Street tube/rail.* **Open** 9am-5pm Mon-Fri. **Map** p400 P3.
A national organisation for disabled voluntary groups publishing books and the bimonthly magazine *New Bulletin* (£35/yr).

Tourism for All *0845 124 9971, www.tourismforall.org.uk.* **Open** *Helpline* 9am-5pm Mon-Fri.
Information for older people and people with disabilities in relation to accessible accommodation and other tourism services.

Wheelchair Travel & Access Mini Buses *1 Johnston Green, Guildford, Surrey GU2 9XS (01483 233640, www.wheelchair-travel.co.uk).*
Hires out converted vehicles (driver optional), plus cars with hand controls and wheelchair-adapted vehicles.

DRUGS

Illegal drug use remains higher in London than the UK as a whole, though it's becoming less visible on the streets and in clubs. Despite fierce debate, cannabis has been reclassified from Class C to Class B (where it rejoins amphetamine), but possession of a small amount might attract no more than a warning for a first offence. More serious Class B and A drugs (ecstasy, LSD, heroin, cocaine and the like) carry stiffer penalties, with a maximum of seven years in prison for possession.

ELECTRICITY

The UK uses the European 220-240V, 50-cycle AC voltage. British plugs use three pins, so travellers with two-pin European appliances should bring an adaptor, as should anyone using US appliances, which run off 110-120V, 60-cycle.

EMBASSIES & CONSULATES

American Embassy *24 Grosvenor Square, Mayfair, W1A 2LQ (7499 9000, http://london.usembassy.gov). Bond Street or Marble Arch tube.* **Open** 8.30am-5.30pm Mon-Fri. **Map** p398 G7.
Australian High Commission *Australia House, Strand, Holborn, WC2B 4LA (7379 4334, www.uk.embassy.gov.au). Holborn or Temple tube.* **Open** 9am-5pm Mon-Fri. **Map** p399 M6.
Canadian High Commission *38 Grosvenor Street, Mayfair, W1K 4AA (7258 6600, www.canada.org.uk). Bond Street or Oxford Circus tube.* **Open** 9.30am-4pm Mon-Fri. **Map** p398 H7.
Embassy of Ireland *17 Grosvenor Place, Belgravia, SW1X 7HR (7235 2171, 7373 4339 passports & visas, www.embassyofireland.co.uk). Hyde Park Corner tube.* **Open** 9.30am-5pm Mon-Fri. **Map** p398 G9.
New Zealand High Commission *New Zealand House, 80 Haymarket, St James's, SW1Y 4TQ (7930 8422, www.nzembassy.com). Piccadilly Circus tube.* **Open** 9am-5pm Mon-Fri. **Map** p399 K7.

EMERGENCIES

In the event of a serious accident, fire or other incident, call **999** – free from any phone, including payphones – and ask for an ambulance, the fire service or police. For hospital Accident & Emergency departments, *see right*; for helplines, *see p371*; for police stations, *see p373*.

GAY & LESBIAN

For information on gay and lesbian life in London, *see p257-263*. The phonelines below offer help and information; for HIV and AIDS, *see p371*.

London Friend *7837 3337, http://londonfriend.org.uk.* **Open** 7.30-9.30pm Mon-Wed.
London Lesbian & Gay Switchboard *0300 330 0630, www.llgs.org.uk.* **Open** 10am-11pm daily.

HEALTH

British citizens or those working in the UK can go to any general practitioner (GP). People ordinarily resident in the UK, including overseas students, are also permitted to register with a National Health Service (NHS) doctor. If you fall outside these categories, you will have to pay to see a GP. Your hotel concierge should be able to recommend one.

A pharmacist may dispense medicines on receipt of a prescription from a GP. NHS prescriptions cost £7.85; under-16s and over-60s are exempt from charges. Contraception is free for all. If you're not eligible to see an NHS doctor, you'll be charged cost price for any medicines prescribed.

Free emergency medical treatment under the NHS is available to:

- EU nationals and those of Iceland, Norway and Liechtenstein; all may also be entitled to state-provided treatment for non-emergency conditions with an EHIC (European Health Insurance Card)
- nationals of New Zealand, Russia, most former USSR states and the former Yugoslavia
- residents (irrespective of nationality) of Anguilla, Australia, Barbados, the British Virgin Islands, the Falkland Islands, the Isle of Man, Montserrat, Poland, Romania, St Helena and the Turks & Caicos Islands
- anyone who has been in the UK for the previous 12 months, or who has come to the UK to take up permanent residence
- students and trainees whose courses require more than 12 weeks in employment in the first year
- refugees and others who have sought refuge in the UK
- people with HIV/AIDS at a special STD treatment clinic

There are no NHS charges for:

- treatment in A&E wards
- emergency ambulance transport to a hospital
- diagnosis and treatment of certain communicable diseases
- family planning services
- compulsory psychiatric treatment

Accident & emergency

Listed below are most of the central London hospitals that have 24-hour Accident & Emergency (A&E) departments.

Charing Cross Hospital *Fulham Palace Road, Hammersmith, W6 8RF (3311 1234, www.imperial.nhs.uk). Hammersmith tube.*
Chelsea & Westminster Hospital *369 Fulham Road, Chelsea, SW10 9NH (8746 8000, www.chelwest.nhs.uk). South Kensington tube.* **Map** p394 C12.
Royal Free Hospital *Pond Street, Hampstead, NW3 2QG (7794 0500, www.royalfree.nhs.uk). Belsize Park tube or Hampstead Heath rail.*
Royal London Hospital *Whitechapel Road, Whitechapel, E1 1BB (3416 5000, www.bartshealth.nhs.uk). Whitechapel tube.*
St Mary's Hospital *Praed Street, Paddington, W2 1NY (3312 6666, www.imperial.nhs.uk). Paddington tube/rail.* **Map** p393 D5.
St Thomas' Hospital *Lambeth Palace Road, Lambeth, SE1 7EH (7188 7188, www.guysandstthomas.nhs.uk). Westminster tube or Waterloo tube/rail.* **Map** p399 L9.
University College Hospital *235 Euston Road, NW1 2BU (3456 7890, www.uclh.nhs.uk). Euston Square or Warren Street tube.* **Map** p396 J4.

Contraception & abortion

Family planning advice, contraceptive supplies and abortions are free to British citizens on the NHS, and to EU residents and foreign nationals living in Britain. Phone 0845 122 8690 or visit www.fpa.org.uk for your local Family Planning Association. The 'morning after' pill (around £25), effective up to 72 hours after intercourse, is available over the counter at pharmacies.
British Pregnancy Advisory Service *0845 730 4030, www.bpas.org.* **Open** *Helpline* 8am-9pm Mon-Fri; 8.30am-4pm Sat, Sun. Callers are referred to their nearest clinic for treatment.
Brook Advisory Centre *7284 6040, 0808 802 1234 helpline, www.brook.org.uk.* **Open** *Helpline* 11am-3pm Mon-Fri. Information on sexual health, contraception and abortion, plus free pregnancy tests for under-25s.
Marie Stopes House *Family Planning Clinic/Well Woman Centre, 108 Whitfield Street, Fitzrovia, W1T 5BE (0845 300 8090, www.mariestopes.org.uk).*

Warren Street tube. **Open** *Clinic* 8.30am-5pm Mon, Wed, Fri; 9.30am-6pm Tue, Thur; 9am-4pm Sat. *Helpline* 24hrs daily. **Map** p396 J4. Contraceptive advice, emergency contraception, pregnancy testing, an abortion service, cervical and health screening or gynaecological services. Fees may apply.

Dentists

Dental care is free for resident students, under-18s and people on benefits. All others must pay. To find an NHS dentist, contact the local Health Authority or a Citizens' Advice Bureau (*see right*).

Dental Emergency Care Service *Guy's Hospital, St Thomas Street, Borough, SE1 9RT (7188 8006). London Bridge tube/rail.* **Open** 9am-5pm Mon-Fri. **Map** p402 Q8. Queues start forming at 8am; arrive by 10am if you're to be seen at all.

Hospitals

For a list of hospitals with Accident & Emergency departments, *see p370*; for other hospitals, check www.yell.com.

Pharmacies

Also called 'chemists' in the UK. Branches of Boots (www.boots.com) and larger supermarkets have a pharmacy. Most keep shop hours (9am-6pm Mon-Sat) but the Boots store at 44-46 Regent Street, W1B 5RA, (7734 6126), opens until midnight (6pm Sun).

STDs, HIV & AIDS

NHS Genito-Urinary Clinics (such as the Centre for Sexual Health) are affiliated to major hospitals. They provide free, confidential STD testing and treatment, as well as treating other problems such as thrush and cystitis. They also offer counselling about HIV and other STDs, and can conduct blood tests.

The NHS website www.nhs.uk/worthtalkingabout also has information, including clinic locations. For helplines, *see right*; for abortion and contraception, *see p370*.

Mortimer Market Centre for Sexual Health *Mortimer Market, off Tottenham Court Road, WC1E 6JB (3317 5100). Goodge Street or Warren Street tube.* **Open** 9am-6pm Mon, Thur; 9am-7.15pm Tue; 1-6pm Wed; 8.15am-3pm Fri. **Map** p396 J4.

Terrence Higgins Trust Lighthouse *314-320 Gray's Inn Road, King's Cross, WC1X 8DP (0808 802 1221, www.tht.org.uk). King's Cross St Pancras tube/rail.* **Open** *Helpline* 10am-8pm Mon-Fri. **Map** p397 M5. Advice for those with HIV/AIDS, their relatives, lovers and friends. It also offers free leaflets about AIDS and safer sex.

HELPLINES

Helplines dealing with sexual health issues are listed under STDs, HIV & AIDS (*see above*).

Alcoholics Anonymous *0845 769 7555, www.alcoholics-anonymous.org.uk.* **Open** 10am-10pm daily.

Citizens' Advice Bureaux *www.citizensadvice.org.uk.* The council-run Citizens' Advice Bureaux offer free legal, financial and personal advice. Check the phone book or see the website for the address of your nearest office.

Missing People *0500 700 700, www.missingpeople.org.uk.* **Open** 24hrs daily. Information on anyone reported missing.

NHS Direct *111, www.nhsdirect.nhs.uk.* **Open** 24hrs daily. A free, first-stop service for medical advice on all subjects.

Rape & Sexual Abuse Support Centre *0808 802 9999, www.rapecrisis.org.uk.* **Open** noon-2.30pm, 7-9.30pm daily. Information and support.

Samaritans *0845 790 9090, www.samaritans.org.* **Open** 24hrs daily. General helpline for those under emotional stress.

Victim Support *0845 303 0900, www.victimsupport.org.uk.* **Open** 9am-9pm Mon-Fri; 9am-7pm Sat, Sun. **Map** p396 H5. Emotional and practical support to victims of crime.

ID

Passports and photographic driver's licences are acceptable forms of ID.

INTERNET

Most hotels have free high-speed internet (though some of the more expensive ones still charge a fee) and establishments all over town, especially cafés, have wireless access, usually free. Even the Tube is wired: see www.tfl.gov.uk/wifi.

LEFT LUGGAGE

Airports

Gatwick Airport *01293 502014 South Terminal, 01293 569900 North Terminal.*
Heathrow Airport *8759 3344.*
London City Airport *7646 0000.*
Stansted Airport *01279 663213.*

Rail & bus stations

Security precautions mean that London stations tend to have left-luggage desks rather than lockers. Call 0845 748 4950 for details.

Charing Cross *7930 5444.* **Open** 7am-11pm daily.
Euston *7387 1499.* **Open** 7am-11pm daily.
King's Cross *7837 4334.* **Open** 7am-11pm daily.
Paddington *77262 0344.* **Open** 7am-11pm daily.
Victoria *7963 0957.* **Open** 7am-midnight daily.

LEGAL HELP

Those in difficulties can visit a Citizens' Advice Bureau (*see left*) or contact the groups below. Try the **Legal Services Commission** (0845 345 4345, www.legalservices.gov.uk) for information. If you're arrested, your first call should be to your embassy (*see p370*).

Law Centres Federation *7839 2998, www.lawcentres.org.uk.* **Open** 11am-5.30pm Mon-Fri. Free legal help for people who can't afford a lawyer and live or work in the immediate area; this office connects you with the nearest centre.

LOST PROPERTY

Always inform the police if you lose anything, if only to validate insurance claims. Only dial 999 if violence has occurred; use 101 for non-emergencies. Report lost passports both to the police and to your embassy (*see p370*).

Airports

For items left on the plane, contact the relevant airline. Otherwise, phone the following:

Gatwick Airport *01293 503162.*
Heathrow Airport *0844 824 3115.*
London City Airport *7646 0000.*
Luton Airport *01582 395219.*
Stansted Airport *01279 663293.*

Public transport

If you've lost property in an overground station or on a train, call 0870 000 5151, and give the operator the details.

Transport for London *Lost Property Office, 200 Baker Street, Marylebone, NW1 5RZ (0343 222 1234, www.tfl.gov.uk/lost property). Baker Street tube.* **Open** 8.30am-4pm Mon-Fri. **Map** p396 G4. Allow two to ten working days from the time of loss. If you lose something on a bus, call 0343 222 1234 and ask for the numbers of the depots at either end of the route. For tube losses, pick up a lost property form from any station.

Taxis

The Transport for London office (*see above*) deals with property found in registered black cabs. Allow two to ten days from the time of loss. For items lost in a minicab, contact the relevant company.

MEDIA

Magazines & newspapers

Time Out remains London's only quality listings magazine – and it's free. If you want to know what's going on and whether it's any good, this is the place to look. It's widely available in central London every Tuesday. The capital's main daily paper (also free) is the sensationalist *Evening Standard*, published Monday to Friday. In the mornings, in tube station dispensers and discarded in the carriages, you'll find *Metro*, a free *Standard* spin-off.

Radio

The stations below are broadcast on standard wavebands as well as digital, where they are joined by some interesting new channels (mostly from the BBC).

Absolute *105.8 FM.* Laddish rock.
BBC Radio 1 *98.8 FM.* Youth-oriented pop, indie and dance.
BBC Radio 2 *89.1 FM.* Bland during the day; better after dark.
BBC Radio 3 *91.3 FM.* Classical music dominates, but there's also discussion, world music and arts.
BBC Radio 4 *93.5 FM, 198 LW.* The BBC's main speech station is led by news agenda-setter *Today* (6-9am Mon-Fri, 7-9am Sat).
BBC Radio 5 Live *693, 909 AM.* Rolling news and sport. Avoid the morning phone-ins.
BBC London *94.9 FM.* All things to do with the capital.
BBC World Service *648 AM.* Some repeats, some new shows, transmitted globally.
Capital FM *95.8 FM.* Pop and chat.
Classic FM *100.9 FM.* Easy-listening classical.
Heart FM *106.2 FM.* Capital for grown-ups.
Kiss *100 FM.* Dance music.
LBC *97.3 FM.* Phone-ins and talk.
Magic *105.4 FM.* Familiar pop.
Smooth *102.2 FM.* Aural wallpaper.
Resonance *104.4 FM.* Arts radio – an inventively oddball mix.
XFM *104.9 FM.* Alternativish rock.

Television

With a multiplicity of formats, there are plenty of pay-TV options. However, the relative quality of free TV keeps subscriptions from attaining US levels.

The five main free-to-air networks are as follows:

BBC1 The Corporation's mass-market station. Relies too much on soaps, game shows and lifestyle TV, but does have quality offerings. As with all BBC stations, there are no commercials.
BBC2 A reasonably intelligent cultural cross-section, but now upstaged by BBC4.
ITV1 Monotonous weekday mass-appeal shows. ITV2 produces similar shows.
Channel 4 Extremely successful US imports, more or less unwatchable home-grown entertainments and the occasional great documentary.
Five From high culture to lowbrow filth. A strange, unholy mix.

Satellite, digital and cable channels include the following:

BBC3 Often appalling home-grown comedy and dismal documentary.
BBC4 Highbrow stuff, including fine documentaries and dramas.
BBC News Rolling news.
BBC Parliament Live debates.
CBBC, CBeebies Children's programmes, the latter is younger.
Discovery Channel Science and nature documentaries.
E4, More4, Film4 Channel 4's entertainment and movie channels.
Fiver US comedy and drama, plus Australian soaps.
ITV2, ITV3, ITV4 US shows on 2, British reruns on 3 and 4.
Sky News Rolling news.
Sky One Sky's version of ITV.
Sky Sports Four channels.

MONEY

Britain's currency is the pound sterling (£). One pound equals 100 pence (p). Coins are copper (1p, 2p), silver (round: 5p, 10p; seven-sided: 20p, 50p), yellowy-gold (£1) or silver in the centre with a yellowy-gold edge (£2). Paper notes are blue (£5), orange (£10), purple (£20) or red (£50). You can exchange foreign currency at banks, bureaux de change and post offices; there's no commission charge at the last of these (for addresses of the most central, *see p373*). Many large stores also accept euros (€).

Western Union *0808 234 9168, www.westernunion.co.uk.*
The old standby. Chequepoint (*see p373*) also offers this service.

Banks & ATMs

ATMs can be found inside and outside banks, in some shops and in larger stations. Machines in many commercial premises levy a charge for each withdrawal, usually £1.85. If you're visiting from outside the UK, your card should work via one of the debit networks, but check charges in advance. ATMs also allow you to make withdrawals on your credit card if you know your PIN; you'll be charged interest plus, usually, a currency exchange fee. Generally, getting cash with a card is the cheapest form of currency exchange but there are hidden charges, so do your research.

Credit cards, especially Visa and MasterCard, are accepted in most shops (except small corner shops) and restaurants (except caffs). However, American Express and Diners Club tend to be accepted only at more expensive outlets. You will usually have to have a PIN number to make a purchase.

No commission is charged for cashing sterling travellers' cheques if you go to one of the banks affiliated with the issuing company. You do have to pay to cash travellers' cheques in foreign currencies, and to change cash. You will always need to produce ID to cash travellers' cheques.

Bureaux de change

You'll be charged for cashing travellers' cheques or buying and selling foreign currency at bureaux de change. Major stations have bureaux, and there are many in tourist areas and on major shopping streets. Most open 8am-10pm.

Chequepoint *550 Oxford Street, W1C 1LY (7724 6127, www.chequepoint.com). Marble Arch tube.* **Open** 24hrs. **Map** p396 G6. **Other locations** throughout the city.
Covent Garden FX *30A Jubilee Market Hall, Covent Garden, WC2E 8BE (7240 9921, www.coventgardenfx.com). Covent Garden tube.* **Open** 9am-6pm Mon-Fri; 10am-4pm Sat. **Map** p399 L7.
Thomas Exchange *13 Maddox Street, Mayfair, W1S 2QG (7493 1300, www.thomasexchange.co.uk). Oxford Circus tube.* **Open** 9am-6pm Mon-Fri. **Map** p396 J6.

Lost/stolen credit cards

Report lost or stolen credit cards both to the police and the 24-hour phone lines listed below.

American Express *01273 696933, www.americanexpress.com.*
Diners Club *0845 862 2935, www.dinersclub.co.uk.*
MasterCard *0800 964767, www.mastercard.com.*
Visa *0800 891725, www.visa.co.uk.*

Tax

With the exception of food, books, newspapers and a few other items, purchases in the UK are subject to Value Added Tax (VAT), aka sales tax. The rate is currently set at 20%. VAT is included in all prices quoted by mainstream shops, although it may not be included in hotel rates.

Foreign visitors may be able to claim back the VAT paid on most goods that are taken out of the EC (European Community) as part of a scheme generally called 'Tax Free Shopping'. To be able to claim a refund, you must be a non-EC visitor to the UK, or a UK resident emigrating from the EC. When you buy the goods, the retailer will ask to see your passport, and will then ask you to fill in a simple refund form. You need to have one of these forms to make your claim; till receipts alone will not do. If you're leaving the UK direct for outside the EC, you must show your goods and refund form to UK customs at the airport/port from which you're leaving. If you're leaving the EC via another EC country, you must show your goods and refund form to customs staff of that country.

After customs have certified your form, get your refund by posting the form to the retailer from which you bought the goods, posting the form to a commercial refund company or handing your form at a refund booth to get immediate payment. Customs are not responsible for making the refund: when you buy the goods, ask the retailer how the refund is paid.

OPENING HOURS

Government offices close on bank (public) holidays (*see p34*), but big shops often remain open, with only Christmas Day sacrosanct. Most attractions remain open on the other public holidays.

Banks 9am-4.30pm (some close at 3.30pm, some 5.30pm) Mon-Fri; some also Sat mornings.
Businesses 9am-5pm Mon-Fri.
Post offices 9am-5.30pm Mon-Fri; 9am-noon Sat.
Pubs & bars 11am-11pm Mon-Sat; noon-10.30pm Sun.
Shops 10am-6pm Mon-Sat, some to 8pm. Many also open on Sun, usually 11am-5pm or noon-6pm.

POLICE

For emergencies, call **999**. The non-emergency number is **101**.

London's police are used to helping visitors. If you've been robbed, assaulted or a victim of crime, go to your nearest police station. (We've listed a handful in central London; look under 'Police' in Directory Enquiries or call 118 118, 118 500 or 118 888 for more.)

If you have a complaint, ensure that you take the offending officer's identifying number (it should be displayed on his or her epaulette). The Independent Police Complaints Commission website, www.ipcc.gov.uk, has details of how to complain to the relevant police force.

Belgravia Police Station *202-206 Buckingham Palace Road, Pimlico, SW1W 9SX (111). Victoria tube/rail.* **Map** p398 H10.
Holborn Police Station *10 Lambs Conduit Street, Bloomsbury, WC1N 3NR. Holborn tube.* **Map** p397 M5.
Charing Cross Police Station *Agar Street, Covent Garden, WC2N 4JP (111) . Charing Cross tube/rail.* **Map** p399 L7.
Chelsea Police Station *2 Lucan Place, Chelsea, SW3 3PB (111). South Kensington tube.* **Map** p395 E10.
Islington Police Station *2 Tolpuddle Street, Islington, N1 0YY (111). Angel tube.* **Map** p400 N2.
Kensington Police Station *72 Earl's Court Road, Kensington, W8 6EQ (111). High Street Kensington tube.* **Map** p394 B11.
Paddington Green Police Station *2-4 Harrow Road, Paddington, W2 1XJ (111). Paddington tube/rail.* **Map** p393 E5.
West End Central Police Station *27 Savile Row, Mayfair, W1S 2EX (111). Oxford Circus tube.* **Map** p398 J7.

POSTAL SERVICES

The UK has a fairly reliable postal service. If you have a query, contact Customer Services on 0845 774 0740. For business enquiries, call 0845 795 0950.

Post offices are usually open 9am-5.30pm during the week and 9am-noon on Saturdays, although some post offices shut for lunch and smaller offices may close for one or more afternoons each week. Some central post offices are listed below; for others, call the **Royal Mail** on 0845 611 2970 or check online at www.royalmail.com.

You can buy individual stamps at post offices, and books of four or 12 first- or second-class stamps at newsagents and supermarkets that display the appropriate red sign. A first-class stamp for a regular letter costs 60p; second-class stamps are 50p. It costs 88p to send a postcard abroad. For details of other rates, see www.royalmail.com.

Post offices

Post offices are usually open 9am-5.30pm Mon-Fri and 9am-noon Sat, with the exception of Lower Regent Street Post Office (11 Lower Regent Street, SW1Y 4LR, 0845 611 2970), which opens 8am-6.30pm Mon-Fri; 9am-5.30pm Sat; noon-4pm Sun. Listed below are the other main central London offices. For general enquiries, call 0845 611 2970 or consult www.postoffice.co.uk.

Albemarle Street *nos.43-44, Mayfair, W1S 4DS. Green Park tube.* **Map** p398 J7.
Baker Street *no.111, Marylebone, W1U 6SG. Baker Street tube.* **Map** p396 G5.
Great Portland Street *nos.54-56, Fitzrovia, W1W 7NE. Oxford Circus tube.* **Map** p396 H4.
High Holborn *no.181, Holborn, WC1V 7RL. Holborn tube.* **Map** p397 L6.

Poste restante

If you want to receive mail while you're away, you can have it sent to Lower Regent Street Post Office (*see p373*), where it will be kept for a month. Your name and 'Poste Restante' must be clearly marked on the letter. You'll need ID to collect it.

PUBLIC HOLIDAYS

On public holidays (bank holidays), many shops remain open, but public transport services generally run to a Sunday timetable. On Christmas Day, almost everything, including public transport, closes down. For the dates for 2014 and 2015, *see p34*.

RELIGION

Times may vary; phone to check.

Anglican & Baptist

Bloomsbury Central Baptist Church *235 Shaftesbury Avenue, Covent Garden, WC2H 8EP (7240 0544, www.bloomsbury.org.uk). Tottenham Court Road tube.* **Services & meetings** 11am, 5.30pm Sun. **Map** p397 Y1.
St Paul's Cathedral *For listings, see p176.* **Services** 7.30am, 8am, 12.30pm, 5pm Mon-Sat; 8am, 10.15am, 11.30am, 3.15pm, 6pm Sun. **Map** p402 O6.
Westminster Abbey *For listings, see p76.* **Services** 7.30am, 8am, 12.30pm, 5pm Mon-Sat; 8am, 10.15am, 11.30am, 3.15pm, 6pm Sun. **Map** p399 K9.

Buddhist

Buddhapadipa Thai Temple *14 Calonne Road, Wimbledon, SW19 5HJ (8946 1357, www.buddhapadipa.org). Wimbledon tube/rail then bus 93.* **Open** *Temple* 9-5pm Sat, Sun. *Meditation retreat* 7-9pm Tue, Thur.
London Buddhist Centre *51 Roman Road, Bethnal Green, E2 0HU (0845 458 4716, www.lbc.org.uk). Bethnal Green tube.* **Open** 10am-5pm Mon-Sat.

Catholic

Brompton Oratory *For listings, see p94.* **Services** 7am, 8am (Latin mass), 10am, 12.30pm, 6pm Mon-Fri; 7am, 8am, 10am, 6pm Sat; 8am, 9am (tridentine), 10am, 11am (sung Latin), 12.30pm, 4.30pm, 7pm Sun. **Map** p395 E10.
Westminster Cathedral *For listings, see p78.* **Services** 7am, 8am, 10.30am, 12.30pm, 1.05pm, 5.30pm Mon-Fri; 8am, 9am, 10.30am, 12.30pm, 6pm Sat; 8am, 9am, 10.30am, noon, 5.30pm, 7pm Sun. **Map** p398 J10.

Islamic

East London Mosque *82-92 Whitechapel Road, Whitechapel, E1 1JQ (7650 3000, www.eastlondonmosque.org.uk). Aldgate East tube.* **Services** times vary; check website for details. **Map** p403 S6.
Islamic Cultural Centre & London Central Mosque *146 Park Road, Marylebone, NW8 7RG (7724 3363, www.iccuk.org). Baker Street tube or bus 13, 113, 274.* **Services** times vary; check website for details.

Jewish

Liberal Jewish Synagogue *28 St John's Wood Road, St John's Wood, NW8 7HA (7286 5181, www.ljs.org). St John's Wood tube.* **Services** 6.45pm Fri; 11am Sat.
West Central Liberal Synagogue *21 Maple Street, Fitzrovia, W1T 4BE (7636 7627, www.wcls.org.uk). Warren Street tube.* **Services** 3pm Sat. **Map** p396 J4.

Methodist & Quaker

Methodist Central Hall *Central Hall, Storey's Gate, Westminster, SW1H 9NH (7222 8010, www.methodist-central-hall.org.uk). St James's Park tube.* **Services** 12.45pm Wed; 11am, 6.30pm Sun. **Map** p399 K9.
Religious Society of Friends (Quakers) *173-177 Euston Road, Bloomsbury, NW1 2BJ (7663 1000, www.quaker.org.uk). Euston tube/rail.* **Meetings** 6.30pm Thur; 11am Sun. **Map** p397 K3.

SAFETY & SECURITY

Despite the riots during 2011, there are no real 'no-go' areas in London, and you're much more likely to get hurt in a car accident than as a result of criminal activity, but thieves haunt busy shopping areas and transport nodes as they do in all cities.

Use common sense and follow some basic rules. Keep wallets and purses out of sight, and handbags securely closed. Never leave bags or coats unattended, beside, under or on the back of a chair – even if they aren't stolen, they're likely to trigger a bomb alert. Don't put bags on the floor near the door of a public toilet. Don't take short cuts through dark alleys and car parks. Keep your passport, cash and credit cards in separate places. Don't carry a wallet in your back pocket. And always be aware of your surroundings.

SMOKING

July 2007 saw the introduction of a ban on smoking in all enclosed public spaces, including pubs, bars, clubs, restaurants, hotel foyers and shops, as well as on public transport. Smokers now face a penalty fee of £50 or a maximum fee of £200 if they are prosecuted for smoking in a smoke-free area. Many bars and clubs offer smoking gardens or terraces.

TELEPHONES

Dialling & codes

London's dialling code is 020; standard landlines have eight digits after that. You don't need to dial the 020 from within the area, so we have not given it in this book.

If you're calling from outside the UK, dial your international access code, then the UK code, 44, then the full London number, omitting the first 0 from the code. For example, to make a call to 020 7813 3000 from the US, dial 011 44 20 7813 3000. To dial abroad from the UK, first dial 00, then the relevant country code from the list below. For more international dialling codes, check the phone book or see www.kropla.com/dialcode.htm.

Australia 61
Canada 1
New Zealand 64
Republic of Ireland 353
South Africa 27
USA 1

Mobile phones

Mobile phones in the UK operate on the 900 MHz and 1800 MHz GSM frequencies common throughout most of Europe. If you're travelling to the UK from Europe, your phone should be compatible; if you're travelling from the US, it may not be. Either way, check your phone is set for international roaming, and that your service provider at home has a reciprocal arrangement with a UK provider.

The simplest option may be to buy a 'pay-as-you-go' phone (about £10-£200); there's no monthly fee, you top up talk time using a card. Check before buying whether it can make and receive international calls.

Operator services

Call 100 for the operator if you have difficulty in dialling; for an alarm call; to make a credit card call; for information about the cost of a call; and for help with international person-to-person calls. Dial 155 for the international operator if you need to reverse the charges (call collect) or if you can't dial direct; this service is very expensive.

Directory enquiries

This service is now provided by various six-digit 118 numbers. They're pretty pricey to call: dial (free) 0800 953 0720 for a rundown of options and prices. The best known is 118 118, which charges £1.59 per call, then £1.99 per minute thereafter; 118 888 charges 59p per call, then £1.99 per minute; 118 811 charges 50p per call. Online, the www.ukphonebook.com offers ten free credits a day to UK residents; overseas users get the same credits if they keep a positive balance in their account.

Yellow Pages This 24-hour service lists phone numbers of businesses in the UK. Dial 118 247 (£1.50p connection charge plus 70p/min) and identify the type of business you require, and where in London. Online, try www.yell.com.

Public phones

Public payphones take coins or credit cards (sometimes both). The minimum cost is 60p (including a 40p connection charge), local and national calls are charged at 60p for 30mins then 10p for each subsequent 15mins. Some payphones, such as the counter-top ones found in pubs, require more. International calling cards, offering bargain minutes via a freephone number, are widely available.

TIME

London operates on Greenwich Mean Time (GMT), five hours ahead of the US's Eastern Standard time. In spring (30 March 2014) the UK puts its clocks forward by one hour to British Summer Time. In autumn (26 October 2014), the clocks go back to GMT.

TIPPING

In Britain it's accepted that you tip in taxis, minicabs, restaurants (some waiting staff rely heavily on tips), hotels, hairdressers and some bars (not pubs). Around 10% is normal, but some restaurants add as much as 15%. Always check whether service has been included in your bill: some restaurants include an automatic service charge, but also leave space for a gratuity on your credit card slip.

TOILETS

Pubs and restaurants generally reserve the use of their toilets for customers. However, all mainline rail stations and a few tube stations – Piccadilly Circus, for one – have public toilets (you may be charged a small fee). Department stores usually have loos that you can use free of charge, and museums (most of which no longer charge an entry fee) generally have good facilities. At night, options are worse. The coin-operated toilet booths around the city may be your only option.

THE LOCAL CLIMATE

Average temperatures and monthly rainfall in London.

	High (°C/°F)	Low (°C/°F)	Rainfall (mm/in)
Jan	6 / 43	2 / 36	54 / 2.1
Feb	7 / 44	2 / 36	40 / 1.6
Mar	10 / 50	3 / 37	37 / 1.5
Apr	13 / 55	6 / 43	37 / 1.5
May	17 / 63	8 / 46	46 / 1.8
June	20 / 68	12 / 54	45 / 1.8
July	22 / 72	14 / 57	57 / 2.2
Aug	21 / 70	13 / 55	59 / 2.3
Sept	19 / 66	11 / 52	49 / 1.9
Oct	14 / 57	8 / 46	57 / 2.2
Nov	10 / 50	5 / 41	64 / 2.5
Dec	7 / 44	4 / 39	48 / 1.9

TOURIST INFORMATION

In addition to the tourist information centres listed below, there are travel information centres, selling tickets for travel and London attractions, at King's Cross St Pancras, Liverpool Street and Victoria stations, and at Piccadilly Circus tube station.

City of London Information Centre *St Paul's Churchyard, City, EC4M 8BX (7332 1456, www.cityoflondon.gov.uk).* **Open** 9.30am-5.30pm Mon-Sat; 10am-4pm Sun. **Map** p402 O6.

Greenwich Tourist Information Centre *Discover Greenwich, Pepys House, 2 Cutty Sark Gardens, SE10 9LW (0870 608 2000, www.visitgreenwich.org.uk). Cutty Sark DLR.* **Open** 10am-5pm daily. **Map** p405 X1.

Holborn Information Kiosk *Kingsway, outside Holborn tube, Holborn, WC2B 6BG (no phone).* **Open** 9am-6pm Mon-Fri. **Map** p397 L5.

Twickenham Visitor Information Centre *44 York Street, Twickenham, Middx, TW1 3BZ (8734 3363, www.visitrichmond.co.uk). Twickenham rail.* **Open** 9am-5.15pm Mon-Thur; 9am-5pm Fri.

WEIGHTS & MEASURES

The UK is moving slowly towards full metrication. Distances are still measured in miles but all goods are officially sold in metric quantities, with no legal requirement for the imperial equivalent to be given. Nonetheless, imperial measurements are still more commonly used, so we use them in this guide.

Below are listed some useful conversions, first into the metric equivalents from the imperial measurements, then from the metric units back to imperial:

1 inch (in) = 2.54 centimetres (cm)
1 yard (yd) = 0.91 metres (m)
1 mile = 1.6 kilometres (km)
1 ounce (oz) = 28.35 grams (g)
1 pound (lb) = 0.45 kilograms (kg)
1 UK pint = 0.57 litres (l)
1 US pint = 0.8 UK pints or 0.46 litres

1 centimetre (cm) = 0.39 inches (in)
1 metre (m) = 1.094 yards (yd)
1 kilometre (km) = 0.62 miles
1 gram (g) = 0.035 ounces (oz)
1 kilogram (kg) = 2.2 pounds (lb)
1 litre (l) = 1.76 UK pints or 2.2 US pints

Further Reference

BOOKS

Fiction

Peter Ackroyd *Hawksmoor*; *The House of Doctor Dee*; *The Great Fire of London* Intricate fiction about the arcane city.
Martin Amis *London Fields* Darts and drinking way out east.
Anthony Burgess *Dead Man in Deptford* A fictionalised life of Marlowe.
Norman Collins *London Belongs to Me* A witty saga of 1930s Kennington.
Sir Arthur Conan Doyle *The Complete Sherlock Holmes* Reassuring sleuthing shenanigans.
Joseph Conrad *The Secret Agent* Anarchism in seedy Soho.
Charles Dickens *Oliver Twist*; *David Copperfield*; *Bleak House* Three of the Victorian master's most London-centric novels.
Anthony Frewin *London Blues* Kubrick assistant explores the 1960s Soho porn movie industry.
Jeremy Gavron *An Acre of Common Ground* The best of the glut of Brick Lane fiction.
Graham Greene *The End of the Affair* Adultery, Catholicism and the Blitz.
Patrick Hamilton *Twenty Thousand Streets Under the Sky* Dashed dreams at the bar of the Midnight Bell in Fitzrovia.
Neil Hanson *The Dreadful Judgement* Embers of the Great Fire.
Melissa Harrison *Clay* South London nature encounters.
Alan Hollinghurst *The Swimming Pool Library; The Line of Beauty* Gay life around Russell Square; metropolitan debauchery.
BS Johnson *Christie Malry's Own Double Entry* A London clerk plots revenge on… everybody.
Doris Lessing *The Golden Notebook; The Good Terrorist* Nobel winner's best London books.
Colin MacInnes *City of Spades*; *Absolute Beginners* Coffee 'n' jazz, Soho 'n' Notting Hill.
Gautam Malkani *Londonstani* A violent tale of South Asian immigrants in Hounslow.
Michael Moorcock *Mother London* A roomful of psychiatric patients live a love letter to London.
Alan Moore *From Hell* Dark graphic novel on the Ripper.
Derek Raymond *I Was Dora Suarez* The blackest London noir.
Nicholas Royle *The Matter of the Heart*; *The Director's Cut* Abandoned buildings and secrets.
Iain Sinclair *Downriver*; *White Chappell/Scarlet Tracings* *Heart of Darkness* on the Thames; the Ripper and book dealers.
Sarah Waters *The Night Watch* World War II Home Front.
Virginia Woolf *Mrs Dalloway* A kind of London *Ulysses*.

Non-fiction

Peter Ackroyd *London: The Biography*; *Thames: Sacred River* Loving and obscurantist histories of the city and its river.
Richard Anderson *Bespoke: Savile Row Ripped and Smoothed* Inside story of a Savile Row tailor.
Nicholas Barton *The Lost Rivers of London* Classic studies of old watercourses.
David Bownes, Oliver Green & Sam Mullins *Underground* Illustrated celebration of 150 years of the Tube.
Paul Du Noyer *In the City* London in song.
Ed Glinert *A Literary Guide to London; The London Compendium* Essential London minutiae.
Sarah Hartley *Mrs P's Journey* Biography of the woman who created the *A–Z*, now a musical.
Leo Hollis *The Stones of London* A superb take on the city's history – through 12 of its key buildings.
Edward Jones & Christopher Woodward *A Guide to the Architecture of London* A brilliant exploration.
Jenny Landreth *The Great Trees of London* Ancient trees in famous and unlikely city locations.
Jenny Linford *London Cookbook* Unsung producers and chefs share their food secrets.
Jack London *The People of the Abyss* Poverty in the East End.
Anna Minton *Ground Control* Important questions about Canary Wharf-style developments – including the Olympic Park.
HV Morton *In Search of London* A tour of London from 1951.
George Orwell *Down and Out in Paris and London* Waitering, begging and starving.
Samuel Pepys *Diaries* Plagues, fires and bordellos.
Cathy Phillips (ed) *London through a Lens*; *Londoners through a Lens* Captivating photographs of the city from the Getty archive.
Roy Porter *London: A Social History* An all-encompassing work.
Steen Eller Rasmussen *London: The Unique City* London buildings through a visitor's eyes.
Sukhdev Sandhu *Night Haunts* London and Londoners after dark.
Iain Sinclair *Lights Out for the Territory*; *London Orbital* Time-warp visionary crosses and then circles London.
Adrian Tinniswood *His Invention So Fertile* Biography of Sir Christopher Wren.
Richard Trench & Ellis Hillman *London under London: A Subterranean Guide* Tunnels, lost rivers, disused tube stations, military bunkers.
Ben Weinreb & Christopher Hibbert (eds) *The London Encyclopaedia* Indispensable reference guide.
Jerry White *London in the 19th Century*; *London in the 20th Century* How London became a global city.

FILMS

Alfie *dir Lewis Gilbert, 1966* What's it all about, Michael?
Blow-Up *dir Michelangelo Antonioni, 1966* Unintentionally hysterical film of Swinging London.
Bourne Ultimatum *dir Paul Greengrass, 2007* Pacy thriller with brilliantly staged CCTV scene in Waterloo Station.
Death Line *dir Gary Sherman, 1972* The lost Victorian cannibal race is discovered in Russell Square tube.
Dirty Pretty Things *dir Stephen Frears, 2002* Body organ smuggling.
Fires Were Started *dir Humphrey Jennings, 1943* Drama-doc war propaganda about the London Fire Brigade.
The Look of Love *dir Michael Winterbottom, 2013* Steve Coogan as Paul Raymond, Soho sleaze king.

The Krays *dir Peter Medak, 1990* The life and times of the most notorious of East End gangsters.
The Ladykillers *dir Alexander Mackendrick, 1951* Classic Ealing comedy.
Life is Sweet; Naked; Secrets & Lies; Vera Drake; Happy-Go-Lucky *dir Mike Leigh, 1990-2008* Metroland; urban misanthropy; familial tensions; sympathy for post-war abortionist; day and night with a north London optimist.
Lock, Stock & Two Smoking Barrels; Snatch; RocknRolla *dir Guy Ritchie, 1998-2008* Former Mr Madonna's cheeky London faux-gangster flicks.
London; Robinson in Space *dir Patrick Keiller, 1994, 1997* Arthouse documentaries tracing London's lost stories.
London River *dir Rachid Bouchareb, 2010* French African man and Guernsey widow brought together by 7 July 2005 bombings.
The Long Good Friday *dir John MacKenzie, 1989* Classic London gangster flick.
Oliver! *dir Carol Reed, 1968* Fun musical Dickens adaptation.
Passport to Pimlico *dir Henry Cornelius, 1949* Superb Ealing comedy.
Peeping Tom *dir Michael Powell, 1960* Powell's creepy serial killer flick.
Performance *dir Nicolas Roeg & Donald Cammell, 1970* Cult movie to end all cult movies.
Sex & Drugs & Rock & Roll *dir Mat Whitecross, 2009* Delirious biopic of splenetic rocker Ian Drury.
Skyfall *dir Sam Mendes, 2012* See the SIS building blown up and Bond nearly run over by a Tube.
28 Days Later *dir Danny Boyle, 2002* Post-apocalyptic London, with bravura opening sequence.
We Are the Lambeth Boys *dir Karel Reisz, 1959* 'Free cinema' classic doc on Teddy Boy culture.
Withnail & I *dir Bruce Robinson, 1987* Classic Camden lowlife comedy.
Wonderland *dir Michael Winterbottom, 1999* Love, loss and deprivation in Soho.

MUSIC

Blur *Parklife* Key London Britpop.
Billy Bragg *Must I Paint You a Picture? The Essential Billy Bragg* The bard of Barking's greatest hits.
Burial *Untrue* Dubstep's finest.
Chas & Dave *Don't Give a Monkey's* Cockney singalong.
The Clash *London Calling* Era-defining punk classic.
Dizzee Rascal *Boy in Da Corner* Rough-cut sounds and inventive lyrics from a Bow council estate.
Ian Dury *New Boots & Panties!!* Cheekily essential listening from the Essex pub maestro.
Hot Chip *The Warning* Wonky electro-pop.
The Jam *This is the Modern World* Weller at his fiercest and finest.
The Kinks *Something Else* 'Waterloo Sunset' and all.
Linton Kwesi Johnson *Dread, Beat an' Blood; Forces of Victory; Bass Culture* Angry reggae from the man Brixton calls 'the Poet'.
Madness *Ultimate Madness* The Nutty Boys' wonderful best.
Melt Yourself Down *Melt Yourself Down* Wigged-out psych-jazz-funk supergroup.
Public Service Broadcasting *Inform–Educate–Entertain* Documentary narration set to music – shouldn't work, but it does.
Saint Etienne *Tales from Turnpike House* Kitchen-sink opera by London-loving indie dance band.
Squeeze *Greatest Hits* Lovable south London geezer pop.
The Streets *Original Pirate Material* Pirate radio urban meets Madness on Mike Skinner's debut.
The xx *Coexist* More shiny, slinky melancholia from the 2010 Mercury Prize winners.

WEBSITES

www.bbc.co.uk/london News, travel, weather, sport.
www.britishpathe.com Newsreels, from spaghetti-eating contests to pre-war Soho scenes.
www.classiccafes.co.uk Fascinating archive of the city's best 1950s and '60s caffs.
http://diamondgeezer.blogspot.com Superb blogger.
www.filmlondon.org.uk London's cinema organisation.
http://greatwenlondon.wordpress.com Fun, engaged, often thought-provoking blog, by our 'London Today' chapter's author.
www.hidden-london.com Undiscovered gems.
www.londoneater.com Passionate food reviews.
www.london-footprints.co.uk Free walks and event listings.
www.london.gov.uk The Greater London Assembly's official website.
http://londonist.com News, culture and things to do.
http://london.randomness.org.uk Review site-cum-wiki of interesting London places.
http://londonreconnections.blogspot.com Transport projects.
www.londonremembers.com Plaques and statues.
http://londonreviewofbreakfasts.blogspot.com Start the day in pun-tastic style.
http://london-underground.blogspot.com Annie Mole's fun and informative daily tube blog.
http://mappinglondon.co.uk Best maps – and ways of mapping – the city.
www.nickelinthemachine.com Terrific blog on history, culture and music of 20th-century London.
http://spitalfieldslife.com Key London blog: focused, charming, informative and very human.
www.timeout.com A vital source: eating and drinking reviews, features and events listings.
www.tfl.gov.uk/tfl Information, journey planners and maps from Transport for London, the city's central travel organisation.

APPS

Hackney Hear (free) Hyperlocal – and totally brilliant – audio guide to London Fields in Hackney.
Hailo (free) Calls a black cab, tells you how long it will be, and deducts the meter fare from your account – but there's no call-out fee.
iCockneyDialect (free) Talk like a local – over 800 translations into London's traditional rhyming slang.
London Cycle: Maps & Routes (free) Most popular of many apps showing the nearest Boris Bike.
London Bus Live (free) Tells you how far away your next bus is.
London Jigsaw (69p) Excellent mix of puzzle and trivia challenge.
Mission:Explore London (free) Fun for kids and adults – very silly challenges around the city.
Street Art London (£2.99) The city's graffiti artists and their work.
StreetMuseum (free) Brilliant Museum of London app – archive shots geolocated to where you're standing, with informative captions.
StreetMuseum Londinium (free) StreetMuseum, but for Romans.
Time Out London Magazine (free) Indispensable guide to the week's happenings in the capital.
Time Travel Explorer (£1.99) Overlays your location with any of four historic maps, the oldest from 1746; a slider blends old and new.
Toiluxe – central London (69p) Where's the nearest public loo? Never be caught short.
Tube Deluxe (69p) There are free apps, but not with departure boards, travel news and journey planning.

Index

INDEX

INDEX

INDEX

INDEX

Q

R

S

Advertisers' Index

Please refer to the relevant pages for contact details.

Explore

Arts and Entertainment

Essential Information

DIANA PRINCESS OF WALES
MEMORIAL WALK
TRAFALGAR SQUARE
NKMENT
CHARING CROSS

Maps

CABINET WAR ROOMS
WESTMINSTER
WESTMINSTER ABBEY
OUSES OF PARLIAMENT

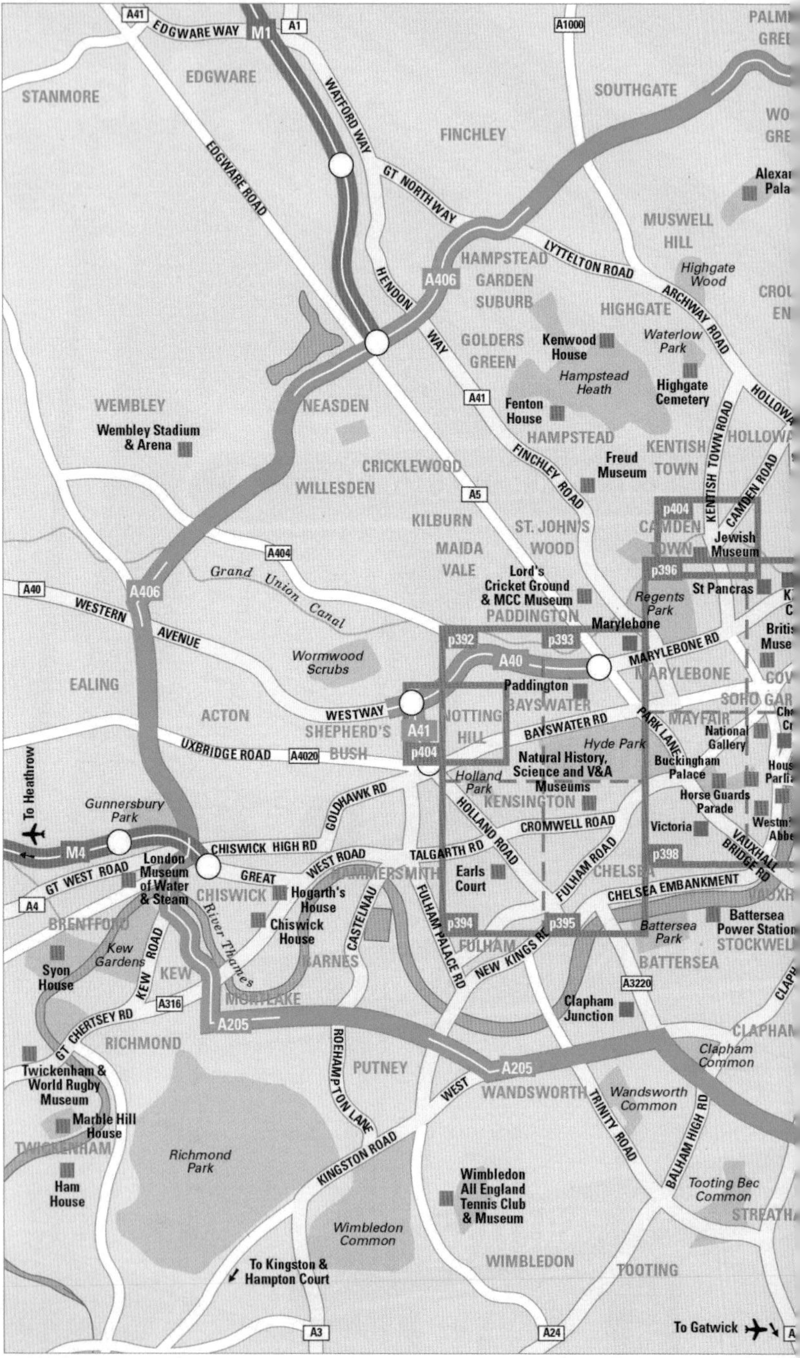
A41
EDGWARE WAY
M1
A1
A1000
STANMORE
EDGWARE
WATFORD WAY
SOUTHGATE
FINCHLEY
EDGWARE ROAD
GT NORTH WAY
MUSWELL HILL
HAMPSTEAD GARDEN SUBURB
LYTTELTON ROAD
Highgate Wood
A406
HENDON WAY
ARCHWAY ROAD
HIGHGATE
GOLDERS GREEN
Kenwood House
Waterlow Park
Hampstead Heath
Highgate Cemetery
WEMBLEY
NEASDEN
A41
Fenton House
Wembley Stadium & Arena
HAMPSTEAD
KENTISH TOWN
KENTISH TOWN ROAD
CAMDEN ROAD
FINCHLEY ROAD
Freud Museum
CRICKLEWOOD
WILLESDEN
A5
p404
KILBURN
ST. JOHN'S WOOD
CAMDEN TOWN
Jewish Museum
MAIDA VALE
A404
p396
Grand Union Canal
Lord's Cricket Ground & MCC Museum
St Pancras
A40
A406
WESTERN AVENUE
Regents Park
PADDINGTON
Marylebone
p392
p393
Wormwood Scrubs
A40
MARYLEBONE RD
MARYLEBONE
EALING
Paddington
BAYSWATER
WESTWAY
ACTON
NOTTING HILL
MAYFAIR
SOHO
SHEPHERD'S BUSH
A41
BAYSWATER RD
PARK LANE
Hyde Park
National Gallery
UXBRIDGE ROAD
A4020
p404
Natural History, Science and V&A Museums
Buckingham Palace
Holland Park
To Heathrow
Gunnersbury Park
GOLDHAWK RD
KENSINGTON
Horse Guards Parade
HOLLAND ROAD
CROMWELL ROAD
Victoria
M4
CHISWICK HIGH RD
London Museum of Water & Steam
TALGARTH RD
WEST ROAD
Earls Court
FULHAM ROAD
GREAT WEST ROAD
HAMMERSMITH
CHELSEA
p398
VAUXHALL BRIDGE RD
GT WEST ROAD
CHISWICK
Hogarth's House
CHELSEA EMBANKMENT
A4
CASTELNAU
FULHAM PALACE RD
BRENTFORD
Chiswick House
River Thames
p394
p395
Battersea Park
Battersea Power Station
Kew Gardens
KEW ROAD
FULHAM
NEW KINGS RD
STOCKWELL
Syon House
KEW
BARNES
BATTERSEA
A3220
A316
MORTLAKE
Clapham Junction
GT CHERTSEY RD
A205
RICHMOND
CLAPHAM
Clapham Common
ROEHAMPTON LANE
A205
Twickenham & World Rugby Museum
PUTNEY
WEST
WANDSWORTH
TRINITY ROAD
Wandsworth Common
Marble Hill House
BALHAM HIGH RD
TWICKENHAM
Richmond Park
KINGSTON ROAD
Ham House
Wimbledon All England Tennis Club & Museum
Tooting Bec Common
Wimbledon Common
WIMBLEDON
TOOTING
To Kingston & Hampton Court
A3
A24
To Gatwick

To Stansted
EDMONTON
WOODFORD
CHIGWELL
TOTTENHAM
William Morris Gallery
FOREST ROAD
Epping Forest
HARRINGAY
WALTHAMSTOW
EASTERN AVE
STAMFORD HILL
LEYTONSTONE
CAMBRIDGE PARK
Wanstead Park
WANSTEAD
STOKENEWINGTON
CLAPTON
LEYTON
ILFORD
FOREST GATE
DALSTON
HACKNEY
STRATFORD
HIGHBURY
Sutton House
Queen Elizabeth Olympic Park
River Lea
West Ham Park
BARKING
HOXTON
Victoria Park
BOW
WEST HAM
EAST HAM
PLAISTOW
Museum of Childhood
MILE END
SHOREDITCH
BETHNAL GREEN
Ragged School Museum
NEWHAM
NEWHAM WAY
Liverpool Street
STEPNEY
CANNING TOWN
BECKTON
CITY
WHITECHAPEL
EAST INDIA DOCK ROAD
Blackwall Tunnel
Emirates Air Line
ExCeL
London City Airport
Tower of London
LIMEHOUSE
Museum of London Docklands
Canary Wharf
WAPPING
The Shad
O2 Arena
THAMES-MEAD
Imperial War Museum
River Thames
ROTHERHITHE
ISLE OF DOGS
Thames Barrier
Woolwich Ferry
BERMONDSEY
WOOLWICH
Maryon Park
Old Royal Naval College
CHARLTON
KENNINGTON
DEPTFORD
Cutty Sark
National Maritime Museum
CAMBERWELL
GREENWICH
Greenwich Park
PLUMSTEAD
Royal Observatory
PECKHAM
NEW CROSS
Oxleas Woods
NUNHEAD
BLACKHEATH
BRIXTON
LEWISHAM
Dulwich Picture Gallery
Peckham Rye
ELTHAM
DULWICH
Horniman Museum
SOUTH CIRCULAR ROAD
FOREST HILL
CATFORD
SIDCUP ROAD
Crystal Palace Park
CRYSTAL PALACE
BROMLEY
0 1 2 3 miles
0 1 2 3 4 5 km
© Copyright Time Out Group 2014

MAPS

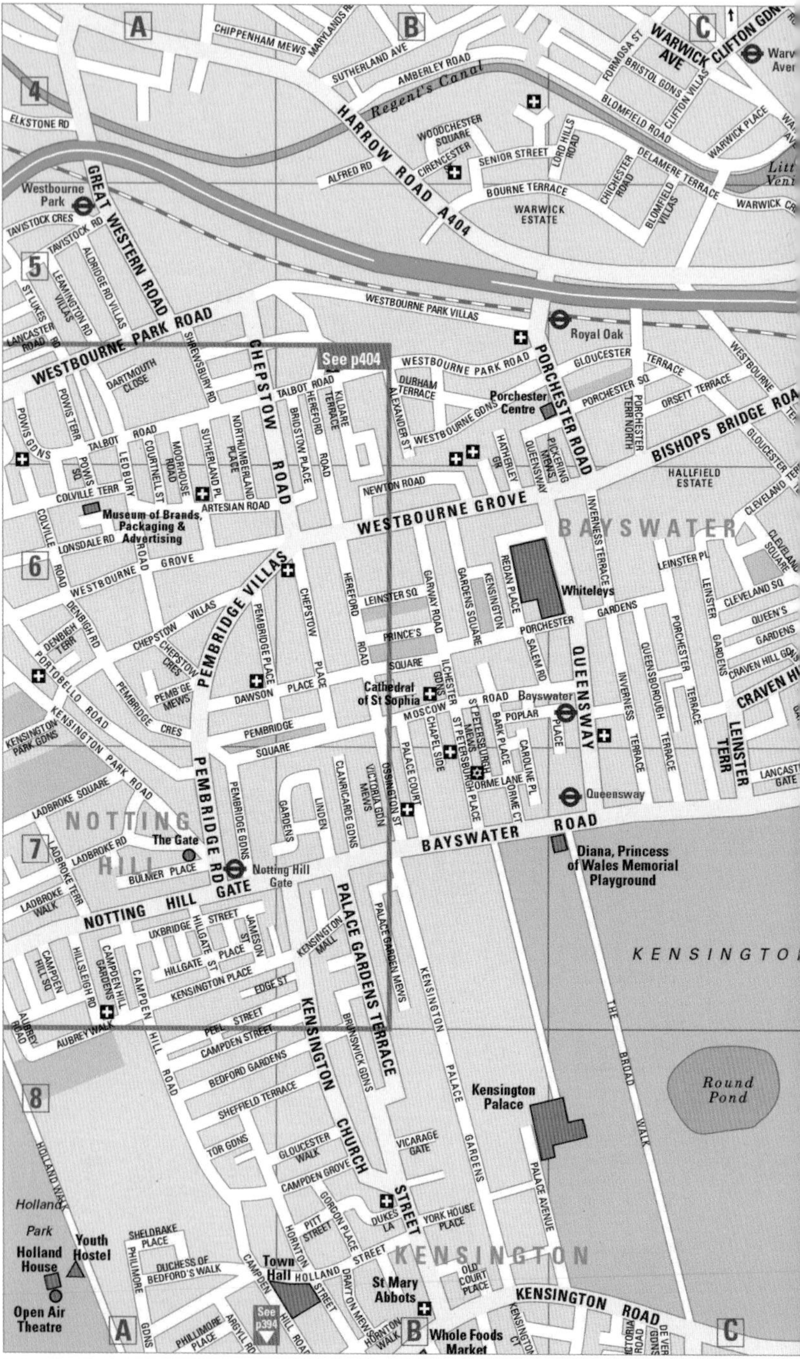
A
B
C
4
5
6
7
8
CHIPPENHAM MEWS
MARYLANDS RD
SUTHERLAND AVE
AMBERLEY ROAD
Regent's Canal
FORMOSA ST
WARWICK AVE
CLIFTON GDNS
BRISTOL GDNS
CLIFTON VILLAS
BLOMFIELD ROAD
WARWICK PLACE
ELKSTONE RD
HARROW ROAD A404
WOODCHESTER SQUARE
CIRENCESTER ST
SENIOR STREET
LORD HILLS ROAD
CHICHESTER ROAD
DELAMERE TERRACE
ALFRED RD
BOURNE TERRACE
WARWICK ESTATE
BLOMFIELD VILLAS
WARWICK CRES
Westbourne Park
GREAT WESTERN ROAD
TAVISTOCK CRES
TAVISTOCK RD
ALDRIDGE RD VILLAS
LEAMINGTON RD VILLAS
ST LUKES RD
LANCASTER ROAD
WESTBOURNE PARK VILLAS
Royal Oak
WESTBOURNE PARK ROAD
SHREWSBURY RD
CHEPSTOW ROAD
See p404
TALBOT ROAD
KILDARE TERRACE
DARTMOUTH CLOSE
DURHAM TERRACE
ALEXANDER ST
PORCHESTER ROAD
GLOUCESTER TERRACE
Porchester Centre
PORCHESTER SQ
PORCHESTER TERR NORTH
ORSETT TERRACE
WESTBOURNE TERRACE
BISHOPS BRIDGE ROAD
POWIS GDNS
POWIS TERR
TALBOT ROAD
COURTNELL ST
MOORHOUSE ROAD
SUTHERLAND PL
NORTHUMBERLAND PLACE
BRIDSTOW PLACE
HEREFORD ROAD
WESTBOURNE GDNS
HATHERLEY GR
QUEENSWAY
PICKERING MEWS
HALLFIELD ESTATE
GLOUCESTER TERRACE
POWIS SQ
LEDBURY
COLVILLE TERR
ARTESIAN ROAD
NEWTON ROAD
CLEVELAND TERR
Museum of Brands, Packaging & Advertising
WESTBOURNE GROVE
BAYSWATER
INVERNESS TERRACE
COLVILLE ROAD
LONSDALE RD
WESTBOURNE GROVE
PEMBRIDGE VILLAS
CHEPSTOW VILLAS
PEMBRIDGE PLACE
CHEPSTOW PLACE
HEREFORD ROAD
LEINSTER SQ
PRINCE'S SQUARE
GARWAY ROAD
GARDENS SQUARE
KENSINGTON
REDAN PLACE
Whiteleys
PORCHESTER GARDENS
LEINSTER PL
CLEVELAND SQUARE
CLEVELAND SQ
QUEEN'S GARDENS
LEINSTER GARDENS
CRAVEN HILL GDNS
CRAVEN HILL
DENBIGH RD
DENBIGH TERR
PORTOBELLO ROAD
CHEPSTOW CRES
PEMB'GE MEWS
PEMBRIDGE CRES
DAWSON PLACE
Cathedral of St Sophia
ILCHESTER GDNS
MOSCOW ROAD
Bayswater
SALEM RD
POPLAR PLACE
QUEENSBOROUGH TERRACE
PORCHESTER TERRACE
LEINSTER TERR
KENSINGTON PARK GDNS
KENSINGTON PARK ROAD
PEMBRIDGE SQUARE
CHAPEL SIDE
ST PETERSBURGH MEWS
ST PETERSBURGH PLACE
BARK PLACE
CAROLINE PL
ORME LANE
ORME CT
LANCASTER GATE
LADBROKE SQUARE
NOTTING HILL
PEMBRIDGE RD
PEMBRIDGE GDNS
GARDENS
LINDEN
CLANRICARDE GDNS
VICTORIA GDN MEWS
OSSINGTON ST
PALACE COURT
Queensway
The Gate
LADBROKE RD
LADBROKE TERR
BAYSWATER ROAD
Diana, Princess of Wales Memorial Playground
BULMER PLACE
Notting Hill Gate
GATE
LADBROKE WALK
NOTTING HILL
UXBRIDGE ST
HILLGATE ST
STREET
JAMESON ST
KENSINGTON MALL
PALACE GARDENS TERRACE
PALACE GARDEN MEWS
KENSINGTON PALACE GARDENS
KENSINGTON GARDENS
CAMPDEN HILL SQ
HILLSLEIGH RD
CAMPDEN HILL GARDENS
HILLGATE PLACE
KENSINGTON PLACE
EDGE ST
AUBREY ROAD
AUBREY WALK
CAMPDEN HILL ROAD
PEEL STREET
CAMPDEN STREET
BEDFORD GARDENS
SHEFFIELD TERRACE
KENSINGTON CHURCH STREET
BRUNSWICK GDNS
THE BROAD WALK
Round Pond
Kensington Palace
HOLLAND WALK
Holland Park
TOR GDNS
GLOUCESTER WALK
VICARAGE GATE
CAMPDEN GROVE
PALACE AVENUE
DUKES LA
YORK HOUSE PLACE
Youth Hostel
Holland House
SHELDRAKE PLACE
PHILLIMORE
PITT STREET
GORDON PLACE
HORNTON STREET
KENSINGTON
DUCHESS OF BEDFORD'S WALK
Town Hall
HOLLAND STREET
DRAYTON MEWS
St Mary Abbots
OLD COURT PLACE
KENSINGTON ROAD
Open Air Theatre
GDNS
PHILLIMORE PLACE
ARGYLL RD
See p394
HILL ROAD
HORNTON WALK
Whole Foods Market
KENSINGTON CT
VICTORIA ROAD
DE VERE GDNS

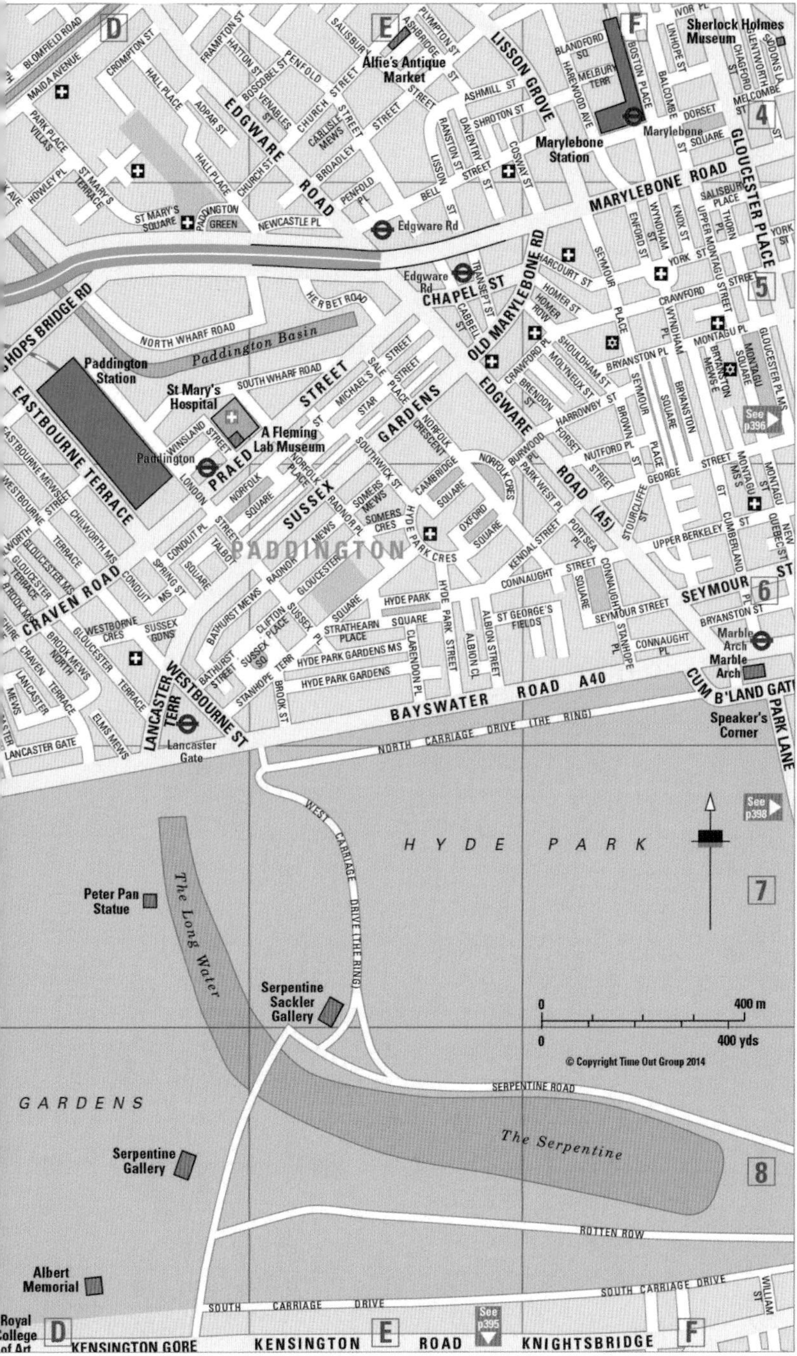
D
E
F
4
5
6
7
8
Sherlock Holmes Museum
Alfie's Antique Market
Marylebone Station
Marylebone
Edgware Rd
Paddington Station
St Mary's Hospital
A Fleming Lab Museum
Paddington
Paddington Basin
PADDINGTON
Marble Arch
Speaker's Corner
Lancaster Gate
HYDE PARK
GARDENS
Peter Pan Statue
The Long Water
Serpentine Sackler Gallery
The Serpentine
Serpentine Gallery
Albert Memorial
Royal College of Art
BLOMFIELD ROAD
MAIDA AVENUE
CROMPTON ST
HALL PLACE
FRAMPTON ST
HATTON ST
BOSCOBEL ST
PENFOLD
SALISBURY
ASHBRIDGE
PLYMPTON ST
LISSON GROVE
BLANDFORD SQ
HAREWOOD AVE
MELBURY TERR
BOSTON PLACE
LINHOPE ST
BALCOMBE
IVOR PL
CHAGFORD ST
GLENTWORTH ST
MELCOMBE ST
DORSET SQUARE
GLOUCESTER PLACE
MARYLEBONE ROAD
EDGWARE ROAD
CHURCH STREET
CARLISLE MEWS
BROADLEY
ASHMILL ST
SHROTON ST
RANSTON ST
DAVENTRY STREET
COSWAY ST
BELL ST
NEWCASTLE PL
PADDINGTON GREEN
ST MARY'S SQUARE
PARK PLACE VILLAS
HOWLEY PL
ST MARY'S TERRACE
ADPAR ST
HERBET ROAD
NORTH WHARF ROAD
SOUTH WHARF ROAD
CHAPEL ST
TRANSEPT ST
CABBELL ST
OLD MARYLEBONE RD
HARCOURT ST
HOMER ST
HOMER ROW
CRAWFORD PL
SHOULDHAM ST
MOLYNEUX ST
BRENDON ST
HARROWBY ST
FORSET ST
NUTFORD PL
BURWOOD PL
PARK WEST PL
ENFORD ST
WYNDHAM ST
KNOX ST
UPPER MONTAGU STREET
SALISBURY PLACE
THORN PL
YORK ST
CRAWFORD STREET
MONTAGU PL
BRYANSTON PL
BRYANSTON MEWS E
BRYANSTON SQUARE
MONTAGU SQUARE
SEYMOUR PLACE
BROWN ST
GEORGE STREET
STOURCLIFFE ST
UPPER BERKELEY ST
CUMBERLAND GT
QUEBEC ST
SEYMOUR ST
SEYMOUR PL
BRYANSTON ST
CONNAUGHT STREET
CONNAUGHT SQUARE
CONNAUGHT PL
STANHOPE PL
SEYMOUR STREET
PORTSEA PL
KENDAL STREET
ST GEORGE'S FIELDS
ALBION STREET
ALBION CL
HYDE PARK STREET
HYDE PARK CRES
OXFORD SQUARE
CAMBRIDGE SQUARE
NORFOLK CRES
NORFOLK CRESCENT
SOUTHWICK ST
SOMERS MEWS
SOMERS CRES
RADNOR PL
SUSSEX GARDENS
NORFOLK PLACE
NORFOLK SQUARE
STAR ST
MICHAEL'S ST
SALE PLACE
PRAED STREET
WINSLAND STREET
LONDON ST
EASTBOURNE TERRACE
EASTBOURNE MEWS
WESTBOURNE STREET
CHILWORTH STREET
CHILWORTH MS
GLOUCESTER MS
GLOUCESTER TERRACE
CRAVEN ROAD
CONDUIT PL
CONDUIT MS
SPRING ST
TALBOT SQUARE
RADNOR MEWS
GLOUCESTER SQUARE
HYDE PARK SQUARE
STRATHEARN PLACE
HYDE PARK GARDENS MS
HYDE PARK GARDENS
CLARENDON PL
BATHURST MEWS
BATHURST STREET
CLIFTON PLACE
SUSSEX PL
SUSSEX SQ
STANHOPE TERR
BROOK ST
WESTBORNE CRES
SUSSEX GDNS
BROOK MEWS NORTH
GLOUCESTER TERRACE
CRAVEN TERRACE
LANCASTER MEWS
LANCASTER GATE
ELMS MEWS
LANCASTER TERR
WESTBOURNE ST
BAYSWATER ROAD A40
CUM B'LAND GATE
PARK LANE
NORTH CARRIAGE DRIVE (THE RING)
WEST CARRIAGE DRIVE (THE RING)
SERPENTINE ROAD
ROTTEN ROW
SOUTH CARRIAGE DRIVE
WILLIAM ST
KENSINGTON GORE
KENSINGTON ROAD
KNIGHTSBRIDGE
(A5)
See p396
See p398
See p395
0
400 m
0
400 yds
© Copyright Time Out Group 2014

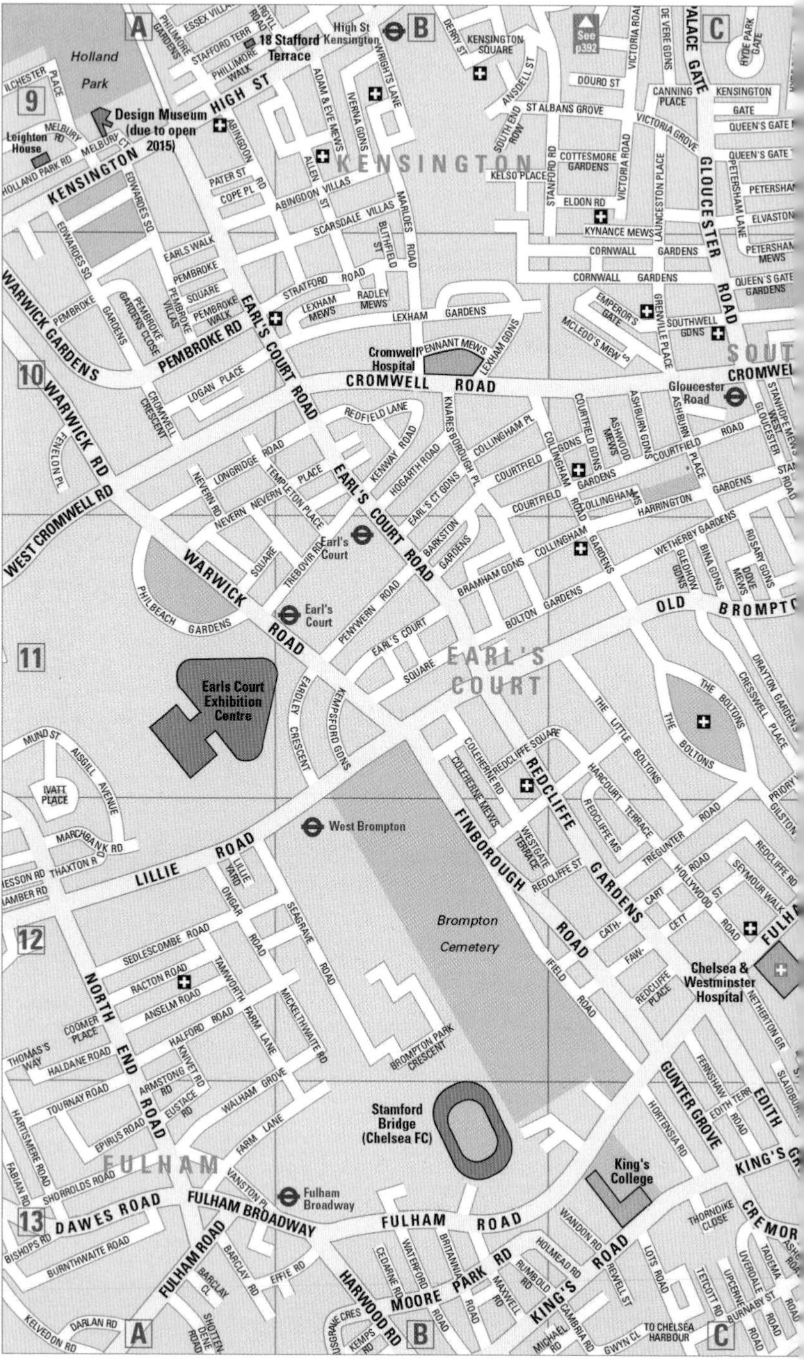

A
B
C
9
10
11
12
13
Holland Park
Design Museum (due to open 2015)
Leighton House
18 Stafford Terrace
High St Kensington
See p392
KENSINGTON
KENSINGTON HIGH ST
CROMWELL ROAD
Cromwell Hospital
Gloucester Road
EARL'S COURT ROAD
WARWICK ROAD
WEST CROMWELL RD
WARWICK GARDENS
PEMBROKE RD
Earl's Court
EARL'S COURT
Earls Court Exhibition Centre
West Brompton
LILLIE ROAD
OLD BROMPTON
REDCLIFFE GARDENS
FINBOROUGH ROAD
Brompton Cemetery
Chelsea & Westminster Hospital
NORTH END ROAD
Stamford Bridge (Chelsea FC)
King's College
Fulham Broadway
FULHAM BROADWAY
FULHAM ROAD
FULHAM
DAWES ROAD
KING'S ROAD
MOORE PARK RD
HARWOOD RD
GUNTER GROVE
EDITH GROVE
TO CHELSEA HARBOUR

MAPS

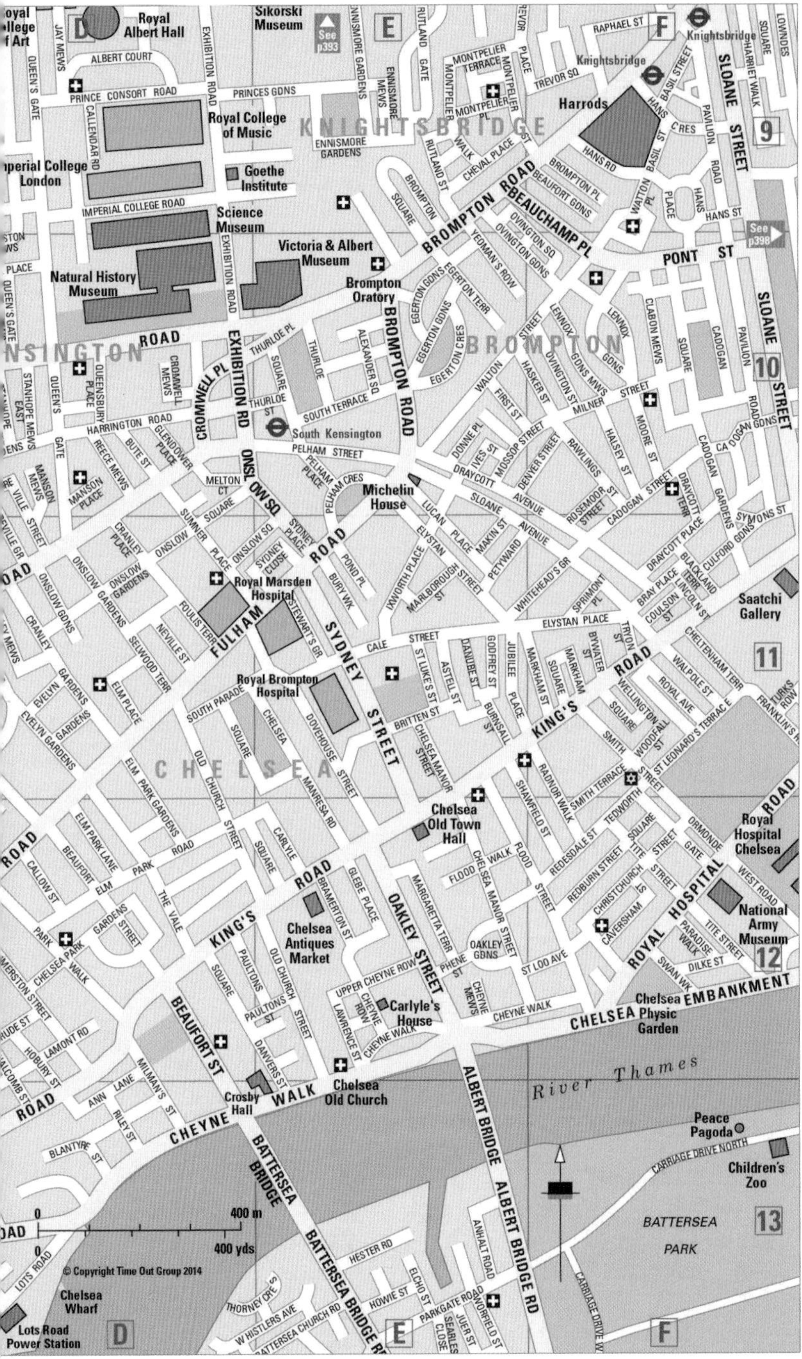

© Copyright Time Out Group 2014

MAPS

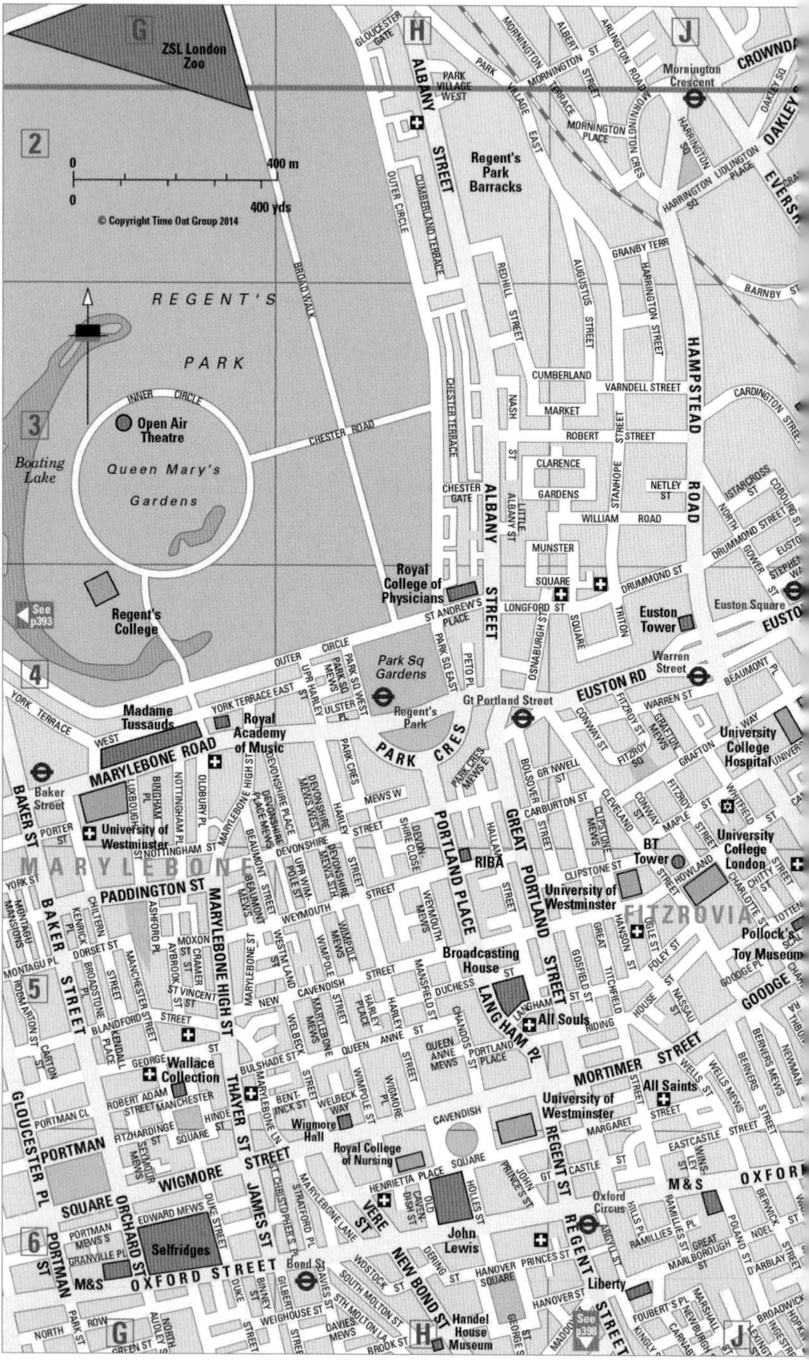
G
H
J
2
3
4
5
6
ZSL London Zoo
0
400 m
0
400 yds
© Copyright Time Out Group 2014
REGENT'S PARK
Boating Lake
INNER CIRCLE
Open Air Theatre
Queen Mary's Gardens
CHESTER ROAD
BROAD WALK
Regent's College
See p393
OUTER CIRCLE
YORK TERRACE
YORK TERRACE EAST
Madame Tussauds
Royal Academy of Music
MARYLEBONE ROAD
Baker Street
BAKER ST
University of Westminster
MARYLEBONE
PADDINGTON ST
MARYLEBONE HIGH ST
Wallace Collection
THAYER ST
PORTMAN SQUARE
WIGMORE STREET
Selfridges
M&S
OXFORD STREET
Bond St
GLOUCESTER PL
ORCHARD ST
JAMES ST
GLOUCESTER GATE
ALBANY STREET
PARK VILLAGE WEST
PARK VILLAGE EAST
Regent's Park Barracks
OUTER CIRCLE
CUMBERLAND TERRACE
CHESTER TERRACE
CHESTER GATE
Royal College of Physicians
ST ANDREW'S PLACE
Park Sq Gardens
Regent's Park
PARK CRES
Gt Portland Street
PORTLAND PLACE
GREAT PORTLAND STREET
RIBA
Broadcasting House
LANGHAM PL
All Souls
Wigmore Hall
Royal College of Nursing
CAVENDISH SQUARE
John Lewis
NEW BOND ST
Handel House Museum
MORNINGTON CRESCENT
Mornington Crescent
ARLINGTON ROAD
MORNINGTON PLACE
HARRINGTON SQ
OAKLEY SQ
CROWNDALE
GRANBY TERR
REDHILL STREET
AUGUSTUS STREET
HARRINGTON STREET
HAMPSTEAD ROAD
CUMBERLAND MARKET
VARNDELL STREET
ROBERT STREET
CLARENCE GARDENS
NETLEY ST
WILLIAM ROAD
MUNSTER SQUARE
DRUMMOND ST
LONGFORD ST
Euston Tower
Euston Square
Warren Street
EUSTON RD
WARREN ST
FITZROY SQ
University College Hospital
CARBURTON ST
BT Tower
University College London
University of Westminster
FITZROVIA
Pollock's Toy Museum
GOODGE ST
MORTIMER STREET
All Saints
University of Westminster
REGENT ST
Oxford Circus
M & S
OXFORD
Liberty
See p398
HANOVER SQUARE
PRINCES ST
CARDINGTON STREET
BEAUMONT PL
GRAFTON WAY
CLEVELAND ST
CHARLOTTE ST
BERNERS ST
WELLS ST
NEWMAN ST
MARGARET ST
GREAT TITCHFIELD ST
MARLBOROUGH ST
POLAND ST
BERWICK ST
ARGYLL ST

K
L
M
St Pancras Gardens
St Pancras Old Church
Camley St Natural Park
Regent's Canal
Battle Bridge Basin
Kings Place
London Canal Museum
CAMLEY ROAD
GOODS WAY
NEW WHARF ROAD
ALL SAINTS ST
KILLICK ST
CARNEGIE ST
CHARLOTTE TERR
MURIEL ST
WYNFORD ROAD
2
GOLDINGTON CRES
GOLDINGTON ST
MEDBURN ST
PLATT ST
CHARRINGTON ST
PURCHESE STREET
COOPERS LANE
ST PANCRAS ROAD
BATTLE BR RD
CRINAN ST
WHARFEDALE ROAD
CALEDONIAN ROAD
PRIORY GREEN
RODNEY ST
CALSHOT STREET
COLLIER STREET
DONEGAL ST
CUMMING ST
CYNTHIA ST
YORK WAY
RAILWAY ST
BALFE ST
King's Cross Station
KEYSTONE CRES
NORTHDOWN ST
CALEDONIA ST
St Pancras International Station
MIDLAND ROAD
BRILL PLACE
CHALTON ST
ALDENHAM ST
POLYGON ROAD
SOMERS TOWN
PHOENIX ROAD
British Library
OSSULSTON STREET
PENTONVILLE ROAD
KING'S CROSS RD
LORENZO ST
WESTON RISE
PENTON RISE
King's Cross St Pancras
CRESTFIELD ST
BIRKENHEAD STREET
ST CHAD'S PLACE
LEEKE ST
BRITANNIA STREET
WICKLOW ST
VERNON RISE
PERCEY CIRCUS
GREAT PERCY ST
3
DRUMMOND CRES
Euston Station
DORIC WAY
CHURCHWAY
CHALTON STREET
EUSTON ROAD
BELGRAVE ST
ST CHAD'S ST
ARGYLE SQ
ARGYLE ST
ARGYLE STREET
SWINTON ST
ACTON ST
WHARTON ST
Euston
GRAFTON PL
JUDD STREET
BIDBORO' ST
TONBRIDGE ST
WHIDBORNE ST
CROMER STREET
GRAY'S INN ROAD
FREDERICK ST
CUBITT STREET
GRANVILLE SQUARE
DUKE'S RD
FLAXMAN TERR
HASTINGS ST
SANDWICH ST
THANET ST
CARTWRIGHT GARDENS
HARRISON STREET
SEAFORD ST
AMPTON ST
UPR WOBURN PL
WOBURN WALK
BURTON STREET
LEIGH ST
REGENT SQUARE
SIDMOUTH ST
See p400
ENDSLEIGH GDNS
ENDSLEIGH ST
WAKEFIELD ST
TAVISTOCK PL
HEATHCOTE ST
Wellcome Collection
Eastman Dental Hospital
PAKENHAM ST
TAVITON ST
GORDON ST
KENTON ST
HUNTER ST
St George's Gardens
MECKLENBURGH
HANDEL ST
Foundling Museum
DOUGHTY STREET
WREN ST
CALTHORPE ST
University College London
TAVISTOCK PLACE
TAVISTOCK SQUARE
WOBURN PLACE
HERBRAND ST
MARCHMONT STREET
Brunswick Centre
GRENVILLE ST
BRUNSWICK SQUARE
Coram's Fields
SQUARE
Mount Pleasant Sorting Office
GORDON SQUARE
CORAM ST
LANSDOWNE TERR
BROWNLOW MEWS
GOUGH ST
PHOENIX PL
4
GOWER STREET
Petrie Museum of Egyptian Archaeology
WOBURN SQUARE
BEDFORD WAY
BERNARD STREET
COLONNADE
GUILFORD STREET
Great Ormond St Hospital
LAMB'S CON
DOUGHTY M'S
MILLMAN ST
Charles Dickens Museum
ROGER ST
COLEY ST
MOUNT PLEASANT
CHENIES M
HUNTLEY ST
TORRINGTON PLACE
MALET STREET
TORRINGTON SQUARE
University of London
RUSSELL SQUARE
Russell Square
QUEEN SQUARE
GREAT ORMOND STREET
CONDUIT
JOHN'S MEWS
JOHN ST
NORTH MEWS
ELM ST
KING'S MEWS
NORTHINGTON ST
GRAY'S INN ROAD
RIDGMOUNT GDNS
BLOOMSBURY
ORDE HALL ST
RUGBY ST
EMERALD ST
GT JAMES ST
CHENIES ST
RIDGMOUNT ST
NORTH CRESCENT
Senate House
SQUARE
OLD GLOUCESTER ST
BOSWELL ST
NEW NORTH ST
DOMBEY ST
HARPUR ST
THEOBALD'S ROAD
Goodge Street
Drill Hall
KEPPEL ST
MONTAGUE PL
BEDFORD PLACE
SOUTHAMPTON ROW
BEDFORD ROW
JOCKEY'S FIELD
RAYMOND BUILDINGS
Gray's Inn Gardens
New London Architecture
ALFRED PL
GOWER MS
COURT ROAD
STORE ST
SOUTH CRESCENT
BEDFORD SQUARE
British Museum
MONTAGUE ST
BLOOMSBURY SQUARE
RED LION SQUARE
PRINCETON ST
LION ST
5
Gray's Inn
SANDLAND ST
BROWNLOW ST
BAYLEY ST
MORWELL ST
BLOOMSBURY ST
GREAT RUSSELL STREET
DRAKE ST
FISHER ST
PROCTER ST
EAGLE ST
CHANCERY LANE
BEDFORD AVE
Cartoon Museum
MUSEUM ST
GILBERT PL
BURY PL
BLOOMSBURY WAY
SICILIAN AVE
CATTON ST
STEPHEN ST
GRESSE ST
RATHBONE PLACE
GREAT RUSSELL ST
DYOTT ST
STREATHAM ST
COPTIC ST
BARTER ST
SOTON PL
HIGH HOLBORN
Holborn
Sir John Soane's Museum
WHETSTONE PK
HOLBORN
STONE BUILDINGS
HANWAY PL
HANWAY ST
BAINBRIDGE ST
NEW OXFORD STREET
WEST CENTRAL ST
NEWTON ST
LINCOLN'S INN FIELDS
REMNANT ST
Tottenham Court Road
ANDREW BORDE ST
ST GILES
BUCKNALL ST
GRAPE ST
STUKELEY ST
MACKLIN ST
PARKER ST
Lincoln's Inn Fields
Lincoln's Inn
SUTTON ROW
SOHO SQUARE
ST GILES HIGH ST
CHARING CROSS RD
DENMARK ST
NEW COMPTON ST
FLITCROFT ST
COVENT GARDEN
DRURY LANE
Freemasons' Hall
GT QUEEN STREET
WILD CT
KINGSWAY
Hunterian Museum
PORTUGAL ST
SERLE STREET
NEW SQUARE
BELL YD
DEAN ST
CARLISLE ST
GOSLETT YD
MANETTE ST
SOHO
SHAFTESBURY AVE
MONMOUTH ST
ENDELL ST
BETTERTON ST
ARNE ST
WILD STREET
KEELEY ST
KEMBLE ST
KEAN ST
LSE
CLEMENT'S INN
GRANGE CT
CAREY ST
6
Royal Courts of Justice
ST ANNE'S CT
FRITH ST
GREEK ST
BATEMAN ST
PHOENIX ST
SHORTS GDNS
NEAL ST
Covent Garden
DRURY LANE
Royal Opera House
SEVEN DIALS
EARLHAM ST
MOOR ST
OLD COMPTON ST
CAMBRIDGE CIRCUS
MEARD ST
TOWER ST
MERCER ST
SHELTON ST
LONG ACRE
BOW ST
RUSSELL ST
See p399
ALDWYCH
St Clement Danes
See p404

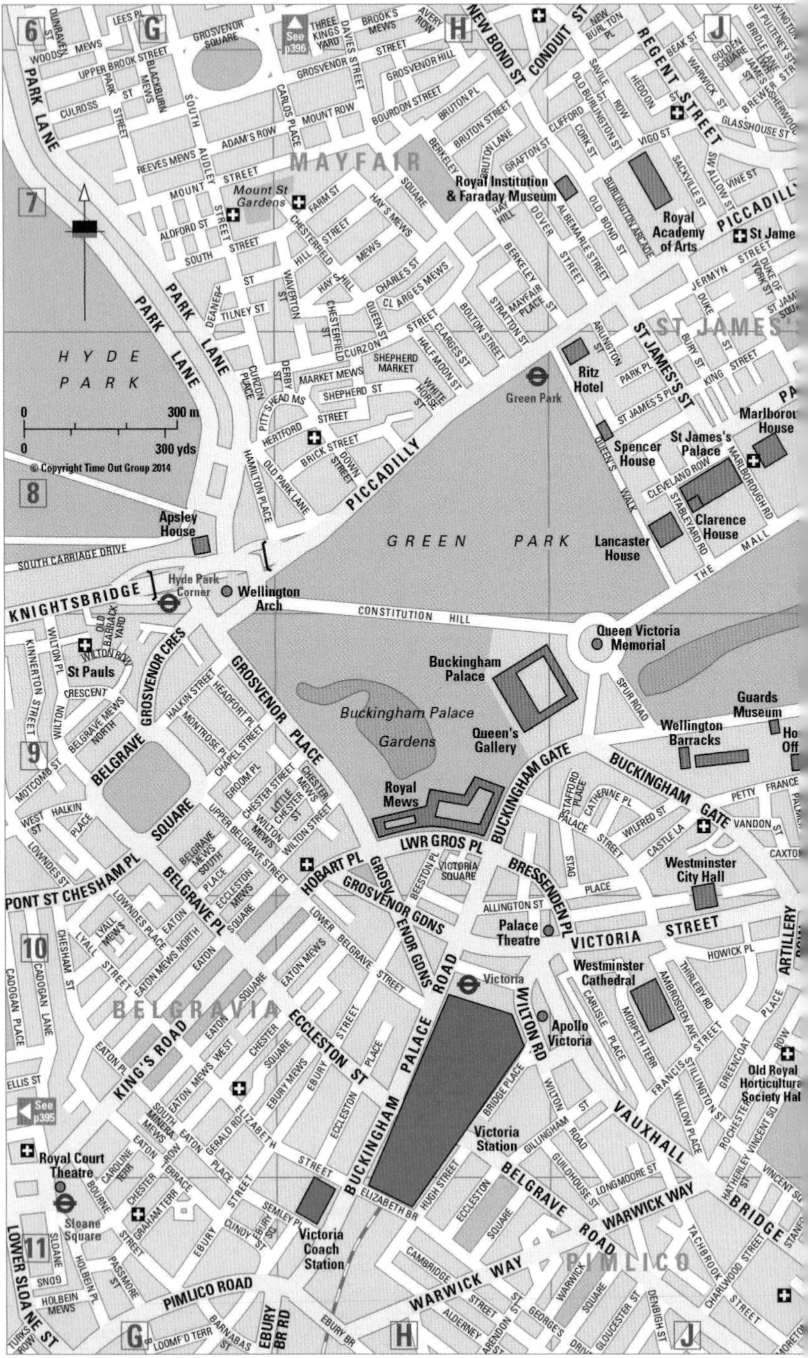
MAYFAIR
HYDE PARK
GREEN PARK
BELGRAVIA
PIMLICO
ST JAMES'
Buckingham Palace Gardens
Mount St Gardens
Royal Institution & Faraday Museum
Royal Academy of Arts
Ritz Hotel
Green Park
Spencer House
St James's Palace
Marlborough House
Clarence House
Lancaster House
Apsley House
Hyde Park Corner
Wellington Arch
Queen Victoria Memorial
Buckingham Palace
Queen's Gallery
Royal Mews
Guards Museum
Wellington Barracks
Westminster City Hall
Palace Theatre
Westminster Cathedral
Victoria
Apollo Victoria
Victoria Station
Victoria Coach Station
Royal Court Theatre
Sloane Square
Old Royal Horticultural Society Hall
St Pauls
See p396
See p395
0 300 m
0 300 yds
© Copyright Time Out Group 2014
PARK LANE
PICCADILLY
KNIGHTSBRIDGE
CONSTITUTION HILL
SOUTH CARRIAGE DRIVE
THE MALL
REGENT STREET
NEW BOND ST
CONDUIT ST
GROSVENOR SQUARE
GROSVENOR STREET
GROSVENOR PLACE
GROSVENOR CRES
BELGRAVE SQUARE
BUCKINGHAM GATE
BUCKINGHAM PALACE ROAD
VICTORIA STREET
VAUXHALL BRIDGE ROAD
WARWICK WAY
BELGRAVE ROAD
ECCLESTON ST
KING'S ROAD
PIMLICO ROAD
LOWER SLOANE ST
CHESHAM PL
PONT ST
LWR GROS PL
HOBART PL
BRESSENDEN PL
WILTON RD
ST JAMES'S ST
JERMYN STREET
CURZON ST
MOUNT STREET
SOUTH AUDLEY STREET
BERKELEY SQUARE
DOVER STREET
ALBEMARLE STREET
OLD BOND ST
SACKVILLE ST
VIGO ST
EBURY BR RD
ELIZABETH BR
6
7
8
9
10
11
G
H
J

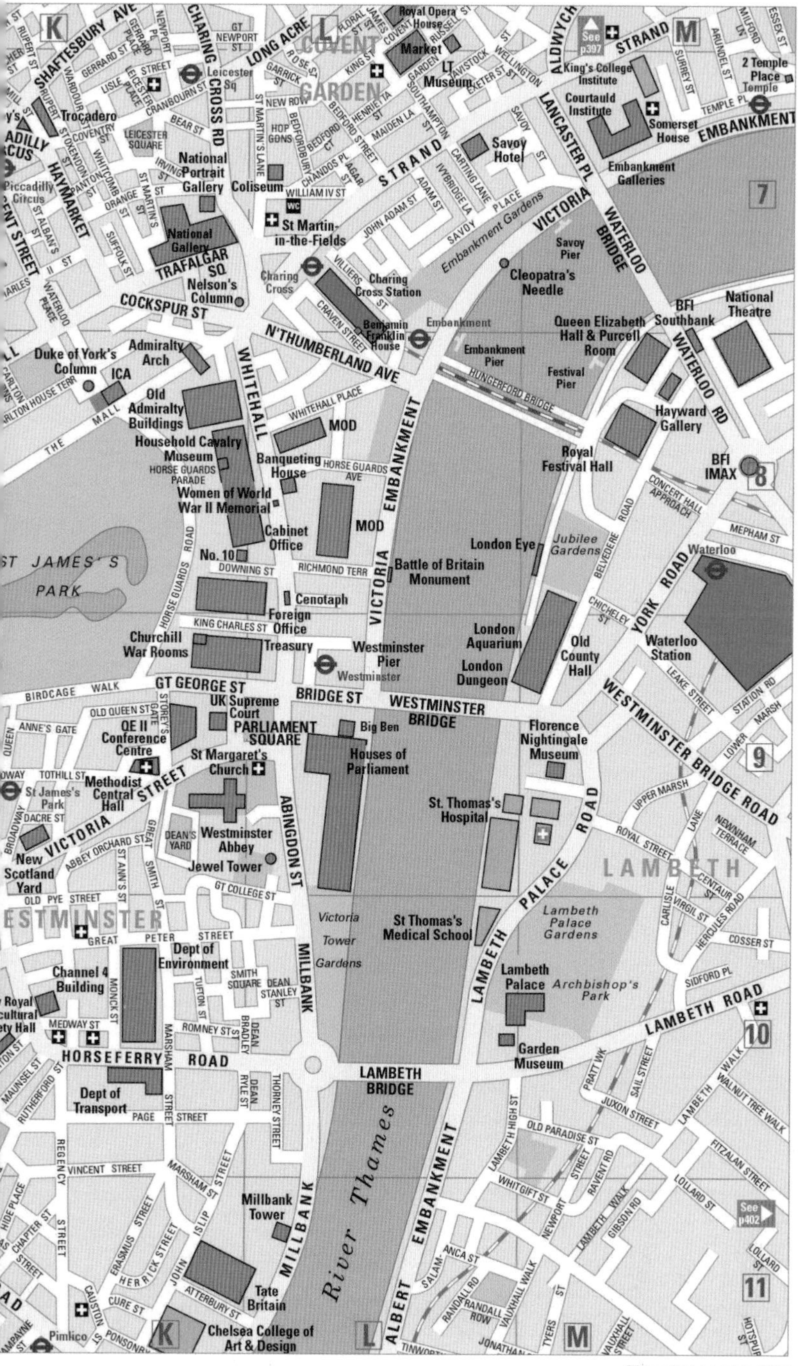
K
L
M
SHAFTESBURY AVE
COVENT GARDEN
Royal Opera House
Market
LT Museum
LONG ACRE
CHARING CROSS RD
Leicester Sq
Trocadero
LEICESTER SQUARE
National Portrait Gallery
Coliseum
National Gallery
TRAFALGAR SQ
Nelson's Column
St Martin-in-the-Fields
Charing Cross
Charing Cross Station
STRAND
ALDWYCH
See p397
King's College Institute
Courtauld Institute
Somerset House
2 Temple Place
Temple
EMBANKMENT
Savoy Hotel
Embankment Galleries
LANCASTER PL
WATERLOO BRIDGE
VICTORIA
Embankment Gardens
Savoy Pier
Cleopatra's Needle
Embankment
Benjamin Franklin House
Embankment Pier
Festival Pier
HUNGERFORD BRIDGE
Queen Elizabeth Hall & Purcell Room
BFI Southbank
National Theatre
Hayward Gallery
Royal Festival Hall
BFI IMAX
WATERLOO RD
7
8
9
10
11
HAYMARKET
Piccadilly Circus
COCKSPUR ST
N'THUMBERLAND AVE
Admiralty Arch
Duke of York's Column
ICA
THE MALL
Old Admiralty Buildings
WHITEHALL
WHITEHALL PLACE
MOD
Household Cavalry Museum
HORSE GUARDS PARADE
Banqueting House
HORSE GUARDS AVE
Women of World War II Memorial
Cabinet Office
No. 10
DOWNING ST
RICHMOND TERR
ST JAMES'S PARK
HORSE GUARDS ROAD
VICTORIA EMBANKMENT
Battle of Britain Monument
London Eye
Jubilee Gardens
Waterloo
Cenotaph
Foreign Office
KING CHARLES ST
Churchill War Rooms
Treasury
Westminster Pier
Westminster
London Aquarium
London Dungeon
Old County Hall
YORK ROAD
Waterloo Station
BIRDCAGE WALK
GT GEORGE ST
BRIDGE ST
WESTMINSTER BRIDGE
UK Supreme Court
PARLIAMENT SQUARE
Big Ben
Houses of Parliament
QE II Conference Centre
Florence Nightingale Museum
WESTMINSTER BRIDGE ROAD
St Margaret's Church
Methodist Central Hall
VICTORIA STREET
St James's Park
Westminster Abbey
Jewel Tower
ABINGDON ST
St. Thomas's Hospital
LAMBETH
New Scotland Yard
LAMBETH PALACE ROAD
WESTMINSTER
Victoria Tower Gardens
St Thomas's Medical School
Lambeth Palace Gardens
Dept of Environment
MILLBANK
LAMBETH
Lambeth Palace
Archbishop's Park
Channel 4 Building
SMITH SQUARE
LAMBETH ROAD
HORSEFERRY ROAD
Garden Museum
LAMBETH BRIDGE
Dept of Transport
PAGE STREET
ALBERT EMBANKMENT
River Thames
VINCENT STREET
Millbank Tower
See p402
Tate Britain
Chelsea College of Art & Design
Pimlico

MAPS

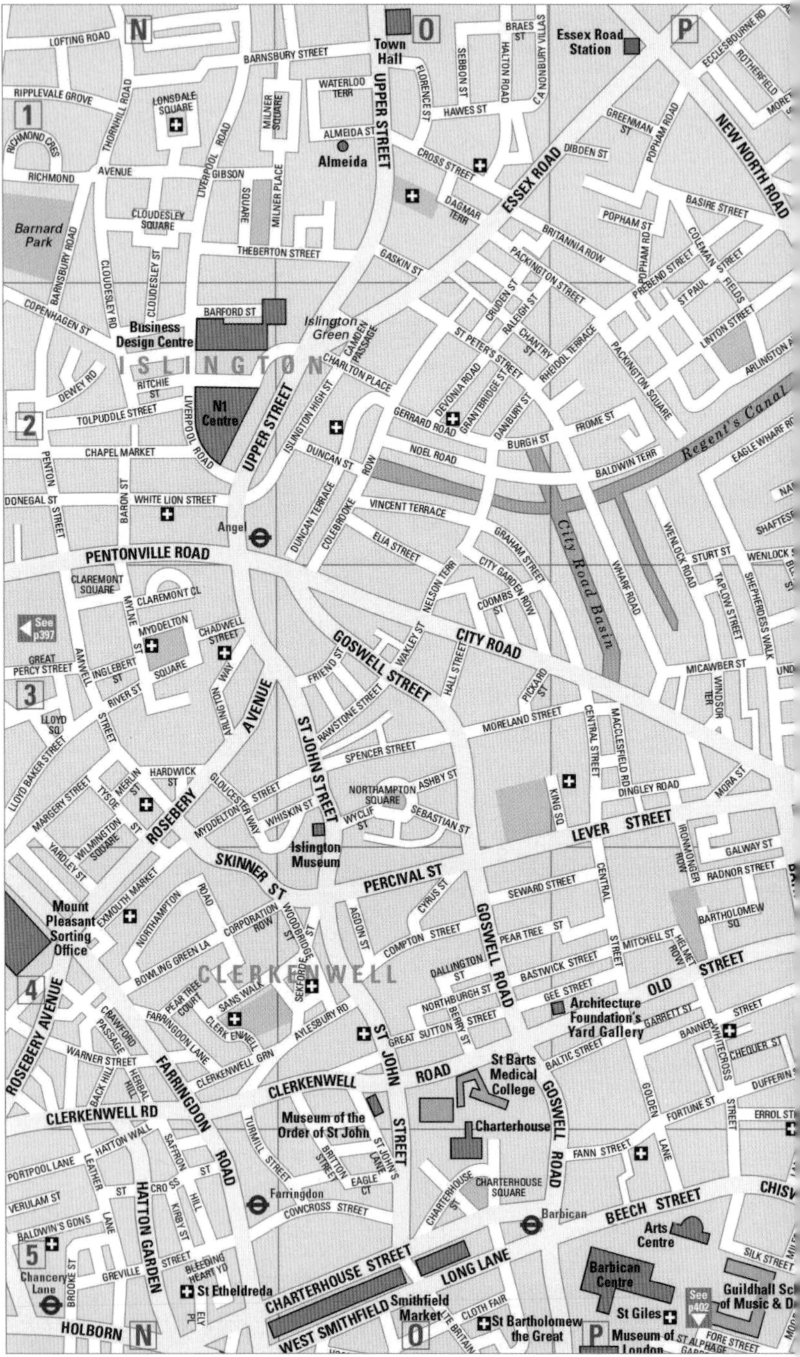
N
O
P
1
2
3
4
5
Town Hall
Essex Road Station
Almeida
Barnard Park
Business Design Centre
Islington Green
ISLINGTON
N1 Centre
Angel
Islington Museum
Mount Pleasant Sorting Office
CLERKENWELL
Architecture Foundation's Yard Gallery
St Barts Medical College
Charterhouse
Museum of the Order of St John
Farringdon
Barbican
Arts Centre
Barbican Centre
St Giles
Museum of London
Smithfield Market
St Bartholomew the Great
St Etheldreda
Chancery Lane
Guildhall School of Music & D
Regent's Canal
City Road Basin
See p397
See p402
LOFTING ROAD
BARNSBURY STREET
RIPPLEVALE GROVE
THORNHILL ROAD
LONSDALE SQUARE
RICHMOND CRES
RICHMOND AVENUE
LIVERPOOL ROAD
GIBSON SQUARE
MILNER SQUARE
MILNER PLACE
WATERLOO TERR
ALMEIDA ST
UPPER STREET
FLORENCE ST
SEBBON ST
HALTON ROAD
BRAES ST
CANONBURY VILLAS
HAWES ST
CROSS STREET
DAGMAR TERR
ESSEX ROAD
DIBDEN ST
GREENMAN ST
POPHAM ROAD
NEW NORTH ROAD
ECCLESBOURNE RD
ROTHERFIELD ST
BASIRE STREET
POPHAM ST
COLEMAN FIELDS
CLOUDESLEY SQUARE
CLOUDESLEY ST
CLOUDESLEY RD
BARNSBURY ROAD
THEBERTON STREET
GASKIN ST
BRITANNIA ROW
PACKINGTON STREET
PREBEND STREET
ST PAUL STREET
COPENHAGEN ST
BARFORD ST
CAMDEN PASSAGE
CHARLTON PLACE
CRUDEN ST
RALEIGH ST
ST PETER'S STREET
CHANTRY ST
RHEIDOL TERRACE
PACKINGTON SQUARE
LINTON STREET
ARLINGTON AVE
DEWEY RD
RITCHIE ST
TOLPUDDLE STREET
ISLINGTON HIGH ST
DEVONIA ROAD
GRANTBRIDGE ST
DANBURY ST
GERRARD ROAD
FROME ST
EAGLE WHARF RD
CHAPEL MARKET
DUNCAN ST
NOEL ROAD
BURGH ST
BALDWIN TERR
PENTON STREET
DONEGAL ST
BARON ST
WHITE LION STREET
DUNCAN TERRACE
COLEBROOKE ROW
VINCENT TERRACE
ELIA STREET
GRAHAM STREET
WENLOCK ROAD
WHARF ROAD
SHAFTESBURY
PENTONVILLE ROAD
CLAREMONT SQUARE
CLAREMONT CL
NELSON TERR
CITY GARDEN ROW
COOMBS ST
STURT ST
TAPLOW STREET
SHEPHERDESS WALK
WENLOCK ST
MYLNE ST
MYDDELTON SQUARE
CHADWELL STREET
GOSWELL STREET
WAKLEY ST
FRIEND ST
CITY ROAD
HALL STREET
GREAT PERCY STREET
AMWELL STREET
INGLEBERT ST
RIVER ST
ARLINGTON WAY
AVENUE
ST JOHN STREET
RAWSTONE STREET
PICKARD ST
MICAWBER ST
WINDSOR TER
LLOYD SQ
LLOYD BAKER STREET
MORELAND STREET
CENTRAL STREET
MACCLESFIELD RD
SPENCER STREET
HARDWICK ST
MARGERY STREET
TYSOE ST
MERLIN ST
ROSEBERY AVENUE
GLOUCESTER WAY
MYDDELTON STREET
WHISKIN ST
NORTHAMPTON SQUARE
ASHBY ST
WYCLIF ST
SEBASTIAN ST
KING SQ
DINGLEY ROAD
MORA ST
WILMINGTON SQUARE
YARDLEY ST
SKINNER ST
PERCIVAL ST
LEVER STREET
IRONMONGER ROW
GALWAY ST
RADNOR STREET
EXMOUTH MARKET
NORTHAMPTON ROAD
CORPORATION ROW
WOODBRIDGE ST
AGDON ST
CYRUS ST
SEWARD STREET
GOSWELL ROAD
BARTHOLOMEW SQ
COMPTON STREET
PEAR TREE ST
MITCHELL ST
HELMET ROW
OLD STREET
BOWLING GREEN LA
SEKFORDE ST
DALLINGTON ST
BASTWICK STREET
PEAR TREE COURT
SANS WALK
NORTHBURGH ST
GEE STREET
CRAWFORD PASSAGE
FARRINGDON LANE
CLERKENWELL CLOSE
AYLESBURY RD
GREAT SUTTON STREET
BERRY ST
GARRETT ST
BANNER ST
WHITECROSS STREET
WARNER STREET
FARRINGDON ROAD
CLERKENWELL GRN
CLERKENWELL ROAD
BALTIC STREET
CHEQUER ST
DUFFERIN ST
BACK HILL
HERBAL HILL
CLERKENWELL RD
TURNMILL STREET
GOLDEN LANE
FORTUNE ST
ERROL ST
HATTON WALL
SAFFRON HILL
ST JOHN'S LANE
BRITTON STREET
FANN STREET
PORTPOOL LANE
LEATHER LANE
EAGLE CT
CHARTERHOUSE SQUARE
CHARTERHOUSE ST
CHISWELL
VERULAM ST
CROSS ST
KIRBY ST
HATTON GARDEN
COWCROSS STREET
BEECH STREET
BALDWIN'S GDNS
SILK STREET
GREVILLE STREET
BLEEDING HEART YD
CHARTERHOUSE STREET
LONG LANE
BROOKE ST
ELY PL
CLOTH FAIR
HOLBORN
WEST SMITHFIELD
FORE STREET
ST ALPHAGE GARDENS

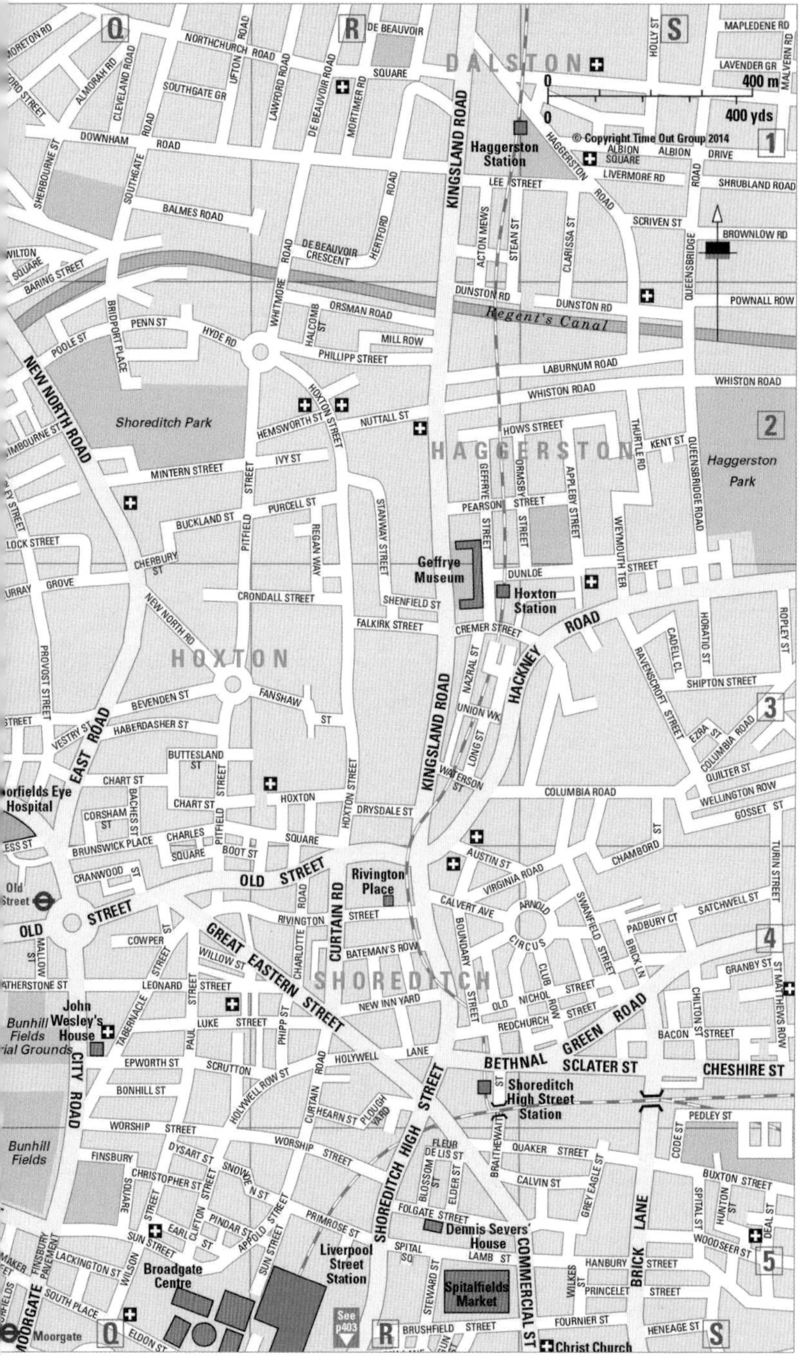
Q
R
S
DALSTON
HAGGERSTON
HOXTON
SHOREDITCH
0
400 m
0
400 yds
© Copyright Time Out Group 2014
1
2
3
4
5
Haggerston Station
Hoxton Station
Geffrye Museum
Shoreditch Park
Haggerston Park
Regent's Canal
KINGSLAND ROAD
HACKNEY ROAD
OLD STREET
GREAT EASTERN STREET
CITY ROAD
EAST ROAD
NEW NORTH ROAD
SHOREDITCH HIGH STREET
COMMERCIAL ST
BETHNAL GREEN ROAD
SCLATER ST
CHESHIRE ST
BRICK LANE
COLUMBIA ROAD
Rivington Place
Shoreditch High Street Station
Dennis Severs' House
Spitalfields Market
Christ Church
Liverpool Street Station
Broadgate Centre
Moorgate
Old Street
John Wesley's House
Bunhill Fields
Moorfields Eye Hospital
See p403

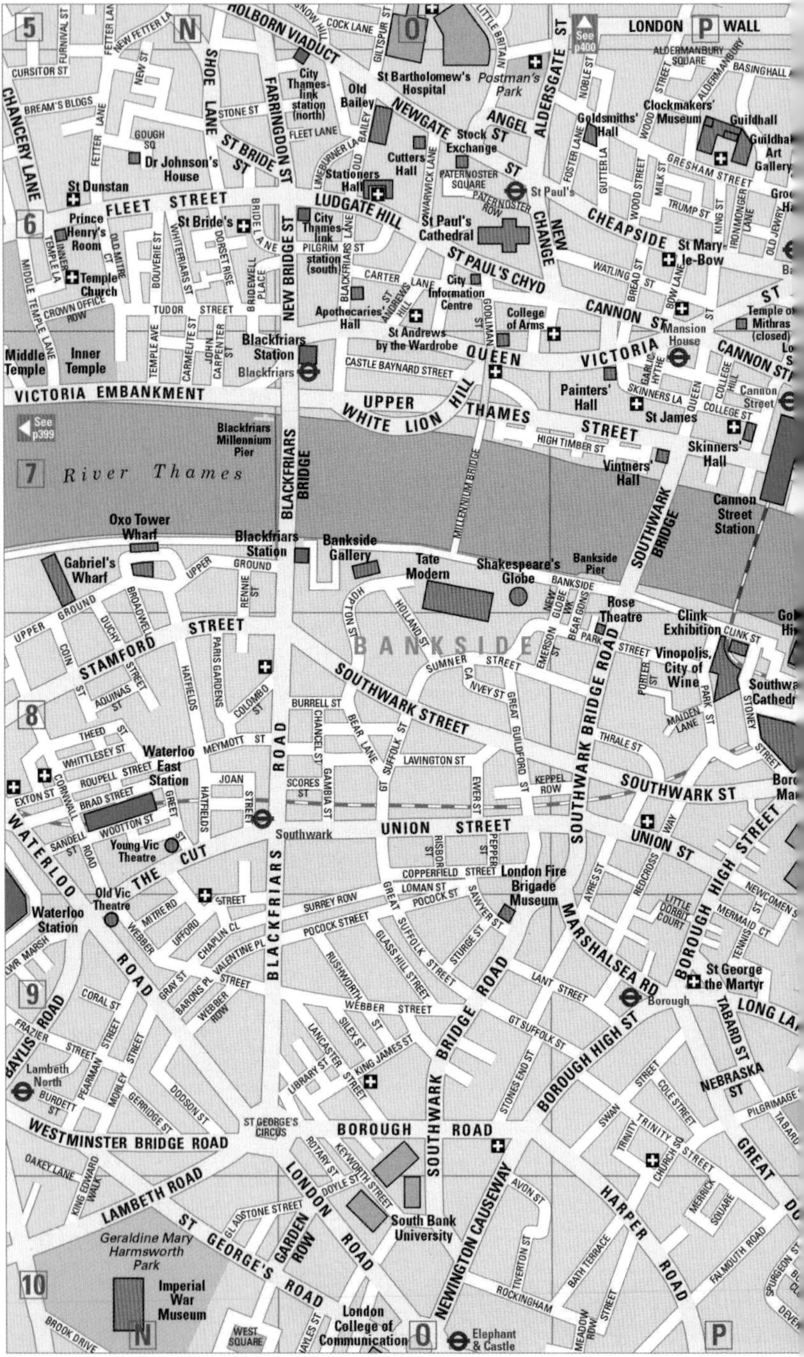
5
N
O
P
6
7
8
9
10
See p400
See p399
HOLBORN VIADUCT
LONDON WALL
CURSITOR ST
CHANCERY LANE
BREAM'S BLDGS
FETTER LANE
NEW FETTER LA
FURNIVAL ST
NEW ST
SHOE LANE
FARRINGDON ST
STONE ST
GOUGH SQ
Dr Johnson's House
ST BRIDE ST
COCK LANE
GILTSPUR ST
LITTLE BRITAIN
City Thameslink station (north)
Old Bailey
St Bartholomew's Hospital
Postman's Park
ALDERSGATE ST
NOBLE ST
ALDERMANBURY SQUARE
ALDERMANBURY
BASINGHALL
Clockmakers' Museum
Guildhall
Guildhall Art Gallery
Goldsmiths' Hall
NEWGATE ST
ANGEL ST
Stock Exchange
Cutters Hall
FLEET LANE
OLD BAILEY
LIMEBURNER LA
WARWICK LANE
PATERNOSTER SQUARE
PATERNOSTER ROW
St Paul's
Stationers Hall
FOSTER LANE
GUTTER LA
WOOD STREET
MILK ST
GRESHAM STREET
TRUMP ST
KING ST
IRONMONGER LANE
OLD JEWRY
St Dunstan
FLEET STREET
St Bride's
BRIDE LANE
NEW BRIDGE ST
LUDGATE HILL
City Thameslink station (south)
PILGRIM ST
St Paul's Cathedral
NEW CHANGE
CHEAPSIDE
St Mary-le-Bow
WATLING ST
BREAD ST
BOW LANE
Prince Henry's Room
INNER TEMPLE LA
MIDDLE TEMPLE LANE
OLD MITRE CT
WHITEFRIARS ST
BOUVERIE ST
DORSET RISE
BRIDEWELL PLACE
BLACKFRIARS LANE
CARTER LANE
ST PAUL'S CHYD
City Information Centre
Temple Church
CROWN OFFICE ROW
TUDOR STREET
Apothecaries' Hall
ST ANDREWS HILL
GODLIMAN ST
College of Arms
CANNON ST
Temple of Mithras (closed)
Mansion House
TEMPLE AVE
CARMELITE ST
JOHN CARPENTER ST
Blackfriars Station
Blackfriars
St Andrews by the Wardrobe
QUEEN
VICTORIA
CANNON ST
Middle Temple
Inner Temple
CASTLE BAYNARD STREET
Painters' Hall
GARLIC HYTHE
SKINNERS LA
COLLEGE HILL
Cannon Street
VICTORIA EMBANKMENT
UPPER
WHITE LION HILL
THAMES
STREET
St James
COLLEGE ST
QUEEN
Blackfriars Millennium Pier
BLACKFRIARS BRIDGE
HIGH TIMBER ST
Skinners' Hall
River Thames
MILLENNIUM BRIDGE
Vintners' Hall
SOUTHWARK BRIDGE
Cannon Street Station
Oxo Tower Wharf
Blackfriars Station
Bankside Gallery
Tate Modern
Shakespeare's Globe
Bankside Pier
Gabriel's Wharf
UPPER GROUND
RENNIE ST
HOPTON ST
HOLLAND ST
BANKSIDE
NEW GLOBE WK
BEAR GDNS
Rose Theatre
Clink Exhibition
CLINK ST
BROADWALL
DUCHY
STREET
PARK
EMERSON ST
UPPER GROUND
COIN
STAMFORD STREET
PARIS GARDENS
HATFIELDS
COLOMBO ST
SUMNER STREET
CANVEY ST
STREET
Vinopolis, City of Wine
PORTER ST
Southwark Cathedral
STONEY STREET
PARK ST
MAIDEN LANE
AQUINAS ST
SOUTHWARK STREET
BURRELL ST
BEAR LANE
GREAT GUILDFORD ST
SOUTHWARK BRIDGE ROAD
THRALE ST
THEED ST
WHITTLESEY ST
MEYMOTT ST
CHANCEL ST
SUFFOLK ST
LAVINGTON ST
Waterloo East Station
ROUPELL STREET
CORNWALL
EXTON ST
BRAD STREET
WOOTTON ST
JOAN STREET
SCORES ST
GAMBIA ST
GT SUFFOLK ST
EWER ST
KEPPEL ROW
SOUTHWARK ST
Borough Market
GREET
HATFIELDS
ROAD
Southwark
UNION STREET
UNION ST
WAY
WATERLOO ROAD
SANDELL ST
Young Vic Theatre
THE CUT
RISBOR ST
PEPPER ST
BOROUGH HIGH STREET
Old Vic Theatre
COPPERFIELD STREET
LOMAN ST
POCOCK ST
London Fire Brigade Museum
AYRES ST
REDCROSS
LITTLE DORRIT COURT
NEWCOMEN ST
MERMAID CT
Waterloo Station
MITRE RD
STREET
SURREY ROW
SAWYER ST
WEBBER
UFFORD
CHAPLIN CL
POCOCK STREET
GLASS HILL STREET
SUFFOLK STREET
STURGE ST
MARSHALSEA RD
TENNIS ST
LWR MARSH
VALENTINE PL
BLACKFRIARS ROAD
RUSHWORTH STREET
St George the Martyr
ROAD
GRAY ST
BARONS PL
STREET
WEBBER ROW
LANT STREET
Borough
LONG LA
CORAL ST
WEBBER STREET
SILEX ST
TABARD ST
BAYLIS ROAD
FRAZIER STREET
STREET
STREET
LANCASTER STREET
GT SUFFOLK ST
BOROUGH HIGH ST
Lambeth North
PEARMAN
MORLEY
KING JAMES ST
LIBRARY ST
STONES END ST
NEBRASKA ST
BURDETT ST
GERRIDGE ST
DODSON ST
SOUTHWARK BRIDGE ROAD
STREET
COLE STREET
PILGRIMAGE
WESTMINSTER BRIDGE ROAD
ST GEORGE'S CIRCUS
BOROUGH ROAD
SWAN
TRINITY ST
TRINITY CHURCH SQ
STREET
GREAT DOVER
OAKEY LANE
KING EDWARD WALK
ROTARY ST
KEYWORTH STREET
DOYLE ST
SOUTH
MERRICK SQUARE
LAMBETH ROAD
LONDON ROAD
AVON ST
HARPER ROAD
GLADSTONE STREET
South Bank University
NEWINGTON CAUSEWAY
FALMOUTH ROAD
ST GEORGE'S ROAD
GARDEN ROW
Geraldine Mary Harmsworth Park
TIVERTON ST
BATH TERRACE
SPURGEON ST
Imperial War Museum
ROCKINGHAM
ROAD
BROOK DRIVE
WEST SQUARE
London College of Communication
Elephant & Castle
MEADOW ROW
STREET

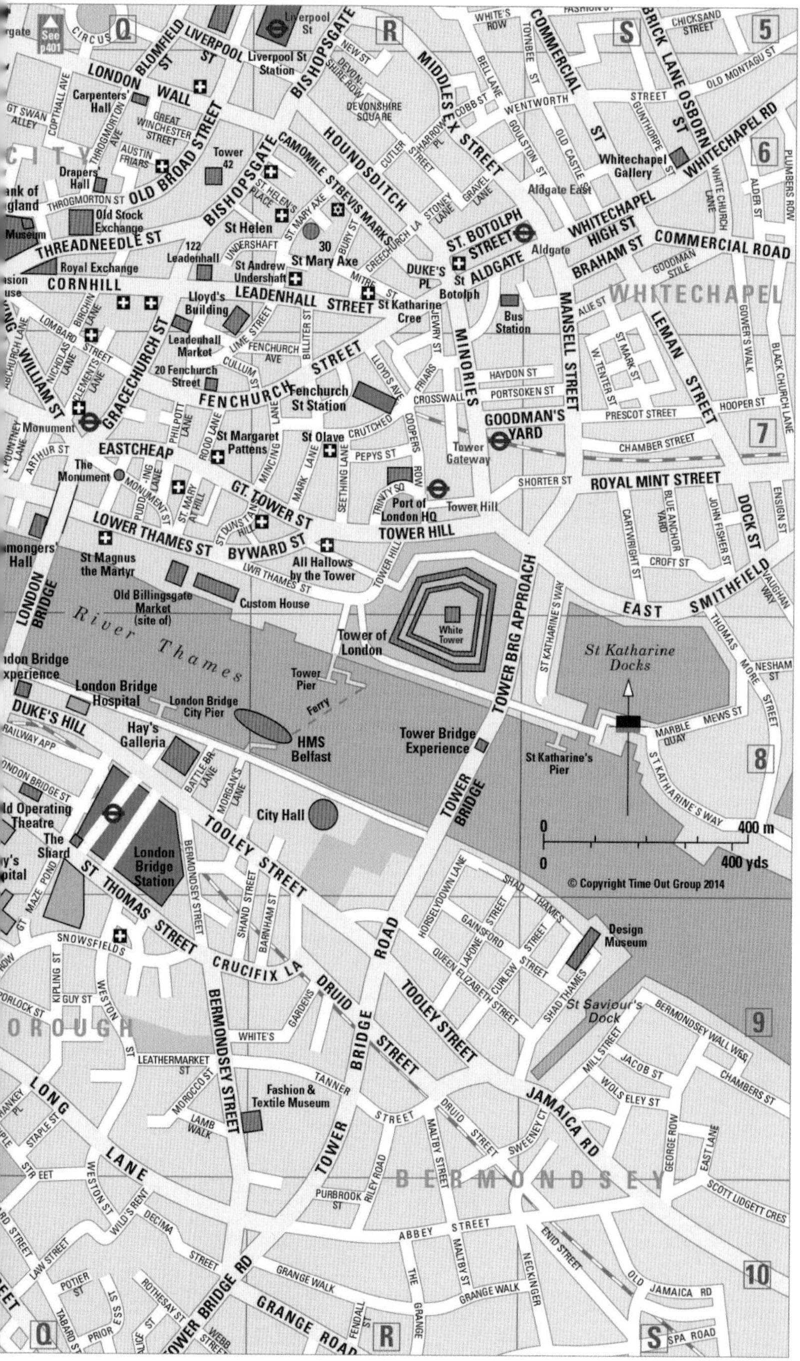
Q
R
S
5
6
7
8
9
10
See p401
CIRCUS
Liverpool St
LIVERPOOL ST
Liverpool St Station
BLOMFIELD ST
LONDON WALL
Carpenters' Hall
BISHOPSGATE
NEW ST
DEVONSHIRE ROW
DEVONSHIRE SQUARE
MIDDLESEX STREET
WHITE'S ROW
TOYNBEE ST
BELL LANE
COMMERCIAL ST
FASHION ST
BRICK LANE
CHICKSAND STREET
OLD MONTAGU ST
OSBORN ST
WENTWORTH STREET
COBB ST
GUNTHORPE ST
GT SWAN ALLEY
COPTHALL AVE
THROGMORTON AVE
GREAT WINCHESTER STREET
AUSTIN FRIARS
OLD BROAD STREET
Tower 42
CAMOMILE ST
HOUNDSDITCH
CUTLER ST
HARROW PL
GOULSTON ST
OLD CASTLE ST
Whitechapel Gallery
WHITECHAPEL RD
PLUMBERS ROW
CITY
Drapers' Hall
Bank of England
THROGMORTON ST
Old Stock Exchange
Museum
ST HELEN'S PLACE
ST MARY AXE
BEVIS MARKS
STONEY LANE
GRAVEL LANE
Aldgate East
WHITE CHURCH LANE
ALDER ST
THREADNEEDLE ST
St Helen
UNDERSHAFT
BURY ST
CREECHURCH LA
ST. BOTOLPH STREET
WHITECHAPEL HIGH ST
COMMERCIAL ROAD
122 Leadenhall
30 St Mary Axe
Aldgate
Royal Exchange
St Andrew Undershaft
DUKE'S PL
ALDGATE
BRAHAM ST
GOODMAN STILE
Mansion House
CORNHILL
MITRE ST
St Botolph
LEADENHALL STREET
St Katharine Cree
WHITECHAPEL
Lloyd's Building
LIME STREET
Bus Station
MANSELL STREET
ALIE ST
LEMAN STREET
GOWER'S WALK
BLACK CHURCH LANE
LOMBARD ST
BIRCHIN LANE
GRACECHURCH ST
Leadenhall Market
FENCHURCH AVE
BILLITER ST
JEWRY ST
MINORIES
ST MARK ST
W. TENTER ST
KING WILLIAM ST
NICHOLAS LANE
CLEMENTS LANE
ABCHURCH LANE
20 Fenchurch Street
CULLUM ST
STREET
LLOYDS AVE
FRIARS
HAYDON ST
PORTSOKEN ST
CROSSWALL
FENCHURCH
Fenchurch St Station
HOOPER ST
Monument
PHILPOTT LANE
ROOD LANE
St Margaret Pattens
MINCING LANE
St Olave
CRUTCHED
COOPERS ROW
GOODMAN'S YARD
PRESCOT STREET
POUNTNEY LANE
ARTHUR ST
EASTCHEAP
MARK LANE
SEETHING LANE
PEPYS ST
Tower Gateway
CHAMBER STREET
The Monument
MONUMENT ST
PUDDING LANE
ST MARY AT HILL
GT. TOWER ST
TRINITY SQ
Port of London HQ
Tower Hill
SHORTER ST
ROYAL MINT STREET
LOWER THAMES ST
ST DUNSTAN'S HILL
BYWARD ST
TOWER HILL
CARTWRIGHT ST
BLUE ANCHOR YARD
JOHN FISHER ST
DOCK ST
ENSIGN ST
Fishmongers' Hall
St Magnus the Martyr
All Hallows by the Tower
LWR THAMES ST
CROFT ST
LONDON BRIDGE
Old Billingsgate Market (site of)
Custom House
TOWER BRG APPROACH
ST KATHARINE'S WAY
EAST SMITHFIELD
VAUGHAN WAY
River Thames
White Tower
Tower of London
St Katharine Docks
THOMAS MORE STREET
NESHAM ST
London Bridge Experience
Tower Pier
London Bridge Hospital
London Bridge City Pier
Ferry
DUKE'S HILL
RAILWAY APP
Hay's Galleria
HMS Belfast
Tower Bridge Experience
St Katharine's Pier
MARBLE QUAY
MEWS ST
ST KATHARINE'S WAY
LONDON BRIDGE ST
BATTLE BR LANE
MORGAN'S LANE
TOWER BRIDGE
Old Operating Theatre
City Hall
0
400 m
400 yds
The Shard
TOOLEY STREET
London Bridge Station
Guy's Hospital
BERMONDSEY STREET
HORSELYDOWN LANE
SHAD THAMES
© Copyright Time Out Group 2014
ST THOMAS STREET
MAZE POND
SHAND STREET
BARNHAM ST
GAINSFORD STREET
LAFONE STREET
QUEEN ELIZABETH STREET
CURLEW STREET
Design Museum
SNOWSFIELDS
ROAD
CRUCIFIX LA
KIPLING ST
WESTON ST
GUY ST
DRUID ST
TOOLEY STREET
St Saviour's Dock
PORLOCK ST
BOROUGH
GARDENS
WHITE'S
BRIDGE
BERMONDSEY WALL WEST
LEATHERMARKET ST
STREET
MILL STREET
JACOB ST
CHAMBERS ST
MOROCCO ST
Fashion & Textile Museum
TANNER STREET
JAMAICA RD
WOLSELEY ST
LONG LANE
LAMB WALK
TOWER
DRUID STREET
SWEENEY CT
MALTBY STREET
GEORGE ROW
EAST LANE
STAPLE ST
RILEY ROAD
BERMONDSEY
SCOTT LIDGETT CRES
WESTON ST
PURBROOK ST
WILD'S RENT
DECIMA STREET
ABBEY STREET
ENID STREET
LAW STREET
GRANGE WALK
NECKINGER
POTIER ST
ROTHESAY ST
MALTBY ST
THE GRANGE
OLD JAMAICA RD
TOWER BRIDGE RD
GRANGE ROAD
FENDALL ST
SPA ROAD
TABARD ST
PRIOR ST
WEBB STREET

MAPS

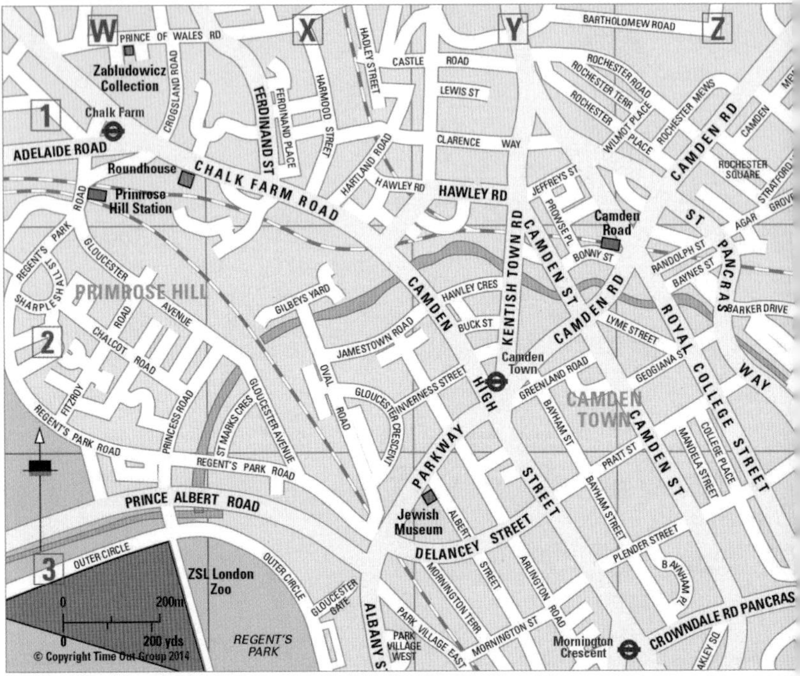
W
X
Y
Z
1
2
3
PRINCE OF WALES RD
Zabludowicz Collection
CROGSLAND ROAD
FERDINAND ST
FERDINAND PLACE
HARMOOD STREET
HADLEY STREET
CASTLE ROAD
LEWIS ST
BARTHOLOMEW ROAD
ROCHESTER ROAD
ROCHESTER TERR
ROCHESTER PLACE
WILMOT PLACE
ROCHESTER MEWS
CAMDEN RD
ROCHESTER SQUARE
STRATFORD
Chalk Farm
ADELAIDE ROAD
Roundhouse
CHALK FARM ROAD
Primrose Hill Station
HARTLAND ROAD
HAWLEY RD
CLARENCE WAY
HAWLEY RD
JEFFREYS ST
PROWSE PL
Camden Road
BONNY ST
AGAR GROVE
ST PANCRAS WAY
RANDOLPH ST
BAYNES ST
BARKER DRIVE
REGENT'S PARK ROAD
ST GEORGE'S TERRACE
SHARPLESHALL ST
GLOUCESTER AVENUE
PRIMROSE HILL
ROAD
CHALCOT ROAD
FITZROY
PRINCESS ROAD
ST MARKS CRES
GLOUCESTER AVENUE
GILBEYS YARD
JAMESTOWN ROAD
OVAL ROAD
GLOUCESTER CRESCENT
INVERNESS STREET
CAMDEN HIGH STREET
HAWLEY CRES
BUCK ST
KENTISH TOWN RD
CAMDEN ST
CAMDEN RD
LYME STREET
ROYAL COLLEGE STREET
Camden Town
GREENLAND ROAD
GEOGIANA ST
CAMDEN TOWN
BAYHAM ST
CAMDEN ST
MANDELA STREET
COLLEGE PLACE
PRATT ST
REGENT'S PARK ROAD
PARKWAY
Jewish Museum
ALBERT STREET
DELANCEY STREET
BAYHAM STREET
PLENDER STREET
BAYNHAM PL
PRINCE ALBERT ROAD
OUTER CIRCLE
ZSL London Zoo
GLOUCESTER GATE
ALBANY ST
PARK VILLAGE EAST
PARK VILLAGE WEST
MORNINGTON TERR
MORNINGTON ST
ARLINGTON ROAD
Mornington Crescent
CROWNDALE RD
PANCRAS
OAKLEY SQ
REGENT'S PARK
0
200m
0
200 yds
© Copyright Time Out Group 2014

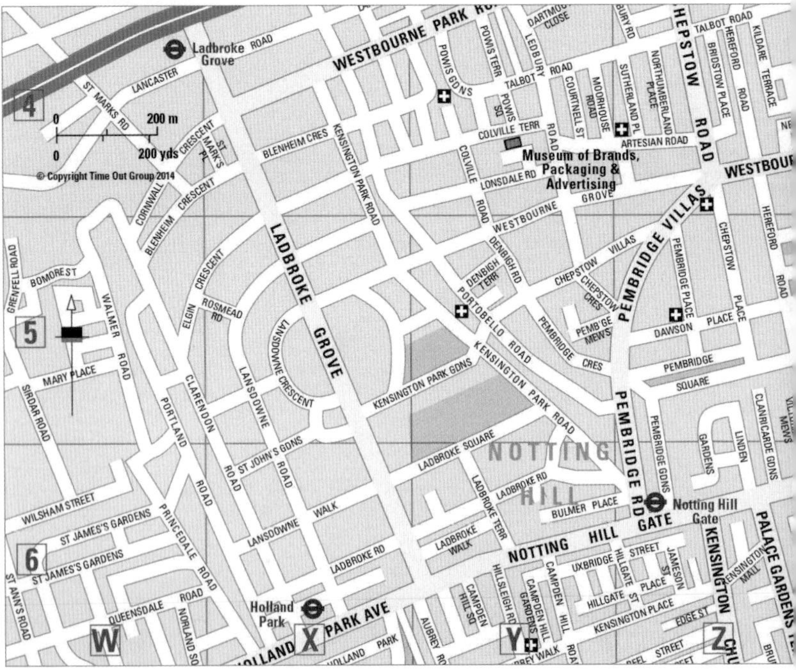
4
5
6
W
X
Y
Z
Ladbroke Grove
LANCASTER ROAD
WESTBOURNE PARK RD
POWIS GDNS
POWIS TERR
POWIS SQ
DARTMOUTH CLOSE
LEDBURY ROAD
TALBOT ROAD
COURTNELL ST
MOORHOUSE ROAD
SUTHERLAND PL
NORTHUMBERLAND PLACE
CHEPSTOW ROAD
TALBOT ROAD
HEREFORD ROAD
BRIDSTOW PLACE
KILDARE TERRACE
ST MARKS RD
0
200 m
0
200 yds
© Copyright Time Out Group 2014
CRESCENT
ST MARK'S PL
BLENHEIM CRES
KENSINGTON PARK ROAD
COLVILLE TERR
COLVILLE ROAD
ARTESIAN ROAD
Museum of Brands, Packaging & Advertising
LONSDALE RD
WESTBOURNE GROVE
WESTBOURNE GROVE
CORNWALL CRESCENT
BLENHEIM CRESCENT
PEMBRIDGE VILLAS
CHEPSTOW PLACE
HEREFORD ROAD
GRENFELL ROAD
BOMORE ST
ELGIN CRESCENT
ROSMEAD RD
LADBROKE GROVE
LANSDOWNE CRESCENT
DENBIGH TERR
DENBIGH RD
PORTOBELLO ROAD
CHEPSTOW VILLAS
CHEPSTOW CRES
PEMBRIDGE CRES
PEMB'GE MEWS
PEMBRIDGE PLACE
DAWSON PLACE
WALMER ROAD
MARY PLACE
SIRDAR ROAD
PORTLAND ROAD
CLARENDON ROAD
LANSDOWNE ROAD
KENSINGTON PARK GDNS
KENSINGTON PARK ROAD
PEMBRIDGE SQUARE
PEMBRIDGE RD
PEMBRIDGE GDNS
LINDEN GARDENS
CLANRICARDE GDNS
ST JOHN'S GDNS
LADBROKE SQUARE
NOTTING HILL
LADBROKE RD
LADBROKE TERR
BULMER PLACE
Notting Hill Gate
WILSHAM STREET
ST JAMES'S GARDENS
PRINCEDALE ROAD
LANSDOWNE WALK
LADBROKE WALK
NOTTING HILL GATE
UXBRIDGE STREET
HILLGATE ST
JAMESON ST
HILLGATE PLACE
KENSINGTON PLACE
EDGE ST
KENSINGTON CHURCH
KENSINGTON MALL
PALACE GARDENS
ST ANN'S ROAD
ST JAMES'S GARDENS
QUEENSDALE ROAD
NORLAND SQ
LADBROKE RD
Holland Park
HOLLAND PARK AVE
HOLLAND PARK
AUBREY RD
HILLSLEIGH RD
CAMPDEN HILL SQ
CAMPDEN HILL GARDENS
CAMPDEN HILL

MAPS

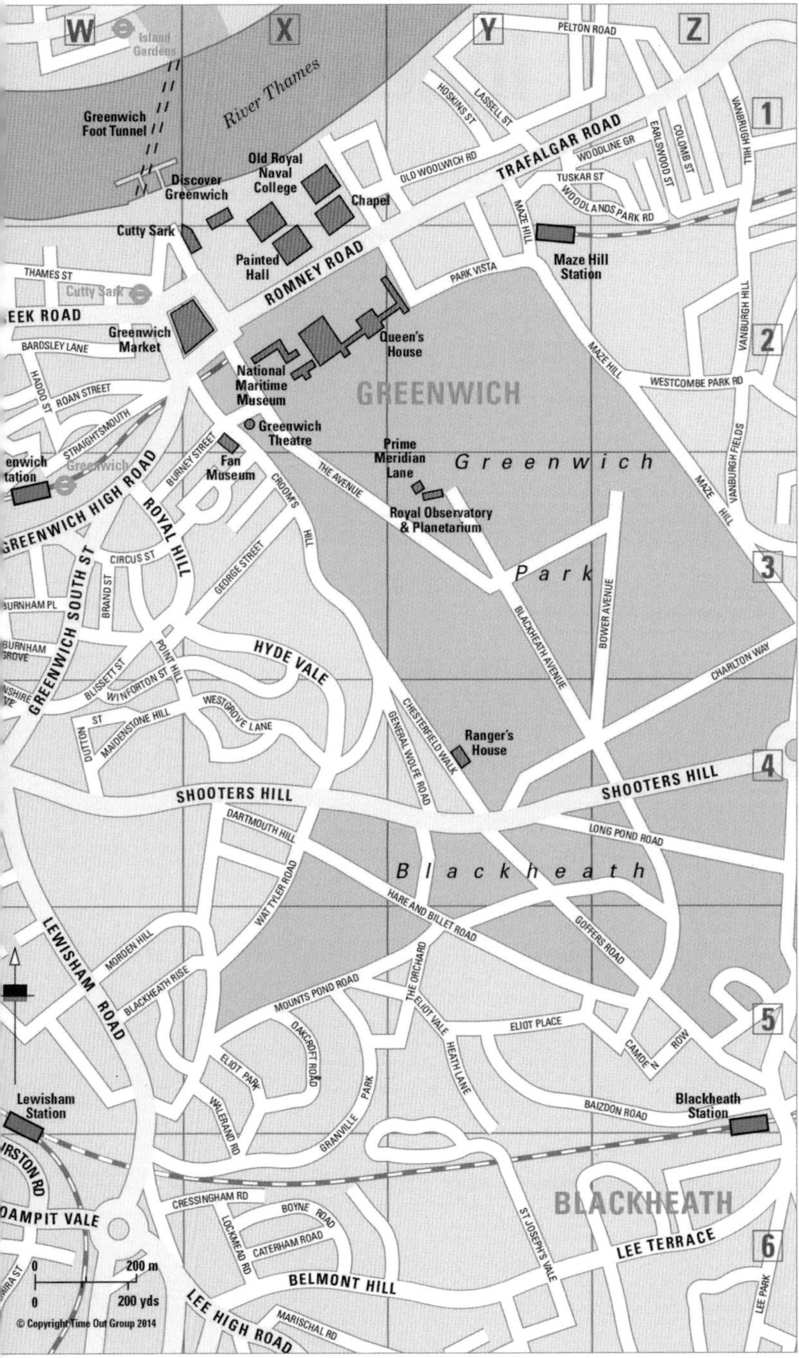
W
X
Y
Z
1
2
3
4
5
6
Island Gardens
River Thames
Greenwich Foot Tunnel
Discover Greenwich
Old Royal Naval College
Chapel
Cutty Sark
Painted Hall
ROMNEY ROAD
TRAFALGAR ROAD
PELTON ROAD
HOSKINS ST
LASSELL ST
OLD WOOLWICH RD
WOODLINE GR
EARLSWOOD ST
COLOMB ST
VANBRUGH HILL
TUSKAR ST
WOODLANDS PARK RD
MAZE HILL
Maze Hill Station
PARK VISTA
THAMES ST
Cutty Sark
EEK ROAD
Greenwich Market
BARDSLEY LANE
Queen's House
National Maritime Museum
GREENWICH
WESTCOMBE PARK RD
HADDO ST
ROAN STREET
STRAIGHTSMOUTH
Greenwich Theatre
BURNEY STREET
Fan Museum
enwich tation
Greenwich
GREENWICH HIGH ROAD
ROYAL HILL
CROOM'S HILL
THE AVENUE
Prime Meridian Lane
Greenwich
Royal Observatory & Planetarium
VANBURGH FIELDS
CIRCUS ST
BRAND ST
GEORGE STREET
Park
BURNHAM PL
BURNHAM GROVE
GREENWICH SOUTH ST
BLACKHEATH AVENUE
BOWER AVENUE
CHARLTON WAY
HYDE VALE
POINT HILL
BISSETT ST
WINFORTON ST
WESTGROVE LANE
DUTTON ST
MAIDENSTONE HILL
CHESTERFIELD WALK
GENERAL WOLFE ROAD
Ranger's House
SHOOTERS HILL
SHOOTERS HILL
DARTMOUTH HILL
LONG POND ROAD
WAT TYLER ROAD
Blackheath
HARE AND BILLET ROAD
GOFFERS ROAD
LEWISHAM ROAD
MORDEN HILL
BLACKHEATH RISE
MOUNTS POND ROAD
THE ORCHARD
ELIOT VALE
HEATH LANE
ELIOT PLACE
CAMDEN ROW
OAKCROFT ROAD
ELIOT PARK
WALERAND RD
GRANVILLE PARK
Lewisham Station
BAIZDON ROAD
Blackheath Station
THURSTON RD
BLACKHEATH
LOAMPIT VALE
CRESSINGHAM RD
BOYNE ROAD
LOCKMEAD RD
CATERHAM ROAD
ST JOSEPH'S VALE
LEE TERRACE
LEE PARK
BELMONT HILL
0
200 m
0
200 yds
LEE HIGH ROAD
MARISCHAL RD
© Copyright Time Out Group 2014

MAPS

Street Index

STREET INDEX

STREET INDEX

STREET INDEX

STREET INDEX

STREET INDEX

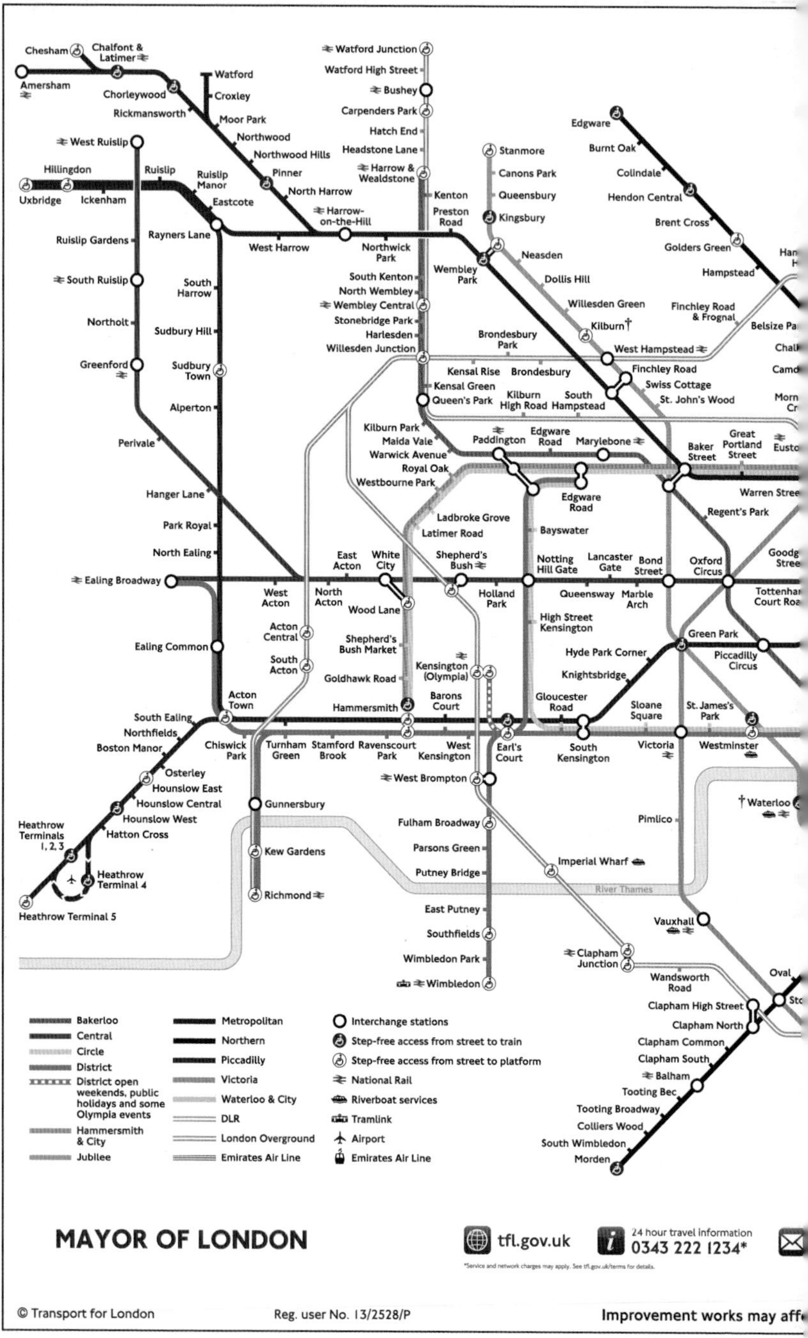
Chesham
Chalfont & Latimer
Amersham
Chorleywood
Rickmansworth
Watford
Croxley
Moor Park
Northwood
Northwood Hills
Pinner
North Harrow
Harrow-on-the-Hill
West Harrow
Watford Junction
Watford High Street
Bushey
Carpenders Park
Hatch End
Headstone Lane
Harrow & Wealdstone
Kenton
Preston Road
Northwick Park
South Kenton
North Wembley
Wembley Central
Stonebridge Park
Harlesden
Willesden Junction
Wembley Park
Stanmore
Canons Park
Queensbury
Kingsbury
Neasden
Dollis Hill
Willesden Green
Kilburn
West Hampstead
Finchley Road
Swiss Cottage
St. John's Wood
Edgware
Burnt Oak
Colindale
Hendon Central
Brent Cross
Golders Green
Hampstead
Finchley Road & Frognal
Belsize Pa
West Ruislip
Hillingdon
Uxbridge
Ickenham
Ruislip
Ruislip Manor
Eastcote
Rayners Lane
Ruislip Gardens
South Ruislip
South Harrow
Northolt
Sudbury Hill
Greenford
Sudbury Town
Alperton
Perivale
Hanger Lane
Park Royal
North Ealing
Ealing Broadway
West Acton
North Acton
East Acton
White City
Wood Lane
Shepherd's Bush
Holland Park
Notting Hill Gate
Queensway
Lancaster Gate
Marble Arch
Bond Street
Oxford Circus
Tottenham Court Road
Goodge Street
Warren Street
Regent's Park
Baker Street
Great Portland Street
Euston
Kensal Rise
Brondesbury
Brondesbury Park
Kensal Green
Queen's Park
Kilburn High Road
South Hampstead
Kilburn Park
Maida Vale
Warwick Avenue
Paddington
Edgware Road
Marylebone
Royal Oak
Westbourne Park
Ladbroke Grove
Latimer Road
Bayswater
Acton Central
South Acton
Ealing Common
Shepherd's Bush Market
Goldhawk Road
Hammersmith
Kensington (Olympia)
High Street Kensington
Hyde Park Corner
Knightsbridge
Green Park
Piccadilly Circus
Gloucester Road
Sloane Square
St. James's Park
Westminster
Victoria
South Kensington
Earl's Court
Barons Court
West Kensington
Ravenscourt Park
Stamford Brook
Turnham Green
Chiswick Park
Acton Town
South Ealing
Northfields
Boston Manor
Osterley
Hounslow East
Hounslow Central
Hounslow West
Hatton Cross
Heathrow Terminals 1, 2, 3
Heathrow Terminal 4
Heathrow Terminal 5
Gunnersbury
Kew Gardens
Richmond
West Brompton
Fulham Broadway
Parsons Green
Putney Bridge
East Putney
Southfields
Wimbledon Park
Wimbledon
Imperial Wharf
River Thames
Clapham Junction
Wandsworth Road
Pimlico
Vauxhall
Waterloo
Oval
Clapham High Street
Clapham North
Clapham Common
Clapham South
Balham
Tooting Bec
Tooting Broadway
Colliers Wood
South Wimbledon
Morden
Bakerloo
Central
Circle
District
District open weekends, public holidays and some Olympia events
Hammersmith & City
Jubilee
Metropolitan
Northern
Piccadilly
Victoria
Waterloo & City
DLR
London Overground
Emirates Air Line
Interchange stations
Step-free access from street to train
Step-free access from street to platform
National Rail
Riverboat services
Tramlink
Airport
Emirates Air Line
MAYOR OF LONDON
tfl.gov.uk
24 hour travel information
0343 222 1234*
*Service and network charges may apply. See tfl.gov.uk/terms for details.
© Transport for London
Reg. user No. 13/2528/P
Improvement works may aff

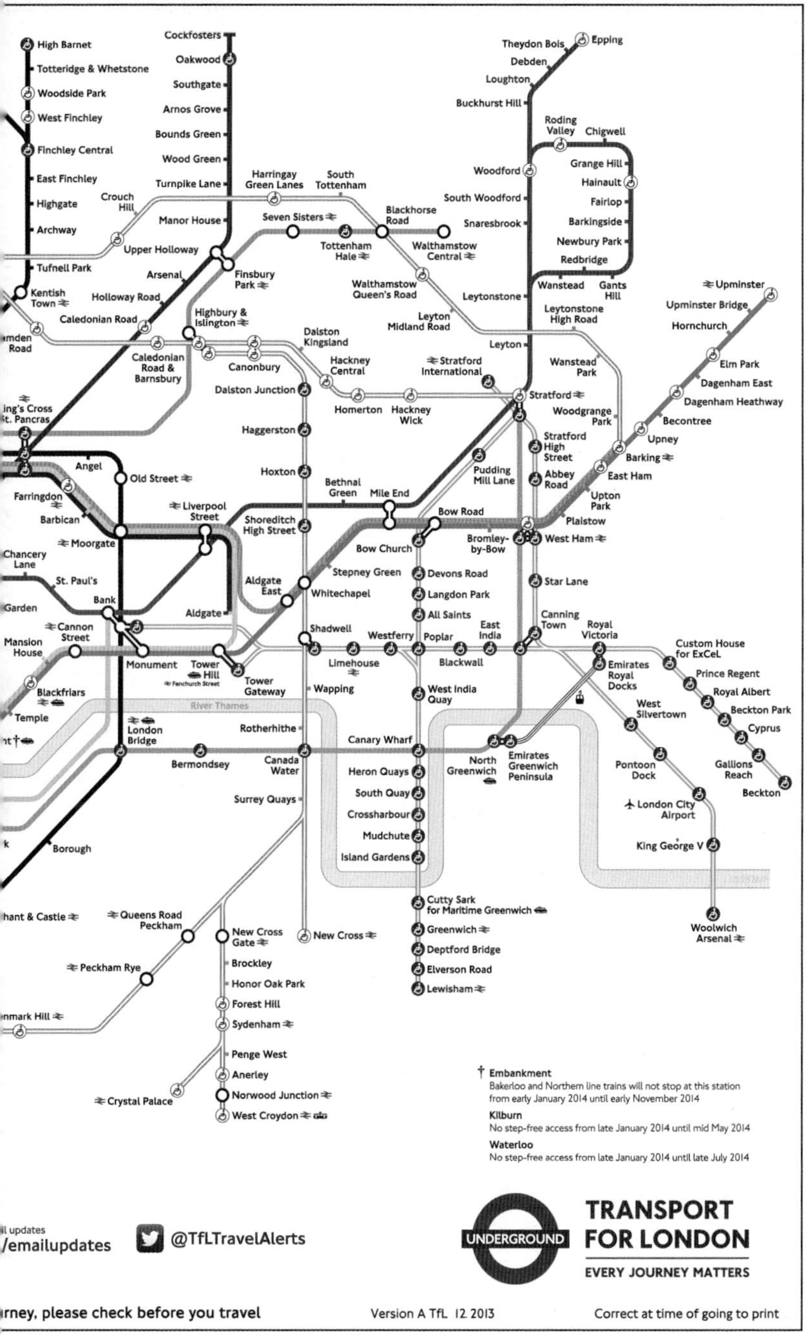
High Barnet
Totteridge & Whetstone
Woodside Park
West Finchley
Finchley Central
East Finchley
Highgate
Archway
Tufnell Park
Kentish Town
Cockfosters
Oakwood
Southgate
Arnos Grove
Bounds Green
Wood Green
Turnpike Lane
Manor House
Crouch Hill
Harringay Green Lanes
South Tottenham
Seven Sisters
Tottenham Hale
Blackhorse Road
Walthamstow Central
Walthamstow Queen's Road
Leyton Midland Road
Upper Holloway
Arsenal
Finsbury Park
Holloway Road
Caledonian Road
Highbury & Islington
Caledonian Road & Barnsbury
Canonbury
Dalston Kingsland
Dalston Junction
Hackney Central
Homerton
Hackney Wick
Haggerston
Hoxton
Shoreditch High Street
Theydon Bois
Epping
Debden
Loughton
Buckhurst Hill
Roding Valley
Chigwell
Grange Hill
Hainault
Fairlop
Barkingside
Newbury Park
Redbridge
Woodford
South Woodford
Snaresbrook
Wanstead
Gants Hill
Leytonstone
Leytonstone High Road
Leyton
Wanstead Park
Stratford International
Stratford
Woodgrange Park
Stratford High Street
Pudding Mill Lane
Abbey Road
Upminster
Upminster Bridge
Hornchurch
Elm Park
Dagenham East
Dagenham Heathway
Becontree
Upney
Barking
East Ham
Upton Park
Plaistow
West Ham
Star Lane
Bromley-by-Bow
Bow Road
Bow Church
Mile End
Bethnal Green
Old Street
Angel
Farringdon
Barbican
Liverpool Street
Moorgate
Chancery Lane
St. Paul's
Bank
Aldgate
Aldgate East
Whitechapel
Stepney Green
Devons Road
Langdon Park
All Saints
Cannon Street
Mansion House
Monument
Tower Hill
Fenchurch Street
Tower Gateway
Shadwell
Limehouse
Westferry
Poplar
Blackwall
East India
Canning Town
Royal Victoria
Custom House for ExCeL
Prince Regent
Royal Albert
Beckton Park
Cyprus
Gallions Reach
Beckton
Emirates Royal Docks
West Silvertown
Pontoon Dock
London City Airport
King George V
Woolwich Arsenal
Blackfriars
Temple
London Bridge
Bermondsey
River Thames
Wapping
Rotherhithe
Canada Water
Surrey Quays
Canary Wharf
West India Quay
Heron Quays
South Quay
Crossharbour
Mudchute
Island Gardens
Cutty Sark for Maritime Greenwich
Greenwich
Deptford Bridge
Elverson Road
Lewisham
North Greenwich
Emirates Greenwich Peninsula
Borough
Queens Road Peckham
Peckham Rye
New Cross Gate
New Cross
Brockley
Honor Oak Park
Forest Hill
Sydenham
Penge West
Anerley
Norwood Junction
West Croydon
Crystal Palace
† Embankment
Bakerloo and Northern line trains will not stop at this station from early January 2014 until early November 2014
Kilburn
No step-free access from late January 2014 until mid May 2014
Waterloo
No step-free access from late January 2014 until late July 2014
/emailupdates
@TfLTravelAlerts
UNDERGROUND
TRANSPORT FOR LONDON
EVERY JOURNEY MATTERS
Version A TfL 12 2013
Correct at time of going to print

MAPS

DISCOVER THE
PRIDE OF LONDON
Disney PRESENTS
THE LION KING
Visit www.thelionking.co.uk or call +44 (0) 20 7091 8870
LYCEUM THEATRE
21 Wellington Street Covent Garden
Photos by Simon Turtle. © Disney